WILLIAM I. SALMON
University of Utah

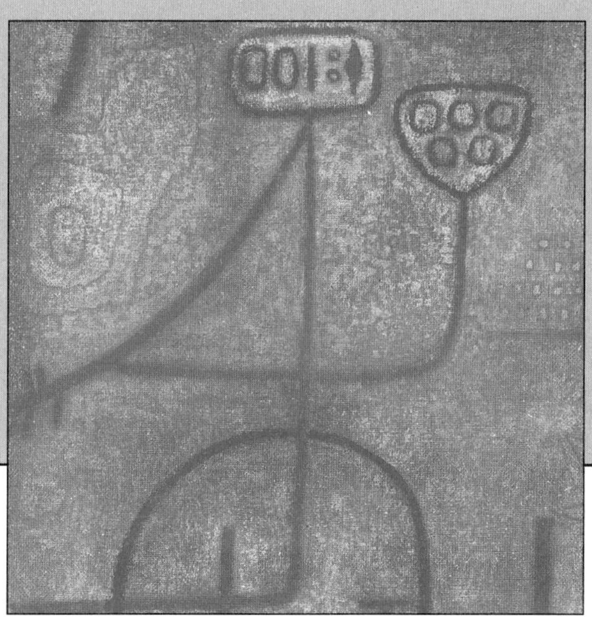

STRUCTURES AND ABSTRACTIONS
An Introduction to Computer Science with Pascal

Second Edition

IRWIN
Burr Ridge, Illinois
Boston, Massachusetts
Sidney, Australia

Dedicated to
the Spirit of Liberal Education,
wherever it survives.

This symbol indicates that the paper in this book is made of recycled paper. Its fiber content exceeds the recommended minimum of 50% waste paper fibers as specified by the EPA.

© RICHARD D. IRWIN, INC., 1992 and 1994

All rights reserved. No part of this publication may be reproduced, stored in a retrieval system, or transmitted, in any form or by any means, electronic, mechanical, photocopying, recording, or otherwise, without the prior written permission of the publisher.

Cover painting:
Copyright 1992 by VAGA New York
Paul Klee (1879–1940)
La belle jardiniere
(ein Biedermeiergespenst), 1939.1237
Reproduced by permission.

Senior sponsoring editor: Tom Tucker
Developmental editor: Lena Buonanno
Marketing manager: Robb Linsky
Project editor: Denise Santor
Production manager: Laurie Kersch
Page designer: Michael Warrell
Compositor: Bill Salmon, *Interactive Educational Systems*
Cover designer: Amy Osborne
Printer: Von Hoffman Press

The programs in this book have been included for instructional use only. They have been carefully tested but are not guaranteed for any particular use. The author and the publisher accept no liabilities for the use of the programs.

Library of Congress Cataloging-in-Publication Data

Salmon, W. (William I.)
Structures and abstractions : an introduction to computer science with Pascal / William I. Salmon. — 2nd ed.
p. cm.
Includes index.
ISBN 0-256-12666-6
1. Pascal (Computer program language) 2. Data structures (Computer science) 3. Abstract data types (Computer science)
I. Title.
QA76.73.P2S253 1994
005.26'2—dc20 93–21441

Printed in the United States of America
1 2 3 4 5 6 7 8 9 0 VH 8 7 6 5 4 3 2 1

Preface

It is a pleasure to respond to the teachers and students who used this book in its first edition and to incorporate many of the improvements they suggested. As in the first edition, this book is intended for a first college-level course in computer science, emphasizing modern software engineering practice. The main issues are procedural and data abstraction, modular and hierarchic software design, program structures and data structures, and first glimpses of informal verification and complexity analysis. The goal is to provide a survey of the important concepts in our field, suitable for courses lasting from one quarter to two semesters. Pascal is the illustrative programming language, but the language is not the main mission, and there is no attempt to cover all of Pascal's syntax. The spirit here has been much influenced by the new ACM/IEEE curriculum guidelines.

What's new in this edition?

The general principles of software engineering and abstraction are introduced at the beginning of Chapter 2, as a lead-in to the explicit techniques for problem solving. The problem-solving techniques now make explicit use of procedural abstraction and encapsulation. New case studies in this chapter set up the solutions of two problems to be attacked in Pascal in later chapters.

The material on text files has been removed from Chapters 4 and 10 and placed in Chapter 17, although it still features a modular, three-level organization. The new organization allows text file material to be taught either early or late in the course, at the discretion of the instructor. To introduce text files early, simply cover Sections 17.1 and 17.2 right after Sections 4.3 and 4.4, respectively, and Sections 17.3–17.6 right after 10.3. (This sequencing is clearly marked in the text and Table of Contents.) Then the remaining sections of Chapter 17 can be covered any time after Chapter 14. Further details appear after this preface, under the heading *Teaching from This Text*.

The sections on testing and debugging, at the ends of many chapters, now contain extensive lists of actual error messages resulting from example errors, using a real-world compiler (Borland/Turbo Pascal 7.0). Other Pascal systems give similar messages in most cases.

An optional Section 5.6 has been added, explaining how to avoid global variables entirely, when this is desired.

A new Chapter 6 introduces the `IF..THEN..ELSE` and `WHILE..DO` control structures, so that students can use decisions and loops at an earlier point in the course. This is done with minimum syntax, to keep attention focused on procedural abstraction at this point in the course.

An optional Section 6.5 introduces the concept of recursion, for those instructors wishing to raise the issue this early, and for those students who wonder what happens if a procedure calls itself. The full treatment of recursion appears in Chapter 12, right after the full treatment of iteration. The chapter on recursion provides more exercises and projects than before.

The coverage of `CASE` structures has been expanded in Section 9.4.

In Sections 11.1–11.4, the explanations of loop invariants have been rewritten to make it clearer how a loop is designed to terminate correctly.

A case study on selection sorting has been added to the chapter on arrays (Chapter 14). The chapter on searching and sorting (Chapter 19) now has a section on insertion sort. This means that the text now provides complete coverage of selection, insertion, and quicksorts. Chapter 19 can now be covered right after Chapter 14 if the instructor desires.

The first example of an abstract data type is now a `Fraction` type instead of `String` (Section 16.2).

Section 19.3, on big-oh notation, now provides an informal heuristic explanation in addition to the formal mathematical one.

In the Turbo Pascal edition, Chapter 21 now introduces object-oriented programming (OOP), using lists, stacks, and queues as examples.

About a third of the questions, exercises, and projects in the book are new.

There are 14 new sidebars, averaging almost a page in length, providing a glimpse of some of the frontiers in computer science. These are substantial quotes from journals, magazines, and books, chosen for their provocative, often controversial ideas and engaging writing styles. They are intended to convey the excitement and rapid changes in computer science, while showing the pervasive effects of computing on our everyday lives and even on our philosophical outlooks.

Themes that continue from the first edition

- Students practice procedural abstraction from the beginning of the course. Algorithms are presented from a hierarchical viewpoint that encourages modular design from the very beginning, with constant emphasis. Unlike most other books, there is no need to apologize later for early monolithic programs, or to "unteach" early bad habits.
- Chapter 2 provides eight explicit problem-solving techniques before students begin Pascal coding. These techniques are used repeatedly throughout the rest of the book and become so ingrained that they provide a foundation for creative solutions to new problems.
- Students are taught to picture both the data structures and the actions that occur in a program. The book contains many "animations" (snapshot sequences) of program execution and pictures of the data structures—380 diagrams in all. (For an example, see Section 6.4.)

- Good programs don't work correctly by luck; they are engineered so that they have to work correctly. We introduce simple techniques for checking the correctness of algorithms before writing programs (Chapter 11).
- Recursion is not more mysterious or difficult than iteration—it's just less familiar. These two techniques for repetition are equally important and each illuminates the other. Therefore, we present recursion and iteration side by side, with frequent comparisons, beginning in Chapter 12.

Meeting the ACM/ IEEE guidelines for the 1990s

Structures and Abstractions satisfies the new curriculum recommendations of the Association for Computing Machinery (ACM) and the Institute of Electrical and Electronic Engineers (IEEE) for a first course in computer science (CS1). In addition, Parts 4 and 5 of the book overlap the latest ACM/IEEE guidelines for CS2 (data structures) courses. In particular, the book emphasizes the three processes of theory, abstraction, and design, while being accessible to first-year students. (See the publication, *Computing Curricula 1991*, ACM Order Number 201910 or IEEE Computer Society Press Order Number 2220.)

Structures and Abstractions provides enough material for a variety of introductory courses, ranging from a single quarter to two semesters in length. There is considerable optional material to allow for various approaches in different teaching situations. Some of the teaching options are discussed under the heading, *Teaching from This Text*, following the preface.

The standard edition of *Structures and Abstractions* uses (except in one appendix) only ISO/ANSI Standard Pascal. All examples have been tested in several typical Pascal environments to ensure that they run correctly. A separate edition is available for those preferring a treatment specific to Borland International's Turbo Pascal and Borland Pascal, using compilation units and objects to implement abstract data types.

Who can read this book?

The reader needs no previous programming experience, but should be computer-literate, with enough experience in mathematics to appreciate the need for rigorous thought and to understand algebraic proofs. *I have found that the best predictors of success in a CS1 course are skills in mathematical proofs and word problems and an ability to communicate clearly in writing.*

Specific features

Consistent emphasis on engineering and design: *Structures and Abstractions* places heavy emphasis on the fundamental techniques for proper software engineering, including procedural and data abstraction, top-down modular design, incremental testing, the use of assertions and loop invariants, and elementary running-time analysis. Modular, hierarchical design is constantly emphasized from Section 2.2 onward, even before we begin to introduce the Pascal language. Chapters 3 and 4 introduce Pascal by means of parameterless procedures, real-number data, and simple I/O, while constantly emphasizing procedural design—an emphasis that continues through Chapters 5–7. The consistent early emphasis on procedural abstraction has the advantage that hardly any monolithic programs appear in the book. Students learn good design practices from the very beginning. Similarly with data abstraction, which begins in Chapter 16: Once we begin to use abstract data types, we continue to use them in Chapters 18, 20, and 21.

Classic algorithms: A first course should introduce its students to many of the classic algorithms on which later courses will build. This book includes base conversion, case mapping, counting characters and words in text, exponentiation, greatest common divisor, square roots, Towers of Hanoi, expression parsing, line drawing, string manipulations, binary search, selection sort, insertion sort, quicksort, list processing, evaluation of postfix expressions, pseudorandom number generation, and simulation. Additional case studies are provided in the lab manual.

Style: The book itself reflects the rules of good programming style. For example, subjects like modularity, procedural abstraction, data abstraction, recursion, loop invariants, and dynamic data structures are introduced by themselves in their own sections and chapters, so that the reader can focus full attention on them. Then each topic is learned "bottom up," with a sequence of stepped examples that gradually increase in complexity and abstraction. Like the programs themselves, chapters are short and modular, divided into short sections with clear goals. More advanced topics likely to be skipped in shorter courses are isolated in optional sections, often toward the ends of chapters or in later chapters. The modular design of the book results in more chapters, sections, and subsections, but these are shorter, clearer, and more flexible in use.

Explicit problem-solving techniques: Classroom testing has proven that students benefit from the presentation and repeated use of explicit methods for problem solving. Chapter 2 presents eight of the most generally useful. These techniques are illustrated with two nontrivial case studies in Chapter 2, and then are used repeatedly throughout the following chapters. By seeing the same techniques applied in various situations, readers gradually learn their use.

A spiral, not a "peek-a-boo" approach: Students need to see why the rules of practice and style are necessary. The book introduces techniques when they are needed, then uses them persistently and consistently. The reader never loses sight of a topic while seeing it unfold, because an important topic is never dropped after being introduced. The gradual deepening and continual exposure to abstraction deepens readers' understanding and appreciation of each topic.

Pedagogical aids

Chapter outlines and summaries: Each chapter begins with a few introductory paragraphs connecting the chapter with previous material and outlining the topics to be covered. The chapter ends with a summary of the main points that were made.

Important terms defined: Important technical terms are shown in boldface when they first appear. If they are likely to be unfamiliar, they are defined in the margin and listed in the glossary. Many are also listed at the end of each chapter, where they serve as a guide to concepts that should be reviewed for exams.

Visualization: Sequences of execution during procedure calls, iteration, recursion, and other complex actions are "animated" by sequences of diagrams acting as "snapshots" of the execution process. Altogether, there are more than 35 such animations, containing more than 195 diagrams. In addition, there are hundreds of diagrams of syntax and data structures—over 380 in all.

Exercises and programming projects: Questions and exercises are distributed throughout the chapters, immediately after material requiring practice and reinforcement. The questions tend to be of the simple, self-check type. Exercises range in difficulty from trivial syntax practice to typical debugging experiences and short programming assignments. Major programming projects are found at the ends of the chapters. I have tried to provide a wide range of problems to meet the needs of various introductory courses. Altogether, there are more than 650 problems, occupying over 100 pages.

Case studies: Important programming issues are illustrated by application to typical problems in computer science. These include first glimpses of many of the kinds of problems to be encountered in later courses, and are used to teach explicit techniques of problem solving as well as informal methods of verification and analysis. (Additional case studies can be found in the companion lab manual.)

Debugging aids: Debugging techniques and examples are discussed frequently. In addition to standard techniques involving modular testing and intermediate output, typical interactive debugging tools are described. Always, the reader is reminded that it is most important to prevent bugs in the first place, by good engineering practices. (The companion lab manual also provides considerable guidance with debugging, along with instructions for using the THINK and Borland/Turbo debuggers.)

Sidebars on important issues: At the ends of many chapters, you will find sidebars illustrating some of the issues that swirl through computer science. These extended quotes from a variety of professional and popular sources are intended to stir discussions in class and to encourage readers to examine their own attitudes toward important computer-related issues of our time.

Acknowledgments

Many reviewers have helped to shape this new edition. Their detailed and thoughtful suggestions along the way are much appreciated. We thank

Jay Martin Anderson, Franklin and Marshall College
Laurie Benaloh, Clarkson University
David Berque, Colgate University
Jack V. Briner, Jr., University of North Caroline–Greensboro
David T. Brown, Ithaca College
John F. Buck, Indiana University, Bloomington
Deborah L. Byrum, Texas A&M University
Adair Dingle, Lehigh University
Ron Gilster, Walla Walla Community College
Wilbur Goltermann, University of Colorado–Denver
Ramon P. Hernandez, Mesa Community College
Kip Irvine, Miami-Dade Community College
Danny Kopec, Carleton University
Cary Laxer, Rose-Hulman Institute of Technology
Lewis Lum, The University of Portland
Rebekah D. May, Ashland Community College
Jack Mostow, Rutgers, The State University of New Jersey
Debbie Noonan, College of William and Mary
Jandelyn Plane, University of Maryland–College Park
Dennis E. Ray, Old Dominion University
Charles W. Reynolds, James Madison University
Ali Salehnia, South Dakota State University
Louis Steinberg, Rutgers, The State University of New Jersey
Christopher J. Van Wyk, Drew University

In addition, the influence of the first-edition reviewers is still felt, and we thank them again: Robert B. Anderson, University of Houston; Brent Auernheimer, California State University, Fresno; Anthony Q. Baxter, University of Kentucky; Louise M. Berard, Wilkes College; David Alan Bozak, SUNY College at Oswego; Larry C. Christensen, Brigham Young University; Robert A. Christiansen, University of Iowa; Denis A. Conrady, University of North Texas; Cecilia Daly, University of Nebraska–Lincoln; Douglas Dankel II, University of Florida; Edmund I. Deaton, San Diego State University; H. E. Dunsmore, Purdue University; Suzy Gallagher, University of Texas; David Hanscom, University of Utah; Robert M. Holloway, University of Wisconsin–Madison; Ronald P. Johnson, Evangel College; George F. Luger, University of New Mexico; William E. McBride, Baylor University; Michael G. Main, University of Colorado at Boulder; Andrea Martin, Louisiana State University; Jane Wallace Mayo, University of Tennessee–Knoxville; Kenneth L. Modesitt, Western Kentucky University; David Phillips, University of Pennsylvania; George A. Novacky, Jr., University of Pittsburgh; David L. Parker, Salisbury State University; Theresa M. Phinney, Texas A&M University; V. S. Sunderam, Emory University; Stephen F. Weiss, University of North Carolina–Chapel Hill; Laurie White, Armstrong State College; Stephen G. Worth III, North Carolina State University–Raleigh; and Marvin Zelkowitz, University of Maryland.

Many teaching assistants and students have helped with the evolution of this book. I would particularly like to thank my teaching assistants, Rich Thomson, Cliff Miller, Elena Driskill, Rory Cejka, Mark Ellens, Mike Stephenson, and Lynn Eggli. I would also like to thank all the students who made suggestions and corrections, especially Alexander Kratsov, Randy Veigel, Mark Nolan, Blair Brandenberg, Ian Adams, David Swingle, and Lisa Clarkson. Over the years, I have received many helpful suggestions from John Halleck and LeRoy Eide, of the University of Utah Computer Center and from my wife, Lydia Salmon. They too deserve effuse thanks.

For many years, I have received encouragement and inspiration from Dave Hanscom, the Undergraduate Coordinator in the University of Utah's Computer Science Department. I also owe a special debt to my son, Edward Salmon, whose superb sense of design influenced the cover and several of the diagrams and projects in this book.

Many thanks to the talented people at Richard D. Irwin, Inc., who provided more support and help than I thought possible. I particularly thank Sheila Glaser, Max Effenson, and Lena Buonanno, the developmental editors, who cheered me along while trying to convince me that *but* is only a conjunction.

But I should also mention Jackson P. Slipshod, who makes frequent appearances in the questions and exercises in this book. To the best of my knowledge, he made his first appearance in a chemistry book by Joseph Nordmann, published many years ago by John Wiley & Sons, Inc. Thanks to Dr. Nordmann's fine book, Jackson has been dogging me ever since.

Questions? Requests?

I enjoy feedback from readers, and have received some of the best suggestions in this way. You can send comments, gripes, corrections, and compliments to the following e-mail addresses. (But please don't ask me to help with your homework!)

William I. Salmon
Internet address: salmon@cs.utah.edu
CompuServe address: 71565,135

TEACHING FROM THIS TEXT

This book supports a variety of college-level courses, from one quarter to two semesters in duration. The flexibility is achieved by designing the book around a core of essential chapters—Chapters 3–10 and 13–15—while also supplying a number of more independent chapters that cover discretionary topics required by some courses but not others. Few instructors will want to cover the whole book, so the following explanations are intended to help in choosing material to suit particular courses and teaching styles.

Chapter 1: Computing and Computation

The goals of the first chapter are to define and explain the concept of an algorithm, to explain what it means to say that a computer is a general-purpose symbol-manipulating machine, and to introduce the kinds of software used in translating algorithms into programs, compiling them into machine language, and executing the resulting machine code. Many but not all of the terms in this chapter should be familiar from previous computer literacy experiences, but this chapter is necessary in order to establish a common vocabulary and conceptual basis for the rest of the book. In my one-quarter classes, time does not allow me to lecture on this material, but I assign it for outside reading, warning students that they will be responsible for the contents of the chapter. Of course, I answer in class any questions that arise from the readings.

Chapter 2: Abstraction, Problem Solving, and Algorithm Design

Sections 2.1 and 2.2 introduce the complexity of modern commercial software systems and the need for abstraction to handle such complexity. In particular, Section 2.2 describes procedural abstraction, describing how actions are encapsulated in procedures. We then apply this way of thinking while introducing (in Sections 2.3–2.12) eight explicit techniques for inventing algorithms to solve problems. One of the techniques is the important principle of top-down design. Sections 2.3–2.6 begin a Fahrenheit-to-Celsius temperature conversion case study, which uses real-number data. This evolving case study is used to provide a unifying thread in Sections. 4.1, 4.5, 4.6, 4.7, 5.1, 5.2, 6.1, 6.2, and 6.7, as the topic of procedural abstraction is pursued more deeply. Section 2.7 applies further problem-solving techniques to the problem of sorting three numbers. This second case study is a setup for Section 6.3, where the algorithm is coded into Pascal. Often, I do not lecture explicitly about this chapter, assigning it, along with Chapter 1, for reading during the first week of class.

Chapter 3: Program Structures

Chapter 3 is where I usually start explicit coverage in class. This chapter uses the abstraction concepts and problem-solving techniques of Chapter 2 while introducing the syntax of Pascal programs. The goal is to show how procedural abstraction is practiced in a programming language, and to show how procedural abstraction involves modularity and hierarchy. Pascal procedures are used, but without parameters. The procedures draw pictures but do not use numeric or character data. I do not give formal lectures on syntax as I cover this material; instead, I act out the solution of the problems in great detail. To cover Section 3.4, for example, I state the problem, then I describe how the output might look (one of the explicit problem-solving techniques of

Chapter 2), then I describe the sequence of steps in executing an appropriate program, then I outline the algorithm, and finally, I build the syntax of a program. The last stage of this process will generate many questions about syntactic details, and I answer all of these, also discussing alternatives at every stage.

Chapter 4: Real Data and I/O

Here we introduce real-number data, explaining how it is stored, why this results in roundoff error, and how we perform real-number input and output (I/O). The goal is to introduce a data type and explain its use without distracting from the emphasis on procedural abstraction. (If we introduced integer, character, and boolean data at this point, together with their associated syntax, we would sacrifice the constant emphasis on procedural abstraction and encapsulation.) The chapter ends with the beginnings of a modularized program for Fahrenheit-to-Celsius conversion, as a motivator for the parameters to be introduced in Chapter 5. Again, I teach this material by acting out the solutions of the problems. When I get to the Pascal-coding stage, I often make "accidental" syntax or semantic errors to show what happens, how I locate the errors, and how I fix them. (I use a microcomputer with LCD overhead projection whenever possible, so that students can see me do these things in real time. When I have no projector, I simulate events on the blackboard.)

Instructors who prefer to introduce text file I/O can do so at this point. Although all file I/O material is collected in Chapter 17, it is designed for flexible use. Sections 17.1 and 17.2 are designed so that they can be covered immediately after Sections 4.3 and 4.4, if desired.

Chapter 5: Procedures with Parameters

Now we take the procedural syntax and top-down design principles from Chapter 3, combine them with the real-number example from Chapter 4, and add new syntactical material on using parameters with procedures. The first case study is the Fahrenheit-to-Celsius problem carried over from Chapter 4. This modularized version is now to the point where it needs protection from bad input data, and this brings up the need for control structures, which will be the topic of Chapter 6. Section 5.4 introduces the important concept of program states, explaining that the purpose of a procedure is to map a precondition state into a postcondition state. Pre- and postconditions are written for most procedures from this point on, allowing students to ease into this idea before we use it in the introduction of loop invariants in Chapter 11. Instructors who don't plan to cover invariants can downplay the emphasis on pre- and postconditions. (In my experience, students have no trouble ignoring topics for which they are not held responsible!)

Chapter 6: Controlling Execution

Section 6.1 introduces a simple form of the `IF..THEN..ELSE` control structure and uses it to protect Chapter 5's Fahrenheit-to-Celsius program from bad input data. This improvement works, but what we really need is a controlled way to repeat execution. Section 6.2 therefore introduces a simple version of the `WHILE..DO` control structure and uses it to build a final version of the F-to-C program. Section 6.3 examines in Pascal the problem of sorting three numbers, which was attacked in Section 2.7 as an example of algorithm design. This case study is the vehicle for introducing the use of stubs and drivers when practicing incremental testing of programs during construction. It also provides an unusually good example of what is involved when one tries to test a program with all possible combinations of input data, and it motivates the need for the more formal verification methods to be introduced in Chapter 11. Chapter 6 also shows how nested procedure calls work, because this issue arises naturally in the three-number sorting problem. The chapter ends with an optional section on recursion because students often ask at this point what happens if a procedure calls itself.

Chapter 7: Functions

After a short introduction of the concept of a function, Section 7.2 contrasts the data-return mechanism of a Pascal function with that of a procedure. Section 7.3 explains how to decide which to use in a given case. The chapter is located here because functions are needed in Sections 8.2, 8.5, and 8.7.

Chapter 8: Ordinal Data Types

Now we have finished introducing procedural abstraction and have practiced top-down, hierarchical design, so we are free to wade through the syntax associated with all the ordinal data types. Section 8.3 presents a major case study (decimal-to-binary conversion) using integer data. The algorithm design involves careful specification of pre- and postconditions for all procedures and functions, together with specifications of the encapsulations in each and descriptions of the state transitions. (Pre- and postconditions were introduced in Section 5.4; encapsulation has been emphasized since Chapter 2.) The development of the Pascal code emphasizes incremental testing with a stubs and a driver, a concept that was introduced in Section 6.3. We also discuss how we know that a loop will necessarily terminate (a major topic of the optional Chapter 11). Section 8.5 works out a case study involving characters, functions, stubs, and an `IF..THEN..ELSE` structure. It also provides a set-up for the boolean expressions introduced in Sections 8.6 and 8.7. The case study on character-property functions (Section 8.7) is a further example of hierarchical design and the replacement of decision structures with boolean expressions. The chapter ends with a thorough explanation of operator precedence, involving all simple data types.

Chapter 9: Decision Structures Again

With the presentation of procedural abstraction complete, Chapters 9 and 10 cover decision structures (`IF..THEN..ELSE` and `CASE`) and repetition structures (`WHILE..DO`, `FOR..DO`, and `REPEAT..UNTIL`) in complete detail. (Simple forms of `IF..THEN..ELSE` and `WHILE..DO` were introduced in Chapter 6. The complete treatment takes 62 pages and would have distracted considerably from the presentation of procedural abstraction if introduced then.) Section 9.1 presents a second version of the `Sort3` procedure, using the nested procedure calls from Section 6.4 and now some new `IF..THEN..ELSE` syntax. Boolean expressions are used to replace `IF..THEN..ELSE` structures in Section 9.1, as they were in Section 8.7. Nested decisions are introduced in Section 9.2 because they are needed in the menu case study of Section 9.3. This case study in turn leads into a discussion of Pascal's `CASE` structure in Section 9.4, and this in turn leads to a need for guard loops, as introduced in Chapter 10.

Chapter 10: Repetition by Iteration

When `WHILE` loops are re-examined in Section 10.1, we can discuss their use of boolean expressions, which was not possible in Section 6.2. We then consider how to count characters in input, using a sentinel to control the loop. This case study involves the concept of the `Input` file and file buffer (Section 4.4) and uses a stub and driver in the testing of the code. Section 10.4 discusses counter-driven pretest loops, as a motivation for the `FOR` structure introduced in Section 10.5. The importance of top-down design comes up again. The `FOR` loop example in Section 10.6 involves ordinal values and character data. Section 10.7 presents a case study involving a Monte Carlo calculation, and is optional. The case study is our first example of using a pseudorandom number generator, a topic that comes up in several later programming projects and in Chapter 21. The `REPEAT..UNTIL` structures of Section 10.8 are applied to the problem of processing menu selections, completing some work that began in Section 9.3. Like Chapter 9, this one will be covered completely in most courses.

Instructors who wish to use text file I/O at this point can cover Sections 17.3–17.6 following Section 10.3. Chapter 17 has been designed to allow this option.

Chapter 11: Iteration by Design (Optional)

This is an optional chapter that introduces the rudiments of formal loop design, using loop invariants and termination conditions. A variety of case studies is provided to meet the needs of different instructors. One-quarter or one-semester courses will probably not have time to cover more than Section 11.1 and one of the other case studies.

Section 11.5 is distinct from the rest of the chapter. It shows how the running times of nested loops can be expressed as functions of loop parameters, and is intended as early preparation for those intending to cover big-oh notation in Section 19.3.

Don't try to cover too much in this chapter, and allow sufficient time for the material you do cover. The chapter applies mathematics in ways that will be new to many students, and the material will take time to assimilate. Instructors preferring to skip this chapter can do so without losing continuity.

Chapter 12: Repetition by Recursion (Optional)

Recursion takes a long time to sink in, so it is introduced in Chapter 12 and revisited frequently, with heavy use of animation diagrams like those used earlier for nested procedure calls. Iteration and recursion are treated as equally important techniques for repetition, and often, both recursive and iterative versions of an algorithm are examined.

Some instructors prefer to postpone this topic, but others (including me) prefer to present recursion and iteration side by side, for direct comparison. In presenting recursion, I emphasize repeatedly that there is nothing new here: A procedure is calling a procedure, as in previous chapters, but now the procedure being called happens to have the same name and to contain the same code as the caller. Working carefully through the execution snapshots (the "animations") of Section 12.1 and one of the case studies goes a long way toward dispelling the mystery that many students attach to this subject. As with the previous chapter, this one provides more material than any one instructor is likely to use, in order to allow flexibility and choice. In my one-quarter course, I usually skip Sections 12.4 and 12.6, but I make sure to mention that every loop can be rewritten recursively, and vice versa; and that some problems are more easily and clearly coded iteratively, while others are more easily and clearly coded recursively. I also always discuss comparative running times, as in Table 12.3.1 and Section 12.7.

Chapter 13: Programmer-Defined Types

Sections 13.1 and 13.2 must be covered before the next chapter, because subrange types are used for array indexes in Chapter 14. The material on enumerated types could be postponed, but why bother? Chapter 13 doesn't require much time in class, so I cover it by working out a couple of case studies.

Chapter 14: Arrays

This is a large chapter with several options. After one-dimensional arrays (Sections 14.1–14.3), many instructors like to discuss sorting, so Section 14.4 examines the selection sort algorithm. If the instructor wants to delve deeper into this subject, Chapter 19 can be covered next, providing complete discussions of sequential search, binary search, big-oh notation, insertion sort, and quicksort. Otherwise, the course can go on directly to the other topics in Chapter 14: string arrays, parallel arrays, multidimensional arrays. In my course, I usually cover most of Chapter 14 through examples worked out in class, leaving the complete treatment of searching and sorting for the next course.

Chapter 15: Records

The core issues in this chapter are presented in Sections 15.1-15.4, so shorter courses may want to skip Sections 15.5 and 15.6. If the goal is to cover some data abstraction at the end of the first quarter or semester, don't spend too much time on Chapter 15, but regard it as a preparation for the `Fraction` ADT in Section 16.2.

Chapter 16: Data Abstraction (Optional)

At this point, we enter the part of the book consisting of topics sometimes reserved for a second course or a second semester. Chapter 16 explains the central issues in the design and construction of abstract data types, and Sections 16.1 and 16.2 are prerequisite to material in Sections 18.4 (`Set` ADT), Chapter 20 (`List` ADT and `BinarySearchTree` ADT), and Chapter 21 (`Stack` and `Queue` ADTs).

Chapter 16 emphasizes the distinction between an ADT's interface and its implementation. Although Standard Pascal does not provide the tools to build a proper ADT, most commercial compilers do. Some general comments about this appear in Section 16.2, with detailed instructions for using units in Turbo and THINK Pascal provided in Appendix H. Instructors preferring to skip ADTs can skip Chapters 15, 20, and 21, and cover only the early sections of Chapter 18 and whatever portions of Chapter 17 and 19 they desire.

Chapter 17: Files (Optional)

There is considerable disagreement among instructors over when to introduce text file I/O. Some instructors want students to use text files as early as Chapter 4, while others save it until late in the CS1 course or even postpone it until the second course. In order to meet all needs, I have chosen to collect all file I/O material in Chapter 17, but to organize it in a three-level presentation. Sections 17.1 and 17.2 can be covered immediately after Sections 4.3 and 4.4, respectively, and Sections 17.3–17.6 can be covered right after Section 10.3, if desired.

Chapter 18: Sets (Optional)

Only the longer CS1 courses are likely to cover this chapter in depth, but enough material is provided here for two-semester courses. Note that Section 18.4 requires that Chapter 16 has been covered previously.

Chapter 19: Algorithms for Searching and Sorting (Optional)

This chapter is unusually complete, and provides enough material for both CS1 and CS2 courses; the instructor should choose from what is offered. The treatment of big-oh notation in Section 19.3 provides both a heuristic and a formal discussion to suit courses at different levels.

Chapter 20: Pointers and Dynamic Data Structures (Optional)

Much of this chapter will be saved for a second course, but Sections 20.1–20.3 are often covered in CS1, and some of Section 20.6. A complete coverage is provided to allow choice and to provide material for longer courses. Except for the first section, most of this chapter draws on the ADT concept introduced in Chapter 16.

Chapter 21: Stacks and Queues (Optional)

This is traditionally CS2 material, but is provided here for use in longer courses. Again, it uses the ADT concept introduced in Chapter 16.

Teaching Aids

Computer science is learned with hands on the machine, not while reading a book. Therefore a lab manual is available as a companion to this text. It provides detailed, hands-on instructions for using MS-DOS and Apple Macintosh operating systems and both Borland/Turbo and THINK Pascal systems. There are step-by-step guided lessons in debugging, and a number of guided case studies in problem solving and program design, including

- Dealing with roundoff error.
- Program animation.
- Experiments with integer, character, and boolean data and with parameters and control structures.
- Calendar programs.
- Testing loop invariants.
- Estimating the readability of text.
- Animating recursion.
- Making change.
- Cellular automata.

- Drawing Sierpinski curves (fractals).
- Simulating a Turing machine.
- Simulating a psychiatrist.
- Animating sorting.
- Building linked lists.

An instructor's manual is also available to interested teachers, containing

- Tips on teaching the course.
- Sample course outlines.
- Solutions to exercises and projects.
- Sample exam questions.

A bank of test questions is also available separately. The latter two items can be obtained by writing to the publisher on a school letterhead.

Sequencing of material

The diagrams on the next two pages show how *Structures and Abstractions* can be used in courses as short as one quarter or as long as two quarters.

Short Course

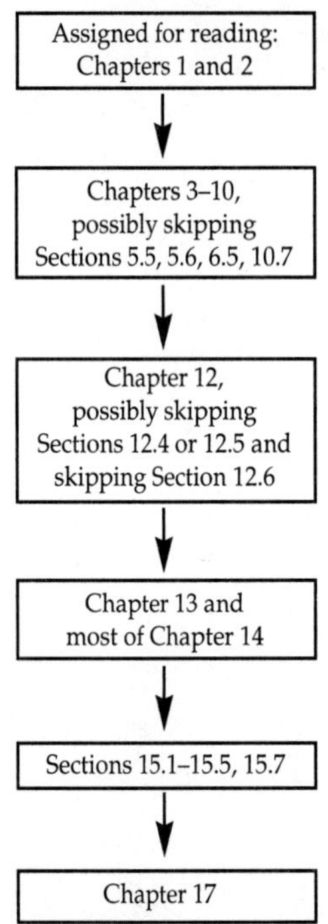

One Quarter or Semester

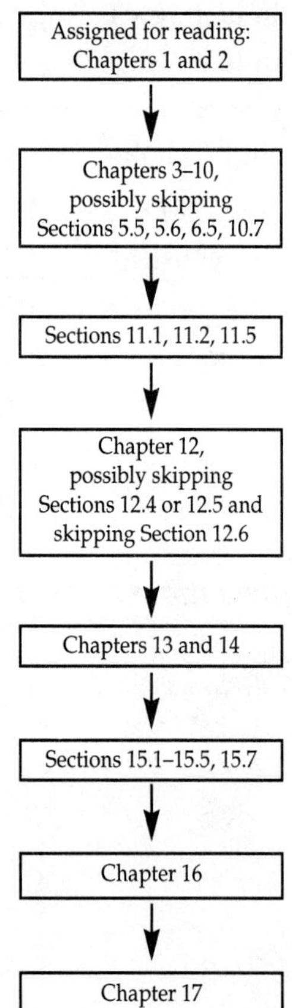

In two semesters, the entire book can be covered. For instructors who wish to change the sequencing of material, this diagram shows dependencies.

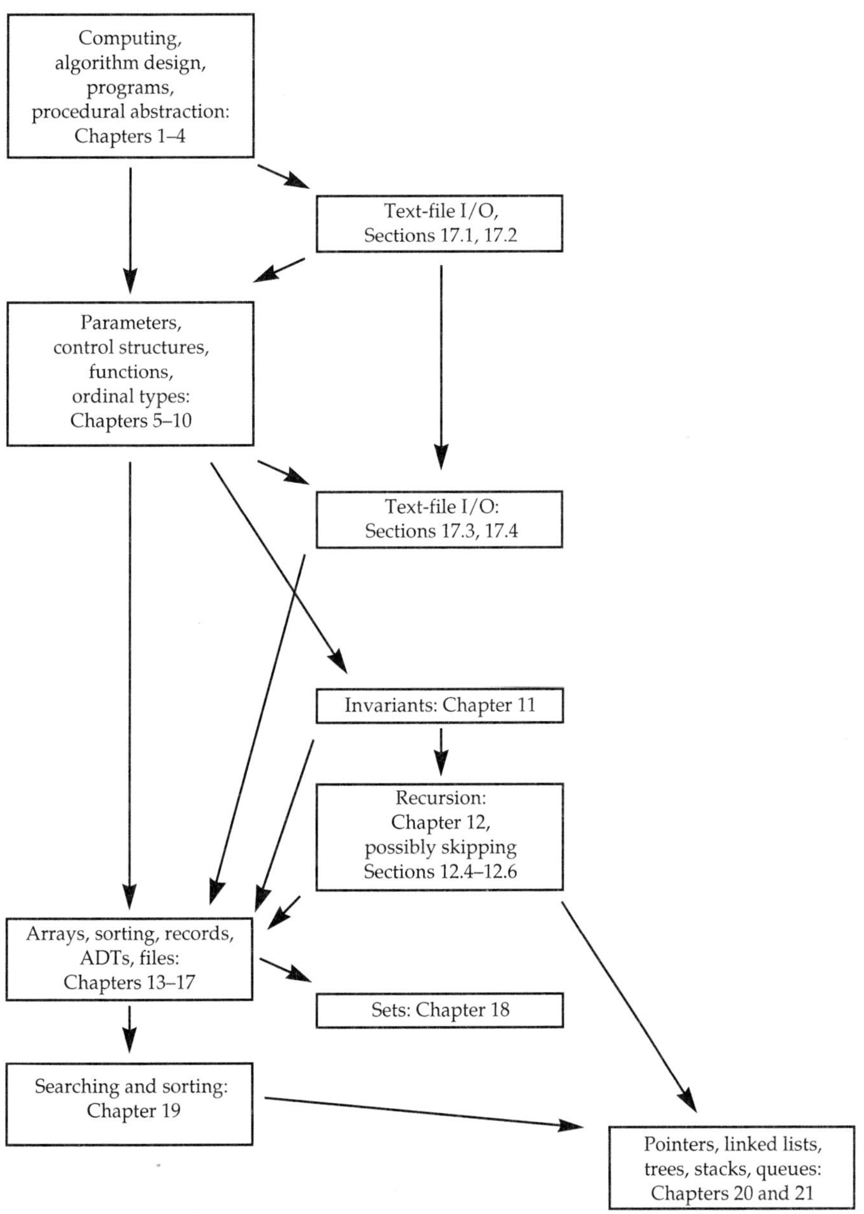

Acknowledgments

Chapter 1, pages 30–31, *The Turing Test for Machine Intelligence.* Excerpt from A. M. Turing, "Computing Machinery and Intelligence," *Mind,* October 1950, volume 59, pages 433–60. Reprinted by permission of Oxford University Press.

Chapter 2, page 52, *Plan to Throw One Away.* Quoted from Frederick P. Brooks, *The Mythical Man-Month: Essays on Software Engineering,* page 116. © 1975 by Addison-Wesley Publishing Company. Reprinted by permission.

Chapter 4, page 93, *Fatal Error: How Patriot Overlooked a Scud.* Quoted from Eliot Marshall, *SCIENCE,* March 13, 1992, page 1347. Copyright 1992 by the American Association for the Advancement of Science. Reprinted by permission.

Chapter 4, page 117, *The Effect of Computers on Structural Engineering.* Copyright © 1982, 1983, 1984, 1985 by Henry Petroski. From the book *To Engineer Is Human,* pages 193–95. Reprinted with permission from St. Martin's Press, Inc., New York.

Chapter 6, page 197, *Answers We Deserve to Get.* Quoted from Elting E. Morison, *Men, Machines, and Modern Times,* page 79. Copyright © 1966 by The MIT Press. Reprinted by permission.

Chapter 8, page 260, *Why Do People Write Programs?* Quoted from Frederick P. Brooks, *The Mythical Man-Month: Essays on Software Engineering,* pages 7–8. © 1975 by Addison-Wesley Publishing Company. Reprinted by permission.

Chapter 10, page 322, *Bumper-Sticker Computer Science.* Quoted from Jon Bentley, *More Programming Pearls,* pages 58–65. © 1988 by Addison-Wesley Publishing Company. Reprinted by permission.

Chapter 12, page 390, *Recursion in Everyday Life.* Excerpt from *Godel, Escher, Bach: An Eternal Golden Braid,* page 127, by Douglas R. Hofstadter. Copyright © 1979 by Basic Books, Inc. Reprinted by permission of BasicBooks, a division of HarperCollins Publishers Inc.

Chapter 14, page 469, *Minds, Brains, and Programs.* Quoted from John R. Searle, "Minds, Brains, and Programs," *The Behavioral and Brain Sciences,* volume 3. © 1980 Cambridge University Press. Reprinted by permission.

Chapter 16, page 553, *Software Design Is a Communications Craft.* Reprinted from *The Elements of Friendly Software Design, The New Edition,* pages 112–13, by Paul Heckel. By permission of SYBEX Inc. Copyright 1991 SYBEX, Inc. All rights reserved. Reprinted by permission.

Chapter 17, page 601, *Control Leads to Obligations.* Quoted from Edsger W. Dijkstra, *A Discipline of Programming,* ©1976, pages 209–210. Reprinted by permission of Prentice Hall, Englewood Cliffs, New Jersey.

Chapter 18, page 642, *The Artichoke Theory.* Quoted from Nolan Bushnell, *BYTE Magazine,* September, 1992, page 378. © by McGraw-Hill, Inc., New York. All rights reserved. Reprinted by permission.

Chapter 19, page 687, *Technology Is Burning the Social Fabric.* Quoted from Jacques Vallee, *The Network Revolution: Confessions of a Computer Scientist,* pages 84–85. © 1982 AND/OR Press. Reprinted by permission.

Chapter 20, page 751. Quoted from Guy L. Steele, Jr., Donald R. Woods, Raphael A. Finkel, Mark A. Crispin, Richard M. Stallman, and Geoffrey S. Goodfellow, *The Hacker's Dictionary,* pages 49– 50, 61, 75–76, 86. © 1983 Harper & Row. Reprinted by permission.

Contents

PART 1: COMPUTING AND PROBLEM SOLVING

PART 2: PROGRAM STRUCTURES AND DATA TYPES

PART 3: CONTROL STRUCTURES

PART 4: DATA STRUCTURES AND DATA ABSTRACTIONS

PART 5: ADVANCED TOPICS

APPENDIXES

PART ONE

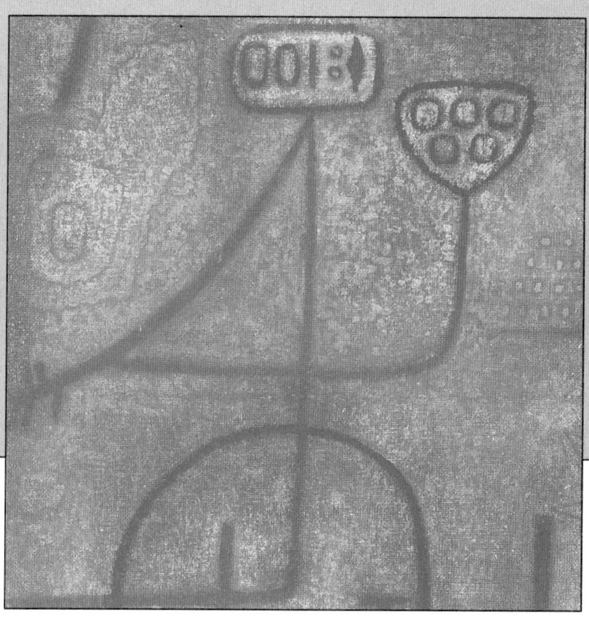

COMPUTING AND PROBLEM SOLVING

CHAPTER

1

Computers and Computation

CHAPTER CONTENTS

INTRODUCTION

We humans communicate by means of **symbols** to which we ascribe meanings. We use many kinds of symbols: characters, numbers, diagrams, icons, spoken words and music, facial expressions, gestures, clothing, and many others. Many of us work at jobs in which we deal all day with a flood of words, numbers, and statistics, a flood that is now so heavy that we need machines to deal with it. The most revolutionary of these machines is the computer.

Symbol: A mark or sign that stands for something else because humans ascribe a meaning.

Computer science is the study of the automation of symbol processing. This includes the design and construction of symbol-processing machines (**hardware**) and of the instructions that control the machines (**software**). Computing is still an infant science. We know how to design machines that are many times faster than those of a decade ago, and we know how to design **programs** to handle a much wider range of problems. Still, we are unable to solve many important data-processing problems. We seek better ways to design programs, better ways to represent data symbolically, better ways to design and control machines, and better ways to analyze performance and prove correctness. These areas of study involve mathematics, physical science, and engineering. They even involve psychology, philosophy, and linguistics, because we study the possibility of "artificial intelligence," develop theories of the nature of information, and seek more appropriate ways to control the complexity of the symbolic information we use.

Hardware: The physical parts of a computer system.

Software: The instructions that control a computer system, provided in the form of programs.

Program: A sequence of instructions provided to a computer.

This book will lay a foundation for your lifetime use of computers. The goals are to equip you with a fundamental understanding of modern computer systems, to help you learn to design programs to solve problems, and to help you appreciate the modes of thought used in the automation of symbol processing. We begin by examining how problems can be solved by devising step-by-step plans called algorithms.

In this chapter, we will:

- Explain what an algorithm is and and how it differs from a program.

- Describe the hardware and software components of a modern digital computer system.
- Show how bit patterns are used to symbolize various types of data.
- Explain the differences among machine languages, assembly languages, and high-level programming languages.
- Explain the steps involved in creating a computer program.

1.1 ALGORITHMS, MACHINES, AND PROGRAMS

The term **algorithm** comes from the name of the ninth-century Arabian mathematician, Mohammed ibn Musa Abu Djefar Al-Khwarizmi, who wrote an important treatise on arithmetic and algebra entitled *Kitab al-gebr we' l mukabala*—"Treatise on Calculation by Restoration and Balancing." The word *al-gebr*, from which the English *algebra* is derived, means *restoration*, and originally referred to Al-Khwarizmi's system of adding or subtracting the same number from both sides of an equation. In his book, Al-Khwarizmi presented the Hindu/Arabian system for decimal numbers, combined Hindu algebra with methods of proof from the ancient Greeks, and also described some routine processes for arithmetic and for solving quadratic equations. The work was eventually translated into Latin and was a major influence in converting European mathematics to the decimal number system, which became known as the Arabic system. (Previously, Europeans had used Roman numerals.) For many years, decimal arithmetic was known as *algorism*, meaning "the art of Al-Khwarizmi." Eventually, the term *algorithm* came to mean a routine process for computation.

Algorithm: A sequence of step-by-step instructions for performing some task, usually a computation.

Today we understand "algorithm" to mean a finite ordered sequence of precise, step-by-step instructions for performing some task. Many of the recipes and procedures in everyday life are algorithms in an informal sense. For example, if you ask me how to get to Charleston Street, and I say, "Go straight ahead to the first traffic light, turn left, go three blocks to Delancy Street, then turn right and go one mile," I have given you an algorithm to find Charleston Street.

The idea of an algorithm is to describe a process so precisely and so unambiguously that it becomes mechanical in the sense that it doesn't require much intelligence, so that it can be performed by rote or by a machine. Formally, an algorithm has at least three necessary qualities:

1. It must accomplish the task.
2. It must be clear and unambiguous.
3. It must define the sequence of steps needed for accomplishing the task. That is, it must specify the steps *in order*.

Finite: Limited in size; neither infinite nor infinitesimal.

Computer scientists usually also require that an algorithm be **finite** in the following two senses:

4. The number of steps must be finite. (That is, the algorithm must **terminate** eventually.)
5. Each step must require only finite time and finite computational resources.

Requirements 4 and 5 are needed to guarantee that the algorithm can be accomplished in finite time, with finite machinery. In human life, we do not have infinite patience, infinite time, or infinite computer hardware. Algorithms satisfying only conditions 1–3 are called *partial algorithms;* those satisfying conditions 4 and 5 as well are called *total algorithms.*

Examples of algorithms

The oldest known arithmetic algorithm was reported around 300 BC by Euclid (who may have gotten it from Eudorus), and is a method for computing the **greatest common divisor** (**GCD**) of two whole numbers. The greatest common divisor is the largest whole number that divides both numbers without remainders. If the two numbers are called A and B, Euclid's algorithm is

1. Compute the remainder of the division of A by B.
2. Replace A by B.
3. Replace B by the remainder computed in step 1.
4. Repeat steps 1 through 3 until B is zero.
5. The *gcd* is the final value of A.

As an example of how this works, consider finding the greatest common divisor of 24 and 9. To begin with, A is 24 and B is 9. Then

1. The remainder of (24 / 9) is 6.
2. A becomes 9.
3. B becomes 6.

Since B was not zero, we repeat steps 1–3 with the new values of A and B:

1′. The remainder of (9 / 6) is 3.

2′. A becomes 6.

3′. B becomes 3.

Since B was not zero, we repeat steps 1–3 with the new values of A and B:

1″. The remainder of (6 / 3) is 0.

2″. A becomes 3.

3″. B becomes 0.

Now B is zero, so the repetition ceases and the greatest common divisor of 24 and 9 is found to be 3.

It will be proven in Section 11.3 that this process always terminates, and that it always gives the correct answer. Thus the process is a total algorithm.

Since ancient times, many such algorithms have been developed to aid frequent calculations and to reduce the likelihood of error. Another famous algorithm is for computing the positive square root of a number, and dates back to perhaps 200 BC. If we seek the square root of N, the algorithm goes like this:

1. Make a rough estimate, $r > 0$, of the square root.
2. Replace r by the quantity $[\ r + (N\ /\ r\ )\ ]\ /\ 2$.
3. Repeat step 2 until r has stopped changing very much.

This algorithm differs from the first in that it doesn't automatically terminate. Instead, it terminates when "r has stopped changing very much," which will occur after a number of repetitions that depends on the initial estimate of r and the precision required. However, if the initial estimate is positive, the algorithm will take us closer and closer to the true square root, and rather rapidly, as it turns out. (This is discussed in detail in Section 11.4.)

Machines

As a natural outcome of the human desire for labor-saving devices, it didn't take long after the Renaissance for mathematicians to dream of machines that could carry out dreary mechanical computations. In addition, there was a real need to improve the reliability of number-crunching. Ships were the primary transporters of raw materials and manufactured goods between Europe and the rest of the world. Ocean travel required accurate navigation, however, which in turn required accurate numerical tables. These tables were computed by humans and were riddled with errors. As a result, ships often found themselves at the wrong places at the wrong times, and many lives and cargoes were lost. A major mathematical priority of the period from 1820 to 1940 was to develop better algorithms for computing numeric tables and to find a way to automate the process in order to reduce errors.

Another pressure in the same direction came from the bureaucratic need to gather and process social and financial data. In the United States, the 1880 census was performed largely by hand, and was barely completed before time for the next census. To prevent a census pileup, the government encouraged inventors to find a way to automate census-taking.

Surprisingly, the concept of automation goes back at least to the time of Homer (ca. 800 BC), who described in the *Iliad* how the gods' food was delivered on automatic "tea-carts" built by Hephaistos. From that time on, inventors have been intrigued by the idea that self-controlled mechanical systems might be used to perform tasks formerly requiring human or animal power. The weight-driven clock was the first automatic man-made device to have a major effect on history. Clocks made it possible to synchronize the activities of many people, allowing smooth intercity commerce, which led to widespread trade, which in turn led to European empire building.

Wind and water were harnessed to perform physical work, first in mills to grind grain, and then, by 1800, along with steam power, for the factories of the Industrial Revolution. The first programmed machine appeared in France in 1801, when Joseph-Marie Jacquard introduced an attachment for silk looms that used patterns of punched holes in steel cards to automatically control the pattern of weaving. This invention revolutionized the textile industry. A decade later, 11,000 Jacquard looms were in use in France, enabling France to outstrip England in textile production. Thousands of French weavers lost their jobs to the new machines, and Europeans had had their first taste of the social problems that can come with automation.

Shortly afterward in England, a mathematician named Charles Babbage sought a way to automate the calculation and printing of navigation tables. He dreamed of building a steam-powered, gear-driven calculating machine controlled by punched cards like those in Jacquard's looms. By 1840, Babbage was planning an "Analytical Engine" to be controlled by three sets of punched cards: one set to provide the data, another to provide instructions for manipulating the data, and a third for controlling storage of intermediate results. Together with Augusta Ada, Countess of Lovelace (1815–52), an amateur mathematician and the daughter of the poet, Lord Byron, Babbage conceived many of the fundamental ideas for modern computer algorithms. His machine was never built because its gearwork construction lay beyond the capabilities of Victorian engineering, but Babbage and Lady Lovelace had shown the way to the Information Age and a new understanding of the power of machines.

> *The analytic engine weaves algebraical patterns, just as the Jacquard loom weaves flowers and leaves.*
>
> —*Augusta Ada, Countess of Lovelace*

Programs

In their dreams of an Analytical Engine, Babbage and Lady Lovelace invented one of the deepest ideas of the Information Age. A computing machine processes data in the form of symbols. In doing this, it is controlled by instructions that make up its algorithm. But the instructions must be provided to the machine also, and they can be provided as sequences of symbols. All that was needed was a language for symbolizing the instructions, and the computing machine could be provided with a *programme*, as Babbage called it, for its activities.

Today we distinguish between an algorithm and a **program**. A program is an expression of an algorithm in a precise language that can be made understandable to a computing machine. The language itself is called a **programming language**.

Questions

1. What is the difference between an algorithm and a program?
2. Who coined the term *program*, as it is used today in programming? Who were the first two people to conceive of programming a machine to manipulate symbols?
3. Using dictionaries and other reference books available to you, define the term *science* as it applies to subjects like mathematical sciences, cognitive science, and computer science, as well as natural sciences like biology, geology, chemistry, and physics. In what ways does computer science differ from natural sciences? In what ways is computer science more nearly a branch of engineering?
4. Which of the following are algorithms? Explain your reasoning.
   a. A recipe for baking a cake.
   b. A code of ethics.
   c. The instructions for filling out an income tax form.
   d. The rules for base-10 multiplication, as they are taught in elementary school.
5. According to the text, is the square-root algorithm a *total* algorithm? Why or why not?
6. What kinds of symbols are commonly manipulated by computers? What kinds of symbols do *not* lend themselves to computer manipulation?
7. In the greatest-common-divisor algorithm, if the "*B* is not zero" test is eliminated, what error will result when the algorithm is carried out?

1.2 COMPUTER SYSTEMS

Programmable: Controlled by instructions that can be changed while the machine is running.

The modern digital computer is a general-purpose, **programmable**, symbol-manipulating machine. It can receive a set of symbols representing characters, numbers, pictures, sound, or some other kind of data, and receive a list of instructions describing operations to be performed on these symbols, and then **execute** (carry out) these instructions, producing (usually) new symbols from the old ones. The original symbols are called the **input** data, while the resulting ones are called the **output**. The list of instructions is called a program. This much gives us an **input/output (I/O)** model of computation, as shown in Figure 1.2.1.

The data are said to be **processed** by the computer, and the computer is referred to as a **data processor**. Many types of processing are possible, including reception, transmission, storage, and various transformations of the symbols. The symbols that come out need not be the same kind that went in. For example, sounds could go in and numbers come out; or numbers could go in and characters come out.

Digital versus analog computers

Analog: Smoothly variable; capable of continuous variations of physical state.

The first computing machines represented symbols by the rotational positions of gears or by continuously variable voltages in electrical circuits. Such machines were said to be **analog** devices, and they were a natural outcome of the desire to model the smoothly varying properties of physical systems. Early examples included astrolabes, orreries, and other astrological and astronomical devices, some of which date back more than 2,000 years. During the Renaissance, ingenious gearwork calculators were devised by mathematicians like Blaise Pascal (1623–62). By World War II, electronic analog computers were in use, solving differential equations and computing the values of integrals. But while analog computers nicely represent smoothly changing values, their disadvantage is that no value can be represented exactly because the physical state of such a machine cannot be made perfectly precise.

Digital: Assuming only distinct states, as opposed to a continuous range of states.

By 1950, the tide had turned in favor of **digital** electronic computers, in which symbols are represented by electronic circuitry allowing only a few (often two) distinct voltage states, and none in between. Digital computers allow faster computations, with a greater degree of precision. But they have the disadvantage that only a finite number of symbols can be represented exactly. Digital and analog signals are compared in Figure 1.2.2.

Central processing unit (CPU) and main memory

To process data, computers contain a **central processing unit (CPU)**, a complex electronic circuit that will, when instructed to, carry out primitive logical operations on symbols. Today a CPU may contain over a million transistors, packaged together in one

Figure 1.2.1 *Input/output model.*

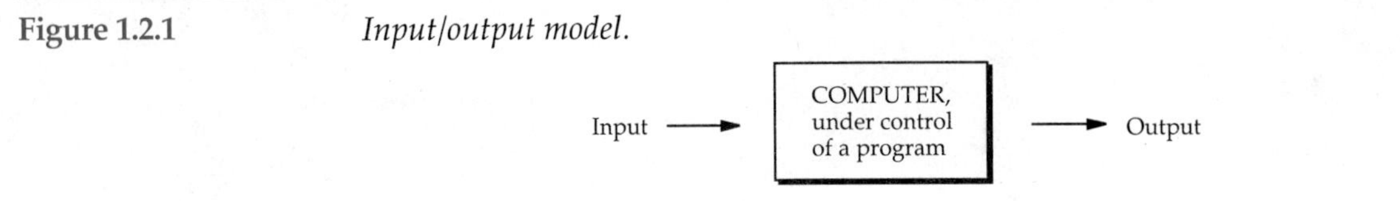

Analog signals are smoothly varying, while digital signals have only discrete values. **Figure 1.2.2**

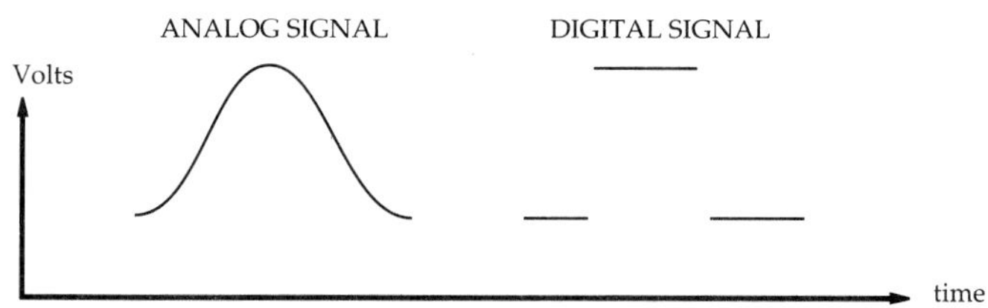

or more integrated-circuit chips (Figure 1.2.3). The design of better and faster CPUs is a continuing concern in computer science, as is the use of multiple CPUs in a single computer system. Although multiple CPUs are becoming more common, the programming language used in this book assumes only a single CPU, so that is what we will assume throughout the book.

A single CPU has a major limitation: *It can perform only one operation at a time*. Because of this, the computer system must also contain devices for storing input symbols, both data and instructions, until the CPU can use them, and for storing output symbols until the CPU signals for them to be transmitted to their final destinations. Temporary storage occurs in electronic circuits called **main memory** or **random-access memory (RAM)**. The data and instructions for a particular program are loaded into main memory. Then the CPU begins to execute the instructions one by one, operating on the data.

Main-memory circuits are made up of millions of transistors used as electronic switches, grouped in integrated circuit chips. At any particular moment, each transistor is either turned on or turned off, and the pattern of on/off voltages in the memory circuits is the computer hardware's way of representing stored data. Each on/off voltage is conceptually the smallest unit of stored data, and is called a **bit**. A group of eight bits is called a **byte**. A group of two or more bytes is often called a **word**; the size of a word depends on the computer system being used. The pattern of on/off voltages representing a datum is called a **bit pattern** (Figure 1.2.4). Thus we can speak of four-bit patterns, two-byte patterns, one-word patterns, and so on.

Bit: An on/off voltage.

Byte: Eight bits.

Word: Two or more bytes.

In most computers, main memory is erased if the computer system loses power. The main memory is said to be **volatile**. For this reason, data needed for more than one computing session must be stored elsewhere in the computer system. For this, computer systems usually provide a relatively large amount of **secondary memory** (also called

A microcomputer CPU on a single integrated circuit chip, with a dime for comparison. 
Figure 1.2.3

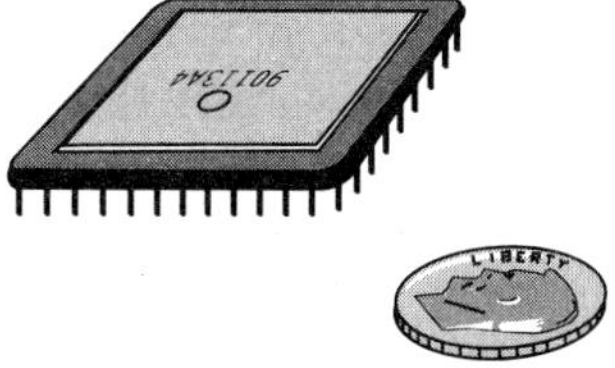

Figure 1.2.4 *A bit pattern is caused by switch settings in transistors, allowing a pattern of current flow in a group of wires. The pattern shown consists of eight bits, or one byte.*

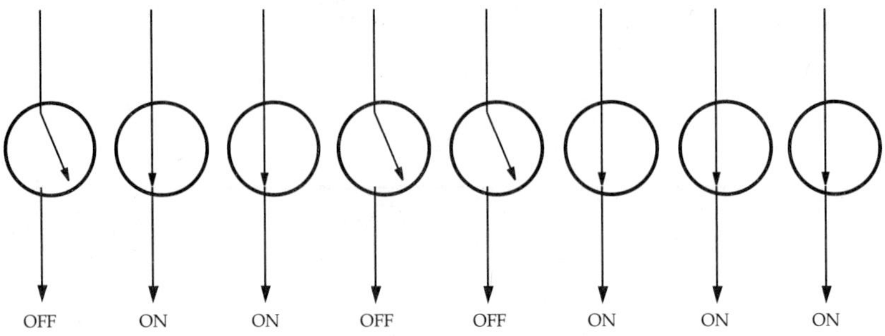

Nonvolatile storage: Storage that is not erased when power is turned off.

mass storage) that is **nonvolatile**. This usually takes the form of magnetic or optical disk storage, as described below.

There is also the little problem of how to turn the computer on. If a computer contains no instructions when it is first turned on, it will not know how to start up, or how to read programs from secondary storage. Therefore, every computer system contains some start-up programs permanently recorded in special nonvolatile electronic memory circuits called **read-only memory (ROM)**. The ROM circuits are contained in integrated-circuit chips on the main circuit boards, near the RAM chips.

Hardware components of a computer system

One of the reasons that so many people find it difficult to imagine how a computer works is that there are no moving parts in the circuitry of the CPU and main memory, so it is impossible to see the computations being done. Another is that computers come in wildly different configurations and look very different from each other. They all share certain key parts, however, so they can all be understood in the same way. It might help to show how the parts are connected.

Returning to our input/output model of the computer system, we first show the CPU in control of incoming data, outgoing data, and main memory. Incoming data are directed to main memory, from which the CPU fetches them for processing. Intermediate or final results are returned to main memory temporarily. When data are to be sent out of the computer for display, printing, communication, or permanent storage, the CPU directs them to be copied from main memory to the output channel. The CPU and main memory (and some other circuitry not shown here) comprise the computer proper (Figure 1.2.5).

Of course, the input data must come from somewhere. They come from devices that represent data as electrical signals that can be understood as bit patterns by the computer. Such input devices include keyboards, mice, trackballs, light pens, touch-sensitive screens, scanners, fax machines, modems, disk drives, and CD (compact disc) players.

Similarly, output data are sent to devices that display, speak, or print; to devices that transmit over communications lines; or to devices that record the data in some way. Common output devices include screens, printers, voice synthesizers, musical inter-

Figure 1.2.5

Input/output model of a computer, showing flow of data from input to main memory, from main memory to CPU, from CPU back to main memory, and from main memory to output.

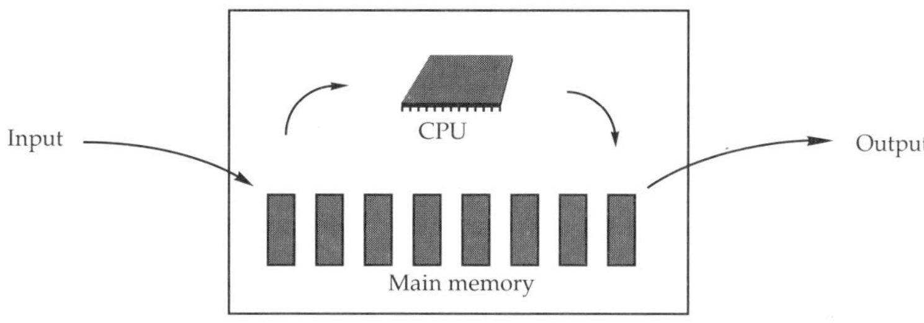

faces, modems, and disk drives (Figure 1.2.6). Notice that mass storage devices serve for both input and output.

These input and output devices lie outside the computer proper, and are called **peripheral devices** or **peripherals**. Of course, in many computer systems, some of the peripherals are packaged so intimately with the computer proper that they appear to be one unit. No matter how these parts are packaged, however, the computer system operates according to the input/output model described above.

Secondary storage

Most computer systems provide some kind of magnetic or optical medium for permanent storage of data and programs. Even the smallest computers commonly use the **floppy disk**, a thin, flexible disk of mylar plastic with a magnetizable coating of iron

Figure 1.2.6

A microcomputer system with a keyboard for input and a screen for output. In this computer, the CPU, RAM, and mass storage are all located in the box under the video monitor. The video monitor is the output device.

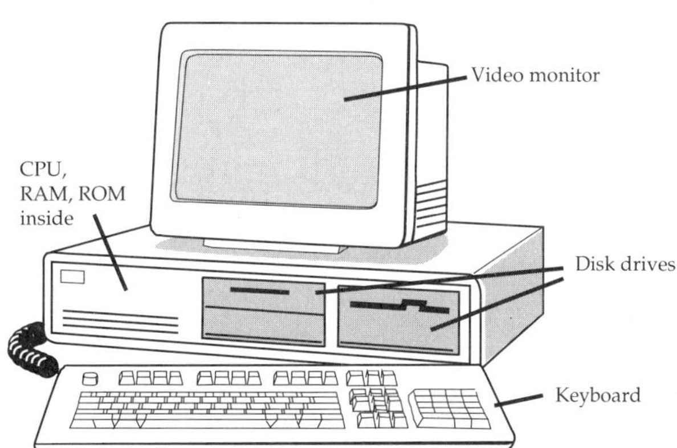

oxide. The delicate disk has a stiff or rigid cover for protection, and ranges in size from two to eight inches. It is used in a floppy **disk drive**, which can write bit patterns onto the disk or read them back. A floppy disk holds up to 1.5 million bytes of data and programs and can be easily carried from one machine to another.

Larger computer systems make heavy use of **hard disk** drives, which contain large-capacity rigid metal or glass disks with magnetic coatings. The advantages of such disks is that they hold 20 million to billions of bytes of data or programs, and can be read from and written to faster than floppy drives. The main disadvantages are that hard disk drives are expensive and the recording media are often not removable. A computer system with a nonremovable hard disk also requires a floppy drive or optical drive for efficient delivery of software.

Optical disks are now coming into widespread use. They are written and read more slowly than hard disks, but they are small and removable, yet offer enormous storage. So far, they have been used primarily for large-scale data and software distribution and to store duplicate copies of important data and programs.

Until recently, many computer systems used **magnetic tape** similar to that used for audio or video recording. The disadvantage of tape storage is that it is **sequential**: To reach a particular datum on a tape, the tape drive must read its way through all intervening data, or must fast-forward to the desired datum. This is much slower than finding data on a disk, which accesses data randomly, so tape storage is used today mostly for backup purposes.

In all of these secondary storage media, data and programs are stored as **disk files**—collections of bit patterns stored together under one filename. Each disk file is listed in a directory of files stored on the disk, and the operating system can quickly locate any file by name when you ask for it. This is the equivalent of conventional files stored in a filing cabinet, but the computer's version is much quicker and can store many times more information.

Hardware versus software

The *physical devices* described above—CPU, main memory, ROM, other electrical circuits, mass-storage devices and media, and peripherals—are called hardware. The instructions that control the hardware, and the data symbols that are manipulated by it, are called software. Up to this point in the book, we have talked mostly about hardware. The rest of the book is concerned mainly with the software. A **computer system**, of course, consists of both hardware and software because either is useless without the other.

Mainframes, minis, and micros

The physical size and configuration of a computer system depends very much on its intended uses. If a computer system is designed to serve hundreds of users simultaneously, it will necessarily contain a great deal of circuitry to handle the communications traffic. It will also need great computational speed, and may have multiple CPUs. Such machines are called **mainframes**, and commonly occupy an entire room, consume tens of thousands of watts of electrical power, and cost hundreds of thousands or even millions of dollars. Needless to say, such machines are used primarily for the most computationally intense applications, especially in organizations doing a great deal of computing.

At the other end of the scale, there are **microcomputers**, also called **personal**

computers or **PCs** (Figure 1.2.6). These are small, cost only hundreds or thousands of dollars, are usually designed to serve only one user at a time, and usually emphasize ease of use. The smallest of these are called **laptops** or **notebook computers**, and are integrated into portable units about 1.5 x 8.5 x 11 inches, weighing less than seven pounds. The most powerful microcomputers are often called **workstations**, and usually feature high-speed CPUs, graphics displays, and very large hard disks. Workstations, like most PCs, sit on desks and feature separate keyboards and monitors (screens). Microcomputers have replaced both typewriters and mainframes for many routine uses, and their uses continue to grow as their hardware speeds increase and as new kinds of software are developed for them.

In between the huge mainframes and the tiny microcomputers are the **minicomputers**. These share many of the mainframe's capabilities, but on a smaller scale. A minicomputer typically serves dozens of users simultaneously, costs on the order of $100,000, and takes up only a small room.

Most of the computers we use in everyday life, however, fall in none of these classes; in fact, they are completely invisible. These are the computers that run your car's ignition and fuel systems or keep its brakes from locking up, the computers that control the dishwasher or microwave oven, and the computers that keep an aircraft in stable flight. Such computers are called **embedded systems**. They are hard-wired into another device and dedicated to a specific task. More and more, our everyday activities and even our lives depend on the correct and speedy operations of such computers.

Computing today

In the 40 years since its first commercial use, computing has passed through several stages of development. First there was the age of the mainframe, in which computing customers submitted their data to professionals, who ran the programs for them. The professionals were like a breed apart—high priests of the machine—and they were the only ones who got to touch the "electronic brains," as computers were sometimes called in those days.

Then in the late 1970s came the age of the hobbyist microcomputer. Suddenly, microcomputers were available for a few thousand rather than a few million dollars and technical enthusiasts could afford machines of their own. During this period, the needed software often was homebrewed, and many microcomputer owners learned to program in simplified programming languages on machines with very little memory of any kind. During this period, the early, clumsy word-processing programs and crude screen graphics made people aware that computers might have many personal uses if they could be made easier to use.

Who needs to understand programming?

At the beginning of the 1980s, many computing professionals were predicting that powerful, friendly programs could be written for everyday use, and that these would make it unnecessary for most users to write their own programs. This period saw the rise of the first powerful business application programs—the word processors, spreadsheets, and database managers.

Today, we realize that every professional person needs to use computers. Most tasks can be done by wide-use commercial programs, but occasionally there is a need for a customized program. Sometimes, computer users write their own programs, but often,

Bug: An error or malfunction.

Debug: To correct an error or malfunction.

they need to hire professional programmers to do custom work. In either of these situations, users need to understand the nature of programming and the ways in which programs are designed, written, tested, and **debugged**. So programming as well as computing has become an important part of our culture, involving most professionals.

Computing tomorrow

Meanwhile, computer scientists are working to make computers more powerful, easier to use, and easier to program. By learning to divide tasks among many CPUs, we can build faster computers for applications that are hopelessly slow today. By studying user interfaces or human/computer interactions, we can make computer usage more intuitive. By studying algorithmic design and program construction, we can learn to make programming more productive and more dependable. By studying how people solve problems, we can learn to make programming languages more powerful and more natural to use. Little by little, we are approaching a day when programming as well as computer use will be an integral part of the professional workday. It will be a new literacy.

Questions

8. Explain the difference between analog and digital signals.

9. What do the acronyms I/O, RAM, CPU, and ROM stand for?

10. Which of the following are hardware, as opposed to software?

- **a.** Floppy disk.
- **b.** CPU.
- **c.** Program.
- **d.** Data.
- **e.** RAM.
- **f.** ROM.
- **g.** Bit patterns.
- **h.** Secondary storage.

11. Which of the following are digital signals, as opposed to analog signals?

- **a.** A bit.
- **b.** A sound wave.
- **c.** A whole number.
- **d.** A color.
- **e.** A traffic signal.

12. Which of these modern devices often contain computers? What are the computers used for?

- **a.** Cash registers.
- **b.** Typewriters.
- **c.** Sewing machines.
- **d.** Telephones.
- **e.** Televisions.
- **f.** Clocks.

1.3 DATA AND STORAGE

Today, we use computers to manipulate numbers, words, pictures, and even sounds. It isn't obvious at first sight how to represent all these kinds of data with two-way electrical signals like "on" and "off." Let's take a first look at some of the most common simple data types and how they are stored in a computer.

Integer data

It is clear that *on* and *off* can be interpreted as the binary digits 1 and 0, respectively, so that the one-byte pattern shown in Figure 1.2.4,

off on on off off on on on,

can be understood by humans as representing the binary number

```
01100111
```

which is the same as the decimal (working from the right) $2^0 + 2^1 + 2^2 + 2^5 + 2^6 = 1 + 2 + 4 + 32 + 64 = 103$. (Binary-decimal conversion is reviewed in Appendix J.) With an extension of this method of interpretation to allow for negative numbers as well as positive ones, we have a method for encoding **integer** data as bit patterns. The binary representation of integers was the first data storage representation used in modern digital computers, and the word *bit* was coined as a contraction of "binary digit."

When an integer is stored in four bytes, there are 32 bits to represent it, each of which can be either on or off. Thus there are $2^{32} = 4{,}294{,}967{,}296$ distinct bit patterns available for symbolizing integers. In other words, only a finite subset of the mathematical integers can be symbolized in the computer.

Obviously, some applications require a wide range of integer values, while other applications use a very narrow range. Typically, integer storage in the Pascal programming language occupies two or four bytes, as explained in Section 8.2 and Appendix K.

Character data

Today, computers are used more often for word processing than for number-crunching. If we want to store characters in the computer for word processing, we can establish a table of **character codes** in which each needed character is associated uniquely with a bit pattern. But how many characters will we need to represent? In English, there are 26 lowercase letters, 26 uppercase letters, the 10 numerals from 0 through 9, plus about 35 special characters used for punctuation and so on. This is almost 100 characters. In addition, there is a need for some special "control characters" that can be used to signal various events to a word-processing program or to the computer hardware. So we end up needing over 100 character codes altogether. Since six bits are capable of only $2^6 = 64$ different bit patterns, while seven bits are capable of $2^7 = 128$ patterns, we see that seven bits are the minimum needed to represent a reasonably complete set of characters in a computer's memory. Some character code systems use eight bits, to allow for more special characters, for graphics symbols, or for error checking. For this reason, computers normally allot one byte, or eight bits, of storage for each character. In Pascal, such storage is called **char** for short.

The standard American code of this sort (See Appendix C) uses only the rightmost seven bits of the byte, and includes the associations shown in Table 1.3.1.

Table 1.3.1 *Representing characters by bit patterns.*

Bit pattern								Character
off	on	on	off	on	off	off	off	**h**
off	on	on	off	off	on	on	on	**g**
off	on	on	off	off	on	on	off	**f**

When we are using this association, we interpret the bit pattern

off on on off off on on on,

which can also be written as

```
01100111
```

as representing the letter *g*. This is the same bit pattern we formerly interpreted as representing the integer 103. In other words, when we are doing text processing, the bit pattern has an entirely different meaning to humans than it does when we are doing arithmetic.

Computers don't interpret data.

But what about other kinds of data? If each "on" signal is understood to represent "yes" and each "off" represents "no," and a bit pattern is understood to represent a pizza, where pizza options are listed in the order

anchovies	green pepper	pineapple	sausage	mushrooms	pepperoni	onions	double cheese

then the same bit pattern shown earlier,

off on on off off on on on,

would represent a pizza with double cheese, onions, pepperoni, pineapple, and green pepper, but without mushrooms, sausage, or anchovies. Clearly, a bit pattern means whatever you, as a human, choose to make of it. *Computers know nothing of human interpretations.* They simply store bit patterns and process them according to the instructions they are given. If you give the computer the wrong bit pattern or the wrong instructions for manipulating it, the computer will merrily produce the wrong results. As programmers say, "Garbage in, garbage out."

Computer data are finite and discrete.

As you can see from the examples above, there are fundamental limitations on the kinds of symbols that can be stored as bit patterns. A data value is stored as a pattern of bits, each of which can be switched only two ways—on or off. There are only a finite number of bits in a computer. Therefore there are only a finite number of bit patterns available for representing data in the computer. It follows that *computer data can take on only a finite number of values*. This means that a digital computer cannot represent all of the points on a number line or number plane, or all the subtleties in a visual scene, or all the nuances in a musical chord.

Furthermore, the bit patterns are all distinct. If there is to be a one-to-one relationship between bit patterns and the symbols they represent, the symbols must be distinct too. We will not be able to store a continuous spread of values, but only a finite number of distinct values with separations in between. We say that *the data must be* **discrete**.

Floating-point numbers

As you can imagine, these properties of storage make it difficult to represent **real numbers** in the computer. After all, there are infinitely many real numbers between any two real numbers, and we simply cannot represent these in memory.

Still, we need to perform real-number arithmetic. In fact, in science, we need to use an extremely wide range of real numbers, from subatomic masses to astronomical distances. The best way to handle such a range in the computer is to store the numbers in a binary version **scientific notation**. As a simple example, suppose we want to store –1.75, which is – (1 + 1/2 + 1/4), represented in binary as –1.11 (Figure 1.3.1 and Appendix J). Rather than store this directly, the computer system first converts the number to binary scientific notation. Normalizing so that the highest nonzero bit is just to the right of the binary point, the number is rewritten as -0.111×2^1. The sign, the binary significand, and the power-of-2 exponent are stored individually:

–	.111	1
Sign	Significand	Exponent

The negative sign can be stored as a single "on" bit, followed by the significand and then the exponent, all in four bytes. If the exponent is given eight bits of its own, the whole bit pattern is

1	11100000000000000000000	00000001
sign	23-bit significand	8-bit exponent with sign

Regrouping bytewise from the left, we have 11110000 00000000 00000000 00000001.

Because scientific notation allows the position of the decimal point to "float," adjusting the exponent to compensate, storage that uses such notation is often called **floating-point** storage by programmers. In Pascal, it is called **Real** storage, and is described in more detail in Section 4.1 and Appendix K.

The binary number 1.11 means 1 + (1/2) + (1/4) or, in decimal, 1.75. **Figure 1.3.1**

2^0 2^{-1} 2^{-2}

↓ ↓ ↓

1 . 1 1

Problems with real-number storage

We have two important problems with real-number storage:

1. Because there are only a finite number of bits, only a finite number of distinct real-number values can be stored. This means that most of the infinitely many real numbers cannot be stored exactly, but must be rounded off to the nearest storable floating-point value. When this happens, there is **roundoff error** when the number is stored. As you will see in Section 4.2, roundoff errors can accumulate during a calculation to cause big trouble.
2. Because the stored values are discretely spaced in value, there will be a smallest nonzero magnitude that can be stored. If the computer attempts to store a positive number less than this, we have what is called an **underflow error** as the computer system either stores a zero (losing all significant figures in the result), or issues an error message, or both. Similarly, there will be an upper limit to the numbers that can be stored. If the computer calculates a result larger than this, the result will not be storable and we will have what is called an **overflow error**.

Memory cells

In order for a computer to find the individual data values stored in memory, there must be some way of knowing where one data value ends and the next begins. Computer memory is organized either into eight-bit *bytes*, or in larger machines, into groups of bytes called *words*. The number of bytes in a word depends on the machine; it is common to have 2-, 4-, 8-, or 12-byte words. But some data values will occupy more than one byte or word, while others will occupy as little as one bit, so it is not always easy to know where a given datum begins and ends in the bytes of memory.

Most programming languages allow for several predefined **types of data**. Integer, floating-point, and character data are the most common types. For data values of each of these types, the programming language provides a standard-sized chunk of memory, called a **memory cell**. For integer data, a two- or four-byte memory cell is often used. For real numbers, the memory cell is often four or eight bytes long. For a character, the cell is a single byte.

Precision

Sometimes, numeric data are required to be precise. That is, they are required to be accurate to many significant digits. For example, there was a time when the US National Debt was a mere $17,383,444,386,952.37. The Department of the Treasury had to know this figure right down to the exact penny, so the number had to be recorded with all 16 significant digits. Obviously, it takes a lot more bits of computer storage to store these digits than it does to store, say, the average pay of a college teacher.

The number of bits of storage devoted to a given data value is called its **precision**. Standard Pascal typically stores a real number in four bytes = 32 bits, of which 23 bits are typically devoted to storing the significand, or significant digits. Since it takes an average of 3.3 bits to store a decimal digit in the encoding scheme usually used, this means that Pascal typically stores about seven decimal digits of a real number, the rest being rounded off. For applications that require more precision than this, some Pascals provide a special **double-precision** data type with memory cells at least eight bytes wide.

Figure 1.3.2

An integer variable named Count, containing the value 1031; a character variable named FirstLetter, containing the value 'A'; and a real-number variable named Weight, containing the value 1031.0. The different types of variables have different widths and use different schemes for encoding the bit patterns.

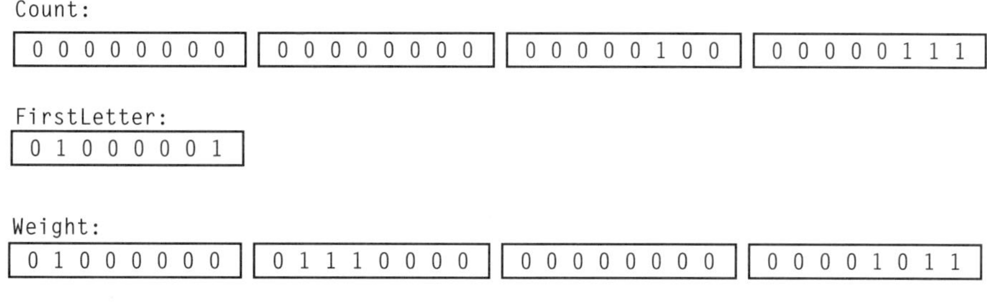

Variables

Variable: A named memory cell in which the stored value can be changed.

Programming languages usually allow you to *name* each memory cell. A named memory cell in which the stored value can be changed by the program is called a **variable**, in analogy to the variables in algebra (Figure 1.3.2). In programming, a variable is like a container for a bit pattern. When you store a value in the variable, you are storing that value's bit pattern in the named memory cell. The bit pattern you store replaces the previous bit pattern in the cell (Figure 1.3.3).

Figure 1.3.3

When a new bit pattern is stored in a variable, it replaces the bit pattern previously stored there.

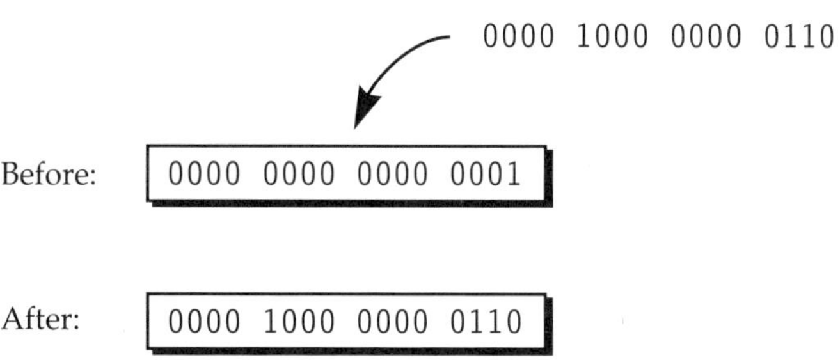

Exercises

13. How many distinct integer values can be encoded as binary bit patterns in memory cells of the following widths? (That is, how many distinct bit patterns can be displayed?)

   a. One bit.

   b. One byte.

   c. One 16-bit word.

   d. Two 16-bit words.

14. In a computer using the ASCII character code (Appendix C), what one-byte bit patterns would be used to store the following characters?

a.	s	**c.**	!	**e.**	9
b.	B	**d.**	line feed	**f.**	~

15. In your own words, what are "overflow error" and "underflow error"?

16. What nonnegative integers are represented by the two-byte binary bit patterns shown below?

```
0000 0010 1100 0101
0100 0000 0000 0000
0000 0000 1111 1111
0000 0001 0000 0000
```

17. What ASCII characters are stored as the following bit patterns?

```
0100 0101
0010 0001
0111 1111
0000 1110
```

18. In your own words, explain what is meant by "roundoff error."

19. The text asserts that it typically takes 3.3 bits to store each significant decimal digit of a floating-point number. Show that this is true. (Hint: Use the fact that the number of significant digits is equal to the base-10 logarithm of the significand.)

20. A portion of RAM, called video RAM, is reserved for storage of the screen image. Imagine that each pixel (each "dot") is represented in storage by four bits and that each bit pattern in the four bits represents a different brightness level in the corresponding pixel. Then how many "shades of gray" can a given pixel have?

1.4 PROGRAMS

A **program** is an algorithm written in a form that is understandable to a computer system. The problem is that a human-described algorithm is too abstract for a CPU to understand.

Program: An algorithm expressed in the unambiguous grammar and vocabulary of a language that can be made understandable to a computer.

Each CPU is designed to execute a very simple collection of instructions called its **primitive instruction set** or its **machine-language instruction set**. Such primitive instructions differ with the design of the CPU, but a typical set consists of the following classes of instructions:

- Copying data from one storage location to another, from the input port to main memory, from main memory to the output port, from main memory to the CPU, or from the CPU to main memory.
- Logical operations, in which two-bit patterns are combined by means of the AND, OR, XOR, NAND, or NOR operations of symbolic logic, or in which a single-bit pattern is inverted by the logical NOT operation.
- Arithmetic operations, in which bit patterns are added, subtracted, multiplied, divided, or compared for relative magnitude.
- Branching instructions, telling the CPU to execute an instruction at some stated point in the program.
- Bit-shift operations, in which the bits of a given bit pattern are shifted left or right or rotated.
- A halt instruction, telling the CPU to halt its execution of a program.

A CPU understands *only* instructions that are expressed on this primitive level, and is therefore unable to follow directly an ordinary human description of an algorithm. There are two things we can do when we want to give commands to a CPU: We can write our instructions directly in the machine language of the CPU, or we can write them in some other language that can be *translated* to the machine's language. Either way, the languages we use are called **programming languages**.

Programming language: A language in which algorithms can be expressed unambiguously in a form that can be made understandable to a computer.

Machine languages versus assembly languages

As already mentioned, a program, along with its data, is loaded into the computer's main memory in preparation for its execution. The data and the program instructions are both stored as bit patterns. This means that *the machine-language instructions obeyed by the CPU are themselves bit patterns.* If we use 1s and 0s to represent bits turned on and off, a typical machine-language instruction might look like this:

```
01000001 01101110 10001110 00001010
```

In the early days of digital computing, programmers actually wrote instructions in this form, and the bits were entered into the machine by plugging and unplugging wires in large panels that looked like telephone switchboards, or by flipping toggle switches. Needless to say, this was a tedious and error-prone task, so programmers soon invented a better way. They invented **assembly languages**, in which each machine-language instruction was symbolized by an easy-to-remember abbreviation called a *mnemonic* (from the Greek for "aid to memory"). In a typical assembly language, an instruction to add the integer in a memory location called X to the integer in a memory location called Y might look like this:

```
ADD X, Y
```

Assembler: A program that translates assembly language instructions into machine language.

An assembly-language program consisting of such mnemonics would then be submitted as data to a program called an **assembler**, which would then translate the mnemonics into machine language. The resulting machine-language instructions, called **machine code** or **object code**, would then be saved in secondary storage and/or executed directly.

The stored-program concept

At this point, we glimpse one of the subtle and deep points about modern computing. *Programs and data are both represented in the computer by symbols, so both can be stored as bit patterns. But if programs are stored like data, they can be treated like data when it is appropriate to do so.* Thus a program, which is just a sequence of symbols, can be acted upon by another program for the purpose of translation or other processing, as we have just seen. Computers can help to create their own programs.

This concept was developed at the Moore School of Electrical Engineering of the University of Pennsylvania between 1943 and 1945, by a team including J. Presper Eckert, John Mauchly, and John von Neumann. Von Neumann, who was one of this century's greatest mathematicians, first described the idea in print in 1945, and to this day, computers that conform to the input/output model, single-CPU, stored-program design are called **von Neumann machines**. Today, computer science is investigating more advanced machines with multiple CPUs that can act in tandem to perform *parallel operations* on data. But most programming in the real world still conforms to the von Neumann model of computation, so that is the one we will emphasize in this text.

High-level languages

By the mid-1950s, some programmers were urging the need for **high-level programming languages** that would allow algorithms to be described more nearly as humans think about them. Within a few years, the FORTRAN (FORmula TRANslation) language had been invented for scientific programming and the COBOL (COmmon Business Oriented Language) had been invented for business programming. These became popular in the 1960s as programmers realized that a program called a **compiler** could translate high-level programs written in these languages into machine-level code that would execute nearly as fast as hand-written machine code. It was found too that high-level code in FORTRAN or COBOL could be written more quickly than machine-level or assembly code, and with fewer errors. This point is extremely important. Without high-level languages, it would be prohibitively difficult to write and debug many of today's complex programs.

Compiler: A program that translates high-level language instructions into a lower-level language, usually machine language.

As it became easier to write large, complex programs, new problems were encountered. A large, complex program was hard to understand and therefore hard to write correctly. Many such programs were being used in critical applications—air-traffic control, spacecraft, defense systems—in which people's very lives depended on the correctness of the programs. By the 1960s, program correctness was an issue of great concern, and computer scientists sought new programming language features that would aid correct programming. One of the first new high-level languages to exploit such features was named after the French mathematician, Blaise Pascal, who designed a mechanical calculator about 1644. The **Pascal language** was designed about 1970 by Niklaus Wirth, a Swiss computer scientist. It was intended to be a small, easily learned language, with features for data organization and algorithmic design that would encourage clear, correct programming. It was not intended to be the final word in professional programming languages, but a teaching language that would lead to experimentation and further development along the lines of clarity and correctness. Its features were constrained by Wirth's demands that the language be simple and easily compiled, that the compiler should clearly indicate grammatical errors in the program it is translating, and that the compiled programs run efficiently (with good speed and efficient use of memory). Pascal has proven so effective in all these ways that it has spread to the world of professional software development. But more importantly, it has spawned a generation of new languages in which clarity and correctness are more easily attained. (A good example is the new US Department of Defense language, named Ada, after Lady Lovelace.) Whatever programming languages you might use in the future, you can be sure that experience with Pascal will be a good foundation.

Pascal: A relatively simple high-level programming language designed by Niklaus Wirth about 1970 for instruction in computer science.

The operating system

By now you can appreciate that hardware without software is useless. Of course, you want your own custom programs for your own special tasks. But to create your own programs, you need a text-processing program called an **editor**. To translate your programs to machine language, you need another program called a *compiler*. And in fact, to run all the hardware devices and to provide an interactive environment in which you can give commands to the machinery, you need a large set of programs called the **operating system** (or OS).

Operating system (OS): The large set of programs that controls the hardware of a computer system, providing an interactive environment in which the user can give commands.

If you think of your hardware system as a collection of technical resources for computing, then the operating system is your resource manager. The operating system supplies the instructions to keep the various hardware components operating in synchrony and concert. It provides a more or less conversational environment in which you can use an input device to give commands, and the system will reply on some output device. It provides special programs to facilitate the various activities involved in creating programs and recording data. It manages the data files in mass storage. It provides an environment in which you can run and test your programs.

An operating system for a large, multiuser computer system is necessarily more complicated. Ideally, such a system must give each user the illusion of being alone on the machine. It does this by **timesharing**: The operating system services the needs of one user for a moment, then, in the fraction of a second while that user is reading the screen, or in the fraction of a second between keystrokes, the operating system runs a task for another user. If there are multiple CPUs in the machine, the operating system may divide them up among various users. If the operating system and the hardware are well designed, the illusion of single use may be quite good.

How is the operating system loaded into memory?

When a computer system is turned on, the computer hardware "wakes up" with only the software that is wired into special memory circuits called read-only memory (ROM). Usually, these relatively few instructions serve only to generate an initial screen display and to command that the computer copy the rest of the operating system from a disk drive. By this means, using the ROM and then a disk drive, the computer system "pulls itself up by its bootstraps." We say that the system **boots** itself.

1.5 EDIT, COMPILE, LINK, AND EXECUTE

Editor: A text-processing program that lets you key in, modify, and save the texts of your programs.

A Pascal program consists of text created by means of a simple text-processing program called an **editor**. The editor allows text to be entered into main memory from the keyboard or from a disk file, and then allows deletions, insertions, and changes to be made. When the program is satisfactory, the programmer commands the editor to copy the text from main memory into a disk file. This is called **saving** the text.

Here, for example, is a really short Pascal program. It is named `Simple` and uses the standard `Output` device, which is usually the screen. Its purpose is to write a line of text on the screen, a task that is performed by a `WriteLn` instruction:

```
PROGRAM Simple ( Output );
BEGIN

   WriteLn( 'Does this really work?' )

END.
```

It would be good practice to run the editor on your computer system and enter this program from the keyboard. Don't worry about why the program looks as it does; just key it in as it is shown, being very careful to *get the spellings, spaces, and punctuation exactly the same as shown*. When you are satisfied that your program is correct, give the command to make your editor save the text in a disk file. The editor will require a filename and may also require an extension to the filename. For example, on many systems, it might be appropriate to name the file `PROG1.PAS`, where `.PAS` is called a *filename extension*, and is used to indicate that the file contains a Pascal program. (On UNIX systems, it would be appropriate to name the file `prog1.p`, in lowercase.) Check your local reference manual for details on your system. When you have saved your Pascal program, **quit** the editor (that is, stop its execution) and return to the operating system.

Compiling your Pascal program

Source code: Instructions written in a higher-level language.

Object code: The lower-level instructions, usually in machine language, resulting from the compilation of source code.

Your Pascal program cannot be executed directly because the CPU does not understand Pascal instructions. First the Pascal must be translated into the CPU's machine language. To do this, you run the Pascal *compiler* program, telling it the name of the file containing your Pascal text, which is called the **source code**. If the compiler succeeds in translating your program, it will save the resulting machine-language version, called the *object code*, in another file (Figure 1.5.1). Again, the details will depend upon your computer system and compiler, so check your reference manual for local details.

If your Pascal program contained typographic errors, the compiler will display their locations, together with more or less informative **error messages**. For example, if you

Figure 1.5.1 *The compiler translates source code into object code.*

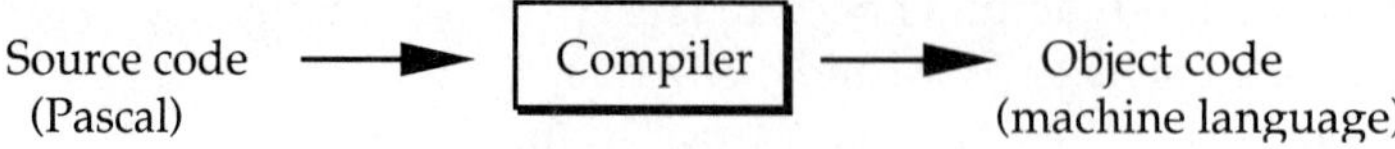

forgot the period at the end of the program, you might see a marker and message like this:

```
END
   ^
Period required following last END of file.
```

If there are any errors, you will have to run the editor again, to correct your source code. Then save the corrected code, quit the editor, and run the compiler again. When the program is **syntactically** correct, the compiler will perform the translation and save your object code in another file.

Syntax: The vocabulary and grammar of a language.

Compiling is a complicated process. The compiler translates each Pascal instruction into a sequence of primitive machine-language instructions that can be understood by the CPU. Some compilers do this by first translating the Pascal into assembly-language instructions, and then translating each assembly-language instruction into the corresponding machine-language instruction. It helps to have a mental picture of the process like the one shown in Figure 1.5.2.

Figure 1.5.2

Pascal must be translated to machine language before it can be executed by the computer. The translation is performed by a compiler or, in some systems, by a compiler followed by an assembler. A typical Pascal instruction translates into several assembly language or machine-language instructions, as shown in this example.

Pascal instruction:

```
WriteLn( 'Does this really work?' )
```

Translated to assembly language by compiler

Assembly-language instructions:

```
PEA  SIMPLE + 0032
JSR  -$3104
PEA +$002A
CLR  -(A7)
.
.
.
```

Translated to machine language by compiler or assembler

Machine-language instructions:

```
01100111 11000011 10100000 00100000
10010001 11001110 00110001 00000100
01100111 11000011 00000000 00101010
01110111 10100111 10100111 01111111
.
.
.
```

Figure 1.5.3 *The linker combines your program's object code with the object codes for any library procedures or functions used by your program, producing a complete machine-language program that can be executed by the CPU.*

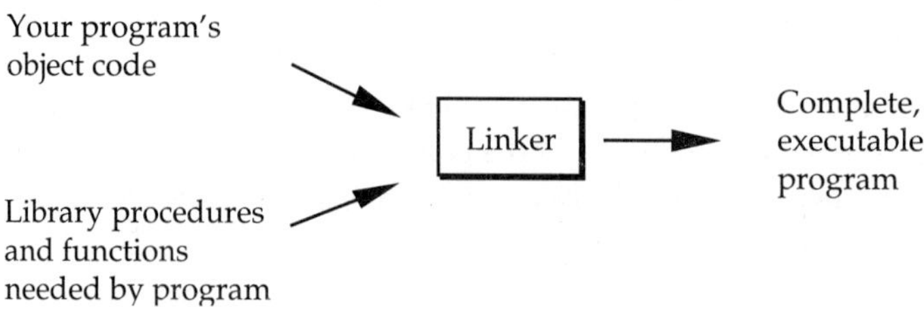

Wait! You still have to link the object code.

The compiled object code is still incomplete. It contains the machine-level translations of the Pascal instructions you wrote, but does not contain the machine code for any standard procedures or functions you used. In the example above, our only instruction is to invoke a standard procedure called `WriteLn`, which "writes a line" of text on the screen. The machine code for the `WriteLn` procedure is found within a disk file called the Pascal Library. By running a program called the **linker**, telling it to **link** your object code, you are hooking up your machine code to some of the library code to create a complete program. The linker saves the result in yet another file. It is this last file that is **executable** by the CPU—that is, it can be executed by the CPU. See Figure 1.5.3.

In some systems, the linker is run automatically and therefore seems invisible. In other systems, you must give a command to run it. Check your reference manual to see how this works on your system.

Now you can run your program

After linking, you can **execute** your program. How you do this will, of course, depend upon your computer system. Give the command to run the program saved by the linker, and your program should run, displaying the message

```
Does this really work?
```

Hopefully, it did work. If so, congratulations. You've just created your first Pascal program!

Batch versus interactive processing

In some computer systems, particularly large multiuser systems, a program and its data are prepared ahead of time and then presented to the system for automatic compilation, linking, and execution at some later time, when the user is usually not present. This mode of operation is called **batch processing**, and was standard operating procedure in the days when programs were punched into cards. (In those days, programmers "wrote" their programs on a separate machine called a card punch, then gave the deck of cards to computer center personnel for compilation and execution.) Batch processing is still used on heavily loaded large computer systems when runs need to be prioritized, or where some runs will use a large percentage of the hardware resources. Because a batch run cannot "talk" back and forth with its user, its program must be written so that all input and output (I/O) can be performed without human intervention.

By contrast, the arrival of personal computing has brought us an era of **interactive processing**, in which the computer user or programmer talks directly with the machine, controlling editing, compilation, linking, and execution as they happen. In this book, the emphasis is on interactive processing except in a few cases in which programs need to read large collections of preassembled data.

LOOKING BACK

The modern digital computer is a programmable symbol-processing machine, transforming its input symbols to produce output symbols. In this book, we imagine the computer to have one central processing unit (CPU) and a main memory. Both data and programs are stored as bit patterns in main memory. Peripheral to the computer proper, we imagine secondary storage and input/output (I/O) devices. A stored-program computer of this kind, with a single CPU, is called a von Neumann machine.

The symbols to be processed must be finite and discrete. Such symbols are stored as bit patterns in the computer's main memory, where they are not interpreted by the computer. That is, the computer has no idea what a given bit pattern means; it merely processes the bit pattern according to instructions it has received.

To control the machine, we design *algorithms*, which are clear, unambiguous, step-by-step instructions for performing computational tasks. After designing an algorithm, we express it in the vocabulary and grammar of a *programming language*. This expression of the algorithm, called a *program*, can be translated automatically by another program, called a *compiler*, into the machine language of the CPU. A third program called a *linker* then "hooks up" the object code produced by the compiler to machine code from the language library, to produce an executable program. This is saved in a disk file for later execution.

Modern computer software and hardware are the most complex systems ever designed by humans—so complex, in fact, that they constantly stretch our abilities to manage their complexities. Computer scientists are trying to develop methods for software engineering that will help us design programs that are easily understood, easily maintained, and provably correct. We have a long way to go, but modern techniques do lead to more useful and more dependable programs. This book emphasizes such techniques.

One of the primary techniques for dealing with complexity is one that we use in everyday life: abstraction. We practice procedural abstraction when we give a name to a procedure and think of it as a single event, without for the moment considering its encapsulated details. We practice object abstraction when we consider an object as a whole, understanding it in terms of the processes it can undergo, without for the moment considering the internal construction of the object or the internal details of its processes. These two kinds of abstraction will be practiced throughout this book, as we deal with the complexities of computer software.

TERMS EMPHASIZED IN THIS CHAPTER

Algorithm 4–6
Analog 8
Assembler 22
Assembly language 21–22
Batch processing 26
Binary 15
Bit 9, 15
Bit pattern 9–10, 15–20
Boot 23
Bug 14
Byte 9
Central processing unit (CPU) 8
Character code 16
Character data 15–16
Compiler 22–24
Computer science 3
Computer system 12
Data 15–20
Debug 14
Digital 8
Discrete 17
Disk file 12
Editor 24
Embedded systems 13
Error message 24–25
Euclid's algorithm 5
Executable 26
Execute 8, 26
Exponent 17
File 12
Filename 12, 24
Finite 4, 16–17
Floppy disk 11–12
Greatest common divisor (GCD) 5
Hard disk 12
Hardware 3, 12
High-level language 22
Input 8, 10–11
Integer data 15
Interactive processing 27
I/O (input/output) 8
Laptop 13
Linker 26
Machine code 22
Machine language 21, 25
Magnetic tape 12
Mainframe 12
Main memory 9
Mass storage 9–10
Memory cells 18–19
Microcomputer 12–13
Minicomputer 13
Nonvolatile memory 10
Notebook computer 13
Object code 22, 24
Operating system 23
Optical disk 12
Output 8, 10–11
Overflow error 18
Parallel operations 22
Partial algorithm 5
Pascal language 22–23
Peripheral device 11
Personal computer (PC) 13
Precision 18
Primitive instruction set 21
Processing 8
Program 3, 7, 21
Programmable 8
Programming language 7, 21
Quitting 24
Random-access memory (RAM) 9
Read-only memory (ROM) 10
Real numbers 17–18
Roundoff error 18
Saving 24
Scientific notation 17
Secondary memory 9
Sequential 12
Significand 17
Software 3, 12
Source code 24
Symbol 3
Terminate 4
Timesharing 23
Total algorithm 5
Types of data 18
Underflow error 18
User interface 23
Variable 19
Volatile 9
Von Neumann machine 22
Word 9, 18
Workstation 13

PROJECTS

1. Answer the following questions about your Pascal system:
   a. Are you using a microcomputer, mainframe, or mini?
   b. Does your system run in interactive or batch mode?
   c. How do you invoke the editor?
   d. How do you invoke the Pascal compiler?
   e. How do you invoke the linker (or is it automatic)?
   f. How do you execute a program after it is compiled and linked?
2. Which of the following are software?
   a. CPU.
   b. Editor.
   c. Compiler.
   d. Main memory.
   e. Peripheral.
   f. Bit pattern.
   g. Operating system.
   h. Hard disk.
   i. Program.
   j. Floppy disk.
3. What are the differences among high-level programming languages, assembly languages, and machine languages?
4. What are the functions of the editor, compiler, and linker programs?
5. What is a von Neumann computer?
6. What is the difference between batch-mode and interactive-mode computing?
7. What is an operating system?
8. As explained in the text, three disk files are saved along the route from source code to machine-executable code. What are these three files, and what are the differences among them?
9. Look up Charles Babbage in the library, and write a paragraph describing the differences between modern digital computers and his plan for the Analytical Engine. In what ways were the machines similar? What contributions were made to the concept by Augusta Ada, Countess of Lovelace?
10. Look up some information on the history of digital computers between 1940 and 1950, and write a page explaining the contributions of Alan Turing, John Atanasoff, J. Presper Eckert, John Mauchly, and John von Neumann to the design of the modern computer system.
11. Edit, compile, link, and execute the sample program from this chapter on your system. Turn in a paper *listing* of your source code along with a *screen dump* (a paper copy of the screen) after execution if this is possible on your system.
12. Consider making a telephone call as an example of procedural abstraction. Describe the procedural details encapsulated in the abstraction of a "phone call."
13. We often refer to "making change" as though it were a simple procedure. In fact, there are fairly many steps in calculating the change to give a customer. Describe the steps encapsulated in the procedure of "making change" when given $1 for a purchase costing no more than 99 cents.

14. Describe a push-button ballpoint pen as an example of object abstraction. That is, describe it as an object to be used, listing the procedures involved in using it, but ignoring the internal constructional details of the pen and the details encapsulated in the procedures for using it.

15. Describe a television set as an example of object abstraction. That is, describe it as an object to be used, listing the procedures involved in using it, but ignoring the internal constructional details of the device and the details encapsulated in the procedures for using it.

16. Considering a television set as an abstract object, give a definition of the object itself, together with a list of the procedures involved in using the object. Describe in detail the encapsulated algorithm for one of the procedures.

17. Considering a bank checkbook as a data abstraction, give a definition of the data object itself, together with a list of the procedures involved in using the object. Describe in detail the encapsulated algorithm for one of the procedures.

18. Considering a telephone book as a data abstraction, give a definition of the data object itself, together with a list of the procedures involved in using the object. Describe in detail the encapsulated algorithm for one of the procedures.

19. List ten devices you encounter every day that contain *embedded computer systems*.

REFERENCES

An engaging and readable discussion of the nature of computing and the design of algorithms can be found in David Harel's book *Algorithmics: The Spirit of Computing* (Addison-Wesley Publishing, 1987) and the abridged edition, which is called *The Science of Computing* (Addison-Wesley Publishing, 1989). Much of the material in these books bears on topics examined in this text, from a different point of view. A broader historical and philosophical perspective is provided by *Turing's Man* by J. David Bolter (University of North Carolina Press, 1984).

A brief explanation of the thinking behind the Pascal programming language can be found in Niklaus Wirth, "An Assessment of the Programming Language Pascal," *Proceedings of the International Conference on Reliable Software*, April 21–23, 1975, pages 23–30. This article was reprinted in the book, *Comparing and Assessing Programming Languages*, edited by Alan Feuer and Narain Gehani (Prentice Hall, 1984). The latter book also provides critiques of Pascal by other authors and comparisons with the C and Ada languages.

The Turing Test for Machine Intelligence

I propose to consider the question "Can machines think?" . . . Instead of attempting [to answer the question directly] I shall replace the question by another, which is closely related to it and is expressed in relatively unambiguous words.

The new form of the problem can be described in terms of a game which we call the "imitation game." It is played with three people, a man (A), a woman (B), and an interrogator (C) who may be of either sex. The interrogator stays in a room apart from the other two. The object of the game for the interrogator is to determine which of the other two is the man and which is the woman. He knows them by labels X and Y, and at the end of the game he says either "X is A and Y is B" or "X is B and Y is A." The interrogator is allowed to put questions to A and B thus:

C: Will X please tell me the length of his or her hair?

Now suppose X is actually A, then A must answer. It is A's object in the game to try to cause C to make the wrong identification. His answer might therefore be

"My hair is shingled, and the longest strands are about nine inches long."

In order that tones of voice may not help the interrogator the answers should be written, or better still, typewritten. The ideal arrangement is to have a teleprinter communicating between the two rooms. Alternatively the question and answers can be repeated by an intermediary. The object of the game for the third player (B) is to help the interrogator. The best strategy for her is probably to give truthful answers. She can add such things as "I am the woman, don't listen to him!" to her answers, but it will avail nothing as the man can make similar remarks.

We now ask the question, "*What will happen when a machine takes the part of A in this game?*" Will the interrogator decide wrongly as often when the game is played like this as he does when the game is played between a man and a woman? These questions replace our original, "Can machines think?"

. . . The new problem has the advantage of drawing a fairly sharp line between the physical and the intellectual capacities of a man . . . . The form in which we have set the problem reflects this fact in the condition which prevents the interrogator from seeing or touching the other competitors, or hearing their voices. Some other advantages of the proposed criterion may be shown up by specimen questions and answers. Thus:

Q: Please write me a sonnet on the subject of the Forth Bridge.
A: Count me out on this one. I never could write poetry.
Q: Add 34957 to 70764.
A: (Pause about 30 seconds and then give as answer) 105621.
Q: Do you play chess?
A: Yes.
Q: I have K at my K1, and no other pieces. You have only K at K6 and R at R1.
It is your move. What do you play?
A: (After a pause of 15 seconds) R–R8 mate.

. . . I believe that in about fifty years' time it will be possible to programme computers, with a storage capacity of about 10^9 [bits], to make them play the imitation game so well that an average interrogator will not have more than 70 per cent chance of making the right identification after five minutes of questioning. The original question, "Can machines think?" I believe to be too meaningless to deserve discussion. Nevertheless I believe that at the end of the century the use of words and general educated opinion will have altered so much that one will be able to speak of machines thinking without expecting to be contradicted.

–A.M. Turing, "Computing Machinery and Intelligence," *Mind* 59, October 1950, pages 433–60. Reprinted in Douglas R. Hofstadter and Daniel C. Dennett, *The Mind's I: Fantasies and Reflections on Self and Soul* (Basic Books, 1981), pages 53-57.

[A reply to this line of thought is given by John R. Searle at the end of Chapter 14.]

CHAPTER 2

Abstraction, Problem Solving, and Algorithm Design

CHAPTER CONTENTS

INTRODUCTION

Inventing algorithms is the central task of computer science. The goal is to take a problem, decompose it into simpler parts, and then to imagine a sequence of steps by means of which a machine can generate a solution. This requires both analysis of the problem and synthesis of a solution—relatively sophisticated thinking.

Some of the computer software you encounter in everyday life—operating systems, airline scheduling software, library databases—are among the most complex systems ever designed and constructed by humans. They are so complex, in fact, that they cannot be completely understood by a single human mind. As a result, we have developed new methods for dealing with such complexity. The first two sections of this chapter will introduce you to the methodology of modern software engineering and the use of abstraction to reduce the complexity of a problem. Such techniques will appear repeatedly in later chapters.

Once the complexity of a problem is under control, we can begin to work out an algorithm that solves the problem. There are distinct stages in the algorithm design, and the purpose of this chapter is to make the steps explicit, so that you will recognize them when they are used in later chapters, and be able to apply them to new problems. First we will examine the steps as they appear in the solution of a simple problem, then we will tackle a harder one.

2.1 THE NEED FOR SOFTWARE ENGINEERING

Beginning programmers seldom realize how large and complex commercial programs can be, but in fact, *modern software systems are the most complex inventions ever conceived by humans*. Consider these examples:

- One early large programming project, the writing of the operating system for the IBM System/360 mainframe in the 1960s, consumed more than 5,000 programmer-years of effort. Approximately 1,000 people were involved in developing the initial release, and 900 were employed thereafter for debugging and refinement. Similar software today is even larger and more complex.
- On January 15, 1990, the AT&T long-distance telephone network suffered massive gridlock because of a *single error in over 2 million lines of programming code* controlling switching in the phone system. Even though AT&T located and fixed the error within 36 hours, businesses lost millions of dollars because their calls could not be completed.
- Today, the US Department of Defense spends more than $30 billion annually for software to control weapons systems. *These systems are often so complex that there is no known way to check their correct functioning in all circumstances.* Yet the lives of many people depend on these systems.
- In large corporations, 90 percent of the cost of running management information systems departments is spent on software; of this, *one-third to one-half is spent on debugging* (defect removal).
- Because of the widespread use of computers in automobiles, aircraft, air traffic control systems, and defense systems, our very lives—even in peacetime—often depend on the correct operation of software. During the Gulf War, a Patriot missile failed to intercept a Scud because of a simple numeric roundoff error (Section 4.2). As a result, the Scud destroyed an Allied barracks at Dhahran, Saudi Arabia, killing 28 soldiers and wounding 98 more.

Software engineering: The study and development of techniques to improve the efficient construction of reliable software.

Clearly, it is vital that important software systems work reliably. But just as clearly, software systems are getting more complex and therefore more difficult to design correctly. To meet the need, computer scientists are developing techniques to help ensure the efficient design and construction of reliable software that is easy to debug, use, and improve. This field of work is called **software engineering**.

Hacking versus engineering

Hack: To write programs quickly, without proper regard for their reliability, maintainability, or portability.

Throughout the 1950s and 1960s, most software was created by self-taught programmers who loved problem solving and were fascinated with all the neat tricks that could be performed with computers. The programs were often "cobbled together" or **hacked** in extremely clever and intricate ways. These programs might be useful and might work most of the time, but they were such intricate puzzles in themselves that nobody but the original programmer could understand their inner construction.

To **port** a program: To move a program to another hardware/software system, getting it to run there.

Unfortunately, all useful programs become unsatisfactory after a while, even if they are satisfactory at first. Either the users discover bugs that were unnoticed at first, or changing circumstances generate demands for new features in the program, or the program must be **ported** (moved or transported) to newer hardware. For a variety of such reasons, existing successful software will *always* have to be modified eventually.

By the time this happens, the original programmer is very likely to have moved on to a new job elsewhere. Even if he or she is still available to modify the program, the programmer will no longer remember all those neat tricks that made the program so intricate. So now, the company that owns the software has a serious and expensive problem: how to modify intricate, complex software that nobody fully understands. Before anybody can make the necessary changes, much time will need to be spent in figuring out how the software worked in the first place.

In the old days, which unfortunately still exist in a few places, programs usually lacked adequate documentation, so it was hard to recover an understanding of an existing program that had not been worked on recently. The programs were hacked, not engineered, so they did not have a clear design that could be easily understood. Furthermore, the intricacy of the programs usually made it impossible to assure users that the algorithms would work correctly in all circumstances.

Such designs are just not good enough in an age when our lives and welfare depend on correct software. We must be able to verify the correctness of our programs. We must be able to modify our software so that its errors can be corrected, so that it can be given new features, and so that it can be ported to new hardware. In other words, the software must be **verifiable**, **modifiable**, and **portable**. These concerns are what software engineering is all about; the old days of hacking are over.

The software life cycle

Because of the almost constant need to modify software—either to add new features or to port it to new hardware—the lifetime of a single program version is usually very short. The revision process can be divided into six stages, called the **software life cycle**:

1. A software *planning phase*, during which the users' needs are determined, program development resources are estimated, and development cost and schedule are roughly predicted. The purpose of this phase of development is to determine whether the software (or revision) will be economically feasible. This requires close cooperation between developers and prospective users.
2. A *requirements analysis and specifications phase*, during which the functions of the proposed software are designed in detail, with attention to how the parts of the program might work together. A system is designed for validating the proper functioning of each part of the software package, and for assembling the parts to make a dependable whole. The result of this phase is to produce detailed specifications for the overall functioning of the software. This too requires close cooperation between the developers and users to ensure that users will be satisfied with the final product.
3. A *software design phase*, in which the overall software package is designed to meet the specifications resulting from phase 2. The overall package is broken into parts called *modules*, each of which will be assigned to a programming team with a team leader. The skeleton of each module is written and tested with dummy data to ensure that data will transfer correctly from module to module, and that the overall program will work as planned. The validation system invented in phase 2 is put into action.
4. A *coding phase*, in which the program segments of the modules are actually written in a programming language. If steps 1–3 have been carried out correctly, the coding phase of the project should be relatively smooth, because it was tightly defined by the design phase.

At this point, a program exists, so you might be tempted to believe that the process is over. The fun is only just beginning, however. The two most important phases are yet to come:

5. A *validation phase,* in which the software is tested to make sure that it works as intended. There are actually three stages in this phase. First, *unit testing* determines whether each separate software module works correctly on its own. When the modules are separately correct, *integration testing* determines whether the set of modules assemble correctly into a complete program that works as designed. Finally, *validation testing* determines whether all of the original software requirements have been met.
6. After all of this work comes the most expensive phase in a software package's life: the phase in which the software is used and maintained. This *maintenance phase,* as it is called, involves producing complete, readable, and correct documentation for the software; locating, identifying, and repairing bugs that appear once the software is in use; and identifying shortcomings in performance. *This phase in the software life cycle often consumes more than half of the software budget of a large computing operation.*

After all this, if the users like the software, they will almost certainly request additional features. Then the whole process begins again!

Software engineering is more than programming.

Today's large software projects require the careful engineering approach outlined above because experience has shown that software that is merely "hacked" is unreliable. It may fail because of outright bugs. Even if it works correctly, it will probably be impossible to revise and augment it without introducing bugs or without incurring unreasonable cost. Instead, the large programming projects of the future will increasingly rely upon the meticulous techniques outlined above and described more completely in the following chapters. These are the techniques of software engineering, and their goal is to help produce correctly designed, easily understood, and provably correct programs. We will emphasize this approach throughout the book.

Before we do, however, you ought to know something about the methods we will use to deal with the complexities that arise in programming problems. These methods all involve the concept of *abstraction.*

2.2 ABSTRACTION AND THE CONTROL OF COMPLEXITY

Computing isn't the only human activity that's complex—even everyday life is more complex than we ordinarily think. To get through a normal day, we simplify the way we think about the things we deal with and the actions we perform. The key is that *we pay attention to what is immediately important while ignoring everything else.*

Procedural abstraction

Suppose you are going to drive to work, and you begin by "starting the car." Because you have driven the car many times, you think of "starting the car" as though it were a simple action. However, this action is actually a sequence of steps that someone had to teach you when you first learned to drive:

"Starting the (stick-shift) car" means:
Insert the key into the ignition switch.
Depress the clutch pedal.
Hold the clutch pedal fully depressed.
Move the gear-shift lever to the "neutral" position.
Turn the key to the start position.
Release the key when you hear the engine "catch."
Release the clutch pedal when the engine is running smoothly.

If you had to think about this much detail while performing every driving procedure, you wouldn't be able to pay enough attention to traffic. (Remember the first time you drove?) To handle all the complexity, you learn operations so thoroughly that you internalize them and, eventually, they become automatic. Later, as an experienced driver, you simply think of "turning right" or "passing another car," without thinking explicitly of all the details in such procedures. The details are **encapsulated** inside the procedure, as we say in computer science. When you refer to a procedure by name, concealing the complexity of its encapsulated details, you are practicing what is called **procedural abstraction** (Figure 2.2.1).

Object abstraction in everyday life

The "car" itself is an extremely complex object, but its complexity doesn't concern you at the moment because you are thinking of the car merely as transportation. Thus, the "car" itself is another kind of abstraction:

Car = "A four-wheeled passenger vehicle"

Again, the abstraction conceals complexity. A typical car has perhaps 10,000 parts and is much more complicated to build or repair than it is to drive. Fortunately, you needn't be concerned about this while driving (except when the car breaks down).

Figure 2.2.1

When we name a procedure, the name stands for all the actions that are encapsulated in the procedure.

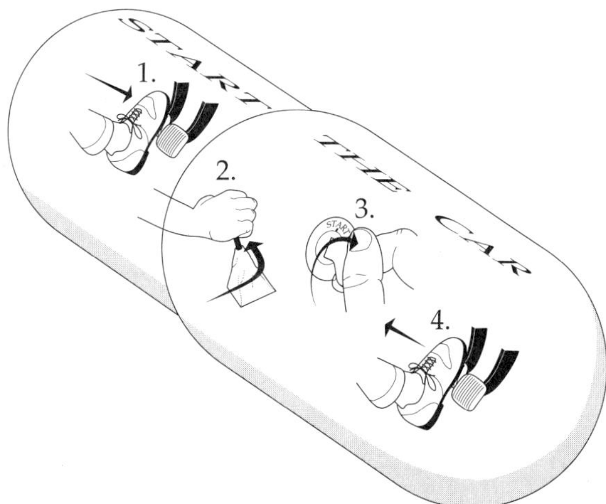

Usually, you can simplify your life by thinking of the car in terms of the *procedures involved in driving it*. In particular, you can think of the car as the object itself, capable of the driving procedures:

Car = A four-wheeled passenger vehicle,
capable of the following driving procedures:
- Starting.
- Accelerating.
- Changing gears.
- Decelerating.
- And so on.

An object that encapsulates in this way the procedures that act on it is said to be an **abstract object** or an **object abstraction** (Figure 2.2.2).

Data objects and procedural abstraction in computer science

These techniques from everyday life are also used to control complexity in computer programming. In programming, we deal with **data objects** that often have complex structures—a list of names, a spreadsheet, formatted text, or an array of pixels on a screen. We manipulate the data by means of complex sequences of instructions to the computer. Very soon, we find ourselves faced with too much complexity to comprehend at once. So we give names to the major data operations, thinking of them as separate **procedures**. For example, if our purpose is to maintain a mailing list of names and addresses, we need to be able to create a mailing list and revise it. Here are some of the procedures we need:

Add a name and address to the list.

Delete a name and address from the list.

Check whether a given name and address is already in the list.

Figure 2.2.2 *An abstract object consists of the object itself together with the operations (procedures) that make the object meaningful.*

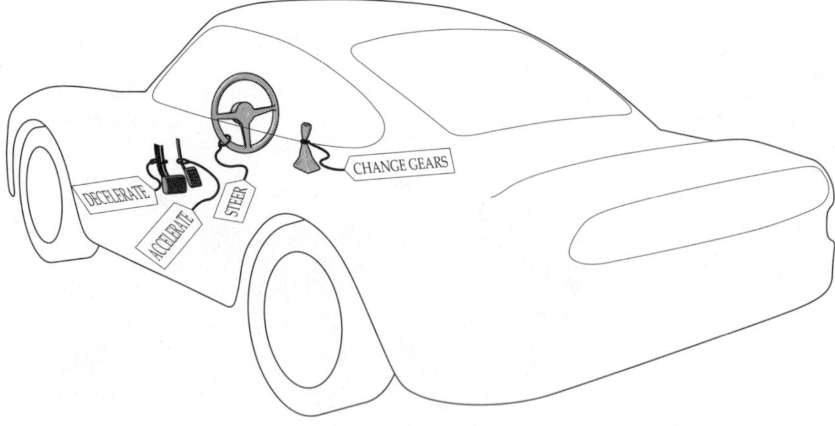

Sort the list (that is, put it in order).

Remove duplicates from the list.

Display the whole list on the screen, one screenful at a time.

Print the whole list on paper.

Save the current list as a mass storage file.

Load a list from a mass storage file into main memory.

The process of naming such operations and referring to them as prefabricated procedures is called *procedural abstraction*, and it is the main topic of chapters 3–6. By building procedures, we encapsulate the detailed computer instructions needed to accomplish the corresponding task, freeing the user from dealing with unnecessary detail while thinking in terms of the purposes of the procedures. Once we have built the procedures, we can carry them out (that is, *execute* them) merely by referring to them by name.

Data abstraction in computer science

The procedures are used to manipulate data objects. In our previous example, the name/address list was the data object. However, a data object is meaningful primarily in terms of the manipulations you can perform on it. Therefore, we package a data object together with the operations that can be performed on it, and give the whole thing a name. This process is called **data abstraction**, and will be a major subject of chapters 16–21. For example, we might define the name/address list as a data abstraction in the following way:

Name/address list (data abstraction):
A list of names and associated addresses, which are to be manipulated by means of the following procedures:
- Add a name and address to the list.
- Delete a name and address from the list.
- Check whether a given name and address is already in the list.
- Sort the list (that is, put it in order).
- Remove duplicates from the list.
- Display the whole list on the screen, one screenful at a time.
- Print the whole list on paper.
- Save the current list as a mass-storage file.
- Load a list from a mass storage file into main memory.

Together, these twin topics of procedural and data abstraction will be a dominant theme throughout the book, leading to a discipline of *object-oriented programming* in later computer science courses.

Questions

1. What does the word *abstraction* mean in the senses used in this book? (Note that only the most recent dictionaries list a definition close to the computer science meaning.)

2. "Both procedural abstraction and object abstraction are used to conceal unnecessary details when those details are not needed." What does this remark mean and why is it important?

3. Which object abstractions would you say do the most to simplify your everyday life? List three of them, and for each, describe the object itself from the user's point of view and list the procedures that make that object useful.
4. Consider a bicycle as an abstract object. How would you define the object itself for a potential user who had never seen one? What procedures are involved in using the object?
5. Consider a single-knob water faucet as an abstract object. How would you define the object itself for a potential user who had never seen one? What procedures are involved in using the object?
6. One of the procedures in using a single-knob water faucet is to adjust the water temperature. Describe the encapsulated algorithm for such a procedure in enough detail that, in principle, a robot could carry out the actions.

2.3 A CASE STUDY IN PROBLEM SOLVING

It might seem obvious, but the first step in solving a problem is to state clearly what the problem is. Most people who have trouble with problem solving have failed to take this first step. For our first example of problem-solving techniques, consider this rough statement of a simple problem: *to convert Fahrenheit temperatures to Celsius.*

2.4 CLARIFY THE PROBLEM; BE SPECIFIC; DESCRIBE WHAT SHOULD HAPPEN IN EXCEPTIONAL CASES.

The initial description of the sample problem leaves a lot unspecified. Where does the Fahrenheit temperature come from? How do we perform the conversion? What do we do with the resulting Celsius temperature? Let's suppose that we want the user of our program to enter a Fahrenheit temperature at the keyboard, then we want to convert this temperature to Celsius and display the result on the screen.

The Fahrenheit-to-Celsius conversion itself is not difficult because we learned the rule in school: "Subtract 32 from the Fahrenheit temperature, then multiply the result by 5/9 in order to get the Celsius temperature."

The original statement of the problem fails to specify what we should do if the user playfully or ignorantly enters a Fahrenheit temperature outside the range of possible values. It is not possible to have a temperature below absolute zero, the temperature at which all molecular vibration ceases, which is -459.7 degrees Fahrenheit. We can, for example, have the program display an error message if the given Fahrenheit temperature is lower than this. (Other possibilities will be examined later.)

After all these considerations, we have a decent specification of the problem:

> *Get a Fahrenheit temperature from the keyboard. If this temperature is below -459.7, display a message telling the user that the temperature is below absolute zero; otherwise, convert the temperature to Celsius and display the results.*

2.5 PLAN THE USER INTERFACE FIRST.

Before designing the algorithm, it helps to plan the **user interface**—that is, the way the program should interact with the user while running. This will help you form a mental picture of the stages required in the algorithm. In our example problem, we might imagine the input and output to look as shown below. (Keyboard entries are highlighted in color.)

User interface: The way in which a program interacts with the user while running.

```
CONVERTING FAHRENHEIT TO CELSIUS

Fahrenheit temperature? 212
212.0 deg. F. = 100.0 deg. C.
```

If the user enters a Fahrenheit temperature that is below absolute zero, the input and output might look like this:

```
CONVERTING FAHRENHEIT TO CELSIUS

Fahrenheit temperature? -500
Temperature is below absolute zero (-459.7 deg.F.).
```

It isn't difficult to imagine this much; you needn't be a programmer to be able to imagine how you would like a program to behave. And even this little bit of progress helps to clarify the required algorithm. There are four main steps:

1. Announce the purpose of the program.
2. Ask for the Fahrenheit temperature and read the user's keyboard entry.
3. Compare the temperature to absolute zero.
4. If the temperature is less than absolute zero, display an error message; otherwise, convert it to Celsius and display the result.

At this stage, many programmers prefer to write a succinct outline in an informal quasi-language called **pseudocode**, which lies somewhere between a formal programming language and everyday English. Here is an example of how one programmer outlined the algorithm described above:

Pseudocode: An informal shorthand language, used for outlining algorithms for human readers.

```
Show purpose;
Get Fahrenheit temperature;
If Fahrenheit < AbsoluteZero then
        Display error.
otherwise
        Convert to Celsius;
        Display temperature
```

The pseudocode outline is an informal technique for planning the sequence of actions that should occur when the program executes. You can think of it as a kind of "table of contents" for a computer program—an outline of the main actions.

The main actions—"Show purpose," "Get Fahrenheit temperature," "Display error," "Convert to Celsius," and "Display temperature"—are examples of the *procedural abstraction* we discussed in Section 2.2. That is, each of these actions has a name and can be thought of as a procedure whose details need not concern us at this stage. (Programmers say that we **hide the information** about the inner workings of these procedures until we need to see it.) The important thing right now is that we have decomposed the

Information hiding: Concealing details until the reader or user needs to know about them.

Figure 2.5.1 *The hierarchy of the second-stage algorithmic plan, as we begin to picture the hierarchy of procedural abstraction. The main algorithm controls the use of five procedures. The arrows indicate data flow to and from the various procedures.*

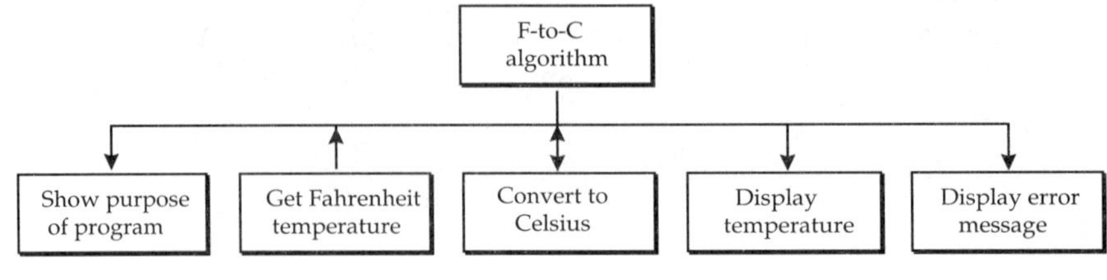

overall Fahrenheit-to-Celsius problem into a sequence of procedures, each of which is carried out under the control of the main algorithm. This is pictured as a procedural **hierarchy diagram** in Figure 2.5.1.

Hierarchy: A layered structure in which items are ranked one above the other.

The pseudocode outline is only a rough draft of our algorithm, listing the major steps in solving the problem. Next we must refine the description of each step.

2.6 DIVIDE UNTIL TRIVIAL; THEN CONQUER.

The previous stage of the design process—planning the input and output—served to clarify both the steps in the overall algorithm and the hierachy of procedural abstraction. In doing this, it revealed how the algorithm decomposes into a succession of five major tasks. In our example, most of these are trivial, but the second step requires a little more detail than we have discussed so far. To "get a Fahrenheit temperature from the keyboard," we first need to ask the user for the data. This is called **prompting** the user. Then we need to **read** a real number from the keyboard. So "Get Fahrenheit" actually involves two smaller steps.

Prompt: *v.* To ask the user for input. *n.* A message asking for input.

Read: To copy data into the computer's main memory from a peripheral device.

Similarly, the "Convert to Celsius" step requires that we take the Fahrenheit temperature, which presumably is stored in a variable, and compute the corresponding Celsius temperature according to the formula

$$\text{Celsius} = (5/9)\cdot(\text{Fahrenheit} - 32)$$

As you can see, we are decomposing the problem into subtasks simple enough for easy programming—that is, we **divide and conquer** until each subtask is trivial. We now have a more complete pseudocode outline, fleshing out the procedures to show what is contained (*encapsulated*) in each:

The ShowPurpose procedure encapsulates:

Display the message,
"CONVERTING FAHRENHEIT TO CELSIUS,"
with a blank line under the message.

The GetFahrenheit procedure encapsulates:

Display the prompt, "Fahrenheit?" (including the space after the question mark). Then read a number from the keyboard into a variable named Fahrenheit.

The ConvertToCelsius procedure encapsulates:
Compute Celsius = (5.0 / 9.0) · (Fahrenheit – 32.0)

The DisplayTemperature procedure encapsulates:
Display both Fahrenheit and Celsius temperatures, like this:
```
212.0 deg. F. = 100.0 deg. C.
```

The DisplayError procedure encapsulates:
Display the message,
```
Temperature is below absolute zero (-459.7 deg. F.)
```

The main algorithm invokes the procedures:
```
ShowPurpose;
GetFahrenheit;

If Fahrenheit < -459.7 then
        DisplayError
otherwise
        ConvertToCelsius;
        DisplayTemperature
```

This is all very informal. We are not writing a computer program at this stage— just a *design* for a computer program, an *algorithm*. During this design stage, the exact notation we use for outlining the design doesn't matter. What does matter is that we have planned the algorithm in such detail that the later conversion from algorithm to Pascal program will be relatively trivial. We will perform that conversion in Chapter 4.

As a final note about the F-to-C algorithm, we might mention that the method we have shown for protecting the algorithm from Fahrenheit temperatures below absolute zero is not the only method we could use. See Project 15 at the end of the chapter.

2.7 A SECOND CASE STUDY: SORTING THREE NUMBERS

Our second example involves the process called **sorting**. Suppose a procedure is given three real numbers and is supposed to arrange them so that they are listed in *increasing order*. For example, if the given numbers are 1.7, 0.9, and 0.55, the procedure must rearrange them so that 0.55 is listed first, then 0.9, and finally 1.7.

To sort: To arrange data in a specified order.

Our previous example of problem solving taught us to make the problem **specification** complete and specific before trying to solve the problem. This means that, in addition to being clear, we must specify what should be done in exceptional circumstances. For example, what should happen if two or even all three of the numbers are the same? In that case, the procedure should arrange the numbers in *nondecreasing order*. For example, if the given numbers are 3.2, 1.9, and 3.2, the sorting procedure should put them in the order 1.9, 3.2, 3.2. In general, we can state the specification like this: If the given numbers are stored in variables called N_1, N_2, and N_3, the sorting procedure should result in $N_1 \le N_2 \le N_3$.

Specification: A detailed, precise statement of the requirements for something to be designed.

Only after all these considerations do we have a decent specification of the problem:

> *Design an algorithm that arranges any three given numbers N_1, N_2, and N_3 so that $N_1 \le N_2 \le N_3$.*

As in our previous case study, we begin by planning the **user interface**. Suppose we want the screen to look like this as the program executes in a typical run:

Figure 2.7.1

In the first-stage plan, the main algorithm uses four procedures, but we have not yet planned the actions to be encapsulated in each procedure. The arrows indicate data flow between the main algorithm and the various procedures.

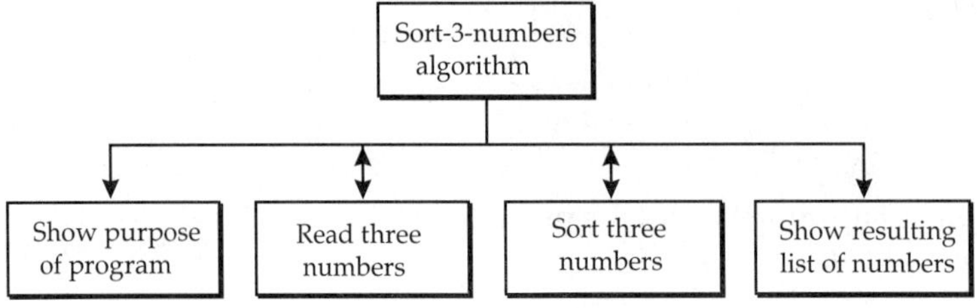


```
SORTING THREE NUMBERS

First number:  3.2
Second number: -1.9
Third number:  3.2

Sorted list: -1.9   3.2   3.2.
```

By the time we've imagined this much, we have an idea of the major steps in the required algorithm:

ShowPurpose;
Get3Nums;
Sort3Nums;
Show3Nums.

The algorithm thus makes use of four procedures, as shown in the *hierarchy diagram* of Figure 2.7.1. The prompt-and-read procedure, Get3Nums, is like the one we had in the previous example, so we know what it encapsulates:

The Get3Nums procedure encapsulates:
Prompt for first number;
Read number from keyboard into Num1 variable;
Prompt for second number;
Read number from keyboard into Num2 variable;
Prompt for third number;
Read number from keyboard into Num3 variable.

There is also a Show3Nums procedure, which will display the reordered numbers:

The Show3Nums procedure encapsulates:
Display message, "Sorted list: ";
Display first number;
Display three spaces;
Display second number;
Display three spaces;
Display third number;

That leaves us with the Sort3Nums procedure, which performs the actual sorting and is therefore the most complicated procedure. We attack it next. Meanwhile, a diagram of the present stage of our hierarchy is shown in Figure 2.7.2.

The hierarchy of the second-stage algorithmic plan, as we begin to plan how each second-level procedure does its work.

Figure 2.7.2

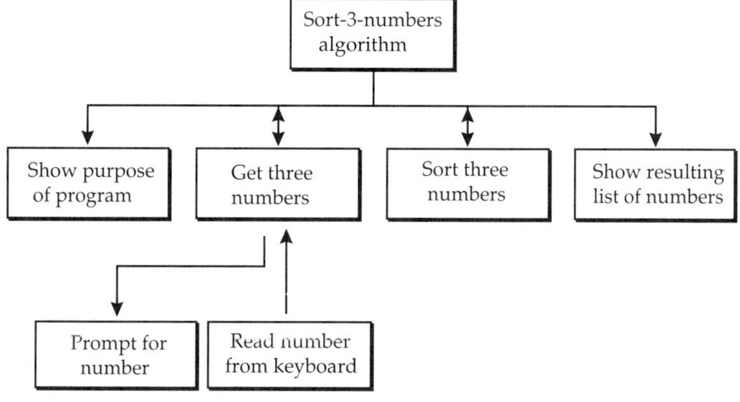

2.8 TOP-DOWN DESIGN

The manner in which we have decomposed the sorting problem is quite deliberate. First the problem was broken down into its four main tasks. Now we are breaking down each of those tasks into subtasks. We will continue this process until we have decomposed the problem into subtasks so small that each one is relatively trivial. This process is called **top-down design** because we deal first with the top-level or major tasks of the problem, and only afterwards break these into smaller and smaller tasks. The term *top down* implies a stratified design in which the major tasks are resolved "downward" into "lower-level" or smaller tasks, as indicated in the hierarchy diagrams.

Top-down design: A design technique in which the overall problem is attacked first, by breaking it down into smaller problems. These smaller problems are dealt with later, by breaking them down into still smaller ones. This process continues until the remaining problems are trivial.

Divide and conquer.

Now we turn to the design of the Sort3Nums procedure, which is the sorting process itself. Proceeding as we did before, we will break this task down, starting at the top. In order to get started, consider how you might divide the three-number sorting problem into smaller problems. Ask yourself this:

Is there a way to sort three numbers by making a series of two-number swaps? Of course there is. If Num1 is greater than Num2, these two values should be swapped. This brings the larger of the two to the second position in the list. After doing this, if the new Num2 is greater than Num3, these should be swapped. This would bring the largest value all the way to the end of the list (the third position). The only remaining task would be to make sure the first two values are still in the correct order.

Work some examples by hand.

For example, if the three numbers are 14.7, 3.3, and 3.0, the process would proceed as shown on the next page:

After swapping the first and second:	3.3	14.7	3.0
After swapping the second and third:	3.3	3.0	14.7
After swapping the first and second:	3.0	3.3	14.7

There needn't always be three swaps, however. If the initial order is 14.7, 3.0, 3.3, we need only two swaps:

After swapping the first and second:	3.0	14.7	3.3
After swapping the second and third:	3.0	3.3	14.7

(This time a third swap is not needed.)

We always need to make three comparisons, however, and these can be accomplished as follows:

If *Num1 is greater than Num2* then
  swap Num1 and Num2;
otherwise,
  don't swap.
Result: Num1 ≤ Num2.

If *Num2 is greater than Num3* then
  swap Num2 and Num3;
otherwise,
  don't swap.
Result: Num3 is the maximum value.

The first two values may still be out of order, so
if *Num1 is greater than Num2* then
  swap Num1 and Num2;
otherwise,
  don't swap.
Result: Num1 ≤ Num2 ≤ Num3.

To make this work, the Sort3Nums procedure must be able to call on a Swap2Nums procedure, which we haven't designed yet. This will add one more box on the third level of our hierarchy diagram, as shown in Figure 2.8.1.

Figure 2.8.1 *Now the hierarchy diagram includes some detail regarding the sorting process itself.*

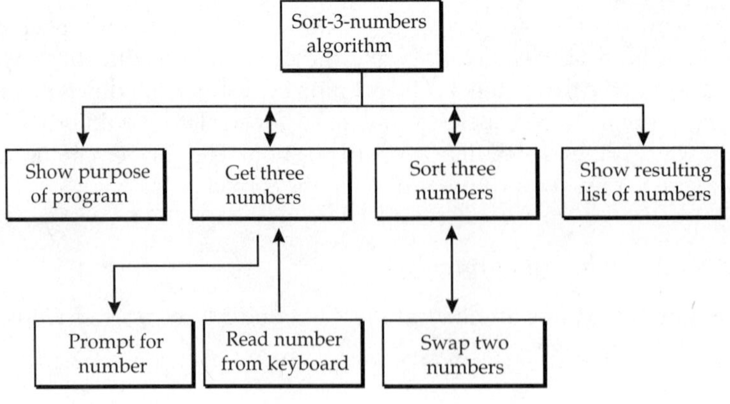

2.9 USE DIAGRAMS.

It is not difficult to design the Swap2Nums procedure, but perhaps not as obvious as it seems at first. Beginners are often tempted to say, "You just swap them," and imagine an algorithm like this:

Copy Num2 into Num1;
Copy Num1 into Num2.

But this overlooks the way computer variables work. *You've got to have a picture in your mind of how the variables work.* Programming is a visual as well as verbal activity, and programmers must have mental pictures of how the algorithms work and how the data are manipulated. *Get in the habit of drawing pictures of your algorithms and data.*

In the present problem, picture the two numbers to be swapped, say 14.7 and 3.3, stored in two variables:

Num1	Num2
14.7	3.3

Now picture what happens if you start to swap them by copying Num2 into Num1. The value being copied into Num1 overwrites (replaces) the value previously stored there:

Num1	Num2
3.3	3.3

Then, of course, if we try to complete the swap by copying Num1 into Num2, the values in the two variables remain the same, and we have lost forever the original value in Num1, which was overwritten in the first step.

Therefore, the Swap2Nums algorithm has to be a little more complicated than it first appeared. We need another variable for temporary storage; we will call it Temp. We begin the swap by copying Num1 into Temp:

Num1	Num2	Temp
14.7	3.3	14.7

Then we can copy Num2 into Num1. We overwrite the previous value in Num1, but we still have the backup copy stored in Temp:

Num1	Num2	Temp
3.3	3.3	14.7

Then we copy Temp into Num2:

Num1	Num2	Temp
3.3	14.7	14.7

And that completes the Swap2Nums process. Here's what we need in the procedure:

The Swap2Nums procedure encapsulates:
Copy Num1 variable into Temp variable;
Copy Num2 variable into Num1 variable;
Copy Temp variable into Num2 variable.

Notice how much the diagrams help in getting the algorithm right. Another kind of diagram that can help is one that shows the overall effect of a **procedure**, considering the procedure as a mathematical **mapping** (or **relation**) from a set of input data to a set of output data. The Swap2Nums procedure takes as its inputs a couple of numbers in variables, and returns (that is, produces as output) swapped values in the two variables:

Mapping or **relation** (mathematics): A correspondence between the members of one set with the members of another set, such that each member of the first set is associated with a member of the second set.

Similarly, the Sort3Nums procedure receives three inputs and returns them in sorted order:

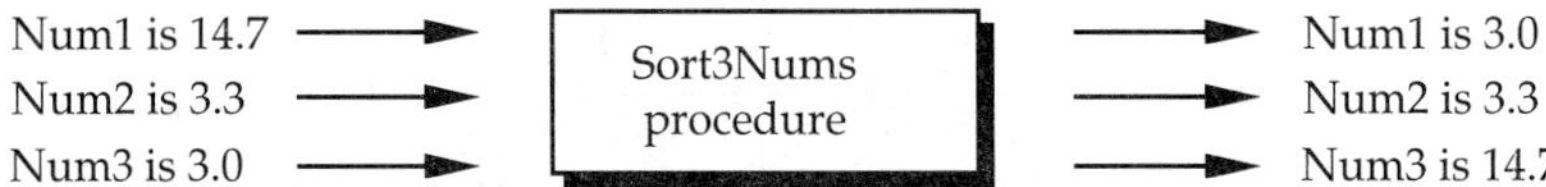

Diagrams like these show the flow of data through a procedure, and are therefore sometimes called **dataflow diagrams**.

2.10 BUILD ON PREVIOUS WORK.

The hierarchical breakdown of computing problems has many advantages. Clearly, it helps us solve difficult problems. But less obviously, it leads to the realization that *algorithms for solving important computing problems often have common parts. Once we have built up a library of common procedures, we will be able to assemble many programs by plugging together procedures we have already built.* At least, we will be able to do this if we have carefully built those procedures as separate modules that can be plugged together easily.

Reusable procedures: Commonly useful procedures that are designed as separate modules to be plugged together when building various programs.

Thus one of the most important lessons in problem solving is that a hierarchical breakdown of problems into pieces can lead us to easily built algorithms that are constructed of **reusable procedures**. This is much easier (and more reliable) than reinventing the wheel whenever we design a program.

2.11 STRUCTURE THE DATA.

The structure of the problem determines the structures of algorithms (typically there will be more than one) that solve the problem. In turn, the nature of a given algorithm determines how the data should be organized to facilitate a solution. Suppose we wanted to sort a list of 25 numbers instead of just three. To do it, we would need 25 variables to hold the numbers, plus an extra Temp variable for use by the Swap2Nums procedure. If you think about generalizing the Sort3Nums algorithm, you will find that the instructions to the computer will be made awkward by the need to refer to 25 different variable names. The algorithm would be much easier to describe if the numbers were stored in a subscripted variable, called an **array**, in which subscripts can be used to address particular numbers in the list: Num_1, Num_2, Num_3, Num_4, and so on.

The general idea of structuring the data, and the idea of the array in particular, will become a central issue in the book when we reach Chapter 14.

2.12 DON'T BE SATISFIED WITH YOUR FIRST IDEA.

We all tend to be inordinately proud of anything we create. (This goes for parenthood as well as algorithm design.) Once you have battled your way to an algorithm that works, you will be inclined to sit back and gloat a little. You may even be resentful when another programmer criticizes your algorithm.

But you must realize that *there is almost always a better algorithm.* In fact, this is the exciting thing about computer science: There is almost always an opportunity to do it better. Sure, you should have pride in your first solution to a problem. Then take the time to rethink the solution later, looking for other ways of attacking the problem; you may come up with something better. As you will see in Chapters 14 and 19, there are more subtle ways to attack the sorting problem than you have glimpsed here. There is even a better version of the Fahrenheit-to-Celsius algorithm; see Project 15.

It is just as important to be willing to rethink a problem when you get stuck. Sometimes your idea just won't pan out, no matter how hard you work on it. The trick is to be able to recognize such a situation. Be suspicious when your algorithm gets so complicated that you are having trouble ensuring that it works correctly. At the very least, this is a sign that you designed the algorithm poorly. It may even mean that the algorithm does *not* work correctly. When you find yourself in such a situation, go back to the very beginning and question your premises. By completely rethinking the problem with an open mind, you may discover an entirely new approach.

Imagination is required.

In this chapter, a number of problem-solving techniques have been illustrated in application to a couple of sample problems. Don't get the idea that all problems are solved in exactly these ways, using these particular techniques in a particular order. This chapter has merely listed some of the more important techniques used in solving programming problems; there are as many other techniques as there are inventive programmers.

George Polya, in his famous book, *How to Solve It*, wrote

> *The first rule of discovery is to have brains and good luck. The second rule of discovery is to sit tight and wait till you get a bright idea.*
>
> *It may be good to be reminded somewhat rudely that certain aspirations are hopeless. Infallible rules of discovery leading to solutions of all possible mathematical problems would be more desirable than the philosophers' stone, vainly sought by the alchemists. Such rules would work magic; but there is no such thing as magic.*

In the rest of this book, you will encounter many illustrations of problem solving. In each case, the problem is defined and at least one approach to its solution is shown. In many cases, other approaches might work just as well, and I strongly recommend that you try to find such alternate approaches. You will see as we work through various problems that there's always more than one way to do it.

LOOKING BACK

The chapter began by giving real-world examples of the need to use careful software engineering rather than just "hacking" programs into shape. It also provided an introduction to the concepts of procedural and data abstraction. Then, by means of two case studies, it presented eight fundamental techniques for breaking down problems and designing algorithms to solve them:

- Clarify the problem, being very specific and precise, and specifying how to deal with exceptional cases.
- First, plan the input and output (the I/O).
- Then divide the problem until the individual pieces are trivial.
- Break down problems from the top level downward, using procedural abstraction. This means breaking the initial problem down first into major tasks, then breaking those down into smaller tasks, then breaking those down into still smaller tasks, until you get down to the level in which the subtasks are easily solved.
- Use diagrams to help yourself understand how the input data for any step should be transformed into the output data. Use diagrams to help yourself understand how any given step works internally.
- Build on previous work. By accumulating a collection of interchangeable algorithmic parts, you will be equipped to build new programs by plugging together prefabricated subalgorithms.
- Structure the data to facilitate the solution. Data can be organized in various ways, and often an algorithm will require a special organization of data. This will become more apparent after Chapter 13.
- Don't be satisfied with your first solution. Be willing to start over, rethinking the problem from scratch, with an open mind.

The two case studies presented in this chapter will be developed into complete programs in later chapters. The Fahrenheit-to-Celsius program will be completed in Chapters 4–6. The program to sort three numbers will be completed in Section 6.3.

TERMS EMPHASIZED IN THIS CHAPTER

PROJECTS

The following exercises ask you to write algorithms for humans (or quasi-humans) to use in carrying out some task. In each case, be sure that your algorithm terminates.

1. You have just built a robotic Bride of Frankenstein. She is eating you out of house and home. But being the concerned scientist you are, you are worried about her dental health. Write an algorithm for B.O.F., showing her how to brush her teeth. This is more complicated than it sounds. You have to explain how to open the toothpaste, what to do if the tube is empty, how to put toothpaste on the brush, and so on.
2. Write an algorithm for looking up a name in a phone book.
3. Write an algorithm for frying scrambled eggs.
4. A program receives integers from the keyboard as three-digit sequences of characters, from left to right. That is, the integer 147 is received as the character "1," followed by the character "4" and then the character "7." Similarly, the integer 47 will be received as "0," "4," "7." Design and write an algorithm describing how a human would add any pair of such numbers, assuming that all integers are positive. Show the encapsulation in each procedure.
5. Similarly, write an algorithm to subtract a smaller integer from a larger one. Show the encapsulation in each procedure.
6. Similarly, write an algorithm to multiply two integers, paying attention to their signs. Assume that you already have a procedure for adding, and build on this. Show the encapsulation in each procedure.
7. Write an algorithm for converting Roman numerals to Arabic decimal numbers. Show the encapsulation in each procedure.
8. Write an algorithm for making change when paid with a dollar bill for a purchase of less than a dollar. Show the encapsulation in each procedure.
9. A prime number is a whole number greater than 1 that is exactly divisible only by 1 and by itself. Except for 2, all the prime numbers are necessarily odd because even numbers are divisible by 2. Design an algorithm that starts at 3, working its way upward through the odd numbers, identifying and displaying all primes. Such an algorithm was devised by Eratosthenes in the third century BC, and works like this: Assume that 3 is prime and consider only odd numbers above 3. Then multiples of 3 cannot be prime, so rule them out. Then look through the list for the first number that hasn't been ruled out, which must be a prime. Rule out all its multiples. The algorithm should continue like this until it has found all primes less than 1,000. Write this algorithm in terms of procedures. For each procedure, show the encapsulation.
10. Write an algorithm to find the roots of a quadratic equation of the form $ax^2 + bx + c = 0$, using the familiar formula

    $$\frac{-b \pm \sqrt{b^2 - 4ac}}{2a}$$

    The algorithm must take account of the fact that a or b or c, or any two of these, or all three, may be zero. It must also allow for the possibility that the discriminant, $b^2 - 4ac$, might be negative. Show the encapsulation in each procedure.
11. Write an algorithm to teach a human how to sort a deck of cards so that aces come first, followed by numbered cards in order, followed by jacks, queens, kings, and finally, jokers. Within a group of the same value, the suits should come in the order clubs, diamonds, hearts, spades. Show the encapsulation in each procedure.

12. Write an algorithm to convert an eight-bit binary integer to decimal. Again, assume that you already have the integer; describe how to convert it. Show the encapsulation in each procedure. (Binary notation is reviewed in Appendix J.)
13. Design an algorithm that searches an unordered list of numbers for a given number. If found, the number's position in the list should be reported; if not found, the algorithm should report the pseudo-position zero. Show the encapsulation in each procedure.
14. How would the algorithm of Exercise 13 differ if the list were initially in order? Would it be an advantage or disadvantage to start with an ordered list? Explain your thinking.
15. The Fahrenheit-to-Celsius algorithm can be protected from Fahrenheit temperatures below absolute zero in a different way than shown in Section 2.4. The GetFahrenheit procedure can check the incoming temperature and, if it is lower than absolute zero, can prompt again for the temperature, and this can continue until the user supplies a meaningful temperature. Outline such an approach in pseudocode.

REFERENCES

The classic textbook on problem-solving techniques is *How to Solve It*, by G. Polya (Doubleday, 1957). A later book of this type is Wayne A. Wickelgren's *How to Solve Problems* (Freeman, 1974). Another useful book with a slightly different emphasis is Daniel Solow's *How to Read and Do Proofs* (John Wiley & Sons, 1982). These three books are highly recommended.

Sorting algorithms has been the subject of much study, and will be discussed further in Chapters 14 and 19. The Sort3Nums algorithm discussed in this chapter is a small version of an algorithm known more generally as *bubble sort*. An interesting discussion of this algorithm (and its drawbacks) is found in David Harel's book, *Algorithmics: The Spirit of Computing* (Addison-Wesley, 1987).

Plan to Throw One Away

In most projects, the first system built is barely usable. It may be too slow, too big, too awkward to use, or all three. There is no alternative but to start again, smarting but smarter, and build a redesigned version in which these problems are solved. The discard and redesign may be done in one lump, or it may be done piece-by-piece. But all large-system experience shows that it will be done. Where a new system concept or new technology is used, one has to build a system to throw away, for even the best planning is not so omniscient as to get it right the first time.

The management question, therefore, is not *whether* to build a pilot system and throw it away. You *will* do that. The only question is whether to plan in advance to build a throwaway, or to promise to deliver the throwaway to customers. Seen this way, the answer is much clearer. Delivering a throwaway to customers buys time, but it does so only at the cost of agony for the user, distraction for the builders while they do the redesign, and a bad reputation for the product that the best redesign will find hard to live down.

Hence *plan to throw one away; you will, anyhow.*

—Frederick P. Brooks, *The Mythical Man-Month* (Addison-Wesley, 1975), page 116.

PART TWO

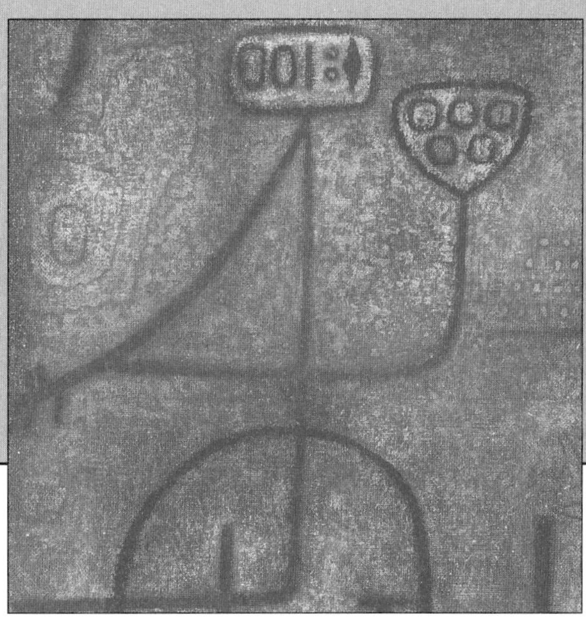

PROGRAM STRUCTURES AND DATA TYPES

Chapter 3
Program Structures

Chapter 4
Real Data and I/O

Chapter 5
Procedures with Parameters

Chapter 6
Controlling Execution

Chapter 7
Functions

Chapter 8
Ordinal Data Types

CHAPTER

3

Program Structures

CHAPTER CONTENTS

INTRODUCTION

From reading the previous two chapters, you know something about problem solving, algorithms, and procedural abstraction. Now it's time to build and run some actual Pascal programs that use these ideas. Chapters 3–10 will gradually introduce the features of the Pascal programming language that make it possible to implement algorithms on the computer.

The first step is to understand the structure of Pascal programs, which are not as simple as the algorithm outlines we showed in Chapter 2. A Pascal program must define its data objects, constants, variables, and procedures, and then must command the actions of the algorithm in the right order. There is always a **main program** containing the instructions to command the main actions. This is the part of the program that runs first. Usually, there are also **subprograms**, called **procedures** and **functions**, which perform actions under the overall command of the main program. Subprograms cannot run by themselves; they require a main program. The main program and the subprograms are the two kinds of **program units** that make up a complete program.

In this chapter, we will begin with a simple example program, and then progress to programs containing a few subprograms. Our main goals are

- To understand the syntactic structures of simple programs.
- To learn how syntax diagrams are used to determine the correct syntax for parts of Pascal programs.
- To learn to build simple programs containing a main program and subpro grams.

Bear in mind that syntax is not the central issue in programming. The main effort in programming is to break an overall task down into subtasks, and then to build a program from a **hierarchy** of **modular** procedures, each of which carries out a distinct subtask. A programmer who understands modularity and hierarchy will be able to easily adapt to various programming languages as the need arises.

3.1 A PASCAL PROGRAM

A Pascal program consists of a *header*, *declarations*, and a sequence of instructions called *statements*. The program must end with a period. Here's the **program structure** in detail:

PROGRAM *ProgramName* (*FileList*);

Declarations, if any

BEGIN

StatementSequence

END.

The first line, called the *program header*, gives the name of the program and lists the data files it uses. After the header come the definitions of constants, types of storage, variables, procedures, and functions used in the program. These definitions are called *declarations*. Finally comes a sequence (list) of instructions, called *statements*, telling the CPU what actions to take, step by step. This last part, from the BEGIN to the END, is called the **main program**. No matter how many procedures and functions are declared in the program, the program always executes the main program first.

Reserved words; case-insensitivity

In this book, Pascal words shown in capital letters, like PROGRAM, BEGIN, and END, have special meanings in the language and cannot be used for any other purpose. These are called **reserved words**, and are listed in Appendix A. (Although they are shown in uppercase in this book in order to point out which words are reserved, and although some Pascal editors distinguish them in some such way, the standard Pascal language does not require that they be entered in any special way in your source code. In fact, Pascal makes no distinction between upper- and lowercase.)

Metawords are placeholders for actual names.

Italicized words like *ProgramName* and *FileList* do not appear themselves in the program, but merely mark the spots where specific things will have to be inserted in specific programs. Such words are sometimes called **metanames** or **metawords** because they are placeholders for actual names to be inserted. (*Meta-* is from the ancient Greek for "behind" or "beyond.")

Here is a simple example of an actual Pascal program. It is explained line by line in the text that follows.

```
PROGRAM Monolithic ( Output );
BEGIN

   {--Show purpose of program }
   WriteLn( 'DRAWING A BIG L:' );
   WriteLn;
```

```
    {--Draw a big L }
    WriteLn( '|' );
    WriteLn( '|' );
    WriteLn( '|' );
    WriteLn( ' ___' )

END.
```

Program header

First comes the **program header**,

```
PROGRAM Monolithic ( Output );
```

announcing to the compiler that the name of this program is `Monolithic`, and that the program will send data to the standard `Output` file. The name `Output` is predefined in Pascal, and indicates the data file that goes out to the screen. When listed in the parentheses of the program header, this name is called a **program parameter**. (Similarly, there is a standard `Input` file that comes in from the keyboard, but it is not used by this program, and therefore not listed in the program header.) In International Standard Pascal, but not some particular Pascal systems, all external files used in the program must be listed inside the parentheses of the program header with commas between the file names. The program header must always be followed by a semicolon (;).

Declarations

After the header come *declarations* (i.e., definitions) of constants, variable types, variables, procedures, and functions, if any. In this program, there are no declarations. If there were any, each would be followed by a semicolon.

Main program; sequence of execution

After the declarations, if any, comes the *main program*, which tells the CPU what actions are to be carried out, and in what order. The list of **statements** (instructions) in the main program must be prefaced by the reserved word `BEGIN` and followed by the reserved word `END`, after which *a period is required*. Between the `BEGIN` and the `END`, the statements in the sequence must be separated by semicolons. No semicolon is required after the last statement in the sequence, just before the `END`. Note that *the statements in the main program are executed by the CPU in the order in which they are listed.*

Semicolons

Note that semicolons are used *between* successive statements. Semicolons are not used to mark the end of statements, so they do not appear after every statement.

Comments

There are two lines in the sample program that are not actually compiled as instructions to the CPU. Instead, they are intended merely as explanations for human readers, and are marked by enclosing them within curly { } braces. Characters within a pair of braces are ignored by the compiler and are called **comments**. Pascal also allows comments to begin with the two-character sequence of a left parenthesis and an asterisk `(*` and end with an asterisk and right parenthesis `*)`, and some programmers prefer to use these instead of braces. (But I don't; it's twice as many keystrokes!)

The executable statements

The statements between `BEGIN` and `END` are executed in sequence, and are called **executable statements**. In our sample program, the first is a `WriteLn` statement (pronounced "write-line"):

```
WriteLn( 'DRAWING A BIG L:' );
```

This writes the message "`DRAWING A BIG L:`" on the screen, leaving the cursor on the next line. *Single quotes (apostrophes) are required at the beginning and end of a string of characters to indicate that the string is data, and not the names of constants, variables, or something else in the program.*

Notice that we have not explained to the CPU how to execute a `WriteLn`. In fact, `WriteLn` is the name of a *procedure* already written for us and built into the Pascal language. What we are actually doing here is calling upon the `WriteLn` procedure. This is an example of how we build our programs from prefabricated parts already constructed by us or by other programmers. This is called **modular programming**.

The second executable statement is simply another call to `WriteLn`, but this time without data to send to the screen:

```
WriteLn;
```

This writes a blank line on the screen, leaving the cursor on the next line.

Then come three `WriteLns`, each of which writes a vertical bar on the screen and moves the cursor to the next line:

```
Write( '|' );
Write( '|' );
Write( '|' );
```

Finally, there is a `WriteLn` that writes a space followed by three dashes. As the program ends, the screen looks like this:

```
DRAWING A BIG L:

|
|
|
 ---
```

Formatting source code with indentation and whitespace

Pascal does not require the comments, the indentation, or the blank lines shown in the sample program, but these are common practice, to make the source code more readable. They help to divide the program into "paragraphs," with each paragraph corresponding to one of the program's tasks. There is a paragraph in which the program announces its purpose and another in which it accomplishes its purpose. This division into paragraphs has no effect on the compilation of the program, but is good style because it makes the program easier to read and understand. Readability is an important issue because programmers usually spend more time reading programs than executing them.

Pitfalls, debugging, and learning from experience

To get practice in running your Pascal system, you should compile, link, and run this program to see if it behaves as shown above. Consult your reference manual or instructor if you need help. Be careful to key in the program exactly as shown, or you will discover that the compiler is intolerant of what may seem to be trivial errors.

Be careful to spell the reserved words and identifiers correctly. Put semicolons and the period where they belong and nowhere else. Errors of spelling, punctuation, and "Pascal grammar" are called **syntax errors**. If you make these kinds of errors, the compiler will display error messages and refuse to compile the program. (A foolish consistency is the hobgoblin of people who use compilers, as Emerson might have said.)

> The Pascal compiler is a great help in finding syntax errors, so use it freely to test your code as you build programs.

If you make mistakes, don't get upset—most of us make mistakes in most programs, and beginners make many mistakes. Think of the compiler as a tool to help you find some of your mistakes. Study the error messages you see when the compiler detects your errors, and try to learn the kinds of errors that generate each message. Try to learn something from each error. After repairing your typos and other mistakes, the program should run correctly. Run the program to get a feel for how it behaves.

Then introduce a few deliberate syntax errors in your source code. (See Section 3.6.) Put a semicolon in the wrong place; delete one of the braces from a comment; misspell an identifier or reserved word. Recompile and notice which error messages appear, and where the errors are flagged. You will see that the compiler often gives very helpful and exact information about syntax errors, but sometimes gets so confused by the errors that its messages are not directly helpful. Make a correction and recompile. Sometimes this has the effect of revealing new error messages. Make another correction, recompile, and keep going until you have eliminated the errors.

> Experiences gained from deliberate errors can be an enormous help later, when you make unintentional errors.

Questions

1. What words are predefined and cannot be used for other purposes by the programmer?
2. What is the first line of a Pascal program?
3. What is the *last* line of a Pascal program?
4. What goes between the `BEGIN` and `END` of a Pascal program?

5. As far as Pascal is concerned, what is the difference between `Monolithic` and `MONOlithiC`?
6. What two kinds of program units are used in a Pascal program?
7. What are Pascal's two kinds of subprograms?

Exercise

8. Remove the apostrophes in the first `WriteLn` of the example program. What error message do you see when you compile? Next, restore the apostrophes but also remove the "O" in the word `PROGRAM` in the program header. Now what error message do you see when you compile? Finally, restore the program to its correct form but remove the period from the last line. What error messages do you see when you compile?

3.2 SYNTAX DIAGRAMS

As you can see from working through the previous example, the Pascal compiler is very picky about the **syntax** of the language: You have to get the vocabulary and grammar just right, or your program won't compile. In learning the syntax, it helps to have a quick-reference guide, so we will use **syntax diagrams** to show the rules succinctly. The diagrams appear in syntax summary boxes within the chapters, and are collected in Appendix F. Syntax diagrams look like railroad tracks seen from the air. *Any path through the diagram represents a legal construction in the Pascal language. Thus the diagram is a visual summary of all syntactically correct structures of a given kind.*

We begin with the syntax diagram for a program, shown in Figure 3.2.1. This diagram indicates that a program consists of a program header followed by a **block**, followed by a period. There is only one path through the diagram, so all three of these elements are required. The terms *ProgramHeader* and *Block* are in italics to indicate that they are meta-names. That is, they are not themselves names in the program, but only placeholders for the actual names.

To see what a program header is, we look at Figure 3.2.2. This diagram has more than one path, so we have options in constructing a header. The reserved word `PROGRAM` is required, as is a program name. Then comes an optional part, which is a pair of parentheses containing a list of all external file variables used by the program. (The option is that the list of file variables can be omitted if the program does not perform input or output.) At the end of the header, a semicolon (;) is required.

After the program header comes a block. A block is defined by Figure 3.2.3. It consists of declarations followed by a *compound statement*. Declarations are definitions of labels (for `GoTo` statements, not discussed in this book), constants, types of storage, variables, and any procedures and functions (i.e., subprograms) written by us. *The declarations must be listed in the order shown in Figure 3.2.4.*

Figure 3.2.1 *Program syntax: A program consists of a ProgramHeader followed by a Block, followed by a period.*

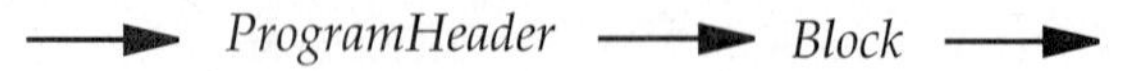

Figure 3.2.2

ProgramHeader syntax in Standard Pascal: the word PROGRAM, followed by the ProgramName, followed optionally by parentheses containing a list of FileVariables, followed by a semicolon. Some Pascal compilers do not require the list of file variables.

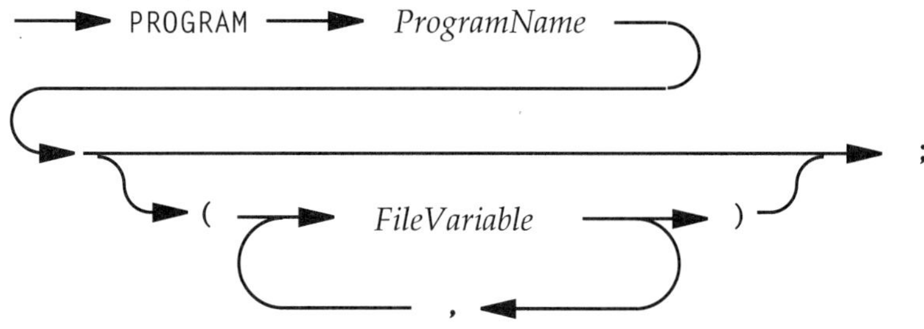

In addition to the declarations, a block contains a **compound statement**, which consists of the reserved word `BEGIN`, then a sequence of statements separated by semicolons, and finally the reserved word `END`. This is shown in Figure 3.2.5.

Putting together all these elements of the syntax, we arrive at the following structure for a complete program:

PROGRAM *ProgramName* (*FileList*);

Label Declarations, if any
Constant Declarations, if any
Type Declarations, if any
Variable Declarations, if any
Procedure and Function Declarations, if any

BEGIN

Statement;
Statement;
...
Statement

END.

The metaword *Statement* stands for the various kinds of Pascal statements that can be used to command various actions. These are shown in Figure 3.2.6 as a preview of the kinds of statements to be described in the next several chapters.

You might wonder at this point why we need all the diagrams when we can express the syntax of a program in a single outline like this. The reason is that several of the building blocks—the declarations, the block, the compound statement—can appear in

Figure 3.2.3

Block syntax: a Block consists of Declarations followed by a CompoundStatement.

Figure 3.2.4

Declarations syntax. Note the required order of the declarations.

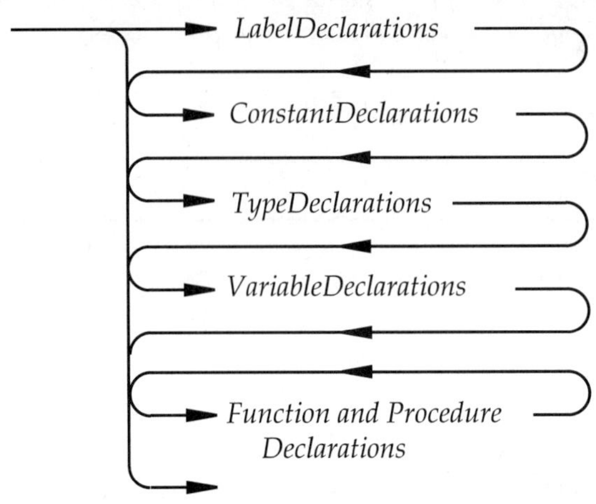

other contexts within a program. By providing separate syntax diagrams for each of these modules, it will be easier to use them in new contexts later in your studies. In fact, what you are seeing is that programs *are built from separate* ***modules*** *that "plug together" in various ways*. This is an important concept.

Questions

9. What things are required in a program header? What part of the program comes immediately after the program header?

10. How many distinct paths conform to the syntax diagram of Figure 3.2.4?

11. How many distinct paths conform to the syntax diagram of Figure 3.2.5?

12. How many distinct paths conform to the syntax diagram of Figure 3.2.6?

13. Do the following Pascal programs conform to the syntax diagrams of this section? If not, why not?

a.
```
PROGRAM One; BEGIN Statement; END;
```

b.
```
PROGRAM Two;
VariableDeclarations
BEGIN;
   Statement;
   Statement
END.
```

Figure 3.2.5

CompoundStatement syntax.

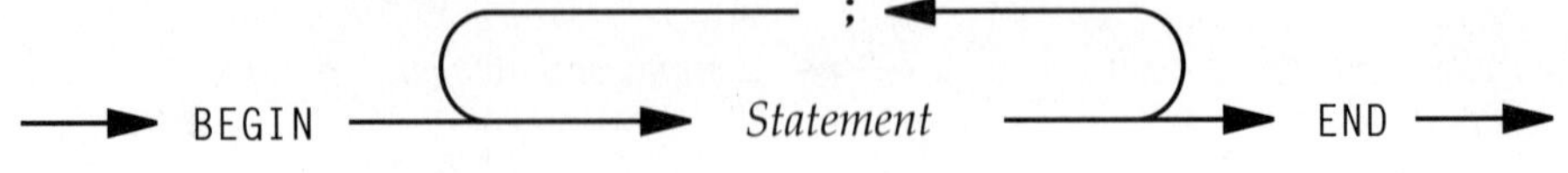

Statement syntax. Pascal features 11 kinds of statements. Procedure calls are introduced in this chapter; the others (except for labels) in the next several chapters.

Figure 3.2.6

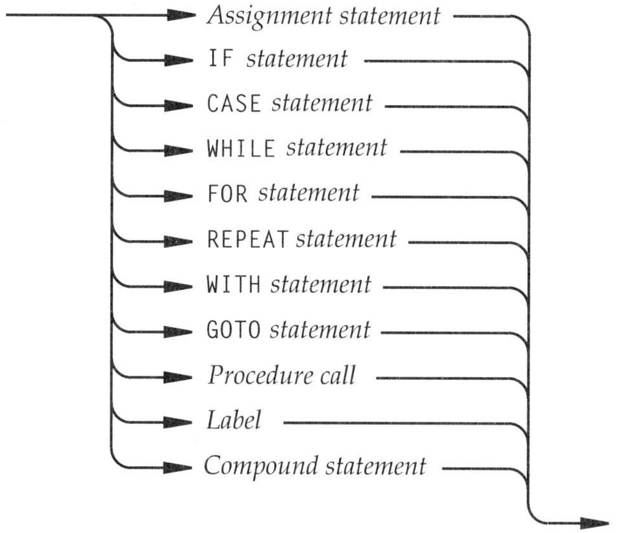

3.3 IDENTIFIERS

There are many names in a program: The program itself has a name, the constants and variables have names, storage types have names, and procedures and functions have names. By giving well-chosen names to the constants, variables, and program units, we make the program easier to read and understand. These names are called **identifiers**. The syntax of an identifier is shown in Figure 3.3.1.

A Pascal identifier must begin with a letter; the rest of the identifier can contain any number of letters or digits. But no other characters are allowed: no special symbols, punctuation marks, underlines, spaces, and so on. (Some Pascals relax this rule.) In addition, reserved words cannot be used as identifiers. Here are examples of legal identifiers in Standard Pascal:

```
A     Average     AnalogSignal     AverageOfManyNumbers

Ch    Digit1      Sort3Numbers
```

Again, Pascal is not case-sensitive, so `Digit1`, `digit1`, and `DIGIT1` are all identical as far as the compiler is concerned.

The following identifiers, however, are *illegal* for the reasons listed:

`Program`	(Cannot use a reserved word as an identifier)
`4F`	(Cannot start with a digit)
`Far_Out`	(Cannot contain characters other than letters and digits)
`Wow!`	(No special characters allowed)
`Yes No`	(No spaces allowed)

Figure 3.3.1 *Identifier syntax: An identifier consists of a letter, optionally followed by digits and/or letters.*

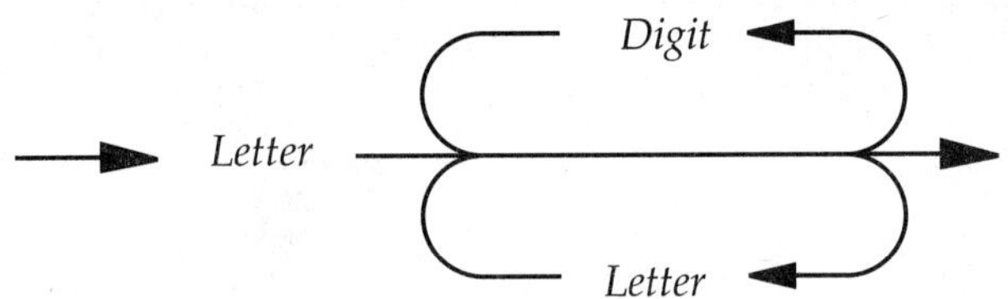

Some Pascal compilers place a limit on the number of characters that can be contained in an identifier. Some count only a few characters as being **significant** in the identifier. For example, some Pascal compilers make use of only the first eight characters, and would therefore treat `AdvancedCalculus` and `AdvancedPhysics` as the same identifier. This can be really confusing when debugging programs, so check the reference manual or perform an experiment to see if your compiler has this limitation.

Some identifiers have been predefined, and should not be redefined by your program, even though it is not actually illegal to do so. These **standard identifiers** are listed in Table 3.3.1. It is illegal to use identifiers that are reserved words, but you can use identifiers that contain embedded reserved words. Thus, `End` is an illegal identifier, but `EndOfTheGame` is not.

Questions

14. What is an identifier? Is the word `BEGIN` an identifier? Why or why not?

Table 3.3.1 *Standard identifiers.*

The following identifiers have predefined meanings in Pascal, and should not be redeclared in your program:

Constants:
```
False, MaxInt, True
```
Types:
```
Boolean, Char, Integer, Real, Text
```
Program parameters:
```
Input, Output
```
Functions:
```
Abs, ArcTan, Chr, Cos, Eof, Eoln, Exp, Ln, Odd,
Ord, Pred, Round, Sin, Sqr, Sqrt, Succ, Trunc
```
Procedures:
```
Get, New, Pack, Page, Put, Read, ReadLn, Reset,
Rewrite, Unpack, Write, WriteLn
```

15. Which of these identifiers are illegal in Standard Pascal? Explain why.

`ZippideeDooDah`	`4Dimensional`	`FarOut`
`Begin`	`eecummings`	`yesno`
`X`	`e.e.cummings`	`Yes/No`
`XSquared`	`X2`	`2X`
`X_Squared`	`Character`	`Char`

Exercise

16. Write and compile small programs to see whether your compiler allows nonstandard identifiers of the following kinds. Report on what you find out.
    a. An underline character used as a word separator in an identifier; for example, `Far_Out`.
    b. An identifier containing more than 255 characters.
    c. Two identifiers differing only in characters beyond the eighth position; for example, `ZippideeDooDah` and `ZippideeHooHah`.
    d. An identifier identical to a reserved word.

3.4 MODULARITY AND HIERARCHY

The `Monolithic` program of Section 3.1 consists of just a main program that calls upon one of Pascal's built-in procedures for output. When this program is executed, the main program commands the actions, which in this example, are all carried out by calling on Pascal's built-in `WriteLn` procedure. `WriteLn` *encapsulates* the details of writing characters on the screen, so our main program doesn't need to concern itself with those details; the main program just calls on the procedure whenever it needs to. Here we have an example of procedural abstraction at work.

Monolithic program: A program consisting of only a main program and no procedures or functions. This is bad programming style because there are no reusable modules..

This was **modular construction** (or **modularity**) too—construction of a program by using a prefabricated procedure. Modular construction will be emphasized throughout the book. All along, we will be trying to assemble a library of useful procedures for use and reuse in a variety of programs. Our first step is to see how we can build our own procedures.

Modular construction or **modularity**: Construction from individually distinct program units, treated as plug-together building blocks.

Writing procedures

The `Monolithic` program consists of two tasks: displaying the purpose of the program and displaying a "big L." Each of these tasks is carried out by an appropriate procedure. If we call the first procedure `ShowPurpose` and the second procedure `DrawL1`, we can describe the procedures in a notation similar to that used in Chapter 2:

The ShowPurpose procedure encapsulates:

```
WriteLn( 'DRAWING A BIG L:' );
WriteLn
```

The DrawL1 procedure encapsulates:

```
WriteLn( '|' );
WriteLn( '|' );
WriteLn( '|' );
WriteLn( ' ---' );
```

Writing a procedure

In Pascal, we practice procedural abstraction by writing **procedures**. A procedure is a sequence of statements grouped together and given a name. The syntax for doing this is very much like that for a program. There is a **procedure header**, followed by any declarations required within the procedure, followed by a compound statement containing the statements that make up the procedure. However, a **procedure declaration** ends with a *semicolon* instead of a period. This is shown in the syntax box below.

For example, to give the first two `WriteLn`s the name `ShowPurpose`, we simply declare

```
PROCEDURE ShowPurpose;
BEGIN

  WriteLn( 'DRAWING A BIG L:' );
  WriteLn

END;
```

Syntax for Declaring a Parameterless Procedure

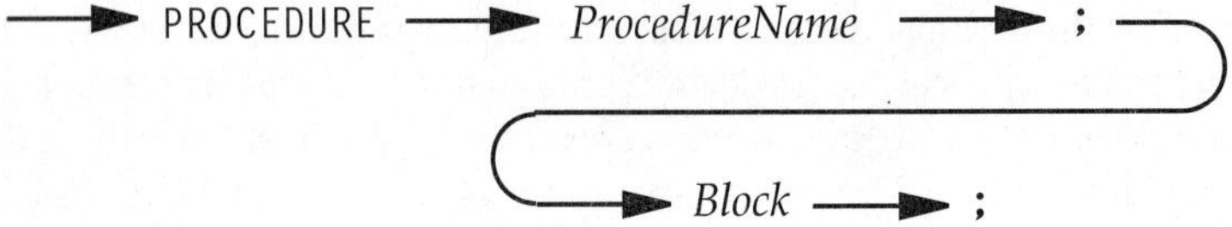

Pseudocode:

PROCEDURE *ProcedureName*;
Block;

Notes:

- A *Block* consists of declarations and a compound statement, as defined in Figure 3.2.3.
- The procedure declaration must appear in the declarations part of the program block, after the declarations of variables, as shown in Figure 3.2.4.

Similarly, to give the last four `WriteLns` the name `DrawL1`, we declare

```
PROCEDURE DrawL1;
BEGIN

   WriteLn( '|' );
   WriteLn( '|' );
   WriteLn( '|' );
   WriteLn( ' ---' )

END;
```

We have now defined how to "show purpose" and how to "draw L1." In effect, we have defined new verbs in Pascal. *These procedures are not stand-alone programs that can be executed by themselves. Instead, they are named groups of statements that can be executed by invoking their names in a program.* In the language of computer science, we **call** a procedure whenever we want to execute it. To call the DrawL1 procedure, we simply execute the statement

To **call** a procedure: To invoke a procedure by name, causing it to execute.

```
   DrawL1
```

whenever we want a "big L" to be drawn.

The declaration of a procedure must appear before the call to that procedure. Specifically, it must appear in the declarations part of a block containing the call statement. A complete program using the two procedures is shown below:

```
PROGRAM ShowL1( Output );


PROCEDURE ShowPurpose;
BEGIN

   WriteLn( 'DRAWING A BIG L:' );
   WriteLn

END;


PROCEDURE DrawL1;
BEGIN

   WriteLn( '|' );
   WriteLn( '|' );
   WriteLn( '|' );
   WriteLn( ' ---' )

END; { PROCEDURE DrawL1 }


BEGIN { main program }

   ShowPurpose;
   DrawL1

END. { main program }
```

Syntax for Calling a Parameterless Procedure

A procedure is executed whenever we state its name.

Pseudocode:
ProcedureName

Note:

- A procedure must be declared in the program before the point where it is called.

When this program is run (Do it!), the main program calls first procedure `ShowPurpose`, which in turn makes two calls to `WriteLn`. Then the main program calls procedure `DrawL1`, which in turn makes four calls to `WriteLn`. Note that one procedure can call another. The hierarchy of calls is shown in Figure 3.4.1.

Hierarchy

But why go to the extra trouble to write a program that does no more than the original, shorter, `Monolith` program? One reason is that *prefabricated procedures make it easier to build more complicated programs.* Another reason is that *a procedure, once declared, can be called any number of times without writing its code again.* (It's *reusable code.*) To see the importance of these advantages, let's embellish the program. In addition to the original L shape, we can make procedures that draw three mirror-reflected variants. We can think of the first shape as fitting the first quadrant of two-dimensional space, which in fact is why it is named `L1`. The other shapes can be named after their respective quadrants:

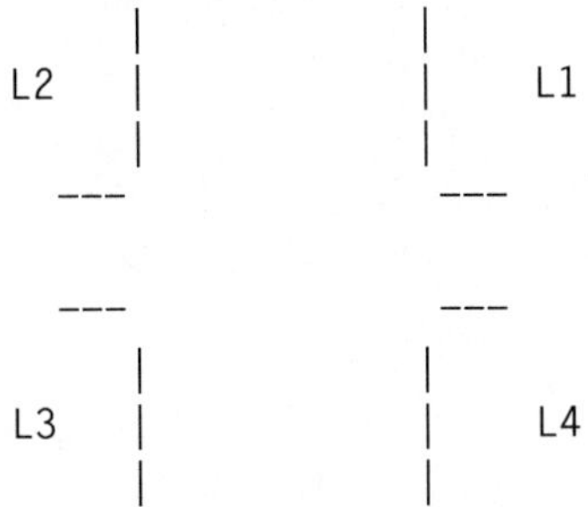

Of course, the procedures for drawing `L2`, `L3`, and `L4` are very much like that for `L1`. The advantage of having all four is that we can easily draw many patterns on the screen. For example, the pattern

Figure 3.4.1 *The hierarchy of the ShowL1 program. The main program calls ShowPurpose and then DrawL1, each of which in turn calls WriteLn.*

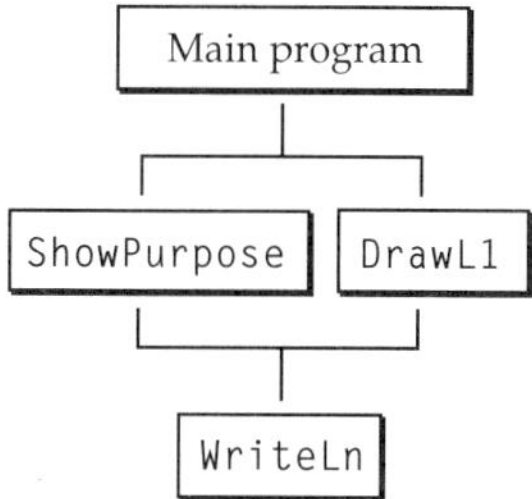


```
|
|
|
 ---
 ---
    |
    |
    |
|
|
|
 ---
 ---
    |
    |
    |
```

can be drawn by having the main program call `DrawL1`, then `DrawL3`, then `DrawL1`, and then `DrawL3` again. The whole program would look like this:

```
PROGRAM ShowPattern ( Output );


PROCEDURE DrawL1;
BEGIN

   WriteLn( '|' );
   WriteLn( '|' );
   WriteLn( '|' );
   WriteLn( ' ---' )

END; { PROCEDURE DrawL1 }
```

```
PROCEDURE DrawL3;
BEGIN

   WriteLn( ' ---' );
   WriteLn( '    |' );
   WriteLn( '    |' );
   WriteLn( '    |' )

END; { PROCEDURE DrawL3 }


BEGIN {main program}

   DrawL1;
   DrawL3;
   DrawL1;
   DrawL3

END. {main program}
```

Sequence of execution

As our programs get more complicated, it is important that you clearly understand the order in which statements are executed. The main program runs first, executing its statements, one after another. In the example above, each statement in the main program calls a procedure. Therefore, procedure `DrawL1` is executed, then `DrawL3`, then `DrawL1` again, and then `DrawL3` again. Even though the procedures are *declared* before the main program, they are not *executed* until they are called. They can be called as many times as you wish.

How the hierarchy works

In this program, the main program calls `DrawL1` and `DrawL3`, and those procedures both call `WriteLn`. The hierarchy of calls is shown in Figure 3.4.2.

Figure 3.4.2 *The hierarchy of the ShowPattern program. The main program calls DrawL1 and DrawL3, which in turn call WriteLn.*

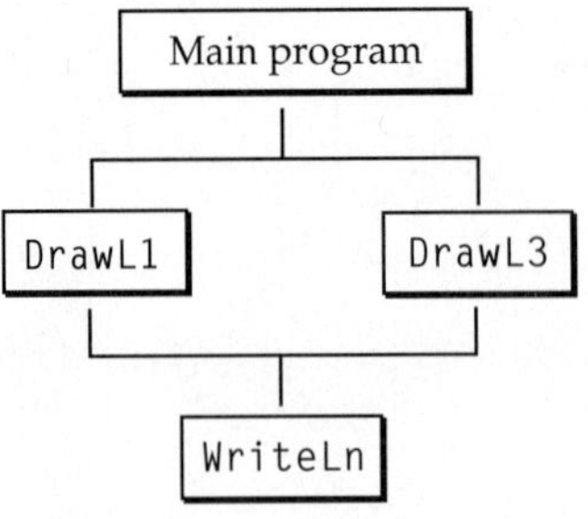

Exercises

17. Write and test programs to draw the patterns shown below.

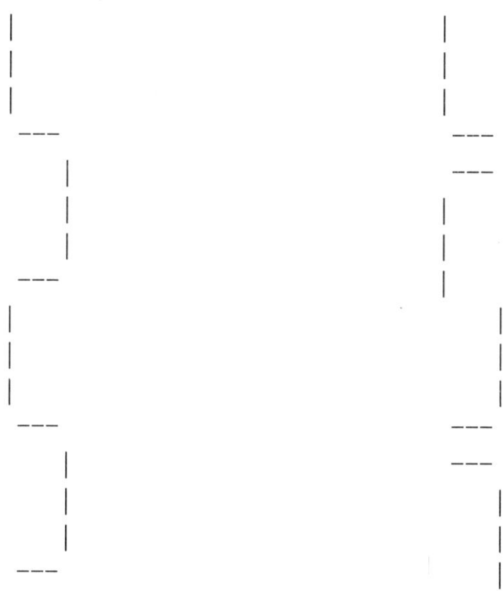

18. The four procedures `DrawL1`, `DrawL2`, `DrawL3`, and `DrawL4` can all be built from three more primitive procedures that draw a horizontal bar and right- and left-aligned vertical bars. Design such procedures, then build them into the `ShowPattern` program so that the `DrawL1` and `DrawL3` procedures call these new procedures instead of calling `WriteLn` directly.

3.5 HIERARCHICAL DESIGN

Now that you know how to use L-shapes to build more complicated patterns, you can encapsulate those in their own procedures, too. This allows us to refer to the more complicated patterns by name. For example, the program shown above draws a picture that is really two patterns like

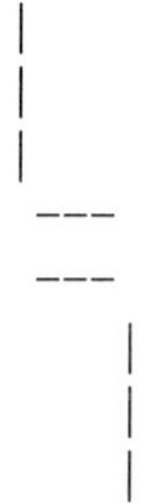

in succession. To give this pattern a name, you define a new procedure to draw it:

```
PROCEDURE DrawL1L3;
BEGIN

   DrawL1;
   DrawL3

END;
```

Then the original program can be rewritten to use this procedure. *Since* `DrawL1L3` *calls both* `DrawL1` *and* `DrawL3`*, those two procedures must be declared before* `DrawL1L3` *is declared.* The whole program would look like this:

```
PROGRAM ShowPattern( Output );


PROCEDURE DrawL1;
BEGIN

   WriteLn( '|' );
   WriteLn( '|' );
   WriteLn( '|' );
   WriteLn( ' ---' )

END; { of procedure DrawL1 }


PROCEDURE DrawL3;
BEGIN

   WriteLn( ' ---' );
   WriteLn( '    |' );
   WriteLn( '    |' );
   WriteLn( '    |' )

END; { of procedure DrawL3 }


PROCEDURE DrawL1L3;
BEGIN

   DrawL1;
   DrawL3

END; { of procedure DrawL1L3 }


BEGIN { main program }

   DrawL1L3;
   DrawL1L3

END. { main program }
```

Now the main program calls `DrawL1L3` twice. Each time `DrawL1L3` is called, it calls `DrawL1` and then `DrawL3`. The result is the same as in the previous version, but now we have a procedure that can be used more easily to generate bigger patterns.

The sequence of execution

Since this is our first program with more than two levels of hierarchy, it might be helpful to "animate" the sequence of execution that occurs. We will use a sequence of five diagrams, to be thought of as frames from a motion picture.

As the main program begins to run, the first statement executed is a call to the `DrawL1L3` procedure:

```
BEGIN { main program }

   DrawL1L3;
   DrawL1L3

END. { main program }
```

When `DrawL1L3` is called, execution of the main program is suspended while the procedure starts to run:

```
BEGIN { main program }

   DrawL1L3;
   DrawL1L3

END. { main program }
```

```
PROCEDURE DrawL1L3;
BEGIN

   DrawL1;
   DrawL3

END; { of procedure DrawL1L3 }
```

The first statement in `DrawL1L3` is a call to the `DrawL1` procedure, so execution of `DrawL1L3` is suspended while the called procedure starts to run. Now both the main program and `DrawL1L3` are suspended:

```
BEGIN { main program }

   DrawL1L3;
   DrawL1L3

END. { main program }
```

```
PROCEDURE DrawL1L3;
BEGIN

   DrawL1;
   DrawL3

END; { of procedure DrawL1L3 }
```

```
PROCEDURE DrawL1;
BEGIN

   WriteLn( '|' );
   WriteLn( '|' );
   WriteLn( '|' );
   WriteLn( ' ---' )

END; { of procedure DrawL1 }
```

The first thing the `DrawL1` procedure does is call `WriteLn`, telling it to send a `'|'` character to the screen. So the execution of `DrawL1` is suspended while `WriteLn` runs:

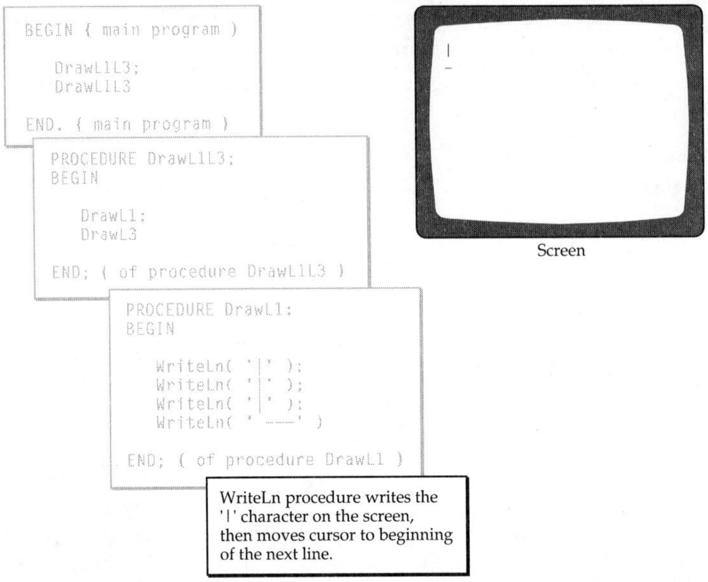

```
BEGIN { main program }

   DrawL1L3;
   DrawL1L3

END. { main program }
```

```
PROCEDURE DrawL1L3;
BEGIN

   DrawL1;
   DrawL3

END; { of procedure DrawL1L3 }
```

```
PROCEDURE DrawL1;
BEGIN

   WriteLn( '|' );
   WriteLn( '|' );
   WriteLn( '|' );
   WriteLn( ' ---' )

END; { of procedure DrawL1 }
```

WriteLn procedure writes the '|' character on the screen, then moves cursor to beginning of the next line.

Screen

After the `WriteLn` finishes, execution returns to `DrawL1`, which calls `WriteLn` three more times. Then `DrawL1` has finished its work, and execution returns to the `DrawL1L3` procedure, which had called `DrawL1` in the first place:

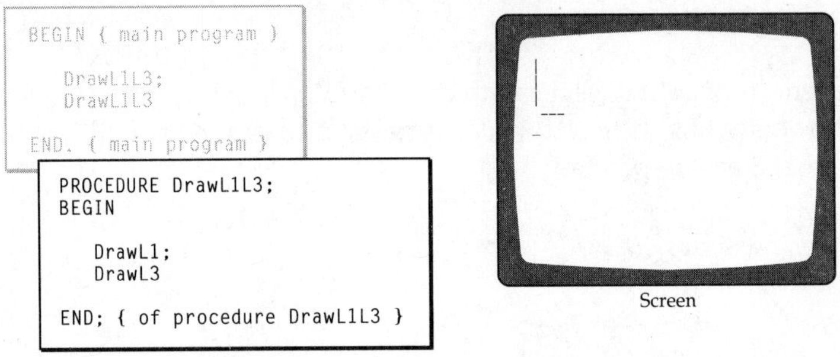

```
BEGIN { main program }

   DrawL1L3;
   DrawL1L3

END. { main program }
```

```
PROCEDURE DrawL1L3;
BEGIN

   DrawL1;
   DrawL3

END; { of procedure DrawL1L3 }
```

Screen

Then `DrawL1L3` calls `DrawL3`, which in turn, calls `WriteLn` four times. This process is similar to the one we've illustrated. After all of `DrawL1L3`'s actions are completed, execution returns to the main program, which calls `DrawL1L3` a second time.

Hierarchical design: The planning of a hierarchy, in which the designed items are ranked one above another.

In writing this program, we have practiced what is called **hierarchical design**. The main program controls the overall task of drawing the whole pattern, so it is said to be at the top of the hierarchy. The main program calls the `DrawL1L3` procedure, so `DrawL1L3` is subordinate to the main program: It is lower in the hierarchy. `DrawL1L3` draws half of the overall pattern. It in turn calls on `DrawL1` and then `DrawL3` to draw pieces of each half of the pattern. `DrawL1` and `DrawL3` each call `WriteLn`, which calls no further procedures. Thus the hierarchy has `WriteLn` on the lowest level and `DrawL1` and `DrawL3` on the next lowest, as shown in Figure 3.5.1.

Figure 3.5.1

Now we have a program in which the main program calls DrawL1L3, which calls DrawL1 and DrawL3, each of which calls WriteLn.

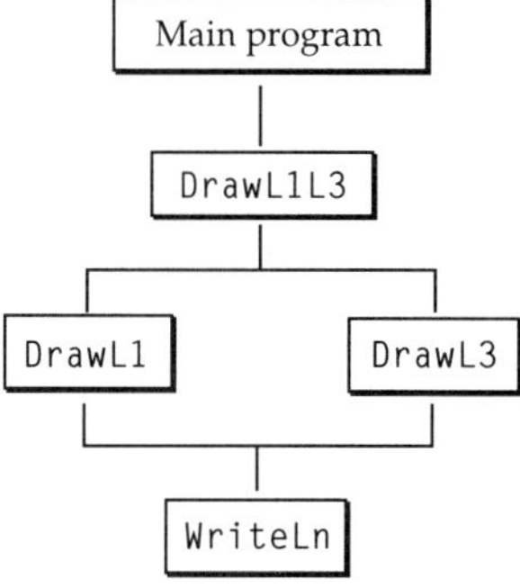

Bottom-up versus top-down design

In this section and in Section 3.4, we designed the lowest-level procedures first, then worked our way up the hierarchy. This is called **bottom-up construction**. It worked in these examples only because it was easy to imagine the breakdown of the problem into its constituent pieces. This made it possible to start off with the smallest piece, and then use it to build the bigger pieces. In large, complex programs this might not have worked. In such cases, it is usually better to begin with the specification of the top-level procedures, then progressively decompose these into smaller and smaller procedures, until the procedures are small enough for easy mental grasp. This is called **top-down design**, and we will practice it more and more as the problems become more difficult.

Top-down design: A design technique in which the main program is designed first, followed by the highest-level subprograms, and so on, moving downwards in the hierarchy.

Question

19. How are the ideas of modularity and hierarchical design used in the automobile and home construction industries? What have been the benefits?

Exercises

20. Redesign the `ShowPattern` program above so that the main program calls a single procedure just once to display the pattern.

21. Design and test a modular, hierarchical program to draw the big "S" shown below. Use the "L" procedures from this section plus any new procedures you need.

22. Invent a pattern you like, and write a modular program to draw it on the screen.

23. (Suggested by John Halleck) Design procedures called `DrawEyes`, `DrawNose`, and `DrawMouth`, so that a face can be drawn by calling the procedure shown below:

```
PROCEDURE DrawFace;
BEGIN

   DrawEyes;
   DrawNose;
   DrawMouth

END; { of procedure DrawFace }
```

Then build all this into a program that draws a face.

3.6 TESTING AND DEBUGGING

As you begin programming in Pascal, it is important to realize that there are three aspects to correctness in a program:

Syntax: Will the compiler understand the intent of the program?

Semantics: Does the program always produce the correct results?

Pragmatics: Is the program useful and easily used?

> A good program succeeds in all three areas. It doesn't matter whether the program compiles if it gives the wrong answers. And even if it gives the right answers, it won't succeed in the real world if it is clumsy, hard to understand, or difficult to use.

Syntax: the vocabulary and grammar of a language

In the beginning, correct *syntax* will be a problem. The syntax of a language consists of its vocabulary and grammar. In the case of Pascal, correct syntax involves all those little picky issues the compiler complains about: the exact spelling of reserved words and identifiers, the exact placement of parentheses and semicolons, and the declaration of identifiers before they are used. If your program contains *syntax errors*, the compiler will

Figure 3.6.1 *Most error messages from the compiler will correctly mark the position and nature of a syntax error.*

```
Semicolon required after last statement

PROGRAM Debug3 ( Output );

BEGIN

   WriteLn( 'Oh,' )
   WriteLn( 'wow!' )

END.
```

Figure 3.6.2

Occasionally, a spurious error message will appear long after the position of the actual error. This indicates that the compiler was really confused by the error. Look for the error before the position of the error message. If not immediately before the message, it may be quite far back.

```
Semicolon required after last statement

PROGRAM TestSayWhat ( Output );

PROCEDURE SayWhat;
BEGIN

   WriteLn( 'Say what?' );

BEGIN

   SayWhat

END.
```

not understand your source code, and will therefore fail to translate it to object code. Code with syntax errors is not even a program, because it cannot be compiled, linked, or executed. Fortunately, syntax errors are relatively easy to correct because the compiler tells you where most of them are. Most error messages will be easy to understand, reading `Semicolon missing`, or `BEGIN required`, or something like that. The exact wording of the message will depend on your compiler (Figure 3.6.1).

Occasionally, a syntax error will confuse the compiler so badly that spurious error messages will appear, or error messages will appear considerably after the actual point of error. An example is shown in Figure 3.6.2.

If you are unable to understand what is wrong, or if you are sure that the error message is incorrect, try "commenting out" whole portions of the program by placing braces around code that you think might be incorrect. This will reduce the amount of

Figure 3.6.3

Here, the procedure declaration has been commented out, leaving only the main program to be compiled. The change in the error message indicates that the commented-out area contains at least one error. (The error is that the procedure lacks an END statement and a semicolon.)

```
SayWhat has not been declared

PROGRAM TestSayWhat ( Output );
{
PROCEDURE SayWhat;
BEGIN

   WriteLn( 'Say what?' );
}
BEGIN

   SayWhat

END.
```

code that the compiler sees. Does this cause a change in the error messages? For example, Figure 3.6.3 shows the same program as in the previous figure, but with the procedure declaration commented out so that the compiler sees only the main program. The change in the error message indicates that the commented-out area contained at least one error.

As mentioned in Section 3.1, one of the best ways to increase your skill at finding and identifying syntax errors is to introduce single deliberate errors into an otherwise correct program, then compile and notice the correlation between the error and the resulting error message. Examples of such tests are shown in Table 3.6.1 for the `TestSayWhat` program used in the accompanying figures. Although the error messages shown were generated by the Turbo Pascal 6.0 compiler, similar messages can be expected from other compilers. Be sure to perform your own tests; there's no substitute for direct experience!

> Debugging is a process of dividing and conquering. Here are two basic techniques to help you find syntax errors:
>
> 1. Compile your program incrementally. That is, write and compile the skeleton of your program before adding the procedures. When the skeleton is correct, add one procedure and compile again. Don't add more code until the previous portion compiles and runs correctly, and never add much code before compiling again.
> 2. When you are unable to spot a syntax error after looking carefully for it, and especially if the error messages don't make sense, comment out part of the program and recompile. Did the error messages change?

To learn to debug, you must be willing to play with Pascal, trying things out just to see what will happen. You need to let the compiler help to teach you the syntax of the language. Table 3.6.1 shows examples of the error messages that resulted with one compiler when deliberate errors were inserted in the `TestSayWhat` program. The table is not a dictionary for interpreting error messages, however. A given error message can result from a variety of errors.

Table 3.6.1 *Examples of syntax errors in the TestSayWhat program.*

Syntax error	**Error message from Turbo Pascal**
Keyword `PROGRAM` missing or misspelled.	`BEGIN expected.`
Space in middle of program identifier.	`";" expected.`
Missing semicolon at end of program header.	`";" expected.`
Keyword `PROCEDURE` missing or misspelled.	`BEGIN expected.`
Missing semicolon at end of procedure header.	`";" expected.`
Standard identifier `WriteLn` misspelled.	`Unknown identifier.`
Missing `BEGIN` in procedure or main program.	`BEGIN expected.`
Missing `END` in procedure or main program.	`";" expected.`
Missing semicolon after `END` of procedure.	`";" expected.`
Missing period at end of program.	`Unexpected end of file.`

Semantics: the meaning of what you say

A program may compile but give the wrong results. When this happens, it means that your Pascal code made sense linguistically, but its *meaning* was wrong. You said "do this and then this," when you should have said "do this and then *that*." No compiler can help you with problems of this kind. To find **semantic errors** (sometimes called **logic errors**), you will have to test whether the program produces correct results when it runs. Semantic errors may or may not produce error messages while the program is running, depending on the nature of the error. When there are semantic errors, it is often helpful to resort to a third classic debugging technique:

> **3.** When a program produces strange results, insert extra output statements to write out *all intermediate results*. Then you will be able to see in more detail what happened during execution.

Pragmatics: the usefulness of what you say

A program may compile and also give the correct results, but it may still be unacceptable because it is too hard to read, too hard to understand, too hard to modify, or too hard to use. Any of these failures would make the program unpragmatic—impractical for programmers or users. As an extreme example, how would you like to spend your working day reading code that is formatted like this?

```
PROGRAM ShowPattern( Output ); PROCEDURE DrawL1; BEGIN WriteLn( '|'
); WriteLn( '|' ); WriteLn( '|' ); WriteLn( ' ---' ) END; PROCEDURE
DrawL3; BEGIN WriteLn( ' ---' ); WriteLn( '    |' ); WriteLn( '
|' ); WriteLn( '    |' ) END; PROCEDURE DrawL1L3; BEGIN DrawL1;
DrawL3 END; BEGIN DrawL1L3; DrawL1L3 END.
```

This is legal but awful Pascal; it is too hard to read.

Exercises

24. Try the program of Figure 3.6.1 with your compiler. What error message do you see? Check that the program compiles and runs correctly if a semicolon is added after the first `WriteLn` call.

25. Try compiling the program shown in Figure 3.6.2. Does your compiler give the same message? Try commenting out the procedure as shown in Figure 3.6.3. What message do you see now? Check that the program compiles and runs correctly when an `END` and semicolon are added at the end of the procedure declaration, before the `BEGIN` of the main program.

26. Find the errors in the following program:

```
PROGRAM Bad ( Output )
BEGN
   WriteLn( 'This program contains four errors.' )
END
```

LOOKING BACK

This chapter has been concerned mostly with program structure. The main points were these:

- A program contains one and only one main program. This is the part of the program that runs first.
- In addition to the main program, a program may contain subprograms, which are of two kinds: procedures and functions. Subprograms are distinct from the main program, and run only when called on.
- The main program and subprograms are the program units that make up a complete program.

By good use of subprograms, we make a program modular. This has several advantages:

- *The program is more clearly organized and therefore easier to understand and debug.*
- *Subprograms are easily reused* in a variety of programs. This is called *modular construction.*
- *Code need not be repeated every time a task needs to be performed.* Once a subprogram is available, its task can be repeated by merely calling the procedure repeatedly.
- *Testing is facilitated.* When an algorithm's hierarchy is relatively simple, the lowest-level subprograms may be constructed and tested first. This is called *bottom-up construction.* But when the hierarchy is complex, we are better off designing and testing the main program first, then designing and testing the top-level subprograms, working our way level by level down the hierarchy of the program. This is called *top-down design.*

We outlined the syntax of Pascal programs, using syntax diagrams to define the structure required. We saw examples of syntax errors and how the compiler might respond to them by displaying error messages during compilation. Programs can suffer from three kinds of errors:

1. Syntax errors are errors in the vocabulary, spelling, punctuation, or declarations in a program. These prevent a program from compiling.
2. Semantic errors are errors in the meaning of a program. These produce occasional or consistent incorrect results when the program is executed.
3. Pragmatic errors make the program inconvenient or impractical for users or programmers. These may be errors of style or of design.

The main effort in programming, however, is not the syntax of a programming language. The programmer's most important job is to break an overall task down into well-chosen subtasks, and then to build a program from a hierarchy of modules, each of which carries out one of the subtasks. A programmer who understands modularity and hierarchy can easily adapt to different programming languages as the need arises.

TERMS EMPHASIZED IN THIS CHAPTER

Block 60–61
Bottom-up construction 75
Calling a procedure 67–68
Case insensitivity 56, 63
Comment 57–58
Compound statement 60–62
Debugging 78
Declarations 56–57
Executable statements 58
Formatting source code 58–59
Hierarchical design 74
Hierarchy 68
Hierarchy diagram 69
Identifiers 63–64
Indentation 58–59
`Input` 57
Logic error 79
Main program 55–57
Metaname or metaword 56
Modular programming 58, 65
Modularity 65
Module 62
`Output` 57
Parameterless procedure 66, 68
Pragmatics 76, 79
Procedure 66
Procedure declaration 66
Procedure header 66
Program header 56–57, 60–61
Program parameters 57
Program structure 56
Program unit 55
Reserved word 56, 64
Semantic error 79
Semantics 76, 79
Semicolons 57
Sequence of execution 70
Significant characters 64
Standard identifier 64
Statements 56–57, 61–63
Subprogram 55
Syntax 60, 76
Syntax diagram 60
Syntax error 59,76–78
Top-down design 75
Variable declarations 61–63

REFERENCES

This book provides syntax diagrams for most of the ISO Standard Pascal language, both in the chapters and in Appendix F. However, some readers may prefer to have a complete Pascal reference manual as well. The best are Doug Cooper's *Standard Pascal User Reference Manual* (Norton, 1983) and the *Pascal User Manual and Report*, third edition, by Kathleen Jensen and Niklaus Wirth (Springer-Verlag, 1985).

It is not easy to learn style in any creative endeavor. To a great degree, style emerges with the ability to design, and both are learned partly by studying examples. There are, however, some books that can help. A classic for programmers is *The Elements of Programming Style* by Brian Kernighan and P. J. Plauger (McGraw-Hill, 1978). A more recent and more advanced book is Henry Ledgard's *Professional Pascal: Essays on the Practice of Programming* (Addison-Wesley Publishing, 1986). By the time you get most of the way through the present book, you should be ready for these.

CHAPTER 4

Real Data and I/O

CHAPTER CONTENTS

INTRODUCTION

The simple programs of Chapter 3 illustrated modular, hierarchical design and gave a taste of how programs can be assembled from previously written procedures. But now it's time to address some issues that did not arise in those programs:

- How does a program receive data from the keyboard? How does it write data to the screen or to disk files?
- How does a program store and manipulate data?
- How do the various program units communicate with each other when data must be transferred?

To get answers for these questions, we need to study how a data type is used in Pascal, and how the standard input/output (I/O) procedures work in detail. You will find that more is going on than is apparent at first sight. This chapter discusses five issues:

1. The real-number data type, used to store numbers with a fractional part and a floating decimal point.
2. The roundoff errors that occur when real numbers are stored in a computer.
3. How data are sent to Pascal's standard output procedures for transmission to the screen.
4. How data are received from the keyboard by means of Pascal's standard input procedures.
5. How the ideas of Chapters 2 and 3 can be applied to the design of interactive programs using real-number data.

4.1 REAL-NUMBER DATA

One of the ways in which the structure of a program is more complicated than the structure of an algorithm outline is that a program must declare its identifiers before they can be used. In fact, most of a program is taken up with the declarations of constants, variables, procedures, and other things to be covered later. When a program uses data, the types of the data objects must be declared. A **data type** is a specification of both the internal storage representation (Appendix K) and the operations that are allowed to act on the data.

Data type: A specification of the properties of the data and the operations they can undergo. Examples are real numbers, integers, and characters.

There are many types of data in computing: numbers, characters, true/false values, lists, vectors, matrices, and so on. In our early programming examples, we will use real numbers, the most familiar type for most beginners. In Pascal, a **real number** is a number written with a whole-number part and either a fractional part or an exponent or both. In mathematics, it is one of the continuously spread values "on the real-number line." In computing, the term refers to a discrete representation of such a value, *stored in a kind of scientific notation*. (This was discussed briefly in Chapter 1.) The number is thought of in terms of its significant digits and its exponent:

$$12.34 = \underbrace{0.1234}_{\text{Significant digits (significand)}} \times \underbrace{10^2}_{\text{Exponent}}$$

When writing **real constants** in Pascal, the whole-number part *must* be shown, but either the fractional part or the exponent (not both) may be omitted when unnecessary. The following constants are legal real numbers in Pascal:

```
 3.1        (That is, 3.1 × 10^0; the exponent of 10 is 0.)
 3.0
-3.1
-3.0
+3.1
 1.234567
```

Such constants are said to be written in **fixed-point notation** because the decimal point is shown in a fixed position, relative to the significant digits. This is similar to the *fix mode* used on some calculators.

Alternatively, constants can be expressed in scientific notation (often called **floating-point notation**), with a floating decimal point and a power-of-10 scaling factor. In Pascal, the letter *e* or *E* in such a constant means "multiplied by 10 raised to the following power" ("E" for *exponent of 10*). The following are also legal:

`3.1e0`	(3.1×10^0: could also be written `3.1`)
`0.31E1`	(Again, could also be written as `3.1`)
`1.1e1`	(1.1×10^1: could be written as `11.0`)
`1.1e+1`	(1.1×10^1: could be written as `11.0`)
`1.1e+01`	(1.1×10^1: could be written as `11.0`)
`1.1e-01`	(1.1×10^{-1}: could be written as `0.11`)
`-1.1E-1`	(-1.1×10^{-1}: could be written as `-0.11`)
`1e1`	(1.0×10^1: could be written as `10.0`)
`0.01234567e+2`	(Could also be written `1.234567`)

Figure 4.1.1

Real-number syntax: A real number consists of an optional sign, followed by a whole-number part, followed by a period and fractional part, or an exponential part, or both.

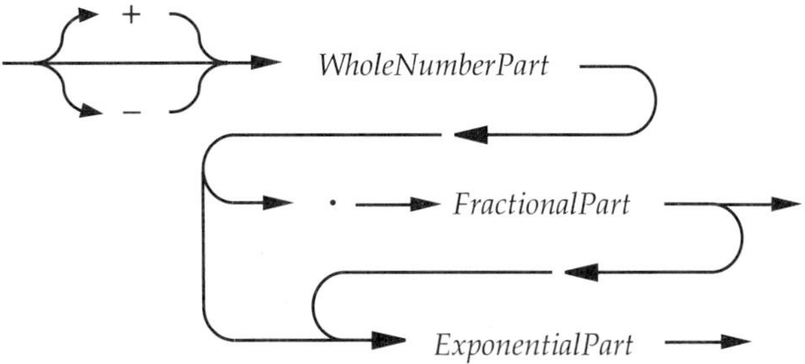

On the other hand, the following are *illegal* as real constants:

`3`	(No fractional part or exponent; just a whole number)
`3.`	(No fractional part or exponent)
`.11`	(No whole-number part; should be written as `0.11`)
`1,234.0`	(Commas not allowed)

Refer to Figure 4.1.1 for a diagram of real-number syntax.

Declaring real constants

The constants shown up to this point are called **literal constants**. Next we show a way to declare a name for a literal constant, creating what is called a **named constant**. *A constant declaration simply gives a name to a value that remains constant throughout execution of the program.* Named constants are declared in the declarations part of the program unit, after the program header but before the declarations of variables:

```
CONST
   Pi = 3.1415927;
   AbsoluteZero = -459.7;   { Fahrenheit }
```

These examples declare that `Pi` and `AbsoluteZero` are synonyms for the corresponding numbers. Because they are declared as constants and not variables, `Pi` and `AbsoluteZero` cannot be given new values during the running of the program. The syntax for declaration of a real constant is shown in Figure 4.1.2.

Figure 4.1.2

Declaring constants.

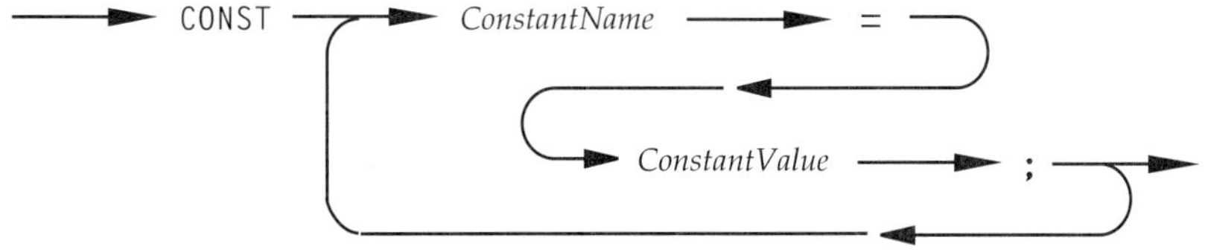

Figure 4.1.3 *Declaring variables.*

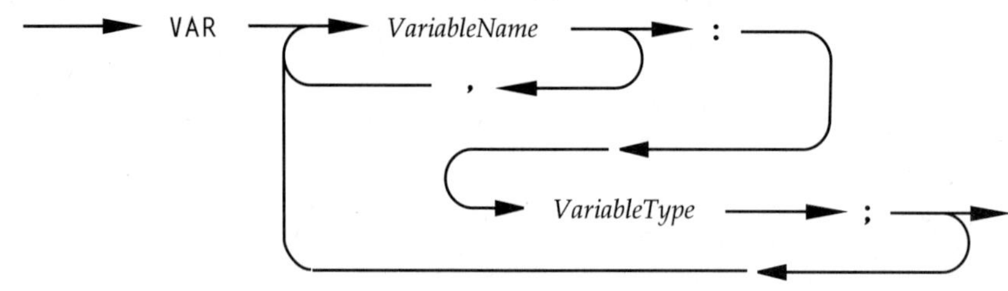

Declaring real variables

In computing, a **variable** is a memory cell to which a name has been attached, and in which the value stored can be changed during execution of the program. Variables must be declared after any constants, but before the word `BEGIN` in the program unit. To declare two **real variables**, `Fahrenheit` and `Celsius`, you can write

```
VAR
    Fahrenheit : Real;
    Celsius    : Real;
```

or, more succinctly,

```
VAR
    Fahrenheit,
    Celsius     : Real;
```

or, more succinctly yet,

```
VAR
    Fahrenheit, Celsius : Real;
```

All three versions are equivalent. The effect of the variable declarations is to create two real-coded memory cells as the program starts to execute.

Initialization of variables

The declaration of a variable just defines the name; it does not give a value to the variable. When the program begins running, a variable contains whatever bit pattern was left in

Figure 4.1.4 *As a program begins running, its variables contain arbitrary bit patterns. The variables are said to contain garbage.*

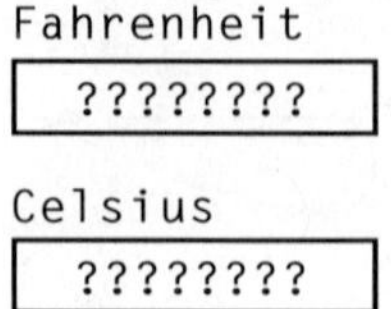

Real operators. **Table 4.1.1**

Operation	Type of operation	Symbol	Purpose
Identity	Unary	+	No change
Negation	Unary	–	"Takes the negative"
Addition	Binary	+	Yields sum
Subtraction	Binary	–	Yields difference
Multiplication	Binary	*	Yields product
Real division	Binary	/	Yields quotient

the memory cell from previous use. Such a bit pattern is meaningless now, and is therefore called **garbage**. See Figure 4.1.4.

If you want a particular value in a variable, your program has to put it there, a process called **initialization** of the variable. There are two ways to place a value in a variable: by reading a value from a file (e.g., the standard `Input` file), and by assigning a value to a variable by means of an assignment statement. You will see examples of both in this chapter.

Real operations

Pascal provides six *operations* on real data. Most of these are familiar from mathematics. There are two **unary operators** (operators taking a single operand) and four **binary operators**, taking two operands. These are shown in Table 4.1.1.

In addition to these, Pascal provides a number of standard functions that can operate on real numbers. These are discussed in Chapter 7, Appendix B, and Endpaper 1. But note that there is no exponentiation operation. Later, we will show how to fill this gap.

Real expressions

An **expression** is a combination of values and operators yielding a net value. A **real expression** is an expression having a real value. Table 4.1.2 shows some very simple examples, some with constants and some with variables.

Real expressions. **Table 4.1.2**

Expression	Value
`3.0 + 4.1`	`7.1`
`Weight1 + Weight2`	Sum of values of `Weight1` and `Weight2`
`4.0 * Celsius`	Product of `4.0` and value of `Celsius`
`3.0 / 4.0`	`0.75`

Things get more interesting when an expression involves several operators. Some rules are obvious:

- One operator cannot immediately follow another. Thus, expressions like `2.5 + -3.6` are illegal. If the intent was to write `2.5 + (-3.6)`, it must be written that way, with parentheses insulating the minus sign from the addition operator.
- In an expression like `2.0 * (4.0 + 3.0)`, the operation within the parentheses is performed first. If parentheses are nested, the expression within the innermost parentheses is performed first. Thus `2.0 + (3.0 * (4.0 - 1.0))` has the value `2.0 + (3.0 * 3.0) = 11.0`.

But expressions can look ambiguous. In the expression `3.0 + 1.0 * 4.0`, is the value `(3.0 + 1.0) * 4.0 = 16.0` or is it `3.0 + (1.0 * 4.0) = 7.0`? The expression can be written with parentheses to force one operation to be performed before the other, but what if the parentheses are omitted? In such cases, we rely on the precedence of the operators.

Order of precedence of real operators

The order of application of operators in an expression is decided automatically by the compiler, according to a "pecking order" among operators called the **order of precedence**. The compiler uses three rules:

1. Operations within parentheses are applied first. If there are nested parentheses, operations within the innermost parentheses are applied first.
2. Within a set of parentheses, or in the absence of parentheses, operators with higher precedence are applied first.
3. If there are several operators with the same precedence, these are applied in left-to-right order.

Table 4.1.3 shows the precedence levels of the real operators. For example, in the expression `3.0 * 2.0 - 7.0 / 2.0`, the multiplication and division are performed first, as though we had written `(3.0 * 2.0) - (7.0 / 2.0)`. This yields 6.0 – 3.5, or 2.5. Similarly, `7.0 / 2.0 + 4.0` is evaluated as though we had written `(7.0 / 2.0) + 4.0`, so the value is 7.5.

Style in expressions

Expressions like these, relying on the order of precedence to determine the value, are hard for humans to check and are therefore error-prone. *Good practice dictates that you use enough parentheses to make the expression unambiguous to human readers.* For example, don't

Table 4.1.3 *Order of precedence of real operators.*

Level of precedence	Operators
Highest	* /
Lowest	+ – (either unary or binary)

write `3.0 * 2.0 - 7.0 / 3.0`; instead write `(3.0 * 2.0) - (7.0 / 3.0)`. Don't write `7.0 / 3.0 + 4.0`; write `(7.0 / 3.0) + 4.0`.

Assigning a value to a variable

One of the ways to store a value in a real variable is to **assign** the value to the variable by means of an **assignment statement**. Such a statement takes the form

VariableName := *RealExpression*

where := is called the **assignment operator**, even though it is not an operator that can appear in an expression. Consider, for example, the code

```
CONST
   Factor = 0.555556;   { 5.0 / 9.0 }

VAR
   Fahrenheit, Celsius : Real;

BEGIN

   Fahrenheit := 212.0;
   Celsius := Factor * ( Fahrenheit - 32.0 );
   .
   .
```

This code assigns the literal constant `212.0` to the `Fahrenheit` variable, and then `0.555556 * (212.0 - 32.0)`, or 100.0, to the `Celsius` variable.

Two warnings about assignment statements are needed:

- Only a variable name can appear to the left of the assignment operator (:=).
- The expression on the right of the assignment operator must produce a value that can be stored in the variable named on the left. You cannot, for example, assign character data to a real variable. More about this later.

Assignment is not equality

The assignment statement

```
Celsius := 0.555556 * ( Fahrenheit - 32.0 )
```

does *not* say that `Celsius` equals (is the same as) 0.555556 times `(Fahrenheit - 32.0)`. That is, the execution of this statement does not permanently tie the value of `Celsius` to the value of `Fahrenheit`. The value of `Fahrenheit` can be changed later without any effect on the value of `Celsius`. *Assignment is not equality.*

As a further example of the difference, consider this statement:

```
Celsius := Celsius + 1.0
```

This is perfectly legal. It says to make a copy of the value stored in `Celsius`, add 1.0 to it, and then store the result back in `Celsius`, replacing its previous value. The net effect is to add 1.0 to the value of `Celsius`. (This is called **incrementing** the value by 1.0.) On the other hand, if the statement were interpreted as an equality, it would make no sense.

Increment: To add to the value of a variable.

Questions

1. In Pascal, what is a real number?
2. How are real constants and real variables declared? Give examples. Which declaration must come first?
3. Compare Table 4.1.1 and the list of standard functions in Appendix B and Endpaper 1. What important real-number operations does Pascal *not* provide?
4. Write your own description of the ways in which Pascal evaluates real expressions, taking into account the effects of parentheses, operator precedence, and left-to-right order.
5. How does the Pascal assignment operator, :=, differ from an equality sign?
6. Are real variables automatically initialized by Pascal? What happens if you use them without initializing them in your program?
7. In Pascal, the type of a constant does not need to be declared, but the type of a variable *does* need to be declared. Why is this?

Exercises

8. Which of the following are *illegal* as real constants? Explain why.

```
1.e-2          1e-2          1.234567e+13
-1e+3          -1.2e2        1.5
.5             2.            1,000.50
```

9. Find the syntax errors in the following program. Try to compile it on your Pascal system, correct the errors, recompile it, and run it.

```
Program Whazzit? ( Output );

CONST
   Whee := 6.12345;

VAR
   Stuff, Nonsense : Real

BEGIN
   Stuff := 12345.6;
   Whee  := 0.0;
   1.1   := Nonsense
END
```

10. Assuming that `Weight` and `Velocity` have the values 1.0 and 2.0, respectively, what are the values of the following expressions?

    a. `8.0 - 4.0 * Weight / Velocity`

    b. `Weight / Velocity * Velocity / Weight`

    c. `((Weight + 2.0) * Velocity + 2.0) * Velocity`

    d. `Weight + 2.0 * Velocity + 2.0 * Velocity`

e. `(Weight + 1.0) / (Velocity - Weight)`

f. `Weight + 1.0 / Velocity - Weight`

g. `1.0 / 6.0 + 1.0 / 6.0 + 1.0 / 6.0 + 1.0 / 6.0`

4.2 ROUNDOFF ERROR

The advantage of real-number storage is that a very wide range of numbers can be stored. The disadvantage is that only a finite number of them can be stored exactly in a computer; the rest are only approximated. (See Appendix K.) The error in storing most real numbers is called **roundoff error** or **representation error**.

Roundoff error is a serious problem in computing, and it will haunt us in several algorithms in this book. One of the situations in which it causes trouble is when adding numbers that are very different in size. Suppose that a program is adding 1×10^{10} and 4.0. These numbers must be converted to the same exponent before they can be added:

$$\begin{array}{rl} & 1.0000000 \quad\quad \times 10^{10} \\ + & 0.0000000004 \times 10^{10} \end{array}$$

Let us assume for the sake of an example that only eight significant figures are stored in the computer. Then the last three digits of the sum will be lost, and the sum will be stored erroneously as 1.0000000×10^{10}, as though we had added zero to the first addend. Thus roundoff error has led to **loss of significance** in our sum.

Now consider the effect this would have on a more complicated calculation. Suppose the program is attempting to solve the quadratic equation

$$ax^2 + bx + c = 0,$$

where $a = 1.0$, $b = 1 \times 10^5$, and $c = -1.0$.

If the program uses the standard formula

$$x = \frac{-b + \sqrt{b^2 - 4ac}}{2a}$$

it computes

$$x = \frac{-10^5 + \sqrt{10^{10} + 4}}{2}$$

$$\approx \frac{-10^5 + \sqrt{10^{10}}}{2} \qquad \text{(loss of significance)}$$

$$= \frac{-10^5 + 10^5}{2} = 0.0$$

This is a really bad result because, when plugged back into the original equation, it gives $-1 = 0$.

There is a way to compute a much more accurate result, however. By multiplying both numerator and denominator of the formula by the quantity $-b - \sqrt{b^2 - 4ac}$, we obtain the new formula

$$x = \frac{\left[-b+\sqrt{b^2-4ac}\right]\left[-b-\sqrt{b^2-4ac}\right]}{2a\left[-b-\sqrt{b^2-4ac}\right]}$$

$$= \frac{\left[b^2-\left(b^2-4ac\right)\right]}{2a\left[-b-\sqrt{b^2-4ac}\right]}$$

$$= \frac{\left[b^2-b^2+4ac\right]}{2a\left[-b-\sqrt{b^2-4ac}\right]}$$

$$= \frac{4ac}{2a\left[-b-\sqrt{b^2-4ac}\right]}$$

$$= \frac{2c}{\left[-b-\sqrt{b^2-4ac}\right]}$$

Using this new formula, the program computes

$$x = \frac{-2}{\left[-10^5-\sqrt{10^{10}+4}\right]}$$

$$\approx \frac{-2}{\left[-10^5-10^5\right]}$$

$$= \frac{-2}{\left[-2\times 10^5\right]} = 1\times 10^{-5}$$

This is a much more accurate value for x, as can be seen by plugging it back into the original equation. It gives $10^{-10} = 0$.

The difference in accuracy between these two computations is striking. Both computations involved the erroneous sum $(10^{10} + 4) = 10^{10}$, but the first formula subtracted the inaccurate $\sqrt{10^{10}}$ from the exact 10^5, giving an erroneous 0 in the numerator. In other words, all of the numerator's significant digits were canceled out. The second formula instead added the inaccurate $\sqrt{10^{10}}$ to the exact 10^5 to get an inexact 2×10^5 in the denominator. This number, while inexact, had not lost all its significant digits.

The moral is that there is always more than one way to write an algorithm, and in real-number calculations it can be important to use the best one. This can take considerable knowledge and skill. *One rule of thumb, among many, is to avoid subtracting real numbers that have almost the same value, for many of the significant figures can cancel out.* Later in the book, you will see other examples of the hazards of roundoff errors. Although we will discuss such problems to some extent, a complete treatment must await a more advanced course in numerical methods or **numerical analysis**. Some good textbooks are cited at the end of the chapter.

Fatal Error: How Patriot Overlooked a Scud

Even a minute mathematical error can lead to tragedy in the computer age, as confirmed by a report on the Patriot missile issued by the General Accounting Office (GAO) . . . . The report describes how a minor bug in Patriot's software allowed an Iraqi Scud missile to slip through Patriot defenses [on 25 February 1991] and hit U. S. Army barracks in Dhahran, Saudi Arabia, killing 28 servicemen.

According to the GAO report, the Patriot's electronic brain—now 20 years old—would have performed well in the task it was designed to do, which was to track and shoot down relatively slow-moving aircraft. But it ran into trouble when it was pressed into service in the Persian Gulf to defend against high-speed ballistic missiles. The main flaw was in the way the Patriot battery's missile-tracking computers processed timing information, which affected its ability to pinpoint the location of fast-moving targets.

The computer's tracking calculations depended on signals from its internal clock, which it translated into a "floating point" mathematical value. Because the computer could handle only relatively small chunks of data (by today's standards), it was forced to truncate this time value slightly, creating a slight error. By itself, the flaw would not have been fatal, but the Patriot software was written in a way that caused the error to increase steadily as time passed on the computer's clock.

That's what happened on the night of 25 February 1991. A Scud missile launched from Iraq popped over the horizon in Saudi Arabia and was picked up by a Patriot's radar, which was then performing a wide scan of the sky. The Patriot locked onto this target and calculated a "track" that was an approximation of the path it would follow to the ground. To confirm that this was truly an enemy Scud, the computer was programmed to get a second radar sighting to determine whether the object was following the path expected of a ballistic missile. If it was not, the signal would be rejected as a false alarm. And to speed up the process, the software told the computer to analyze only data from a small portion of the radar beam—the portion within a mathematically limited zone (the "range gate") centered on the path that a ballistic missile would be expected to follow. If the computer found a target within this range gate, it would know that the attack was real and would launch a Patriot missile. Sadly, in this case the computer miscalculated the position of the range gate, failed to see the Scud, and ruled that the original signal was a false alarm.

The mistake occurred because this particular Patriot battery had been running continuously for about 100 hours. According to GAO, its logic had built up a timing lag of 0.3433 second. That may sound trivial, but when tracking targets at ballistic speeds the error was fatal, for it caused the computer to shift the range gate 687 meters, letting the Scud pass unnoticed.

—Eliot Marshall, "Fatal Error: How Patriot Overlooked a Scud," *SCIENCE*, 13 March 1992, page 1347.

Questions

11. Why do real numbers in a computer behave differently from real numbers in mathematics? Explain in your own words.

12. In mathematics, real-number arithmetic obeys the laws of association, distribution, and commutation. (Review these in a college algebra book if you need to.) Do these laws hold when dealing with real numbers in a computer? Explain your answer, being specific and giving examples.

Exercises

13. A scientific calculator is actually a very small computer, and therefore subject to the roundoff error discussed in this section. Test your calculator and see if you can find values of x for which the following mathematical equalities fail badly. Use trial and error.

a. exp(ln x) = x

b. $10^{\log x} = x$

c. sqrt(x^2) = x

14. Find the largest real number, x, such that your calculator claims that $1.0 + x = 1.0$. This number is called the *machine epsilon*.

15. The average of the n real numbers $x_1, x_2, \ldots, xn$ is often calculated from the formula

average = $(x_1 + x_2 + x_3 + \ldots + xn) / n$

Can you propose a more accurate way to calculate the average? It might make a significant difference when n is very large. Explain why.

16. The standard deviation of a sequence of real numbers $x_1, x_2, \ldots, xn$ is a measure of how widely these numbers typically deviate from their average. The formula most often given for the sample standard deviation, σ, is

$$\sigma^2 = \frac{1}{n(n-1)}\left[n\sum_{i=1}^{n} x_i^2 - \left(\sum_{i=1}^{n} x_i\right)^2 \right]$$

This uses the sum of the data values and the sum of the squares of the data values. These sums are easy to compute on most scientific calculators. Try out this formula on your calculator. Find s for the following sequences of three numbers:

a. 1.00000, 1.00001, 1.00002

b. 1.0000000, 1.0000001, 1.0000002

c. 1.000000000, 1.000000001, 1.000000002

Explain your results. If your calculator has a built-in standard deviation function, compare its results with the ones given by our formula. Is it better? (A better algorithm for this calculation is described in Chapter 14's Projects.)

4.3 USING PARAMETERS WITH WRITE AND WRITELN

Standard Pascal provides two **output procedures**, by means of which a program can display data on the standard output device, which we will assume is a screen. These procedures are called `Write` and `WriteLn`, and are similar in their operation. Both are used to display a sequence of data values on one line of the screen. The difference is that `WriteLn` afterwards moves the cursor to the beginning of the next line, so that subsequent output will appear on a new line.

The syntax for calling these two output procedures is to specify the procedure name, followed by parentheses containing a list of the data values to be written on the screen. The data values are separated in the list by commas. These data values will be displayed in the order they are listed. Such values will be expressions of some kind; that is, they will be literal or named constants, or variables, or more complicated expressions.

Suppose, for example, that we have the following declarations and initializations:

```
CONST
   One = 1.0;

VAR
   Two : Real;

BEGIN

   Two := 2.0 * One;
```

Then, if the program calls

```
   Write( One, Two );
```

the screen will display something like

```
 1.0000000000E+00 2.0000000000E+00_
```

and the cursor will remain on the same line, after the last output value. (Your system may show a different number of digits, but the display should be similar.) On the other hand, if we call

```
   WriteLn( One, Two );
```

the cursor will end up at the beginning of the next line:

```
 1.0000000000E+00 2.0000000000E+00

_
```

We can also send literal constants (as opposed to named constants) to the output procedures. For example, we might send a literal string constant, followed by the value of a named real constant:

```
   Write( 'One = ', One );
```

This displays

```
One =  1.0000000000E+00_
```

On the other hand, we might send a literal real constant and the value of a variable. The call

```
   Write( 1.0, '    ', Two );
```

displays

```
 1.0000000000E+00     2.0000000000E+00_
```

The expressions whose values are to be displayed can be as complicated as you want. For example, the call

```
   WriteLn( 2.0 * ( One - ( Two / 3.0 ) ) );
```

writes the value of the expression

```
2.0 * ( One - ( Two / 3.0 ) ),
```

and therefore displays

```
 6.6666666667E-01

_
```

Syntax for Calling Write and WriteLn

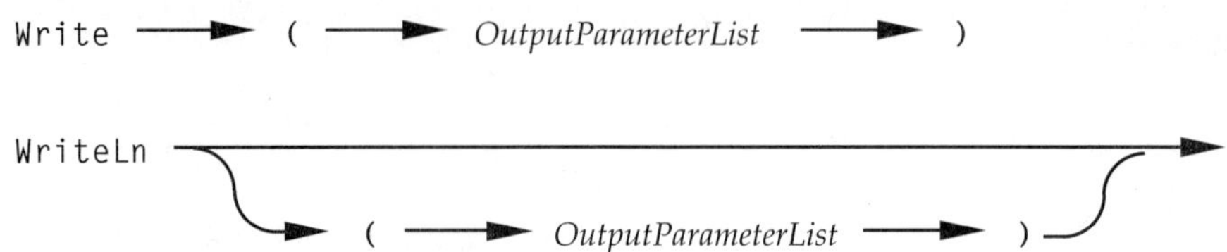

Pseudocode:

```
Write( OutputParameterList )
WriteLn( OutputParameterList )
WriteLn
```

where *OutputParameterList* is a list of output values, separated by commas. The output values are the values of expressions; that is, they can be specified as literal or named constants, or variables, or more complicated expressions.

Notes:

- `Write` transmits the *OutputParameterList* values to the screen in the order listed, then leaves the cursor immediately after the last value, on the same line of output.
- `WriteLn` transmits the *OutputParameterList* values to the screen in the order listed, then transmits an `<EOLn>` to move the cursor to the beginning of the next line.
- If *OutputParameterList* is omitted from a call to `WriteLn`, a blank line is sent to the screen. (*OutputParameterList* cannot be omitted from a call to `Write`.)
- The appearance of output values can be specified in the `Write` or `WriteLn` call. This is called *formatting*, and is explained on the next page.

Screen output consists of characters.

When you send a real number to the screen, the real number is not displayed directly. Real numbers are stored in the computer's memory in a binary-encoded scientific notation that cannot be displayed. (See Appendix K.) Therefore, the output procedure must translate such numbers to character representations in order to display them. Displaying a real number therefore involves three steps:

1. The calling program unit—main program or subprogram—sends a copy of a real number to `Write` or `WriteLn`.
2. The output procedure translates the number into a string of characters that symbolizes the number. For example, the number `-123.4` might be translated into the string of characters `'-1.2340000000E+02'`. This is a string of 17 character codes and *not* the memory representation of a real number.
3. The output procedure transmits the resulting string of characters to the screen in left-to-right order.

Figure 4.3.1

In the call WriteLn(1.23, 2.34), WriteLn receives two real parameters, translates them to character strings, and sends the strings to the screen.

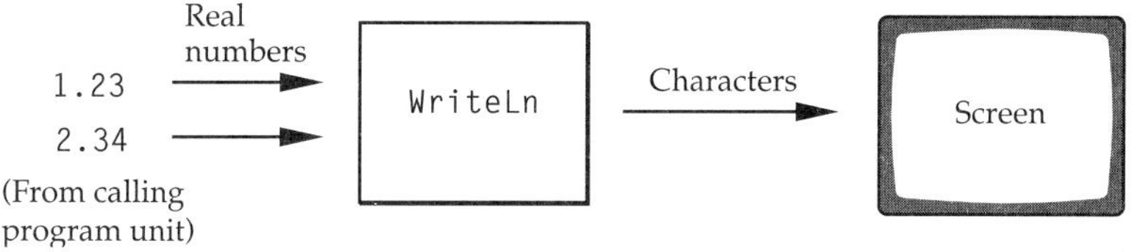

Output values are in-parameters of the output procedure.

The values sent to `Write` or `WriteLn` for display are called **in-parameters** of the procedure. These values are copied by the calling program unit into storage cells that belong to the procedure. The procedure then uses the copied values as data for display.

In summary, the output procedure receives parameters from the calling program unit, converts these parameters to character-string representations, then sends the strings to the screen. This is diagrammed in Figure 4.3.1.

Formatting real-number output

In the examples shown above, no control was exercised over the appearance of the real numbers on the screen. They just printed however the Pascal system decided to do it, in the **default format**. But we can specify the format in the `Write` or `WriteLn` call if we want. This is called **formatting the output**. There are two ways to specify the output format of a real number. The simplest is to specify just the **field width**, which is the number of characters to be used in displaying the number, including the decimal point:

```
RealExpression : FieldWidth
```

If the specified field width is greater than that required to display the number, the number is shown *left-aligned* in the field. If the specified field width is less than enough to display the number, some of the right-hand digits may be chopped off; the results depend on your Pascal system.

Suppose, for example, that `Two` has the value 2.0, as before. Then

`Write( Two )`	will print	`Δ2.0000000000E+00`
`Write( Two : 8 )`	will print	`Δ2.0E+00`
`Write( Two : 10 )`	will print	`Δ2.0E+00ΔΔ`

(Here, the Δ symbols indicate the locations of blanks.)

This kind of output is said to be in **floating-point format** because scientific notation is used to allow the decimal point to "float."

There is also a way to specify what is called **fixed-point format**; that is, the everyday notation for real numbers, in which the decimal point has a fixed position among the digits. This is accomplished similarly, but with a second specifier for the number of digits that should appear to the right of the decimal point:

```
RealExpression : FieldWidth : FractionalDigits
```

With this kind of formatting, the number is *right-aligned* in the field. Again suppose that Two has the value 2.0. Then

```
Write( Two : 6 : 1 )       will print    ΔΔΔ2.0
Write( Two : 3 : 1 )       will print    2.0
Write( Two : 5 : 2 )       will print    Δ2.00
Write( Two : 10 : 2 )      will print    ΔΔΔΔΔΔ2.00
```

Output to the screen is actually a text file.

Data sent to the screen is, as we have said, a stream (or sequence) of characters. To be more precise, it is a stream of characters organized into lines of text. Pascal refers to this as a **text file.** Pascal's standard output text file is associated with the predefined Output file variable declared in the program header. In fact, the way we have used Write and WriteLn so far is very similar to the way we will later write data to an external text file stored on a disk drive. This will be discussed further in Chapter 17. (For those who want to know more about this, Sections 17.1–17.2 are designed so that they can be studied immediately after the present chapter.)

End-of-line signals in output

<EOLn>: The end-of-line signal.

The stream of characters sent to the Output file can include special control characters that are used to control the appearance of the screen. The most common example is the control signal sent by WriteLn at the end of a line, the so-called **end-of-line signal**. We will indicate this signal in the book by the symbol <EOLn>. In some Pascal systems, the end-of-line signal is a single control character. (In ASCII, it would be character 13, called *carriage return.*) In Turbo Pascal, the end-of-line signal is a sequence of two characters: ASCII character 13 (carriage return) followed by ASCII character 10 (line feed). Consult your reference manual or instructor for details about your Pascal system.

Questions

17. What is the difference between writing the variable Two and writing the string 'Two' to the screen?

18. When the Write or WriteLn procedure writes real numbers to the screen, it writes *characters.* For example, when 1.1 is written, what gets written is the string ' 1.1000000000E+00', for example, and not the real number 1.1. What is the distinction being made here?

19. When the following stream of characters goes to the Output file, what does the screen look like? Also, show the final position of the cursor.

```
Key F for first name<EOLn>or  L for last name<EOLn>
```

Exercises

20. What is written to Output by the following program? (Show *exactly* what will be displayed on your system.)

```
PROGRAM Test1( Output );

CONST
   FourThirdsPi = 4.1887902;
```

```
VAR
   Radius, Volume : Real;

BEGIN
   WriteLn( 'VOLUME OF A SPHERE' );
   WriteLn;

   Radius := 1.1;
   Volume := FourThirdsPi * Radius * Radius * Radius;

   WriteLn( 'Radius = ', Radius:4:1 );
   WriteLn( 'Volume = ', Volume:8:2 )
END.
```

21. What is written to `Output` by the following program? (Show *exactly* what will be displayed on your system.)

```
PROGRAM Test2( Output );

CONST
   PlancksConstant = 6.626176e-34; { Joule-sec }

VAR
   Frequency, Energy : Real;

BEGIN
   WriteLn( 'FREQUENCY-ENERGY RELATION' );
   WriteLn;

   Frequency := 6.0e+14;
   Energy    := PlancksConstant * Frequency;

   Write( 'For a frequency of ', Frequency:10, '/sec,' );
   WriteLn( ' energy = ', Energy:10, ' Joules' )
END.
```

22. What is written to `Output` by the following program? (Show *exactly* what will be written on your system.)

```
PROGRAM Test3( Output );

VAR
   Mass1, Mass2 : Real;

BEGIN
   WriteLn( 'AVERAGE OF TWO MASSES' );
   WriteLn;

   Mass1 := 1.23;
   Mass2 := 2.659;

   WriteLn( 'Average of masses ', Mass1:5:2, ' and ', Mass2:5:2 );
   WriteLn( 'is ', ( 0.5 * (Mass1 + Mass2) ):5:2 )
END.
```

23. Write a small program that writes the message

```
The magic number<EOLn>7.0,<EOLn>plus or minus 2.0<EOLn>
```

to the screen. Write the two numbers as formatted real output.

24. What is written to `Output` by the following program? (Show *exactly* what will be written on your system.)

```
PROGRAM Test4( Output );

VAR
   FocalLength, Diameter, FNumber : Real;

BEGIN

   WriteLn( 'F-NUMBER' );

   FocalLength := 105.0;
   Diameter    := 4.77;
   FNumber     := FocalLength / Diameter;

   WriteLn( 'f = ', FocalLength:8:2 );
   WriteLn( 'd = ', Diameter:8:2 );
   WriteLn( 'gives f/', FNumber:4:1 )

END.
```

4.4 USING PARAMETERS WITH READ AND READLN

To complement the standard `Output` file, which is a stream of characters going to the screen, Pascal also has a standard `Input` file, which is a stream of characters coming from the keyboard. A pair of input procedures, `Read` and `ReadLn`, are used to copy data from the `Input` file into program variables. (`Read` is used to read the next datum from the current line of input; `ReadLn` reads the rest of the current line.) We specify the variables to receive data by listing them as parameters for the input procedures. For example, if a program unit has declared a real variable `Fahrenheit`, the call `ReadLn(Fahrenheit)` will read a real number from the keyboard and store it in the `Fahrenheit` variable. This is shown in Figure 4.4.1.

The `Read` and `ReadLn` procedures can get input values for as many variables as you wish; just list them as parameters. Note that `Read` and `ReadLn` *parameters must be variables;* they cannot be constants or more general expressions.

The Input text file

The `Input` file is a text file. Therefore, when `Read` and `ReadLn` read from the keyboard, they are reading *characters*. If the strings of characters symbolize real-number data, then

Figure 4.4.1 *Reading a real number from the keyboard and storing it in the caller's Fahrenheit variable.*

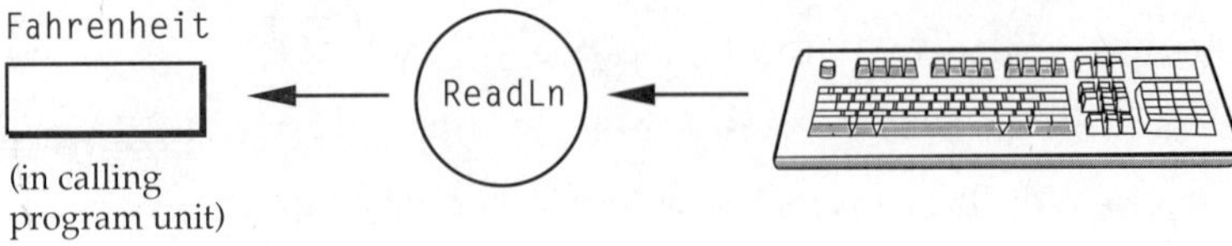

the input procedure will have to convert the strings to real numbers. This, of course, is the reverse of the conversion performed by output procedures.

The input process for a single real number involves four stages:

1. Leading whitespace characters (blanks, tabs, end-of-line characters) are skipped.
2. The input procedure reads the string of numeric characters, terminating input when it encounters a character that cannot be part of the real number. Such a character is called a **delimiter**. The normal delimiters are whitespace characters.
3. The received string of characters is translated into a real-number value.
4. The resulting real number is stored in the corresponding parameter variable.

Delimiter: A symbol used to mark the beginning or end of data.

Figure 4.4.2 shows the input process for real numbers.

In-parameters versus out-parameters

As you have seen in the discussions of this section and the last, parameters can be used to transmit data in two directions:

- An **in-parameter** is used to copy a value *into* a procedure. In this way, the calling program unit sends data to the procedure that is called. This is what happens when the program calls Write or WriteLn.
- An **out-parameter** is used to return a value *from* a procedure to a variable in the program unit that called the procedure. This is how Read and ReadLn return values.

Later in this chapter, and even more in the next chapter, we will examine how you can write your own procedures that receive and return parameters. You will find that the syntax when calling your own procedures is similar to that used when calling `WriteLn` and `ReadLn`.

I/O buffering

Data do not travel directly from the keyboard to the variables that are parameters of the `Read` or `ReadLn` statement; this would be too hardware-inefficient. Human fingers and keyboards are so much slower than the normal operations of the CPU and main memory that if the CPU communicated directly with them, its activities would be greatly disrupted.

Translating a string of keyboard characters into a real number and storing the number in a parameter variable. **Figure 4.4.2**

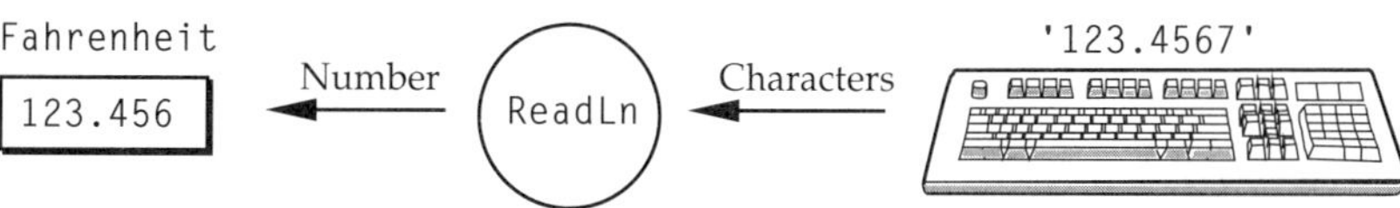

Figure 4.4.3 *Data are transferred to and from external devices by way of buffers, which are holding areas in main memory. Here we see an input buffer providing temporary storage for data traveling from the keyboard to variables called Fahrenheit and Celsius.*

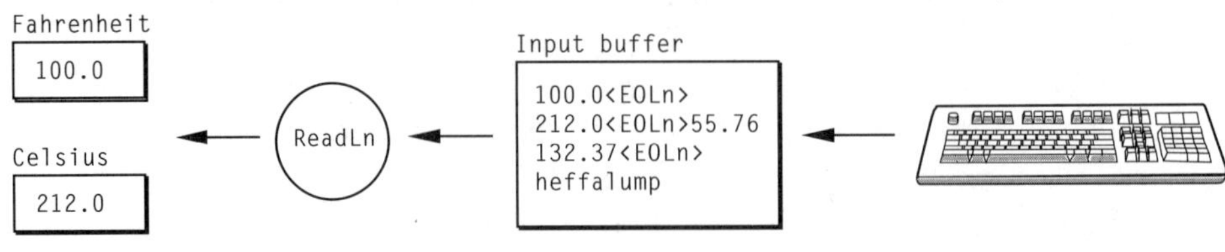

When the `Input` or `Output` files are automatically opened as the program begins, the program is connected to the file by means of a storage area in main memory called a **file buffer**. The buffer acts like a temporary way station on the way to or from the peripheral devices, and is usually big enough to hold several hundred characters worth of data. Thus data are transferred in two stages on the way from variables to output devices, and on the way from input devices to variables. An example is shown in Figure 4.4.3.

The advantage of buffering is that data are transferred to or from the relatively slow external devices in large chunks, without distracting the CPU. However, the memory-to-memory transfer between variables and buffer can occur quickly, whenever required by the input or output procedures.

When a program reads from a file like `Input`, the data are copied immediately from the file into the **input buffer** for that file. However, the Pascal Standard does not say whether these data will be transferred immediately from the buffer to the input variables specified in the call to `Read` or `ReadLn`. In fact, the results may vary with the Pascal system being used; in general, we can only say that the variables receive values whenever the Pascal system gets around to transferring them—whenever the buffer is **flushed**, as programmers say. In many Pascal systems, flushing occurs when an input operation encounters the *end-of-line signal*, `<EOLn>`, which is signaled by the user pressing the RETURN key (marked ENTER on some keyboards). For this reason, interactive programs that call the `Read` procedure behave strangely under some Pascal systems. *In this book, we will largely avoid this problem by using* `ReadLn` *for most input operations.*

Similar problems may occur with output. When does the output from a `Write` or `WriteLn` arrive in the external file? Whenever the **output buffer** is flushed, which may not be until the next `<EOLn>` is transmitted to the output buffer. This is not often a problem with modern Pascal systems, but if you should have problems with screen output not arriving promptly on the screen from `Write` statements, try changing the `Write` to a `WriteLn`.

The end-of-file signal

<EOF>: The end-of-file signal.

Another special signal that may arrive from the `Input` file is the so-called end-of-file signal, which is symbolized `<EOF>` in this book. The end-of-file signal indicates to the program that there will be no more inputs. In Chapter 17, you will see in detail how this signal can be detected by a program and how it can be used. In Turbo Pascal, `<EOF>` is signaled by pressing Control-Z on the keyboard. (Hold down the CONTROL key while pressing the Z key.) For other systems, check with your instructor or reference manual.

Syntax for Calling Read and ReadLn

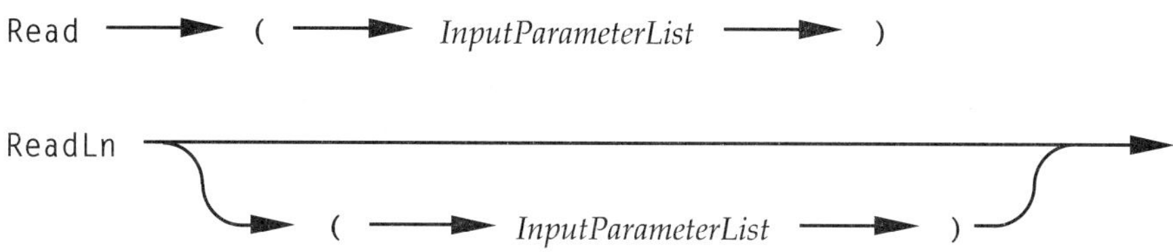

Pseudocode:

```
Read( InputParameterList )
ReadLn( InputParameterList )
ReadLn
```

Here *InputParameterList* is a list of the names of the variables to receive values from the keyboard. The variable names are separated by commas.

Notes:

- The `Read` and `ReadLn` parameters are the variables in which input values are to be stored. Therefore, these parameters must be *variables*, not constants or expressions. Thus,

  `Read( Variable1, Variable1 )`

  or

  `ReadLn( Variable1, Variable2 )`

  will copy the first input value into *Variable1* and the second input value into *Variable2*.
- If not enough inputs are provided, `Read` or `ReadLn` will wait for the rest, and the program will not continue until those values are provided.
- If more values are provided than there are variables to receive them, `Read` will leave the remaining values in the input stream, to be read by later calls to `Read` or `ReadLn`. Under the same circumstances, `ReadLn` will discard all extra values remaining on the current line of input, along with the `<EOLn>`.

What happens to the last data left in a buffer?

It may happen that characters remain in input and output buffers when a Pascal program reaches the end of execution. In order that these data will reach their final destinations before the program terminates, Pascal always flushes the buffers at the end of execution, as part of the process of closing the files. Any extra characters remaining in input buffers, and not corresponding to `Read` or `ReadLn` parameters, are discarded.

Questions

25. When you enter a real number at the keyboard, you are pressing keys that send character codes to your Pascal program. How, then, does your program know that your keystrokes are supposed to symbolize a real number?

26. What is the difference between `Read` and `ReadLn`?

27. How do the Read and ReadLn procedures differ from the Write and WriteLn procedures in the way they use their parameters?

28. Why is it often safer to use ReadLn than Read?

Exercises

29. Jackson P. Slipshod has been trying to compile this program for the past five hours. (He's not bright, but he's determined.) Find all of his syntax errors.

```
PROGRAM SlipshodTest( Input );
VAR
   Millimeters = Real;
BEGIN
   Write( 'Number of millimeters? ' );
   ReadLn( Millimeters:6:2 );
   WriteLn( 'I read ', Millimeters:6.2, ' mm.' )
END.
```

30. If the user enters the characters

```
68.5<EOLn>20.3<EOLn>
```

then what will be displayed on the screen by the following program? (Show *exactly* what will be written on your system.)

```
PROGRAM Test6( Input, Output );
VAR
   Fahrenheit, Celsius : Real;

BEGIN
   Write( 'Fahrenheit temperature? ' );
   ReadLn( Fahrenheit );
   Write( 'Celsius temperature? ' );
   ReadLn( Celsius );
   WriteLn;
   WriteLn( Fahrenheit:6:2, ' F.' );
   WriteLn( Celsius:6:2, ' C.' )
END.
```

31. Cora Meltdown has written this appalling program, intending it to display two numbers in the reverse of the order in which they were entered. When the program runs, it prints gibberish for Num2. Why? Show Cora how to improve her program.

```
PROGRAM Meltdown1( Input, Output );
VAR
   Num1, Num2 : Real;

BEGIN
   WriteLn( Num2 );
   ReadLn( Num1, Num2 );
   WriteLn( Num1 )
END.
```

32. Suppose you run this program:

```
PROGRAM Test5( Input, Output );
VAR
   Mass1, Mass2 : Real;

BEGIN

   ReadLn( Mass1, Mass2 );
   WriteLn( Mass1:6:2, Mass2:6:2 )

END.
```

Suppose that the screen output looks like this:

```
ΔΔ1.23Δ12.34
```

where the Δ symbol indicates a blank. Then which of the following *cannot* have been the input? *Explain your answers.*

a. `0.123e1Δ1.234e1`

b. `1.233333Δ12.34e0`

c. `1.233333..12.34e0`

d. `Δ1.23<EOLn>12.34321`

4.5 DESIGNING AN INTERACTIVE PROGRAM

For a simple example of a complete program involving real numbers and interactive I/O, consider the problem we worked on in Sections 2.3–2.6: converting Fahrenheit temperatures to Celsius. We want a user-friendly, useful program, and we want the program to be modular.

Plan the I/O first.

As you recall, we want the I/O to look like this when the program is running:

```
CONVERTING FAHRENHEIT TO CELSIUS

Fahrenheit temperature? 212

212.0 deg. F. = 100.0 deg. C.
```

(Color indicates what the user enters from the keyboard.)

Leaving aside for the moment the question of how the program should deal with inappropriate inputs, we have a pseudocode outline like this (see Section 2.4):

The ShowPurpose procedure encapsulates:
Display the message,
"CONVERTING FAHRENHEIT TO CELSIUS,"
with a blank line after the message.

The GetFahrenheit procedure encapsulates:
Display the prompt, "Fahrenheit? " (including the space after the question mark). Then read a number from the keyboard into a variable named `Fahrenheit`.

The ConvertToCelsius procedure encapsulates:
Compute Celsius = 0.555556 · (Fahrenheit – 32.0)

The ShowTemperature procedure encapsulates:
Display both Fahrenheit and Celsius temperatures, like this:
`212.0 deg. F. = 100.0 deg. C.`

The main algorithm invokes the procedures:
ShowPurpose;
GetFahrenheit;
ConvertToCelsius;
ShowTemperature

Write and test a skeleton.

This time around, you know enough Pascal to start translating the algorithm into a program. First, write the skeleton, with just comments to outline the main tasks:

```
PROGRAM FahrenheitToCelsius ( Input, Output );
{
  Converts Fahrenheit temperatures to Celsius.
  SKELETON ONLY.
}
VAR
   Fahrenheit, Celsius : Real;

BEGIN

   {--Show purpose of program }
   {--Get Fahrenheit temperature }
   {--Convert to Celsius }
   {--Display both Fahrenheit and Celsius }

END.
```

> It is important to compile and test the program skeleton at this early stage, before adding code to accomplish the four tasks. It is far easier to find errors in a small chunk of code than in a larger chunk. (This is called *incremental testing*.)

Plan the flow of data, using parameters.

Before going further, think about the flow of data between the main program and the procedures. First, the main program calls `ShowPurpose` to display the purpose of the program. No data are sent from the main program to `ShowPurpose` or returned by `ShowPurpose` to the main program, so the procedure call is simply

```
ShowPurpose;
```

After calling `ShowPurpose`, the main program calls the `GetFahrenheit` procedure, which prompts for a Fahrenheit temperature, reads one from the keyboard, and then returns the value to the main program. This means that `GetFahrenheit` will use an *out-parameter* to return a value to the main program. The procedure will be called by

```
GetFahrenheit( Fahrenheit );
```

Next, the main program sends the value of `Fahrenheit` to the `ConvertToCelsius` procedure and the procedure returns a `Celsius` value to the main program. `Fahrenheit` is an *in-parameter* but `Celsius` is an out-*parameter*, and the procedure call is

```
ConvertToCelsius( Fahrenheit, Celsius );
```

Finally, the main program sends the values of `Fahrenheit` and `Celsius` *to* the `ShowTemperature` procedure:

```
ShowTemperature( Fahrenheit, Celsius )
```

Since these two values are sent into the procedure, but the procedure returns no values to the main program, both parameters here are *in-parameters*.

The hierarchy of procedures in this program and the flow of data are both shown in Figure 4.5.1.

The hierarchy of the FahrenheitToCelsius program, as it will be when completed. The arrows indicate directions of data flow. Figure 4.5.1

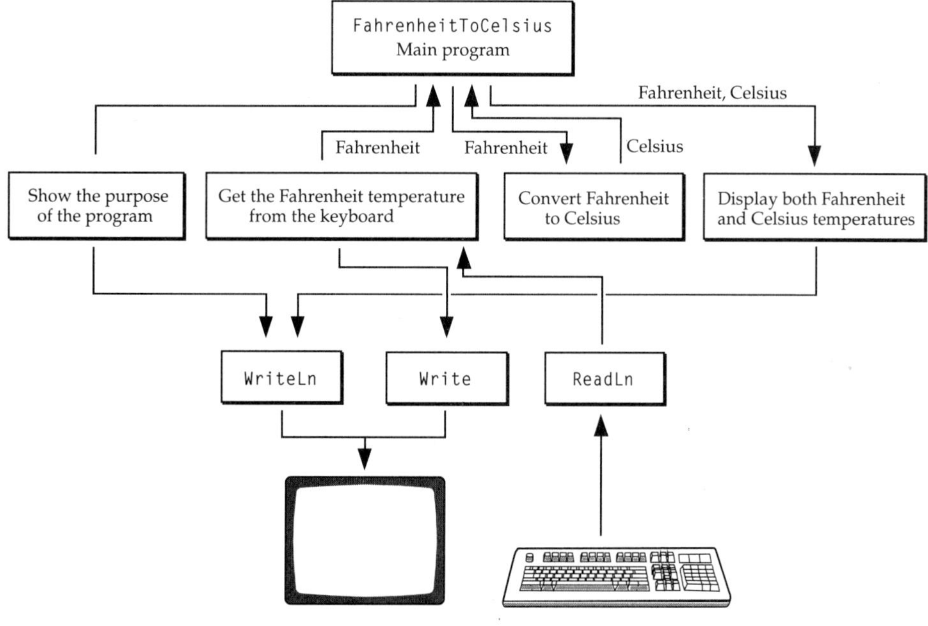

Now we can complete the main program.

With the skeleton compiled and checked and the data flow planned, we can complete the code in the main program and describe the procedures more completely:

```
PROGRAM FahrenheitToCelsius ( Input, Output );
{ Converts Fahrenheit temperatures to Celsius. }

VAR
   Fahrenheit, Celsius : Real;
{
  INCOMPLETE--
  The following procedures need to be declared here:

  ShowPurpose procedure:
     (no parameters)
  ShowPurpose encapsulates
     WriteLn( 'CONVERTING FAHRENHEIT TO CELSIUS' );
     WriteLn;

  GetFahrenheit procedure:
     (out-parameter) Fahrenheit
  GetFahrenheit encapsulates
     Write( 'Fahrenheit temperature? ' );
     ReadLn( Fahrenheit );

  ConvertToCelsius procedure:
     (in-parameter) Fahrenheit
     (out-parameter) Celsius
  ConvertToCelsius encapsulates
     Celsius := (5.0 / 9.0) * ( Fahrenheit - 32.0 );

  ShowTemperature procedure:
     (in-parameter) Fahrenheit
     (in-parameter) Celsius
  ShowTemperature encapsulates
     WriteLn;
     WriteLn( Fahrenheit:6:1, ' deg. F.  =  ',
              Celsius:6:1, ' deg. C.' )
}
BEGIN

   {-- Show purpose of program }
   ShowPurpose;

   {-- Get Fahrenheit temperature }
   GetFahrenheit( Fahrenheit )

   {-- Convert to Celsius }
   ConvertToCelsius( Fahrenheit, Celsius );

   {-- Display Fahrenheit and Celsius }
   ShowTemperature( Fahrenheit, Celsius )

END.
```

This is top-down design.

We are practicing *top-down design* here, and haven't yet filled in the procedure declarations, so of course, the program is still not complete. Therefore, if you compile the program at this stage (Come on, do it!), you will see error messages saying that the identifiers `ShowPurpose`, `GetFahrenheit`, `ConvertToCelsius`, and `ShowTemperature` have not been defined. The declarations for these procedures are complicated by their parameters, and we have not yet explained how to put parameters in the declarations. That's the subject of the next chapter.

4.6 WHY BOTHER WITH PROCEDURES?

At this point, you might be wondering why we go to so much trouble to build a modular program. After all, we aren't required to use procedures; we can just put all the code right into the main program in place of the corresponding procedure calls. If we do, the `FahrenheitToCelsius` program is this simple:

```
PROGRAM FahrenheitToCelsius ( Input, Output );
{
  Converts Fahrenheit temperatures to Celsius.
  MONOLITHIC VERSION,
  ILLUSTRATING POOR PROGRAMMING STYLE.
}

VAR
   Fahrenheit, Celsius : Real;

BEGIN

   {-- Show purpose of program }
   WriteLn( 'CONVERTING FAHRENHEIT TO CELSIUS' );
   WriteLn;

   {-- Get Fahrenheit temperature }
   Write( 'Fahrenheit temperature? ' );
   ReadLn( Fahrenheit );

   {-- Convert to Celsius }
   Celsius := (5.0 / 9.0) * ( Fahrenheit - 32.0 );

   {-- Display Fahrenheit and Celsius }
   WriteLn;
   WriteLn( Fahrenheit:6:1, ' deg. F.  =  ',
            Celsius:6:1, ' deg. C.' )

END.
```

This program is complete. Compile, link, and run it, and you will see that it acts as we planned. Not only does the program work, but you will see many programs similar to this listed in older programming books. Nevertheless, *it is poor programming style to put all the program code into the main program.*

There are six potential advantages to using procedures:

- By giving a task a name, we make it easier to refer to. Code that calls clearly named procedures is easier to understand than code in which all tasks are described in the main program. Programs that use procedures are easier to design because of the way they "divide and conquer" the whole problem. On the other hand, if all the code were in the main program, we would be faced with the full complexity of the program even at first glance; there would be no procedural abstraction to reduce the initial apparent complexity.
- Naming the tasks reduces the need for comments; if well done, it makes the code more "self-documenting."
- By having a procedure perform the task, we can perform the task many times in the same program by simply invoking the procedure repeatedly. The code for the task need not be reproduced every time we need it.
- A procedure can be saved in a library of useful subprograms and plugged into any program that needs it. Thus a procedure is *reusable* in many programs—an important point in professional programming.
- Once a procedure is written and properly tested, we can use the procedure without any further concern for its inner workings. In other words, we can think of it in terms of *what* it does rather than *how* it does what it does. Thus the procedure has become an *abstraction*, to be invoked whenever needed, as though it were a part of the programming language. In this sense, *it extends the language.*
- Large, complicated programs are written by teams of programmers. By making a program modular, it can be divided up into modules small enough to be worked on by one team. Each of these modules in turn can be broken down into submodules small enough to be designed by an individual programmer.

Although a monolithic programming style was typical three decades ago and is still used by some programmers, it is not good enough for today's complex programming tasks. Therefore, we will not use it in this book.

4.7 TESTING AND DEBUGGING

This is a good time to review the suggestions of Section 3.6 regarding incremental testing and divide-and-conquer debugging. The discipline of *incremental testing* is often hard to adopt until you've been up half the night hunting for a bug in a program that must be finished by tomorrow morning. When you notice that programmers who use incremental testing tend to finish their debugging much more quickly, you realize the importance of good technique.

Section 3.6 also mentioned the fact that debugging is a divide-and-conquer activity. When looking for a semantic error, you need to know what part of the program it is in.

Compiler error message indicating a failure to declare an identifier. **Figure 4.7.1**

```
"Fahrenheit" not declared

PROGRAM FahrenheitToCelsius ( Input, Output );
BEGIN

   Write( 'Fahrenheit temperature? ' );
   ReadLn( Fahrenheit );
   ...
```

The first step is to know what part of the program it is *not* in. How far does the program run before giving erroneous results? You'll know only if you have had your program print out all its intermediate results, or if your Pascal system supplies a debugger (a special testing program) that lets you examine the contents of your variables at every stage of execution. As Sherlock Holmes said in *A Scandal in Bohemia*, "It is a capital mistake to theorize with no data." Don't try to *guess* where your error is; try to gather evidence indicating where it *must* be.

This chapter has introduced new syntax that can, of course, lead to new errors, both syntactic and semantic. Here are a few tips.

Failure to declare an identifier

A failure to declare an identifier is a syntax error and will generate a compiler error message. An example is shown in Figure 4.7.1.

Failure to initialize variables

Because Pascal does not initialize variables automatically, you must initialize them deliberately, either by assignment or by Read or ReadLn procedures. If you forget to do this, a variable will contain garbage (a random bit pattern), and your results will be garbage. ("Garbage in, garbage out," as mentioned earlier.) This is not a syntax error but a *semantic error*. Sometimes you will notice that your results are nonsensical, but sometimes you won't notice. On some Pascal systems, if you make the same run several times with an uninitialized variable, your program may give several different results (Figure 4.7.2). This is because different memory cells may be allocated for the same variable on successive runs. On other computer systems, this won't happen.

Figure 4.7.2

What's wrong with this program? It compiles, but when it runs on some Pascal systems, the Fahrenheit temperature is garbage.

```
PROGRAM FahrenheitToCelsius ( Input, Output );
VAR
   Fahrenheit, Celsius : Real;

BEGIN

   WriteLn( 'CONVERTING FAHRENHEIT TO CELSIUS' );
   WriteLn;

   Celsius := (5.0 / 9.0) * ( Fahrenheit - 32.0 );

   WriteLn;
   WriteLn( Fahrenheit:6:1, ' deg. F.  =  ', Celsius:6:1, ' deg. C.' )

END.
```

The data must have the same type as the variable.

In an assignment statement, the expression must have a value of the same type as the variable to which the value is being assigned. If this is not the case, you have a *syntax error.* An example is shown in Figure 4.7.3.

When reading a value from the keyboard, the program cannot force the user to enter a value of the correct type. If the program asks for a Fahrenheit temperature, for example, there is no way to keep the user from entering the string `'212.0'` instead of the real number `212.0`. If a `ReadLn` sees a string in apostrophes when it was told to read a real number, it will generate a **run-time error** message, saying something like `TYPE MISMATCH` or `INPUT ERROR`. There is really nothing we can do to prevent user errors of this kind, short of writing our own input procedures with elaborate protection schemes.

Figure 4.7.3

Attempting to compile a program that uses a string in a real expression.

```
Type incompatibility

Celsius := (5.0 / 9.0) * ( Fahrenheit - '32.0' );
...
```

Examples of syntax errors in Turbo Pascal 6.0. **Table 4.7.1**

Syntax error	Error message from compiler
Real constant has no whole-number part.	`Error in expression.`
Real constant contains comma.	`";" expected.`
`CONST` declaration after `VAR` declaration.	(no message)
Procedure declaration before `CONST`.	(no message)
`CONST` declaration uses : instead of =	`Invalid subrange base type.` (!?)
`VAR` declaration uses = instead of :	`":" expected.`
Missing semicolon at end of declaration.	`";" expected.`
Assignment statement uses = instead of :=	`":=" expected.`
Two contiguous operators in real expression.	`Error in expression.`
Nonvariable on left of assignment operator.	`Error in statement.`
Semicolon instead of comma in list of `Write`, `WriteLn`, `Read`, or `ReadLn` parameters.	`")" expected.` (!?)
Missing left apostrophe enclosing string constant.	`Unknown identifier.`
Missing right apostrophe enclosing string constant.	`String constant exceeds line.`
Period instead of colon in `WriteLn` formatting.	`Invalid qualifier.`
Parameter to `Read` or `ReadLn` is not a variable.	`Variable identifer expected.`
Identifier is not declared before use.	`Unknown identifier.`
`IF` structure has semicolon before `ELSE`.	`Error in statement.`

(Notice that the Turbo Pascal compiler does not flag everything that would be a syntax error in Standard Pascal. Note also that other compilers will give somewhat different error messages.)

LOOKING BACK

This chapter began by introducing our first Pascal data type, real numbers. We described how real constants and variables are declared in a program, how real operations are performed, and the fact that most real numbers are only approximated in a computer.

We then examined how real numbers are read into variables from text files, and how they are written to text files. This led to a detailed examination of how parameters are used in Pascal's standard input and output procedures. We found that some parameters are used to transmit values into a procedure, while other parameters are used to return values from a procedure.

Here is a reprise of the main points, topic by topic:

Real numbers

- Real constants are written in either fixed-point or floating-point notation.
- Constants must be declared before variables.
- Named constants are just synonyms for literal constants. The value of a constant cannot be changed during the running of the program.
- The declaration of a variable does not initialize the variable; the variable initially contains garbage. To give a variable a particular value, we must either assign a value to it or read a value into it.
- In evaluating a real expression, the operations in parentheses are performed first. If parentheses are nested, the operations inside the innermost parentheses are performed first. Among operators at the same level of parentheses-nesting, higher-precedence operators are applied first. Multiplication and division operators have highest precedence, followed by additive and subtractive operators.
- It is bad style to write expressions that rely on order of precedence; instead, use enough parentheses to make your intentions clear.
- Real numbers are usually rounded off when stored in a computer. This means that most real numbers in a computer are only approximations of their correct values. We say that these numbers suffer roundoff error. Roundoff error can cause serious loss of significant digits during a calculation.

Standard output procedures

- The standard `Output` file is connected to the screen. This file is a text file; that is, it is a stream of characters, divided into lines. Lines are separated by end-of-line signals, denoted by `<EOLn>`.
- The `Write` procedure transmits to the screen the character representations of its parameter values in the order in which these parameters are listed in the procedure call. It then leaves the screen cursor immediately after the last value, on the same line.
- The `WriteLn` procedure transmits to the screen the character representations of its parameter values in the order in which these parameters are listed in the procedure call. It then writes an `<EOLn>` to the file, moving the screen cursor to the beginning of the next line.
- The appearance of the characters representing output data can be controlled by formatting the outputs.

Standard input procedures

- The standard `Input` file is connected to the keyboard. This file is a text file; that is, it is a stream of characters, divided into lines. Lines are separated by `<EOLn>` signals.
- The `Read` and `ReadLn` procedures receive characters from the keyboard. The characters are translated to the appropriate data types, then copied into the variables listed as parameters.

- The `Read` procedure gets input values for each of its parameters in the order in which these parameters are listed. `Read` leaves unread values in the input stream, to be read by later `Read`s or `ReadLn`s.
- The `ReadLn` procedure gets input values for each of its parameters in the order in which these parameters are listed. `ReadLn` discards unread values remaining on the current line of input, along with the following `<EOLn>`.

TERMS EMPHASIZED IN THIS CHAPTER

PROJECTS

1. Design a modular, interactive program that reads a purchase price, computes the 6.75 percent sales tax, and displays the purchase price, tax, and total price. Use a modular style similar to that shown in the book. Test the skeleton; the procedures will be completed as a project in Chapter 5.

2. Design a modular, interactive program that reads three real numbers from the keyboard, calculates the sample standard deviation according to the formula of Exercise 16, and then displays the result. How does this result compare with the one from your calculator? Use a clear, modular style in your program. (Hint: The sums in the formula can be built up term by term as the numbers are entered.) Test the skeleton; the procedures will be completed as a project in Chapter 5.

3. Horse-race betting is usually on the pari-mutuel system, in which the total amount wagered, minus a percentage for the management and the government, is divided among those who bet on the horses in the first three places in proportion to the amounts bet.

   Design a Pascal program that calculates the amount of payoff owed to a bettor who places a $2 bet on one of the first three horses in a race. Before the money is distributed to the winners, the government takes 14 percent of the total wagered amount and the track operators take 9 percent. The purse—the amount left after the government and operators are paid—is split up among the winning bettors as follows: 50 percent to those who bet on the first-place horse, 30 percent to those who bet on the horse who came in second, and 20 percent to those who bet on the third horse. Within these categories, bettors are paid in proportion to the amounts they bet. Input to your program will be the total amount wagered on the race, the identifying numbers of the three winning horses, and the amount bet on each. The output will be a list of the three horses and the payoff per each $2 bet on each horse. You may assume that the program's user will enter quantities that make sense; for example, the amounts bet on each horse will be positive and the total amount wagered will exceed the sum of the bets on the winning three horses. Test the skeleton of your program; the procedures will be completed as a project in Chapter 5.

REFERENCES

Real-number storage and internal operations are discussed at length in textbooks on computer arithmetic. An excellent example is the book by Joseph J. F. Cavanagh, *Digital Computer Arithmetic* (McGraw-Hill, 1984). One of the best introductions to roundoff error is in *Essentials of Numerical Analysis with Pocket Calculator Demonstrations* by Peter Henrici (John Wiley & Sons, 1982). All textbooks on numerical methods and numerical analysis cover this topic.

The finer points of Pascal's I/O procedures are described in two standard reference works that should be at the elbows (why elbows?) of all serious Pascal programmers: Doug Cooper's *Standard Pascal User Reference Manual* (Norton, 1983) and the *Pascal User Manual and Report*, third edition, by Kathleen Jensen and Niklaus Wirth (Springer-Verlag, 1985).

Robert Pirsig's autobiographical novel, *Zen and the Art of Motorcycle Maintenance* (Morrow, 1973) is not really about Zen or about motorcycles, but it is about both, which is saying the same thing. (Understand?) Whatever it is about, it offers considerable insight into the discipline and frame of mind required for debugging and repair.

The Effect of Computers on Structural Engineering

The computer enables engineers to make more calculations more quickly than was conceivable with either the slide rule or the calculator, hence the computer can be programmed to attack problems in structural analysis that would never have been attempted in the pre-computer days. If one wished to design a complicated structure of many parts, for example, one might first have made educated guesses about the sizes of the various members and then calculated the stresses in them. If these stresses were too high, then the design had to be beefed up where it was overstressed; where some calculated stresses were too low, then those understressed parts of the structure could be made smaller, thus saving weight and money. However, each revision of one part of the structure could affect the stresses in every other part. If that were the case, the entire stress analysis would have to be repeated. Clearly, in the days of manual calculation with a slide rule—wooden or electronic—such a process would be limited by the sheer time it would consume, and structures would be generally overdesigned from the start and built that way. Furthermore, excessively complex structures were eschewed by designers because the original sizing of members might be too difficult to even guess at, and calculations required to assure the safety of the structure were simply not reasonable to perform. Hence engineers generally stuck with designing structures that they understood well enough from the very start of the design process.

Now, the computer not only can perform millions of simple, repetitive calculations automatically in reasonable amounts of time but also can be used to analyze structures that engineers of the slide rule era found too complex. The computer can be used to analyze these structures through special software packages, claimed to be quite versatile by their developers, and the computer can be instructed to calculate the sizes of the various components of the structure so that it has minimum weight since the maximum stresses are acting in every part of it. That is called optimization. But should there be an oversimplification or an outright error in translating the designer's structural concept to the numerical model that will be analyzed through the automatic and unthinking calculations of the computer, then the results of the computer analysis might have very little relation to reality. . . .

What is commonly overlooked in using the computer is the fact that the central goal of design is still to obviate failure, and thus it is critical to identify exactly *how* a structure may fail. The computer cannot do this by itself, although there are attempts to incorporate artificial intelligence into the machine to make it an "expert system". . . . However, until such a farfetched notion becomes reality, the engineer who employs the computer in design must still ask the crucial questions: Will this improperly welded pipe break if an earthquake hits the nuclear reactor plant? Will this automobile body crumple in this manner when it strikes a wall at ten miles per hour? Will any one of the tens of thousands of metal rods supporting this roof break under heavy snow and cause it to fall into the crowded arena?

—Henry Petroski, *To Engineer Is Human* (St. Martin's Press, 1985), pages 193–95.

CHAPTER 5

Procedures with Parameters

CHAPTER CONTENTS

INTRODUCTION

Chapter 2 showed that the process of dividing a problem into subproblems results in an algorithm divided into procedures. Thus, the structure of the problem is reflected in the structure of its solution. Chapter 3 began to show how this structuring can be implemented in a Pascal program. Chapter 4 continued by showing how parameters are sent to and from Pascal's standard I/O procedures. By the end of Chapter 4, we had written most of an interactive program for Fahrenheit to Celsius conversion, outlining several of our own procedures.

Now we complete the F-to-C program by declaring procedures with parameters. As you know from the previous chapter, some parameters are sent *into* a procedure, while others may be used to return values *from* the procedure. In this chapter, we will learn how to use both kinds in Pascal. Here are your major goals for the chapter:

- To understand the mechanism by which some Pascal parameters are transmitted into a procedure, but not back out. In Pascal, these in-parameters are called *value parameters*.
- To understand the mechanism by which other parameters can be used to transmit values both into and out of a procedure. In Pascal, these in-and-out parameters are called *variable parameters* or *VAR parameters*.
- To understand that the purpose of a procedure is to change the *state* of the program.
- To learn to write *pre- and postconditions* as part of the specification of a procedure.
- To learn the difference between *global and local scope*, and to understand why global variables should seldom be used.

5.1 PROCEDURES WITH VALUE PARAMETERS

In our plan for the `FahrenheitToCelsius` program, we use a procedure to display the Fahrenheit and Celsius temperatures. To do this, the main program sends the values of the `Fahrenheit` and `Celsius` variables into the procedure when it calls the procedure:

```
ShowTemperature( Fahrenheit, Celsius )
```

(This is analogous to the way we sent values into the `WriteLn` procedure in the previous chapter.)

Declaring a procedure with parameters is almost the same as declaring a parameterless procedure, which we discussed in Section 3.4. The new feature is that *the parameters must be declared in the procedure header*. If we use the encapsulated code written in Section 4.5 for the `ShowTemperature` procedure, we have this declaration:

```
PROCEDURE ShowTemperature( Fahrenheit : Real;
                           Celsius    : Real );
BEGIN

   WriteLn;
   WriteLn( Fahrenheit:6:1, ' deg. F. = ',
            Celsius:6:1, ' deg. C.' )

END;
```

Identifiers declared in the procedure belong to the procedure.

`Fahrenheit` and `Celsius` are *in-parameters* when they are declared as shown here. (We'll see how to declare in-and-out parameters later.) In-parameters are created by the procedure and exist only when the procedure is running, and *there is no need for the parameters' names to be the same in the procedure as they are outside*. We can just as well change the parameters' names to `F` and `C` inside the procedure:

```
PROCEDURE ShowTemperature( F : Real;
                           C : Real );
BEGIN

   WriteLn;
   WriteLn( F:6:1, ' deg. F. = ',
            C:6:1, ' deg. C.' )

END;
```

Association of actual and formal parameters

When you send `Fahrenheit` and then `Celsius` to the `ShowTemperature` procedure, which has the header

```
PROCEDURE ShowTemperature( F, C : Real );
```

you are associating the main program's `Fahrenheit` variable with the procedure's `F` variable, and the main program's `Celsius` variable with the procedure's `C` variable:

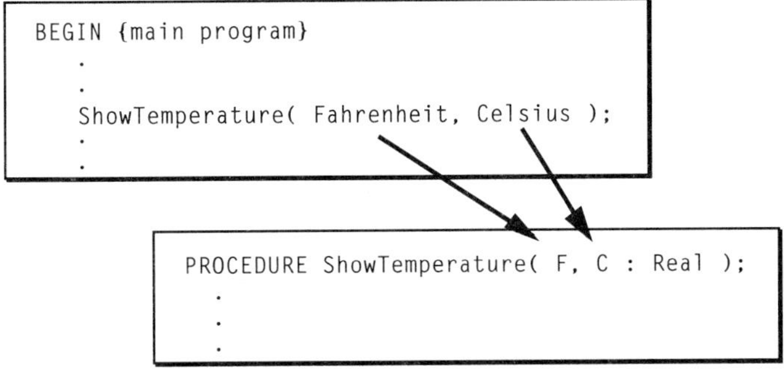

`Fahrenheit` and `Celsius`, whose values are transmitted to the procedure, are called the **actual parameters** of the procedure; they are the names of the actual values sent to the procedure. The `F` and `C` variables listed in the procedure header are called the **formal parameters** of the procedure. When the main program calls the procedure, the first actual parameter value, `Fahrenheit`, is copied into the procedure's first formal parameter, `F`, and the second actual parameter value, `Celsius`, is copied into the procedure's second formal parameter, `C`. The copying occurs just before the procedure begins to run.

> An **actual parameter** (or **argument**) is a value sent to a subprogram or received from a subprogram; it is listed in the statement that *calls* the subprogram.
>
> A **formal parameter** is a variable appearing in the parameter list of a subprogram header, acting as a placeholder or dummy variable for the actual value being transmitted to or from the caller.

Value parameters

Inside the procedure, the two formal parameters, `F` and `C`, are variables that come into existence when the procedure is called. Values are copied into these variables from the main program's `Fahrenheit` and `Celsius` variables, respectively. As the procedure begins to run, it has *copies of the values* of the actual parameters, but does not use the actual parameter variables, `Fahrenheit` and `Celsius`, because those exist in a block of memory used by the main program and not by the procedure. Since the procedure receives only copies of the *values* of `Fahrenheit` and `Celsius`, the parameters are said to be **passed by value**, and we say that the parameters are **value parameters**. The copying process is *one-way*: It copies values into the procedure, but not back out.

> Value parameters (parameters passed by value) are Pascal's version of the **in-parameters** we discussed in Chapter 4.

Sequence of events

Here's the sequence of events when `ShowTemperature` is called by the main program. First, the main program makes copies of the two actual parameters being transmitted to the procedure:

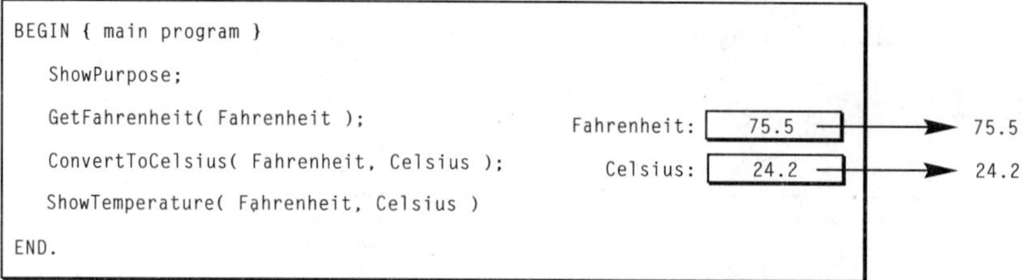

Then the main program suspends execution while the procedure starts to run. The copies of the actual parameter values, `Fahrenheit` and `Celsius`, are copied into the procedure's `F` and `C` variables, respectively:

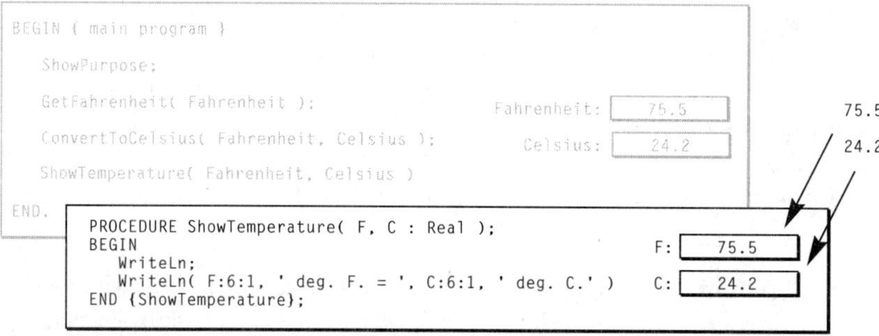

Then `ShowTemperature` executes, calling `WriteLn` twice. When `ShowTemperature` terminates, the main program resumes. But there is no more code to execute in the main program, so the program terminates.

A procedure must be declared before it is used.

Pascal requires that all procedures and functions not provided by the system be declared before they are called. A procedure is declared by writing its code into the declarations section of the program, before the main program's `BEGIN`. If one procedure or function calls another, the called subprogram must be declared before it is called. This may force a certain order of declarations. (You will see examples shortly.)

The form of a program with procedures

A program containing subprograms has the same structure as shown before, but the subprograms must be declared in the declarations part of the program, before they are used:

`PROGRAM` *ProgramName*`(` *FileList* `);`

ConstantDeclarations
TypeDeclarations
VariableDeclarations

Declarations of procedures and functions,
each declared before it is called.

```
BEGIN
   StatementSequence
END.
```

Options in declaring the formal parameters

The two parameters in our `ShowTemperature` procedure are both value parameters and both real variables. Therefore, their declarations take the same form, and they can be declared together if desired. The following procedure headers are all equivalent:

```
PROCEDURE ShowTemperature( F : Real;
                           C : Real );

PROCEDURE ShowTemperature( F : Real; C : Real );

PROCEDURE ShowTemperature( F, C : Real );
```

The choice among these three versions is a matter of taste. The rules for declaring a procedure with value parameters are shown in the accompanying syntax summary.

Syntax for declaring a procedure with value parameters

Procedure declaration:

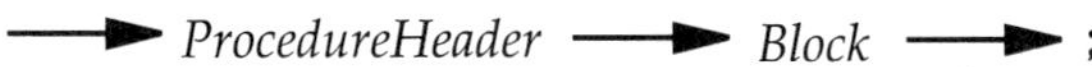

Procedure header:

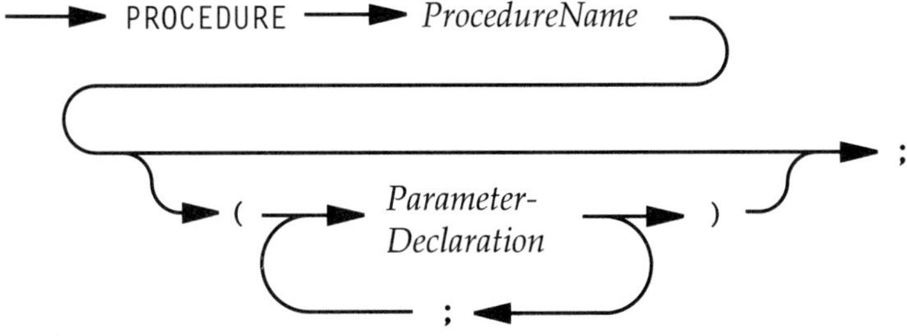

Parameter declaration:

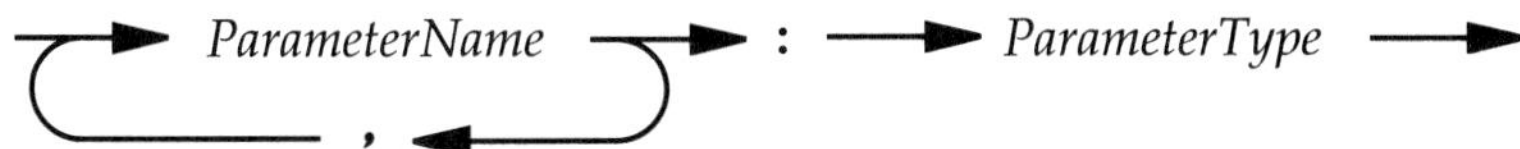

Pseudocode:

```
PROCEDURE ProcedureName( FormalParameterList );
   OtherDeclarations
BEGIN
   StatementSequence
END;
```

Notes:

- The *FormalParameterList*, if any, contains declarations of formal parameters, separated by semicolons. Each declaration is of the form

  ParameterName : *TypeName*

  where *ParameterName* is the identifier to be used within the procedure. (This name is known only within the procedure.) *TypeName* is the name of a built-in type or a previously declared type.
- If several parameters are of the same type, they can be declared together in a single declaration of the form

  Parameter1, Parameter2, . . . , ParameterN : *TypeName*

  with commas between parameters that share the single declaration.
- Distinct declarations are separated by semicolons.
- If there are no formal parameters, the parentheses should be omitted.
- The *OtherDeclarations* are declarations of constants, types, variables, functions, and procedures to be used within the procedure, but which are not parameters of the procedure. The syntax for such declarations is the same as that used in a main program.
- Except for the name of the procedure itself, identifiers declared within a procedure, including its formal parameters, are *local* to that procedure. That is, they are known within the procedure but unknown outside the procedure. This means that different procedures can reuse the same variable or constant name for different purposes, with no conflict.

Naming the formal value parameters

In our example, the main program's `Fahrenheit` and `Celsius` variables are distinct from the procedure's `F` and `C` variables and are different storage cells, so *it is actually better style to give them different names in the procedure.*

Confirming that value parameters are in-parameters

To confirm that value parameters are in-parameters, perform an experiment. Add a pair of spurious statements to the `ShowTemperature` procedure to make it change the values of `F` and `C`. Also add to the main program a final `WriteLn` that displays the values of `Fahrenheit` and `Celsius` after the procedure returns execution to the main program:

```
PROGRAM Experiment1 ( Input, Output );
{
  Confirming that ShowTemperature cannot modify
  its actual arguments
}
VAR
   Fahrenheit, Celsius : Real;
```

```
PROCEDURE ShowPurpose;
BEGIN

   WriteLn( 'CONVERTING FAHRENHEIT TO CELSIUS' );
   WriteLn

END; { ShowPurpose }


PROCEDURE ShowTemperature( F, C : Real );
BEGIN

   WriteLn;
   WriteLn(F:6:1, ' deg. F. = ', C:6:1, ' deg. C.');

   {--If the formal parameters are modified,  }
   {  will the actual parameters be modified? }
   F := 999.9;
   C := 999.9

END; { ShowTemperature }


BEGIN { main program }

   ShowPurpose;

   Fahrenheit := 212.0;
   Celsius := ( 5.0 / 9.0 ) * ( Fahrenheit - 32.0 );

   ShowTemperature( Fahrenheit, Celsius );

   {-- Were the actual parameters modified? }
   WriteLn( 'Final values: ',
            Fahrenheit:6:1, '    ', Celsius:6:1 )

END.
```

Compile, link, and run this program. You will see

```
CONVERTING FAHRENHEIT TO CELSIUS

 212.0 deg. F. =  100.0 deg. C.
Final values:  212.0    100.0
```

This proves that the `ShowTemperature` procedure, which modified its formal parameters `F` and `C`, was unable to transmit the new values to the main program's actual parameters, `Fahrenheit` and `Celsius`.

Expression values can be copied by value.

The actual parameter associated with a formal value parameter can be the value of an expression. For example, the main program of `FahrenheitToCelsius` can be simplified slightly, eliminating the `Celsius` variable and `ConvertToCelsius` procedure:

```
ShowPurpose;

GetFahrenheit( Fahrenheit );

ShowTemperature( Fahrenheit,
            ( 5.0 / 9.0 ) * ( Fahrenheit - 32.0 ) )
```

Questions

1. How do you call a procedure named `Ready`, sending to it the values of the variables `Set` and `Go`?
2. What is the difference between *actual* and *formal* parameters?
3. Why is a value parameter also called an *in-only* parameter?
4. Where is the code for a procedure inserted into a program that calls the procedure?
5. How do the separators between actual parameters in a procedure call differ from the separators between formal parameters in the procedure header?

Exercises

6. What is printed by the following program?

```
PROGRAM FiveSix( Output );
VAR
   This : Real;

PROCEDURE WingDing( That, TheOther : Real );
BEGIN
   WriteLn( That:6:1, TheOther:9:1 )
END; { WingDing }

BEGIN { main program }
   This := 1.1;
   WingDing( 2.2, This );
   WriteLn( This:6:1 )
END.
```

7. Write a procedure named `ShowCost`, with one formal parameter named `TotalPrice`, that prints the following output when sent the actual parameter value 120.95:

```
TOTAL PRICE
$ 120.95, including sales tax.
```

Be sure to use output formatting so that the real number will be displayed in this form. Test your procedure by writing a main program to go with it, and compiling and running the whole program.

8. Similar to Exercise 7, except that this time, use two parameters named `NetPrice` and `SalesTax`. The output should look like this:

```
Net price $ 119.95
Sales tax $   8.10
------------------
TOTAL     $ 128.05
```

9. Write a `ConvertInchesToMillimeters` program that uses procedures. The main program and its two procedure calls are shown below.

```
PROGRAM ConvertInchesToMillimeters ( Input, Output );
CONST
   MmPerInch = 25.4;

VAR
   Inches : Real;

{ Add declarations for the procedures            }
{ ShowPurposeOfProgram and DisplayResults here. }

BEGIN

   ShowPurposeOfProgram;

   {-- Get number of inches from keyboard }
   Write( 'Number of inches: ' );
   ReadLn( Inches );

   {-- Convert inches to millimeters }
   DisplayResults( Inches, (MmPerInch * Inches) )

END.
```

Your completed program should display output in the following form:

```
CONVERTING INCHES TO MILLIMETERS
--------------------------------

Number of inches: 1.5

 1.5 inches = 38.1 millimeters
```

5.2 PROCEDURES WITH VARIABLE PARAMETERS

In the FahrenheitToCelsius program, we need a GetFahrenheit procedure that prompts for and reads a temperature, and then returns it to the main program to be stored in the Fahrenheit variable. To do this, the procedure will need an *in-and-out parameter* that transmits a value from the procedure back to the main program. Such a procedure is called in the usual way:

```
GetFahrenheit( Fahrenheit );
```

The procedure declaration differs, however, in the way the parameter is declared in the procedure header:

```
PROCEDURE GetFahrenheit( VAR F : Real );
BEGIN

   Write( 'Fahrenheit? (Must be <= -459.7) ' );
   ReadLn( F )

END;
```

The word VAR before the name of the F variable declares that it is an in-and-out parameter, which Pascal calls a **variable parameter**. A variable parameter transmits values both into and out of a subprogram. (Pascal does not have out-only parameters: just in-only and in-and-out parameters.) In GetFahrenheit, we will use the parameter only for returning values (transmitting values out) to the main program.

Variable (VAR) parameter: A parameter that transmits a value both into and out of a subprogram.

> Variable parameters (parameters passed by reference) are Pascal's version of the in-and-out parameters we discussed in Chapter 4.

Introducing our new procedure into FahrenheitToCelsius, we have a nearly complete program:

```
PROGRAM FahrenheitToCelsius2 ( Input, Output );
{
  Second version, nearly complete;
  ConvertToCelsius still undeclared.
}
VAR
   Fahrenheit, Celsius : Real;


PROCEDURE ShowPurpose;
BEGIN

   WriteLn( 'CONVERTING FAHRENHEIT TO CELSIUS' );
   WriteLn

END; { ShowPurpose }
```

```
PROCEDURE GetFahrenheit( VAR F : Real );
BEGIN

   Write( 'Fahrenheit? (Must be <= -459.7) ' );
   ReadLn( F )

END;


{
  Procedure ConvertToCelsius:
     (in-parameter)  Fahrenheit
     (out-parameter) Celsius
  ConvertToCelsius encapsulates:
     Celsius := ( 5.0 / 9.0 ) * ( Fahrenheit - 32.0 )
}


PROCEDURE ShowTemperature( F, C : Real );
BEGIN

   WriteLn;
   WriteLn( F:6:1, ' deg. F. = ', C:6:1, ' deg. C.' )

END { ShowTemperature };


BEGIN { main program }

   {--Display the purpose of the program }
   ShowPurpose;

   {--Get Fahrenheit temperature from keyboard }
   GetFahrenheit( Fahrenheit );

   {--Convert Fahrenheit to Celsius }
   ConvertToCelsius( Fahrenheit, Celsius );

   {--Display the results }
   ShowTemperature( Fahrenheit, Celsius )

END.
```

How the VAR parameter works in this example

The VAR formal parameter (the one in the procedure) is actually *the same memory cell* as the actual parameter (the one in the calling program unit). In other words, F is actually *the same memory cell* as Fahrenheit; the memory cell is called Fahrenheit by the main program but called F by the procedure. In other words, F and Fahrenheit are actually two **aliases** for the same memory cell, which was created by the main program. The procedure does not allocate its own storage for the VAR parameter (Figure 5.2.1).

Alias: A name used for an entity in a certain context.

Figure 5.2.1 *Because F is a variable parameter, F is just another name for the memory cell called Fahrenheit in the main program.*

```
BEGIN                                          Fahrenheit: [ ]
   ShowPurpose;
   GetFahrenheit( Fahrenheit );

    PROCEDURE GetFahrenheit( VAR F : Real );
    BEGIN                                                  F:

       Write( 'Fahrenheit? (Must be >= -459.7) ' );
       ReadLn( F )

    END; { GetFahrenheit }
```

VAR parameters are passed by reference.

As you can see from this example, a VAR parameter's value is not actually copied from the subprogram to the caller or vice versa. Instead, the caller simply tells the subprogram which of the caller's variables to use for storage of the parameter value. To be precise, the subprogram is given a **reference** to the caller's variable—that is, the address of the caller's variable—and we say that the parameter is **passed by reference**. The only thing that is actually passed to the subprogram is the address of the actual parameter storage cell in the caller's memory area.

Naming a formal VAR parameter

Because a formal VAR parameter is actually another name for the actual VAR parameter and both of these names denote the same storage cell, it is good style to use the same name in the subprogram and the calling program unit when this is practical.

Confirming that VAR parameters are passed both in and out

To confirm that VAR parameters are in-and-out parameters, modify the test program from Section 5.1 so that it displays the value of Fahrenheit before, during, and after the execution of the GetFahrenheit procedure. This is left as Exercise 11.

Protecting the procedure from inappropriate input

Our plan of Section 2.4 called for the GetFahrenheit procedure to prompt repeatedly for a Fahrenheit temperature until receiving one that is at least as great as absolute zero. The present version of the procedure fails to do this, but we will correct this shortcoming in the next chapter, when we discuss how to control execution within a program.

Syntax for declaring a procedure with a variable (VAR) parameter

Procedure declaration:

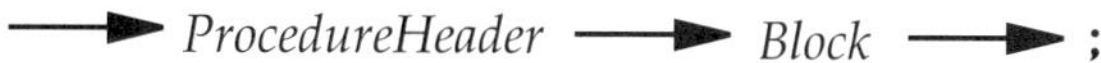

Procedure header:

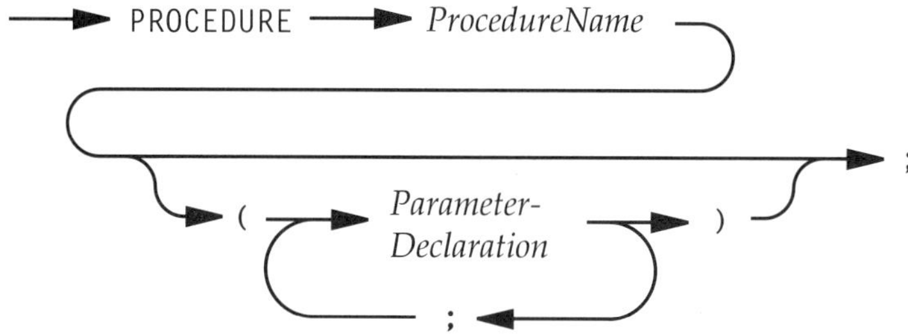

VAR parameter declaration:

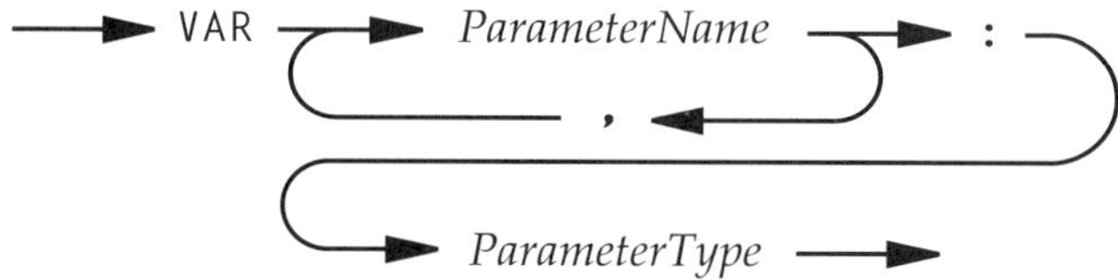

Notes:

- The declaration of a VAR parameter is identical to the declaration of a value parameter except for the reserved word VAR prefixed to the declaration.
- A VAR formal parameter is actually the same storage cell as the corresponding actual parameter. Therefore, changes in the value of the formal parameter are actually changes in the value of the corresponding actual parameter.

Exercises

10. Modify the FahrenheitToCelsius2 program so that the GetFahrenheit procedure uses the same name for its VAR parameter as is used in the main program. Explain why it is considered good style to use the same name for actual and formal VAR parameters, but different names for actual and formal value parameters.

11. Modify the Experiment1 program of Section 5.1 so that it demonstrates experimentally that a VAR parameter is passed into and out of a subprogram that uses it.

5.3 A PROCEDURE WITH BOTH VALUE AND VAR PARAMETERS

We have one more procedure to implement in the `FahrenheitToCelsius` program. We need a Fahrenheit-to-Celsius conversion procedure that receives a Fahrenheit temperature as its input, returning the corresponding Celsius temperature as its output. Since one parameter will be an in-parameter while the other will be an out-parameter, we need both a value parameter and a `VAR` parameter. The resulting `ConvertToCelsius` procedure is shown in the completed program below:

```
PROGRAM FahrenheitToCelsius3 ( Input, Output );
{ First fully modular version }

VAR
   Fahrenheit, Celsius : Real;


PROCEDURE ShowPurpose;
BEGIN

   WriteLn( 'CONVERTING FAHRENHEIT TO CELSIUS' );
   WriteLn

END; { ShowPurpose }


PROCEDURE GetFahrenheit( VAR F : Real );
BEGIN

   Write( 'Fahrenheit? (Must be >= -459.7) ' );
   ReadLn( F )

END; { GetFahrenheit }


PROCEDURE ConvertToCelsius( F            : Real;
                            VAR Celsius : Real );
BEGIN

   Celsius := ( 5.0 / 9.0 ) * ( F - 32.0 )

END; { ConvertToCelsius }


PROCEDURE ShowTemperature( F, C : Real );
BEGIN

   WriteLn;
   WriteLn( F:6:1, ' deg. F. = ', C:6:1, ' deg. C.' )

END; { ShowTemperature }
```

```
BEGIN { main program }

   {-- Display purpose of program }
   ShowPurpose;

   {--Get Fahrenheit temperature }
   GetFahrenheit( Fahrenheit );

   {--Convert Fahrenheit to Celsius }
   ConvertToCelsius( Fahrenheit, Celsius );

   {--Display both Fahrenheit and Celsius }
   ShowTemperature( Fahrenheit, Celsius )

END.
```

Now (finally!) you can compile, link, and run the program in a fully modular form. When you do, you should get the output we planned:

```
CONVERTING FAHRENHEIT TO CELSIUS

Fahrenheit? (Must be >= -459.7) 212

 212.0 deg. F. =  100.0 deg. C.
```

A shortcoming

In its present form, the program demands a Fahrenheit temperature greater than or equal to –459.7 degrees, but does nothing to force the user to enter such a value. If the user enters a value less than absolute zero, the program will compute a nonsense Celsius value. In the next chapter, you will learn how to prevent such problems.

Experimenting with the VAR parameter

To convince yourself that only `VAR` parameters can change the value of an actual parameter, try removing the `VAR` declaration from the `C` parameter in the `Convert` procedure. When you run the altered program, the output will show that `Celsius` no longer receives a value from `Convert`, but instead contains garbage because it was never initialized by the program.

Questions

12. How does a variable parameter differ from a value parameter? How do their uses differ?

13. Since `VAR` parameters are in/out parameters, they have the potential to be general-purpose parameters. Why don't we make *all* parameters `VAR` parameters?

Exercises

14. Jackson P. Slipshod has written the following program, which seems to have a bug, since it won't compile. Please tell Jackson what his error is:

```
PROGRAM Bad12 ( Output );
VAR
   Stuff : Real;

PROCEDURE Trubble( Junk         : Real;
                   VAR Nonsense : Real );
BEGIN
   Nonsense := Junk + Nonsense;
   WriteLn( Junk:6:2, Nonsense:9:2 )
END;

BEGIN
   Stuff := 111.1;
   Trubble( Stuff, Stuff );
   WriteLn( Stuff:6:2, Junk:9:2 )
END.
```

15. If `Fahrenheit` and `Celsius` are reversed in the call to `ShowTemperature` on the previous page, and if no other change is made in the program, what output will result if `Fahrenheit` is 212.0?

16. If `Fahrenheit` and `Celsius` are reversed in the call to `ConvertToCelsius` on the previous page, and if no other change is made in the program, what will happen when the program is executed? Why?

17. Yesterday morning, one share of common stock in the Zidsdorf Corporation was worth the `OpeningPrice`; at the end of the day, it was worth the `ClosingPrice`. Write a procedure that receives these two values as input parameters, and returns the change in price and the percentage of change. [Percentage of change equals `100.0 * (ClosingPrice - OpeningPrice) / OpeningPrice`.] Write a main program and test your procedure.

18. Write a procedure that receives the radius of a circle as an input parameter, returning the area and circumference of the circle as output parameters. Write a main program and test your procedure.

19. No matter what Num is sent to the following procedure, it always returns 5.00. Why?

```
PROCEDURE DoMagic (Num        : Real;
                   VAR Result : Real);
VAR
  OldNum : Real;
BEGIN
  OldNum := Num;
  Num := Num + (Num + 1);
  Num := Num + 9.0;
  Num := Num / 2.0;
  Result := Num - OldNum
END; { DoMagic }
```

20. Enter and run the following program, and observe the output. Then change the parameters of the TwoParams procedure to be VARs. Does the output look the same as before? Why?

```
PROGRAM TestPassing( Output );
VAR
   One : Real;

PROCEDURE TwoParams( X, Y : Real );
BEGIN
   WriteLn( X:4:1, Y:7:1 );
   Y := 0.0;
   WriteLn( X:4:1, Y:7:1 )
END; { TwoParams }


BEGIN { main program }
   One := 1.0;
   TwoParams( One, One );
   WriteLn( One:4:1 )
END.
```

5.4 PROGRAM STATES; PRE- AND POSTCONDITIONS

Program state: The set of values stored in all variables and files at a particular time during execution.

The **state** of a program is the set of values stored in all variables and files at a particular time during execution. In simple terms, the program state is "the state of affairs" at a particular time, expressed as a "snapshot" of all the variables and files.

Our `FahrenheitToCelsius3` program starts out in the initial state shared by all programs:

State 1: Variables uninitialized; no input or output.

Then, after the execution of the `ShowPurpose` procedure, the program is in

State 2: Variables uninitialized; no input;
purpose of program displayed on the screen.

After `GetFahrenheit` has executed, the program reaches

State 3: `Fahrenheit` variable has received a value from the keyboard; `Celsius` variable uninitialized;
purpose of program still displayed on the screen.

After `ConvertToCelsius` has executed, the program is in

State 4: `Fahrenheit` variable has a value;
`Celsius` variable has a value;
purpose of program still displayed on the screen.

Finally, after `ShowTemperature` has executed, the program is in

State 5: `Fahrenheit` variable has a value;
`Celsius` variable has a value;
purpose of program and both `Fahrenheit` and `Celsius` values displayed on the screen.

As this indicates, a procedure carries the program from one state to another. In fact, the *meaning* of a procedure is synonymous with the change in program state that it causes. Changes in program state are called **state transitions**, and are often shown in what is called a **state transition diagram**. A diagram for the `FahrenheitToCelsius3` program is shown in Figure 5.4.1, on the next page.

Specifying pre- and postconditions

In order to accomplish its purpose, a procedure may require certain conditions to exist in the program state just before the procedure executes. These conditions are called **preconditions** of the procedure. If the prior program state does not meet the stated preconditions, a procedure may produce meaningless results or encounter an error during execution. It might even crash.

On the other hand, if the preconditions are appropriate, a procedure should produce the desired conditions in the program state just *after* the procedure executes. These are called the procedure's **postconditions**. *Thus a procedure makes a sort of contract with the program: "If you give me the right preconditions, I guarantee to produce the right postconditions."*

The purpose of the GetFahrenheit procedure is to prepare the preconditions for the ConvertToCelsius procedure. If `ConvertToCelsius` is given a physically meaningless Fahrenheit temperature, it will calculate a meaningless Celsius temperature. Although

State transition diagram for FahrenheitToCelsius3. **Figure 5.4.1**

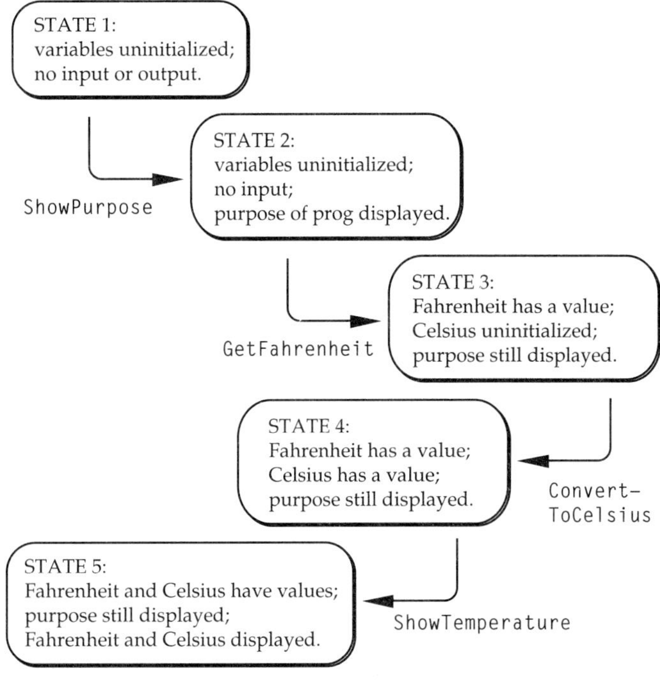

temperatures below absolute zero will cause no computational error when running the program, we should assert that `ConvertToCelsius`'s precondition for correct results is that `Fahrenheit` be greater than or equal to absolute zero. With this in mind, we can write the pre- and postconditions as **assertions** in the procedure. These serve as important documentation, stating what is required and what is produced by the procedure.

Assertion: A comment asserting conditions in the program at that point. That is, a comment asserting the program state.

Adding pre- and postcondition assertions to all the procedures in the program, here is a better-documented version of the `FahrenheitToCelsius` program:

```
PROGRAM FahrenheitToCelsius4 ( Input, Output );
{ Fully modular version }

VAR
   Fahrenheit, Celsius : Real;


PROCEDURE ShowPurpose;
{
  PRECONDITION:
  None.

  POSTCONDITION:
  The purpose of the program is displayed on the screen.
}
```

```
BEGIN

   WriteLn( 'CONVERTING FAHRENHEIT TO CELSIUS' );
   WriteLn

END; { ShowPurpose }


PROCEDURE GetFahrenheit( VAR F : Real );
{
  PRECONDITION:
  None.

  POSTCONDITION:
  The parameter contains a Fahrenheit temperature.
}
BEGIN

   Write( 'Fahrenheit? (Must be >= -459.7) ' );
   ReadLn( F )

END; { GetFahrenheit }


PROCEDURE ConvertToCelsius( F     : Real;
                            VAR C : Real );
{
  PRECONDITION:
  F >= AbsoluteZero.

  POSTCONDITION:
  C contains the Celsius temperature
  corresponding to the given F temperature.
}
BEGIN

   C := ( 5.0 / 9.0 ) * ( F - 32.0 )

END; { ConvertToCelsius }


PROCEDURE ShowTemperature( F, C : Real );
{
  PRECONDITION:
  F and C contain corresponding Fahrenheit and Celsius values.

  POSTCONDITION:
  The values of F and C are displayed on the screen.
}
BEGIN

   WriteLn;
   WriteLn( F:6:1, ' deg. F. = ', C:6:1, ' deg. C.' )

END; { ShowTemperature }
```

```
BEGIN { main program }

   {-- Display purpose of program }
   ShowPurpose;

   {--Get Fahrenheit temperature }
   GetFahrenheit( Fahrenheit );

   {--Convert Fahrenheit to Celsius }
   ConvertToCelsius( Fahrenheit, Celsius );

   {--Display both Fahrenheit and Celsius }
   ShowTemperature( Fahrenheit, Celsius )

END.
```

Two of these procedures demand no preconditions. In the future, we will not bother to list "`PRECONDITION: None`" for such procedures. Similarly, you will notice that we have not bothered to state as preconditions facts that are evident from the procedure's parameter declarations. There is no reason, for example, to state in `GetFahrenheit` that the variable `F` must exist before the procedure can accomplish its goal.

Throughout the rest of the book, we will design each program as a sequence of states, and design each procedure as a mapping, or transformation, from a precondition state to a postcondition state (Figure 5.4.2). In doing this, we will find ourselves led to clearer programs that more often work correctly as soon as we get them built.

5.5 GLOBAL AND LOCAL SCOPE

As you recall, a Pascal program consists of a header followed by a block:

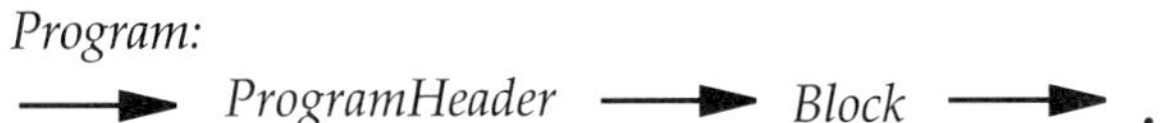

A *Block* contains declarations followed by a compound statement:

In other words, a block contains the declarations that pertain to the following compound statement, which is the body of the program. But those declarations may

A procedure is a mapping from the preconditions to the postconditions. **Figure 5.4.2**

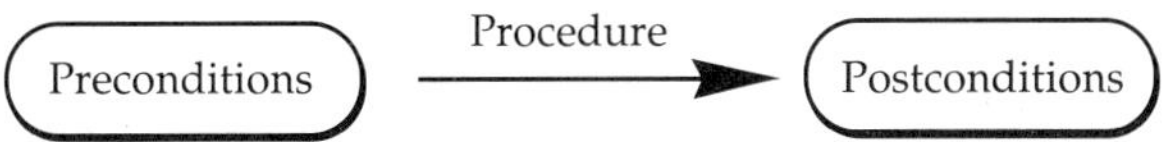

include subprograms, which in turn contain their own blocks. After all, a procedure has the structure

Procedure:

→ *ProcedureHeader* → *Block* → ;

And a procedure's block again contains declarations and a compound statement:

Block:

→ *Declarations* → *CompoundStatement* →

This means that a procedure's block is contained within the program's block, which in turn means that the program's declarations are still in effect within the procedure. This is what we mean when we say that Pascal is a **block-structured language**.

We consider again the Fahrenheit-to-Celsius conversion program of Section 5.4, of which a portion is shown on the next page. Look in particular at the variables declared by the main program and at the `ConvertToCelsius` procedure:

```
PROGRAM FahrenheitToCelsius4 ( Input, Output );

VAR
   Fahrenheit, Celsius : Real;
.
.
PROCEDURE ConvertToCelsius( F     : Real;
                            VAR C : Real );
{
  PRECONDITION:
  F >= -459.69 degrees.

  POSTCONDITION:
  C contains the Celsius temperature corresponding
  to the given F temperature.
}
BEGIN

   C := ( 5.0 / 9.0 ) * ( F - 32.0 )

END; { ConvertToCelsius }
.
.

BEGIN { main program }

   ShowPurpose;
   GetFahrenheit( Fahrenheit );
   ConvertToCelsius( Fahrenheit, Celsius );
   ShowTemperature( Fahrenheit, Celsius )

END.
```

Figure 5.5.1

The Fahrenheit and Celsius variables declared in the main program have global scope, extending over the whole program. The F and C variables declared in the Convert-ToCelsius procedure have only local scope, extending only through the procedure in which they are declared.

```
PROGRAM FahrenheitToCelsius ( Input, Output );

VAR
   Fahrenheit, Celsius : Real;
.
.
PROCEDURE ConvertToCelsius( F     : Real;
                            VAR C : Real );
BEGIN

   C := ( 5.0 / 9.0 ) * ( F - 32.0 )

END; { ConvertToCelsius }
.
.
BEGIN { Main program }

   ShowPurpose;
   GetFahrenheit( Fahrenheit );
   ConvertToCelsius( Fahrenheit, Celsius );
   ShowTemperature( Fahrenheit, Celsius )

END.
```

Scope of local variables, F and C

Scope of global variables, Fahrenheit and Celsius

Here the names `Fahrenheit` and `Celsius` are declared by the program, so they are available throughout the program, even inside the procedure. The region of the program over which identifiers are defined is called the **scope** of the identifiers, and the `Fahrenheit` and `Celsius` identifiers are said to have **global scope** or to be **global identifiers**.

On the other hand, the names `F` and `C` are declared within the `ConvertToCelsius` procedure, and they have scope extending only through that procedure. They are therefore said to have **local scope**, relative to the global scope of `Fahrenheit` and `Celsius`, and are said to be **local identifiers**. (Later on, when we have more complicated programs with procedures within procedures, we will speak of **relatively global** or **relatively local scopes**.) The scopes of the variables in the `FahrenheitToCelsius4` program are shown in Figure 5.5.1.

What if local variables have the same names as global variables?

Several interesting and important programming issues are related to this idea of scope. Let's consider them one by one.

Suppose the program is rewritten so that the `ConvertToCelsius` procedure declares local `Fahrenheit` and `Celsius` identifiers:

```
PROGRAM FahrenheitToCelsius ( Input, Output );

VAR
   Fahrenheit, Celsius : Real;
.
.

PROCEDURE ConvertToCelsius( Fahrenheit   : Real;
                            VAR Celsius  : Real );
BEGIN

   Celsius := ( 5.0 / 9.0 ) * ( Fahrenheit - 32.0 )

END; { ConvertToCelsius }

.
.
.

BEGIN { main program }

   ShowPurpose;
   GetFahrenheit( Fahrenheit );
   ConvertToCelsius( Fahrenheit, Celsius );
   ShowTemperature( Fahrenheit, Celsius )

END.
```

The two parameters are declared within the procedure, and these local declarations override, within the procedure, any global declarations of the same identifiers. In other words, within the procedure, `Fahrenheit` and `Celsius` are *local identifiers*, just as they were when named `F` and `C`. Now the program has two pairs of variables named `Fahrenheit` and `Celsius`. The ones declared by the procedure exist only while the procedure is running, and are located in the part of memory used by that procedure. The ones declared by the main program exist throughout the running of the program, and are located in the part of memory occupied by the main program.

Why declare parameters if we have global variables?

Looking at the program above, you might wonder why we bother to have parameters in the `ConvertToCelsius` procedure. After all, the global declarations of `Fahrenheit` and `Celsius` have scope over the entire program, including the procedure, so it is redundant to declare such variables within the program, right?

Wrong! Suppose the program were written like this:

```
PROGRAM FahrenheitToCelsius ( Input, Output );

VAR
   Fahrenheit, Celsius : Real;
.
.
PROCEDURE ConvertToCelsius;
{ Receives Fahrenheit temperature;            }
{ returns corresponding Celsius temperature }

BEGIN

   Fahrenheit := Fahrenheit - 32.0;
   Celsius := ( 5.0 / 9.0 ) * Fahrenheit

END; { ConvertToCelsius }
.
.

BEGIN { main program }

   ShowPurpose;
   GetFahrenheit( Fahrenheit );
   ConvertToCelsius( Fahrenheit, Celsius );
   ShowTemperature( Fahrenheit, Celsius )

END.
```

Now `ConvertToCelsius` simply reuses the global variables declared by the main program; we have no extra variables, and the program seems more efficient. But *this program now runs incorrectly*. Here's some sample I/O:

```
CONVERTING FAHRENHEIT TO CELSIUS

Fahrenheit temperature? 212

 180.0 deg. F. = 100.0 deg. C.
```

Of course, the 180.0 printed in the last line is incorrect. The problem is that the procedure now not only computes a value for `Celsius`, but also subtracts 32.0 from the global value of `Fahrenheit`. Then, when `ShowTemperature` displays the final value of `Fahrenheit`, it shows 180.0 instead of 212.0.

In this example, we say that the `ConvertToCelsius` procedure has a **side effect** because, in addition to computing the `Celsius` temperature as it is supposed to, the procedure also modifies `Fahrenheit`. It was able to do this because we let it play around with *global identifiers*.

Side effect: An effect of a subprogram, other than the effect that was obviously intended.

Using value parameters to avoid side effects.

Another way to have trouble with side effects is to use VAR parameters too freely. Suppose the previous version of the ConvertToCelsius procedure is changed to

```
PROCEDURE ConvertToCelsius( VAR F, C : Real );
BEGIN

   F := F - 32.0;
   C := ( 5.0 / 9.0 ) * F

END; { ConvertToCelsius }
```

We still have the same side effect. The procedure modifies both F and C, and because these are both variable parameters of the procedure, both changes are transmitted to the main program. (Again, the procedure is directly modifying the global storage cells, but this time the procedure is using different names for those cells.)

Of course, one way to remove the side effect is to get rid of the spurious assignment statement in the procedure, changing the second assignment statement to read

```
   C := ( 5.0 / 9.0 ) * ( F - 32.0 )
```

In order to absolutely prevent any possibility of side effects, we should make F *a value parameter.* This restrains the scope of the F identifier to the procedure itself, and also makes the associated storage cell distinct from the global storage cell associated with the name Fahrenheit. By writing the procedure header

```
PROCEDURE ConvertToCelsius( F     : Real;
                            VAR C : Real );
```

we make it impossible for the procedure to modify the actual parameter corresponding to F.

Tips for self-documenting code

The proper use of parameters is an important contribution to self-documenting code. The parameter list should tell the reader at a glance what data are transferred in and out of a procedure. The value parameters are obviously transferred into the procedure, but not back out. The VAR parameters are obviously intended for two-way transfer. The names of the parameters should indicate their meaning in the procedure. Close attention to these details makes the program easier to understand at a glance, and this in turn leads to more reliable programming.

Tips for the prevention of side effects

The proper use of parameters can prevent dangerous side effects:

- Use value parameters for data that are to be sent into a subprogram, but not to be modified by the subprogram.

- Use variable parameters only when you intend the subprogram to modify them and to transmit the changes to the caller.
- Don't let a procedure use global variables. (For more on this, see Section 5.6.)

Side effects are dangerous because they allow errors that are extremely hard to track down. In addition, there are two other reasons why you should not allow subprograms to modify global variables:

- It is easier for a programmer to understand what a procedure does if its parameters are declared explicitly. Value parameters are obviously intended to send data into the subprogram, but not back out. Variable parameters are obviously intended to return changed values. But if a subprogram is allowed to modify globals as well as parameters, then we can never be sure what all the effects of the subprogram are, until we carefully check all of its inner workings.
- If written with carefully used parameters, procedures can be unplugged from their test programs and saved in libraries as prefabricated program parts, to be plugged together to build many other programs. With all of a procedure's inputs and outputs clearly stated in the parameter list, modular construction is much easier.

Throughout the book, we will emphasize that procedures and functions should be self-contained, modular, and self-documenting. And we will always try to minimize side effects. These are important elements of craftsmanship, enabling us to develop subprograms that are true building blocks for sizable programs.

Exercises

21. Consider the following program:

```
PROGRAM OneTwoThree( Output );
VAR
   Y : Real;

PROCEDURE C ( VAR X : Real );
BEGIN
   WriteLn( X:3:1 );
   X := X + 2.0
END; { C }

PROCEDURE B ( X : Real );
BEGIN
   X := X + 1.0;
   C( X );
   WriteLn( X:3:1 )
END; { B }
```

```
PROCEDURE A ( X : Real );
BEGIN

   WriteLn( X:3:1 );
   B( X + 1.0 );
   WriteLn( X:3:1 )

END; { A }


BEGIN

  Y := 1.0;
  A( Y )

END.
```

a. What is the scope of X in procedure C? In procedure B? In procedure A? What is the scope of the Y variable?

b. What is displayed when the program runs? Explain the output.

c. If the Y identifier is changed to X, will the program's output change? Explain.

22. Consider the following program:

```
PROGRAM ThreeTwoOne( Output );
VAR
   X, Y : Real;


PROCEDURE C ( One, Two : Real );
BEGIN

   One := One + 1.0;
   Two := Two + 2.0

END; { C }


PROCEDURE B ( VAR One, Two : Real );
VAR
   Three : Real;

BEGIN

   Three := One;
   One   := Two;
   Two   := Three;
   WriteLn( One:3:1, '      ', Two:6:1 );
   C( One, Two )

END; { B }
```

```
PROCEDURE A ( VAR One, Two : Real );
BEGIN
   WriteLn( Two:3:1, '   ', One:6:1 );
   B( One, Two );
   WriteLn( Two:3:1, '   ', One:6:1 )
END; { A }

BEGIN
  X := 1.0;
  Y := 2.0;
  WriteLn( X:3:1, '   ', Y:6:1 );
  A( X, Y );
  WriteLn( X:3:1, '   ', Y:6:1 )
END.
```

a. What is the scope of `One` and `Two` in procedure `C`? In procedure `B`? In procedure `A`? What is the scope of `X` and `Y`?

b. What is displayed when the program runs? Explain the output.

23. What is printed by the following program? Explain the output.

```
PROGRAM GlobalTrouble ( Output );
VAR
   Global : Real;

PROCEDURE A ( VAR G : Real );
VAR
   Global : Real;
BEGIN
   WriteLn( G:3:1, '   ', Global:6:1 );
   Global := G + 1.0;
   WriteLn( G:3:1, '   ', Global:6:1 )
END; { A }

BEGIN
  Global := 1.0;
  WriteLn( Global:3:1 );
  A( Global );
  WriteLn( Global )
END.
```

5.6 ADVANCED TOPIC: AVOIDING GLOBAL VARIABLES

As you saw in the previous section, the variables declared in a Pascal main program are global to the entire program. This is a shortcoming in the Pascal language, making it more difficult than it ought to be to prevent procedures from having unintended side effects. Some programmers feel so strongly that global variables are to be avoided that they use a programming trick to deal with the problem:

If the main program does nothing but call a procedure named Main, then this procedure can act as the effective main program. Variables declared within the Main procedure will be local to that procedure.

Here's what the `FahrenheitToCelsius` program looks like when rewritten in this way:

```
PROGRAM FahrenheitToCelsius5 ( Input, Output );
{ This version avoids global variables altogether.}


PROCEDURE ShowPurpose;
{
  POSTCONDITIONS:
  The purpose of the program has been displayed.
}
BEGIN

   WriteLn( 'CONVERTING FAHRENHEIT TO CELSIUS' );
   WriteLn

END; { ShowPurpose }


PROCEDURE GetFahrenheit( VAR Fahrenheit : Real );
{
  POSTCONDITIONS:
  A physically meaningful value of Fahrenheit
  has been obtained from the keyboard.
}
BEGIN

   Write( 'Fahrenheit? (Must be >= -459.7) ' );
   ReadLn( Fahrenheit )

END; { GetFahrenheit }


PROCEDURE ConvertToCelsius( F     : Real;
                            VAR C : Real );
{
  PRECONDITIONS:
  F has been initialized.
```

```
  POSTCONDITIONS:
  Celsius temperature C has been computed from the
  Fahrenheit temperature F.
}
BEGIN

   C := ( 5.0 / 9.0 ) * ( F - 32.0 )

END; { ConvertToCelsius }


PROCEDURE ShowTemperature( F, C : Real );
{
  PRECONDITIONS:
  F and C have been initialized.

  POSTCONDITIONS:
  F and C have been displayed.
}
BEGIN

   WriteLn;
   WriteLn( F:6:1, ' deg. F. = ', C:6:1, ' deg. C.' )

END; { ShowTemperature }


PROCEDURE Main;
{
  PRECONDITIONS:
  None.

  POSTCONDITIONS:
  Purpose of program has been displayed.
  Fahrenheit temperature has been read from keyboard
  and converted to Celsius.
  Results have been displayed.
}
VAR
   Fahrenheit, Celsius : Real;

BEGIN

   {--Display purpose of program }
   ShowPurpose;

   {--Get Fahrenheit temperature from keyboard }
   GetFahrenheit( Fahrenheit );

   {--Convert Fahrenheit to Celsius }
   ConvertToCelsius( Fahrenheit, Celsius );

   {--Display both Fahrenheit and Celsius }
   ShowTemperature( Fahrenheit, Celsius )

END; { Main }
```

```
BEGIN { main program }

   Main

END.
```

In this version of the program, the `Fahrenheit` and `Celsius` variables are declared within the `Main` procedure, and are therefore local to the procedure. We have no global variables whatsoever. Because of this and the way we've carefully controlled the use of `VAR` parameters, we have greatly reduced the danger of unintended side effects.

On the other hand, we've paid for this advantage by having a do-nothing main program that looks artificial. Some serious software engineers believe that the advantage is well worth the price. Others disagree. It's a matter of style that you will have to decide for yourself.

5.7 TESTING AND DEBUGGING

One of the most common errors with procedures often gives no error message, but instead gives unpredictable variable values. Here is a simple example; see if you can spot the error.

```
PROGRAM Bug5A ( Input, Output );
{
  This contains a common error in using a procedure.
}
VAR
   Angle: Real;


PROCEDURE GetAngle( Angle : Real );
BEGIN

   Write( 'Angle in radians? ' );
   ReadLn( Angle )

END; { GetAngle }


BEGIN { main program }

   GetAngle( Angle );

   WriteLn;
   WriteLn( 'Main has angle = ', Angle : 6 : 2,
            ' radians' )

END.
```

When this program is run, the I/O might look like this:

```
Angle in radians? 1.5

Main has angle =   0.00 radians
```

The user entered an angle of 1.5 radians, but the main program did not receive that value. This implies that something interfered with proper transmission of the `Angle` parameter from the `GetAngle` procedure to the main program. If we look at the program with that idea, we quickly see that `GetAngle` cannot return a value because its parameter is a *value* parameter rather than a *variable* parameter. The word `VAR` is missing in front of the parameter declaration in the procedure header.

In the run shown above, no error occurred. But if the main program had divided some number by the angle, a divide-by-zero error would have occurred, and this error would have been the first symptom noticed by the programmer. The tricky thing about missing-`VAR` mistakes is that they don't always cause the same symptoms. The lesson is that when your program is behaving strangely, you should check the values of all variables, either by printing them out as we did here, or by using a debugger to track the values.

The order of actual and formal parameters must match.

If the actual parameters are not in the same order as the corresponding formal parameters, often there will be no error message, but the program will produce crazy results. This happens, for example, if you call

```
PROCEDURE ShowTemperatures( F, C : Real );
```

by means of the statement

```
ShowTemperatures( Celsius, Fahrenheit )
```

Such a mistake would cause output like this:

```
100.0 deg. F. =  212.0 deg. C.
```

This output is clearly nonsensical, but if you aren't checking it carefully, you may overlook it. The lesson: never trust a program; check it carefully.

Figure 5.7.1

Attempting to compile a program in which the actual and formal parameters differ in number.

```
"," expected

PROCEDURE GetCoords( VAR Angle  : Real;
                     VAR Radius : Real );
BEGIN
.
.
END; { GetCoords }

BEGIN { main program }

   GetCoords( Angle[)];
   .
   .
```

Parameters must match in number and in type.

If there are not the same number of actual parameters as there are formal parameters, your Pascal system will issue an error message and refuse to run the program. An example is shown in Figure 5.7.1.

A similar error is to send the wrong type of value to a formal parameter. With `VAR` parameters, the actual and formal parameters must be of the same type. (After all, they refer to the same storage cell.) With value parameters, the requirement is that the actual parameter value be a type that can be assigned to the formal parameter. For example, an integer value can be sent to a real formal parameter, but a real value cannot be sent to an integer formal parameter. A mistake of this kind results in an "`Incompatible types`" error message.

Table 5.7.1 *Examples of syntax errors in Turbo Pascal 6.0.*

Syntax error	Error message from compiler
Procedure not declared before use.	`Unknown identifier.`
Keyword `PROCEDURE` missing or misspelled in procedure header.	`":" expected.`
Semicolon missing from end of procedure header.	`";" expected.`
Keyword `BEGIN` missing or misspelled in procedure.	`BEGIN expected.`
Keyword `END` missing or misspelled in procedure.	`Unknown identifier or BEGIN expected.`
Semicolon missing from end of procedure.	`";" expected.`
Comma instead of semicolon between formal parameter declarations.	`")" expected.`
More actual parameters than formal parameters.	`")" expected.`
Fewer actual parameters than formal parameters.	`"," expected.`
Actual parameter differs in type from formal parameter.	`Type mismatch.`

The most important tips on debugging

- Test one procedure at a time. Don't add a second procedure until you are sure that the first one is working correctly.
- First write a driver and test the procedure as a stub. When this much is working correctly, add code to the procedure and test again.
- Check to see that every identifier is declared before it is used.
- Don't use global variables. Instead, send all values into and out of procedures as parameters.
- Use a value parameter when you want an *in-only* parameter.
- Use a `VAR` parameter only when you want an in-and-out parameter.
- Use `VAR` parameters only when necessary.
- Make sure that all formal parameters have the correct data type.
- Make sure that actual parameters agree with the formal parameters in number, in order, and in type.

LOOKING BACK

Most procedures need to receive data for processing and/or need to return the results of processing, so procedures usually need transmission mechanisms for receiving and returning data. They do this by means of their parameters.

First we examined value parameters:

- Value parameters are transmitted to a procedure by copying their actual values into the formal parameters. This method of transmission is one-way: The procedure can receive the copied values, but cannot return new values to the calling program unit.
- A formal value parameter is a different storage cell from the actual value parameter, located in a different part of memory.

Then we examined variable parameters:

- Formal variable parameters (or VAR parameters) are the same storage cells as the corresponding actual parameters.
- A variable parameter can therefore be modified by the procedure, and the modified value will be available afterwards to the calling program unit. Thus variable parameters are two-way: They transmit values both into and out of a procedure.

We studied the concept of program state, which is the condition of the variables and files at a given moment in the execution of the program. We discussed the fact that a procedure can be viewed as a process that changes the program state. In this vein, we wrote pre- and postconditions for procedures.

- The preconditions of a procedure are the data conditions that must exist in order for the procedure to run correctly.
- The postcondition of a procedure is the program state that results from the procedure's execution.

- The pre- and postconditions constitute a "contract" that the procedure makes with the program: "If the program gives me the right preconditions, I will produce the promised postconditions."

Finally, we discussed the scope of constant and variable identifiers:

- A local identifier is known only within the subprogram in which it is declared.
- A global identifier is declared at the top of the program and is known throughout.

We emphasized that global variables (variables having global identifiers) are dangerous because they often cause side effects. Therefore, we discourage their use except in exceptional cases. Global constants are often useful, however, as a way of making the constants of a program more self-documenting.

TERMS EMPHASIZED IN THIS CHAPTER

PROJECTS

1. Write the beginnings of a credit-card account program. Your program should prompt for and read the previous balance and the amount of the current charge. Then it should display the new balance. The I/O should look like this:

```
CREDIT CARD STATEMENT
---------------------
Previous balance? $ 601.57
Charge? $ 14.23

New balance: $ 615.80
```

   Your program should be fully modular, with procedures for all of the main tasks.

2. Write a procedure that receives as parameters two times given in 24-hour format, in the form Hours1, Minutes1, Hours2, Minutes2. The procedure should compute and display the difference between the two times, in hours and fractional hours. For example, if

   Hours1 = 13.0, Minutes1 = 15.0,
   Hours2 = 15.0, Minutes2 = 45.0,

   the first time is understood to be 13:15, the second time is understood to be 15:45, and the difference is 2.50 hours. On the other hand, if

   Hours1 = 3.0, Minutes1 = 15.0,
   Hours2 = 2.0, Minutes2 = 45.0,

   the two times are 3:15 and 2:45, respectively, and the difference is –0.50 hours. Your procedure should call another procedure to convert hours and minutes to a single real number representing hours and *fractional hours*. Write a driver and test your procedure.

3. Complete the purchase price/tax/total price program that was begun in Project 1 of Chapter 4.

4. Complete the standard deviation program that was begun in Project 2 of Chapter 4.

5. Complete the pari-mutuel program that was begun in Project 3 of Chapter 4.

REFERENCES

The mechanisms used for parameter passing in Pascal are not the only ones that have been used in programming languages. See, for example, the discussion in Section 7–8 of Terrence W. Pratt's book *Programming Languages*, second edition (Prentice-Hall, 1984). Also see pages 215–16 of Bruce J. MacLennan's *Principles of Programming Languages*, second edition (Holt, Rinehart and Winston, 1987).

An interesting brief history of the concept of scope is found in Chapter 10 of Edsger Dijkstra's *A Discipline of Programming* (Prentice-Hall, 1976). Dijkstra is one of the originators of the ideas now called *structured programming*.

A provocative development of the use of procedures and procedural abstraction is found in Part 1 of *Structure and Interpretation of Computer Programs* by Harold Abelson, Gerald Jay Sussman, and Julie Sussman (MIT Press, 1985). This covers material appearing in our Chapters 1 through 12, but in terms of the LISP language.

CHAPTER 6

Controlling Execution

CHAPTER CONTENTS

INTRODUCTION

Up to this point, our programs have consisted of "straight-line code"; that is, the instructions were always executed one after another, in the order listed. There was no way for a program to change or control its execution according to data received or computed during a run. For example, there was no way for the program to choose whether to execute a statement, and no way to repeat the execution of a group of statements. Yet decisions and repetition are important aspects of most algorithms, so we take the time now to show some simple ways to make them happen in Pascal programs.

As our first example, we give the Fahrenheit-to-Celsius program the ability to protect itself from inappropriate input data. We will do that by building **control structures** into the program—special instructions that let the program control its own execution according to conditions that occur during a run. After we improve the F-to-C program, we will design a program to sort three numbers. In addition to showing an important use of control structures, this program will provide an example of nested procedure calls.

We have four main goals in this chapter:

- To learn how to build a **decision structure** into a program, so that the program can decide for itself whether to execute this group of statements or that one.
- To learn how to build a **repetition structure** into a program, so the program can repeatedly execute the same group of statements.
- To work through a top-down design problem involving **nested procedure calls**.
- To catch a first glimpse of what happens when a procedure calls itself, and to see why that might be useful.

6.1 STRUCTURES THAT MAKE DECISIONS

Before we leave the Fahrenheit-to-Celsius program we developed earlier, we ought to say something about how it can be made to protect itself from inappropriate input data.

Control structure: A statement that controls the execution of other statements.

Pascal provides some statements that are used to control the execution of other statements. These are called **control structures**. For a simple example, let's make the `GetFahrenheit` procedure check for a physically impossible Fahrenheit temperature coming in from the keyboard (that is, for a temperature below absolute zero). In order to perform the check, we want the algorithm to work like the pseudocode outline shown in Section 2.4:

```
If Fahrenheit < AbsoluteZero then
      DisplayError

otherwise
      ConvertToCelsius;
      ShowTemperature
```

The Pascal version of this is very similar. If we assume that an `AbsoluteZero` constant has been defined, the Pascal control structure has the general form

```
IF Fahrenheit < AbsoluteZero THEN
   Statement1

ELSE
   Statement2
```

Decision structure: A control structure that makes decisions.

Here we have an example of a **decision structure**, a control structure that makes a decision. This particular one creates a two-way fork in the execution: If `Fahrenheit` is less than `AbsoluteZero`, *Statement1* is executed; otherwise, *Statement2* is executed. *Statement1* and *Statement2* are said to be *conditionally executed*. One way to represent the action diagramatically is shown in Figure 6.1.1.

IF..THEN..ELSE is a single statement.

Note that the entire `IF..THEN..ELSE` structure is a single Pascal statement. *There is no semicolon after* `THEN` *or between Statement1 and* `ELSE`. If another statement follows the `IF..THEN..ELSE` structure, however, there must be a semicolon after *Statement2*. (Note

Figure 6.1.1

The flow of execution through an IF..THEN..ELSE decision structure. If the tested condition is true, Statement1 is executed; if it is false, Statement2 is executed instead.

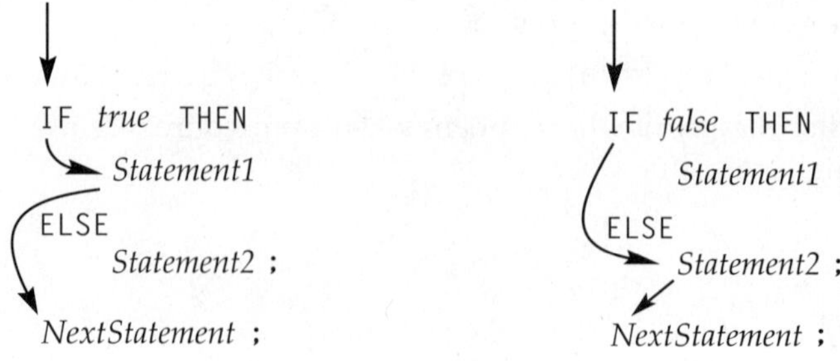

also that we call this an `IF..THEN..ELSE` structure rather than an `IF...THEN...ELSE` structure; Pascal uses two-dot ellipses rather than the three dots used in English to symbolize missing words.)

Relational operators

The < (less than) operator is one of six **relational operators** that can be used in this kind of decision structure. Here's the complete list:

<	means	"less than."	<>	means	"not equal to."
<=	means	"less than or equal to."	>=	means	"greater than or equal to."
=	means	"equal to."	>	means	"greater than."

(A complete treatment of all of Pascal's logical operators and decision structures will be given in Chapters 9 and 10.)

Conditionally executed statements can be simple or compound.

To implement our particular algorithm, we need to plug in an appropriate *Statement1* and *Statement2*. The syntax of Pascal allows these to be either simple statements or compound statements, whichever is needed in a particular case. (Compound statements were defined in Section 3.2.) In our case, we need only a simple *Statement1*, but we need a compound *Statement2*, as shown in the sample program below. Note also that we have to define the `AbsoluteZero` constant before we can use it:

```
PROGRAM FahrenheitToCelsius ( Input, Output );

CONST
   { Lowest meaningful Fahrenheit temperature }
   AbsoluteZero = -459.7;

VAR
   Fahrenheit, Celsius : Real;


PROCEDURE ShowPurpose;
{
  PRECONDITION:
  None.

  POSTCONDITION:
  The purpose of the program is displayed on the screen.
}
BEGIN

   WriteLn( 'CONVERTING FAHRENHEIT TO CELSIUS' );
   WriteLn

END; { ShowPurpose }
```

```
PROCEDURE GetFahrenheit( VAR F : Real );
{
  PRECONDITION:
  None.

  POSTCONDITION:
  The parameter contains a Fahrenheit temperature.
}
BEGIN

   Write( 'Fahrenheit? (Must be >= -459.7) ' );
   ReadLn( F )

END; { GetFahrenheit }


PROCEDURE ShowError;
{
  PRECONDITION:
  The temperature is below absolute zero.

  POSTCONDITION:
  An appropriate error message has been displayed on the screen.
}
BEGIN

   WriteLn( 'Temperature is below absolute zero (-459.7 F.)' );
   WriteLn

END; { ShowError }


PROCEDURE ConvertToCelsius( F     : Real;
                            VAR C : Real );
{
  PRECONDITION:
  F >= AbsoluteZero.

  POSTCONDITION:
  C contains the Celsius temperature corresponding to
  the given F temperature.
}
BEGIN

   C := ( 5.0 / 9.0 ) * ( F - 32.0 )

END; { ConvertToCelsius }
```

```
PROCEDURE ShowTemperature( F, C : Real );
{
  PRECONDITION:
  F and C contain corresponding Fahrenheit and Celsius values.

  POSTCONDITION:
  The values of F and C are displayed on the screen.
}
BEGIN

   WriteLn;
   WriteLn( F:6:1, ' deg. F. = ', C:6:1, ' deg. C.' )

END; { ShowTemperature }


BEGIN

   {-- Show purpose of program }
   ShowPurpose;

   {--Prompt for and read a Fahrenheit temperature }
   GetFahrenheit( Fahrenheit );

   IF Fahrenheit < AbsoluteZero THEN
      ShowError

   ELSE
   BEGIN
      ConvertToCelsius( Fahrenheit, Celsius );
      ShowTemperature( Fahrenheit, Celsius )
   END

END.
```

When this program is given a Fahrenheit temperature below absolute zero, we see the corresponding error message:

```
CONVERTING FAHRENHEIT TO CELSIUS

Fahrenheit? -500

Temperature is below absolute zero (-459.7 F.)
```

When the program is given a reasonable temperature, we see the correct F-to-C conversion:

```
CONVERTING FAHRENHEIT TO CELSIUS

Fahrenheit? 212

 212.0 deg. F. =  100.0 deg. C.
```

Syntax for IF..THEN..ELSE structures

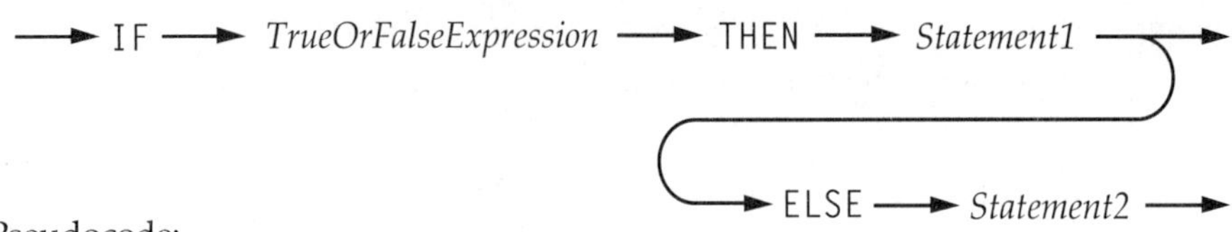

Pseudocode:

```
IF TrueOrFalseExpression THEN
   Statement1
ELSE
   Statement2
```

If the *TrueOrFalseExpression* is true, *Statement1* is executed but not *Statement2*. If the *TrueOrFalseExpression* is false, *Statement2* is executed but not *Statement1*. Afterwards, execution passes to the next statement after the control structure.

Notes:

- *Statement1* and *Statement2* can be either simple or compound statements.
- The `ELSE` clause is optional.

Further details will be discussed in Section 9.1.

Semicolons in the IF..THEN..ELSE structure

It is easy to forget that Pascal's semicolons go between the statements in a sequence, and not at the end of every line. If you forget this, you might be tempted to put a semicolon at the end of an `IF..THEN` line, causing some strange results. For example, if you write

```
IF Fahrenheit < AbsoluteZero THEN;
   ShowError

ELSE
BEGIN
   ConvertToCelsius( Fahrenheit, Celsius );
   ShowTemperature( Fahrenheit, Celsius )
END
```

the extra semicolon after `THEN` terminates the `IF..THEN` structure, leaving the ELSE clause orphaned. The result is a syntax error and your program will not compile.

In an IF..THEN structure without an ELSE clause, the result is even worse, because the program will compile but will execute incorrectly. You will see an example of this in Section 6.3.

Indentation as an element of good style

Pascal does not require the indentation shown in this book, but good taste demands *some* sort of indentation. Any useful program will be read not only by the original programmer, but by other programmers who need to add to it or build upon it. *If it is useful, it will be read many times.* Therefore, it should be written to be readable.

Indentation makes decision structures easier to read and understand. Surely

```
IF Fahrenheit < AbsoluteZero THEN
   ShowError

ELSE
BEGIN
   ConvertToCelsius( Fahrenheit, Celsius );
   ShowTemperature( Fahrenheit, Celsius )
END
```

is more readable than

```
IF Fahrenheit < AbsoluteZero THEN
ShowError
ELSE
BEGIN
ConvertToCelsius( Fahrenheit, Celsius );
ShowTemperature( Fahrenheit, Celsius )
END
```

or worse yet,

```
IF Fahrenheit < AbsoluteZero THEN ShowError ELSE BEGIN
ConvertToCelsius( Fahrenheit, Celsius ); ShowTemperature(
Fahrenheit, Celsius ) END
```

(These are all equally legal as far as the compiler is concerned.)

This is not to say that the indentation and whitespace conventions of this book are better than all others. Seek your own clear style; try it out on other programmers; refine it. Your goal is to make your subprograms easy for other programmers to read and use. This will make it easy to share code, build large programs in team efforts, and debug and extend large programs.

Decisions without an ELSE clause

We might mention here that a decision structure of the form

IF relation is true THEN
    do something
ELSE
    do nothing

(which did not arise in our example) can be implemented in Pascal by omitting the `ELSE` clause and writing

`IF` relation is true `THEN`
  do something;

This situation will arise in Section 6.3.

There are more subtleties to the use of decision structures, but that's enough for now; a more complete treatment will be found in Chapter 9.

Questions

1. Which of the listed statements are correct in reference to the following structure?

   ```
   IF Fahrenheit < AbsoluteZero THEN
       Statement1
   ELSE
       Statement2
   ```

   a. Either *Statement1* or *Statement2* is executed, but not both.

   b. It is possible that neither *Statement1* nor *Statement2* will be executed.

   c. It is possible that both *Statement1* and *Statement2* will be executed.

   d. *Statement1* and *Statement2* are executed zero or more times.

2. In which of the following structures is *Statement1* executed?

   a.
   ```
   IF AbsoluteZero = AbsoluteZero THEN
       Statement2
   ELSE
       Statement1
   ```

   b.
   ```
   IF AbsoluteZero < AbsoluteZero THEN
       Statement1
   ELSE
       Statement2
   ```

   c.
   ```
   IF AbsoluteZero <> AbsoluteZero THEN
       Statement2;
   Statement1
   ```

   d.
   ```
   IF -1.0 < 0.0 THEN Statement2; Statement1
   ```

Exercises

3. Write an `IF..THEN..ELSE` structure that enacts the following logic: "If Fahrenheit is greater than or equal to zero, write the word 'NONNEGATIVE' on the screen; otherwise, write the word 'NEGATIVE'." Write a simple program to test your decision structure.

4. Design an `IF..THEN..ELSE` structure that tells the user whether or not a real variable, *X*, contains a value equal to that in another real variable, *Y*. Test your structure in a simple program.

5. Without running it, predict what will be printed by the following procedure if `Love` is 37.7777:

   ```
   PROCEDURE ForEsme ( Love : Real );

   CONST
      Squalor = 42.2222;
   ```

```
BEGIN
   IF Love <= Squalor THEN
      WriteLn( 'I''m quite communicative for my age.' )
   ELSE
      WriteLn( 'I prefer stories about squalor.' )
END; { ForEsme }
```

6. What will happen if a semicolon is added to the decision structure of Exercise 5, as shown below?

```
   IF Love <= Squalor THEN
      WriteLn( 'I''m quite communicative for my age.' );
   ELSE
      WriteLn( 'I prefer stories about squalor.' )
```

7. What is printed by the following (horrible) procedure if JD is 1952.0?

```
PROCEDURE Bananafish ( JD : Real ); CONST Salinger = 1948.0;
BEGIN IF JD = Salinger THEN
Write('He says he doesn''t want a lot of fools looking at his tattoo');
WriteLn END; { Bananafish }
```

6.2 STRUCTURES THAT REPEAT EXECUTION

The Fahrenheit-to-Celsius program is still unsatisfactory because it terminates if it is given a physically impossible Fahrenheit temperature. A more desirable behavior would be to prompt repeatedly for a Fahrenheit temperature until the user enters a reasonable one, as in the following example:

```
Fahrenheit temperature? (Must be >= -459.7) -600
Fahrenheit temperature? (Must be >= -459.7) -460
Fahrenheit temperature? (Must be >= -459.7) -459
-459.0 deg. F. = -273.2 deg. C.
```

This would require the program to execute the prompt and ReadLn repeatedly until the Fahrenheit temperature is at least as great as absolute zero.

A group of statements executed repeatedly is called a **loop**, and the process of repeated execution is called **looping** or **iteration**. We create a loop by placing the statements to be repeated inside a control structure that causes execution to "loop backwards": a so-called **loop structure**. Assuming that an AbsoluteZero constant has been declared and a value has been stored in the Fahrenheit variable, we can write a loop structure of the form

Loop: A group of statements executed repeatedly.

Iteration: Looping.

```
WHILE Fahrenheit < AbsoluteZero DO
   Statement
```

With values in both Fahrenheit and AbsoluteZero, the WHILE structure executes Statement (which is called the **loop body**) if and only if Fahrenheit is less than AbsoluteZero, after which execution returns ("loops back") to the WHILE statement, to test again whether Fahrenheit is less than AbsoluteZero. If Fahrenheit is in fact less, Statement is executed again and execution loops back again to the WHILE statement.

Loop body: The simple or compound statement that is executed repeatedly by the loop structure.

Figure 6.2.1

A WHILE loop structure executes Statement repeatedly as long as the loop condition is true. When the loop condition becomes false, execution skips to the next statement after the loop structure.

This continues until `Fahrenheit` is no longer less than `AbsoluteZero`. Figure 6.2.1 shows one way to diagram the flow.

Infinite loop: A loop that repeats forever.

If `Fahrenheit` never becomes greater than or equal to `AbsoluteZero`, the loop continues forever, a condition known as an **infinite loop**. On the other hand, if `Fahrenheit` is already greater than or equal to `AbsoluteZero` when execution first reaches the loop structure, the `Statement` comprising the body of the loop is never executed; execution simply skips immediately to whatever lies beyond the loop structure.

Using a loop in the GetFahrenheit procedure

Of course, `Statement` can be either a simple statement or a compound statement. In our particular case, we want to prompt for and read a Fahrenheit temperature, and then continue to prompt and read until we get a meaningful value, so we can write, for example,

```
Write( 'Fahrenheit temperature? (Must be >= -459.7) ' );
ReadLn( Fahrenheit );

WHILE Fahrenheit < AbsoluteZero DO
BEGIN
   Write( 'Fahrenheit temperature? (Must be >= -459.7) ' );
   ReadLn( Fahrenheit );
END
```

We can use this in the `GetFahrenheit` procedure to ensure a meaningful input value. Then we no longer need the decision structure in the main program or the `ShowError` procedure:

```
PROGRAM FahrenheitToCelsius ( Input, Output );

CONST
   { Lowest meaningful Fahrenheit temperature }
   AbsoluteZero = -459.7;
```

```
VAR
   Fahrenheit, Celsius : Real;


PROCEDURE ShowPurpose;
{
  PRECONDITION:
  None.

  POSTCONDITION:
  The purpose of the program is displayed on the screen.
}
BEGIN

   WriteLn( 'CONVERTING FAHRENHEIT TO CELSIUS' );
   WriteLn

END; { ShowPurpose }


PROCEDURE GetFahrenheit( VAR F : Real );
{
  PRECONDITION:
  None.

  POSTCONDITION:
  The parameter contains a Fahrenheit temperature >= -459.7.
}
BEGIN

   Write( 'Fahrenheit temperature? (Must be >= -459.7) ' );
   ReadLn( F );
   WHILE Fahrenheit < AbsoluteZero DO
   BEGIN
      Write( 'Fahrenheit temperature? (Must be >= -459.7) ' );
      ReadLn( F )
   END

END; { GetFahrenheit }


PROCEDURE ConvertToCelsius( F     : Real;
                            VAR C : Real );
{
  PRECONDITION:
  F >= AbsoluteZero.

  POSTCONDITION:
  C contains the Celsius temperature corresponding to
  the given F temperature.
}
BEGIN

   C := ( 5.0 / 9.0 ) * ( F - 32.0 )

END; { ConvertToCelsius }
```

```
PROCEDURE ShowTemperature( F, C : Real );
{
  PRECONDITION:
  F and C contain corresponding Fahrenheit and Celsius values.

  POSTCONDITION:
  The values of F and C are displayed on the screen.
}
BEGIN

   WriteLn;
   WriteLn( F:6:1, ' deg. F. = ', C:6:1, ' deg. C.' )

END; { ShowTemperature }


BEGIN

   {-- Show purpose of program }
   ShowPurpose;

   {--Get a meaningful Fahrenheit temperature }
   GetFahrenheit( Fahrenheit );

   {--Convert to Celsius and show results }
   ConvertToCelsius( Fahrenheit, Celsius );
   ShowTemperature( Fahrenheit, Celsius )

END.
```

Syntax of the WHILE..DO structure

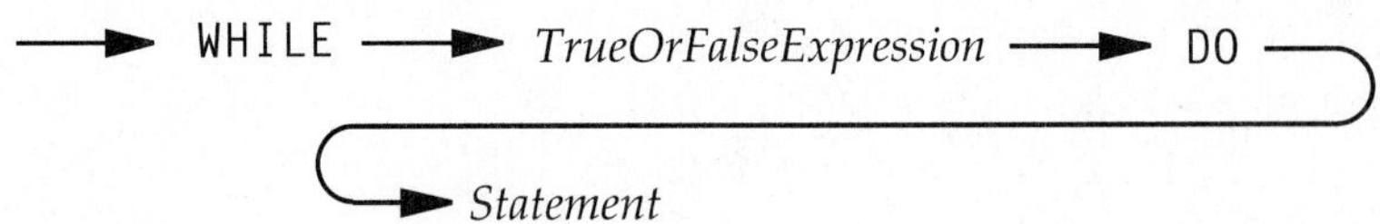

Pseudocode:

`WHILE` *TrueOrFalseExpression* `DO`
    Statement

If *TrueOrFalseExpression* is true, *Statement* is executed, then *TrueOrFalseExpression* is evaluated again. If it is still true, *Statement* is executed again, then *TrueOrFalseExpression* is evaluated again. And so on, until *TrueOrFalseExpression* is found to be false.

Notes:

- *Statement* may be a simple or compound statement, and is called the loop body.
- If *TrueOrFalseExpression* is false when execution first reaches the loop structure, *Statement* is never executed.

You should run the completed program. When you do, you will see repeated prompts for a meaningful Fahrenheit temperature as long as you enter values below absolute zero:

```
CONVERTING FAHRENHEIT TO CELSIUS

Fahrenheit temperature? (Must be >= -459.7) -600
Fahrenheit temperature? (Must be >= -459.7) -460
Fahrenheit temperature? (Must be >= -459.7) -459
-459.0 deg. F. = -272.8 deg. C.
```

Questions

8. Which of the listed statements is correct regarding the following code fragment?

```
Write( 'Fahrenheit? (Must be >= -459.7) ' );
ReadLn( Fahrenheit );
WHILE Fahrenheit < AbsoluteZero DO
BEGIN
   Write( 'Fahrenheit? (Must be >= -459.7) ' );
   ReadLn( Fahrenheit )
END
```

   a. If the user first enters 32.0, the loop body is never executed.
   b. If the user first enters –500.0, the loop body is never executed.
   c. If the user always enters –500.0, the loop never finishes executing.
   d. If the user first enters –500.0, the loop executes until the user enters a value that is at least –459.7.

9. What is the difference in execution between (a) and (b)?

   a.
```
IF Fahrenheit < AbsoluteZero THEN
BEGIN
   Write( 'Fahrenheit? ' );
   ReadLn( Fahrenheit )
END
```

   b.
```
WHILE Fahrenheit < AbsoluteZero DO
BEGIN
   Write( 'Fahrenheit? ' );
   ReadLn( Fahrenheit )
END
```

10. What is printed by the following procedure, if it is called by the statement `Macbeth( 3.0, 1.5 )`?

```
PROCEDURE Macbeth( Count, Finish : Real );
BEGIN
   Write( 'Tomorrow, ' );
   WHILE Count > Finish DO
   BEGIN
      Write( 'and tomorrow, ' );
      Count := Count - 1.0
   END;
   WriteLn;
   WriteLn( 'Creeps in this petty pace from day to day' )
END; { Macbeth }
```

11. In Question 10, if the call were `Macbeth( 2.0, 0.0 )`, would the procedure do the same thing? Could it be counted on to do the same thing, regardless of the computer hardware being used? Why? (Hint: See Section 4.2.)

Exercises

12. How many times is the loop body executed in each of the following code fragments?

a.

```
X := 1.5;
WHILE X >= 0.0 DO
BEGIN
   WriteLn( X:4:1 );
   X := X - 1.0
END;
```

b.

```
X := 1.5;
WHILE X >= 0.0 DO
BEGIN
   WriteLn( X:4:1 );
   X := X + 1.0
END;
```

c.

```
X := -1.5;
WHILE X >= 0.0 DO
BEGIN
   WriteLn( X:4:1 );
   X := X - 1.0
END;
```

6.3 CASE STUDY: SORTING THREE NUMBERS

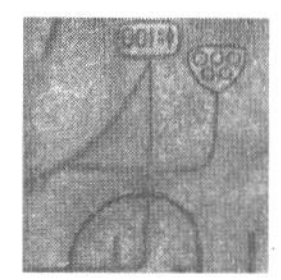

One of the most common tasks in day-to-day computing is to *sort* data into increasing or decreasing order. For example, we often need to sort names into alphabetical order, or money transactions into chronological order, or numbers into increasing order. It has been estimated that as much as one-quarter of all running time on mainframe computers is spent in sorting. In later chapters, we will examine several general sorting algorithms, but before we do so, we should examine the smaller problem of how to sort *three* numbers. The algorithm provides good examples of top-down design, the use of VAR parameters, and the use of decision structures.

We want a procedure that receives three real numbers, and then exchanges them so that the values end up in *increasing order*. (For example, the numbers 3.0, 0.5, and 1.1 will be arranged in the order 0.5, 1.1, 3.0.) If two or more of the numbers are equal, they end up in *nondecreasing order*. (For example, the numbers 1.1, 3.0, 1.1 will end up in the order 1.1, 1.1, 3.0.) We can condense these goals into the following succinct pre- and postconditions:

```
PROCEDURE Sort3Reals( VAR Num1, Num2, Num3 : Real );
{
  PRECONDITIONS:
  Num1, Num2, and Num3 have been initialized.

  POSTCONDITIONS:
  Num1 <= Num2 <= Num3.
}
```

Incremental testing

To write the procedure, we introduce an important technique for minimizing errors. We will first write a *skeleton* for the procedure, called a **stub**. We will test the stub *before adding the code that actually performs the sort*. This testing will be performed by a simple main program called a **driver**. When we are sure the skeleton is syntactically and semantically correct, we will add code to the procedure and test again. This process, called **incremental testing**, makes debugging easier because there is relatively little that can go wrong at any stage. In later chapters, as programs get more difficult, this process will be increasingly important, so it is good to start practicing it now.

Stub: A skeletal subprogram written for first-stage testing.

Driver: A main program written to test a stub.

Incremental testing: A multistage testing process in which only a small amount (an increment) of new code is added before each test.

Here are a driver and stub for a Sort3Reals procedure:

```
PROGRAM TestSort3Reals ( Input, Output );
{ Driver for testing the Sort3Reals procedure. }

VAR
   Num1, Num2, Num3 : Real;
```

```
PROCEDURE Get3Reals( VAR Num1, Num2, Num3 : Real );
{
  POSTCONDITIONS:
  Num1, Num2, and Num3 have been initialized.
}
BEGIN

   Write( 'First real number?  ' );
   ReadLn( Num1 );
   Write( 'Second real number? ' );
   ReadLn( Num2 );
   Write( 'Third real number?  ' );
   ReadLn( Num3 );

END; { Get3Reals }


PROCEDURE Sort3Reals( VAR Num1, Num2, Num3 : Real );
{
  PRECONDITIONS:
  Num1, Num2, and Num3 have been initialized.

  POSTCONDITIONS:
  Num1 <= Num2 <= Num3.
}
BEGIN

   WriteLn( 'Sort3Reals is only a stub.' )

END; { Sort3Reals }


BEGIN { driver }

   Get3Reals( Num1, Num2, Num3 );

   WriteLn;
   WriteLn( 'Before sorting, values are ',
            Num1:6:1, Num2:6:1, Num3:6:1 );
   Sort3Reals( Num1, Num2, Num3 );
   WriteLn( 'After sorting, values are  ',
            Num1:6:1, Num2:6:1, Num3:6:1 )

END.
```

Note that `Sort3Reals`, when completed, will rearrange the values in its three parameters, and these changes must be reflected in the calling program unit, so the parameters must be in-and-out parameters and must be declared as `VAR`s.

If the driver-and-stub combination is entered correctly, it will produce the following output when it runs:

```
First real number?  1.1
Second real number? 3.3
Third real number?  2.2
```

```
Before sorting, values are    1.1   3.3   2.2
Sort3Reals is only a stub.
After sorting, values are     1.1   3.3   2.2
```

Divide and conquer.

Once the driver and stub are working, we can turn to the sorting process itself. Here's an idea:

> *We need to rearrange three numbers; maybe we can do it by swapping two numbers at a time. That would reduce the original problem to a series of smaller problems.*

Design from the top down.

Never mind right now how we will swap two numbers; we'll worry about that later. For now, assume that the swapping can be done somehow. We concentrate on the higher-level problem of the sorting algorithm itself: how to sort three numbers by swapping two at a time.

Work some examples.

It helps to consider some examples. If `Num1` is greater than `Num2`, these two values should be swapped. This brings the larger of the two to the second position in the list. After doing this, if the new `Num2` is greater than `Num3`, these should be swapped. This would bring the largest value all the way to the end of the list (the third position). The only remaining task would be to make sure the first two values are still in the correct order. For example, if the three numbers are 14.7, 3.3, and 3.0,

After swapping the first and second:	3.3	14.7	3.0
After swapping the second and third:	3.3	3.0	14.7
After swapping the first and second:	3.0	3.3	14.7

There needn't always be three swaps, however. If the initial order is 14.7, 3.0, 3.3, we need only two swaps:

After swapping the first and second:	3.0	14.7	3.3
After swapping the second and third:	3.0	3.3	14.7

(This time a third swap is not needed.)

We always need three comparisons, however, and these can be accomplished with three consecutive decision structures. Here's the plan in pseudocode:

If *Num1 is greater than Num2* then
  swap Num1 and Num2;
otherwise, don't swap.
Resulting program state: Num1 ≤ Num2.

If *Num2 is greater than Num3* then
  swap Num2 and Num3;
otherwise, don't swap.
Resulting program state: Num3 is the maximum value.

The first two values may still be out of order, so if *Num1 is greater than Num2* then
swap Num1 and Num2;
otherwise, don't swap.
Resulting program state: Num1 ≤ Num2 ≤ Num3.

Suppose we have a `Swap2Reals` procedure that swaps two real numbers. (We'll build one later.) Then the first decision is whether to swap `Num1` and `Num2`: that is, whether to call `Swap2Reals(Num1,Num2)` or skip calling it. After calling it or not, the program is faced with the second decision, whether to call `Swap2Reals(Num2, Num3)` or skip it. After that, it decides whether to call `Swap2Reals(Num1, Num2)` or skip it. Now we can write the Pascal directly from the pseudocode, using `IF..THEN` structures that lack `ELSE` clauses:

```
PROCEDURE Sort3Reals( VAR Num1, Num2, Num3 : Real );
{
  PRECONDITIONS:
  Num1, Num2, and Num3 have been initialized.

  POSTCONDITIONS:
  Num1 <= Num2 <= Num3.
}
BEGIN

   IF Num1 > Num2 THEN
      Swap2Reals( Num1, Num2 );
   { Assertion: Now Num1 <= Num2 }

   IF Num2 > Num3 THEN
      Swap2Reals( Num2, Num3 );
   { Assertion: Now Num2 <= Num3 }

   { First two nums may be out of order again }
   IF Num1 > Num2 THEN
      Swap2Reals( Num1, Num2 )
   { Assertion: Now Num1 <= Num2 <= Num3 }

END; { Sort3Reals }
```

Incremental testing again

Now, having designed the upper levels of the program hierarchy, we stop and test what we have done so far. Insert the `Sort3Reals` procedure into the program in place of its stub. Then add a stub for the new `Swap2Reals` procedure:

```
PROCEDURE Swap2Reals( VAR FirstNum, SecondNum : Real );
{
  PRECONDITION:
  FirstNum and SecondNum have been initialized.

  POSTCONDITION:
  The values of FirstNum and SecondNum
  have been exchanged.
}
```

```
BEGIN
   WriteLn( 'Swap2Reals is only a stub.' )
END; { Swap2Reals }
```

Compile, link, and run the program again to make sure there are no syntactic errors.

Finally, implement the lowest-level procedure.

Now (and only now) it is time to implement the `Swap2Reals` procedure, which is supposed to exchange two numbers called `FirstNum` and `SecondNum`. We could copy `SecondNum` into `FirstNum`, but that would destroy the original value of `FirstNum`. So we first make a backup copy of `FirstNum` called `OldFirst`, then copy `SecondNum` into `FirstNum`, and finally copy the backup of the old `FirstNum` into `SecondNum`. For example, if `FirstNum` is initially 1.1 and `SecondNum` is initially 2.2, the `Swap2Reals` procedure will pass through the following states:

Initially, we have the *preconditions*:

State 1:	`FirstNum`	= 1.1;
	`SecondNum`	= 2.2;
	`OldFirst`	= ???

After copying `FirstNum` into `OldFirst`,

State 2:	`FirstNum`	= 1.1;
	`SecondNum`	= 2.2;
	`OldFirst`	= 1.1

After copying `SecondNum` into `FirstNum`, overwriting the old value there,

State 3:	`FirstNum`	= 2.2;
	`SecondNum`	= 2.2;
	`OldFirst`	= 1.1

After copying `OldFirst` into `SecondNum`, overwriting the old value there, we have the *postconditions*:

State 4:	`FirstNum`	= 2.2;
	`SecondNum`	= 1.1;
	`OldFirst`	= 1.1

The code to be inserted in `Swap2Reals` therefore uses an `OldFirst` variable that is declared within the procedure:

```
OldFirst  := FirstNum;
FirstNum  := SecondNum;
SecondNum := OldFirst
```

The complete program is shown on the next page.

```
PROGRAM TestSort3Reals ( Input, Output );
{ Driver for testing Sort3Reals }

VAR
   Num1, Num2, Num3 : Real;


PROCEDURE Get3Reals( VAR Num1, Num2, Num3 : Real );
{
  POSTCONDITIONS:
  Num1, Num2, and Num3 have been initialized.
}
BEGIN

   Write( 'First real number?  ' );
   ReadLn( Num1 );
   Write( 'Second real number? ' );
   ReadLn( Num2 );
   Write( 'Third real number?  ' );
   ReadLn( Num3 )

END; { Get3Reals }


PROCEDURE Swap2Reals( VAR FirstNum, SecondNum : Real );
{
  PRECONDITION:
  FirstNum and SecondNum have been initialized.

  POSTCONDITION:
  The values of FirstNum and SecondNum
  have been exchanged.
}
VAR
   OldFirst : Real;

BEGIN

   OldFirst  := FirstNum;
   FirstNum  := SecondNum;
   SecondNum := OldFirst

END; { Swap2Reals }
```

```
PROCEDURE Sort3Reals( VAR Num1, Num2, Num3 : Real );
{
  PRECONDITIONS:
  Num1, Num2, and Num3 have been initialized.

  POSTCONDITIONS:
  Num1 <= Num2 <= Num3.
}
BEGIN

   IF Num1 > Num2 THEN
      Swap2Reals( Num1, Num2 );
   { Assertion: Now Num1 <= Num2 }

   IF Num2 > Num3 THEN
      Swap2Reals( Num2, Num3 );
   { Assertion: Now Num2 <= Num3 }

   { First two nums may be out of order again }
   IF Num1 > Num2 THEN
      Swap2Reals( Num1, Num2 )
   { Assertion: Now Num1 <= Num2 <= Num3 }

END; { Sort3Reals }


BEGIN { driver }

   Get3Reals( Num1, Num2, Num3 );

   WriteLn;
   WriteLn( 'Before sorting, values are ',
            Num1:6:1, Num2:6:1, Num3:6:1 );
   Sort3Reals( Num1, Num2, Num3 );
   WriteLn( 'After sorting, values are  ',
            Num1:6:1, Num2:6:1, Num3:6:1 )

END.
```

Test this completed program. No matter what numbers you give the program, the output should indicate correct sorting:

```
First real number?  3.3
Second real number? 1.1
Third real number?  2.2

Before sorting, values are    3.3   1.1   2.2
After sorting, values are     1.1   2.2   3.3
```

Verifying the algorithm

Having thought out the sorting logic in such detail, complete with step-by-step assertions, we felt certain before writing the Pascal that the algorithm would work as advertised. This kind of **logical verification of algorithms** is very important, as we will often see later.

However, even if we feel certain that the program will run correctly, it is still important to test it thoroughly, in case we overlooked something. We should test it with all possible permutations of the three values. Since the first value can be in any of the three positions, for each of which the second value can be in either of the remaining two positions, for each of which the position of the third value is fixed, there are 3x2x1 = 3! = 6 permutations of three objects. Using the same numbers as before, the six permutations are

14.7	3.0	3.3
14.7	3.3	3.0
3.0	14.7	3.3
3.3	14.7	3.0
3.0	3.3	14.7
3.3	3.0	14.7

Test the program in all of these cases. There are still some **exceptional cases** to test. Will the program work correctly when all three values are equal? What if any two are equal? Check the algorithm and convince yourself that it should work correctly for these cases. Also test it by running the program.

It would be inconvenient to test all possible cases if we had many more values to sort. If there were 25 values, for example, there would be 25! = 1.55×10^{25} possible orderings. A computer that sorted each case in 0.00001 second would take

$$(1.55 \times 10^{25} \text{ cases}) \times (1.0 \times 10^{-5} \text{ sec/case}) \times (3.17098 \times 10^{-8} \text{ years/sec})$$
$$= 4.92 \times 10^{12} \text{ years} = 4{,}920{,}000{,}000{,}000 \text{ years}$$

to work all these cases! This is why we will need to use more subtle verification techniques in later chapters when dealing with more general sorting algorithms.

Pitfall: The mystery of the extra semicolon

As was mentioned in Section 6.1, it is easy to forget that Pascal's semicolons go between the statements in a sequence, and not at the end of every line. This can have an especially bad effect if you put semicolons in the wrong places in `IF..THEN` structures. For example, if you write

```
IF Num1 > Num2 THEN;
   Swap2Reals( Num1, Num2 );
```

the extra semicolon after `THEN` terminates the `IF..THEN` structure, so the effect is the same as if you wrote

```
IF Num1 > Num2 THEN;
Swap2Reals( Num1, Num2 );
```

or equivalently,

```
IF Num1 > Num2 THEN
   ;
Swap2Reals( Num1, Num2 );
```

That is, if Num1 is greater than Num2, the decision structure executes the **empty statement** (**null statement**) following the THEN. Then, after the decision structure has terminated, the swap is always executed, without any control by the decision structure. What a difference a little semicolon can make!

6.4 ANIMATION: NESTED PROCEDURE CALLS

As you have seen several times now, procedures can call procedures, and when this happens, the program executes by a sequence of **nested calls**. Consider the TestSort3Reals program, in which the main program calls the Sort3Reals procedure, which in turn calls the Swap2Reals procedure.

Order of declarations

As you recall, any identifier in a Pascal program must be defined before it can be used. In the TestSort3Reals program, the Sort3Reals procedure calls the Swap2Reals procedure, so Swap2Reals must be declared *before* Sort3Reals.

Sequence of execution

Consider the sequence of execution in this program, and notice how VAR parameters are used to accomplish the sorting. Just before Sort3Reals is called, the program is the *precondition state* for the procedure: The three parameters have been initialized.

```
BEGIN
   Get3Reals( Num1, Num2, Num3 );
   WriteLn;
   WriteLn( 'Before sorting, values are ',
            Num1:6:1, Num2:6:1, Num3:6:1 );
   Sort3Reals( Num1, Num2, Num3 );
```

Num1:	3.3
Num2:	1.1
Num3:	2.2

The main program sends three Real parameters to Sort3Reals, but the parameters are VARs—they are *passed by reference*—so the procedure's three formal parameters are actually the same storage cells allocated by the main program for those three numbers. As the procedure starts to run, the main program is suspended, as we see on the next page.

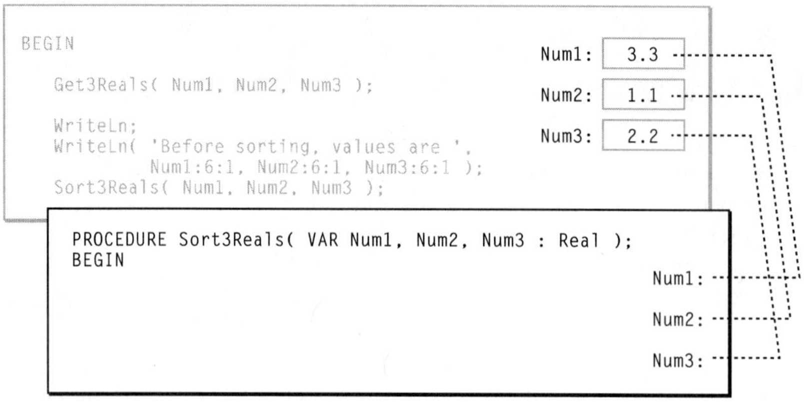

```
BEGIN                                                   Num1: [ 3.3 ]

   Get3Reals( Num1, Num2, Num3 );                       Num2: [ 1.1 ]

   WriteLn;                                             Num3: [ 2.2 ]
   WriteLn( 'Before sorting, values are ',
            Num1:6:1, Num2:6:1, Num3:6:1 );
   Sort3Reals( Num1, Num2, Num3 );

      PROCEDURE Sort3Reals( VAR Num1, Num2, Num3 : Real );
      BEGIN
                                                        Num1:
                                                        Num2:
                                                        Num3:
```

Sort3Reals first checks whether Num1 is greater than Num2. Since it is, the Sort3Reals procedure prepares to call the Swap2Reals procedure. Just before the call is executed, the program is in the precondition state for Swap2Reals: Num1 contains 3.3 and Num2 contains 1.1.

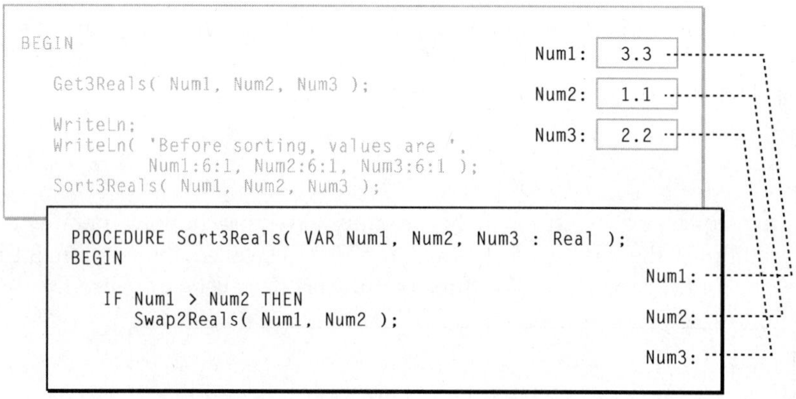

```
BEGIN                                                   Num1: [ 3.3 ]

   Get3Reals( Num1, Num2, Num3 );                       Num2: [ 1.1 ]

   WriteLn;                                             Num3: [ 2.2 ]
   WriteLn( 'Before sorting, values are ',
            Num1:6:1, Num2:6:1, Num3:6:1 );
   Sort3Reals( Num1, Num2, Num3 );

      PROCEDURE Sort3Reals( VAR Num1, Num2, Num3 : Real );
      BEGIN
                                                        Num1:
         IF Num1 > Num2 THEN
            Swap2Reals( Num1, Num2 );                   Num2:

                                                        Num3:
```

Execution of Sort3Reals is suspended while Swap2Reals starts to run. Swap2Reals uses two parameters that are passed by reference. FirstNum is just an alias for the same storage cell that is called Num1 by Sort3Reals and the main program, while SecondNum is an alias for the storage cell that is called Num2 by Sort3Reals and the main program. The Swap3Reals procedure also declares a new local variable, called OldFirst, which contains garbage as the procedure starts to run, as we see on the next page.

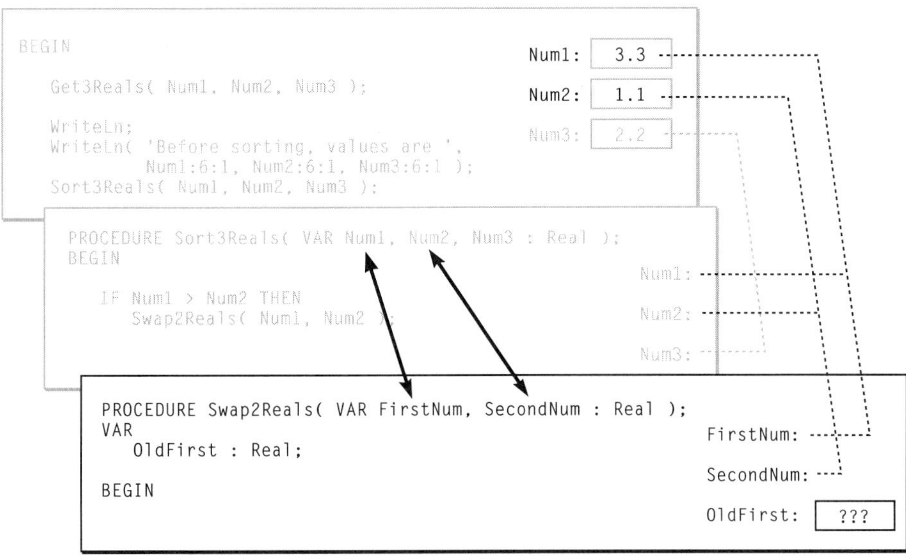

Swap2Reals exchanges the values of its two parameters, satisfying its stated postconditions. As it terminates, the exchanged values are already in the main program's storage cells called Num1 and Num2, because Swap2Reals was using those storage cells directly.

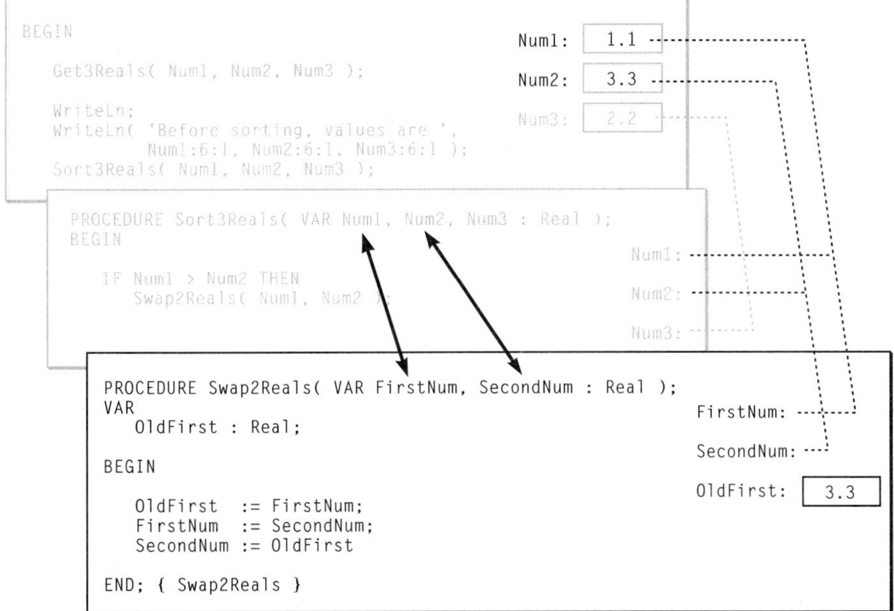

After `Swap2Reals` terminates, the `Sort3Reals` procedure resumes executing where it left off. It checks whether `Num2` is greater than `Num3`:

```
BEGIN                                             Num1: [ 1.1 ]
   Get3Reals( Num1, Num2, Num3 );                 Num2: [ 3.3 ]
   WriteLn;                                       Num3: [ 2.2 ]
   WriteLn( 'Before sorting, values are ',
            Num1:6:1, Num2:6:1, Num3:6:1 );
   Sort3Reals( Num1, Num2, Num3 );

PROCEDURE Sort3Reals( VAR Num1, Num2, Num3 : Real );
BEGIN
                                                  Num1:
   IF Num1 > Num2 THEN
      Swap2Reals( Num1, Num2 );                   Num2:

   IF Num2 > Num3 THEN                            Num3:
      Swap2Reals( Num2, Num3 );
```

Since `Num2` is greater than `Num3`, the `Sort3Reals` procedure calls `Swap2Reals` again. This time, it sends `Num2` and then `Num3` as the actual parameters. As `Swap2Reals` starts to execute, its `FirstNum` identifier is an alias for the storage cell called `Num2` by the main program and `Sort3Reals`. Similarly, `SecondNum` is an alias for the storage cell called `Num3` by the main program and `Sort3Reals`:

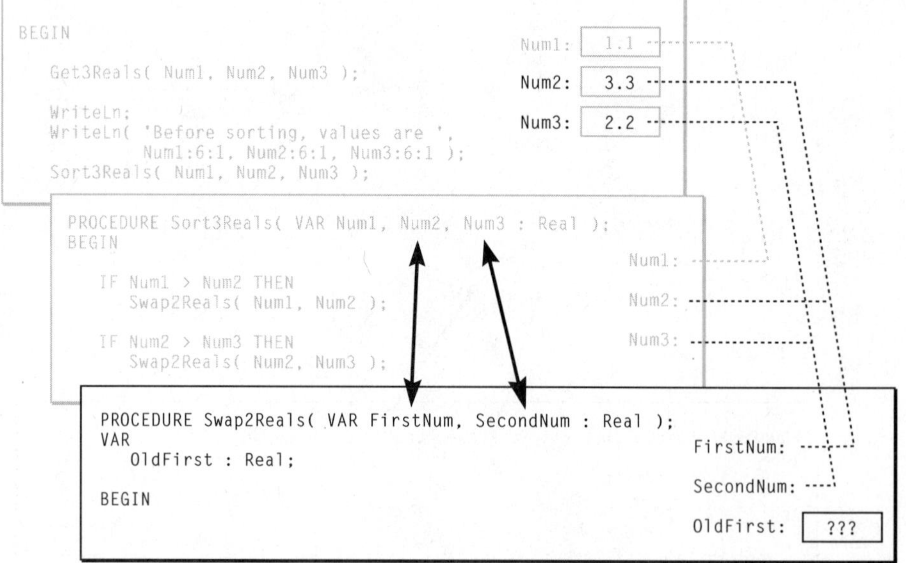

`Swap2Reals` exchanges the values of its two parameters, satisfying its stated postconditions. As it terminates, the exchanged values are already in the main program's storage cells called `Num2` and `Num3`, because `Swap2Reals` was using those storage cells directly.

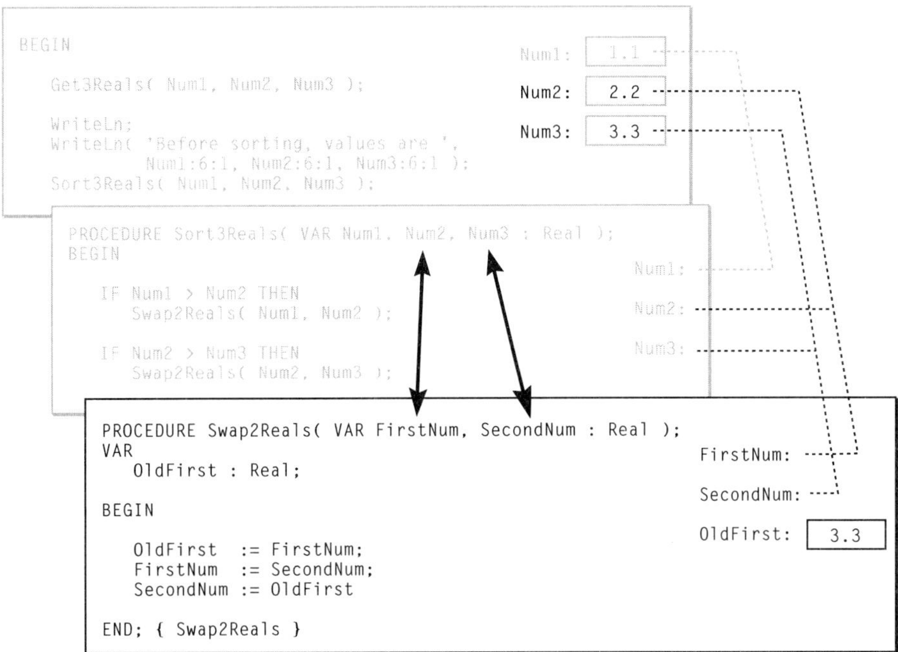

After Swap2Reals terminates, the Sort3Reals procedure resumes executing where it left off. It checks whether Num1 is greater than Num2:

```
BEGIN                                                Num1: [ 1.1 ]

   Get3Reals( Num1, Num2, Num3 );                    Num2: [ 2.2 ]

   WriteLn;                                          Num3: [ 3.3 ]
   WriteLn( 'Before sorting, values are ',
            Num1:6:1, Num2:6:1, Num3:6:1 );
   Sort3Reals( Num1, Num2, Num3 );

PROCEDURE Sort3Reals( VAR Num1, Num2, Num3 : Real );
BEGIN
                                                     Num1:
   IF Num1 > Num2 THEN
      Swap2Reals( Num1, Num2 );                      Num2:

   IF Num2 > Num3 THEN                               Num3:
      Swap2Reals( Num2, Num3 );

   IF Num1 > Num2 THEN
```

Because Num1 is not greater than Num2, the Sort3Reals procedure does not call Swap2Reals again. Instead, Sort3Reals terminates and the main program resumes execution where it was suspended. Note that Sort3Reals' stated postconditions have been satisfied: The values in Num1, Num2, and Num3 are in sorted order. The main program calls WriteLn to display the results:

```
BEGIN

   Get3Reals( Num1, Num2, Num3 );

   WriteLn;
   WriteLn( 'Before sorting, values are ',
            Num1:6:1, Num2:6:1, Num3:6:1 );
   Sort3Reals( Num1, Num2, Num3 );
   WriteLn( 'After sorting, values are  ',
            Num1:6:1, Num2:6:1, Num3:6:1 )

END.
```

Num1:	1.1
Num2:	2.2
Num3:	3.3

Previews of coming attractions

The Sort3Reals procedure would be more generally useful if it would sort three data items of any kind, not just real numbers. We will make just such an improvement in Chapter 8.

Questions

13. In the Swap2Reals procedure, the formal parameters are named FirstNum and SecondNum instead of Num1 and Num2. Which naming convention is better in this case? Why?

14. What is meant by the *state* of a program?

15. In terms of program states, what is the purpose of a procedure?

16. What is meant by a procedure's precondition?

17. What is meant by a procedure's postcondition?

18. What is incremental testing?

19. In terms of incremental testing, what is the reason for using a stub and driver?

20. In the TestSort3Reals program of Section 6.3, what will happen if the Sort3Reals procedure is declared before the Swap2Reals procedure?

21. If procedure Turing calls procedure VonNeumann, which calls procedure Atanasoff, which procedure must be declared first? Which must be declared last?

Exercises

22. Predict the output of this program:

```
PROGRAM Fun ( Output );
VAR
   A, B : Real;

PROCEDURE Zip( VAR Whip : Real );
BEGIN
   Whip := Whip + 3.0;
END; { Zip }

PROCEDURE Flip( VAR Clip : Real );
BEGIN
   WriteLn( Clip );
   Clip := Clip + 2.0;
   Zip( Clip );
   WriteLn( Clip )
END; { Flip }

PROCEDURE Dip( Slip : Real );
BEGIN
   WriteLn( Slip );
   Slip := Slip + 1.0;
   Flip( Slip );
   WriteLn( Slip )
END; { Dip }

BEGIN { main program }
   A := 3.0;
   B := 2.0 * A + 1.0;
   Dip( B );
   WriteLn;
   WriteLn( A, B )
END.
```

23. Consider the following program:

```
PROGRAM OneTwoThree( Output );

PROCEDURE C ( X : Real );
BEGIN
   WriteLn( X:3:1 )
END; { C }

PROCEDURE B ( X : Real );
BEGIN
   WriteLn( X:3:1 );
   C( X + 1.0 )
END; { B }

PROCEDURE A ( X : Real );
BEGIN
   WriteLn( X:3:1 );
   B( X + 1.0 )
END; { A }

BEGIN
   A( 1.0 )
END.
```

When the program is executed, it displays

```
1.0
2.0
3.0
```

Explain in detail why the output looks like this.

24. In the algorithm of this section, if `Num1 > Num2`, then `Num1` and `Num2` are swapped. Then, if `Num2 > Num3`, these two are swapped. This brings the largest of the three values to the end of the list, and we sometimes say that the largest value has "bubbled" to the end of the list. Using pseudocode like that in Chapter 2, design an algorithm that bubbles the largest number to the end of an *N*-number list, and then bubbles the next-to-largest number to the next-to-last position in the list, and so on, until the list is sorted. This technique is called *bubble sorting,* and will be discussed further in Chapter 14's Exercise 25.

6.5 ADVANCED TOPIC: WHEN PROCEDURES CALL THEMSELVES

Section 6.4 has shown in considerable detail what happens when one procedure calls another. If you examine the syntax rules for procedure calls, however, you will find that there is nothing in Pascal that prevents a procedure from calling *itself*. In fact, this process, called **recursion**, can be quite useful as a way of making a program repeat the execution of a procedure. In this section, we take a brief look at recursion; a full treatment appears in Chapter 12.

Recursion: A procedure calling itself.

> When a procedure calls itself, it really calls a *clone* of itself. The process is exactly the same as when one procedure calls another. The only thing new is that both procedures happen to have the same name and the same code.

Consider our original version of the `GetFahrenheit` procedure:

```
PROCEDURE GetFahrenheit( VAR Fahrenheit : Real );
BEGIN

   Write( 'Fahrenheit? (Must be >= -459.7) ' );
   ReadLn( Fahrenheit )

END; { Fahrenheit }
```

The problem in this version of the procedure was that the user was not prevented from entering a value of `Fahrenheit` less than absolute zero. To deal with this possibility, we added a loop to continue prompting for a temperature until an acceptable one was entered (Section 6.2).

But we can accomplish the same thing by having `GetFahrenheit` *call itself* if (and only if) the previous `Fahrenheit` value was unacceptable:

```
PROCEDURE GetFahrenheit( VAR Fahrenheit : Real );
BEGIN

   Write( 'Fahrenheit? (Must be >= -459.7) ' );
   ReadLn( Fahrenheit );

   IF Fahrenheit < AbsoluteZero THEN
      GetFahrenheit( Fahrenheit )

END; { Fahrenheit }
```

Animation of the recursive execution

To understand how such a procedure works, it is necessary to be able to picture the sequence of events when it is called. When the procedure is first called, the `Write` statement is executed, after which the `ReadLn` waits for a real number to be entered at the keyboard:

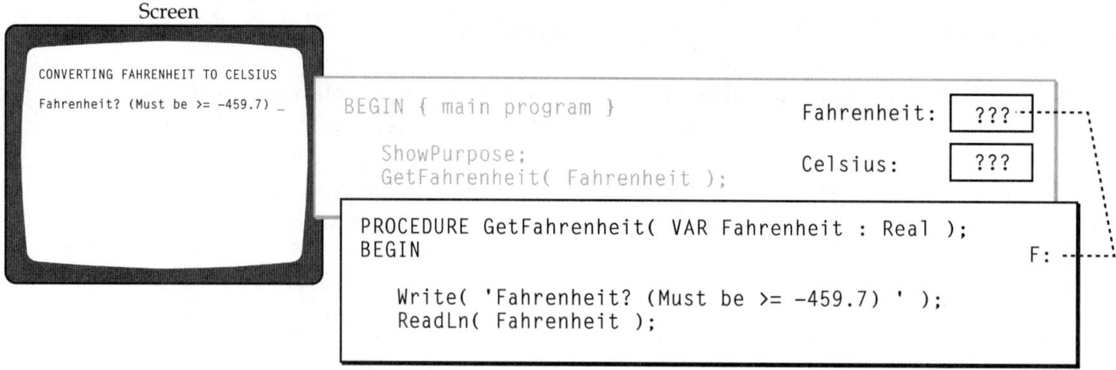

Suppose that the user keys in -500, which is below absolute zero. In that case, the IF structure causes the procedure to call another copy of itself. The first copy of GetFahrenheit is suspended as the second copy begins to execute. The second copy prompts again for a temperature and then the ReadLn waits for a number to be entered:

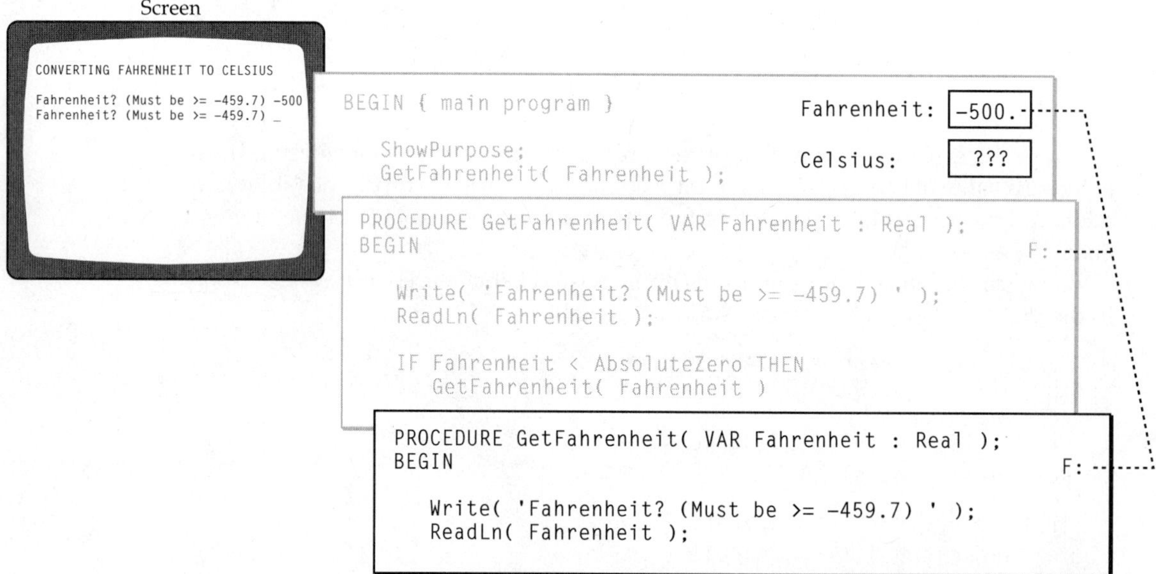

Suppose the user enters 0 this time. Then the IF structure in the second copy of GetFahrenheit determines that Fahrenheit is greater than absolute zero, and does *not* call GetFahrenheit again. The second copy of the procedure terminates, returning execution to the first copy. Since the second copy's Fahrenheit parameter is a VAR parameter, it is actually the same storage cell as the first copy's Fahrenheit variable. Therefore, the number 0.0 is already stored in the Fahrenheit parameter that belongs to the first copy of the procedure:

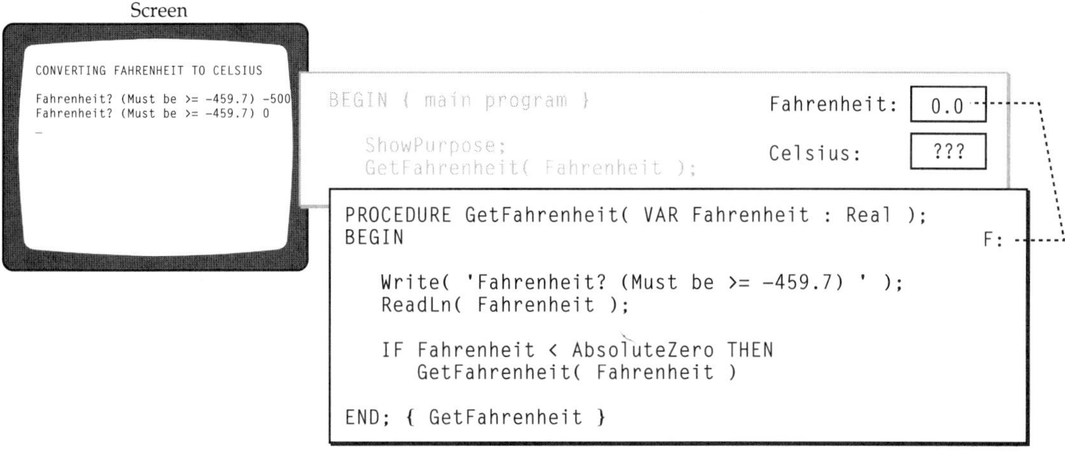

Now the first copy of `GetFahrenheit` terminates because there is no more code for it to execute. Execution returns to the main program, whose `Fahrenheit` variable is actually the same storage cell as the `Fahrenheit` in-and-out parameter in the two copies of the `GetFahrenheit` procedure. The main program is now ready to call the `ConvertToCelsius` procedure:

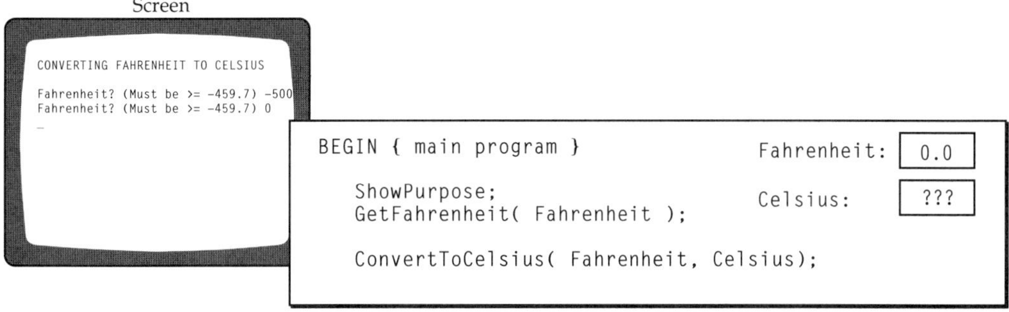

Recursion often confuses beginning programmers unnecessarily. There are really only two main things to remember about it:

- When procedure `A` calls another copy of itself, the process is the same as when procedure `A` calls procedure `B`, except that `B` happens to be the same as `A`.
- If procedure `A` calls another copy of itself, this new copy will call a third copy of itself, and the process will never end unless something stops the process. Therefore, *there must be, somewhere along the line, a decision structure that eventually halts the recursive process.*

These points will be explored in much greater depth in Chapter 12, where you will also find a detailed comparison of recursion and looping. Recursion is mentioned now primarily to dispel the mystery surrounding this important technique and to give a partial answer to those readers who wonder about it at this point.

Questions

25. What is meant by *recursion*?

26. What is needed to keep recursion from being an infinitely repetitive process?

27. What is displayed by the following program?

```
PROGRAM Recursive ( Output );

PROCEDURE Wow( X : Real );
BEGIN

   WriteLn( X:3:1 );

   IF X < 4.0 THEN
      Wow( X + 1.0 )

END; { Wow }

BEGIN

   Wow( 1.0 )

END.
```

6.6 TESTING AND DEBUGGING

This chapter has introduced decision and control structures, which allow a program to control its own execution according to data received or computed during a run. Of course, if the control structures are not constructed correctly, their programs will act differently than you intended. The most interesting errors of this kind are the ones that cause *infinite looping* or *infinite recursion*, both of which result in the program running forever or until you halt it manually, whichever occurs first.

> To deal with infinite loops or infinite recursion, you must know how to stop a runaway program on your computer system. On some systems, keying Control-C will stop a program. (Hold down the CONTROL key while pressing the C key.) In Turbo Pascal, the halt command is Control-Shift-Break. Check your reference manual or ask your instructor for the halt command on your system.

Some of the easiest mistakes with control structures involve missing or misused keywords, or spurious semicolons. Figure 6.6.1 shows a typical syntax error message when the compiler encounters an `IF..THEN..ELSE` structure in which the keyword `THEN` is missing. Figure 6.6.2 shows a typical result when the compiler discovers a spurious semicolon after the `IF..THEN` clause, just before the keyword `ELSE`. Your

Figure 6.6.1

If the keyword THEN is missing from an IF..THEN..ELSE structure, the Pascal compiler will issue a syntax error message and refuse to compile the program.

```
THEN expected.
```

```
IF Fahrenheit < AbsoluteZero
  ShowError

ELSE
BEGIN
   ConvertToCelsius( Fahrenheit, Celsius );
   ShowTemperature( Fahrenheit, Celsius )
END;
```

compiler might not give the same messages shown in the figures, so you should deliberately introduce such errors into working programs to see what error messages result in your Pascal system. Examples are shown in Table 6.6.1 on the next page.

Runtime errors

The two syntax errors shown in the figures cause error messages and failure to compile. A more insidious kind of error gives no messages and no failure to compile, but yields the wrong computed result when the program runs. It can be hard to spot such errors, which are called *runtime errors* or *semantic errors*. Consider this example:

```
IF Fahrenheit < AbsoluteZero THEN
   ShowError

ELSE
   ConvertToCelsius( Fahrenheit, Celsius );
   ShowTemperature( Fahrenheit, Celsius )
```

Figure 6.6.2

A spurious semicolon after the THEN clause will terminate the IF..THEN structure at that point, leaving the ELSE clause dangling beyond the end of the structure. Again, this is a syntax error and the compiler will refuse to compile the program.

```
Error in statement.
```

```
IF Fahrenheit < AbsoluteZero THEN
   ShowError;

ELSE
BEGIN
   ConvertToCelsius( Fahrenheit, Celsius );
   ShowTemperature( Fahrenheit, Celsius )
END;
```

Table 6.6.1 *Examples of IF..THEN..ELSE syntax errors in Turbo Pascal 6.0.*

Syntax Error	Error message from compiler
Condition is not a true/false expression.	`Boolean expression expected.`
Keyword `THEN` is missing.	`THEN expected.`
Spurious semicolon after `THEN`.	`";" expected.` (at ELSE)
Spurious semicolon after *Statement1*, before `ELSE`.	`Error in statement.` (At ELSE)

There is no syntax error here, but the code does not work as intended. If the user provides a Fahrenheit temperature at least as great as `AbsoluteZero`, the control structure works correctly: The Fahrenheit temperature is converted to Celsius, and both numbers are displayed. If the Fahrenheit temperature is below `AbsoluteZero`, however, the control structure calls `ShowError` as it should, but also calls `ShowTemperature`, which displays garbage. This happens because the programmer has forgotten to write the code in the `ELSE` clause as a single compound statement, bracketing it inside a `BEGIN..END` pair. As a result, the decision structure ends with the semicolon following the call to `ConvertToCelsius` and therefore the call to `ShowTemperature` falls after the end of the decision structure. Such an error can be hard to spot, even after noticing the mistake in execution.

Errors with loops

`WHILE` loops are prone to the same kinds of errors as decision structures. Figure 6.6.3 shows a typical compiler reacting to a `WHILE` structure in which the keyword `DO` has been inadvertently replaced with `THEN`. Table 6.6.2 summarizes the most common errors and corresponding typical error messages.

Runtime errors with loops

It's just as easy to make errors with semicolons in `WHILE` loops as in decision structures. The results are sometimes more spectacular, though. Consider this code fragment:

```
Write( 'Fahrenheit? (Must be >= -459.7) ' );
ReadLn( Fahrenheit );

WHILE Fahrenheit < AbsoluteZero DO;
BEGIN
   Write( 'Fahrenheit? (Must be >= -459.7) ' );
   ReadLn( Fahrenheit );
END
```

If the user first enters a number below `AbsoluteZero`, the computer appears to lock up and no further prompts are displayed on the screen. The reason lies in the erroneous line

Figure 6.6.3

If the keyword DO is inadvertently replaced with THEN, the WHILE structure will fail to compile.

```
DO expected.
```

```
Write( 'Fahrenheit? (Must be >= -459.7) ' );
ReadLn( Fahrenheit );

WHILE Fahrenheit < AbsoluteZero THEN
BEGIN
   Write( 'Fahrenheit? (Must be >= -459.7) ' );
   ReadLn( Fahrenheit )
END
```

```
WHILE Fahrenheit < AbsoluteZero DO;
```

The spurious semicolon terminates the WHILE structure, which is effectively the same as

```
WHILE Fahrenheit < AbsoluteZero DO
   ;
```

In other words, the loop executes a null statement. Because the loop body never reads another value for `Fahrenheit`, the loop condition remains true and the loop runs until you give a manual command to halt the program.

Testing control structures with a source-code debugger

When testing to make sure that a control structure works as intended, you need a way to trace the path of execution through the structure in the various cases that may occur. The most convenient technique, if you have it available, is to use a *source-code debugger*—a program that allows you to execute the program in slow motion, while displaying the point of execution, the values in the variables, and the I/O, all at the same time. Using a good interactive debugger is like watching your program run under a microscope; you can see a lot of detail that otherwise might escape your attention. Ask your instructor about the debugger in your Pascal system.

Table 6.6.2

Examples of WHILE..DO syntax errors in Turbo Pascal 6.0.

Syntax Error	Error message from compiler
Condition is not a true/false expression.	`Boolean expression expected.`
Keyword `DO` is missing.	`DO expected.`
`THEN` instead of `DO`.	`DO expected.`

Testing control structures with the help of extra output statements

When you don't have a debugger, you can get similar information about execution by inserting extra output statements in your program, to print out the values of variables and to print messages about the course of execution during the run. Here is an example of a procedure equipped in this way for testing:

```
PROCEDURE Sort3Reals( VAR Num1, Num2, Num3 : Real );
{
  PRECONDITIONS:
  Num1, Num2, and Num3 have been initialized.

  POSTCONDITIONS:
  Num1 <= Num2 <= Num3.
}
BEGIN
   WriteLn( 'Initially, Sort3Reals has' );
   WriteLn( Num1:10:2, Num2:10:2, Num3:10:2 );
   WriteLn;

   IF Num1 > Num2 THEN
   BEGIN
      WriteLn( 'Swapping Num1 and Num2:' );
      Swap2Reals( Num1, Num2 );
      WriteLn( Num1:10:2, Num2:10:2, Num3:10:2 );
      WriteLn
   END;
   { Assertion: Now Num1 <= Num2 }

   IF Num2 > Num3 THEN
   BEGIN
      WriteLn( 'Swapping Num2 and Num3:' );
      Swap2Reals( Num2, Num3 );
      WriteLn( Num1:10:2, Num2:10:2, Num3:10:2 );
      WriteLn
   END;
   { Assertion: Now Num2 <= Num3 }

   { First two nums may be out of order again }
   IF Num1 > Num2 THEN
   BEGIN
      WriteLn( 'Swapping Num1 and Num2:' );
      Swap2Reals( Num1, Num2 );
      WriteLn( Num1:10:2, Num2:10:2, Num3:10:2 );
      WriteLn
   END;
   { Assertion: Now Num1 <= Num2 <= Num3 }

   WriteLn( 'Returning from Sort3Reals...' )

END; { Sort3Reals }
```

This may seem like more work than it's worth, but after you've stayed up half the night searching in vain for an error that's right in front of your eyes, you will become a believer in thorough incremental testing. Don't be reluctant to use your debugger or extra printout; these tools can save you a lot of time.

LOOKING BACK

This chapter has introduced three control structures, each of which is used to control the execution of simple or compound statements:

- The `IF..THEN..ELSE` structure, which chooses between two alternative paths of execution, executing either one statement or another.
- The `IF..THEN` structure, which decides whether to execute a statement. (This is actually an `IF..THEN..ELSE` structure without an `ELSE` clause.)
- The `WHILE..DO` structure, which executes a statement zero or more times.

The `IF..THEN` and `IF..THEN..ELSE` are examples of *decision structures*, while the `WHILE..DO` is an example of a *loop*, also called a *repetition structure* or *iterative structure*.

We worked through four applications of control structures. First, we saw how to use a decision structure and then a repetition structure to protect the Fahrenheit-to-Celsius program from inappropriate inputs. Then we used decision structures to build a procedure to sort three numbers. Finally, we used a decision structure to control repetition by recursion. This has been merely a first taste of these topics; all will receive considerably more discussion in later chapters.

TERMS EMPHASIZED IN THIS CHAPTER

Compound statement 159
Control structure 158
Decision structure 158–163
Divide and conquer 173
Driver 171
Empty statement 179
Exceptional cases 178
Halting execution 190
Incremental testing 171, 174
Indentation 162–163
Infinite loop 166, 190
Iteration 165
Iterative structure 165
Loop 165
Loop body 165
Nested procedure calls 179–184
Pass by reference 179–180
Postconditions 171
Preconditions 171
Program state 173–174
Recursion 187–190
Relational operator 159
Repetition structure 165
Runtime error 191–193
Simple statement 159
Sorting 171
Source-code debugger 193
Stub 171
Top-down design 173
`VAR` parameter 179–180
Verification of algorithms 178

PROJECTS

1. Design a procedure called `MinOf3` that receives three real numbers as parameters, then displays the minimum of the three. Use a driver to test your procedure first as a stub and then as a complete procedure, proving that it works correctly.

2. Design a program that prompts for and reads the three coefficients, A, B, and C, of a quadratic equation

   $$Ax^2 + Bx + C = 0$$

   The program should then tell the user whether the given equation has real roots. (Hint: Test the discriminant, $B^2 - 4AC$.) Make your program modular and hierarchical, and use the top-down design techniques emphasized in this book.

3. Write a modular program that reads nonnegative real numbers from the keyboard until encountering a negative number, and then displays the maximum, the minimum, and the average of the numbers, not counting the negative one. (The negative number, which acts only to mark the end of the input data, is called a *sentinel*.)

4. Write a short, modular program that uses a loop to print out the immortal ditty,

   99 bottles of beer on the wall, 99 bottles of beer;
   if one of those bottles should happen to fall,
   98 bottles of beer on the wall.

   98 bottles of beer on the wall, 98 bottles of beer;
   if one of those bottles should happen to fall,
   97 bottles of beer on the wall.

   (and so on)

   Disclaimer: The author of this book does not often drink beer, and does not advocate that you do so. The ditty merely refers to beer falling off the wall, and was intended as an off-the-wall example.

5. Write a modular program that computes the minimal coins to give in change for any amount less than a dollar. Your program should call a `GetChange` procedure for the total amount of change, which is to be supplied by the user of the program. Then the program should use the following algorithm:

   a. Call a `ShowQuarters` procedure to display the number of quarters to give in change, subtracting the value of the quarters from the total change and returning the amount of remaining change to the main program.

   b. Then call a `ShowDimes` procedure to display the number of dimes to give in the remaining change, subtracting the value of the dimes from the remaining change and returning the result to the main program.

   c. Then call a `ShowNickels` procedure to display the number of nickels to give in the remaining change, subtracting the value of the nickels from the remaining change and returning the result to the main program.

   d. Finally call a `ShowPennies` procedure to display the number of pennies represented by the remaining change.

   Here's how a sample run should look:

```
Total change? (Between 0.0 and 0.99) 0.93
Quarters: QQQ
Dimes:    D
Nickels:  N
Pennies:  PPP
```

Here's a suggestion: If you multiply the total change in the `GetChange` procedure by 100.0 so that the change is a whole number, then define a quarter to be 25.0, a dime to be 10.0, and so on, you can avoid roundoff error in the computation. This is because whole real numbers are stored exactly in the computer.

6. Write a procedure that reverses the order of four `VAR` parameter values. In other words, if the procedure receives the values 1.0, 0.5, 3.0, 2.5, respectively, it should return the values 2.5, 3.0, 0.5, 1.0. Your procedure should call the `Swap2Reals` procedure developed in Section 6.3. Write a driver and test your procedure.

REFERENCES

Detailed instructions for using the source-code debuggers in Turbo Pascal and THINK Pascal can be found in the companion lab manual, *The Structures and Abstractions Labs: Experiments in Pascal and Turbo Pascal.*

Further information on the subtleties of using control structures will be found in Chapters 9 and 10 of the current book. Still more information on the differences among control structures in various programming languages can be found in language-theory textbooks like those listed below:

- Bruce J. MacLennan, *Principles of Programming Languages*, second edition (Holt, Rinehart and Winston, 1987).
- Terrence W. Pratt, *Programming Languages*, second edition (Prentice Hall, 1984).

Answers We Deserve to Get

[L]ike the steam engine, the steel mill, the dynamo, the computer is an opportunity to be exploited, an immensely powerful extension of man's ingenuity and power in the service of his will. But it is also a source, as I have said, of concern. If we put the wrong things into it, if we select the wrong problems or state the right problems incorrectly, we will get unsatisfactory solutions. Perhaps the easiest way to put it is that in using the computer, man will get the answers he deserves to get.

Here it seems to me is the cause for real alarm because of a sad historical fact. On the record men have been luckier in giving answers than in asking the right questions, or at least they have been more skillful in making up half answers they can live with than in putting the full questions accurately framed.

—Elting E. Morison, *Men, Machines, and Modern Times* (MIT Press, 1966), page 79.

CHAPTER

7

Functions

CHAPTER CONTENTS

INTRODUCTION

We have been discussing ways in which actions can be specified in Pascal. First we examined operators and expressions, which are carryovers from algebra. The syntax and semantics are pretty much as in mathematics: Operators act on operands to produce the value of an expression. Then we discussed a couple of Pascal's control structures, which are used to make decisions and control repetition. Control structures are carryovers from logic theory: If such-and-such is true, then do the appropriate thing. We also examined thoroughly the use of procedures, which are, in a sense, more literary than mathematical. They are Pascal's *verbs*, you might say. Executing a procedure is like saying, Go away and carry out this process, and come back when you are finished. When execution returns from a procedure, it may or may not bring back values with it, but in any case, the procedure itself is thought of as an action, and not as having a value.

Both operators and procedures can be thought of in terms of input/output models. An operator receives data inputs and operates on them, producing some output data.

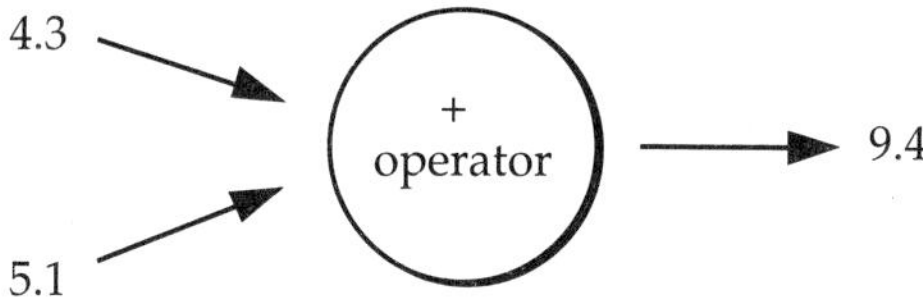

Similarly, a procedure usually receives input parameters, but may or may not return output parameters. We may have, for example, a procedure like `ConvertToCelsius`, which produces an output value:

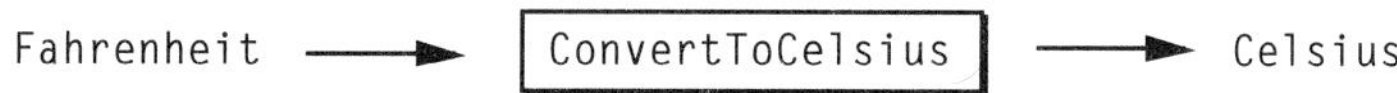

Or we may have a procedure like `ShowTemperature`, which has inputs but no outputs:

There is one more way to specify actions in Pascal and, like the first, it is taken from mathematics. It is the **function**.

Function: (Mathematics) A rule of association between two sets of data, such that each value in the first set is associated with a unique value in the second set.

For example, when you mail a first-class letter at the post office, a function is used to associate the weight of the letter with the cost of postage, according to a table:

Weight not exceeding (oz.)	Postal rate (cents)
1	29
2	52
3	75
4	98
⋮	⋮

This table constitutes a rule for computing a unique postage for any given weight of letter, and therefore constitutes a postage function defined on the set of positive real numbers representing weight. The **domain** of the function is the set of positive real numbers representing weight; the **range** is the set of discrete whole numbers

$$\{29, 52, 75, 98, \ldots\}$$

The syntax for using such a function in mathematics should be familiar. We say that "the postage is the value of the postal rate for the given weight" or, algebraically,

$$\text{Postage} = \text{PostalRate}(\text{Weight}).$$

In Pascal, we use an assignment statement, assigning the value of the postal rate function, whose parameter is the given weight, to the `Postage` variable:

```
Postage := PostalRate( Weight )
```

This syntax differs from that for procedures because *the function itself has a value*. For this reason, functions are traditionally named after the function's value, and *the name is a noun*. Contrast this with procedures, whose names are traditionally verbs, describing the action taken, and whose names are not associated with values.

> A Pascal function is a subprogram that returns a value associated with the function's own name.

7.1 CALLING A FUNCTION

Now let's use a function in the Fahrenheit-to-Celsius conversion program developed earlier. In Section 5.3, we wrote a `ConvertToCelsius` procedure that encapsulated the conversion formula,

```
C := (5.0 / 9.0) * ( F - 32.0 )
```

The procedure was invoked by the statement

```
ConvertToCelsius( Fahrenheit, Celsius );
```

Such syntax is fairly clear. It amounts to the command, "Convert the Fahrenheit temperature to Celsius." Now we can try another way, **calling a function**, which may appeal to those who have used mathematical functions a good deal. We can replace our earlier procedure call with an assignment statement that assigns to `Celsius` the value of a `CelsiusConversion` function when applied to the `Fahrenheit` temperature:

```
Celsius := CelsiusConversion( Fahrenheit );
```

This would be read in English as, "The Celsius temperature is the value of the Celsius conversion function, applied to the Fahrenheit temperature." With this version, the overall program is

```
PROGRAM FahrenheitToCelsius8 ( Input, Output );
{ Modular version, using a conversion function. }
VAR
   Fahrenheit, Celsius : Real;

{ Declarations of function and procedures go here. }

BEGIN { main program }

   ShowPurpose;
   GetFahrenheit( Fahrenheit );
   Celsius := CelsiusConversion( Fahrenheit );
   ShowTemperature( Fahrenheit, Celsius )

END.
```

The program will not compile in this form, however, because the `CelsiusConversion` function has not yet been declared. That is our next step.

Syntax for calling a function

A user-defined function is simply a way of giving a name to the computation of a data value. The function can be called (invoked) in any expression of appropriate type. Wherever the function's value is needed, we insert code of the form

`FunctionName(` *ActualParameterList* `)`

That is, we insert the name of the function followed by the list of parameter values to be sent to the function, enclosed in parentheses. *A function call is an expression*, and therefore can appear wherever expressions of that type are allowed.

Notes:

- The parentheses can be omitted if the function has no parameters.
- If there are several parameter values, they are separated by commas.

7.2 DECLARING A FUNCTION

The `CelsiusConversion` function is supposed to encapsulate a transformation from an initial state in which we have only a Fahrenheit temperature to a final state in which we have both a Fahrenheit temperature and the corresponding Celsius temperature. Declaring the function is like declaring the `ConvertToCelsius` procedure, with only three differences. Two of them appear in the **function header**:

```
FUNCTION CelsiusConversion( F : Real ) : Real;
{
  PRECONDITION:
  F has a value.

  POSTCONDITION:
  Returns the Celsius temperature corresponding
  to the Fahrenheit temperature F.
}
BEGIN

   CelsiusConversion := ( 5.0 / 9.0 ) * ( F - 32.0 )

END;
```

According to the header, which says the function itself is "`: Real`," `CelsiusConversion` computes a real number. In other words, the result of the function's execution is to assign a real-number value to the identifier `CelsiusConversion`.

A function header starts with the reserved word `FUNCTION` and ends with the declaration of the type of value returned by the function. The general syntax for function declarations is shown in the box on the next page.

A value must be assigned to the function identifier.

The function *must* assign a value to the function name. In the example, the value of the expression `( 5.0 / 9.0 ) * ( F - 32.0 )` is assigned to `CelsiusConversion`. Then, when the function has completed its execution, this **value is returned** to the main program as the value of the function. `CelsiusConversion` is actually the name of a temporary storage cell used to return a value to the main program.

Identifiers within the function are local to the function.

The parameter for the `CelsiusConversion` function is a value parameter. The *formal* value parameter is called `F`, while the *actual* value parameter was called `Fahrenheit` by the main program. (See the previous page.) Different names have been chosen for these because the storage cell used for the parameter in the main program is not the same as the storage cell used in the function. When the main program calls `CelsiusConversion( Fahrenheit )`, it sends to `CelsiusConversion` a copy of the actual `Fahrenheit` value. This copy is then stored by `CelsiusConversion` in the `F` variable created when `CelsiusConversion` starts to run. Thus `Fahrenheit` and `F` are two different variables, located at two different places in memory. Since `F` is declared within the

`CelsiusConversion` function and exists only when the `CelsiusConversion` is running, it is said to be *local* to the function. The name `F` is local too; it is defined only within the function in which it is declared. This works the same as it does with value parameters in procedures.

Syntax for declaring a simple function

Function declaration:

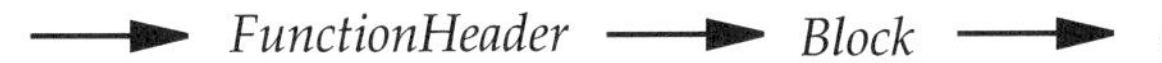

Function header:

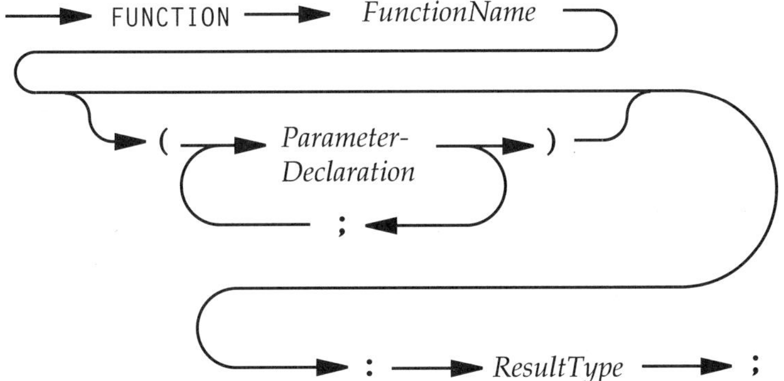

Pseudocode:

```
FUNCTION FunctionName ( FormalParameterList ) : ResultType;
OtherDeclarations
BEGIN
  StatementSequence
END;
```

Notes:

- The *FormalParameterList*, if any, declares parameter types. The individual declarations are separated by semicolons. Each declaration is of the form

  ParameterName : *TypeName* or `VAR` *ParameterName* : *TypeName*

  where *ParameterName* is a parameter name with scope *only* over the function. *TypeName* is a previously declared type name.
- If several parameters are of the same type, they can be declared together in a single declaration, with commas between the parameter names:

  Parameter1, Parameter2, ..., ParameterN : *TypeName*
- Distinct declarations are separated by semicolons.
- If there are no parameters, the parentheses should be omitted.
- *ResultType* is the type of value returned by the function. It must be specified as a previously declared type name, and can refer to any simple type, but not to a composite type.

(syntax, continued)

- *OtherDeclarations* are declarations of constants, types, and variables used within the function, other than parameters. The syntax is like that in a main program. The scope of these declarations extends only over the function in which the declarations are made.
- Somewhere within *StatementSequence*, there must be at least one statement that assigns a value to the *FunctionName*. The last value so assigned during execution of the function will be the value returned by the function to the calling program unit.

Functions usually use value parameters.

A function has a special purpose: to compute a single value to be returned as "the function's value" associated with the function's name. Therefore, a function does not usually return any values by means of its parameter list, and therefore doesn't usually use VAR parameters. Many programmers feel that functions should *never* return any values by means of VAR parameters, as a matter of style. Other programmers feel that, in certain situations, it can be useful to have a function return, for example, an error signal as a VAR parameter. (This would then be an **intended side effect**.) This issue will arise in some later examples, but for the time being, our functions will use only value parameters, and will not return any values by means of the parameter list. When we want a subprogram to return more than one value, we will use a procedure.

Putting it all together

Now we have both the program that calls the function, and the function itself. Here is the complete program:

```
PROGRAM FahrenheitToCelsius8 ( Input, Output );
{ Version 4, using a conversion function }

CONST
   AbsoluteZero = -459.7; { Fahrenheit }

VAR
   Fahrenheit, Celsius : Real;

PROCEDURE ShowPurpose;
{
  POSTCONDITION:
  The purpose of the program is displayed on the screen.
}
BEGIN

   WriteLn( 'CONVERTING FAHRENHEIT TO CELSIUS' );
   WriteLn

END; { ShowPurpose }
```

```
PROCEDURE GetFahrenheit( VAR F : Real );
{
  POSTCONDITION:
  The parameter contains a Fahrenheit temperature.
}
BEGIN

   Write( 'Fahrenheit? (Must be >= -459.7) ' );
   ReadLn( F );

   WHILE F < AbsoluteZero DO
   BEGIN
      Write( 'Fahrenheit? (Must be >= -459.7) ' );
      ReadLn( F )
   END

END; { GetFahrenheit }


FUNCTION CelsiusConversion( F : Real ) : Real;
{
  PRECONDITION:
  F has a value.

  POSTCONDITION:
  Returns the Celsius temperature corresponding
  to the Fahrenheit temperature F.
}
BEGIN

   CelsiusConversion := ( 5.0 / 9.0 ) * ( F - 32.0 )

END; { CelsiusConversion }


PROCEDURE ShowTemperature( F, C : Real );
{
  PRECONDITION:
  F and C contain corresponding Fahrenheit and
  Celsius temperatures.

  POSTCONDITION:
  The values of F and C are displayed on the screen.
}
BEGIN

   WriteLn;
   WriteLn( F:6:1, ' deg. F. = ', C:6:1, ' deg. C.' )

END; { ShowTemperature }
```

```
BEGIN { main program }

   ShowPurpose;
   GetFahrenheit( Fahrenheit );
   Celsius := CelsiusConversion( Fahrenheit );
   ShowTemperature( Fahrenheit, Celsius )

END.
```

The output from this program looks the same as it did in the previous version:

```
CONVERTING FAHRENHEIT TO CELSIUS

Fahrenheit? (Must be >= -459.7) 212

 212.0 deg. F. =  100.0 deg. C.
```

Let's examine the operation of the function in this program. After `GetFahrenheit` has returned a value to the `Fahrenheit` variable, the program executes the assignment statement that calls the function. As always in an assignment statement, the first step is to evaluate the expression on the right of the assignment operator. In the present case, this expression is simply the function call `CelsiusConversion( Fahrenheit )`. In response to the call, the function springs to life in a part of main memory separate from the main program. The main program transmits to the function a copy of the `Fahrenheit` value, then the main program is suspended as the function begins to execute.

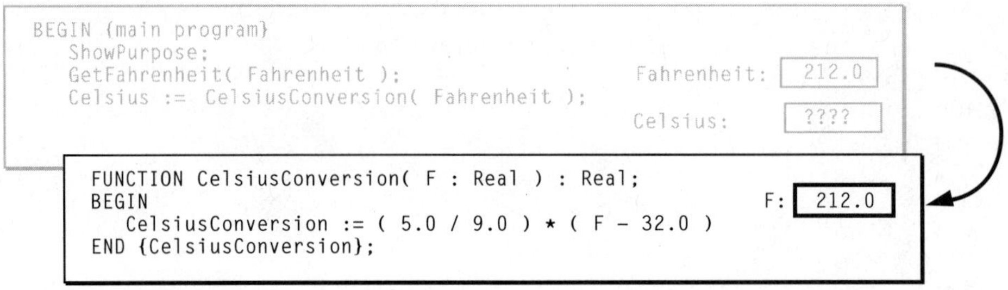

```
BEGIN {main program}
   ShowPurpose;
   GetFahrenheit( Fahrenheit );                         Fahrenheit: [ 212.0 ]
   Celsius := CelsiusConversion( Fahrenheit );
                                                        Celsius:    [ ???? ]

   FUNCTION CelsiusConversion( F : Real ) : Real;
   BEGIN                                                         F: [ 212.0 ]
      CelsiusConversion := ( 5.0 / 9.0 ) * ( F - 32.0 )
   END {CelsiusConversion};
```

The function computes the Celsius temperature equivalent to the given Fahrenheit temperature, and stores the result under the name `CelsiusConversion`.

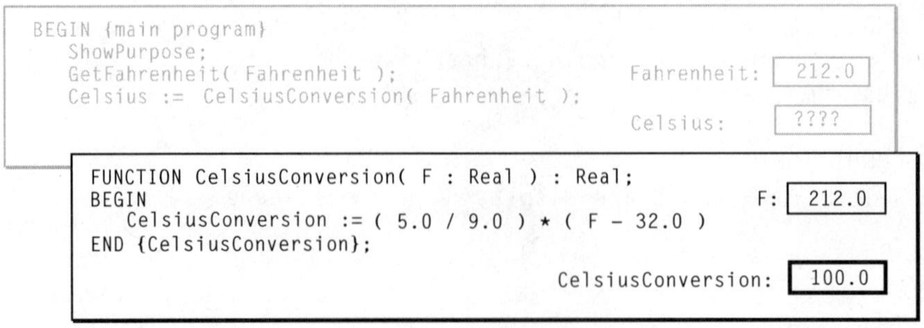

```
BEGIN {main program}
   ShowPurpose;
   GetFahrenheit( Fahrenheit );                         Fahrenheit: [ 212.0 ]
   Celsius := CelsiusConversion( Fahrenheit );
                                                        Celsius:    [ ???? ]

   FUNCTION CelsiusConversion( F : Real ) : Real;
   BEGIN                                                         F: [ 212.0 ]
      CelsiusConversion := ( 5.0 / 9.0 ) * ( F - 32.0 )
   END {CelsiusConversion};
                                         CelsiusConversion: [ 100.0 ]
```

Now the function has finished executing, and the value of `CelsiusConversion` is transmitted to the expression in the main program in which `CelsiusConversion` was called.

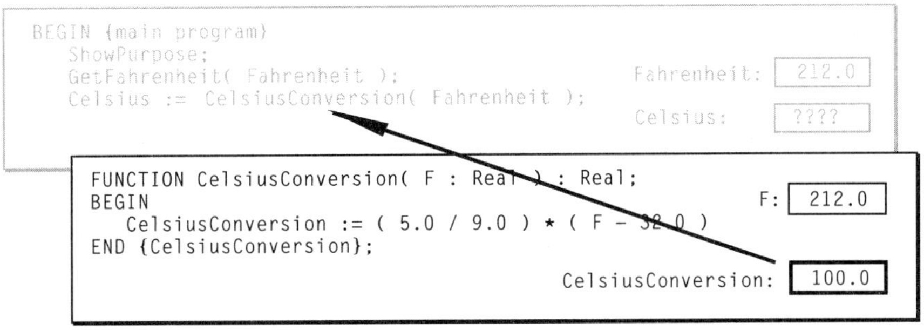

```
BEGIN {main program}
   ShowPurpose;
   GetFahrenheit( Fahrenheit );                    Fahrenheit: [ 212.0 ]
   Celsius := CelsiusConversion( Fahrenheit );
                                                   Celsius:    [ ???? ]

   FUNCTION CelsiusConversion( F : Real ) : Real;
   BEGIN                                                    F: [ 212.0 ]
      CelsiusConversion := ( 5.0 / 9.0 ) * ( F - 32.0 )
   END {CelsiusConversion};
                                        CelsiusConversion: [ 100.0 ]
```

The function ceases to exist in main memory. That is, its memory space is released for other use. The main program continues from the point where it was suspended, assigning the function value to `Celsius`.

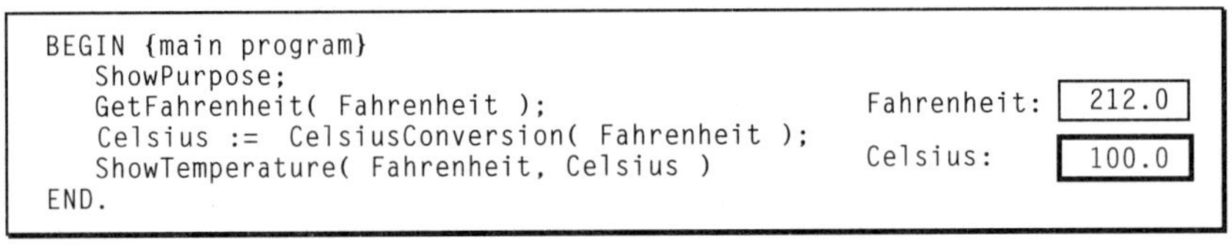

```
BEGIN {main program}
   ShowPurpose;
   GetFahrenheit( Fahrenheit );                    Fahrenheit: [ 212.0 ]
   Celsius := CelsiusConversion( Fahrenheit );
   ShowTemperature( Fahrenheit, Celsius )          Celsius:    [ 100.0 ]
END.
```

The main program then continues from this point, as described in the last chapter.

Try out this version of the program on your own Pascal system. Are there new compilation errors? If so, *they must be in the little bit of code you added since the first test.* Correct any errors and compile again. When all the errors are fixed, recompile and run the program, trying various inputs to see how the program behaves.

Functions are invoked in expressions.

Since a function call is an expression, a function call can be made within any expression of appropriate type, or wherever such an expression is allowed. Here is an example that shortens our main program slightly:

```
BEGIN { main program }

   ShowPurpose;
   GetFahrenheit( Fahrenheit );
   ShowTemperature( Fahrenheit, CelsiusConversion( Fahrenheit ) )

END.
```

Here the function call `CelsiusConversion( Fahrenheit )` is used to directly compute the second actual parameter value to be sent to the `ShowTemperature` procedure, making it unnecessary for the main program to declare a `Celsius` variable. In this example, the function call is contained within a call to a procedure; the two calls are said to be **nested**.

7.3 WHEN DO WE USE A FUNCTION?

A function should be used when the only purpose of the subprogram is to compute a single data value. On the other hand, a procedure is preferred in three situations:

1. A procedure is preferred when no value is returned.
2. A procedure is preferred when more than one value is returned.
3. A procedure is preferred when I/O is performed in addition to returning a value.

In the previous section, a `CelsiusConversion` function was written rather than simply inserting the statement

```
Celsius := ( 5.0 / 9.0 ) * ( Fahrenheit - 32.0 )
```

in the main program, even though it made the program longer.

In this kind of situation, there are three potential advantages to using a function:

1. By giving a name to the computation of a value, we make it easier to refer to that computation. Code that uses clearly named functions is easier to understand than code that performs all computations in the main program.
2. If a function performs the computation, the program can repeat the computation over and over by simply calling the function repeatedly. The code for the computation need not be reproduced every time it is needed.
3. A function can be saved in a library of useful subprograms and plugged into any program that needs it.

There is another task in the `FahrenheitToCelsius` program in which the goal is to return a single value to the main program: the task of prompting for and reading a value for `Fahrenheit`. It might seem natural to replace the procedure call

```
GetFahrenheit( Fahrenheit );
```

with a call to a `FahrenheitTemperature` function in an assignment statement:

```
Fahrenheit := FahrenheitTemperature;
```

Here the function `FahrenheitTemperature` needs no parameters, so we can declare it without a parameter list:

```
FUNCTION FahrenheitTemperature : Real;
{
  POSTCONDITION:
  A Fahrenheit temperature is returned.
}
VAR
   F : Real;

BEGIN

   Write( 'Fahrenheit? (Must be >= -459.7) ' );
   ReadLn( F );
```

```
   WHILE F < AbsoluteZero DO
   BEGIN
      Write( 'Fahrenheit? (Must be >= -459.7) ' );
      ReadLn( F )
   END;

   FahrenheitTemperature := F

END; { FahrenheitTemperature }
```

This will work, but it is not a good use of a function, because we are really performing *two* tasks here: showing output and getting a value for Fahrenheit. According to the third criterion listed above, a procedure would be preferable.

The function identifier does not act as a variable.

The function above raises a frequently-asked question: If a value can be assigned to the function identifier, is the function identifier actually the name of a *variable*? If so, we can shorten the `FahrenheitTemperature` function by making the function identifier do the work of the `F` variable:

```
FUNCTION FahrenheitTemperature : Real;
{
  ERROR: THE FOLLOWING CODE WON'T WORK!
}
BEGIN

   Write( 'Fahrenheit? (Must be >= -459.7) ' );
   ReadLn( FahrenheitTemperature );

   WHILE FahrenheitTemperature < AbsoluteZero DO
   BEGIN
      Write( 'Fahrenheit? (Must be >= -459.7) ' );
      ReadLn( FahrenheitTemperature )
   END

END; { FahrenheitTemperature }
```

However, *this is illegal*. In Pascal, a function identifier cannot be used in an expression inside the function itself. Therefore, the `ReadLn`s and `WHILE` statement shown above are illegal. This was the reason we needed the local `F` variable in the previous version of the function.

Questions

1. What is the conceptual difference (the semantic difference) between a function and a procedure?
2. What is the syntactic difference between a function and a procedure?
3. Where can a function call be used in a program?
4. Under what circumstances is a function inappropriate?

Exercises

5. Write a function called `CToF` that converts Celsius temperatures to Fahrenheit, and write a driver to test it. (Reverse the algebra used for the F-to-C conversion.)

6. Write a function called `FToK` that converts Fahrenheit temperatures to Kelvin. (The Kelvin temperature is 273.15 degrees more than the corresponding Celsius temperature.) Test your function.

7. Write a modular program that converts pounds to kilograms, using a function to calculate the number of kilograms. (1 pound = 0.45359 kilograms.)

8. Write a function named `SalesTax`, with one value parameter named `NetPrice`, which returns a value equal to 6.75 percent of the parameter value. Also write a main program to use in testing, and test your function.

9. Write and test a program containing a function named `AverageOfThree`, which receives three value parameters named `Num1`, `Num2`, and `Num3`, returning their average.

10. Write a function called `CubeOf` that returns the cube of its real argument. For example, `CubeOf( 1.1 )` should be 1.331. Write a driver and test your function.

11. The amount of money accumulated after a principal, P, is invested for n years at a simple annual interest rate of r is $P\,(1 + nr)$. Write and test a function that receives P, n, and r as parameters, returning this amount.

12. Over the period from 1650 to 1972, the population of the world was approximated by the function

$$P(t) = \frac{1.85477 \times 10^{11}}{(2021.55 - t)}$$

where t is the year. Write a population function using this formula, and use it to predict the population of the world in the years 2000, 2010, and 2020.

7.4 STANDARD FUNCTIONS IN PASCAL

Pascal provides 15 functions in the standard library. These are listed in Appendix B. The **standard functions** are invoked in the same way as ones you write yourself: You give the function's name, followed by an appropriate list of actual parameters. Ten of the standard functions perform real-number calculations:

Function	Computes	Constraint
`Abs`	Absolute value	
`ArcTan`	Arc tangent	Result is in radians.
`Cos`	Cosine	Parameter is in radians.
`Exp`	Power of e ($\approx$ 2.7182818)	
`Ln`	Natural (base-e) logarithm	Parameter must be positive.
`Round`	Nearest whole number	
`Sin`	Sine	Parameter is in radians.
`Sqr`	Square	
`SqRt`	Positive square root	Parameter must be nonnegative.
`Trunc`	Whole-number part of real	

Here are some examples of real-number functions at work:

Expression	Value
`Abs( -3.14 )`	3.14
`ArcTan( 1.0 )`	0.78539816
`Cos( 3.1415926 )`	–1.0
`Exp( 1.0 )`	2.7182818
`Ln( 2.7182818 )`	1.0
`Round( 4.53 )`	5.0
`Round( -4.53 )`	–5.0
`Sin( 3.1415926 )`	0.0
`Sqr( 4.0 )`	16.0
`SqRt( 16.0 )`	4.0
`Trunc( 4.53 )`	4.0
`Trunc( -4.53 )`	–4.0

(Your Pascal may give slightly different answers in some cases because of roundoff errors.)

Nested function calls

As mentioned at the end of Section 7.2, a function call can appear as an actual parameter value in another function or procedure call. The most common example occurs when printing out the value of the function:

```
WriteLn( 'The square root of ', X:5:2, ' is ', SqRt(X):5:2 )
```

This displays output of the form

```
The square root of 15.00 is  3.87
```

Similarly, we can have nested function calls. The statement

```
X := Exp( Ln( 2.0 ) )
```

should assign the value 2.0 to X. (Why?) Roundoff error may affect the result slightly; try it on your system and see what happens.

Question

13. Why does `X := Exp( Ln( 2.0 ) )` assign 2.0 to `X`? Explain.

Exercise

14. Predict the output of this program:

```
PROGRAM Whazzit ( Output );
VAR
   Three : Real;
```

```
FUNCTION Zing( Stuff : Real ) : Real;
BEGIN

   Zing := 4.0 + Stuff

END; { Zing }


FUNCTION Ding( Junk : Real ) : Real;
BEGIN

   Ding := Sqr( Zing( Junk ) )

END; {Ding}


BEGIN {main program}

   Three := 3.0;
   WriteLn( Ding( Three ) )

END.
```

7.5 TESTING AND DEBUGGING

Writing functions poses the same problems as writing procedures, with two added pitfalls. Watch out for these:

1. The code within a function must assign a value to the function identifier. Failure to do this is a syntax error in Standard Pascal, and should result in a compiler error message. Some Pascal compilers do not issue such a message, but failure to assign a value to the function identifier will cause trouble because it results in garbage being returned as the value of the function.

2. Within the function, the function identifier is not a variable identifier in the usual sense. In particular, the function identifier *cannot appear in an expression* within the function itself. Thus the following is *illegal*:

```
FUNCTION Hypotenuse( X, Y : Real ) : Real;
BEGIN

   Hypotenuse := (X * X) + (Y * Y);
   Hypotenuse := SqRt( Hypotenuse )  {++ ILLEGAL! ++}

END; { Hypotenuse }
```

You should test your compiler to see if it issues clear error messages when these requirements are violated.

Examples of the error messages issued by a sample compiler are shown in Table 7.5.1.

Examples of syntax errors in Turbo Pascal 6.0. **Table 7.5.1**

Syntax error	Error message from compiler
Function not declared before use.	`Unknown identifier.`
Keyword `FUNCTION` missing or misspelled in function header.	`":" expected.`
Semicolon missing from end of function header.	`";" expected.`
Failure to declare function's return type.	`":" expected.`
Keyword `BEGIN` missing or misspelled in function.	`BEGIN expected.`
Keyword `END` missing or misspelled in function.	`Unknown identifier` or `BEGIN expected.`
Semicolon missing from end of function.	`";" expected.`
Failure to assign a value to function identifier.	(no message)
Comma instead of semicolon between formal parameter declarations.	`")" expected.`
More actual parameters than formal parameters.	`")" expected.`
Fewer actual parameters than formal parameters.	`"," expected.`
Actual parameter differs in type from formal parameter.	`Type mismatch.`
Function identifier is used in an expression within the function itself.	`"(" expected.` (!?)

(Notice that the Turbo Pascal compiler does not flag everything that would be a syntax error in Standard Pascal. Note also that other compilers will give somewhat different error messages.)

LOOKING BACK

A Pascal function is a special subprogram for computing a single value, which is returned as the value of the function itself. We noted the following differences between functions and procedures:

- Unlike a procedure, a function has a type, which is the type of value returned by the function.
- Normally, a function uses only value parameters, and therefore returns no values by means of the parameter list.
- A function is called as it is in mathematics, by naming the function, followed by its actual parameter list.
- A function call can be placed in any expression of the same type, or in any place where such an expression would be appropriate.

Pascal provides 15 standard functions, 10 of which were briefly described in Section 7.4.

TERMS EMPHASIZED IN THIS CHAPTER

Actual parameters 202
Calling a function 200–201, 207
Declaring a function 202–204
Domain 200
Expression, function call is 201, 207
Formal parameters 202
Function 200
Function, advantages of 208
Function header 202
Function identifier 209, 212
Function, value returned by 202–204, 212
Function, when to use 208
Input/output model 199
Intended side effect 204
Local identifier 202–203
Nested call 207, 211
Range 200
Returned value 202–204, 212
Sequence of declarations 203–204
Sequence of execution 206–207
Standard functions 210–211
Subprogram 200
Value parameter 204
Variable (VAR) parameter 204

PROJECTS

1. Heron's formula gives the area of a triangle having sides a, b, and c as

$$\text{Area} = \sqrt{s(s-a)(s-b)(s-c)}$$

where $s = (a + b + c) / 2$. Write and test a fully modular program that reads from the keyboard the three sides, and then predicts the area of any triangle. What does it mean if the area is a complex number? What will the program do in this event?

2. Standard Pascal lacks a base-10 logarithm function, though it does have a base-e logarithm function. Fortunately, you can easily write your own base-10 logarithm function by making use of the fact that

$$\log(x) = \ln(x) / \ln(10)$$

Write a `Log` function along with a driver, and test it.

3. By analogy with Project 2, write a function to compute the base-x logarithm of y, where x and y are parameters of the function.

4. Pascal does not provide an exponentiation operator, so we cannot write expressions of the form x^p directly. On the other hand, such an operation can be carried out by a function, if we use a little algebra. Let $z = x^p$. Then, taking the base-e logarithm of both sides of the equation, we have

$$\ln z = \ln(x^p) = p \ln x.$$

Now, taking the antilogarithm of both sides, we regain z on the left:

$$z = \exp(p \ln x)$$

Since $z = x^p$, we have $x^p = \exp(p \ln x)$. (Of course, x must be positive.) Pascal provides both the `Exp` and `Ln` functions, so it is easy to write a `Power` function that, when called by `Power( X, P )`, where `X` and `P` are both real numbers, returns the real number x^p. Write and test such a function.

5. (Uses function developed in Project 4.) If you invest a certain amount of principal, P, at a daily interest rate r, compounded daily for n days, the return on your investment will be $P(1 + r)^n$. Write a fully modular program that prompts for and reads the values of P, r, and n, and then computes and displays the return on the investment. Use procedures and functions where appropriate.

6. Another way to compute x^p is to sum the series

$$x^p \approx 1 + p\ln(x) + \frac{[p\ln(x)]^2}{2} + \frac{[p\ln(x)]^3}{6} + \frac{[p\ln(x)]^4}{24} + \frac{[p\ln(x)]^5}{120}$$

This method is only approximate, however. Write a function that works in this way, and check its accuracy for several known cases.

7. The factorial, $n!$, of a *large* whole number n, can be approximated by Stirling's formula,

$$\ln(n!) \approx \left(n + \frac{1}{2}\right)\ln(n) - n + \ln\left(\sqrt{2\pi}\right)$$

Use this relationship to write a function that returns an approximation to the factorial of large whole real numbers. Write a driver and test your function in several known cases.

8. Pascal lacks a tangent function but provides both sine and cosine functions. Write your own tangent function, using the fact that

$$\tan(\theta) = \frac{\sin(\theta)}{\cos(\theta)}$$

Write your tangent function so that it accepts angles in degrees. Since Pascal's sine and cosine functions require their angles in radians, you will also need to write a degrees-to-radians conversion function. (360 degrees = 2π radians.) Write a driver and test your functions.

9. The bth root of a real number x is

$$\sqrt[b]{x} = x^{1/b}$$

Write a function `Root` such that `Root( B, X )` is the `B`th root of `X`, computed in this way. (Use the result of Project 4.) Test your function on some known cases.

REFERENCES

In the C and C++ programming languages, there are no procedures, just functions. A procedure is considered to be merely a function that returns the "void" value. For a discussion, see the essays by Alan Feuer and Narain Gehani and by Prabhaker Mateti in the book *Comparing and Assessing Programming Languages: Ada, C, Pascal*, edited by Alan Feuer and Narain Gehani (Prentice Hall, 1984).

The idea of applying functions to data can become the fundamental model of computation. This is known as *functional programming*, and is the basis of a number of modern programming languages, including the LISP language. See the discussion of procedural abstraction in Chapter 1 of Harold Abelson, Gerald Sussman, and Julie Sussman's *Structure and Interpretation of Computer Programs* (MIT Press/McGraw-Hill, 1985). For a deeper study, see Peter Henderson's *Functional Programming* (Prentice Hall, 1980), or the book of the same name by Anthony J. Field and Peter G. Harrison (Addison-Wesley Publishing, 1988).

CHAPTER

8

Ordinal Data Types

CHAPTER CONTENTS

INTRODUCTION

In the early days of computing, the data were numbers and computing meant number-crunching. But today we manipulate many kinds of data—numbers, characters, pictures, sounds—in fact, any kind of discrete, finite data. Of course, we don't perform the same operations on these various kinds of data. We do arithmetic with numbers, word processing with characters, drawing with graphics elements, and so on. In order to facilitate these various kinds of operations, we store different kinds of data in appropriate ways, as mentioned in Chapter 1. This means that computer data must be categorized so that they can be stored appropriately. Thus, we have **data types**, which are categories or classes of data.

Computer scientists invent systematic methods for storing and manipulating various kinds of data, represented by symbols. We invent useful models of the symbolic data to be manipulated, thinking of the data types in terms of their *uses*. Character data, for example, must be suitable for word processing, while numbers must suit arithmetic. Such distinctions are important. A data type not only has its own set of allowed values, but also has *its own allowed operations*.

Considered as an abstraction, data consist of both a *what* and a *how*, you might say. A datum itself is a bit pattern stored in a computer's memory: That's the thing itself, the *what*. But a datum is not useful unless we have a set of operations we can perform on it: That's the *how*. A data type, considered together with its set of meaningful operations, is called a **data abstraction** or **abstract data type**. This concept was introduced in Section 2.2 and will receive a full treatment in Chapter 16. In the present chapter, we are building toward it.

Abstract data type: A set of allowed data values, together with a set of allowed operations.

In this chapter, we will introduce three more of Pascal's built-in data types:

- Integers (whole numbers).
- Characters.
- Booleans (true/false values).

For each of these data types, you will learn, just as you did for real numbers,

- To define constants and variables.
- To use operators.
- To build expressions.
- To build procedures and functions for performing operations not built into Pascal.

You will find that each data type is made meaningful primarily by the operations that can be applied to it.

Finally, you will learn to use type declarations to make procedures and functions useful in manipulating a wide range of data types.

8.1 ORDINAL DATA

These three new data types—integers, characters, and booleans—are characterized by a property that distinguishes them from real numbers. While Pascal's real numbers approximate the continuous spread of numeric values on the real-number line, our new data types represent symbols that are *fundamentally discrete and enumerable* and can therefore be stored exactly, without any roundoff error.

Enumerate: To list in order.

Ordinal data type: A data type whose allowed values can be associated one-to-one with the natural numbers.

Integers, characters, and logical values can be **enumerated**. That is, we can list all possible values in order. We can say which value comes first in the list, which comes second, and so on. Data types whose values can be so listed are called **ordinal data types**. As you can easily imagine, Pascal's integer values have the order `..., -1, 0, 1, 2, 3, ...`. Similarly, Pascal lists characters in alphabetic order, and logical values in the order `False, True`.

A property of such ordered values is that each has a **predecessor** and **successor** in the list, except of course at the ends of the list. Pascal provides standard functions `Pred` and `Succ`, respectively, to compute the predecessor and successor of any given ordinal value. That is, `Pred( Value )` is the predecessor of `Value` in the list of values of that type, while `Succ( Value )` is the successor. For example,

```
Pred( 1 ) is 0; Succ( 1 ) is 2;
Pred( 'B' ) is 'A'; Succ( 'B' ) is 'C';
Pred( 'h' ) is 'g'; Succ( 'g' ) is 'h';
Pred( True ) is False; Succ( False ) is True.
```

In the following three sections, we will explore the properties of these ordinal data types in more detail.

8.2 INTEGER DATA

Integer data values are whole numbers, either positive or negative. In Standard Pascal, the range is from -MaxInt through +MaxInt, inclusive, where MaxInt is a standard predefined constant whose value depends upon the system being used. (Check your compiler reference manual to see what MaxInt is in your Pascal system. Also check the lower limit: Some Pascals allow integers from -MaxInt-1 to +MaxInt.) It is an error to attempt to compute or store an integer value outside this range. Such a value will be too large in magnitude to fit in an integer storage cell, so Standard Pascal will issue an OVERFLOW ERROR message and halt execution of the program. In computing, unlike mathematics, the range of integers is *finite*.

In integer constants, a sign is optional on positive values. The following examples are legal:

```
7    +7    -10000    0    +0    -14
```

An integer constant cannot contain commas, a decimal point, a fractional part, or an exponent. The following are *illegal* as integers, for the reasons given:

10,000	(Contains a comma)
1.0	(Contains a decimal point and fractional part)
1.1	(Same reason)
1.	(Contains a decimal point)
.4	(Contains no whole-number part; also contains a decimal point and fractional part)
1e2	(Contains an exponent)

Declaring integer constants

Integer constants are declared in the same way as real constants, but they are assigned integer values:

```
CONST
   SecondsPerMinute  = 60;
   SecondsPerHour    = 3600;
```

Of course, the declarations of constants come before the declarations of types or of variables.

Declaring integer variables

Variables must be declared after any constants, but before the word BEGIN in the program unit. To declare an integer variable called Age, you would write

```
VAR
   Age : Integer;
```

As with the Real type, the effect of a variable declaration is to create a named memory cell as the program starts to execute. The declaration does not give an initial value to these cells in Standard Pascal. As the program begins running, a variable may contain a garbage value.

Integer operations

There are seven operations on integer data. Most of these are familiar from mathematics and similar to those for real data. First there are two **unary operators** (that is, operators taking a single operand):

Unary operation	Symbol	Purpose
Identity	+	No change
Negation	–	Takes the negative

In addition, there are five **binary operators**, taking two operands:

Binary operation	Symbol	Purpose
Addition	+	Yields sum of addition
Subtraction	–	Yields difference
Multiplication	*	Yields product
Integer division	DIV	Yields quotient of integer division
Modulus	MOD	Yields remainder of integer division

These are integer operators, remember. Integer division yields an *integer-truncated quotient*:

```
 7 DIV 2  =  3
 1 DIV 2  =  0
-5 DIV 2  = -2
```

The modulus operator, when applied to positive operands, yields the *remainder of integer division*:

```
7 MOD 2  =  remainder of 7 DIV 2   =  1
6 MOD 2  =  remainder of 6 DIV 2   =  0
```

Expressions involving MOD must have a positive divisor; it is an error to have a negative or zero divisor.

Why the modulus is not simply the remainder of integer division

When the dividend is negative and the divisor is positive, Standard Pascal's MOD operator returns the true modulus value, which is not the integer remainder in such a case. To see why this is true, let's take a brief look at one of the fundamental laws of arithmetic. Suppose that *Dividend* is a nonnegative integer and *Divisor* is a positive integer. Then the Quotient-Remainder Theorem of integer arithmetic can be stated as follows:

$$Dividend = (Divisor \cdot Quotient) + Remainder \qquad (1)$$

where $0 \leq Remainder < Divisor$, $0 \leq Dividend$, and $0 < Divisor$. For example, in the integer division 5 DIV 3, we have $Dividend = 5$, $Divisor = 3$, $Quotient = 1$, $Remainder = 2$, and $5 = (3 \cdot 1) + 2$.

For any given *Dividend* and *Divisor* satisfying the constraints, it can be proven that *Quotient* and *Remainder* are unique. In particular,

$$\textit{Quotient} = \text{floor}(\textit{Dividend} / \textit{Divisor}) \quad (2)$$

where the floor function is defined as follows.

The floor function

If x is a real number, floor(x) is defined to be the largest integer that is less than or equal to x. For example,

$$\text{floor}(1.67) = 1$$

$$\text{floor}(1.0) = 1$$

$$\text{floor}(-1.67) = -2$$

Note that floor is a *type-transfer function*, converting a real number to an integer.

Type-transfer function: A function that converts a value of one type to a value of another type.

The definition of the modulus

When *Dividend* and *Divisor* are both positive, floor(*Dividend* / *Divisor*) equals *Dividend* `DIV` *Divisor* or `Trunc(` *Dividend* `/` *Divisor* `)`, so Equation (2) is not surprising. You may be surprised, however, to see what happens when we substitute (2) into (1). We obtain

$$\textit{Remainder} = \textit{Dividend} - \textit{Divisor} \cdot \text{floor}(\textit{Dividend} / \textit{Divisor})$$

The remainder shown here is, of course, a function of *Dividend* and *Divisor*, and it is called "*Dividend* modulo *Divisor*," which is usually abbreviated *Dividend* mod *Divisor*. Thus we obtain a *definition of the mod operation*:

$$\textit{Dividend} \bmod \textit{Divisor} = \textit{Dividend} - \textit{Divisor} \cdot \text{floor}(\textit{Dividend} / \textit{Divisor}) \quad (3)$$

Here are some examples:

$$5 \bmod 3 = 5 - 3 \cdot \text{floor}(5/3) = 5 - 3 \cdot 1 = \mathbf{2}$$

$$4 \bmod 3 = 4 - 3 \cdot \text{floor}(4/3) = 4 - 3 \cdot 1 = \mathbf{1}$$

$$3 \bmod 3 = 3 - 3 \cdot \text{floor}(3/3) = 3 - 3 \cdot 1 = \mathbf{0}$$

$$2 \bmod 3 = 2 - 3 \cdot \text{floor}(2/3) = 2 - 3 \cdot 0 = \mathbf{2}$$

$$1 \bmod 3 = 1 - 3 \cdot \text{floor}(1/3) = 1 - 3 \cdot 0 = \mathbf{1}$$

$$0 \bmod 3 = 0 - 3 \cdot \text{floor}(0/3) = 0 - 3 \cdot 0 = \mathbf{0}$$

Note the cyclic behavior of the mod values and the fact that they conform to the inequality stated earlier, $0 \le (\textit{Dividend} \bmod \textit{Divisor}) < \textit{Divisor}$. These properties are useful in many applications involving cyclic phenomena, as we will see shortly.

When *Dividend* is nonnegative and *Divisor* is positive, the definition of *Dividend* mod *Divisor* is familiar: floor(*Dividend* / *Divisor*) is the same as Pascal's *Dividend* `DIV` *Divisor* and *Dividend* `MOD` *Divisor* is just the ordinary remainder of integer division.

The modulus when the dividend is negative

When *Dividend* is negative, however, Pascal systems differ in the way they compute *Dividend* `MOD` *Divisor*. International Standard Pascal uses equation (3)—the correct mathematical definition—so that *Dividend* `MOD` *Divisor* continues the same cyclic pattern into negative values of *i*:

$$-1 \bmod 3 = -1 - 3 \cdot \text{floor}(-1/3) = -1 - 3 \cdot (-1) = \mathbf{2}$$

$$-2 \bmod 3 = -2 - 3 \cdot \text{floor}(-2/3) = -2 - 3 \cdot (-1) = \mathbf{1}$$

$$-3 \bmod 3 = -3 - 3 \cdot \text{floor}(-3/3) = -3 - 3 \cdot (-1) = \mathbf{0}$$

$$-4 \bmod 3 = -4 - 3 \cdot \text{floor}(-4/3) = -4 - 3 \cdot (-2) = \mathbf{2}$$

$$-5 \bmod 3 = -5 - 3 \cdot \text{floor}(-5/3) = -5 - 3 \cdot (-2) = \mathbf{1}$$

$$-6 \bmod 3 = -6 - 3 \cdot \text{floor}(-6/3) = -6 - 3 \cdot (-2) = \mathbf{0}$$

Many Pascal compilers do not conform to this definition, however, preferring to define the `MOD` as the naive remainder of ordinary integer division, even for negative *Dividend*. This results in `-1 MOD 3 = -1`, for example.

Why the true modulus is preferred

Standard Pascal specifies a true modulus rather than a simple remainder because the modulus is useful in many applications involving cyclic phenomena. Consider calculating time as displayed on a dial clock. At three minutes before noon, the time was –3 minutes, relative to noon, and

Hours displayed on clock dial = floor(`-3 / 60`) = –1 hour

Minutes displayed on clock dial = `-3 MOD 60` = +57 minutes

Thus, the clock time would be displayed as –1 hour, +57 minutes on the dial. A compiler that doesn't compute the true modulus might compute `-3 MOD 60` to be –3, giving a result other than the one desired.

Overloaded operators and polymorphism

The operator symbols +, –, and * are used with both integers and real numbers. However, these operators do not mean the same thing when applied to integers as they do when applied to reals. Integer addition, subtraction, and multiplication are, at the machine level, performed differently than the similar operations on reals. Thus, the +, –, and * operators have different meanings, depending on the types of their operands. We say that the operators are **overloaded** or **polymorphic**.

Integer expressions

An **integer expression** is an expression producing an integer value. Here are some very simple examples:

Expression	Value
`3 + 4`	7
`Age + Year`	Sum of values of `Age` and `Year`
`Age * Count`	Product of values of `Age` and `Count`
`3 DIV 4`	0
`3 MOD 4`	3

Operator precedence

With more complicated integer expressions, the order of application of operators is determined by parentheses and precedence in the same way as with real expressions. Again, the multiplication and division operators have higher precedence:

Level of precedence	Operators
Highest	`* DIV MOD`
Lowest	`+ -`

(Notice that the unary minus has the same precedence as subtraction.)

For example, in the expression `3 * 2 - 7 DIV 3`, the multiplication and division are performed first, as though we had written `(3 * 2) - (7 DIV 3)`. This yields `6 - 2`, or `4`. In the expression `7 DIV 3 * 4`, the operators, which have the same precedence, are applied in left-to-right order, as though we had written `(7 DIV 3) * 4`, giving 8. It is poor practice to rely on order of precedence to determine the value of an expression because precedence is hard to check at a glance, and therefore is error-prone. Good practice dictates that you use enough parentheses to make expressions unambiguous to human readers.

Ordinal properties of integers

As mentioned earlier, Standard Pascal's integer values have the order

```
{ -MaxInt, -MaxInt+1,..., -1, 0, 1, 2, 3,..., MaxInt-1, MaxInt}
```

(In some Pascal systems, the list starts with `-MaxInt-1`.) Because the order of values is specified by the Pascal Standard, each integer value has a unique predecessor and successor in the list. Two operators, `Pred` and `Succ`, are provided for computing these:

Expression	Value
`Pred( -MaxInt )`	Predecessor of first value is undefined
`Succ( -MaxInt )`	`-MaxInt+1`
`Pred( 0 )`	`-1`
`Succ( 0 )`	`+1`
`Pred( MaxInt )`	`MaxInt-1`
`Succ( MaxInt )`	Successor of last value is undefined

("Undefined" values are system-dependent and should result in run-time error messages if your system's *range-checking* feature is turned on.)

Other integer functions

Integer data can be sent to the other functions described in Section 7.4: `Abs`, `ArcTan`, `Cos`, `Exp`, `Ln`, `Sin`, `Sqr`, `SqRt`. In addition, there is a function that tells whether an integer is even or odd:

Expression	Value
`Odd( IntExpr )`	Returns the logical value `True` if the integer expression is odd; otherwise, it returns `False`.

There are also type-transfer functions, used to convert real values to integers:

Expression	Value
`Round( RealExpr )`	Returns the integer value closest to the value of the given real expression. For example, `Round( 6.7 )` is 7, `Round( -6.7 )` is –7, and `Round( 6.3 )` is 6.
`Trunc( RealExpr )`	Returns the truncated integer part of the value of the given real expression. For example, `Trunc( 6.7 )` is 6 and `Trunc( -6.7 )` is –6.

Note that `Round( X )` is `Trunc( X + 0.5 )` for $X \geq 0$ and is `Trunc( X - 0.5 )` for $X < 0$.

Converting integers to reals

There is no need for a function to convert integers to reals because an assignment statement can be used for that. For example, the code

```
VAR
   Count  : Integer;
   Weight : Real;

BEGIN
   .
   .
   Count := 6;
   Weight := Count;
```

stores 6 in `Count`, but 6.0 in `Weight`. You cannot, however, assign a real value to an integer variable. You must use `Round` or `Trunc` to extract an integer value, and then assign the result to the integer variable. We say that integer values are **assignment-compatible** with real variables, but that real values are not assignment-compatible with integer variables.

Assignment -compatible: A value is assignment-compatible with a variable if it is legal to assign it to the variable, even if it is a different type.

Formatting integer output

If integers are displayed without formatting, they are printed in a field predefined by the particular Pascal system. The field is often as wide as the widest storable integer. For example, the output from

```
   Count := 4;
   WriteLn( 'The count is ', Count );
```

might be

```
The count is       4
```

To improve the appearance, you can *format* the integer output by specifying the field width after the variable name, separated by a colon. For example,

```
Count := 4;
WriteLn( 'The count is ', Count:1 );
```

will display

```
The count is 4
```

If you specify a field width too small for the number, Standard Pascal will automatically expand the width. If you specify a field wider than necessary, extra spaces will be displayed to the left of the number.

Reading into integer variables

Integers can be read from text files (like the standard `Input` file) by means of `Read` and `ReadLn`, in the same manner as real numbers. When reading into integer variables, the data values read must be integer and not real. The `Read` or `ReadLn` will skip over any leading whitespace and then read the longest unbroken string of characters interpretable as an integer number. Once a character is encountered that cannot be part of an integer number, the string up to that point is converted to an integer value and the result stored in the corresponding `Read` or `ReadLn` parameter. Successive integer values should be separated by whitespace in the input.

For example, suppose we are reading from `Input`, using `ReadLn( Count, Age )`, where `Count` and `Age` are integer variables. If the user enters

ΔΔ+1Δ00027<EOLn>
(where Δ indicates a space)

then `Count` gets the value 1 and `Age` the value 27. If the user enters

Δ-33<EOLn>14W27<EOLn>

then `Count` gets –33 and `Age` gets 14.

A `Read` statement doesn't discard the end of the line. If we are using `Read( Count, Age )` and the user enters

ΔΔ+1Δ00027<EOLn>

then `Count` gets the value 1 and `Age` the value 27, and the last <EOLn> remains in the `Input` stream unread. (It will, then, be the first input to be seen by the next `Read` or `ReadLn`.) On the other hand, if the user enters

Δ-33<EOLn>14W27<EOLn>

then `Count` gets –33 and `Age` gets 14, and W27<EOLn> remains in the `Input` stream unread.

Questions

1. Which of the following are *legal* integer constants? Explain why.

`14`	`14.`	`14.0`	`14.1`	`0`	`0.`
`0.0`	`0.1`	`1,000`	`MaxInt`	∞	`three`

2. Assuming that `Count` is 4 and `Number` is 3, what are the values of the following expressions? Use operator precedence rules where needed. You can, of course, check your answers by running a test program.

   a. `Count + 2 * Number - 1`
   b. `Count * 2 + Number DIV 1`
   c. `(Number + 2) DIV Number - 1`
   d. `Number + 2 DIV Number - 1`
   e. `Count DIV 2 * 2 DIV Count`
   f. `2 + (-Count)`
   g. `2 - (Count + (Number - 1))`
   h. `3 * (-(Count + Number))`
   i. `1 DIV 1 + Count`
   j. `1 DIV (1 + Count) +3`
   k. `Pred( Count ) DIV Succ( Number )`
   l. `Pred( Count ) MOD Succ( Number )`
   m. `Pred( Succ( Number ) )`
   n. `Succ( Pred( Count ) )`
   o. `-Count MOD Number`
   p. `-Number MOD Count`
   q. `Round( -3.6 ) +1`
   r. `Trunc( 9.999999 )`
   s. `Odd( 7 )`
   t. `Odd( 0 )`

3. How do the integer numbers of computing differ from those of mathematics?

4. Real numbers are usually approximated in the computer, while integer values are always stored exactly. However, *whole* real numbers are stored exactly unless they have too many digits. How is this possible?

5. What is the value of `MaxInt` in your Pascal system?

Exercises

6. Write a real function called `FractionalPart` that returns the fractional part of its real-number parameter. That is, `FractionalPart( 12.3456 )` should have the value 0.3456. Write a driver and test your function. (Hint: You may want to use Pascal's `Trunc` function in writing your function.)

7. Design and write a program to investigate what happens in your Pascal system if a program tries to display the values of `Succ( MaxInt )`, `Pred( -MaxInt )`, and `Pred( -MaxInt-1 )`.

8. Design and write a program to investigate whether your Pascal system implements the `MOD` as described in the text, or whether `(I MOD J)` merely computes the remainder.

8.3 CASE STUDY: DISPLAYING INTEGERS IN BINARY

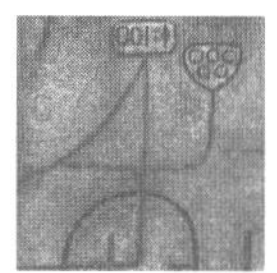

As an example of integer operations encapsulated as procedures, we will design a program that displays nonnegative integers in binary notation. (This is reviewed in Appendix J.) *First we plan the I/O,* which might look like this:

```
CONVERTING DECIMAL TO BINARY

Nonnegative integer? 100

100 decimal = 01100100 binary.
```

Use the I/O to develop a rough plan.

As you can see from the sample I/O, the algorithm will involve four major steps:

1. Show the purpose of the program.
2. Prompt for and read a suitable integer.
3. Convert to binary.
4. Display the results.

Then trace the state transitions and specify the encapsulations.

Looking carefully at this rough plan, we can see that step 2 will return a value to a variable that we will name `DecimalInt`. Step 3 receives this value and converts its value to binary, storing the result in a variable we will name `BinaryInt`. Using these two variables, we can plan the program's state transitions in a little more detail:

1. **Preconditions:** Nothing has been displayed;
   `DecimalInt` and `BinaryInt` contain garbage.

   ShowPurpose procedure
   (no parameters)
   encapsulates:

   ```
   WriteLn( 'CONVERTING DECIMAL TO BINARY' );
   WriteLn
   ```

   Postconditions: Purpose has been announced;
   the variables contain garbage values.

2. **GetDecimal procedure**
   (out-parameter) `DecimalInt`
   encapsulates:

   ```
   Write( 'Nonnegative integer? ' );
   ReadLn( DecimalInt );
   WHILE DecimalInt < 0 DO
   BEGIN
      Write( 'Nonnegative integer? ' );
      ReadLn( DecimalInt )
   END
   ```

   Postconditions: Purpose has been announced;
   `DecimalInt` has a value.

3. **BinaryOf function**
   (in-parameter) `DecimalInt`
   (returned function value) `BinaryOf`
   encapsulates:
   binary conversion of `DecimalInt` (algorithm not yet planned)

   Postconditions: Purpose has been announced;
   `DecimalInt` has a value;
   the bits representing the binary notation for
   `DecimalInt` have been returned and copied into `BinaryInt`.

4. **ShowDecAndBin procedure**
   (in-parameter) `DecimalInt`
   (in-parameter) `BinaryInt`
   encapsulates:

```
WriteLn;
WriteLn( DecimalInt, ' decimal = ',
         BinaryInt, ' binary' )
```

   Postconditions: Purpose has been announced;
   `DecimalInt` and `BinaryInt` have values;
   the bits of `BinaryInt` have been displayed.

Test first with a stub.

At this point, we have enough detail to write the skeleton of the program and to implement the easier procedures. We initially use a stub in place of the decimal-to-binary conversion procedure:

```
PROGRAM DecToBin( Input, Output );
{ Converts a nonnegative decimal integer to binary. }
VAR
   DecimalInt, BinaryInt : Integer;


PROCEDURE ShowPurpose;
{
  POSTCONDITIONS:
  The purpose of the program has been displayed
  on the screen.
}
BEGIN

   WriteLn( 'CONVERTING DECIMAL TO BINARY');
   WriteLn

END; { ShowPurpose }
```

```
PROCEDURE GetDecimal( VAR DecimalInt : Integer );
{
  POSTCONDITIONS:
  DecimalInt has a value.
}
BEGIN

   Write( 'Nonnegative integer: ' );
   ReadLn( DecimalInt );
   WHILE DecimalInt < 0 DO
   BEGIN
      Write( 'Nonnegative integer: ' );
      ReadLn( DecimalInt )
   END

END; { GetDecimal }


FUNCTION BinaryOf( Dec : Integer ) : Integer;
{
  PRECONDITIONS:
  Dec has been initialized.

  POSTCONDITIONS:
  Function returns the binary notation for Dec.
}
BEGIN

   WriteLn( 'BinaryOf IS ONLY A STUB.' );
   BinaryOf := 0

END; { BinaryOf }


PROCEDURE ShowDecAndBin( Dec, Bin : Integer );
{
  PRECONDITIONS:
  Dec and Bin have been initialized.

  POSTCONDITIONS:
  Dec and Bin have been displayed on the screen.
}
BEGIN

   WriteLn;
   WriteLn( Dec, ' decimal = ', Bin, ' binary' )

END; { ShowDecAndBin }
```

```
BEGIN { main program }

   ShowPurpose;
   GetDecimal( DecimalInt );
   BinaryInt := BinaryOf( DecimalInt );
   ShowDecAndBin( DecimalInt, BinaryInt )

END.
```

Incremental testing

Before going further, we compile to check for syntax errors. (Do it!) If all is correct, we run the program and see I/O like this:

```
CONVERTING DECIMAL TO BINARY

Nonnegative integer? 100
BinaryOf IS ONLY A STUB.

     100 decimal =          0 binary
```

The decimal-to-binary conversion

Now comes the hard part: converting a decimal integer *d* to binary. Recall from Appendix J that the lowest bit of binary is the remainder of the division *d* `DIV 2`—that is, *d* `MOD 2`. Then we replace *d* by the quotient *d* `DIV 2` and compute *d* `MOD 2`, which is the next higher bit. We continue in this way until *d* `DIV 2` becomes zero. Then we display the *d* `MOD 2` and quit. Using this method, here's how we convert 12 to binary:

12 `MOD` 2 = 0 (the first and least significant bit);
12 is replaced by (12 `DIV` 2) = 6;

6 `MOD` 2 = 0 (the second bit);
6 is replaced by (6 `DIV` 2) = 3;

3 `MOD` 2 = 1 (the third bit);
3 is replaced by (3 `DIV` 2) = 1;

1 `MOD` 2 = 1 (the fourth and most significant bit);
1 is replaced by (1 `DIV` 2) = 0.

The result is that the decimal integer 12 is written in binary notation as `1100`. Here's the algorithm in pseudocode:

While *d* > 0, do the following:
  Compute the latest bit as *d* `MOD 2`;
  Replace *d* by *d* `MOD 2`.

Then the most significant bit is *d*.

When things get awkward

But wait! There's a problem here. The binary digits are generated from right to left, and we want to display them from left to right. What can we do about this? In Chapter 14, you will see how to store all the bits in a subscripted variable, so they can be displayed in any order by scanning the subscripts. Using only what we know so far, we could use one variable for each bit, but this seems very awkward.

> When an algorithm leads you into an awkward situation, there is probably a better algorithm to be found.

Don't settle for your first idea.

A little thought results in a better idea: If our previous algorithm has yielded its bits in the reverse of the desired order, maybe we can reverse the order in which the bits are generated. A little more thought leads to the realization that, if the bits were generated from left to right, we could display them one by one, as they were generated. Then we wouldn't need to save them before displaying them. The same procedure that generated them could display them, and this would simplify the program.

To start from the most significant end of the bit pattern, we first compute the largest possible power-of-2 contribution to the given number, display it as a 1 or 0, and subtract it from the value of the number. Then we compute the next-largest power-of-2 contribution, display it, subtract it, and so on. For example, if `MaxInt` is 32,767, as it is on many Pascal systems, the largest power of 2 that can contribute to an integer is 16,384, the next largest is 8,192, and so on, through declining powers of 2: 4,096, 2,048, 1,024, 512, 256, 128, 64, 32, 16, 8, 4, and finally, 2. The sequence of computation is:

The leftmost digit is (`Number DIV 16384`); display it.
  The remainder of this division is
    `Remainder := (Number MOD 16384).`

The next digit is (`Remainder DIV 8192`); display it.
  The remainder of this division is
    `Remainder := (Remainder MOD 8192).`

The next digit is (`Remainder DIV 4096`); display it.

And so on, until
The next digit is (`Remainder DIV 2`); display it.
  The remainder of this division is
    `Remainder := (Remainder MOD 2).`

Finally, the last digit is `Remainder`; display it.

An example

For example, if `Number` is 100, the computation produces the results shown in the table on the next page:

Step	Value produced	Bit displayed
`100 DIV 16384`	0	0
`Remainder := 100 MOD 16384`	100	
`100 DIV 8192`	0	0
`Remainder := 100 MOD 8192`	100	

and similarly, all bits are 0 until the power-of-2 divisor becomes 64:

Step	Value produced	Bit displayed
`100 DIV 64`	1	1
`Remainder := 100 MOD 64`	36	
`36 DIV 32`	1	1
`Remainder := 36 MOD 32`	4	
`4 DIV 16`	0	0
`Remainder := 4 MOD 16`	4	
`4 DIV 8`	0	0
`Remainder := 4 MOD 8`	4	
`4 DIV 4`	1	1
`Remainder := 4 MOD 4`	0	
`0 DIV 2`	0	0
`Remainder := 0 MOD 2`	0	
`Remainder is 0`	0	0

With the bits displayed left to right, just as they are generated, the displayed value is `000000001100100`.

Coding this algorithm directly, we can have a somewhat different `ShowDecAndBin` procedure than shown previously:

```
PROCEDURE ShowDecAndBin( Number : Integer );
{
  PRECONDITION:
  Number >= 0;

  POSTCONDITION:
  The decimal and binary representations of Number have been
  displayed on the screen.
}
VAR
   PowerOfTwo, Remainder : Integer;

BEGIN

   WriteLn;
   Write( Number:3, ' is the same as ' );
```

```
   PowerOfTwo := MaxPowerOfTwo;
   Remainder  := Number;
   WHILE PowerOfTwo > 1 DO
   BEGIN
      Write( (Remainder DIV PowerOfTwo):1 );
      Remainder := Remainder MOD PowerOfTwo;
      PowerOfTwo := PowerOfTwo DIV 2
   END;

   Write( Remainder:1, ' binary' )

END; { ShowDecAndBin }
```

Note that this procedure requires a previously defined constant, `MaxPowerOfTwo`, which must be the largest power of 2 that is less than or equal to `MaxInt`.

Sequence of execution and termination of the loop

Consider for a moment how this loop runs. If, for example, `MaxPowerOfTwo` is `16384` and `Number` is `100`, successive trips through the loop body take the following actions:

First trip has `PowerOfTwo = 16384` and `Remainder = 100`:
Write 1;
`Remainder  := 100;`
`PowerOfTwo := 8192`

Second trip has `PowerOfTwo = 8192` and `Remainder = 100`:
Write 1;
`Remainder  := 100;`
`PowerOfTwo := 8192`

and so on. `PowerOfTwo` decreases toward 1, and this eventually stops the loop.

Exercises

9. Replace the `BinaryOf` function and `ShowDecAndBin` procedure in the `DecToBin` program skeleton with the `ShowDecAndBin` procedure shown above, remove the `BinaryInt` variable, and define a `MaxPowerOfTwo` constant. Demonstrate that the program runs correctly.

10. Design and write a procedure that displays a given one-byte integer in octal (base 8) notation. (See Appendix J.) Note that each octal digit corresponds to a group of three bits.

11. Write a procedure that goes with the `ShowDecAndBin` procedure to calculate `MaxPowerOfTwo` automatically from `MaxInt`.

8.4 CHARACTER DATA

Just as Pascal's integer numbers can be enumerated, the characters used in text processing can be enumerated. A **character** is just that: a *single* character: a letter of the alphabet in upper- or lowercase, a punctuation mark or other special symbol, a digit, or a special **control character** (like control-C or control-Z) used to control computer software or hardware. You can use any of the characters defined in the *character set* provided with your Pascal system. Usually, this is the International Standards Organization (ISO) set, of which the American variant is called the American Standard Code for Information Interchange (ASCII, pronounced ass'-key). A few mainframe systems use IBM's Extended Binary-Coded Decimal Interchange Code (EBCDIC, pronounced ebb'-sih-dick) instead. Both of these character sets are listed in Appendix C. In a given character set, the first-listed character has ordinal value 0, the next character has ordinal value 1, and so on. The ASCII set has ordinal values 0 through 127, while the EBCDIC set has ordinal values 0 through 255.

Character constants

A **character constant** is written as a single symbol enclosed in apostrophes:

`'a'`	
`'A'`	
`' '`	(The *space* or *blank* character)
`'1'`	(The numeral "1," distinct from the integer 1)
`'.'`	(The *period* character)
`'"'`	(The *quotation mark* character)

Don't confuse a numeral character like `'1'` and an integer like 1. An integer can be used for arithmetic while a character is intended for text processing. (As we've said before, the real meaning of a data type lies in the operations that can be applied to it.)

The following are *illegal* as character constants in Pascal:

`7`	(This is an integer, not a character.)
`"7"`	(Double quotation marks not allowed; must use apostrophes.)

The apostrophe character

apostrophes

Delimit: To mark off the beginning or end.

The apostrophe character is a special case. Since apostrophes are used to **delimit** (mark off) all character constants, we specify the apostrophe character itself by enclosing within apostrophes *two* apostrophes—an "apostrophe apostrophe." For example, if your program executes `WriteLn( '''' )`, you will see the single character `'` on the screen. If it executes `WriteLn( 'What''s up?' )`, you will see `What's up?` on the screen.

Declaring character constants and variables

Character constants are declared in the same manner as other constants.

```
CONST
   BigH    = 'H';
   LittleH = 'h';
```

Character variables are declared to be of type `Char`. For example, for a variable for storing a person's first initial, the declaration might be

```
VAR
   FirstInitial : Char;
```

The ordinal properties of characters

Pascal's set of characters is system-dependent, but whatever set your system uses, it defines the ordered list of characters for your Pascal compiler. The character set is related to the integers 0, 1, 2, 3, . . . by means of the character code, which associates with each character a code number, called its **ordinal value**. Pascal provides a standard `Ord` function to compute the ordinal value for any character. (Actually, `Ord` can be applied to any ordinal value, whether character, integer, or boolean.) Here are some examples for upper- and lowercase letters and numerals:

Expression	Value when using ASCII	Value when using EBCDIC
`Ord( 'A' )`	65	193
`Ord( 'B' )`	66	194
⋮	⋮	⋮
`Ord( 'Z' )`	90	233
`Ord( 'a' )`	97	129
`Ord( 'b' )`	98	130
⋮	⋮	⋮
`Ord( 'z' )`	122	169
`Ord( '0' )`	48	240
`Ord( '1' )`	49	241
⋮	⋮	⋮
`Ord( '9' )`	57	249

Pascal places few constraints on the ordinal values of characters:

- The numeral digits must be in numerical order and contiguous.
- The uppercase and lowercase letters must be in alphabetic order but not necessarily contiguous.
- There are no other constraints.

There is no requirement that uppercase letters come before lowercase, or that numerals come before letters. As you can see from the table above, ASCII lists numerals before letters, and uppercase letters before lowercase. EBCDIC, on the other hand, lists lowercase letters before uppercase, and uppercase letters before numerals. There is not even a fixed number of characters: the ASCII codes range from 0 through 127, while the EBCDIC codes range from 0 through 255. These differences will cause us some trouble when we try to write **portable** text-processing procedures—procedures that can be run on a wide range of computer systems.

Portable software: Software capable of being used on a wide range of computer systems without change.

Converting characters to integers and vice versa

The `Ord` function performs a character-to-integer conversion. The reverse conversion can be accomplished with the `Chr` function, which converts a nonnegative integer to the character for which it is the code number:

Expression	Value in ASCII	Value in EBCDIC
`Chr(50)`	`'2'`	Undefined
`Chr(67)`	`'C'`	Undefined
`Chr(99)`	`'c'`	Undefined
`Chr(131)`	Undefined	`'c'`
`Chr(209)`	Undefined	`'J'`
`Chr(242)`	Undefined	`'2'`

The `Ord` and `Chr` functions can be considered to be *type-transfer functions*, converting character to integer or integer to character. As with other ordinal types, the `Pred` and `Succ` functions can be used to compute the predecessor and successor of values. For example, `Pred('b')` is `'a'`, while `Succ('b')` is `'c'`.

Formatting character output

When writing characters to `Output`, each character is displayed by default in a field just wide enough for it. However, you can also format output by specifying a wider field width, in which case extra spaces are inserted to the left of the character. For example, the statement `WriteLn( 'A', 'B':2, 'C':3 )` prints `'A'` in a field one space wide, but `'B'` in a field two spaces wide and `'C'` in a field three spaces wide:

```
A B  C
```

One useful application is to insert spaces between data values. For example, the statement

```
WriteLn( 'Name', ' ':6, 'Address' )
```

inserts six spaces between `'Name'` and `'Address'`:

```
Name      Address
```

Reading character data

Reading from text files (like `Input`) into character variables is easy because text files consist entirely of characters, so no conversion is needed. A `Read` or `ReadLn` reads the next character datum into the character parameter variable. Because whitespace characters *are* characters, they are read like any other. Thus, no delimiters are possible between successive character values in a text file.

For example, when using `Read( Ch1, Ch2 )` to read values into character variables `Ch1` and `Ch2`, if the user enters

```
H<EOLn>O<EOLn>W<EOLn>
```

the `Ch1` variable gets the value `'H'` and `Ch2` gets `<EOLn>`, and the next character to be read will be `'O'`. On the other hand, if `ReadLn(Ch1, Ch2)` reads

```
H<EOLn>O<EOLn>W<EOLn>
```

the `Ch1` variable gets the value `'H'` and `Ch2` gets `<EOLn>`, and the `ReadLn` discards everything through the next `<EOLn>`, including the `'O'`. Therefore, the next character to be read later will be `'W'`, not `'O'`.

Reading end-of-line

As an aside, we mention a peculiarity of Pascal's processing of characters when reading from text files. When reading the end-of-line signal `<EOLn>` from the keyboard, most Pascals store a space—ASCII 32—in the variable, not an `<EOLn>`.

8.5 CASE STUDY: MAPPING LOWERCASE LETTERS TO UPPERCASE

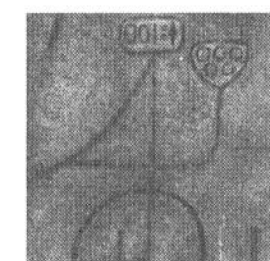

Pascal does not provide many character operations or functions, so we will often need to build our own. As a first example, let's build a function that converts any lowercase letter to uppercase. In working on this function, you will become more familiar with the nonportability of character manipulations in Pascal: that is, the difficulty in getting character manipulations to run the same on different computer systems. We begin by writing a driver to test the proposed function.

```
PROGRAM TestLowerToUpper( Input, Output );
{ Driver for testing the UpperCase function }

VAR
   Letter : Char;


FUNCTION Upper( Ch : Char ) : Char;
{
  PRECONDITION:
  Ch has been initialized.

  POSTCONDITION:
  If Ch is a lower-case letter, Upper is the corresponding
  upper-case letter; otherwise, Upper = Ch.
}
BEGIN

   WriteLn( 'Function Upper is just a stub.' );
   Upper := Ch

END; { Upper }


BEGIN { driver }

   Write( 'Lowercase letter? ' );
   ReadLn( Letter );

   WriteLn( 'Sending ', Letter, ' to Upper...' );
   Letter := Upper( Letter );
   WriteLn( 'Received ', Letter, ' from Upper.' )

END.
```

This driver calls `Upper` in an assignment statement, replacing the old value of `Letter` with the value returned by the function. Initially, we test the driver with a stub function. In order to *really* test the skeleton, the function must assign some value to the function name, so we have chosen for it to return the same character it was given. If everything is okay so far, the program will compile and we will see I/O like the sample below:

```
Lowercase letter? a
Sending a to Upper...
Function Upper is just a stub.
Received a from Upper.
```

When the stub is working, add the encapsulation.

Now it is time to work out code for the operation that should be encapsulated by the function. Notice first of all that the postconditions stated in the skeleton say that the function is supposed to map `Ch` to uppercase only if it is a lowercase letter; otherwise, the function is supposed to return `Ch`. To do this, we need a decision structure:

```
IF Ch is a lowercase letter THEN
   Return the uppercase equivalent of Ch
ELSE
   Return Ch
```

How do we perform the mapping when `Ch` is a lowercase letter? In the character code charts in Appendix C, it is apparent that both ASCII and EBCDIC are designed so that there is a constant shift between lower- and uppercase. In ASCII, we can map a lowercase letter to uppercase by subtracting 32 from its ordinal value. EBCDIC appears more complicated at first because of the gaps between groups of letters, but in fact each uppercase letter can be obtained from the corresponding lowercase letter by adding 64 to its ordinal value. All we need to do in either case is to shift the ordinal value of `Ch` by some constant amount, depending on the character code being used. The ordinal-value shift would be accomplished by

```
Ord( Ch ) + Shift
```

where `Shift` is an appropriate constant. The character corresponding to the shifted ordinal value would be

```
Chr( Ord( Ch ) + Shift )
```

If the program is written in this way, the value of `Shift` will depend on the character code in use, so we will need one version of the function for ASCII and another for EBCDIC. To avoid this, we can compute the shift on the fly:

```
Chr( Ord( LCLetter ) + Ord( 'A' ) - Ord( 'a' ) )
```

The resulting function is shown on the next page:

```
FUNCTION Upper( Ch : Char ) : Char;
{
  PRECONDITION:
  Ch has been initialized.

  POSTCONDITION:
  If Ch is a lowercase letter, Upper is the corresponding
  uppercase letter; otherwise, Upper = Ch.
}
BEGIN

   IF ( 'a' <= Ch ) AND ( Ch <= 'z' ) THEN
      Upper := Chr( Ord( Ch ) + Ord( 'A' ) - Ord( 'a' ) )

   ELSE
      Upper := Ch

END { Upper };
```

Note the expression that controls the decision structure. It uses an AND operator—something we haven't seen before. Expressions like this one are the subject of the next section.

Questions

12. Which of the following are illegal character constants? Why?

    `a   abc   'a'   'abc'   7   '7'   '78'   'A"   "ABC"   '?'`

13. What are the differences among `'7'` stored in a character variable, 7 stored in an integer variable, and `7.0` stored in a real variable? Explain in your own words.

14. In what way does the `Upper` function fail to conform to its stated postconditions when the Pascal system uses EBCDIC?

Exercises

15. What happens on your computer system if a program writes `Chr(7)` to the screen? (If your system uses EBCDIC, send `Chr(47)` instead.)

16. Write a small program that prompts for and reads a character from the keyboard, and then displays the character along with its ordinal value. Such a program is useful when testing control characters, end-of-file signals, etc. See Appendix C for complete lists of the ASCII and EBCDIC character sets, including control characters.

17. Write a function called `Encipherment` that takes a given character and returns the character `Shift` ordinal values above it, where `Shift` is a globally declared constant. In order to prevent the encipherment process from running off the top of the character code chart, you will have to use modulus arithmetic, so that ordinal values higher than the highest possible "wrap around" to the lowest. For example, if your system uses the ASCII code, the ordinal value 128 will have to wrap around to become 0, ordinal value 129 will have to become 1, and so on. Test your function by using it to shift characters by +3, so that the message `'How now?'` becomes, in ASCII, `'Krz#qrzB'`.

18. Write a `Decipherment` function that deciphers the output from the `Encipherment` function described in Exercise 17.

8.6 BOOLEAN DATA

Now we come to a type of data that is less familiar to some readers. `Boolean` data can have only two values: `False` and `True`. In other words, it is "logical" data, used to signal the truth or falsity of some proposition or condition. Thus there are only two `Boolean` constants, having ordinal values 0 and 1, respectively:

```
False
True
```

Note also that the two allowed `Boolean` values are not in apostrophes because they are predefined constants in the Pascal language. (The words themselves are not reserved, but are merely predefined identifiers.)

Because `False` and `True` occur in that order as the only two allowed `Boolean` constants, we have

```
Succ( False ) = True,          Pred( True ) = False,
Ord( False )  = 0,             Ord( True )  = 1.
```

Declaring Boolean constants and variables

`Boolean` constants are declared in the usual way:

```
CONST
  Lie = False;
```

Similarly with variables. If you want a variable named `Finished`, you declare

```
VAR
  Finished : Boolean;
```

Placing values in Boolean variables

In Standard Pascal, you cannot read `Boolean` values from the keyboard. There is no particular reason for this; it is merely a shortcoming of the `Read` and `ReadLn` procedures. (Some Pascal systems allow it.) In the next chapter, you will learn how to design your own input procedures for `Boolean` values. Meanwhile, we will assign values to the variables.

Boolean expressions

Boolean values are usually encountered in programs as the values of `Boolean` expressions, which are Pascal's version of logical propositions. Science is full of propositions. We say, "The angle is less than π radians," or "The weights are not equal," or "Acceleration is positive." Such propositions are either true or false, so they are unambiguous statements of fact. Propositions of this form are simply comparisons (or tests of relationships), and can be evaluated in Pascal by one of the **relational operators** shown in Table 8.6.1. (These were discussed briefly in Section 6.1.)

Relational operators. **Table 8.6.1**

Relational operator	Meaning
=	Equal
<>	Not equal
<	Less than
<=	Less than or equal to
>	Greater than
>=	Greater than or equal to

A relational operator can *compare two values of similar types*. Thus we can compare integers with integers, reals with reals, characters with characters, or booleans with booleans. The only cross-comparison allowed is integers with reals. (This is not good style, however!) Table 8.6.2 shows some legal relational `Boolean` expressions:

Relational expressions involving numbers. **Table 8.6.2**

Expression	Meaning	Value
`4 <= 5`	4 less than or equal to 5	`True`
`4 <> 4`	4 not equal to 4	`False`
`4.0 = 4`	real 4.0 equals integer 4	`True`
`4.0 >= 4.0`	4.0 greater than or equal to 4.0	`True`
`4.0 > 5.0`	4.0 greater than 5.0	`False`

The third example tests for equality between a real 4.0 and an integer 4. The integer number is automatically converted to real before the test is performed.

We can also compare characters for their order in the character code being used. Because of the properties of character sets mentioned in Section 8.4, we have the situations shown in Table 8.6.3:

Relational expressions involving characters. **Table 8.6.3**

Expression	Meaning	Value
`'B' > 'A'`	`'B'` greater than `'A'`	`True`
`'g' < 'h'`	`'g'` less than `'h'`	`True`
`'1' < '2'`	`'1'` less than `'2'`	`True`
`'B' = 'b'`	`'B'` equals `'b'`	`False`
`'B' <> 'b'`	`'B'` not equal to `'b'`	`True`
`'B' > 'a'`	`'B'` greater than `'a'`	(Depends on character code)
`'B' > '1'`	`'B'` greater than `'1'`	(Depends on character code)
`'?' > '!'`	`'?'` greater than `'!'`	(Depends on character code)

Similarly, character strings *of the same length* can be compared in the following sense: String A equals string B only if all the characters are the same; string A is less than string B if, in the first position containing differing characters, the character in A is less than the character in B. The result is a lexical ordering of strings, as shown in Table 8.6.4.

Table 8.6.4 *Relational expressions involving strings.*

Expression	Meaning	Value
'march' > 'april'	'march' greater than 'april'	True because 'm' > 'a'
'apr' > 'may'	'apr' greater than 'may'	False because 'a' < 'm'
'lover' < 'loves'	'lover' less than 'loves'	True because 'r' < 's'
'love' < 'loving'	'love' less than 'loving'	Cannot be compared because lengths differ

Boolean values can be compared because Pascal requires that False and True have ordinal values 0 and 1, respectively. The results are shown in Table 8.6.5.

Table 8.6.5 *Relational expressions involving booleans.*

Expression	Meaning	Value
False < True	False less than True	True
True <= False	True less than or equal to False	False
False <> True	False not equal to True	True
False = False	False equals False	True

Examples of relational Boolean expressions

Returning now to the examples of scientific propositions listed previously, suppose that we have a real constant named Pi and real variables named Angle, Weight1, Weight2, and Acceleration. Assume also that these variables have been assigned values. Then we could compute the True or False values of the propositions by writing appropriate relational expressions, as shown in Table 8.6.6.

Table 8.6.6 *Relational expressions involving variables.*

Proposition	Corresponding Boolean expression
The angle is less than π radians.	Angle < Pi
The weights are not equal.	Weight1 <> Weight2
Acceleration is positive.	Acceleration > 0.0

Formatting Boolean output

The exact form and default field width for printed boolean values is system-dependent. Normally, the words `'True'` and `'False'` are displayed, though the use of upper- or lowercase may vary. You can format Boolean output by specifying the field width. If it is too wide, extra spaces are inserted to the left of the output; if too narrow, only some of the characters are printed. For example, if `Finished` is `True`, then `WriteLn( Finished, ' ':3, Finished:1 )` displays

```
True   T
```

Reading Boolean data

In Standard Pascal, `Boolean` values cannot be read from the keyboard.

Compound Boolean expressions

We often make more complex propositions, as when we say, "The angle is less than π radians *and* the acceleration is positive." This combines two relational propositions by means of the `AND` operator. Or we might say, "The angle is less than π radians *or* the acceleration is positive," which is a different proposition, using the `OR` operator. Or, for a more complicated example, we might say, "It is *not true that* the angle is less than π radians and the acceleration is positive." All of these are compound propositions, in which relational propositions are combined by means of the `Boolean` operators `NOT`, `AND`, and `OR`. These operators will be familiar to readers who have studied logic (Table 8.6.7).

Boolean operators. **Table 8.6.7**

Name of operation	Symbol
Negation	`NOT`
Conjunction	`AND`
Disjunction	`OR`

The **negation operator**, `NOT`, operates on a single `Boolean` operand, and is therefore said to be a *unary* operator: If `B` is a `Boolean` value, the negation of `B` is `NOT B`. The `NOT` operator changes a `True` into a `False`, or a `False` into a `True`. We can summarize this in the form of a table showing the two possibilities. This is called a **truth table**, and is shown in Table 8.6.8.

Truth table for the NOT operator. **Table 8.6.8**

B	NOT B
`True`	`False`
`False`	`True`

Conjunction and **disjunction**, on the other hand, are binary operators, taking two operands. An expression of the form `( Operand1 AND Operand2 )` is `True` only if both `Operand1` *and* `Operand2` are `True`. Thus the truth table for the `AND` operator has four rows, as shown in Table 8.6.9.

Table 8.6.9 *Truth table for the AND (conjunction) operator.*

B1	B2	B1 AND B2
True	True	True
True	False	False
False	True	False
False	False	False

An expression of the form `( Operand1 OR Operand2 )` is `True` if `Operand1` is `True` *or* `Operand2` is `True`, *or both*. Otherwise, this expression is `False`. This is shown in Table 8.6.10.

Table 8.6.10 *Truth table for the OR (disjunction) operator.*

B1	B2	B1 OR B2
True	True	True
True	False	True
False	True	True
False	False	False

Precedence of Boolean operators

There are four levels of precedence among `Boolean` operators, if we include relational operators. These are shown in Table 8.6.11.

Table 8.6.11 *Order of precedence of Boolean operators.*

Precedence	Operators
Highest	`NOT`
	`AND`
	`OR`
Lowest	`=   <>   <   <=   >   >=`

Examples of compound Boolean expressions

Returning to our previous examples, suppose that we have a real constant named `Pi` (which is 3.14159) and real variables named `Angle` and `Acceleration`. Assume also that these variables have the values 1.5 and –15.55, respectively. Then we can evaluate the `Boolean` expressions corresponding to the compound propositions listed earlier:

Proposition:
"The angle is less than π radians *and* the acceleration is positive."
Boolean expression:
`(Angle < Pi) AND (Acceleration > 0.0)`
Value:
`True AND False`, which is `False`.

Proposition:
"The angle is less than π radians *or* the acceleration is positive."
Boolean expression:
`(Angle < Pi) OR (Acceleration > 0.0)`
Value:
`True OR False`, which is `True`.

Proposition:
"It is *not true* that the angle is less than π radians
and the acceleration is positive."
Boolean expression:
`NOT ( (Angle < Pi) AND (Acceleration > 0.0) )`
Value:
`NOT(True AND False)`, which is `NOT(False)`, or `True`.

Try it out!

As always, the best way to become familiar with this is to try it in a program. Run the following program on your Pascal system. See if you can predict its output.

```
PROGRAM Logic ( Output );
VAR
   Logical1, Logical2 : Boolean;

BEGIN
   Logical1 := True;
   Logical2 := NOT Logical1;
   Write( 'Logical1 is ', Logical1 );
   WriteLn( ' and its negation is ', Logical2 );
   WriteLn( '( Logical1 AND Logical2 ) is ',
            Logical1 AND Logical2 );
   WriteLn( '( Logical1 OR Logical2 ) is ',
            Logical1 OR Logical2 );
   WriteLn( 'NOT( Logical1 AND Logical2 ) is ',
            NOT( Logical1 AND Logical2 ) )

END.
```

Since `Logical1` is assigned the value `True`, `Logical2` is assigned the value `NOT True`, which is `False`. So your output should look like this:

```
Logical1 is true and its negation is false
( Logical1 AND Logical2 ) is false
( Logical1 OR Logical2 ) is true
NOT( Logical1 AND Logical2 ) is true
```

Some Pascals will print "T" in place of "true" and "F" in place of "false," but you should see something of this form.

Don't compare real numbers for equality.

This is a good place to reiterate that real numbers are usually rounded off when stored in the computer, and therefore are not stored exactly. As a result, real numbers that are exactly equal in mathematics are often not exactly equal in a computer. For example, the following Boolean expression is likely to be `False`:

```
( (2.0 / 3.0) - (1.0 / 3.0) - (1.0 / 3.0) ) = 0.0
```

Therefore, it is poor style to check two real numbers for equality or inequality.

DeMorgan's laws

In evaluating compound `Boolean` expressions that combine `NOT` with `AND` or `NOT` with `R`, it is often useful to know two equivalencies pointed out by the mathematician Augustus DeMorgan in 1847:

`NOT( B1 AND B2 )` is equivalent to `( NOT B1 ) OR ( NOT B2 )`

`NOT( B1 OR B2 )` is equivalent to `( NOT B1 ) AND ( NOT B2 )`

These are called **DeMorgan's laws**. The first law says that the proposition "It is not the case that both B1 and B2 are true" is the same as asserting that "Either B1 is not true or B2 is not true, or both." The second says that "It is not the case that B1 or B2 is true or that both are true" is the same as "B1 is not true and B2 is not true."

If you think carefully about these English propositions, you can convince yourself that DeMorgan's laws are valid. However, the real reason we know they are valid is that we can *prove* them. Table 8.6.12 demonstrates the validity of the first law by showing that `NOT(B1 AND B2)` has exactly the same truth value as `(NOT B1) OR (NOT B2)`, no matter

Table 8.6.12 *Proving the equivalence of NOT(B1 AND B2) and (NOT B1) OR (NOT B2).*

B1	B2	B1 AND B2	NOT(B1 AND B2)	NOT B1	NOT B2	(NOT B1) OR (NOT B2)
T	T	T	F	F	F	F
T	F	F	T	F	T	T
F	T	F	T	T	F	T
F	F	F	T	T	T	T

(These two columns are equivalent.)

what the values of B1 and B2. Since the two compound expressions have the same truth value in every case, they are logically equivalent.

Boolean functions that detect <EOLn> and <EOF>

Pascal provides two standard Boolean functions that are useful in the control of inputs from files. The first is called EOLn, and is used to detect end-of-line signals, <EOLn>s, in the input stream from a text file. The other is called EOF, and is used to detect end-of-file signals, <EOF>s, in the input stream from any file.

Since the EOLn function detects end-of-line signals, it can be used only with text files like the standard Input file. The EOLn function looks ahead in the text file, examining the next unread datum in the input buffer. If that datum is <EOLn>, the function returns True; otherwise, it returns False. Thus, the following code would read characters from the Input file into the Ch variable and display their ordinal values, up to, but not including, the end-of-line signal:

```
VAR
   Ch : Char;

BEGIN

   WHILE NOT EOLn DO
   BEGIN
      Read( Ch );
      Write( Ord(Ch) )
   END;

   WriteLn;
   ...
```

Similarly, the EOF function looks ahead in the input buffer and reports, True or False, whether the next unread datum in the buffer is the end-of-file signal:

```
   WHILE NOT EOF DO
   BEGIN
      Read( Num );
      ...
   END;
```

We will make some interesting use of this function in Chapter 12.

Exercises

19. Determine the values of the following Boolean expressions, assuming that we have already run the fragment of initialization code shown below. Test your conclusions by compiling and running test programs.

```
VAR
   Year : Integer;
   Cost : Real;
   Ch   : Char;
   Taxpayer : Boolean;
```

```
BEGIN
   Year := 1994;
   Cost := 32.75;
   Ch   := 'h';
   Taxpayer := True;
```

Expression	Value
a. `(Year - 1988) <> 4`	________
b. `(Year - 1988) * Cost <= 200.0`	________
c. `'a' = Ch`	________
d. `(Ord(Ch) - Ord('a')) <> 2`	________

20. Modify the `Logic` program to test the values of `NOT( NOT( Logical2 ) )` and `(NOT( Logical1 )) AND (NOT( Logical2 ))`.

21. Write a small program to test the assertion made in the text, that the ordinal value of `False` is 0 and the ordinal value of `True` is 1.

22. What are the values of the following `Boolean` expressions?

a. `( Length >= 24.0 ) OR ( Length < 24.0 )`

b. `( Class <> 'C' ) AND ( Class = 'C' )`

c. `( Classification = 'S' ) OR ( NOT Precision )`

d. `NOT ( ( Length <> 12.0 ) AND ( Cost < 2.0 ) )`

23. Using a truth table similar to Table 8.6.12, prove that the second of DeMorgan's laws is valid in all possible cases.

24. Write a program to confirm that DeMorgan's laws are valid in all possible cases. Have your program show equivalence by printing a truth table of all possible cases, similar to Table 8.6.12.

25. Write a `Boolean` function called `IsFirstQuadrant` that indicates whether a given real number angle in radians is in the first quadrant. For the purpose of this exercise, all angles from 0 through $\pi/2$, inclusive, are considered to be in the first quadrant. Write a driver and test your function.

26. Match the English sentences to the `Boolean` expressions. Each sentence has one and only one best match.

___ "I don't drink and drive."	**a.** `B1 OR ( NOT B2 )`
___ "B1 but not B2."	**b.** `(NOT Drink) AND (NOT Drive)`
	c. `B1 AND ( NOT B2 )`
	d. `(NOT Drink) OR (NOT Drive)`

27. In evaluating the expression `(B1 AND B2)`, there is no need to evaluate `B2` when `B1` has already been found to be false, for then the whole expression must be false. Similarly, in evaluating the expression `(B1 OR B2)`, there is no need to evaluate `B2` when `B1` has already been found to be true, for then the whole expression must be true. Does your Pascal system take advantage of these shortcuts? (This is called *shortcircuiting the evaluation*.) Devise a way to perform an experimental test and carry it out. Report your findings.

8.7 CASE STUDY: CHARACTER-PROPERTY FUNCTIONS

We can explore the properties of the Boolean operators AND and OR by writing some useful Boolean functions that report on different kinds of characters. In particular, we will create

- IsLowerCase, a Boolean function that reports whether a given character is a lowercase letter.
- IsUpperCase, a Boolean function that reports whether a given character is an uppercase letter.
- IsDigit, a Boolean function that reports whether a given character is one of the digits '0' through '9'.
- IsLetter, a Boolean function that reports whether a given character is a letter.
- IsAlphanumeric, a Boolean function that reports whether a given character is an alphanumeric character, either letter or digit.

There is a hierarchy here because

- IsLetter will be True if and only if IsLowerCase or IsUpperCase is True.
- IsAlphanumeric will be True if and only if IsLetter or IsDigit is True.

At the lowest level of the hierarchy, IsLowerCase, IsUpperCase, and IsDigit each need only one Boolean expression to compute the value of the function. For example, if the Pascal system is using ASCII (see Exercise 30 for EBCDIC), the value of IsLowerCase, operating on a character Ch, is simply the value of the expression ((Ch >= 'a') AND (Ch <= 'z')). This value is then assigned to the IsLowerCase identifier as the value returned by the function. Note the assignment of the value of a Boolean expression to the identifier of the function:

```
FUNCTION IsLowerCase( Ch : Char ) : Boolean;
{
  PRECONDITION:
  Ch has an ASCII value.

  POSTCONDITION:
  IsLowerCase is True if Ch is a lowercase letter,
  and False otherwise. Ch is unchanged.
}
BEGIN

   IsLowerCase := (Ch >= 'a') AND (Ch <= 'z')

END; { IsLowerCase }
```

```
FUNCTION IsUpperCase( Ch : Char ) : Boolean;
{
  PRECONDITION:
  Ch has an ASCII value.

  POSTCONDITION:
  IsUpperCase is True if Ch is an uppercase letter,
  and False otherwise. Ch is unchanged.
}
BEGIN

   IsUpperCase := (Ch >= 'A') AND (Ch <= 'Z')

END; { IsUpperCase }


FUNCTION IsDigit( Ch : Char ) : Boolean;
{
  PRECONDITION:
  Ch has an ASCII value.

  POSTCONDITION:
  IsDigit is True if Ch is a digit,
  and False otherwise. Ch is unchanged.
}
BEGIN

   IsDigit := (Ch >= '0') AND (Ch <= '9')

END; { IsDigit }
```

With these lower-level building blocks, we can easily build the upper-level functions. For example, `IsLetter` should return the value of the `Boolean` expression

```
  (IsLowerCase( Ch ) OR IsUpperCase( Ch ))
```

So the final two functions are

```
FUNCTION IsLetter( Ch : Char ) : Boolean;
{
  PRECONDITION:
  Ch has an ASCII value.

  POSTCONDITION:
  IsLetter is True if Ch is a lower- or uppercase
  letter, and False otherwise. Ch is unchanged.
}
BEGIN

   IsLetter := IsLowerCase( Ch ) OR IsUpperCase( Ch )

END { IsLetter };
```

```
FUNCTION IsAlphanumeric( Ch : Char ) : Boolean;
{
  PRECONDITION:
  Ch has an ASCII value.

  POSTCONDITION:
  IsAlphanumeric is True if Ch is a letter or digit,
  and False otherwise. Ch is unchanged.
}
BEGIN

   IsAlphanumeric := IsLetter( Ch ) OR IsDigit( Ch )

END; { IsAlphanumeric }
```

The functions must be declared in the order shown because of their interdependence.

Exercises

28. Write Boolean expressions to accomplish the following tasks. (Do *not* use decision structures.)

- **a.** If the real Number is nonnegative and Ch has the value 'C', store False in the Boolean variable Error; otherwise, store True.
- **b.** If the real Angle is positive but the real Velocity is greater than 100, store True in the Boolean variable Fast; otherwise, store False.
- **c.** If the integer Count is even and divisible by 3, store True in the Boolean variable TwoAndThree; otherwise, store False.
- **d.** If the character Ch is a space (blank), horizontal tab, carriage return, line feed, vertical tab, or form feed, store the value True in the Boolean variable IsWhiteSpace; otherwise, store False.
- **e.** If it is not true that the angle is nonnegative, store True in the Boolean variable BadAngle; otherwise, store False.

29. Rewrite the IsLowerCase and IsUpperCase functions of this section so that they will work correctly with EBCDIC. (See Appendix C.) This will be more complicated than with ASCII because of gaps in the letter codes.

30. Write a driver and test the five functions of this section.

8.8 OPERATOR PRECEDENCE

In the preceding sections, you have seen operators for the manipulation of Real, Integer, and Boolean values. For each type the order of precedence of its operators was listed. Now we show the levels of precedence of *all* of Pascal's operators in Table 8.8.1.

Table 8.8.1 *Precedence of operators.*

Operators	Category	Precedence level	
`( )`	parentheses	Highest:	1
`NOT`	negation		2
`*, /, DIV, MOD, AND`	multiplicative		3
`+, -, OR`	additive		4
`=, <>, <, <=, >, >=, IN`	relational	Lowest:	5

(The `IN` operator listed here is the set-inclusion operator introduced later, in Section 18.2. It is included here only for the sake of completeness.)

Examples of precedence

If you understand the precedence of these operators, you should have no trouble evaluating mixed expressions. Here are some examples:

```
PROGRAM OpPrecedenceTest ( Output );
VAR
   Yes, No     : Boolean;
   Big, Small  : Integer;

BEGIN

   Yes   := True;
   No    := False;
   Big   := 7;
   Small := 3;

   { Here are some compound Boolean expressions      }
   { written in bad style, without parentheses,      }
   { to show the effects of operator precedence.     }
   { What do the following output statements write? }
   WriteLn( NOT Yes OR No );
   WriteLn( No AND NOT No );
   WriteLn( Small + Big MOD Small > Small DIV Big );
   WriteLn( Yes OR No AND NOT No OR Yes )

END.
```

The first expression is `NOT Yes OR No`. Here the `NOT` operator has highest precedence, and so is applied first. The result is

```
(NOT Yes) OR No  =  (NOT True) OR False
                 =  False OR False  =  False
```

In the second example, the `NOT` operator is again applied first:

```
No AND NOT No  =  No AND (NOT No)
               =  False AND (NOT False)
               =  False AND True  =  False
```

The third example is more complicated. The `MOD` and `DIV` operators have equal precedence on a higher level than the > operator. These two multiplicative operators are applied left-to-right, as though we had written

```
Small + (Big MOD Small) > (Small DIV Big)
```

Of the two remaining operators, the + has higher precedence, as though we had written

```
(Small + (Big MOD Small)) > (Small DIV Big)
 =  (3 + (7 MOD 3)) > (3 DIV 7)
 =  (3 + 1) > (0)
 =  (4 > 0)
 =  True
```

The fourth expression contains a `NOT`, which has highest precedence. Thus the expression is equivalent to `Yes OR No AND (NOT No) OR Yes`. The `AND` is the next operator to be applied, yielding `Yes OR (No AND (NOT No)) OR Yes`. Finally, the two `OR`s are applied in left-to-right order:

```
Yes OR (No AND (NOT No)) OR Yes
=  (Yes OR (No AND (NOT No))) OR Yes
=  (True OR (False AND (NOT False))) OR True
=  (True OR (False AND True)) OR True
=  (True OR (False)) OR True
=  True OR True
=  True
```

Recognizing illegal expressions

If you understand operator precedence, you will be able to recognize ill-formed expressions. Consider, for example, the expression

```
Small < Big OR Small <> Big
```

The `OR` operator has highest precedence, so the expression is equivalent to

```
Small < (Big OR Small) <> Big
```

However, `(Big OR Small)` *makes no sense*. The `OR` operator requires two `Boolean` operands, but `Big` and `Small` are both of type `Real`. If the expression had been written

```
(Small < Big) OR (Small <> Big)
```

it would have made sense and could have been evaluated. (With the initializations in `OpPrecedenceTest`, its value would be `True`.)

Exercises

31. Show that the following (poorly written) `Boolean` expressions have the values shown. Assume that `Yes = True`, `No = False`, `Big = 7`, and `Small = 3`.

	Expression	Value
a.	`True AND NOT False`	`True`
b.	`NOT ( True AND False )`	`True`
c.	`NOT True AND NOT False`	`False`
d.	`NOT True OR True`	`True`
e.	`Yes AND (Big MOD Small <= Small DIV Big)`	`False`
f.	`Yes OR No OR No AND Yes`	`True`
g.	`No OR Yes OR Yes OR No`	`True`
h.	`NOT NOT NOT No OR No`	`True`
i.	`No OR NOT NOT NOT Yes`	`False`
j.	`Big - 1 <> 2 * Small + 1`	`True`

32. Determine which of the following expressions is legal. Explain your answers.

a. `Big DIV Small AND Big`

b. `NOT Big <> Small * Big`

c. `Big MOD Small AND Yes`

d. `No OR Small = (Big - 3) AND Yes`

e. `(Small = Big - 3) OR Yes AND No`

8.9 TYPE DECLARATIONS

Now it's time to take another look at the `Sort3Reals` program from Section 6.3 and ask ourselves if we can improve it in some way. Wouldn't it be nice if we could use it to sort not only numbers, but characters and other data? As it stands, the procedure will work with characters if we go in and change the declaration in `Sort3Real`'s parameter list, and in two places in the `Swap2Reals` procedure. But that's awkward and error-prone. Is there some way to simplify the changes that would be needed to change the type of values?

Yes, there is. We can declare a new type, called `Items`, up at the front of the program, defining it to be (for the moment) the same as type `Real`. Then we can just deal with variables of type `Items` in the procedures. Later, if we want to change the definition of `Items`, we will only have to change one line, right at the beginning of the program. Now we have a program that is more easily adaptable to different situations.

```
PROGRAM TestSort3 ( Input, Output );
{ Driver for testing Sort3Reals }

TYPE
   Items = Real;

VAR
   Val1, Val2, Val3 : Real;


PROCEDURE Get3( VAR Val1, Val2, Val3 : Items );
{
  POSTCONDITIONS:
  Val1, Val2, and Val3 have been initialized.
}
BEGIN

   Write( 'First value?  ' );
   ReadLn( Val1 );
   Write( 'Second value? ' );
   ReadLn( Val2 );
   Write( 'Third value?  ' );
   ReadLn( Val3 )

END; { Get3 }


PROCEDURE Swap2( VAR First, Second : Items );
{
  PRECONDITION:
  First and Second have been initialized.

  POSTCONDITION:
  The values of First and Second have been exchanged.
}
VAR
   OldFirst : Real;

BEGIN

   OldFirst  := First;
   First     := Second;
   Second    := OldFirst

END; { Swap2 }
```

```
PROCEDURE Sort3( VAR Val1, Val2, Val3 : Items );
{
  PRECONDITIONS:
  Val1, Val2, and Val3 have been initialized.

  POSTCONDITIONS:
  Val1 <= Val2 <= Val3.
}
BEGIN

   IF Val1 > Val2 THEN
      Swap2( Val1, Val2 );
   { Assertion: Now Val1 <= Val2 }

   IF Val2 > Val3 THEN
      Swap2( Val2, Val3 );
   { Assertion: Now Val2 <= Val3 }
   { First two nums may be out of order again }

   IF Val1 > Val2 THEN
      Swap2( Val1, Val2 )
   { Assertion: Now Val1 <= Val2 <= Val3 }

END; { Sort3 }


BEGIN { driver }

   Get3( Val1, Val2, Val3 );

   WriteLn;
   WriteLn( 'Before sorting, values are ',
            Val1, '   ', Val2, '   ', Val3 );
   Sort3( Val1, Val2, Val3 );
   WriteLn( 'After sorting, values are  ',
            Val1:10, '   ', Val2:10, '   ', Val3:10 )

END.
```

Type declaration syntax

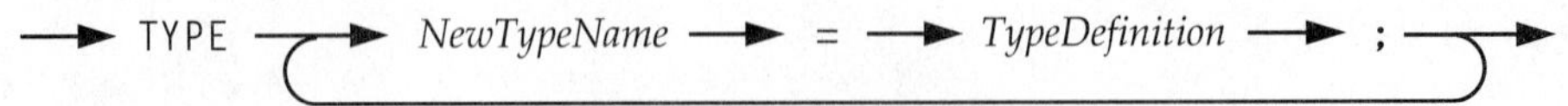

The Pascal declaration:

TYPE
    NewTypeName = *TypeDefinition* ;

A type declaration defines a new type name to be a synonym for an existing type, or as we will see later, a subset or composite involving existing types.

It always pays to make your subprograms as generally useful as possible, so that you can reuse them in other programs. We have succeeded here in making the `Sort3` procedure as useful as possible with simple data types that can be compared by relational operators. Later, we will encounter structured, nonsimple data types which cannot be ordered by means of relational operators, and then we will need to improve `Sort3` again.

Questions

33. Can `Swap2` and `Sort3` be written as functions? If so, why haven't we chosen to do so?

34. Suggest a way to compare values of `Items` type in the event (which will occur later) that such values cannot be compared by means of relational operators.

LOOKING BACK

We examined Pascal's three ordinal data types: `Integer`, `Char`, and `Boolean`. These three types consist of discrete values that are ordered and enumerable. Each value (except the first and last) has a unique predecessor and successor, which can be computed by Pascal's `Pred` and `Succ` functions.

By contrast, real numbers are spread over the continuous range of values on the real-number line and it is not possible to specify the predecessor or successor of a real number. Therefore, real data are not considered ordinal even though these numbers are stored discretely in the computer.

For each of the three ordinal types, we described its operators and standard functions. `Pred` and `Succ` can be applied to all three, but there are other functions that are specific to an individual type, like `DIV` and `MOD` with the `Integer` type, or `NOT`, `AND`, and `OR` with the `Boolean` type. We discussed the evaluation of expressions, including the precedence of operators.

Several case studies were presented: a decimal-to-binary converter, a function to map lowercase letters to uppercase, a set of character-property functions, and a generalized version of `Sort3` . In each case study, we wrote and tested a driver and stub first, then implemented the subprograms. This incremental development technique made it easier to debug the program as we went along, never writing too much code at one time. We also minimized the chance of a semantic error by specifying pre- and postconditions for a subprogram before implementing it. Both of these techniques will be of increasing importance in later chapters.

At the end of the chapter, we looked at an example of how a programmer-defined type can be used to make a program easily reusable with a variety of simple data types. `TYPE` declarations of this kind will often appear in later chapters.

In the next chapter, we will make fuller use of the `Boolean` data type, as we use it to help build more complex decision structures.

TERMS EMPHASIZED IN THIS CHAPTER

PROJECTS

1. Design and write a real function called `NearestCent` that returns its real parameter, rounded to two decimal places. For example, `NearestCent( 1.234567 )` should be 1.23, and `NearestCent( 1.999 )` should be 2.00. Hint: Scale the number up by 100.0, round it, then scale the result back down.

2. Design and test a program that determines experimentally whether your Pascal system uses the ASCII character set.

3. Write a small main program that asks for the user's initials, one at a time, and reads them into character variables. Afterwards, the program should print the initials in the usual format, with periods between them.

4. A certain brand of flashlight batteries indicates the date of manufacture by means of a date code consisting of a capital letter indicating a month, followed by two digits indicating the year. For example, the code `C91` indicates March, 1991. Write a program that reads a date code from the keyboard, displaying the date in the form 3/1991. Do *not* use decision structures or other material not introduced to this point in the book. Use

modularity as appropriate. Your program does not need to cope with dates in the first decade of this century.

5. A year is not really 365 days, but 365.242199 days. In order to keep the calendar in phase with the equinoxes and solstices, Julius Caesar adopted a system adding an extra day to every fourth year, which was called a leap year. This system was not accurate enough, however, and a new calendar system was decreed by Pope Gregory XIII in 1582. According to this system, a year divisible by four is a leap year unless it is a centennial year, in which case it is a leap year only if divisible by 400. Write a `Boolean` function that reports whether a given year is a leap year. Do not use any material not introduced to this point in the book; you can do the computation with one well-designed `Boolean` expression!

6. Design and write a `ChooseFromMenu` procedure that displays a menu and returns a character representing the user's choice from the menu. The menu to be displayed is

```
Key F for first name
or  L for last name:
```

   `ChooseFromMenu` should read a one-character response from the keyboard, then return `'F'` if the user enters `'F'` or `'f'` or return `'L'` if the user enters `'L'` or `'l'`. The procedure should repeatedly display the menu until the user enters one of the required characters. Use good modular design practices. Write a driver and test your procedure.

7. Design and write a function that returns the letter grade corresponding to an exam score, according to the scheme listed below. For the sake of this assignment, we will assume that there are no scores above 99 or below 50. Use a driver to test your function.

Score	**Grade**	**Score**	**Grade**
90–99	A	60–69	D
80–89	B	50–59	E
70–79	C		

8. Write a modular, hierarchical program that proves the equivalence of the following two expressions by printing out their truth tables:

   a. `NOT(( Logical1 AND Logical2 ) OR (NOT( Logical2 )))`

   b. `((NOT( Logical1 )) OR (NOT ( Logical2 ))) AND Logical2`

9. Pascal defines three operators that take Boolean operands: `NOT`, `AND`, and `OR`. However, one properly-chosen Boolean operator will do all that these operators can do. Consider the `NAND` operator defined by the truth table shown below:

Logical1	**Logical2**	**Logical1 NAND Logical2**
`True`	`True`	`False`
`True`	`False`	`True`
`False`	`True`	`True`
`False`	`False`	`True`

   Note that the truth table for `NAND` is identical to that for the negation of `AND`. `NAND` in fact stands for "`NOT-AND`." Use DeMorgan's Laws (Section 8.6) to show that `NAND` can be used to build the `NOT`, `AND`, and `OR` operators.

10. The `NAND` operation was described in Project 9. Design and write a function to implement this operation in Pascal.

11. Modify the `Sort3` procedure by adding a fourth parameter, a `Boolean`, called `SortUp`. If `SortUp = True`, the procedure should sort its first three parameters into nondecreasing order. If `SortUp = False`, the procedure should sort into nonincreasing order. Test your procedure.

REFERENCES

One of the more readable general introductions to the concept of data types is J. Craig Cleaveland's book, *An Introduction to Data Types* (Addison-Wesley Publishing, 1986). A succinct history of the concept is found in Section 5–1 of Terrence W. Pratt's book, *Programming Languages*, second edition (Prentice Hall, 1984).

Why Do People Write Programs?

First is the sheer joy of making things. As the child delights in his mud pie, so the adult enjoys building things, especially things of his own design. I think this delight must be an image of God's delight in making things, a delight shown in the distinctness and newness of each leaf and each snowflake.

Second is the pleasure of making things that are useful to other people. Deep within, we want others to use our work and find it helpful. . . .

Third is the fascination of fashioning complex puzzle-like objects of interlocking moving parts and watching them work in subtle cycles, playing out the consequences of principles built in from the beginning. The programmed computer has all the fascination of the pinball machine or the jukebox mechanism, carried to the ultimate.

Fourth is the joy of always learning, which springs from the nonrepeating nature of the task. In one way or another the problem is ever new, and its solver learns something: sometimes practical, sometimes theoretical, and sometimes both.

Finally, there is the delight of working in such a tractable medium. The programmer, like the poet, works only slightly removed from pure thought-stuff. He builds his castles in the air, from air, creating by exertion of the imagination. Few media of creation are so flexible, so easy to polish and rework, so readily capable of realizing grand conceptual structures. . . .

Yet the program construct, unlike the poet's words, is real in the sense that it moves and works, producing visible outputs separate from the construct itself. It prints results, draws pictures, produces sounds, moves arms. The magic of myth and legend has come true in our time. One types the correct incantation on a keyboard, and a display screen comes to life, showing things that never were nor could be.

Programming then is fun because it gratifies creative longings built deep within us and delights sensibilities we have in common with all men.

—Frederick P. Brooks, Jr., *The Mythical Man-Month: Essays on Software Engineering* (Addison-Wesley, 1975), pages 7–8.

PART THREE

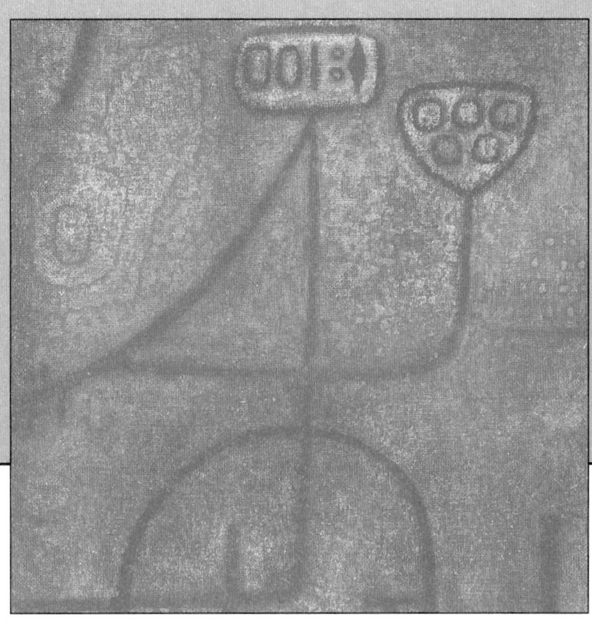

CONTROL STRUCTURES

CHAPTER

9

Decision Structures Again

CHAPTER CONTENTS

INTRODUCTION

Now it is time to examine the full range of Pascal's control structures. In this chapter we discuss the finer points of *decision* or *selection structures*, which are used by a program to decide which statements to execute, often selecting among several groups of statements. The goals of the chapter are

- To review `IF..THEN` and `IF..THEN..ELSE` structures, using `Boolean` expressions in the syntax.
- To show how `Boolean` expressions can often replace complicated decision structures.
- To show how `IF..THEN..ELSE` structures can be nested, one within another.
- To show how a nested `IF..THEN..ELSE` structure sometimes can be replaced by a simpler `CASE` structure.

> IF? . . . Talk'st thou to me of "IFs"?
> Thou are a traitor: Off with his head!
>
> —*William Shakespeare, King Richard III, Act III, Scene iv*

9.1 IF..THEN..ELSE AGAIN

In Section 6.1, we introduced the IF..THEN..ELSE structure, whose syntax can now be described more generally in terms of Boolean expressions. When equipped with the optional ELSE clause, the IF..THEN..ELSE defines a two-way execution path through the code: Either execute *Statement1* or execute *Statement2*, but not both. On the other hand, if we delete the ELSE clause, we have conditional execution of a single statement, whether simple or compound. Both cases are shown in the syntax box on the next page.

Let us now examine some of the finer points about the use of IF..THEN..ELSE and IF..THEN structures.

Conditional execution of a compound statement

Sometimes you want a decision structure to conditionally execute more than one statement. As suggested by the syntax diagram, this is accomplished by having the structure conditionally execute a *compound statement*, a sequence of statements enclosed within a BEGIN–END pair. For example, if you want Sort3 to print a message for every Swap2 it performs, you could write

```
PROCEDURE Sort3( VAR Val1, Val2, Val3 : Items );
BEGIN

   IF Val1 > Val2 THEN
   BEGIN
      Swap2( Val1, Val2 );
      WriteLn( 'Swapped 1 and 2' )
   END;
   { Assertion: Now Val1 <= Val2 }

   IF Val2 > Val3 THEN
   BEGIN
      Swap2( Val2, Val3 );
      WriteLn( 'Swapped 2 and 3' )
   END;
   { Assertion: Now Val3 is the maximum value }

   { First two values may still be out of order }
   IF Val1 > Val2 THEN
   BEGIN
      Swap2( Val1, Val2 );
      WriteLn( 'Swapped 1 and 2' )
   END
   { Assertion: Now Value1 <= Value2 <= Value3 }

END; { Sort3 }
```

Syntax for IF..THEN..ELSE structures

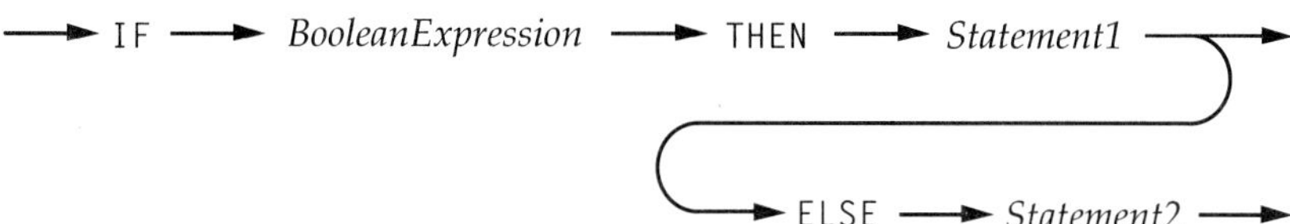

Pseudocode:

IF *BooleanExpression* THEN
    Statement1
ELSE
    Statement2

When the `ELSE` clause is present, execution proceeeds as follows: If *BooleanExpression* is true, *Statement1* is executed, but not *Statement2*. If *BooleanExpression* is false, *Statement2* is executed, but not *Statement1*. Afterwards, execution passes to the next statement after the control structure.

Notes:

- *Statement1* and *Statement2* can be either simple or compound statements.
- The `ELSE` clause is optional. If it is deleted, we have an `IF..THEN` structure, as shown below.

→ IF → *BooleanExpression* → THEN → *Statement1* →

Pseudocode:

IF *BooleanExpression* THEN
    Statement1

In this structure, if *BooleanExpression* is true, *Statement1* is executed; otherwise, *Statement1* is not executed. Afterwards, in either event, execution passes to the next statement after the control structure.

When NOT to use a decision structure

Deciding whether to assign `True` or `False` to a `Boolean` variable is handled more simply and more elegantly with a `Boolean` expression than with an `IF..THEN..ELSE` structure. For example, suppose we want to know whether a given integer is a single-digit positive number. We can write

```
IF ( Num > 0 ) AND ( Num < 10 ) THEN
   SingleDigit := True
ELSE
   SingleDigit := False;
```

but it is simpler and more elegant to write

```
SingleDigit := ( Num > 0 ) AND ( Num < 10 );
```

Use a `Boolean` expression when you can, but when you can't, use a decision structure.

Exercises

1. Simplify the following functions as much as possible, replacing each `IF..THEN..ELSE` structure with a statement that assigns the value of a `Boolean` expression to the `Boolean` variable.

   a.
```
FUNCTION EvenNegative ( Num : Integer ) : Boolean;
BEGIN
   IF ( NOT( Num < 0 ) OR ( NOT( (Num MOD 2) = 0 ) ) ) THEN
      EvenNegative := False
   ELSE
      EvenNegative := True
END { EvenNegative };
```

   b.
```
FUNCTION ForwardAcceleration ( Direction : Integer;
                               Accel     : Real ) : Boolean;
BEGIN
   IF ( Direction < 0 ) OR ( Accel < 0.0 ) THEN
      ForwardAcceleration := False
   ELSE
      ForwardAcceleration := True
END { ForwardAcceleration };
```

2. Complete the following functions by completing the assignment statements.

   a.
```
FUNCTION SevenBits ( Num : Integer ) : Boolean;
{
  POSTCONDITIONS:
  Returns True if -128 <= Num <= 127; otherwise, returns False.
}
BEGIN
   SevenBits :=
END { SevenBits }
```

   b.
```
FUNCTION IsSnowing ( Precip : Boolean;
                     TempF  : Real ) : Boolean;
{
  POSTCONDITIONS:
  Returns True if it is precipitating and Temp < 32.0;
  otherwise, returns False.
}
BEGIN
   IsSnowing :=
END { IsSnowing }
```

3. The `Sort3` procedure in Section 8.9 includes the triple-repetitive code

```
IF Val1 > Val2 THEN
   Swap2( Val1, Val2 );

IF Val2 > Val3 THEN
   Swap2( Val2, Val3 );

IF Val1 > Val2 THEN
   Swap2( Val1, Val2 )
```

Repetitive code like this suggests the need for a procedure. Change this code to read

```
Sort2( Val1, Val2 );
Sort2( Val2, Val3 );
Sort2( Val1, Val2 )
```

Write an appropriate `Sort2` procedure, incorporate it into the program, and compile and test your new version of `TestSort3`.

4. What is printed when the following procedures execute?

a.
```
PROCEDURE Strange;

VAR
   I, J : Integer;

BEGIN

   I := 47;
   J := -I;

   IF J <= I THEN
      WriteLn( 'J <= I' )
   ELSE;
      WriteLn( 'J > I' )

END; {Strange}
```

b.
```
PROCEDURE Mystery;
VAR
   I, J : Integer;

BEGIN

   I := -47;
   J := -I;

   IF J <= I THEN
      WriteLn( 'J <= I' );
      WriteLn( 'J > I' )

END; {Mystery}
```

c.
```
PROCEDURE Hmmm( I, J : Integer );
BEGIN

   IF (J <= I) OR (J >= I) THEN
      WriteLn( 'Condition 1' )
   ELSE
      WriteLn( 'Condition 2' )

END; { Hmmm }
```

d.
```
PROCEDURE Puzzle;
VAR
   I, J : Integer;

BEGIN

   I := 47;
   J := I;

   IF J <= I THEN
      WriteLn( 'J <= I' );
      WriteLn( 'J > I' )

END; { Puzzle }
```

e.
```
PROCEDURE Woof ( I, J : Integer );
BEGIN

   IF (J < I) AND (J > I) THEN
      WriteLn( 'Hmmm...' )

END; { Woof }
```

9.2 NESTED DECISIONS

Some problems require decisions within decisions. Consider how we might find the maximum of three numbers called `Num1`, `Num2`, and `Num3`. First off, it's clear we have to compare the numbers, and that the problem is to find the correct pattern of comparisons.

Let's try to divide and conquer: Can we arrive at the answer by comparing two numbers at a time? If `Num1` is greater than `Num2`, then `Num1` is the biggest considered so far; otherwise `Num2` is the biggest so far. Of course `Num3` is still untested. Up to here, the tentative algorithm is

```
IF Num1 > Num2 THEN
   {-- Maximum is Num1 or Num3 }
ELSE
   {-- Maximum is Num2 or Num3 }
```

In each case, there is still a two-way decision to be made, so we resolve each case by inserting another `IF..THEN..ELSE` structure:

```
    IF Num1 > Num2 THEN
        {-- Maximum is Num1 or Num3 }
        IF Num1 > Num3 THEN
            Maximum := Num1
        ELSE
            Maximum := Num3

    ELSE
        {-- Maximum is Num2 or Num3 }
        IF Num2 > Num3 THEN
            Maximum := Num2
        ELSE
            Maximum := Num3
```

The inner `IF..THEN..ELSE` structures are said to be *nested* within the outer one. `BEGIN`s and `END`s are not needed inside the outer structure because each of the inner `IF..THEN..ELSE` structures is a single statement.

Here is a complete program for testing the algorithm. As always, we build the `MaxOf3` function as an independent module, so that it can be used in other programs after testing.

```
PROGRAM TestMaxOf3( Input, Output );

TYPE
    Items = Real;

VAR
    FirstNumber, SecondNumber, ThirdNumber : Items;


FUNCTION MaxOf3( Num1, Num2, Num3 : Items ) : Items;
{
  PRECONDITIONS:
  Num1, Num2, Num3 have been initialized.

  POSTCONDITIONS:
  MaxOf3 = the largest of the three parameters.
}
BEGIN

    IF Num1 > Num2 THEN
        {-- Maximum is Num1 or Num3 }
        IF Num1 > Num3 THEN
            MaxOf3 := Num1
        ELSE
            MaxOf3 := Num3

    ELSE
        {-- Maximum is Num2 or Num3 }
        IF Num2 > Num3 THEN
            MaxOf3 := Num2
        ELSE
            MaxOf3 := Num3

END; { MaxOf3 }
```

```
BEGIN { driver }

   WriteLn( 'FINDING MAXIMUM OF THREE NUMBERS' );
   WriteLn;

   Write( 'First number:  ' );
   ReadLn( FirstNumber );
   Write( 'Second number: ' );
   ReadLn( SecondNumber );
   Write( 'Third number:  ' );
   ReadLn( ThirdNumber );

   WriteLn;
   WriteLn( 'Max is ',
            MaxOf3( FirstNumber, SecondNumber, ThirdNumber ) )

END.
```

Indentation

Pascal doesn't care about indentation but indentation helps humans understand the code. Programmers disagree, however, on the most readable style of indentation in nested `IF..THEN..ELSE` structures. Some would prefer the code to be written this way, using an `ELSE IF` combination:

```
IF Num1 > Num2 THEN
   {-- Maximum is Num1 or Num3 }
   IF Num1 > Num3 THEN
      MaxOf3 := Num1
   ELSE
      MaxOf3 := Num3

ELSE IF Num2 > Num3 THEN
   {-- Maximum is Num2 or Num3 }
   MaxOf3 := Num2

ELSE
   MaxOf3 := Num3
```

Is it clearer this way? It's a matter of taste. It runs the same either way.

Deep nesting

In Standard Pascal, there is no syntactic limit on the depth to which you can nest `IF..THEN..ELSE` structures, but there is a stylistic limit: Deep nesting is hard to understand. Also, if you nest decision structures very deeply, indenting each level of nesting, your code will move pretty far to the right of the page. In such cases, you will probably prefer the second style of indentation, or to move some of the code into subprograms, or to use a `CASE` structure (Section 9.4). You may also be able to find a simpler way to write your code!

Pitfall: A dangling ELSE

In designing nested decisions, you must be careful to associate each `ELSE` clause with the correct `IF..THEN` and not leave a dangling `ELSE`. Suppose I handed you this unindented fragment of code and asked you what grade it assigns for a score of 85:

```
IF Score >= 80 THEN IF Score >= 90 THEN Grade := 'A' ELSE Grade := 'B'
```

If this code is supposed to be as suggested by the indentation

```
IF Score >= 80 THEN
   IF Score >= 90 THEN
      Grade := 'A'
   ELSE
      Grade := 'B'
```

then it should assign a grade of `'B'` for a score of 85. On the other hand, if it's supposed to be as suggested by the indentation

```
IF Score >= 80 THEN
   IF Score >= 90 THEN
      Grade := 'A'
ELSE
   Grade := 'B'
```

then it should assign no grade at all for a score of 85, and a grade of `'B'` for scores lower than 80.

Presumably the programmer intended the first interpretation, but the original unindented version of the code does not make this clear. The Pascal compiler doesn't care about indentation in any event. It has a rule for resolving ambiguities of this sort: *An* `ELSE` *is associated with the last previous unmatched* `IF..THEN` *unless forced otherwise by the* `BEGIN..END` *block structure.* So in the example above, the compiler would interpret the code (in any of these versions) as implied by the first indented version.

As an example of forcing the `ELSE` to associate with another `IF..THEN`, notice that the second interpretation of the ambiguous code could be forced by writing

```
IF Score >= 80 THEN
BEGIN
   IF Score >= 90 THEN
      Grade := 'A'
END

ELSE
   Grade := 'B'
```

Exercises

5. Correct the syntactic errors in the following nested structures. Assume that `Year` and `Score` are integer variables and `Storage` is a character variable.

   a.
```
IF Year < -45 THEN
   WriteLn( 'Lunar' );
ELSE IF Year < 1582
   WriteLn( 'Julian' )
ELSE
   WriteLn( 'Gregorian' );
```

   b.
```
IF Storage = 'O' THEN
   WriteLn( 'one byte' )
ELSE
   IF Storage = 'F'
      WriteLn( 'four bytes, two''s-complement' )
ELSE IF Storage = 'B' THEN
   WriteLn( 'one byte' )
ELSE
   WriteLn( 'four bytes, real' );
```

   c.
```
IF Score = 5 THEN
   WriteLn( 'Credit' );
ELSE IF Score = 4 THEN
   WriteLn( 'Partial credit' )
ELSE
   WriteLn( 'No credit' );
```

6. If `Phase` is an integer variable and contains the value 4, then what is printed by the following code fragments? Explain your answers.

   a.
```
IF Phase < 4 THEN
   WriteLn( Phase - 1 )
ELSE
   WriteLn( Phase + 2 );
IF Phase = 4 THEN
   WriteLn( Phase );
```

   b.
```
IF Phase < 4 THEN
   WriteLn( Phase - 1 )
ELSE
   IF Phase > 4 THEN
      WriteLn( Phase + 2 )
   ELSE
      WriteLn( Phase );
```

c.
```
IF Phase < 4 THEN
   IF Phase = 4 THEN
      WriteLn( Phase )
ELSE IF Phase > 4 THEN
   IF Phase = 4 THEN
      WriteLn( Phase );
```

7. Write a program that reads an integer score between 0 and 100, sending this score to a character function named `ConvertToGrade`. This function should return to the main program the corresponding letter grade, which should then be displayed on the screen along with the score. Letter grades are associated with scores in the usual way:

Scores	**Grade**
90 through 100	A
80 through 89	B
70 through 79	C
60 through 69	D
Less than 60	F

8. In Chapter 8's Project 5, you wrote a `Boolean` function that determines whether a given year is a leap year. Rewrite this function, using nested decision structures to find the `Boolean` value.

9.3 CASE STUDY: MENUS

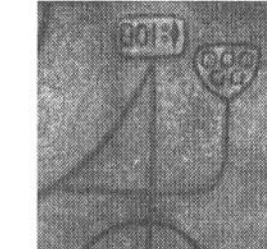

In a program that performs alternate tasks, there must be some way for the user to tell the program what to do. Often a **menu** is the most convenient way for the user to interact with the program. The user sees a list of choices and responses, and enters one of the responses. For example, in a program to perform temperature conversions, the user might be presented with this menu:

```
Enter
  F  to convert Celsius to Fahrenheit,
  C  to convert Fahrenheit to Celsius,
  K  to convert Fahrenheit to Kelvin.

Your choice? _
```

If the user enters `'F'`, `'C'`, or `'K'`, the program is to perform as promised. Otherwise, it should display the message `'CHOICE MUST BE F, C, OR K'`. All of these things can be accomplished with the help of nested `IF..THEN..ELSE` structures. In the following code, `Choice` is a `Char` variable, and it is assumed that we have declared some appropriate conversion functions called `FToC`, `CToF`, and `FToK`.

```
WriteLn( 'Enter' );
WriteLn( '  F to convert from Celsius to Fahrenheit,' );
WriteLn( '  C to convert from Fahrenheit to Celsius,' );
WriteLn( '  K to convert from Fahrenheit to Kelvin.' );
WriteLn;
Write( 'Your choice? ' );
ReadLn( Choice );

IF (Choice = 'F') OR (Choice = 'f') THEN
   Fahrenheit := CToF( Celsius )

ELSE IF (Choice = 'C') OR (Choice = 'c') THEN
   Celsius := FToC( Fahrenheit )

ELSE IF (Choice = 'K') OR (Choice = 'k') THEN
   Kelvin := FToK( Fahrenheit )

ELSE
   WriteLn( 'CHOICE MUST BE F, C, OR K' );
   .
   .
```

The code uses the second form of nested indentation shown in Section 9.2 because it reads better in this case. Notice, too, that the user may enter either upper- or lowercase responses to the menu prompt. After all, the program has no control over the user's SHIFT key, so it should act appropriately in either lower- or uppercase. Similarly, there is no way to keep the user from entering an illegal response, so the code contains an `ELSE` clause to handle that possibility.

Is there a better way?

It is awkward to list both upper- and lowercase responses for each of the three possibilities, so we look for a better way. Remembering the uppercase conversion function from Section 8.5, we use it to map all responses to uppercase in the first place. The code is now a little simpler and a little better:

```
WriteLn( 'Enter' );
WriteLn( '  F to convert from Celsius to Fahrenheit,' );
WriteLn( '  C to convert from Fahrenheit to Celsius,' );
WriteLn( '  K to convert from Fahrenheit to Kelvin.' );
WriteLn;
Write( 'Your choice? ' );
ReadLn( Choice );
Choice := Upper( Choice );

IF (Choice = 'F') THEN
   Fahrenheit := CToF( Celsius )

ELSE IF (Choice = 'C') THEN
   Celsius := FToC( Fahrenheit )

ELSE IF (Choice = 'K') THEN
   Kelvin := FToK( Fahrenheit )
```

```
ELSE
   WriteLn( 'CHOICE MUST BE F, C, OR K' );
   .
   .
```

9.4 CASE STRUCTURES

The deeply nested `IF..THEN..ELSE` structures of the previous section are somewhat cumbersome. This is a common situation, in which a program makes a multiway decision on the basis of the value in an ordinal variable. Such situations are so common that Pascal provides a shorthand syntax called the `CASE` structure—a control structure that says, "If it's this case, then do this; if it's that case, then do that other thing; and so on." The general syntax is shown in the following syntax box on the next page. Briefly, the structure is

```
CASE OrdinalSelector OF
   OrdinalConstantList1  :  Statement1;
   OrdinalConstantList2  :  Statement2;
   .
   .
   OrdinalConstantListN  :  StatementN
END;
```

The idea is simple: The program tests the value of the *OrdinalSelector* variable, and selects which code to execute on the basis of its ordinal value. If *OrdinalSelector* has one of the values in *OrdinalConstantList1*, then the program executes *Statement1*. If it has the a value in *OrdinalConstantList2*, it executes *Statement2* instead; and so on. In this pseudocode outline, *Statement1*, *Statement2*, . . ., *StatementN* can be either simple or compound statements.

An integer example

Suppose we have some code involving an integer variable called `DayNum`:

```
DayNum := 3;
CASE DayNum OF
   1, 7    : WriteLn( 'Resting' );
   2       : WriteLn( 'Back to work' );
   3, 4, 5 : WriteLn( 'Working hard' );
   6       : WriteLn( 'Almost time for a rest' );
END;
```

Then, because `DayNum` was given the value 3, the `CASE` structure displays `Working hard`.

CASE Structure Syntax

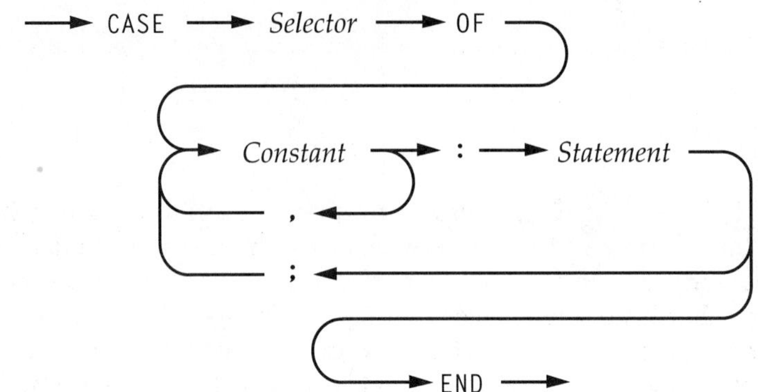

Pseudocode:

```
CASE OrdinalSelector OF
    OrdinalConstantList1 : Statement1;
    OrdinalConstantList2 : Statement2;
    .
    .
    OrdinalConstantListN : StatementN
END
```

Notes:

- The *OrdinalSelector* is an expression of any *ordinal* type: `Integer`, `Char`, `Boolean`, or, as you will see later, enumeration or subrange. It cannot be `Real` because reals are not ordinal.
- The *OrdinalConstantLists* are lists of one or more constants of the same type as the *Selector*. If a list contains more than one constant, these are separated by commas.
- The *Statements* can be simple or compound, or even null.
- In Standard Pascal, it is an error for *OrdinalSelector* to take on a value that does not appear in any of the *OrdinalConstantLists*. However, many Pascal compilers allow an `ELSE` or `OTHERWISE` clause for such cases:

```
CASE OrdinalSelector OF
    OrdinalConstantList1 : Statement1;
    OrdinalConstantList2 : Statement2;
        .
        .
    OrdinalConstantListN : StatementN

ELSE
    Statement

END
```

Check your compiler reference manual to see if an `ELSE` or `OTHERWISE` clause is allowed in your version of Pascal.

Revisiting the menu problem

The menu example of the previous section can also be carried out by a `CASE` structure. In this example, the *OrdinalSelector* is a `Char` variable called `Choice`. The program has displayed the following menu:

```
Enter
  F  to convert Celsius to Fahrenheit,
  C  to convert Fahrenheit to Celsius,
  K  to convert Fahrenheit to Kelvin.

Your choice? _
```

The user's response is stored in the `Choice` variable. If `Choice = 'F'`, we want the program to call a `CToF` procedure; if it is `'C'`, we want the program to call `FToC`, and so on. Here is a `CASE` structure, shown side by side with the equivalent `IF..THEN..ELSE IF` portions of the nested `IF` structures of the previous section:

```
CASE Choice OF
   'F' : Fahrenheit := CToF( Celsius );
   'C' : Celsius    := FToC( Fahrenheit );
   'K' : Kelvin     := FToK( Fahrenheit )
END;
```

```
IF (Choice = 'F') THEN
   Fahrenheit := CToF( Celsius )
ELSE IF (Choice = 'C') THEN
   Celsius := FToC( Fahrenheit )
ELSE IF (Choice = 'K') THEN
   Kelvin := FToK( Fahrenheit );
```

However, the standard `CASE` structure allows no part that corresponds to the `ELSE` clause of the nested `IF` structures, describing what should happen if `Choice` contains a value other than those listed. This is a serious limitation of Standard Pascal's `CASE` structure.

Exceptional selector values cause errors in Standard Pascal.

In Standard Pascal, any *OrdinalSelector* value other than those listed as case constants will cause a runtime error when the `CASE` structure is executed. For example, if a program has `Choice = 'Z'` and executes the `CASE` structure shown above, there will be a runtime error and the program may halt. If **range-checking** is turned on, the program will display an error message like `CASE SELECTOR OUT OF RANGE` or `ILLEGAL VALUE IN SELECTOR`. (You may not see the message if range-checking is turned off.) With or without the message, Standard Pascal does not handle such situations gracefully.

Range-checking: An option in many Pascal systems, by which the runtime package can automatically report data values that go outside the ranges allowed for their types.

Some systems allow a nonstandard ELSE clause.

Many Pascal implementations provide a nonstandard, optional `ELSE` or `OTHERWISE` clause in their `CASE` structures, to handle the possibility that the *OrdinalSelector* may have none of the listed values. An example is shown on the next page:

```
CASE Choice OF
   'F': Fahrenheit := CToF( Celsius );
   'C': Celsius := FToC( Fahrenheit );
   'K': Kelvin := FToK( Fahrenheit )

ELSE
   WriteLn( 'CHOICE MUST BE F, C, OR K' )

END
```

Guarding Standard Pascal's CASE structure with an IF structure

To **guard**: To protect a piece of code from undesirable effects of inappropriate data.

Good programming practice requires that programs be protected from data that might cause a crash. In Standard Pascal, we can **guard** a `CASE` structure by encasing the `CASE` (Pardon the pun!) in an `IF..THEN..ELSE` structure. It isn't elegant, but it does the job:

```
IF (Choice = 'F') OR (Choice = 'C') OR (Choice = 'K') THEN

   CASE Choice OF
      'F' : Fahrenheit := CToF( Celsius );
      'C' : Celsius := FToC( Fahrenheit );
      'K' : Kelvin := FToK( Fahrenheit )
   END;

ELSE
   WriteLn( 'ILLEGAL CHOICE.' );
```

This isn't a very good solution, however. For one thing, it is inelegant; but more importantly, it doesn't allow the program to continue prompting the user until a useful menu choice is made.

Guarding the CASE structure with a loop structure

A better way to guard a menu-processing `CASE` structure from improper selector values would be to encase the menu's prompt-and-answer code in a loop that continues prompting the user for input until an acceptable value is entered. Then, after the program exits the loop, any following `CASE` structure would be guaranteed of having a proper selector value. This is an important technique even if your Pascal system allows an `ELSE` clause in `CASE` structures, and we'll use it in the next chapter.

When do we use a CASE structure?

`CASE` structures are useful when (i) a multiway decision depends on the value in an ordinal variable, and (ii) nested `IF..THEN..ELSE` structures would be harder for the human reader to understand.

On the other hand, when a multiway choice cannot be decided solely according to the value in an ordinal value, a `CASE` structure is not appropriate and nested `IF..THEN..ELSE` structures should be used instead.

Question

9. Describe the differences between CASE structures and IF..THEN..ELSE structures. Explain the shortcomings of CASE structures.

Exercises

10. Imagine that a program has just displayed the menu

```
Enter
  A to add;
  D to delete;
  P to print.
Your choice? _
```

Write a CASE structure that processes the one-character response to this menu as follows: If the response is 'A', the structure adds 1 to a variable named Total; if the response is 'D', the structure subtracts 1 from Total; if 'P', it displays the value of Total.

11. Write a CASE structure that determines whether a given character is a vowel. For the purpose of this exercise, assume that the vowels are a, e, i, o, and u, either upper- or lowercase.

12. Imagine that you are writing a compiler. Write a CASE structure that watches for a sign character in a real expression. If the character is '+' or '-', the structure should display the message 'precedence level 0'; if the character is '*' or '/', it should display the message 'precedence level 1'; if anything else, the structure should do nothing.

9.5 TESTING AND DEBUGGING

The most common errors with decision structures are

- Inappropriate semicolons.
- Incorrect nesting.
- Failure of the selector variable to take on any of the tested values in a CASE structure.

These pitfalls were discussed earlier in the chapter. When you suspect that you are dealing with such an error, a *source-code debugger* can be a big help in pinpointing the location. (See Section 6.6 and the companion lab manual.) A good debugger will let you run your program up to a specified point in the code, called a *breakpoint*, and then execute your statements one by one, a process called *single-stepping* or *tracing*. The debugger can then be made to display the values of the variables in a so-called *watch* or *observe* window, so that you can check quickly for correct values at intermediate points in the execution. Quite often, merely checking a few values will reveal gross errors and lead you to the location of an error. A typical debugger is shown in Figure 9.5.1, indicating that the value in a selector variable is not one of the values listed in the CASE structure.

Figure 9.5.1 *A typical source-code debugger halted at a breakpoint in the code (at the arrow) displaying the value of the Choice variable in a watch window. The value of Choice is 'M', which is not one of the values listed in the CASE structure. This is an error in Standard Pascal.*

```
CODE

──► CASE Choice OF

      'F', 'f' : Fahrenheit := CToF( Celsius );
      'C', 'c' : Celsius := FToC( Fahrenheit );
      'K', 'k' : Kelvin := FToK( Fahrenheit )

    END;
```

```
WATCH
Choice = 'M' { Char }
```

When in doubt, print it out!

If your Pascal system does not provide a debugger, you can get the same information about your program by inserting extra output statements at strategic locations, printing out the values of all suspect variables at intermediate points of execution. The most common mistake of beginning programmers when looking for errors is to not print out enough data about what is really going on. Sherlock Holmes had it exactly right when he said in *A Scandal in Bohemia*, "It is a capital mistake to theorize with no facts." Be sure to gather enough facts before jumping to conclusions about your errors. Often an error is not what you first think it is.

Table 9.5.1 *Examples of syntax errors in CASE structures in Turbo Pascal 6.0, which allows an ELSE clause. (Errors in IF..THEN..ELSE structures were shown in Table 6.6.1.)*

Syntax error	Error message from compiler
Selector is not an ordinal expression.	`Ordinal expression expected.`
Keyword `OF` is missing.	`OF expected.`
Keyword `END` is missing.	`";" expected.`
Constants in a *ConstantList* are separated by a semicolon rather than a comma.	`":" expected.`
Semicolon missing between cases.	`END expected.`
Semicolon before `ELSE` clause or before `END`.	(No message)

LOOKING BACK

This chapter has provided additonal details on Pascal's decision structures: the `IF..THEN` structure, which conditionally executes a simple or compound statement; the `IF..THEN..ELSE` structure, which executes either of two alternative statements, either simple or compound; and the `CASE` structure, which allows multiway decisions that are determined by the value of an ordinal variable.

We used nested `IF..THEN..ELSE` structures to handle a complicated set of decisions in Section 9.2. Nesting can be continued to any desired depth, but the program gets more and more difficult to follow in such code, so it must be carefully planned. Often hierarchical subprogram design or a `CASE` structure can be used to simplify such programs.

The chapter ended with a brief introduction to the use of menus in programs. The example involved character responses from the keyboard, and benefited from using the `Upper` function developed earlier, and by use of a `CASE` structure, especially when the structure allows for a nonstandard `ELSE` or `OTHERWISE` clause. We also recognized a need for repetitive prompting when the user enters illegal responses to a menu. This will be discussed in the next chapter.

TERMS EMPHASIZED IN THIS CHAPTER

Boolean expression 265
Breakpoint 279–280
`CASE` 275–278
Compound statement 264
Conditional execution 264
Dangling `ELSE` 271
Debugger 279–280
Decision structure 263
Guarding a CASE structure 278
`IF..THEN` 265
`IF..THEN..ELSE` 265
Indentation 270
Menu 273–275
Multiway decision structure 268–271, 275–278
Nested decisions 268–271
Observe window 279–280
Selection structure 263
Single-stepping 279
Source-code debugger 279–280
Tracing 279
Two-way decision 264–265
Watch window 279–280

PROJECTS

1. (Suggested by Elena Driskill) Write a program that counsels people about their professional aptitudes. The program should know about the following professions:

Profession	Requirements
Brush salesman	Talkative, likes to travel
Gossip columnist	Either talkative or likes to travel or both
Cruise ship captain	Likes to travel, age between 21 and 60
CIA agent	Not talkative, likes to travel, age 18 or over
Bartender	Age over 21
Grocery bagger	No special requirements

   The program should ask the user some questions about his or her qualifications. On the basis of the answers, it should print out all the listed professions for which the user is qualified. Use a procedure to decide on and print out the recommendations.

2. (Suggested by Rich Thomson) Write a program that plays the Famous Person Guessing Game. The user thinks about one of the people in a list of famous persons known to the computer. The computer asks a series of yes/no questions about the person. Based on the user's answers to the questions, the computer determines which person the user had in mind. Your program should obtain the response from the user as a character (`'Y'` or `'N'`). You will ask three questions and store the results in three `Boolean` variables. Use the `Boolean` value `True` for the answer `'Y'` and the`Boolean False` for the answer `'N'`. Determine which person the user is thinking of by writing a unique `Boolean` expression (involving your three `Boolean` variables) for each famous person. Use this expression in an `IF...THEN` structure that will print out the name of the famous person the user has in mind. The questions are:

   i. Is the person alive?

   ii. Is the person female?

   iii. Is the person a politician?

   The famous people are Bill Clinton, Marie Curie, George Burns, Margaret Thatcher, Abraham Lincoln, Indira Gandhi, Thomas Edison, and Ralph Nader.

3. Write a `ShowHexadecimal` procedure that displays the hexadecimal (base-16) notation for a given one-byte positive integer. In the hexadecimal system, a single digit can have the values 0 through 15. The values 0–9 are written as in the decimal system, but the digit values 10–15 are represented by the capital letters A–F. (See Appendix J.) Thus the hexadecimal notation `C7` corresponds to the decimal number (12 x 16) + (7 x 1) = 199.

4. Write a `GetHex` procedure that reads a two-hex-digit number, and then returns the decimal value of that number. This procedure is the inverse of the one in Project 3.

5. Write a procedure that reads a word of up to four characters, terminated by a space or `<EOLn>`, and then reports a `Boolean` value indicating whether the word is a legal Pascal identifier. Don't worry about whether the word is a reserved word or predefined identifier.

6. The Floor function in mathematics, when applied to a real number, returns the largest integer less than or equal to the real number. That is, the Floor of a real number x has the property that

   $$\text{Floor}(x) \leq x < \text{Floor}(x) + 1.$$

   For example, Floor(1.23) = 1, while Floor(–7.31) = –8 and Floor(3.0) = 3. Design and write a `Floor` function in Pascal.

7. The Ceiling function in mathematics, when applied to a real number, returns the smallest integer greater than or equal to the real number. That is, the Ceiling of a real number x has the property that

   $$\text{Ceiling}(x) - 1 < x \le \text{Ceiling}(x).$$

   For example, Ceiling(1.23) = 2, while Ceiling(–7.31) = –7 and Ceiling(4.0) = 4. Design and write a `Ceiling` function in Pascal.

8. (From Dave Hanscom) Your local bank has assigned you to write a program to help customers calculate how much money they will accumulate in a savings account. The bank pays 7.6 percent interest at the end of each calendar year, on the year-end balance (before adding interest) if that balance is at least $500. If the balance is less than $500, it pays 7.2 percent. Your program must first ask the user to provide a password. If the user enters an incorrect password three times in a row, the program will terminate with an explanatory message. The correct password should be a four-digit integer. Once the user has entered the correct password, the program will ask for the first and last year for which the bank balance is to be calculated. For each year in the range, the program will then run as follows:

   i. It will ask for the total amount of deposits for that year, and the user will enter the amount.

   ii. It will ask for the total of withdrawals for that year, and the user will enter the amount. If the total of withdrawals is greater than the balance in the account, the program will ask for a smaller withdrawal total until such a number is provided.

   iii. It will calculate the closing balance for the year, using an appropriate interest rate.

   iv. It will display the year, the opening balance, the amount of deposits, the amount of withdrawals, the interest rate, and the closing balance, nicely formatted on the screen.

   Your program must check its input data for reasonableness. The program must not crash or give garbage output if the user enters negative numbers, a final year less than the starting year, and so on.

REFERENCES

The design of decision structures has been the subject of much study. Summaries are presented in textbooks on programming language design, such as Bruce J. MacLennan's *Principles of Programming Languages*, second edition (Holt, Rinehart and Winston, 1987), and Terrence W. Pratt's *Programming Languages*, second edition (Prentice-Hall, 1984). The failure of Standard Pascal's `CASE` structure to allow an `ELSE` clause is criticized by Prabhaker Mateti, in "Pascal versus C: A Subjective Comparison," in *Proceedings of the Symposium on Language Design and Programming Methodology*, September 1979 (Springer-Verlag). This article, among others of this type, is reprinted in *Comparing and Assessing Programming Languages: Ada, C, Pascal* (Prentice-Hall, 1984), edited by Alan Feuer and Narain Gehani.

CHAPTER 10

Repetition by Iteration

CHAPTER CONTENTS

INTRODUCTION

Like most labor-saving devices, computers are at their best when performing repetitive tasks. Repetitive data manipulations have a pattern, and the pattern can be exploited by setting up the right kind of iterative control structure, called a *loop*. This idea was introduced in Chapter 6, but now we explore it in much greater depth.

Pascal provides three iterative control structures:

- The `WHILE..DO` structure:
  While some condition is valid, keep executing repeatedly. The condition is tested before each execution of the loop body. (This structure, which is the most general, was introduced in Chapter 6.)
- The `FOR..DO` structure:
  Execute the loop body a preset number of times.
- The `REPEAT..UNTIL` structure:
  Repeat execution of the loop body until some condition occurs. The condition is tested after each execution of the loop body.

This chapter will explore these three structures in depth, examining their relative advantages and disadvantages and working through some typical applications of each.

10.1 THE WHILE . . DO STRUCTURE AGAIN

The `WHILE` structure can be described in English as, "While the conditions remain appropriate, keep repeating this task." The Pascal syntax was introduced in Section 6.2 and is described in greater detail in the box below.

In this chapter, we will examine all three of loop structures. As we do so, remember these unique properties of the `WHILE` structure:

- If *BooleanExpression* is `False` when execution first reaches the `WHILE` structure, *Statement* will never be executed. In other words, it is possible to make *zero* trips through a `WHILE` loop.
- Therefore, a `WHILE` loop is useful when the situation may or may not call for repeated executions of the loop body. (You will see an example on the next page.)
- The `WHILE` structure is Pascal's universal loop structure. As you will see later in the chapter, all loops can be constructed as `WHILE` structures, though it is often more convenient to use a `FOR` or `REPEAT..UNTIL` structure for reasons that will become apparent later.

Syntax of the WHILE..DO structure

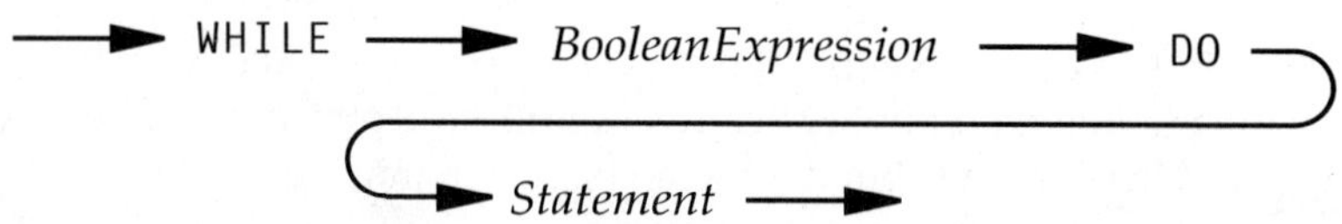

Pseudocode:

```
WHILE BooleanExpression DO
   Statement
```

If *BooleanExpression* is true, *Statement* is executed, then *BooleanExpression* is evaluated again. If it is still true, *Statement* is executed again, then *BooleanExpression* is evaluated again. And so on, until *BooleanExpression* is found to be false.

Notes:

- *Statement* may be a simple or a compound statement. It is called the **body** of the loop because it contains the instructions to be repeatedly executed while *BooleanExpression* is true.
- Each execution of *Statement* is called a **trip or pass** through the loop.
- *BooleanExpression* is called the **loop condition** because it determines whether the loop will continue. *BooleanExpression* is tested before every trip through the loop. If it is `True`, then *Statement* is executed and then *BooleanExpression* is tested again, and so on. If it is `False` when tested, the loop terminates and execution passes on to whatever code lies beyond the loop. If *BooleanExpression* is false when execution first reaches the `WHILE` structure, *Statement* is never executed.
- The `WHILE` structure is said to be a **pretest loop** because *BooleanExpression* is tested at the top of the loop, before each execution of *Statement*.

10.2 CASE STUDY: COUNTING CHARACTERS IN INPUT

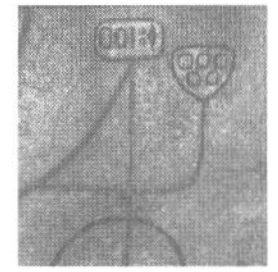

As an example of a situation that calls for a `WHILE` loop, consider how a program might count characters that come in from the standard `Input` file, stopping the count when the user enters some end-of-input signal, say the character `'@'`. A character like this, serving only to mark the end of the actual data, is called a **sentinel**.

Sentinel: A data value serving as a marker; for example, marking the end of input.

To begin the design process, we should first refine the specifications. We want to count characters from the keyboard until we see the sentinel, but the sentinel itself should not be counted. Here is the plan in detail:

1. Initialize the counter to zero.
2. Read a character from the keyboard, using a `ReadLn`.
3. If the current character is not the sentinel, then
   a. Count the character.
   b. Read another character, using a `ReadLn`.
   c. Loop back to the beginning of step 3.

It is possible that the sentinel might be the first character that is read, in which case we should count no characters at all. In such a case, we should never execute the body of the loop in step 3. This is why we test whether the current character is the sentinel at the beginning of step 3, before each execution of the loop body, and this in turn means that a `WHILE` structure is the natural choice for the loop.

Using a `WHILE` structure, we might have this code:

```
CONST
   Sentinel = '@';

VAR
   Count : Integer;
   Ch    : Char;
.
.
Count := 0;
ReadLn( Ch );

WHILE Ch <> Sentinel DO
BEGIN

   Count := Count + 1;
   ReadLn( Ch )

END;
```

The sequence of execution

Characters are being read by calls to `ReadLn`, so the user will have to press the RETURN key after each character, including the final `'@'`. Let us suppose that the user has entered the string

`'H'<EOLn>'e'<EOLn>'l'<EOLn>'l'<EOLn>'o'<EOLn>'@'<EOLn>`

Then when execution reaches the `WHILE` structure, `Count` has the value 0 and the initial `ReadLn` has read `'H'` into `Ch` and has also discarded the `<EOLn>` after the `'H'`. The following diagram shows the situation as the loop begins, when the `Boolean` expression is evaluated. A left-pointing bent arrow ↵ is used to symbolize <EOLn> within the file.

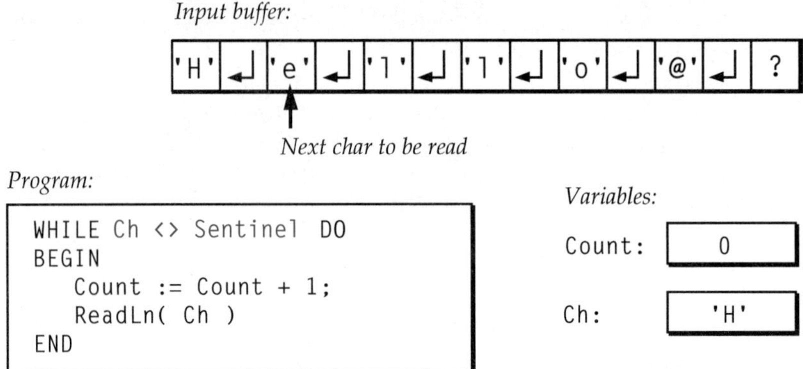

Since `Ch` is not the sentinel, the body of the loop is executed. First `Count` is incremented,

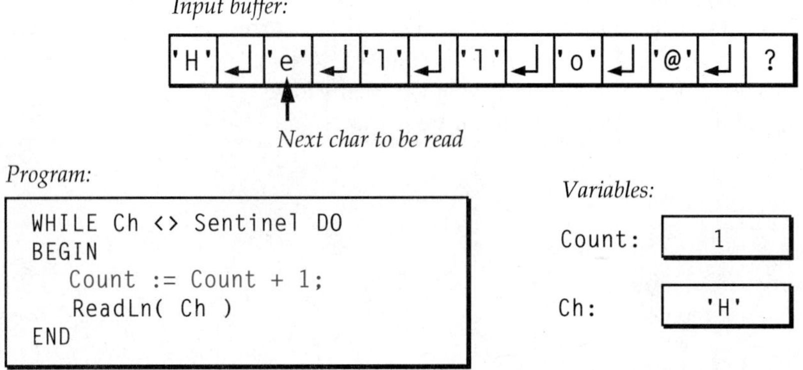

Then another `ReadLn` is executed:

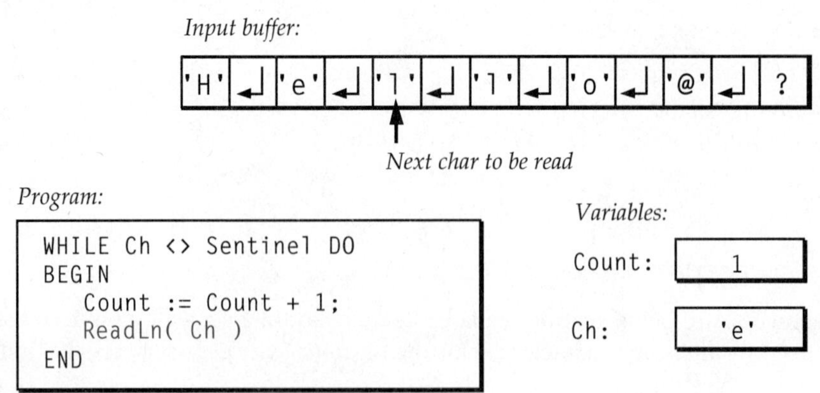

At this point, `Ch` contains `'e'`, `Count` contains `1`, and we have finished the first trip through the loop body. Execution next loops back to the top of the `WHILE` structure and the `Boolean` expression is evaluated again:

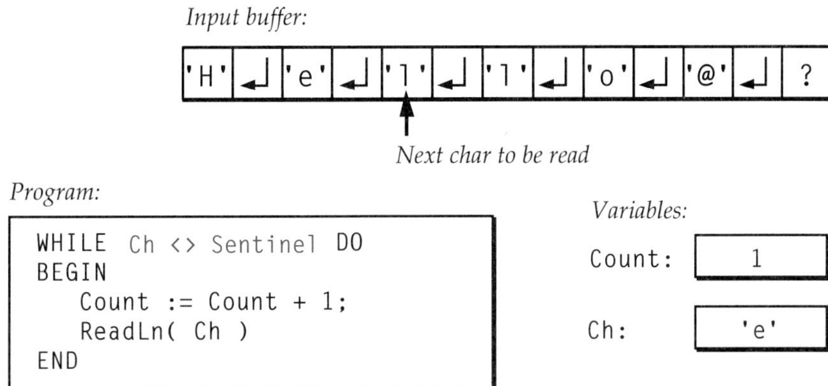

Again, `Ch` does not contain the sentinel, so the loop body is executed a second time. During the second trip, `Count` becomes 2, another character is read into `Ch`, and we loop back again.

This continues until the fifth trip, in which `Count` becomes 5 and the `ReadLn` stores `'@'` in `Ch`. Then we loop back and evaluate the `Boolean` expression for the sixth time:

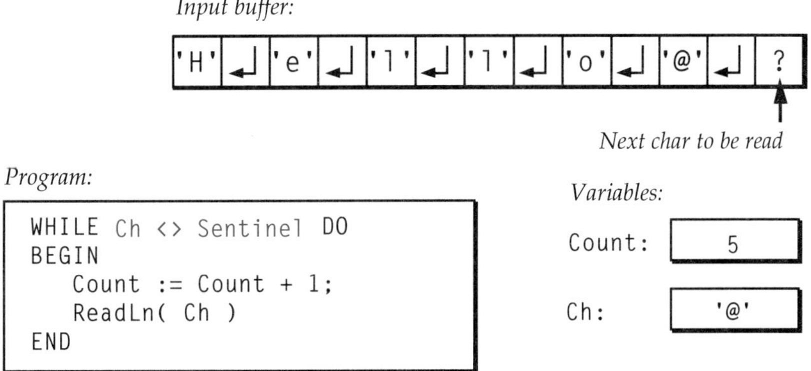

This time `Ch` contains the sentinel, so the loop terminates, with execution passing on to whatever code lies beyond the end of the `WHILE` structure. `Count` contains 5, the number of nonsentinel characters that were read.

What if the first character is the sentinel?

If the user enters no characters before the sentinel, just `'@'` and `<EOLn>`, we arrive at the `WHILE` structure with `Count` containing 0 and `Ch` containing the sentinel character. This is shown at the top of the next page.

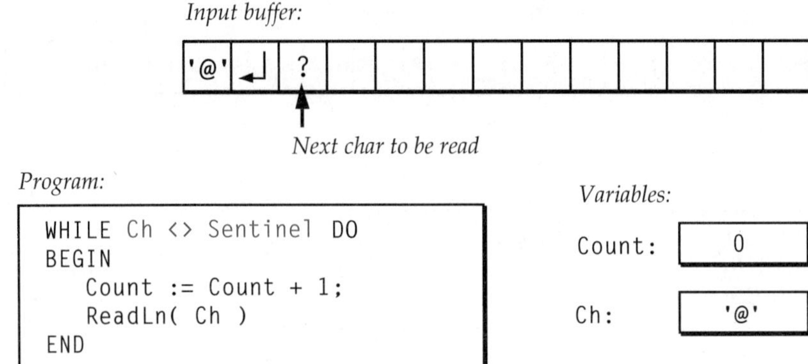

The `Boolean` expression is `False`, so the loop body is never executed; execution passes immediately to the code lying beyond the end of the `WHILE` structure, with `Count` containing 0, the number of nonsentinel characters read.

A procedure or a function?

Should our code be in a procedure or a function? We said in Section 7.3 that *a procedure is preferred when I/O is performed in addition to returning a value*, so we will use a procedure here. We will name it `CountChars`, and make `Count` a `VAR` parameter. We will also inform the reader that each character should be on a separate line, and to terminate the sequence with the sentinel:

```
PROCEDURE CountChars( VAR Count : Integer );
{
   POSTCONDITION:
   Count contains the number of characters received
   from Input, not including the sentinel.
}
CONST
   Sentinel = '@';

VAR
   Ch : Char;

BEGIN
   Count := 0;

   WriteLn( 'Enter each character on a separate line,' );
   WriteLn( 'with ', Sentinel, ' to mark end of sequence:' );
   ReadLn( Ch );

   WHILE Ch <> Sentinel DO
   BEGIN

      Count := Count + 1;
      ReadLn( Ch )

   END

END; { CountChars }
```

Write a driver to test the procedure.

As usual, we set up a driver before running the procedure, and test the driver with a stub in place of the final procedure. For initial testing purposes, the stub returns 0 to the main program:

```
PROGRAM TestCounting (Input, Output);
{Driver for CountChars procedure}

VAR
   NumChars : Integer;


PROCEDURE CountChars( VAR Count : Integer );
{
  POSTCONDITION:
  Count contains the number of characters received
  from Input, not including the sentinel.
}
BEGIN

   WriteLn( 'CountChars is a stub only.' );
   Count := 0

END; { CountChars }


BEGIN { main program }

   WriteLn( 'COUNTING CHARS IN KEYBOARD INPUT' );
   WriteLn;

   {-- Get number of input characters }
   CountChars( NumChars );

   WriteLn;
   WriteLn( 'Number of chars = ', NumChars )

END.
```

As usual, *you should compile and test the driver program at this stage,* before adding the code for the `CountChars` procedure. By removing bugs at this early stage, you make it easier to debug the `CountChars` procedure itself when you get around to adding its code.

Questions

1. When running the `CountChars` procedure, what will happen if the user enters `<EOF>` before entering any other characters? (`<EOF>` was defined in Section 4.4.) Will this cause the procedure to fail? Will the procedure report the correct value of `Count`?
2. In running the `CountChars` procedure, why does the user have to press the RETURN key after every character entered? (Give two reasons.)

Exercises

3. How many times will *Statement* be executed in the following `WHILE` structures?

a.
```
Finished := False;
WHILE NOT Finished DO
BEGIN
   Statement;
   Finished := True
END;
```

b.
```
Finished := True;
WHILE NOT Finished DO
BEGIN
   Statement;
   Finished := False
END;
```

c.
```
Finished := False;
WHILE NOT Finished DO
BEGIN
   Statement
END;
```

d.
```
Finished := True;
WHILE Finished DO
BEGIN
   Statement;
   Finished := False
END;
```

e.
```
Count := 0;
WHILE Count < 6 DO
BEGIN
   Statement;
   Count := Count + 2
END;
```

f.
```
Count := 0;
WHILE Count >= 0 DO
BEGIN
   Statement;
   Count := Count - 1
END;
```

10.3 FENCEPOSTS, SEMICOLONS, AND INFINITE LOOPS

The `CountChars` procedure uses two `ReadLn`s to read its characters. It seems possible to improve the algorithm by rearranging it to use a single `ReadLn`. Here is one possibility, using a `Boolean` variable to keep track of whether more characters remain to be read before the sentinel:

```
VAR
   Ch         : Char;
   MoreToRead : Boolean;

BEGIN
   .
   .
   Count      := 0;
   MoreToRead := True;

   WHILE MoreToRead DO
   BEGIN

      ReadLn( Ch );
      Count := Count + 1;

      IF Ch = Sentinel THEN
         MoreToRead := False

   END;
```

Unfortunately, this stucture suffers from one of the most common errors with loops: an **off-by-one error**, also called a **fencepost error**. The code above counts the sentinel, so its final result is too high by one.

The term *fencepost error* comes from a common problem in everyday counting:

> If fenceposts are 12 feet apart, how many fenceposts are required for 36 feet of fence?

Many people would quickly divide 36 by 12 and leap to the conclusion that we need three fenceposts. But this neglects the fact that there must be posts on *both* ends of the fence, so the correct answer is four.

The fencepost error in our counting-characters code can be fixed by incrementing the counter only if the latest character is not the sentinel:

```
WHILE MoreToRead DO
BEGIN

   ReadLn( Ch );

   IF Ch = Sentinel THEN
      MoreToRead := False

   ELSE
      Count := Count + 1

END;
```

With this version of the loop structure, our procedure looks like this:

```
PROCEDURE CountChars( VAR Count : Integer );
{
  POSTCONDITION:
  Count contains the number of characters received from Input,
  not including the sentinel.
}
CONST
   Sentinel = '@';

VAR
   Ch         : Char;
   MoreToRead : Boolean;

BEGIN

   Count      := 0;
   MoreToRead := True;

   WriteLn( 'Enter each character on a separate line,' );
   WriteLn( 'with ', Sentinel, ' to mark end of sequence:' );

   WHILE MoreToRead DO
   BEGIN

      ReadLn( Ch );

      IF Ch = Sentinel THEN
         MoreToRead := False

      ELSE
         Count := Count + 1

   END

END; { CountChars }
```

Is this version of the procedure better than the one in the last section? There is only one `ReadLn` call, but now there is a `Boolean` variable we didn't have before. Perhaps the first version is easier to understand, but it's a matter of taste.

The mystery of the extra semicolon and the infinite loop

Here's another common error. Suppose the loop structure above were written as follows, with an extra semicolon after the `WHILE..DO`:

```
WHILE MoreToRead DO;
BEGIN
   ReadLn( Ch );

   IF Ch = Sentinel THEN
      MoreToRead := False
   ELSE
      Count := Count + 1
END
```

When this version is executed, the computer just seems to "go away"; no characters are ever read, and the program never ends. What is wrong? Perhaps it would help to point out that the code is the same as if we had indented it this way:

```
WHILE MoreToRead DO
   ;
BEGIN
   ReadLn( Ch );

   IF Ch = Sentinel THEN
      MoreToRead := False
   ELSE
      Count := Count + 1
END
```

The extra semicolon after the `WHILE..DO` statement acts as a separator between the `WHILE..DO` and the next statement, which is now the compound statement `BEGIN..END`. Thus, the entire `WHILE` structure in this version consists of just

```
WHILE MoreToRead DO
   ;
```

This says, "As long as `MoreToRead` is true, keep on executing an empty statement." Since an empty statement cannot modify `MoreToRead`, `MoreToRead` remains true forever, and the loop continues running forever. This is an example of an *infinite loop*, one of the common errors in writing loop structures.

> On some Pascal systems, an infinite loop can be halted by keying Control-C. (Hold down the CONTROL key while pressing the C key.) In Turbo Pascal, the halt command is Control-Shift-Break. (But the system must be configured to recognize the command.) Check your reference manual or ask your instructor for the halt command that works with your system.

10.4 COUNTER-DRIVEN WHILE..DO STRUCTURES

The `Boolean` expression in a `WHILE` structure is often used to test the value of a variable that counts trips through the loop: a so-called **counter variable**. Suppose that you need to print out a table of the ordinal values and characters in your system's character set (Appendix C) from some low ordinal value to some high ordinal value. For example, you might want to print out the ASCII characters from number 33 through number 40. (It could happen!) Suppose that the output should look as shown on the next page:

```
Ord Value   Character

    33          !
    34          "
    35          #
    36          $
    37          %
    38          @
    39          '
    40          (
```

We know that the rows of the table can be printed by the statement

```
WriteLn( OrdValue:5, ' ':11, Chr( OrdValue ) )
```

All we need is a loop that sweeps `OrdValue` from a given low value to a given high value. Assume that we already have these limits. The plan of the loop can be outlined as follows:

1. Write the table header and then skip a line.

2. `OrdValue` is initialized with the value of the given low limit.

3. If `OrdValue` is no greater than the given high limit, then
  a. Write a row of the table.
  b. Increment `OrdValue`.
  c. Loop back to the beginning of step 3.

Now, before writing code, check that this will work even in exceptional cases. We might be given a high limit that is *lower* than the low limit, but that's okay. In such a case, the loop body will never be executed, and an empty table will be displayed. We might be given limits that include control characters as opposed to displayable characters. Some of these control characters may cause weird things to happen when we try to display them. We might, therefore, show the message

```
Not displayable
```

in the table when we encounter these ordinal values. So let's rewrite step **3a** to read

3a. On the current row of the table, display the ordinal value and

If `OrdValue` is in the displayable range, then
  display the character for this `OrdValue`
else
  display the message `Not displayable`

The rest of the algorithm is unchanged.

Here is a procedure that implements the second version of the algorithm:

```
PROCEDURE ShowCharTable( LowLimit, HighLimit : Integer );

VAR
   OrdValue : Integer;

BEGIN

   WriteLn( 'Ord Value', ' ':3, 'Character' );
   WriteLn;

   OrdValue := LowLimit;
   WHILE OrdValue <= HighLimit DO
   BEGIN

      Write( OrdValue:5, ' ':11 );

      IF Displayable( OrdValue ) THEN
         WriteLn( Chr( OrdValue ) )

      ELSE
         WriteLn( 'Not displayable' );

      OrdValue := OrdValue + 1

   END

END; { ShowCharTable }
```

The purpose of this procedure is to write the table, not to figure out if characters are displayable. Therefore, we have not written into this procedure the code to check for displayability. *That's the discipline of top-down design: In this procedure, write only what is required by the task at hand. If we need subtasks done, assume that we can write other subprograms for those. We'll worry later about how to design those other subprograms.*

Exercises

4. Write a driver and a suitable `Displayable` function for the `ShowCharTable` procedure shown above, and test it.

5. Explain why the following loop structures are syntactically illegal. Assume that `Count` is `Integer`, `Ch` is `Char`, and `Finished` is `Boolean`.

   a.
   ```
   WHILE Count DO
      Statement;
   ```

   b.
   ```
   WHILE Count < 10
      Statement;
   ```

   c.
   ```
   WHILE Ch <> 'a' DO
      Statement;
      Statement
   END;
   ```

6. How many times will *Statement* be executed in the following `WHILE` structures?

a.
```
Finished := False;
WHILE NOT Finished DO
BEGIN
   Statement;
   Finished := Succ( Finished )
END;
```

b.
```
Finished := Pred( True );
WHILE Finished DO
BEGIN
   Statement;
   Finished := False
END;
```

c.
```
Count := 10;
WHILE Count > 0 DO
BEGIN
   Statement;
   Count := Count - 3
END;
```

d.
```
Ch := 'A';
WHILE Ch <= 'C' DO
BEGIN
   Statement;
   Ch := Pred( Ch )
END;
```

e.
```
Ch := 'A';
WHILE Ch <= 'C' DO
BEGIN
   Statement;
   Ch := Succ( Ch )
END;
```

f.
```
RNum := 0.0;
WHILE RNum <> 100.0 DO
BEGIN
   Statement;
   RNum := RNum + 0.1
END;
```

7. `WHILE` structures, like all control structures, can be nested. What is printed by the following program fragments?

   a.
```
I := 0;

WHILE I <= 3 DO
BEGIN

   J := 0;

   WHILE J <= 3 DO
   BEGIN
      WriteLn( I:1, ' ':3, J:1 );
      J := J + 1
   END;

   I := I + 1

END;
```

   b.
```
Count := 0;
WHILE Count < 10 DO
   WHILE Count > 10 DO
      Count := Count + 1;
      WriteLn( Count:2 );
```

8. How many times will *Statement* be executed in the following nested `WHILE` structures?

   a.
```
Index := 1;
Limit := 10;

WHILE Index < Limit DO
BEGIN

   Count := 5;

   WHILE Count >= 1 DO
   BEGIN
      Statement;
      Count := Count - 1
   END;

   Index := Index + 1

END;
```

   b.
```
Index := 0;
WHILE Index < 3 DO
BEGIN
   Statement;
   WHILE Index > 3 DO
      Index := Index + 1;
END;
```

10.5 FOR STRUCTURES

Counter-controlled `WHILE` **loops** are so common that Pascal provides a shorthand version. Consider the upward-counting `WHILE` loop in which the integer counter starts at `LowerLimit`, **increments** by 1, and ends at `UpperLimit`:

```
Count := LowerLimit;
WHILE Count <= UpperLimit DO
BEGIN
   Statement;
   Count := Count + 1
END
```

This loop can be written in the alternate `FOR..TO..DO` notation

```
FOR Count := LowerLimit TO UpperLimit DO
   Statement
```

Similarly for the downward-counting `WHILE` loop in which the integer counter starts at `UpperLimit` and **decrements** downward by 1 to `LowerLimit`:

```
Count := UpperLimit;
WHILE Count >= LowerLimit DO
BEGIN
   Statement;
   Count := Count - 1
END
```

This loop can be written in the alternate `FOR..DOWNTO..DO` notation

```
FOR Count := UpperLimit DOWNTO LowerLimit DO
   Statement
```

In both cases, the `FOR` structure is equivalent to a `WHILE` structure that includes

- **Preinitialization** of the counter variable.
- A **pretest loop** in which the counter is compared with a terminal value.
- **Postincrementation** or **postdecrementation**
  (incrementation or decrementation at the bottom of the loop).

There's a limitation: The counter variable, also called the **loop index**, is required to change by *1* after each trip through the loop; no other incrementation or decrementation is allowed. On the other hand, the `FOR` structure allows the loop index to be of *any ordinal type*, and not just integer. The complete syntax is summarized on the next pages.

When to use a FOR loop

A `FOR` loop is appropriate when each iteration is to be associated with a distinct value of a counter variable and the limits of the counter are known before the loop begins.

Syntax of the FOR . . TO . . DO structure

Upward-counting version:

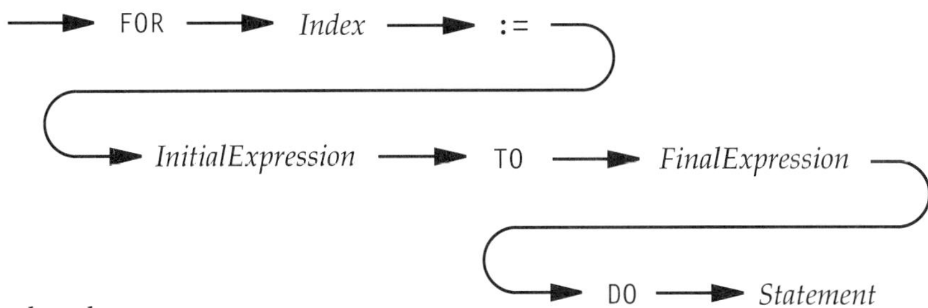

Pseudocode:

```
FOR Index := InitialExpression TO FinalExpression DO
   Statement
```

is shorthand for

```
Index := InitialExpression;
WHILE Index <= FinalExpression DO
BEGIN
   Statement;
   Index := Succ( Index )
END
```

Downward-counting version:

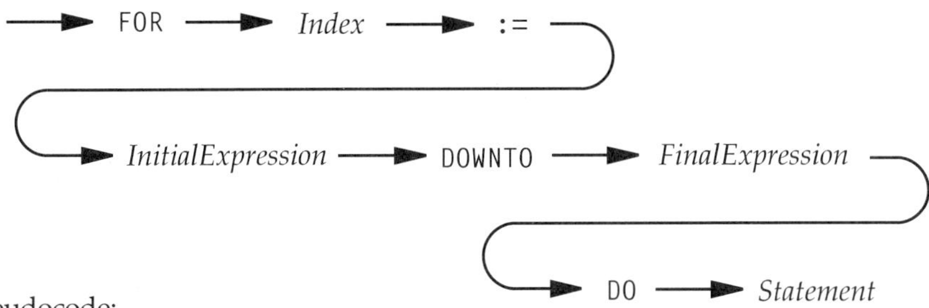

Pseudocode:

```
FOR Index := InitialExpression DOWNTO FinalExpression DO
   Statement
```

is shorthand for

```
Index := InitialExpression;
WHILE Index >= FinalExpression DO
BEGIN
   Statement;
   Index := Pred( Index )
END
```

(Syntax summary continued on the next page)

Syntax of the FOR . . TO . . DO structure (continued from previous page)

Notes:

- *Index* is the name of the counter variable, or loop index, which can be of any *ordinal type*. It doesn't have to be an integer, but it cannot be real. This variable must be declared in the local variable declarations of the program or subprogram that immediately contains it. It cannot be a formal parameter of the subprogram containing the `FOR` structure.
- *InitialExpression* and *FinalExpression* are expressions of a type that is assignment-compatible with *Index*. If the value of *FinalExpression* is less than the value of *InitialExpression* in an upward-counting `FOR` loop, or if the value of *FinalExpression* is greater than the value of *InitialExpression* in a downward-counting `FOR` loop, no trips are executed and the loop is skipped.
- *Statement* comprises the *loop body*. This may be a simple or compound statement.
- The number of trips through the loop is actually calculated before the loop begins. Therefore, the body of the loop cannot alter, *or even threaten to alter*, the number of trips. In Standard Pascal it is therefore illegal to perform the following operations in the body of a `FOR` loop:

  Assigning a value to *Index*.

  Passing *Index* as a `VAR` parameter to a subprogram.

  Reusing *Index* as the counter for a nested `FOR` loop.

  Calling `Read` or `ReadLn` with *Index* as a parameter.
- *Index* is regarded as an artifact of the loop whose value becomes **undefined** after the loop has terminated. That is, the value of *Index* after the loop has ended depends on your Pascal system.
- Because a `FOR` loop's *Index* becomes undefined when the loop terminates, *Index* acts afterwards as though its final incrementation or decrementation had not occurred. This means that *Index* will not go out of range even if *FinalExpression* is equal to the maximum or minimum allowed value for the *Index* type. This allows `FOR` loops to be used in some situations in which the corresponding `WHILE` loop would cause a range error. (See Chapter 14.)

Sequence of execution when counting upward

To fully understand the execution of a `FOR` loop, bear in mind that it is shorthand for a counter-driven `WHILE` loop, as shown above. For example, consider the code

```
FOR Index := 1 TO 2 DO
   WriteLn( Index:1 );

WriteLn( 'Loop has terminated.' );
```

As the loop begins to run, `Index` is initialized to 1. This is the preinitialization step mentioned above:

```
FOR Index := 1 TO 2 DO
   WriteLn( Index:1 );

WriteLn( 'Loop has terminated.' );
```

Then, at the top of the loop, `Index` is compared to 2. (This is the pretest.)

```
FOR Index := 1 TO 2 DO
   WriteLn( Index:1 );

WriteLn( 'Loop has terminated.' );
```

Since the loop is counting upward and `Index` is no greater than 2, the body of the loop is executed; that is, the `WriteLn` displays 1.

```
FOR Index := 1 TO 2 DO
   WriteLn( Index:1 );

WriteLn( 'Loop has terminated.' );
```

Then, as the first trip through the loop body ends, `Index` becomes 2. (This is the post-incrementation.)

```
FOR Index := 1 TO 2 DO
   WriteLn( Index:1 )
   {Index is incremented at bottom of loop};

WriteLn( 'Loop has terminated.' );
```

This ends the first trip.

Back at the top of the loop again, `Index` is compared with 2.

```
FOR Index := 1 TO 2 DO
   WriteLn( Index:1 );

WriteLn( 'Loop has terminated.' );
```

Since it is no greater than 2, the loop body is executed again, displaying 2.

```
FOR Index := 1 TO 2 DO
   WriteLn( Index:1 );

WriteLn( 'Loop has terminated.' );
```

As the second trip ends, `Index` is incremented to 3.

```
FOR Index := 1 TO 2 DO
   WriteLn( Index:1 );
   {Index is incremented at bottom of loop};

WriteLn( 'Loop has terminated.' );
```

Back at the top of the loop again, `Index` is found to be greater than 2,

```
FOR Index := 1 TO 2 DO
   WriteLn( Index:1 );

WriteLn( 'Loop has terminated.' );
```

so the loop terminates and execution passes to the statement following the loop, which displays the message `Loop has terminated`.

```
FOR Index := 1 TO 2 DO
   WriteLn( Index:1 );

WriteLn( 'Loop has terminated.' );
```

The net effect is that this loop displays the output

```
1
2
Loop has terminated.
```

Undefined value: A value that depends on the Pascal system being used, and is therefore undependable.

`Index` may or may not have the value 3 when the loop terminates; it depends on the Pascal system being used. In this sense, the value of the loop index becomes **undefined** on termination of the loop.

Sequence of execution when counting downward

A downward-counting loop is similar. Consider the code

```
FOR Index := 2 DOWNTO 1 DO
   WriteLn( Index:1 );

WriteLn( 'Loop has terminated.' );
```

As the loop begins to run, `Index` is preinitialized to 2.

```
FOR Index := 2 DOWNTO 1 DO
   WriteLn( Index:1 );

WriteLn( 'Loop has terminated.' );
```

Then, at the top of the loop, `Index` is compared to 1.

```
FOR Index := 2 DOWNTO 1 DO
   WriteLn( Index:1 );

WriteLn( 'Loop has terminated.' );
```

Since the loop is counting downward and `Index` is not *less* than 1, the body of the loop is executed; that is, the `WriteLn` displays 2.

```
FOR Index := 2 DOWNTO 1 DO
   WriteLn( Index:1 );

WriteLn( 'Loop has terminated.' );
```

Then, as the first trip through the loop body ends, `Index` is *decremented* to 1 (post-decrementation).

```
FOR Index := 2 DOWNTO 1 DO
   WriteLn( Index:1 )
   {Index is decremented at bottom of loop};

WriteLn( 'Loop has terminated.' );
```

This ends the first trip.

Back at the top of the loop again, `Index` is compared with 1.

```
FOR Index := 2 DOWNTO 1 DO
   WriteLn( Index:1 );

WriteLn( 'Loop has terminated.' );
```

Since it is not less than 1, the loop body is executed again, displaying 1.

```
FOR Index := 2 DOWNTO 1 DO
   WriteLn( Index:1 );

WriteLn( 'Loop has terminated.' );
```

As the second trip ends, `Index` is decremented to 0.

```
FOR Index := 2 DOWNTO 1 DO
   WriteLn( Index:1 );
   {Index is decremented at bottom of loop};

WriteLn( 'Loop has terminated.' );
```

Back at the top of the loop again, `Index` is found to be less than 1,

```
FOR Index := 2 DOWNTO 1 DO
   WriteLn( Index:1 );

WriteLn( 'Loop has terminated.' );
```

so the loop terminates and execution passes to the statement following the loop, which displays the message `Loop has terminated.`

```
FOR Index := 2 DOWNTO 1 DO
   WriteLn( Index:1 );

WriteLn( 'Loop has terminated.' );
```

The net effect is that this loop displays the output

```
2
1
Loop has terminated.
```

`Index` may or may not have the value 0 when the loop terminates; it depends on the Pascal system being used. Again, the value of the loop index becomes *undefined* upon termination of the loop.

10.6 USING FOR STRUCTURES

The last section may mislead you into thinking that `FOR` loops are always driven by integer counter variables, or that they are only useful when a variable increments or decrements by 1. To dispel these possible misconceptions, we examine two more applications.

The loop index can be of any ordinal type.

The index of a FOR loop can be *any ordinal type*: Integer, Char, Boolean, or others you will meet later. Consider an alternate version of the ShowCharTable procedure that receives characters, rather than ordinal values, as parameters. This version generates the same display as before, but by a reverse technique. The loop sweeps through all the characters in the specified range, calculating the ordinal values from the characters:

```
PROCEDURE ShowCharTable2( LowCh, HighCh : Char );

VAR
   Ch       : Char;
   OrdValue : Integer;

BEGIN

   WriteLn( 'Ord Value', ' ':3, 'Character' );
   WriteLn;

   FOR Ch := LowCh TO HighCh DO
   BEGIN

      OrdValue := Ord( Ch );
      Write( OrdValue:5, ' ':11 );

      IF Displayable( OrdValue) THEN
         WriteLn( Ch )
      ELSE
         WriteLn( 'Not displayable' )

   END

END; { ShowCharTable2 }
```

If the call is

```
ShowCharTable2( ' ', '$' )
```

this procedure gives the output shown below:

```
Ord Value   Character

   32
   33           !
   34           "
   35           #
   36           $
```

Again, the index of a FOR loop can be any ordinal type, but *it cannot be real.*

Incrementing or decrementing by something other than 1

Sometimes you want a loop that increments or decrements by a number different from 1, or even by a real number. Neither of these things can be done directly by a Pascal FOR loop, but it isn't difficult to get them done *in*directly. For example, if you want to display a given number of odd positive integers, starting with 1, you need a loop that increments an integer by two during each trip:

```
PROCEDURE DisplayOddPositive( HowMany : Integer );
{
  PRECONDITION:
  0 < HowMany.

  POSTCONDITION:
  Displayed table shows HowMany odd positive integers,
  starting with 1.
}
VAR
   Index, OddInt : Integer;

BEGIN

   WriteLn( 'Odd integers <= ', HowMany:5 );
   WriteLn;

   { -- Start with the first odd positive integer }
   OddInt := 1;

   FOR Index := 1 TO HowMany DO
   BEGIN

      WriteLn( OddInt:5 );
      OddInt := OddInt + 2

   END

END; { DisplayOddPositive }
```

On the first trip through the loop, `OddInt` contains 1. On successive trips, `OddInt` is incremented by 2, so it sweeps upward through the odd integer values. Thus, while the loop index is incremented by 1 after every trip, `OddInt` is incremented differently.

Questions

9. In the `DisplayOddPositive` procedure above, suppose that the initialization of `OddInt` and the `FOR` loop were replaced by

```
FOR Index := 1 TO HowMany DO
   WriteLn( ((2 * Index) - 1):5 )
```

Now the integer to be displayed is calculated directly from `Index` and the code is much shorter. But will this code run as fast as the first version? Why or why not?

10. Suppose that the goal in `DisplayOddPositive` were not to display a given number of odd positive integers, but to display all odd positive integers less than a given number, which is supplied as a parameter. Would a `FOR` loop then be the most appropriate structure, or would a `WHILE` structure be more appropriate? Discuss this.

11. Why is the `OrdValue` variable desirable in the `ShowCharTable2` procedure?

Exercises

12. Standard Pascal decrees that it shall be illegal for the body of a `FOR` loop to modify the loop's index, or even threaten to modify it. Nonetheless, some actual Pascal implementations fail to issue an error message in such cases. What does your Pascal system do with the following loop?

```
FOR Count := 1 TO 5 DO
BEGIN
   WriteLn( Count );
   Count := Count + 5;
   WriteLn( Count )
END;
```

13. What is printed by the following code fragment? Assume that `Index` is `Integer` and `RNum` is `Real`.

```
WriteLn( 'Num   SqRt( Num )' );
WriteLn;

FOR Index := 1 TO 10 DO
BEGIN
   RNum := Index;
   WriteLn( RNum:5:1, ' ':5, SqRt( RNum ):6:3 )
END;
```

14. What would happen if Exercise 12 used the following code?

```
WriteLn( '  Num   SqRt( Num )' );
WriteLn;

FOR RNum := 1.0 TO 10.0 DO
   WriteLn( RNum:5:1, ' ':5, SqRt( RNum ):5:3 );
```

15. How many trips are made through the following loop structures? (Assume ASCII code.)

a.
```
FOR Ch := 'a' TO 'z' DO
   WriteLn( Ch, ' ':3, Ord( Ch ):3 );
```

b.
```
FOR Logical := True DOWNTO False DO
   WriteLn( Logical, ' ':3, Ord( Logical ):1 );
```

c.
```
Low := 1;
High := 2 * Low - 4;
FOR Index := High DOWNTO Low DO
   WriteLn( Index:2 );
```

d.
```
Low := 1;
High := MaxInt - (MaxInt - 1);
FOR Index := Low TO High DO
   WriteLn( Index:2 );
```

16. How many trips are made through the *inner* loop structures? (Assume ASCII.)

a.
```
FOR Ch1 := 'a' TO 'z' DO
   FOR Ch2 := 'a' TO Ch1 DO
      WriteLn( Ch1, ' ':3, Ch2 );
```

b.
```
FOR Ch1 := 'a' TO 'z' DO
   FOR Ch2 := 'a' TO 'z' DO
      WriteLn( Ch1, ' ':3, Ch2 );
```

c.
```
N := 25;
FOR Index := 1 TO N DO
   FOR Count := N DOWNTO 1 DO
      WriteLn( Count:3 );
```

d.
```
N := 25;
FOR Index := 1 TO N DO
   FOR Count := Index DOWNTO 1 DO
      WriteLn( Count:3 );
```

10.7 CASE STUDY: MONTE CARLO CALCULATION OF PI

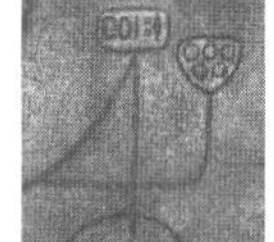

The theory of probability provides techniques for computing numbers from random events. Such calculations are often called **Monte Carlo methods**, after the casino in Monaco. As a simple example of such a calculation, we will compute an estimate of π. The method we are going to discuss is similar to one called "Buffon's needle," described in 1777 by the French mathematician and scientist, George Louis Leclerc, the Comte de Buffon. References are cited at the end of the chapter.

Here is our version of the problem: What is the probability that points distributed randomly inside a square will fall inside a circle inscribed in the square? In particular, suppose we have a 2 x 2 square containing a circle of radius 1, as shown in Figure 10.7.1.

Here's where probability theory comes in. Suppose there are many points, and that these points are distributed randomly within the square. Then the laws of probability predict that the fraction of these points in the square that also fall inside the circle will equal

$$\text{(Area of the circle) / (Area of the square)} = \pi r^2 / 4r^2 = \pi(1)^2 / 4(1)^2 = \pi / 4$$

Figure 10.7.1

What is the probability that points distributed randomly within the 2x2 square will fall inside the inscribed circle, which has radius 1?

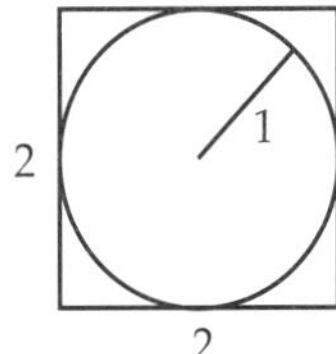

Figure 10.7.2 *The quadrant considered in the calculation has $0 \le x < 1$ and $0 \le y < 1$.*

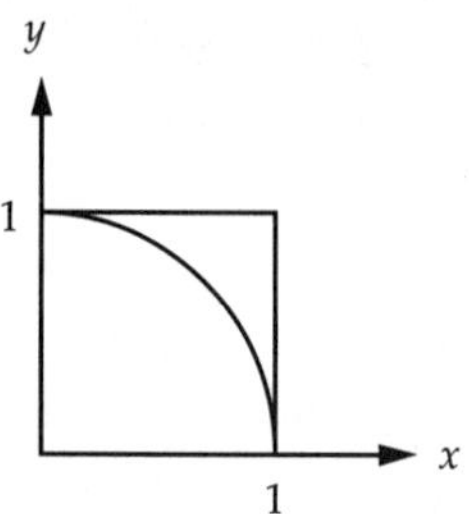

We now have the basis for a nonintuitive but simple way to estimate π: We sprinkle many randomly distributed points into the square, and count the fraction of them that fall inside the circle. This fraction should equal π / 4.

Generating randomly distributed points

To make the calculation easier, let us choose a rectangular coordinate system with the origin at the center of the square. Furthermore, let us consider only the upper-right quadrant, as shown in Figure 10.7.2. Each randomly located point (x,y) in this quadrant will have x and y as random numbers in the ranges $0 \le x < 1,\ 0 \le y < 1$.

Many Pascal systems provide a function called `Random` that returns random numbers in just this range. If your system does not provide such a function, you can use the one described in Appendix I of this book. The `Random` function does not return a truly random number, but a number in a sequence like this one:

0.1230000, 0.4133567, 0.1229731, 0.7231456, 0.056723, . . .

The first number in the sequence is called the **seed**, and is chosen as described below. After the seed, each number in the sequence is calculated from the one before it. Each time you call `Random`, the next number in the sequence is calculated. The numbers are therefore not random, because if you knew the algorithm, you could predict each number from its predecessor in the sequence. But no pattern is obvious when we examine the sequence, so the numbers are said to be **pseudorandom**.

In typical Pascal systems, the sequence of pseudorandom numbers is started by calling a `Randomize` procedure, which generates a seed number or requests one from the user. The `Random` function will then return another number in the sequence every time it is called. Because the sequence is not truly random, the numbers will eventually repeat, with the process cycling through a finite sequence of numbers again and again. But a good pseudorandom number generator will generate many numbers before it repeats.

The syntax for calling `Randomize` and `Random` is worth a comment. The `Random` function is unusual because it not only returns a value, but also produces a new value of the seed, to be used in generating the next number in the sequence. (In other words, it has an *intentional side effect*.) We might, therefore, choose to have the seed as a `VAR` parameter. This would require the following syntax when generating random x and y values:

```
X := Random( Seed );
Y := Random( Seed );
```

Unfortunately, this syntax is likely to suggest that the calling program should produce the `Seed` values. Actually, the `Seed` values are maintained entirely by `Randomize` and `Random`, and should not be the concern of client programs. Therefore, most programmers prefer to hide the `Seed` value within the pseudorandom subprograms, *making* `Seed` *a global variable.* Despite the warnings in this book against using global variables, the pseudorandom number generator is a rare exception to the rule.

Using `Randomize` and `Random`, we can generate 1,000 random points in the upper-right quadrant of our square by writing

```
{ -- Seed the pseudorandom number generator }
Randomize;
.
.
FOR Count := 1 TO 1000 DO
BEGIN

    { -- Calculate next point }
    X := Random;
    Y := Random

END;
```

The fraction of points falling inside the circle

Once we have a point (x, y), we determine whether it falls within the circle by checking whether the radial distance from the origin is less than 1.0:

```
IF ( X * X ) + ( Y * Y ) < 1.0 THEN
    { -- Point lies inside the circle }
```

All that remains is to find the fraction of all points having this property. This fraction should turn out to be about $\pi / 4$, if the total number of points is great enough. (In other words, in the limit as the number of points approaches infinity, the fraction of points falling in the circle approaches $\pi / 4$.)

Putting it together

Now we have a Monte Carlo function that estimates π, using the plan just described. A `FOR` structure is appropriate for generating the pseudorandom points because the number of points to be generated is known before the loop begins. The function is shown on the next page.

```
FUNCTION MonteCarloPi : Real;

CONST
   TotalPoints = 10000;

VAR
   Seed : Real;  { Initial number needed by Random function }
   X, Y : Real;  { Coordinates of pseudorandom point        }

   PointsInCircle : Integer; { Number of points inside the circle }
   Count          : Integer; { Running count of points generated  }

{
  Uses Randomize procedure and Random function.
  If these are not provided by your Pascal system,
  copy here the subprograms described in Appendix I.
}
BEGIN

   { -- Seed the pseudorandom number generator }
   Randomize;

   PointsInCircle := 0;

   WriteLn('Calculating; please wait...');
   FOR Count := 1 TO TotalPoints DO
   BEGIN

      { -- Calculate next point }
      X := Random;
      Y := Random;

      IF (X * X) + (Y * Y) < 1.0 THEN
         { -- Point lies inside the circle }
         PointsInCircle := PointsInCircle + 1

   END;

   MonteCarloPi := 4.0 * (PointsInCircle / TotalPoints)

END; { MonteCarloPi }
```

How well does it work?

It should come as no surprise that a pseudorandom method for approximating π is not very efficient. It takes an enormous number of plotted points before we get a good estimate. Table 10.7.1 shows some typical results, using the pseudorandom number generator described in Appendix I.

Table 10.7.1

Monte Carlo estimates of π with arbitrary seeds.

Number of points plotted	Seed	Estimate of pi
10	0.011	2.8
	0.123	3.6
	0.501	4.0
100	0.011	2.9
	0.123	2.9
	0.501	3.2
1,000	0.011	3.22
	0.123	3.03
	0.501	3.19
10,000	0.011	3.154
	0.123	3.095
	0.501	3.161
100,000	0.011	3.150
	0.123	3.167
	0.501	3.111

(Because of roundoff errors, your system may give different results.)

Clearly, there are more efficient ways to estimate π. (One is mentioned in Project 6 at the end of this chapter.) Our interest in Monte Carlo methods is to show the basic idea in a simple example, and to show the use of a `FOR` structure. Monte Carlo methods are often used in situations where no better method exists; they are a method of last resort.

10.8 REPEAT . . UNTIL STRUCTURES

Sometimes we have a need for at least one iteration of a process that should continue until some event occurs. Such an iteration requires a loop structure that always makes at least one trip, testing at the *bottom* of the loop for the need to make another iteration. Such structures are called **posttest loops** and are implemented in Pascal with the `REPEAT..UNTIL` structure. The syntax is shown on the next page.

Syntax of the REPEAT..UNTIL structure

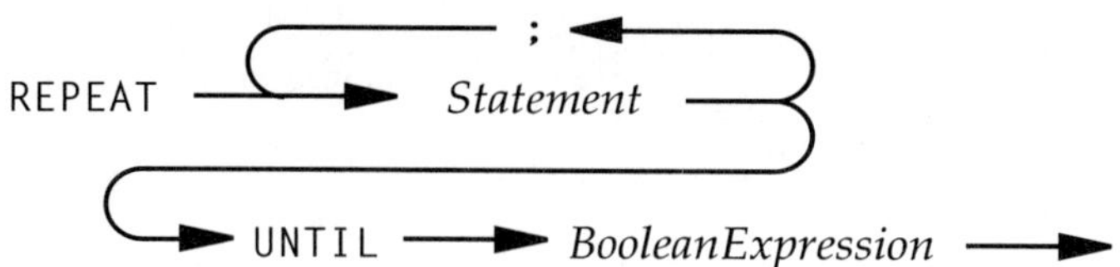

Pseudocode:

```
REPEAT
    StatementSequence
UNTIL BooleanExpression
```

Notes:

- *StatementSequence* is a sequence of one or more simple statements, separated by semicolons. It is called the *body* of the loop because it contains the instructions to be repeatedly executed until *BooleanExpression* becomes true.
- The *BooleanExpression* is called the **exit condition** or **termination test** because it determines whether the loop will terminate. It is tested after every trip through the loop. If it is `True`, the loop terminates and execution passes on to whatever code lies beyond the loop. If it is `False`, then *StatementSequence* is executed again, *BooleanExpression* is tested again, and so on.
- Because the exit condition is tested at the bottom of the loop, a `REPEAT..UNTIL` structure is said to be a *posttest loop*.
- The `REPEAT..UNTIL` structure does not require the `BEGIN` and `END` of a compound statement. In this way, it differs syntactically from the `WHILE` and `FOR` syntax. Note also that the *BooleanExpression* is a termination condition, whereas the `WHILE` structure's *BooleanExpression* is a loop-continuation condition.

The sequence of execution

StatementSequence is first executed, then *BooleanExpression* is evaluated. This ends the first trip through the loop. If *BooleanExpression* is `False`, the second trip begins: *StatementSequence* is executed and then *BooleanExpression* is evaluated. This ends the second trip. This process continues until eventually *BooleanExpression* is found to be `True`; when this happens, the loop terminates and execution passes to the first statement after the `REPEAT..UNTIL` structure.

The termination condition must eventually become true, or the loop will run forever. Whenever you design a loop, make sure that the loop will always terminate.

A simple example

Although `REPEAT..UNTIL` structures are useful in a variety of circumstances, they are especially appropriate when reading data from the keyboard. In this situation, we know that the program should read at least once. For example, a `REPEAT..UNTIL` structure would be useful in preventing errors in the response to a menu:

```
REPEAT

   WriteLn( 'Enter' );
   WriteLn( '  F to convert from Celsius to Fahrenheit,' );
   WriteLn( '  C to convert from Fahrenheit to Celsius,' );
   WriteLn( '  K to convert from Fahrenheit to Kelvin.' );
   WriteLn;
   Write( 'Your choice? ' );
   ReadLn( Choice );
   WriteLn;

   Choice := Upper( Choice )

UNTIL ( Choice = 'F' ) OR ( Choice = 'C' ) OR ( Choice = 'K' );
```

With this structure, the menu is repeated until the user enters one of the three acceptable responses.

Similarly, a `REPEAT..UNTIL` would be particularly appropriate when reading data from the keyboard until encountering a sentinel character.

When to use a REPEAT . . UNTIL loop

A `REPEAT..UNTIL` loop is appropriate in any situation in which at least one trip must be made through the loop body and there is no chance that the loop should be skipped.

Any REPEAT . . UNTIL can be written as a WHILE . . DO.

A `REPEAT..UNTIL` structure always executes its loop body at least once. A `WHILE` structure, on the other hand, may not execute its loop body at all. Therefore, any `REPEAT..UNTIL` can be rewritten as a `WHILE` structure with an extra execution of the loop body out in front of the loop. In particular,

```
REPEAT

   Statement

UNTIL BooleanExpression;
```

has the same effect as

```
Statement;

WHILE NOT BooleanExpression DO
   Statement;
```

Note that the boolean expression must be inverted for the `WHILE` loop.

This equivalence is interesting because it shows that *any* of Pascal's loops can be written as `WHILE` structures if we wish. In fact, it can be shown that all iterative structures in any programming language can be constructed as `WHILE`s. (See the book by Ghezzi and Jazayeri cited at the end of the chapter.) The equivalence is also sometimes useful when proving the correctness of loops, as we will do in the next chapter.

Questions

17. In what ways does a REPEAT..UNTIL structure differ from a WHILE structure?

18. In what situations would a REPEAT..UNTIL structure be more appropriate than a FOR structure or a WHILE structure? In what situations would a FOR or WHILE structure be more appropriate than a REPEAT..UNTIL?

Exercises

19. How many times is the body of the loop executed? (Assume ASCII code where appropriate. Choice is a Char variable, Finished is Boolean, and Index is Integer.)

a.
```
Index := 10;
REPEAT
    WriteLn( 'Index = ', Index:2 );
    Index := Index - 2
UNTIL Index < 1;
```

b.
```
Index := 10;
REPEAT
    WriteLn( 'Index = ', Index:2 );
    Index := Index - 2
UNTIL ( Index < 1 ) OR ( Index >= 1 );
```

c.
```
Ch := 'a';
REPEAT
    WriteLn( Ch );
    Ch := Succ( Ch )
UNTIL Ch = 'z';
```

d.
```
Finished := False;
REPEAT
    Write( '<Y>es or <N>o? ' );
    ReadLn( Choice );
    Finished := NOT Finished
UNTIL Finished;
```

20. Write REPEAT..UNTIL structures that do the same things as the structures shown.

a.
```
Num := MyNumber + 1.0;
WHILE Num <> MyNumber DO
BEGIN
    Write( 'What number am I thinking of? ' );
    ReadLn( Num )
END;
```

b.
```
Sum := 0;
Write( 'Number? ' );
ReadLn( Num );
WHILE Num >= 0 DO
BEGIN
   Sum := Sum + Num;
   Write( 'Number? ' );
   ReadLn( Num )
END;
```

c.
```
Count := 0;
Finished := False;
WHILE NOT Finished DO
BEGIN
   Read( Ch );
   IF Ch = Sentinel THEN
      Finished := True
   ELSE
      Count := Count + 1
END;
```

d.
```
Product := 1;
FOR Index := Num DOWNTO 1 DO
   Product := Product * Index;
```

10.9 TESTING AND DEBUGGING

Whenever you suspect a problem in a loop structure, you should immediately test for

- Correct initializations.
- Correct termination of iteration.
- Correct results.

As mentioned in Chapter 9, many Pascal systems provide a *source-code debugger*, a program that can help you check your program. A good debugger will let you execute your statements one by one, a process called *single-stepping* or *tracing*. The debugger can also run your program up to any specified point in the code, a so-called *breakpoint*, and then pause automatically. Either way, the debugger can be made to display the values stored in variables, so that you can check for correct values at intermediate points in the execution. Quite often, merely checking a few values will reveal gross errors and lead you to the location of your error. Full details and step-by-step examples appear in the companion lab manual cited at the end of this chapter.

Figure 10.9.1 *Using a source-code debugger to stop at the bottom of the loop, displaying the values of variables in a watch window.*

```
CODE

      High := 10.0;

      Sum := 0.0;
      Num := 1.0;
      WHILE Num <> High DO
      BEGIN
         Sum := Sum + Num;
         Num := Num + 0.1
 -->  END;
```

```
WATCH
Num = 10.0000019  { Real }
Sum = 490.499786  { Real }
```

As an example of how this works, Figure 10.9.1 shows a hypothetical but typical debugger in use as we look for the cause of an infinite loop in a program intended to compute the sum

$$1.0 + 1.1 + 1.2 + \ldots + 9.9$$

The loop is a `WHILE` structure, using a real variable called `Num` to count upward from `1.0` to `High` and a running sum to store the latest result of additions. In the figure, the debugger has paused execution at the end of what is supposed to be the last iteration, displaying `Num` and `Sum` in a watch window.

When you don't have a debugger

The same check can be done without the debugger, with a little effort. We can insert extra output statements, so that the loop will automatically print the values of its variables at the end of every trip:

```
High := 10.0;

Sum := 0.0;
Num := 1.0;
WHILE Num <> High DO
BEGIN
   Sum := Sum + Num;
   Num := Num + 0.1;
   WriteLn( Num:11:7, Sum:14:7 )  { OUTPUT FOR DEBUGGING }
END;
```

On one machine, this produced the output

```
  1.1000000      1.0000000
  1.2000000      2.0999999
  1.3000001      3.3000000
  .              .
  .              .
  .              .
  9.8000011    470.7998047
  9.9000015    480.5997925
 10.0000019    490.4997864
  .              .
  .              .
  .              .
```

By either technique, we see that `Num` gets the value 10.0000019 instead of 10.000000 because of roundoff error. Clearly, `Num` will never equal 10.000000, so the ill-designed loop will never terminate. A partial solution is to change the loop structure to read

```
High := 10.0;

Sum := 0.0;
Num := 1.0;
WHILE Num < High DO
BEGIN
   Sum := Sum + Num;
   Num := Num + 0.1
END;
```

This can still result in an off-by-one error, however. (Why?) The real solution is to use an integer counter, converting its value to a real number.

LOOKING BACK

In this chapter, we examined Pascal's three control structures for iteration (looping). These were:

- The `WHILE` structure, a general-purpose pretest loop.
- The `FOR` structure, a counter-driven pretest loop with built-in preinitialization and postincrementation or postdecrementation.
- The `REPEAT..UNTIL` structure, a general-purpose posttest loop.

We saw that if loop structures are not carefully designed, they can fail to terminate (an infinite loop) or fail to execute the correct number of iterations. Loops that execute one too many or one too few iterations are said to exhibit a fencepost error.

We briefly examined three applications of loops. We used a `WHILE` loop to read characters from the keyboard. Later we used a `FOR` loop in a Monte Carlo estimate of the number π. Finally, we used a `REPEAT..UNTIL` loop to force a user to enter a correct response to a menu.

This chapter has been concerned with the syntax and semantics of simple loop structures, but hasn't shown how to guarantee the correctness of loops or how to deal with more complex iterations. Those are the subjects of the next chapter.

TERMS EMPHASIZED IN THIS CHAPTER

PROJECTS

1. Write a program that displays a table of the sums $1 + 2 + 3 + \cdots + N$ for every value of N from 1 through 15.

2. Write a program that reads a sequence of real numbers and computes the maximum, minimum, and average of these. Your program should first ask the user for the number of values in the sequence. Then it should use a `FOR` loop to prompt for and read the numbers in the sequence. Guard against division by zero when computing the average.

3. Write a real function to compute the value of e^x, also written $\exp(x)$, by summing the first 25 terms of the infinite series for e^x,

   $$1 + x + (x^2 / 2!) + (x^3 / 3!) + (x^4 / 4!) + \cdots$$

   Note that 24! is 6.20×10^{23}, so you will not be able to directly compute integer factorials of large integers. Instead, rewrite the series as

   $$1 + (x^1 / 1!) + (x^2 / 2!) + (x^3 / 3!) + (x^4 / 4!) + \cdots$$

   and observe that the nth term in the series is equal to the previous term multiplied by the fraction (x / n). Thus by keeping each new term computed, you can compute the next from it, without computing a factorial. Write a driver to test your function by comparing its result with that obtained from the standard `Exp` function.

4. Rewrite the function of Project 3 so that it sums the terms of the series in reverse order. Compare the results of this new function with those of the previous one for a number of values of x. Do the two functions give the same results? For which values of x do they differ the most? Why do they differ?

5. The arc tangent function is equal to the sum of the infinite series

$$\arctan(x) = x - x^3 / 3 + x^5 / 5 - x^7 / 7 + \cdots$$

when $x^2 < 1$. Write a function that computes the arctan for a given parameter value by summing the first 10 terms of the series. Compare the result to the value of $\arctan(x)$ produced by the standard `ArcTan` function in your Pascal system.

Hints:

a. After the first term, each term can be calculated by multiplying the previous term by $x^2 (i - 2)/ i$, where i is the resulting power of x in the term.

b. Similarly, the sign of each term after the first is the negative of the sign before it.

6. The number pi can be computed from the formula

$$\pi = 24 \arctan(1/8) + 8 \arctan(1/57) + 4 \arctan(1/239).$$

The arctan functions can be computed from the series shown in Project 5. Calculate an estimate of pi by this method. [Reference: D. Shanks and J. W. Wrench, Jr., *Mathematics of Computation*, volume 16, pages 76–99 (1962).]

7. If your computer system features high-resolution graphics, a quick-and-dirty test of a pseudorandom number generator can be made by generating and plotting several thousand random points on the screen. A pattern like pepper sprinkled on the screen indicates a good generator, while banding in the pattern indicates a defective generator. It is interesting that many generators supplied in commercial software fail this test. Try it on the generator supplied with your Pascal system and with the one described in Appendix I. Find out from your instructor or reference manual how to plot points on your screen.

8. Write a program to determine experimentally the largest positive real number `X` such that `X + 1.0 = 1.0` in your computer. This number is called the *machine epsilon*.

9. (From Dave Hanscom) A drunken pirate is staggering up a gangplank from the dock to his ship. The gangplank is 5 paces wide and 15 paces long. We start watching the pirate when he is at the dock end of the gangplank. If he takes more than 2 steps to the left or right, he will fall in the water and drown. If he takes more than 15 steps forward, he will be safely on board his ship. Write a computer program to simulate the pirate's drunken stagger as follows. Read an integer from the keyboard, then repeatedly execute the following steps:

a. If the integer is divisible by 2, the pirate takes a step forward.

b. If the integer is not divisible by 2, but if the integer minus 1 is divisible by 4, the pirate takes a step to the right.

c. Otherwise, the pirate takes a step to the left.

d. Use a pseudorandom number generator to generate a new integer, then repeat from step a.

The terminating conditions are:

1. Entry of a negative integer. (The pirate presumably falls asleep on the gangplank in that case.)

2. The pirate falls over one side of the gangplank and drowns.

3. The pirate makes it safely to his ship.

Have your program display the pirate's progress after each step.

REFERENCES

A good general discussion of control structures, including iterative ones, is found in Chapter 5 of *Programming Language Concepts*, second edition, by Carlo Ghezzi and Mehdi Jazayeri (John Wiley & Sons, 1987). This book discusses the structures used in various programming languages and explains why some are in less favor than others among modern software engineers.

Buffon's needle and Monte Carlo estimates of π receive interesting treatments in Petr Beckmann's *A History of π (PI)* (St. Martin's Press, 1971) and George Gamow's *One Two Three . . . Infinity* (Viking, 1947). Pseudorandom number generators are discussed in Appendix I of the present book.

For detailed, step-by-step instructions on the use of source-code debuggers, see the lab manual written to accompany this book, entitled *The Structures and Abstractions Labs*, second edition (Richard D. Irwin, 1994). This manual describes the debuggers for both Turbo Pascal (under MS-DOS) and THINK Pascal (on the Apple Macintosh).

Bumper-Sticker Computer Science

The sooner you start to code, the longer the program will take.
—*Roy Carlson, University of Wisconsin*

If you can't write it in English, you can't code it.
—*Peter Halpern, Brooklyn, New York*

If the code and comments disagree, then both are probably wrong.
—*Norm Schryer, Bell Labs*

If you have too many special cases, you are doing it wrong.
—*Craig Zerouni, Computer FX Ltd.*

Get your data structures correct first, and the rest of the program will write itself.
—*David Jones, Assen, The Netherlands*

Make a user interface as consistent and predictable as possible.
—*Contributed by several programmers*

Twenty percent of all input forms filled out by people contain bad data.
—*Vic Vyssotsky, Bell Labs*

Eight percent of all input forms ask questions they have no business asking.
—*Mike Garey, Bell Labs*

Don't make the user provide information that the system already knows.
—*Rick Lemons, Cardinal Data Systems*

Bumper-Sticker Computer Science Continued

Of all my programming bugs, 80% are syntax errors. Of the remaining 20%, 80% are trivial logic errors. Of the remaining 4%, 80% are pointer errors. And the remaining 0.8% are hard.
—*Marc Donner, IBM Watson Research Center*

Don't debug standing up. It cuts your patience in half, and you need all you can muster.
—*Dave Storer, Cedar Rapids, Iowa*

Don't get suckered in by the comments—they can be terribly misleading. Debug only the code.
—*Dave Storer, Cedar Rapids, Iowa*

Don't include a sentence in documentation if its negation is obviously false.
—*Bob Martin, AT&T Technologies*

Don't keep doing what doesn't work.
—*Anon*

The first 90% of the code accounts for the first 90% of the development time. The remaining 10% of the code accounts for the other 90% of the development time.
—*Tom Cargill, Bell Labs*

Don't write a new program if one already does more or less what you want. And if you must write a program, use existing code to do as much of the work as possible.
—*Richard Hill, Hewlett-Packard S.A., Geneva, Switzerland*

Furious activity is no substitute for understanding.
—*H. H. Williams, Oakland, CA*

If you lie to the computer, it will get you.
—*Perry Farrar, Germantown, MD*

Keep it simple, stupid. [The KISS Principle]
—*Anon*

Always do the hard part first. If the hard part is impossible, why waste time on the easy part? Once the hard part is done, you're home free.

Always do the easy part first. What you think at first is the easy part often turns out to be the hard part. Once the easy part is done, you can concentrate all your efforts on the hard part.
—*Al Schapira, Bell Labs*

Quoted by Jon Bentley, *More Programming Pearls* (Addison-Wesley, 1988), pages 58–65.

CHAPTER 11

Iteration by Design

CHAPTER CONTENTS

INTRODUCTION

In the previous chapter, we discussed Pascal's three loop structures. If you worked through the examples, exercises, and projects, you undoubtedly found that loops are sometimes hard to build correctly. Often a loop makes too many or too few trips, or it never stops, or its results are incorrect. For these reasons, it isn't good enough to build loops in a haphazard way. We must *engineer* loops so that they will perform as expected, under all conditions. This chapter discusses some basic techniques for doing that.

We begin by examining more carefully what a loop does, using pre- and postconditions to make the loop's specification more precise. Then we introduce the concept of a *loop invariant*, a constant property of a loop that describes how the loop accomplishes its purpose. We will see that the loop invariant and the boolean expression that controls the loop together guarantee the postconditions. The preconditions, loop invariant, and postconditions are written into the program in the form of assertions—comments stating conditions that should hold at specific points during execution. Such careful specifications are a great help in designing loop structures and in making sure they work as intended. The techniques will be developed in the contexts of three typical applications:

- Raising a real number to an integer power.
- Finding the greatest common divisor of two positive integers.
- Iteratively calculating the square root of a positive real number.

We will also compare the running times of various nested loop structures and see how the running times can be expressed as functions of the amount of data processed.

11.1 DESIGNING FOR CORRECTNESS: LOOP INVARIANTS

In the examples of the previous chapter, we invented iterative algorithms seemingly out of thin air, then repaired and refined the structures until they worked correctly. From this, you may have gained the impression that programming is either a haphazard activity or a magical art. But programming done in those ways would be too undependable. In fact, programming can be a completely rational activity when correctness is engineered into algorithms from the start. You have already gotten a taste of this in our use of pre- and postconditions and of assertions in general. Now we apply this kind of thinking to the design of loops.

The purpose of a loop is to repeatedly execute the same operations. *This means that every iteration of a loop makes, in some sense, the same kind of contribution to the net result.* The iterated contribution is the essence of the loop: If you design the iterations correctly, and the loop makes the correct number of iterations, the loop will necessarily build the correct result. There are thus two vital elements to correct loop design:

1. Design correctly the repeated contribution of each iteration, which is fundamentally the same for each iteration.
2. Ensure that the loop makes the correct number of iterations.

As an example, consider summing the positive integers less than or equal to some positive number, *N*. Here is a loop that accomplishes the task correctly; our goal is to discover *why* it is correct.

```
{ ASSERTION: N >= 0 }
Int := 0;
Sum := 0;

WHILE Int < N DO
BEGIN
   Int := Int + 1;
   Sum := Sum + Int
END;
```

The sequences of values in `Int` and `Sum` are shown in Table 11.1.1. These specify the program state before the loop begins, after each iteration, and after the loop terminates.

A constant pattern in the loop's program states

Note the interesting pattern in the values of `Sum` in Table 11.1.1:

```
0
0 + 1
0 + 1 + 2
.
.
0 + 1 + 2 + ... + N
```

All of these expressions are of the form

```
(0 + 1 + 2 + ... + Int)
```

Program states before the loop begins, while it is running, and after it terminates, as specified by the values of the loop variables. **Table 11.1.1**

When?	Int	Sum
Before the first trip	0	0
After the first trip and before the second	1	0 + 1 = 1
After the second trip and before the third	2	0 + 1 + 2 = 3
After the third trip and before the fourth	3	0 + 1 + 2 + 3 = 6
.	.	.
.	.	.
.	.	.
After the Nth trip and at termination	N	0 + 1 + 2 + 3 + ... + N

where `Int` ranges from `0` to `N`. Thus there is a constant pattern in the values of `Sum` as `Int` is changed by the loop. We can use this pattern to better understand why and how the loop works.

Here is the program state just before the loop begins:

```
{
  PRECONDITIONS:
  Int = 0
  and Sum = (0 + 1 + 2 + ... + Int) = 0.
}
```

Here is the program state after the loop terminates:

```
{
  POSTCONDITIONS:
  Int = N
  and Sum = (0 + 1 + 2 + ... + Int)
          = (0 + 1 + 2 + ... + N).
}
```

Between the precondition state and the postcondition state, the loop carries the program through a number of intermediate states by repeatedly executing the same pair of operations:

- Increment `Int` by 1.
- Add the new `Int` to `Sum`.

The changes in state are shown visually in Figure 11.1.1.

Figure 11.1.1 *In each diagram, the area under the whole stair-step curve indicates the desired sum, (0 + 1 + 2 + . . . + N). The sum is built up, integer by integer, in the Sum variable. The current value of the Sum variable is shown as the black area under the curve; the part of the sum still to be added is shown in gray.*

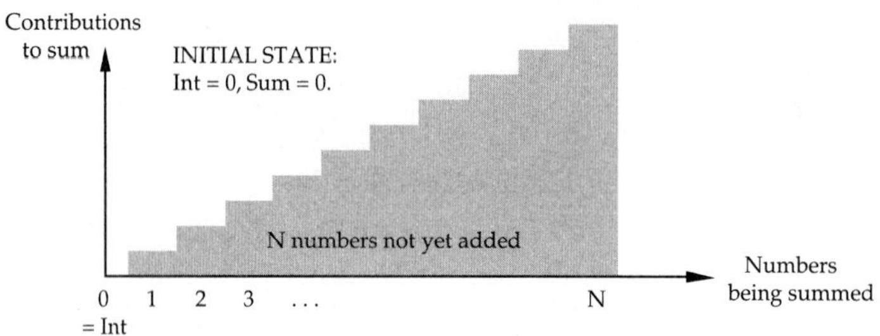

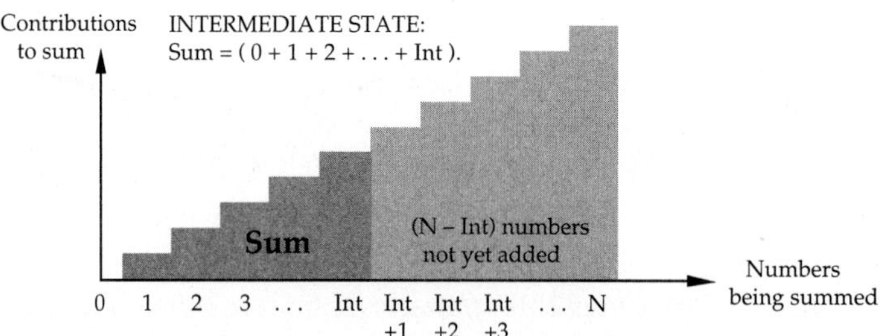

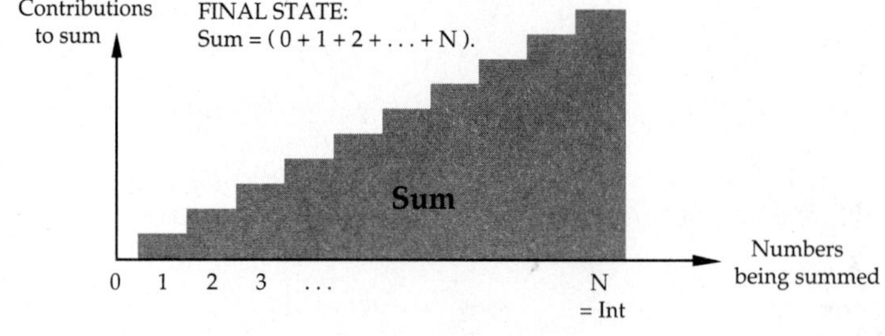

The intermediate program states occurring between iterations show the same pattern as the initial state and the final state. This pattern stays constant because the loop repeatedly executes the same two operations. Thus, we can describe a constant property shared by all of these program states, a property called the **loop invariant**. It is written in the form of an assertion:

Loop invariant: A constant property of the program states at the beginning and end of every iteration of a loop structure.

```
{
  LOOP INVARIANT:
  0 <= Int <= N
  and Sum = (0 + 1 + 2 + ... + Int).
}
```

This assertion is said to be an *invariant* property of the loop's program states because

- It is true of the initial state, when `Int` and `Sum` are both 0.
- It is true of the state at the *end* of each iteration because
    - **a.** `Int` has been incremented but cannot become greater than `N`.
    - **b.** `Int` has been added to `Sum`.
- It is therefore true of the state at the *beginning* of each iteration.

Of course, there is a moment during each iteration, between incrementing `Int` and adding `Int` to `Sum`, when the assertion is untrue, but the following addition to `Sum` immediately corrects that situation. *The behavior of the loop is to restore the validity of the invariant by the end of every iteration.*

What is true when the loop terminates?

The loop iterates as long as the loop condition is satisfied: as long as `Int < N`. The loop terminates when the loop condition becomes negated; that is, when

`( NOT ( Int < N ) )` or, equivalently, `( Int >= N )`

When execution reaches the first statement beyond the loop, it is either because the loop was skipped or because the loop ran but has terminated. In either case, two things are true:

1. *The loop invariant is satisfied* because it is valid at the beginning and end of every iteration. Therefore, `0 <= Int <= N` and `Sum = (0 + 1 + 2 +...+ Int)`.
2. *The loop condition is not satisfied*: that's why the loop is not running (or no longer running). Therefore, `NOT( (Int < N) )` or, equivalently, `(Int >= N)`.

Together, these two facts make up the postconditions of the loop. In our present example, we have the following postconditions:

1a. `0 <= Int <= N`

1b. `Sum = (0 + 1 + 2 + ... + Int)`

2. `( NOT ( Int < N ) )` or, equivalently, `( Int >= N )`

Postcondition **2** is consistent with postcondition **1a** only if `Int = N`. This result, together with postcondition **1b**, gives us `Sum = (0 + 1 + 2 + ... + N)`, so we obtain the postconditions we sought for our loop:

```
{
  POSTCONDITIONS:
  Int = N
  and Sum = (0 + 1 + 2 + ... + Int)
          = (0 + 1 + 2 + ... + N).
}
```

There is an important pattern to the logic at work here. The loop invariant is valid at the beginning and end of every trip through the loop. Therefore, the loop invariant is compatible with both the preconditions and the postconditions. However, when the `WHILE` loop terminates, its loop condition becomes negated. The combination of the invalid loop condition and the valid loop invariant yields the postconditions. You can see this more clearly if we write the preconditions, loop condition, invariant, and postconditions into the code, as shown on the next page:

```
{ ASSERTION: N >= 0 }
Int := 0;
Sum := 0;
{
  PRECONDITIONS:
  Int = 0
  and Sum = (0 + 1 + 2 + ... + Int) = 0.
}

WHILE Int < N DO
{
  LOOP INVARIANT:
  0 <= Int <= N
  and Sum = (0 + 1 + 2 + ... + Int).
}
BEGIN

   Int := Int + 1;
   Sum := Sum + Int

END;
{
  POSTCONDITIONS:
  The loop condition is invalid: Int >= N.
  Also, the invariant is valid:  0 <= Int <= N
                                 and Sum = (0 + 1 + 2 + ... + Int).

  Combining these, we have Int = N and Sum = (0 + 1 + 2 + ... + N).
}
```

The loop invariant shows the same pattern as the pre- and postconditions, indicating how the program state progressively changes from the initial state to the final state. When the loop terminates, the negated loop condition combines with the invariant to change the preconditions into the postconditions, as illustrated in Figure 11.1.2.

Figure 11.1.2 *The loop invariant, combined with a loop condition that has become invalid, changes the preconditions into the postconditions.*

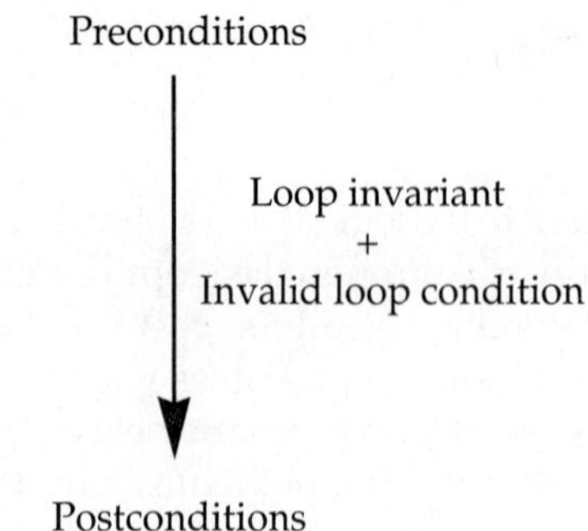

How do we know the loop terminates?

Of course, we will never get to the postconditions if the loop doesn't terminate. In our example, we know that the loop will terminate correctly because of these facts:

- The preconditions assert that `Int = 0` and `N >= 0` before the loop begins. Therefore, `0 <= Int <= N` initially.
- If `N` is initially `0`, the loop body is never executed. In this case, the preconditions are identical to the postconditions, and we end up with `Int = N = 0`.
- When `N > 0`, the loop is executed. During its execution, the loop invariant asserts that `Int` is never greater than `N` after any trip through the loop.
- The loop increments `Int` by 1, so `Int` eventually becomes equal to `N`, if it isn't equal initially. This terminates the loop.

Therefore, one of the postconditions is that `Int = N`, as desired.

How do we know the loop gives the correct result?

We know that the loop gives the correct result because of these facts:

- The preconditions assert that `Int = 0` and `N >= 0` before the loop begins. Therefore, `0 <= Int <= N` initially. Also, `Sum = 0` initially.
- If `N` is initially `0`, the loop is never executed. In this case, the preconditions are identical to the postconditions, and we have `Int = N = Sum = 0`, which is the correct result.
- When `N > 0`, the loop is executed. According to the loop invariant, after every iteration, we have `Int <= N` and `Sum = (0 + 1 + 2 + ... + Int)`.
- When the loop terminates, `Int = N`, so `Sum = (0 + 1 + 2 + ... + N)`.

By showing how the loop builds up the values of both `Int` and `Sum`, the loop invariant and loop condition have given us confidence that the coded loop will necessarily give the correct results under all circumstances.

Pitfalls with loop invariants

It is usually possible to state more than one invariant for a loop. In our example, we could have stated

```
{
  LOOP INVARIANT:
  Int >= 0.
}
```

This invariant is indeed a constant property of the loop, but it is trivial because it does not explain why the loop gives the correct results. *A good loop invariant describes the progression of program states between the preconditions and the postconditions.*

Isn't this overkill?

Our example may seem like overkill. After all, we wrote more assertions than Pascal code! The real advantage of loop invariants is that they aid the correct design of difficult algorithms. In fact, when we make good use of pre- and postconditions and loop invariants *before* writing code, we are led toward control structures that *must* work correctly, rather than cobbled-together code that just *happens* to work correctly. And that's the difference between engineering and hacking.

Invariants in FOR loops

Consider the FOR structure

```
{ ASSERTION: N >= 0. }
Sum := 0;
FOR Int := 1 TO N DO
   Sum := Sum + Int;
```

This loop produces the same result as before, summing the integers from 1 through *N*. The invariant for this loop is almost the same as the invariant for the essentially equivalent WHILE loop, which is

```
{ ASSERTION: N >= 0. }
Sum := 0;
Int := 1;
WHILE Int <= N DO
BEGIN
   Sum := Sum + Int;
   Int := Int + 1
END;
```

There is just one difference. According to the Pascal Standard, the value of a FOR loop index becomes undefined after the loop terminates. In the example, this means that Int has a system-dependent value after the FOR loop terminates, and we therefore cannot specify the final value of Int. Because of this, we write the loop assertions as shown below:

```
{ ASSERTION: N >= 0. }
Sum := 0;
{
  PRECONDITIONS:
  Int = 0
  and Sum = (0 + 1 + 2 + ... + Int) = 0.
}

FOR Int := 1 TO N DO
{
  LOOP INVARIANT:
  1 <= Int <= (N+1)
  and Sum = [0 + 1 + 2 + ... + (Int-1)].
}
   Sum := Sum + Int;

{
  POSTCONDITIONS:
  Int is undefined
  and Sum = (0 + 1 + 2 + ... + N).
}
```

Questions

1. How does a loop invariant express the purpose of a loop?
2. What logical condition terminates a `WHILE` loop?
3. What additional conditions combine with the loop invariant to produce the postconditions?
4. In the `FOR` loop on the previous page, how do the loop condition and invariant combine to guarantee that `Sum = (0 + 1 + 2 +...+ N)` after the loop terminates?

Exercises

5. Run the loop shown above with `N` = 1, 2, 3, 4, and 5. By examining the resulting values of `Sum` in these cases, try to guess a formula for the sum $1 + 2 + 3 + \cdots + N$ as a function of N. (Hint: It is quadratic in N.)
6. Jackson P. Slipshod has written this version of a loop to sum the first N positive integers. Criticize his work. Are his assertions correct? Does his loop give the correct results? Does his invariant clearly show how the preconditions are changed into the postconditions? Does his loop terminate correctly?

```
{
  PRECONDITIONS:
  Int = 1 and Sum = sum of positive integers < Int.
}
Int := 1;
Sum := 0;

WHILE Int <= N DO
{
  LOOP INVARIANT:
  1 <= Int <= N and Sum = (0 + 1 + 2 + ··· + Int).
}
BEGIN
   Sum := Sum + Int;
   Int := Int + 1
END;
{
  POSTCONDITIONS:
  Int = N and Sum = (0 + 1 + 2 + ··· + Int).
}
```

7. Does the following loop correctly sum the first N positive integers? How do you know?

```
Sum := 0;
FOR Int := 1 TO N DO
   Sum := Sum + Int;
```

8. Write preconditions, invariants, and postconditions for these loops:

a.
```
{-- Product of integers up to 10 }
Product := 1;
Int     := 0;

WHILE Int < 10 DO
BEGIN
   Int     := Int + 1;
   Product := Product * Int
END;
```

b.
```
{-- Finding the minimum of five numbers }
Count := 0;

WHILE Count < 5 DO
BEGIN

   ReadLn( Number );
   Count := Count + 1;

   IF Count = 1 THEN
      Min := Number
   ELSE
      IF Number < Min THEN
         Min := Number

END;
```

11.2 CASE STUDY: RAISING A REAL NUMBER TO AN INTEGER POWER

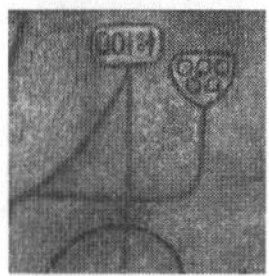

As an example of using preconditions, invariant, loop condition, and postconditions to design a loop, consider the problem of raising a real number to an integer power, an operation not provided by Standard Pascal. Suppose in particular that we want to write a function with the following skeleton:

```
FUNCTION IntPower( Number : Real;
                   Power  : Integer ) : Real;
{
  PRECONDITIONS:
  Number and Power have been initialized.

  POSTCONDITIONS:
  IntPower is assigned the value of the given Number,
  raised to the given Power.
}
BEGIN

   { Computation of given Power of Number }

   IntPower := { result of computation }

END;
```

Divide and conquer.

There is no difficulty if the power is zero, because the zeroth power of any real number is 1.0. Also, there is no difficulty if the power is negative, the result is simply the inverse of the result we would get with a positive power:

$$\text{Number}^{-k} = 1.0 \,/\, (\, \text{Number}^{k}\,)$$

Thus, the only part of the problem requiring much work is to find a *positive* power of a number.

To raise a real number to a positive integer power, the real number must be multiplied by itself that number of times:

$$\text{Number}^{k} = \text{Number x Number x} \ldots \text{x Number} \quad (k \text{ times})$$

Designing the loop

To calculate a positive power of a given number, we need a loop to perform the repeated multiplications, and the loop must be equipped with a counter variable to count the number of multiplications. The loop must satisfy four conditions:

1. Loop variables must be initialized appropriately.
2. The loop itself must perform the correct operations during each trip.
3. The loop must terminate after the correct number of iterations.
4. The final result must equal $\text{Number}^{\text{Power}}$.

The idea is to keep a running product and to use a variable called `Mults` to count the number of multiplications. In order to maintain the running product, it is helpful to note that

$$\text{Number}^{\text{Power}} = 1.0 \text{ x Number x Number x} \ldots \text{x Number}$$
(Multiplying Power times, each time by Number)

This shows more clearly that if `Power` happens to be `0`, the loop will make no trips and the result is simply `1.0`.

The plan is to start with a `Product` of `1.0`, and then have the loop repeatedly multiply `Product` by `Number`, with the total number of multiplications equal to `Power`:

- Initially, `Mults` is 0 and `Product` is 1.0, so that `Product = Number`^{0}.
- After the first iteration, `Mults` is 1 and `Product` is `Number`^{1}.
- After the second iteration, `Mults` is 2 and `Product` is `Number`^{2}.

  .
  .
- After the final iteration, `Mults` is `Power` and `Product` is `Number`^{Power}. (Then the loop should terminate.)
- After the loop terminates, the value of `Product` is assigned to `IntPower`.

In this way, the desired product gradually builds up as the loop iterates. The purpose of the loop is to carry `Product` from its initial value to its final value, as shown in Figure 11.2.1. The process of building up the running product in the loop can be visualized as shown in Figure 11.2.2.

Figure 11.2.1

The purpose of the loop is to carry product from its initial to its final value.

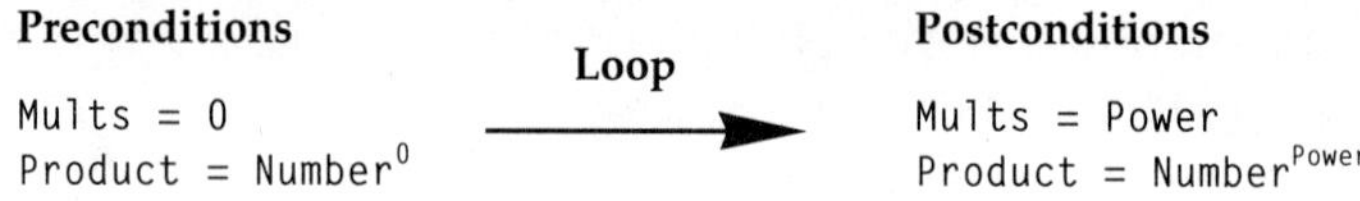

This is very much like our previous example, but with multiplication in place of summation. After all the analysis, we can write the loop's preconditions, invariant, and postconditions. For the time being, we consider only nonnegative powers:

```
{
  PRECONDITIONS:
  0 <= Power and Mults = 0 and
  Product = (Number ** Mults) = (Number ** 0) = 1.0.

  ("**" stands for exponentiation.)
}
{
   LOOP INVARIANT:
   0 <= Mults <= Power and Product = (Number ** Mults).

   LOOP CONDITION:
   Mults < Power.
}
{
  POSTCONDITIONS:
  0 <= Mults <= Power and Product = (Number ** Mults)
  and (NOT (Mults < Power) ) = (Mults >= Power).

  Therefore, Mults = Power and
  Product = (Number ** Mults) = (Number ** Power).
}
```

Figure 11.2.2

At the end of a particular iteration and before the next, Mults numbers have been multiplied to get the running product.

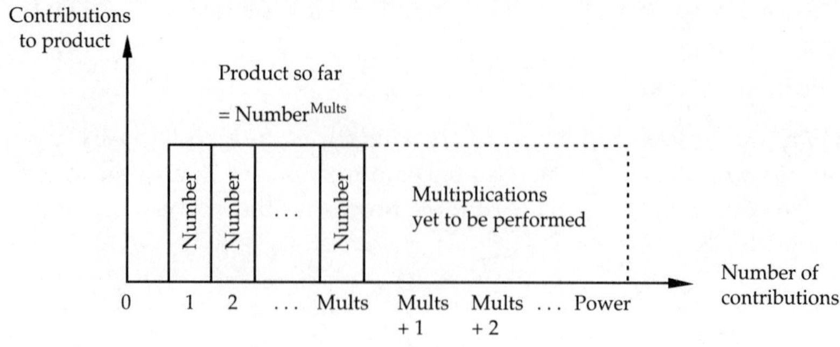

Now that we know in detail what the loop must do, we can write code that satisfies the assertions. The loop condition gives us the boolean expression to test at the top of the loop:

```
Mults   := 0;
Product := 1.0;
{
  PRECONDITIONS:
  0 <= Power and Mults = 0 and
  Product = (Number ** Mults) = (Number ** 0) = 1.0.

  ("**" stands for exponentiation.)
}

WHILE Mults < Power DO
{
   LOOP INVARIANT:
   0 <= Mults <= Power and Product = (Number ** Mults).

   LOOP CONDITION:
   Mults < Power.
}
BEGIN

   Product := Product * Number;
   Mults   := Mults + 1

END;
{
  POSTCONDITIONS:
  0 <= Mults <= Power and Product = (Number ** Mults)
  and (NOT (Mults < Power) ) = (Mults >= Power).

  Therefore, Mults = Power and
  Product = (Number ** Mults) = (Number ** Power).
}

IntPower := Product;
```

Before the loop begins, `Product` is `1.0` and `Mults` is `0`, so the invariant holds: `Product` equals $\texttt{Number}^0$ and `Mults` is in the specified range. At the end of each iteration, `Product` has been multiplied by `Number` and `Mults` has been increased by 1, so the invariant is still true. Therefore the invariant is true at the beginning and end of every iteration. Because the algorithm maintains the validity of this invariant, it works correctly for all nonnegative values of `Power`.

The loop terminates.

If `Power = 0`, the loop is skipped, `Mults = Power = 0`, and the postconditions are satisfied. If `Power > 0`, the loop is executed, with `Mults` initially less than `Power`. Since each iteration adds one to `Mults`, `Mults` will eventually become equal to `Power`. When `Mults` equals `Power`, the loop condition becomes negated and the loop terminates.

Therefore, the loop always terminates correctly when `Power` is nonnegative. We still have to add the ability to handle negative powers.

Handling negative powers

If `Power` is negative, the result should be just the inverse of what it would be if the power were positive. We can do the computation as before, counting up to the *absolute value* of `Power`, and then taking the inverse afterwards. (The absolute value function was introduced in Section 7.4.) A few modifications extend the algorithm for negative powers, and we have the finished function, as shown on the next two pages.

```
FUNCTION IntPower( Number : Real;
                   Power  : Integer ) : Real;
{
  PRECONDITIONS:
  Number and Power have been initialized.

  POSTCONDITIONS:
  IntPower = (Number ** Power), where ** stands for exponentiation.
}
VAR
   Product : Real;     { Running product }
   Mults   : Integer;  { Counts multiplications }

BEGIN

   Mults   := 0;
   Product := 1.0;

   {
     PRECONDITIONS:
     Mults = 0 and
     Product = (Number ** Mults) = (Number ** 0) = 1.0.
   }

   WHILE Mults < Abs( Power ) DO
   {
      LOOP INVARIANT:
      0 <= Mults <= Abs( Power )
      and Product = (Number ** Mults).

      LOOP CONDITION:
      Mults < Abs(Power).
   }
   BEGIN

      Product := Product * Number;
      Mults   := Mults + 1

   END;
```

```
    {
      POSTCONDITIONS:
      The loop invariant is valid:   0 <= Mults <= Abs( Power )
                                     and Product = (Number ** Mults).
      The loop condition is negated: Mults >= Abs( Power ).

      Therefore,
      Mults = Abs( Power )
      and Product = (Number ** Mults) = (Number ** Abs(Power)).
    }

    IF Power >= 0 THEN
       IntPower := Product

    ELSE
       IntPower := 1.0 / Product

END; { IntPower }
```

Questions

9. Why does the function above work correctly when `Power` is zero? Is it explained by the invariant and loop condition?

10. Can the `IntPower` algorithm be written without the local `Mults` variable? Is it as easy to write the loop assertions that way?

Exercises

11. Real powers of a real number can be computed according to the formula

$$x^y = \exp(y \ln x)$$

Write a `RealPower` function that uses this formula, using preconditions, invariant, loop conditions, and postconditions in the design process. Then, by actual experiment, compare the accuracy of this function with that of `IntPower`. Try the powers 1, 2, 4, 8, 16, and 32 of the real number 3.0.

12. Using pre- and postconditions, invariant, and loop condition, design a function that computes the product of two integers, *I* and *J*, by adding *I* to itself *J* times.

13. Write a function that computes `(Int1 DIV Int2)` by repeatedly subtracting `Int2` from `Int1`. Use a precondition, invariant, loop condition, and postcondition in the design process.

11.3 CASE STUDY: THE GREATEST COMMON DIVISOR

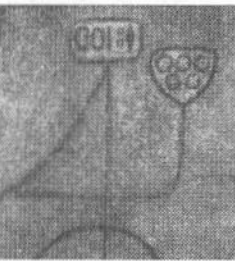

The oldest known algorithm was first recorded by the Greek mathematician, Euclid, around 300 BC, but probably was invented by Euclid's predecessor, Eudorus. The algorithm finds the greatest common divisor (gcd) of two distinct positive integers, called `Larger` and `Smaller`, where (naturally) `Larger` > `Smaller`. We use the notation

gcd(`Larger`, `Smaller`)

for this divisor. Here are some examples:

gcd(12, 4) = 4; gcd(21, 6) = 3; gcd(21, 4) = 1

The Euclid/Eudorus gcd algorithm was briefly described in Chapter 1. To see how this algorithm might be invented, picture the two given numbers as bar graphs, as shown in Figure 11.3.1.

As the diagram indicates, the larger number can be thought of as containing multiples of the smaller number, plus a remainder equal to `(Larger MOD Smaller)`. The greatest common divisor of these two numbers must "fit into" each of these numbers without remainders, as shown in Figure 11.3.2.

As you can see, the gcd of `Larger` and `Smaller` is also the gcd of `Smaller` and `(Larger MOD Smaller)`. Thus, we can replace the original problem by the smaller and therefore easier problem of finding the gcd of `Smaller` and `(Larger MOD Smaller)`:

gcd(`Larger`, `Smaller`)

= gcd(`Smaller`, `(Larger MOD Smaller)`)

Note that the behavior of the `MOD` operator guarantees that `Smaller > (Larger MOD Smaller)`, so the first parameter of the gcd function remains larger than the second parameter. We now rename the two parameters as shown in Figure 11.3.3.

This gives us an iterative method for finding the gcd of two numbers, in which each iteration consists of replacing `Larger` by `Smaller` and replacing `Smaller` by `(Larger MOD Smaller)`. For example,

gcd(21, 6) = gcd(6, 3) = gcd(3, 0)

Defining the greatest common divisor of 3 and 0 to be 3, we have our result:

gcd(21, 6) = 3

Figure 11.3.1 *The two numbers, Larger and Smaller, represented by bar graphs. The smaller number "fits into" the larger number some number of times, with a remainder given by (Larger MOD Smaller).*

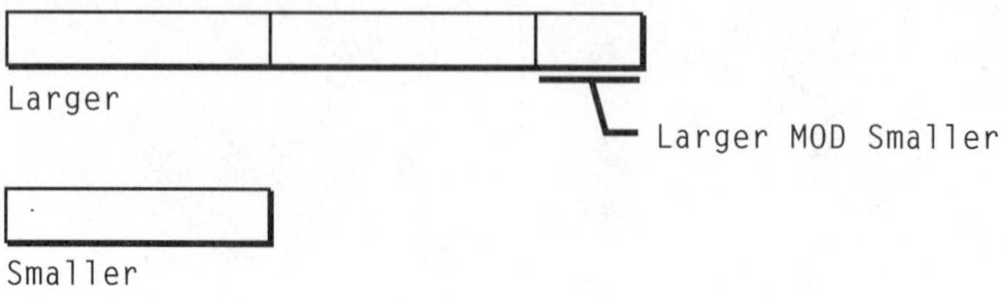

Figure 11.3.2

The greatest common divisor (gcd) of the two numbers, Larger and Smaller, must fit into each of these numbers without remainder. This implies that it also divides into (Larger MOD Smaller) without remainder.

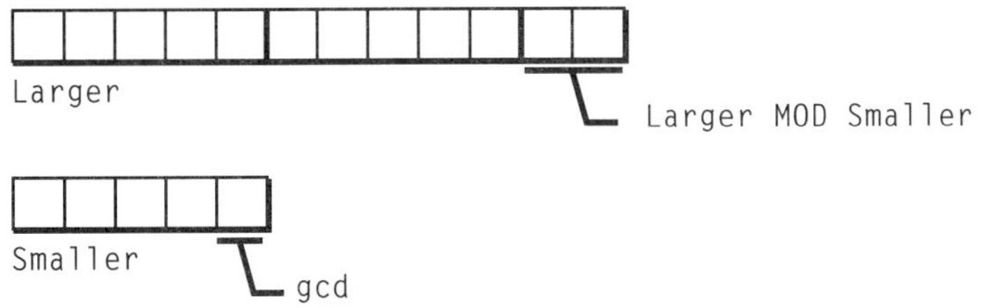

The algorithm always terminates correctly.

Note that the algorithm will always terminate. The quantity (Larger MOD Smaller) is necessarily less than Smaller, so the replacements during each iteration always give smaller numbers than in the previous iteration. But (Larger MOD Smaller) is never less than zero, so the replacements of Smaller cause it to decrease to zero. Since Smaller is initially > 0 and then decreases, it is guaranteed to reach zero eventually, terminating the algorithm.

When Smaller reaches zero, we are left with a problem of the form gcd(N, 0), where N > 0. But this problem is trivial; the greatest common divisor of a positive number and zero is equal to the positive number. When we reach this point, we have discovered that

gcd(Larger, Smaller) = gcd(N, 0) = N

The constant pattern in the program states

The initial conditions are that Smaller and Larger are both positive, with Smaller less than Larger; that is, 0 < Smaller < Larger. We introduce two local variables, called S and L, which start out being equal to Smaller and Larger, respectively:

```
{
  PRECONDITIONS:
  0 < Smaller < Larger, S = Smaller, and L = Larger.
  Therefore 0 < S < L and gcd( Larger, Smaller ) = gcd( L, S ).
}
```

Figure 11.3.3

After replacing the original problem by the smaller problem.

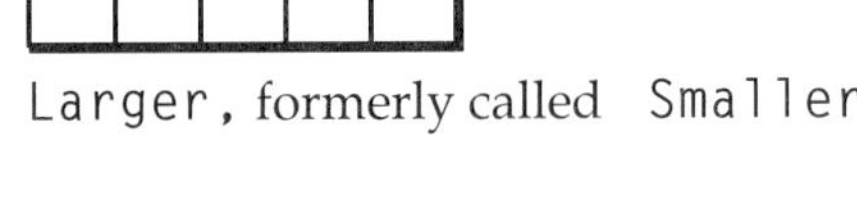

Smaller, formerly called Larger MOD Smaller

By the time we reach the end of the algorithm, L and S will in general have been replaced several times, but in such a way that gcd(L, S) is the gcd we seek, namely gcd(Larger, Smaller). Furthermore, S will have decreased to zero, indicating the end of the process. Thus we can make the following assertion about the final program state:

```
{
  POSTCONDITIONS:
  S = 0 and
  gcd( Larger, Smaller ) = gcd( L, S ) = gcd( L, 0 ) = L <= Larger.
}
```

(Note that if Smaller = 0, no replacements occur and we end up with L = Larger. On the other hand, if Smaller <> 0, replacements occur, causing the final value of L to be < Larger.)

The pattern is expressed in the loop invariant.

By now, the pattern is apparent. S and L are repeatedly replaced as we have described, in such a way that S is always less than L and both are decreasing. But the replacement process has the very special property that gcd(L, S) is always equal to the gcd we seek:

```
{
  LOOP INVARIANT:
  0 <= S < L <= Larger
  and gcd( Larger, Smaller ) = gcd( L, S ).
}
```

Again, you see an example of how the loop invariant specifies the constant property of the progression of program states.

What kind of loop do we need?

When Smaller is greater than zero, we always need to make at least one trip through the loop. Therefore, we choose a REPEAT..UNTIL structure for the loop.

What is the loop condition?

Initially, S is equal to Smaller and therefore greater than zero. As we iterate, S decreases toward zero. We exit the loop when S = 0 because, at that point, the gcd will be equal to L. Therefore, the loop condition—the condition for continuing looping—is that S > 0; the exit condition is that S = 0.

Writing the code

We can now write the code as a direct implementation of the assertions listed above. Carefully compare the comments in the code with the discussion on the past several pages:

```
{ ASSERTION: 0 < Smaller < Larger }
S := Smaller;
L := Larger;

{
  PRECONDITIONS:
  0 < Smaller < Larger, S = Smaller, and L = Larger.
  Therefore 0 < S < L and gcd( Larger, Smaller ) = gcd( L, S ).
}

REPEAT
{
  LOOP INVARIANT:
  0 <= S < L <= Larger
  and gcd( Larger, Smaller ) = gcd( L, S ),

  LOOP CONDITION:
  S > 0.
}

   Remainder := L MOD S;
   L := S;
   S := Remainder

UNTIL S = 0;

{
  POSTCONDITIONS:
  S = 0 and
  gcd( Larger, Smaller ) = gcd( L, S ) = gcd( L, 0 ) = L <= Larger.
}

GCD := L
```

Other cases

The code shown above assumes that `0 < Smaller < Larger`, but consider what happens in the other cases:

- If `Smaller` and `Larger` are equal, `Remainder` is zero when first computed, so `L` becomes `S` and `S` becomes zero, and the loop terminates after one trip. Immediately, we have `GCD = L = Larger = Smaller`. Thus, the algorithm works correctly when `Larger = Smaller` as well as when `Larger > Smaller`.
- If `Larger` is less than `Smaller`, the first trip through the loop merely swaps `L` and `S`, after which the algorithm proceeds as originally designed.

Therefore, the algorithm works for *any* positive values of `Larger` and `Smaller`. The only reason we assumed `Larger` > `Smaller` was to make the pre- and postconditions and loop assertions clear enough and simple enough to help us design the code.

The Pascal procedure

The complete function can now be written to handle *all* positive parameters, but the loop assertions become more general and therefore less specific.

```
FUNCTION GCD( Int1, Int2 : Integer ) : Integer;
VAR
   S, L, Remainder : Integer;

BEGIN

   IF ( Int2 > 0 ) AND ( Int1 > 0 ) THEN
   { -- Inputs are legal }
   BEGIN

      S := Int2;
      L := Int1;
      {
        PRECONDITIONS:
        0 < S = Int2 and 0 < L = Int1.
      }
      REPEAT
      {
        LOOP INVARIANT:
        gcd( Int1, Int2 ) = gcd( L, S )
        and 0 <= S <= max( Int1, Int2 )
        and 0 <= L <= max( Int1, Int2 ).

        LOOP CONDITION:
        S > 0.
      }

         Remainder := L MOD S;
         L := S;
         S := Remainder

      UNTIL S = 0;
      {
        POSTCONDITIONS:
        S = 0 and
        gcd( Int1, Int2 ) = gcd( L, S ) = gcd( L, 0 )
        = L <= max( Int1, Int2 ).
      }

      GCD := L

   END { IF }

   ELSE

      { -- Illegal parameters }
      GCD := 0

END; { GCD }
```

Exercises

14. Jackson P. Slipshod believes that he has discovered a shorter implementation of Euclid's algorithm. Unfortunately, it often gives the wrong result. What is wrong with it?

```
FUNCTION GCD( Larger, Smaller : Integer ) : Integer;
BEGIN
   WHILE Smaller > 0 DO
   BEGIN
      Larger  := Smaller;
      Smaller := Larger MOD Smaller
   END;
   GCD := Larger
END; { GCD }
```

15. Jackson's friend, Cora Meltdown, has another implementation of the algorithm that often fails. What's wrong with this one?

```
FUNCTION GCD( Larger, Smaller : Integer ) : Integer;
VAR
   Remainder : Integer;
BEGIN
   WHILE Remainder > 0 DO
   BEGIN
      Larger  := Smaller;
      Smaller := Remainder;
      Remainder := Larger MOD Smaller
   END;
   GCD := Larger
END; { GCD }
```

16. The following function will not compile. Explain why.

```
FUNCTION GCD( Larger, Smaller : Integer ) : Integer;
BEGIN
   GCD := Larger;
   WHILE Smaller > 0 DO
   BEGIN
      Larger  := Smaller;
      Smaller := GCD MOD Smaller;
      GCD     := Larger
   END
END; { GCD }
```

11.4 CASE STUDY: SQUARE ROOTS BY AN ITERATIVE METHOD

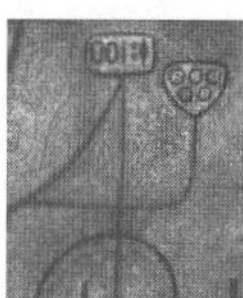

Now we study an **iterative method** for estimating the square root of a given number to any desired accuracy. The method was first reported by a Scottish mathematician, James Gregory, in 1674, but is often called **Newton's method** because it can be derived from the Newton-Raphson method, which is studied in many calculus courses.

Gregory's approach does not require calculus, however—just a little algorithmic thinking. Suppose we are given a positive number, N, and an initial positive estimate of its square root. There are three possibilities regarding the estimate:

- If the estimate is less than the actual square root, then the quotient (N / Estimate) will be greater than the square root.
- If the estimate is greater than the actual square root, then the quotient (N / Estimate) will be less than the square root.
- If the estimate is exactly equal to the square root, then the quotient (N / Estimate) is also equal to the square root.

If the original estimate is too high or too low, the average of the original estimate and (N / Estimate) is closer to the true square root than the original estimate was, so we make this our new estimate. (The fact that the new estimate is closer to the true value follows intuitively from the remarks above, but a proof will be given shortly.) Thus, we can home in on the square root by an iterative process: We replace the original estimate by the new estimate; then we replace that estimate by another estimate made in the same way, and repeat this process until the latest estimate differs from the previous one by less than some desired precision. This is how square roots are computed by calculators and computers. The method converges toward the exact square root quite rapidly, typically requiring only five or six iterations for eight-digit precision if the original estimate is not too far off.

Proving convergence

When an iterative method approaches an exact result more and more closely, we say that it **converges**. The Gregory-Newton method always converges if the initial estimate of the root is positive, as we now show. Suppose we seek the square root, r, of a positive real number, N. We don't know the exact square root, but we guess that it has the value $g > 0$. Suppose that g differs from the actual root, r, by an amount ε, so that

$$g = r + \varepsilon \text{ and } N = r^2 = (g - \varepsilon)^2$$

Then when we apply the Gregory-Newton method, we get a new estimate of the root, called g':

$$g' = \frac{1}{2}\left[g + \frac{N}{g}\right] = \frac{1}{2}\left[g + \frac{(g-\varepsilon)^2}{g}\right] = \frac{1}{2}\left[\frac{g^2 + (g-\varepsilon)^2}{g}\right]$$

$$= \left[\frac{2g^2 - 2g\varepsilon + \varepsilon^2}{2g}\right]$$

$$= g - \varepsilon + \frac{\varepsilon^2}{2g} = r + \frac{\varepsilon^2}{2g}$$

The error in the old estimate is ε, while the error in the new estimate is $\varepsilon^2 / 2g$. Therefore, the method converges if it is always true that

$$\left| \frac{\varepsilon^2}{2g} \right| < |\varepsilon|$$

But g is always positive, so this is equivalent to

$$|\varepsilon| < 2g$$

In other words, the method converges if the magnitude of the error in g is less than twice as large as g itself. Substituting for g, we have this condition for convergence:

$$|\varepsilon| < 2(r+\varepsilon)$$

When ε is nonnegative, $\varepsilon = |\varepsilon|$, so this condition gives the result $|\varepsilon| > -2r$. This doesn't tell us anything because $|\varepsilon| > 0$. When ε is negative, however, $\varepsilon = -|\varepsilon|$. Substituting this in the condition, we get

$$|\varepsilon| < 2(r - |\varepsilon|)$$

$$3|\varepsilon| < 2r$$

$$\text{or} \quad |\varepsilon| < 2r/3$$

Combining this with the equation $g = r + \varepsilon$, we find that the Gregory-Newton method converges to the square root for all $g > r / 3$.

But if $g \le r / 3$, we can show (Exercise 26) that $g' \ge 5r / 3$, after which the method will converge, according to the proof just completed. Therefore, the method converges for all positive initial guesses g.

Convergence is fast.

When g gets close to the actual root, the error ε becomes small. Under these conditions, we have shown that the error in the next iteration is proportional to the *square* of ε, and is therefore considerably smaller. A method that converges in this way is said to be **quadratically convergent**; its consequence is that the Gregory-Newton method can give eight-digit precision in its estimate of the square root in only five or six iterations, starting from an initial $g = N$.

The method terminates.

Once convergence has reduced the change in the root estimate to zero, there will be no further change because another iteration gives the same result. This is because we have only a finite representation of the real numbers, so g actually becomes equal to the square root of N in a finite number of steps, after which

$$g' = \frac{1}{2}\left(g + \frac{N}{g}\right) = \frac{1}{2}\left(\sqrt{N} + \frac{N}{\sqrt{N}}\right) = \sqrt{N}$$

This means that the algorithm can automatically determine when the root has been found by checking to see if the new estimate differs from the old one.

Describe the process more precisely.

In preparing to write a square root function, the first step is to define the Gregory-Newton process in more detail than we did at first. We need two variables, which we may call `OldEstimate` and `NewEstimate`. We found that the process will converge for any positive first estimate, so we can use a rough first guess, even `Number` itself. Then the process is this:

OldEstimate := Some initial estimate, often *Number* itself ;
NewEstimate := [*OldEstimate* + (*Number* / *OldEstimate*)] / 2.0

```
{
  PRECONDITIONS:
  Number > 0 and OldEstimate > 0 and NewEstimate > 0.
}
```

Iterate until *NewEstimate* equals *OldEstimate* within desired precision:

```
{
  INVARIANT:
  0 ≤ |NewEstimate - SqRt(Number)| ≤ |OldEstimate - SqRt(Number)|
}
```

OldEstimate := *NewEstimate*;
NewEstimate := [*OldEstimate* + (*Number* / *OldEstimate*)] / 2.0

```
{
  POSTCONDITION:
  0 ≤ | NewEstimate - SqRt( Number ) | ≤ Allowed error
}
```

Designing the loop structure

The required number of iterations is unknown beforehand; the loop will simply terminate when successive estimates stop changing very much. Therefore, a `FOR` loop is not appropriate. On the other hand, it is possible that `NewEstimate` may equal `OldEstimate` within the desired precision when the loop begins, so we may not need to run the loop at all. So our first idea is that the loop should be a `WHILE` structure rather than a `REPEAT..UNTIL`:

```
OldEstimate := Some initial estimate, often Number itself;
NewEstimate := ( OldEstimate + ( Number / OldEstimate ) ) / 2.0;

WHILE |NewEstimate - OldEstimate| ≥ Desired precision DO
BEGIN

   OldEstimate := NewEstimate;
   NewEstimate := ( OldEstimate + ( Number / OldEstimate ) ) / 2.0

END;

SquareRoot := NewEstimate
```

But according to what we said at the end of Section 10.8, this code is equivalent to the following `REPEAT..UNTIL` structure:

```
NewEstimate := Some initial estimate, often Number itself;

REPEAT

   OldEstimate := NewEstimate;
   NewEstimate := ( OldEstimate + ( Number / OldEstimate ) ) / 2.0

UNTIL |NewEstimate - OldEstimate| < Desired precision;

SquareRoot := NewEstimate
```

Testing for convergence

The remaining problem is to decide when the process has converged to the desired precision. We might quit iterating when the absolute value of the difference between `NewEstimate` and `OldEstimate` becomes less than some small preset number. (This is called an **absolute convergence criterion**.) But this wouldn't give very many significant figures if the root itself turns out to be a very small number.

A better approach is to terminate the loop when the change in the estimate is small relative to the magnitude of the estimate itself. This is called a **relative convergence criterion**. For example, if

```
| NewEstimate - OldEstimate | = 0.1 * | NewEstimate |
```

then we have about one significant digit of precision. If it is a hundredth, we have about two significant digits. We will pick a relative convergence criterion of 1×10^{-8}, to give at least seven significant figures. In other words, we will terminate the iteration when

```
| (NewEstimate - OldEstimate) / NewEstimate | < ConvergenceCriterion
```

Taking the initial estimate to be `Number` itself, and taking into account the outline above, we have the function shown on the next page:

```
FUNCTION SquareRoot( Number : Real ) : Real;
{
  PRECONDITION:
  Number > 0.

  POSTCONDITION:
  Final estimate differs from the previous estimate by less than
  ConvergenceCriterion * NewEstimate.
}
CONST
   ConvergenceCriterion = 1.0e-8;  { Relative convergence criterion }

VAR
   OldEstimate, NewEstimate, RelativeChange : Real;

BEGIN

   {--Pick initial crude estimate }
   NewEstimate := Number;

   {
     PRECONDITIONS:
     Number > 0 and NewEstimate > 0.
   }

   REPEAT
   {
     LOOP INVARIANT:
     0 <= Abs( NewEstimate - SqRt(Number) )
           <= Abs( OldEstimate - SqRt(Number) ).

     LOOP CONDITION:
     RelativeChange >= ConvergenceCriterion.
   }
      OldEstimate := NewEstimate;
      NewEstimate := ( OldEstimate + (Number / OldEstimate) ) / 2.0;
      RelativeChange := Abs((NewEstimate - OldEstimate) / NewEstimate)

   UNTIL RelativeChange < ConvergenceCriterion;

   {
     POSTCONDITION:
     0 <= RelativeChange < ConvergenceCriterion.
   }

   SquareRoot := NewEstimate

END; { SquareRoot }
```

How it runs

By inserting a `WriteLn` to display each successive value of `NewEstimate`, we can watch the method converge on a root. If `Number` is initially 4.0, we see

```
2.50000000
2.04999995
2.00060964
2.00000000
2.00000000
```

Questions

17. What does it mean to say that an iterative method *converges*?

18. What does it mean to say that the Gregory-Newton method for square roots is *quadratically convergent*?

19. How does the loop invariant in the `SquareRoot` function imply the eventual termination of the loop?

20. How does the loop invariant, together with the loop condition, imply the postcondition?

21. What does the Gregory-Newton method do if the initial guess at the root is *zero*?

Exercises

22. By direct substitution in the iteration formula $g' - (g + N/g) / 2$ show that the Gregory-Newton process gives the correct result, $g = r$, when $g = g'$.

23. Write a driver for the `SquareRoot` function and test it. What does it give for the square root of 3? Is this correct?

24. Demonstrate by an actual example how the `SquareRoot` function could fail if the absolute value were not used in computing `RelativeChange`.

25. The Gregory-Newton method for the square root can be simplified by replacing the relative convergence criterion with an equality test:

```
FUNCTION SquareRoot( Number : Real ) : Real;
VAR
   OldEstimate, NewEstimate : Real;

BEGIN

   NewEstimate := Number;

   REPEAT
     OldEstimate := NewEstimate;
     NewEstimate :=  ( OldEstimate + (Number / OldEstimate) ) / 2.0
   UNTIL NewEstimate = OldEstimate;

   SquareRoot := NewEstimate

END; { SquareRoot }
```

Will this version of the function always work? If not, why not? Try it out on your computer. Write an invariant for this loop.

26. Show that when $g = r / 3$ in the Gregory-Newton method, $g' = 5r / 3$. Then show that when $g < r / 3, g' > 5r / 3$. Thus when $g \leq r / 3$, the next estimate is $\geq 5r / 3$, after which the method will necessarily converge according to the proof given in the text. Therefore, the method converges for all positive g.

27. The Gregory-Newton method is said to be quadratically convergent because an error ε is reduced to an error proportional to ε^2 during the next iteration. Show that this means that the number of accurate significant bits in the estimate of the square root doubles at every iteration.

11.5 NESTED LOOPS AND RUNNING TIMES

When a loop structure is executed as part of the body of another loop structure, we say that the loops are **nested**. There are two kinds of nesting: direct and indirect. In **direct nesting**, the inner loop structure is literally one of the statements listed in the body of the outer loop structure. In **indirect nesting**, the outer loop body calls a procedure or function that contains the inner loop structure.

Direct nesting

Here is an example of directly nested loops, used to print an N x $(N-1)$ rectangle of asterisks:

```
{ -- Code segment 11.5.1 }
N := 4;
FOR Row := 1 TO N DO
BEGIN

   FOR Col := 1 TO (N - 1) DO
      Write( '*' );

   WriteLn

END;
```

This code prints the pattern

```
***
***
***
***
```

The outer loop makes four trips, each of which prints a row of output. During each trip through the outer loop, the inner loop makes three trips, each of which prints one asterisk. The resulting output contains $N(N-1) = 4 \times 3 = 12$ asterisks in all.

Indirect nesting

The same effect may be obtained by indirect nesting, in which a procedure is called to print each row:

```
{ -- Code segment 11.5.2 }
PROCEDURE PrintRow( Limit : Integer );
VAR
   Col : Integer;

BEGIN

   FOR Col := 1 TO (Limit-1) DO
      Write( '*' );

   WriteLn

END; { PrintRow }
.
.
N := 4;
FOR Row := 1 TO N DO
   PrintRow( N );
```

Since the `FOR Col` loop in the `PrintRow` procedure runs during execution of the body of the `FOR Row` loop, it is effectively nested within that loop. This version of the code is very slightly slower than the first version because some time is consumed in calling the procedure. The difference is insignificant, though, compared with the total time spent in the `Write` and `WriteLn` procedures, as we now show.

Estimating running time

Although it hasn't mattered in the examples so far, we will later encounter situations in which the running time of an algorithm can be an issue in its design. In a computation involving large amounts of data, one algorithm might require several minutes or even hours to run, while another might require only a few seconds. Often the extra running time in the slower algorithms is spent mostly in nested loops.

The running time of nested loops can be very roughly estimated by counting the number of statements executed when they run. In the directly nested example above, $N(N-1)$ calls are made to the `Write` procedure, plus N calls to `WriteLn`. These $N(N-1) + N = N^2$ calls consume most of the running time, so we expect the total running time of the algorithm to be proportional to N^2. This prediction is confirmed by the actual time measurements shown in Table 11.5.1, measured on a microcomputer.

As N doubles, the running time increases by roughly a factor of four, indicating the roughly quadratic dependence of running time on N. (Small differences are caused by the idiosyncrasies of the system's output buffer.)

Running time (on a microcomputer) of code segment 11.5.1, as a function of N. **Table 11.5.1**

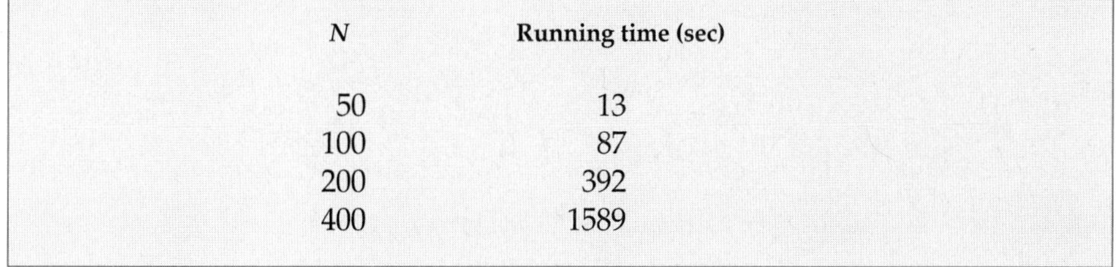

N	**Running time (sec)**
50	13
100	87
200	392
400	1589

Compare this with the running-time dependence when the inner loop does not depend on N:

```
{ -- Code segment 11.5.3 }
N := 4;
FOR Row := 1 TO N DO
BEGIN

   FOR Col := 1 TO 3 DO
      Write( '*' );

   WriteLn

END;
```

Now `Write` is called $3N$ times and `WriteLn` is called N times, so the running time is proportional to N rather than N^2. This is confirmed by the actual times shown in Table 11.5.2. When N doubles, the running time approximately doubles. (Again, small differences from the prediction are caused by peculiarities of the system's output buffer.)

When the inner loop depends on the outer loop's index

The range of the inner loop may depend on the outer loop index. Consider the following code:

```
{ -- Code segment 11.5.4 }
N := 4;
FOR Row := 1 TO N DO
BEGIN

   FOR Col := 1 TO (2 * Row - 1) DO
      Write( '*' );

   WriteLn

END;
```

Each trip through the outer loop prints a row of `(2 * Row - 1)` asterisks:

```
*
***
*****
*******
```

Table 11.5.2 *Running time of code segment 11.5.3, as a function of* N.

N	**Running time (sec)**
50	1.2
100	2.3
200	4.8
400	11.3

The `WriteLn` procedure is called N times. The number of calls to `Write` is equal to the total number of asterisks printed, which is

$$1 + 3 + 5 + \ldots + (2N - 1) = N^2$$

(This formula can be partially confirmed by checking it for a few particular values of N. A general proof is inductive, using the technique described in Appendix G.) Thus the total number of calls to the output procedures is $N^2 + N$, a quadratic function of N. When N is very large, this function is dominated by the N^2 term. Thus, for very large N, we expect the running time of this code segment to quadruple when N is doubled. (Exercise 33 asks you to test this assertion with your computer.)

A more complex example

Lest you think that nested loops are always `FOR` loops or that running times are always proportional to simple powers of the program parameters, consider this code segment:

```
{ -- Code segment 11.5.5 }
WriteLn('N = ', N : 2);

Row := N;
WHILE Row > 0 DO
BEGIN

   Index := Row;
   REPEAT
      Write('*');
      Index := Index * 2
   UNTIL Index > N;

   WriteLn;
   Row := Row DIV 2

END; { WHILE Row }
```

Here is sample output:

```
N =  1
*

N =  2
*
**

N =  3
*
**

N =  4
*
**
***
```

```
N =  5
*
**
***
N =  6
*
**
***
N =  7
*
**
***
N =  8
*
**
***
****
```

The number of trips through the inner loop equals the number of asterisks printed. At first sight, this number appears to be roughly linear, but it is not. Further samples are shown in Table 11.5.3, where the complex behavior is more evident.

To make a long story short, the number of trips through the inner loop is given by $L(L+1)/2$, where L is the biggest exponent of two such that 2^L is no greater than N. As you can see, the running times of nested loops can depend on the data values in complex ways.

Question

28. Cora Meltdown is having trouble understanding why code segment 11.5.3 runs so much faster than segment 11.5.1 when `N` is large. How would you explain this to her?

Table 11.5.3 *Number of trips through inner loop of code segment 11.5.5, for various values of* N.

N	**Trips through inner loop = Asterisks**
1	1
2–3	3
4–7	6
8–15	10
16–31	15
32–63	21
64–128	28

Exercises

29. What is printed by the following nested loop structures? Assume $N = 4$.

a.

```
FOR I := 1 TO N DO
   FOR J := 1 TO N DO
      WriteLn( I, J );
```

b.

```
FOR I := 1 TO N DIV 2 DO
   FOR J := 1 TO N DIV I DO
      WriteLn( I, J );
```

c.

```
I := N;
J := N;

REPEAT

   REPEAT
      Write( I:3 );
      I := I + 1
   UNTIL I > J;
   WriteLn;

   REPEAT
      Write( J:3 );
      J := J - 1
   UNTIL J < I;

   WriteLn

UNTIL J <= 1;
```

30. What is printed by the following code segments?

a.

```
N := 4;

FOR I := 1 TO N DO
BEGIN

   FOR J := N-I DOWNTO 1 DO
      Write( J:3 );

   WriteLn;

   FOR J := 1 TO 2*I-1 DO
      Write( J:3 );

   WriteLn

END;
```

b.
```
Length := 4;

WHILE Length > 0 DO
BEGIN

   FOR Index := 1 TO Length DO
      Write( '*' );

   WriteLn;
   Length := Length DIV 2

END;
```

31. In the following code segments, how many trips are made through the inner loops, as a function of *N*?

a.
```
FOR I := N DOWNTO 1 DO
   FOR J := 2 TO N DO
      WriteLn( I, J );
```

b.
```
FOR I := N DOWNTO 1 DO
   FOR J := 2 TO I DO
      WriteLn( I, J );
```

c.
```
FOR I := N DOWNTO 1 DO
   FOR J := I TO N DO
      WriteLn( I, J );
```

32. In the following code segments, how many times are output procedures called as a function of *N*?

a.
```
FOR I := 1 TO N DO
   FOR J := I DOWNTO 1 DO
      WriteLn( I, J );
```

b.
```
FOR I := 1 TO N-1 DO
   FOR J := I+1 TO N DO
      WriteLn( I, J );
```

c.
```
FOR Row := 1 TO N DO
BEGIN

   FOR Col := 1 TO (N - Row) DO
      Write( ' ' );

   FOR Col := 1 TO (2*Row - 1) DO
      Write( '*' );

   WriteLn

END;
```

33. Time code segments 11.5.1 and 11.5.4 on your computer system for $N = 100, 200, 400,$ and 800, and confirm that the running times approximately quadruple when *N* doubles, indicating that the running times are roughly quadratic functions of *N*.

LOOKING BACK

This chapter has introduced two of the more advanced aspects of loop design and use:

- How a loop structure is designed with the aid of an invariant and loop condition, so that it will yield the desired change in program state, from preconditions to postconditions.
- How the running time of a nested loop structure can be estimated as a function of the size of the data set.

Much of the chapter was devoted to the idea that an iterative structure can be *engineered* so that it will necessarily produce the desired change in program state, rather than just happening to work, more or less by accident. To this end, we carefully constructed pre- and postconditions for a loop, and then determined an invariant and loop condition that would carry the precondition state into the postcondition state. Only after all this did we actually write code. By this time, we were virtually certain that the loop would work as desired.

We also took a first look at a subject that will become of major importance in later chapters: how to predict the running times of nested loop structures, as functions of the amount of data to be processed. We saw examples in which the running time was a quadratic function of the size of the data set, and took a brief look at a somewhat more complicated case.

TERMS EMPHASIZED IN THIS CHAPTER

Absolute convergence criterion 349
Assertion 328
Convergence 346–347, 349
Direct nesting 352
`FOR` loops 332
Greatest common divisor (gcd) 340–344
Gregory-Newton method 346–351
Indirect nesting 352
Invariant 326–332
Iterative method 346, 361
Loop assertions 325
Loop condition 329–331
Loop invariant 326–332
Nested loops 352
Newton's method 346–351
Program state 327–329, 336
Quadratic convergence 347
Raising to a power 334–339
Relative convergence criterion 349
Running-time estimates 353–356
Square roots, method for 346–351
Sum of integers 326–332

PROJECTS

1. The factorial of a nonnegative integer N is defined by $N! = 1 \times 2 \times 3 \times \ldots \times (N-1) \times N$. Design a function to compute the factorial of nonnegative integers, using pre- and postconditions, a loop invariant, and loop condition in the design process. Test your function, but watch out for overflow. If `MaxInt` = 32767, you won't be able to calculate factorials for $N > 7$; if `MaxInt` = 2,147,483,647, you won't be able to use $N > 11$.

2. Napier's number, $e = 2.71828...$ is defined to be the value of $(1 + x)^{1/x}$ as x gets closer and closer to zero. Write a procedure that displays values of this expression for values of x progressively closer to zero, both from above and below. Your output should look like this:

```
Upper X       f(X)      Lower X        f(X)
0.50000000    2.2500    -0.50000000    4.0000
0.05000000    2.6533    -0.05000000    2.7895
0.00500000    2.7115    -0.00500000    2.7251
0.00050000    2.7176    -0.00050000    2.7190
0.00005000    2.7182    -0.00005000    2.7183
0.00000500    2.7183    -0.00000500    2.7183
0.00000050    2.7183    -0.00000050    2.7183
0.00000005    2.7183    -0.00000005    2.7183
```

(Your numbers may not be identical because of different roundoff errors in different systems.) Hint: To raise a real number to a real power, recognize that a^b is the same as `Exp( b * Ln( a ) )`.

3. Using `CountChars` as a starting point, write a `CountWords` procedure that counts the number of words in input. Also write a driver and test your procedure. For the purpose of this project, a word is considered to be a contiguous sequence of printable characters terminated by whitespace.

4. It is a remarkable fact that the Pythagorean Theorem, `Hypotenuse = Sqrt( Side1 * Side1 + Side2 * Side2 )` can be applied without taking a square root. According to C. Moler and D. Morrison, in *IBM J. Res. Develop.* **27** (November, 1983), pages 577–81, the hypotenuse can be computed accurately by a very simple algorithm. First define

```
P := maximum( Side1, Side2 );
Q := minimum( Side1, Side2 );
```

Then perform three iterations of the following steps:

```
R := Sqr( Q / P );
S := R / ( 4.0 + R );
P := P + ( 2.0 * S * P );
Q := S * Q
```

After three iterations of this, the hypotenuse will be closely approximated by `P`. Write a program to test this assertion.

5. Despite the two failures shown in Exercises 14 and 15, it is possible to write a correct implementation of Euclid's algorithm using a `WHILE` structure in place of the `REPEAT..UNTIL`. Write such a function and demonstrate that it works correctly.

6. Write a `GCD` function that returns the greatest common divisor of *three* given positive integers. Hint: `GCD(Int1, Int2, Int3) = GCD(Int1, GCD(Int2, Int3))`.

7. The least common multiple, `LCM`, of two positive integers, I and `J`, is the smallest positive integer such that I divides `LCM` without remainder and `J` divides `LCM` without remainder. For example,

```
LCM( 9, 2 ) = 18
LCM( 7, 11 ) = 77
```

and `LCM( 33, 2 ) = 66`

Write a function that computes the `LCM` of any two given positive integers. Hint: What is the product of the `LCM` and the `GCD`?

8. In the days before computers had circuitry for carrying out real division, an iterative technique was used, requiring only multiplication and subtraction. To calculate the inverse of N, 1.0 / N, each iteration computed a new estimate, g', from the previous estimate, g, by means of the formula

   $$g' = g\,(2 - Ng)$$

   This iterative process can be shown to converge if $0 < g < 2/N$. For example, the calculation of 1.0 / 3.0 would proceed through the following values if the first estimate were 0.5:

   0.5000000, 0.2500000, 0.3125000, 0.3320312, . . .

   Design and write an iterative inverse function similar to the square root function developed in this section, and test your function on various values of N.

9. Show that the iterative method of Project 8 converges for $0 < g < 2/N$.

REFERENCES

Structured programming is the discipline of using only control structures having provable consequences. This is the only way that we can produce verified programs: programs proven to be correct. There is a large literature on this subject, but much of it lies far beyond the level of the present text. For readers curious about the subject, here are some excellent starting sources:

- Edward Nash Yourdon, editor, *Classics in Software Engineering* (Yourdon Press, 1979).
- David Gries, *The Science of Programming* (Springer-Verlag, 1981).
- H. D. Mills, et al., *Principles of Computer Programming: A Mathematical Approach* (Allyn & Bacon, 1987).
- R. C. Linger, H. D. Mills, and B. I. Witt, *Structured Programming* (Addison-Wesley Publishing, 1979).

The fact that all programs can be built from only three control structures—simple sequences, `IF..THEN..ELSE`, and `WHILE`—was first proven in a famous paper by Boehm and Jacopini. The ensuing worldwide discussion of the proper use of control structures in programs included equally famous papers by Dijkstra, Ashcroft and Manna, and others. Many of these papers are collected in the first reference listed above.

With regard to the case studies in this chapter, I have drawn on the particularly lucid treatment of the *gcd* problem that appears in R. G. Dromey's *How to Solve It by Computer* (Prentice-Hall, 1982). This book is highly recommended. The Gregory-Newton method for calculating square roots is a special case of the Newton-Raphson method, which is discussed in virtually every textbook on numerical analysis or numerical methods. A full treatment is given, for example, in *Numerical Analysis*, third edition, by Richard L. Burden and J. Douglas Faires (Prindle, Weber, and Schmidt, 1985).

CHAPTER 12

Repetition by Recursion

CHAPTER CONTENTS

INTRODUCTION

The previous chapter showed how certain control structures can iterate the execution of the same sequence of statements. In addition to iteration, Pascal can repeat an action by *having a subprogram call itself*. This is called **recursion**, and in some situations, it is more suitable than iteration.

Recursion is often regarded as a deep mystery to be reserved for more advanced courses. As you are about to see, there is nothing mysterious about recursion. It works just like the nested procedure calls you studied in Section 6.4, the only new feature being that when procedure A calls procedure B, B and A happen to be *two copies of the same procedure*. If you bear in mind that this is all that is happening, you should have no trouble. We begin with a simple but surprising example.

12.1 THE POWER OF RECURSION

Some problems are almost trivial with the help of recursion, but very difficult to solve by iteration. For example, consider the `Strange` procedure, which reads a stream of characters until encountering `<EOF>`, the end-of-file signal:

```
PROGRAM Surprise ( Input, Output );

PROCEDURE Strange;
VAR
   Ch : Char;

BEGIN

   IF NOT EOF THEN
   BEGIN
      Read( Ch );
      Strange;
      Write( Ch )
   END

END; { Strange }

BEGIN { main program }

   Strange

END.
```

(The end-of-file signal was discussed in Section 4.4. The `EOF` function, which detects the end-of-file signal, is discussed in Section 17.3, which can be read at this point if desired.)

If `Strange` doesn't encounter the end-of-file signal immediately, it reads a character—the letter `'a'`, say—and then calls up a new copy of `Strange`. At that point, the original `Strange` goes into suspension while the new copy starts to run, using its own area of memory:

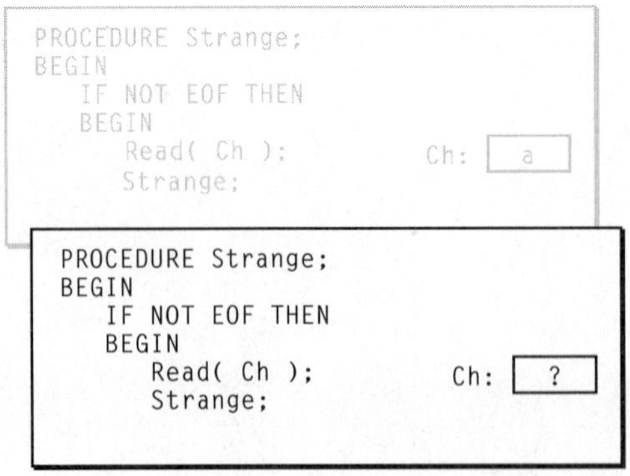

```
PROCEDURE Strange;
BEGIN
   IF NOT EOF THEN
   BEGIN
      Read( Ch );                Ch: [ a ]
      Strange;
```

```
PROCEDURE Strange;
BEGIN
   IF NOT EOF THEN
   BEGIN
      Read( Ch );                Ch: [ ? ]
      Strange;
```

The new copy of `Strange` reads another character, let's say `'b'`, and then calls up a third copy of `Strange`. At that point, the second `Strange` goes into suspension while the third copy starts to run in its own area of memory:

```
PROCEDURE Strange;
BEGIN
   IF NOT EOF THEN
   BEGIN
      Read( Ch );                 Ch: [ a ]
      Strange;

  PROCEDURE Strange;
  BEGIN
     IF NOT EOF THEN
     BEGIN
        Read( Ch );               Ch: [ b ]
        Strange;

    PROCEDURE Strange;
    BEGIN
       IF NOT EOF THEN
       BEGIN
          Read( Ch );             Ch: [ ? ]
          Strange;
```

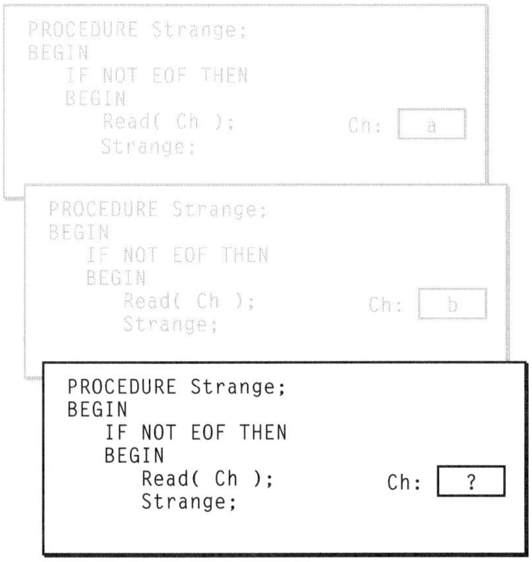

The third copy reads yet another character, which we will pretend is `'c'`, and then calls up a fourth copy of `Strange`. The third copy is suspended while the fourth copy begins to run in its own area of memory:

```
PROCEDURE Strange;
BEGIN
   IF NOT EOF THEN
   BEGIN
      Read( Ch );                 Ch: [ a ]
      Strange;

  PROCEDURE Strange;
  BEGIN
     IF NOT EOF THEN
     BEGIN
        Read( Ch );               Ch: [ b ]
        Strange;

    PROCEDURE Strange;
    BEGIN
       IF NOT EOF THEN
       BEGIN
          Read( Ch );             Ch: [ c ]
          Strange;

      PROCEDURE Strange;
      BEGIN
         IF NOT EOF THEN
         BEGIN
            Read( Ch );           Ch: [ ? ]
            Strange;
```

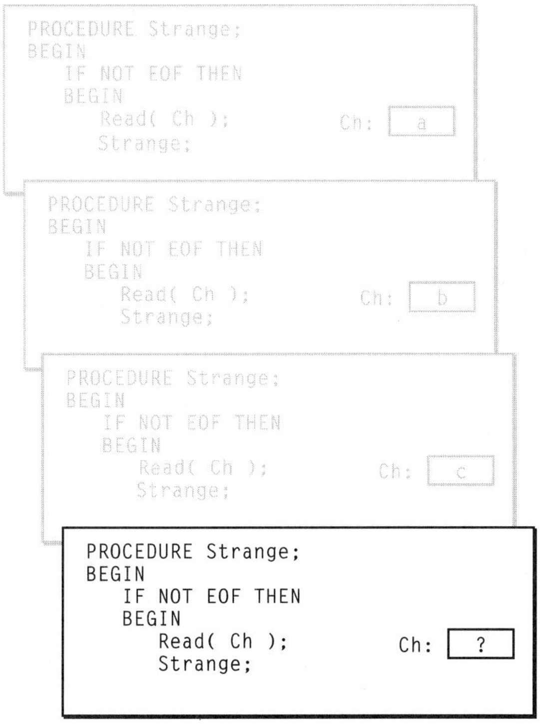

Now suppose that the user presses the end-of-file key. In that case, the boolean expression in

```
IF NOT EOF THEN
```

is `False`, so the conditionally executed code is skipped, and the fourth copy of `Strange` is terminated without doing anything further. The fourth copy of `Strange` goes out of existence, and execution picks up in the third copy where it was suspended.

```
PROCEDURE Strange;
BEGIN
   IF NOT EOF THEN
   BEGIN
      Read( Ch );                Ch: [ a ]
      Strange;

PROCEDURE Strange;
BEGIN
   IF NOT EOF THEN
   BEGIN
      Read( Ch );                Ch: [ b ]
      Strange;

PROCEDURE Strange;
BEGIN
   IF NOT EOF THEN
   BEGIN
      Read( Ch );                Ch: [ c ]
      Strange;
      Write( Ch )
```

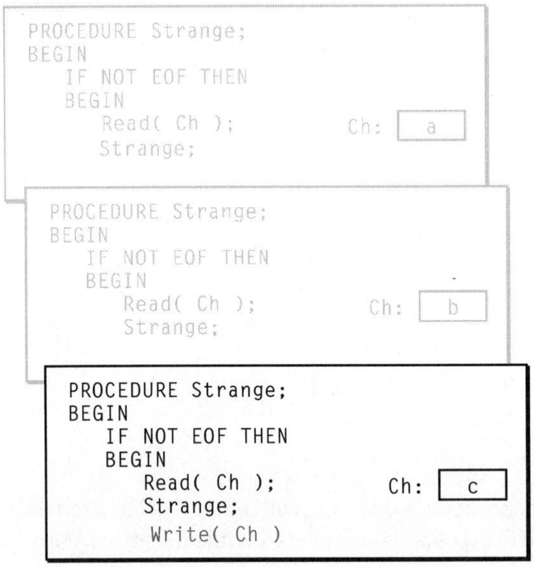

The third copy then writes the value of its local `Ch` variable to the screen:

```
c
```

The third copy of `Strange` then terminates, and execution picks up in the second copy where it was suspended.

```
PROCEDURE Strange;
BEGIN
   IF NOT EOF THEN
   BEGIN
      Read( Ch );                Ch: [ a ]
      Strange;

PROCEDURE Strange;
BEGIN
   IF NOT EOF THEN
   BEGIN
      Read( Ch );                Ch: [ b ]
      Strange;
      Write( Ch )
```

The second copy writes the value of its local `Ch` variable to the screen:

```
cb
```

The second copy of `Strange` then terminates, and execution picks up in the first copy where it was suspended.

```
PROCEDURE Strange;
BEGIN
   IF NOT EOF THEN
   BEGIN
      Read( Ch );                Ch: [ a ]
      Strange;
      Write( Ch )
```

The first copy writes the value of its local `Ch` variable to the screen:

```
cba
```

The first copy of `Strange` terminates, returning execution to the main program where it was suspended. The main program has nothing further to do, so all execution ceases. The net result is that *this program writes the reverse of what was keyed in, no matter how many characters were entered.* But try and write an equally simple *iterative* program that behaves like this one. Just try—and then you will better appreciate the power of recursion.

Another sign of the power of recursion is that very small changes in the algorithm have very big effects on the way it executes. The following version of `Strange` differs only in having two lines swapped:

```
PROCEDURE Strange;
VAR
   Ch : Char;
BEGIN

   IF NOT EOF THEN
   BEGIN
      Read( Ch );
      Write( Ch );
      Strange
   END

END; { Strange }
```

Now the procedure immediately echoes exactly what was keyed in, *without holding it and reversing it!* Little changes can have powerful effects.

12.2 THE STRUCTURE OF A RECURSIVE SUBPROGRAM

As with looping and the danger of infinite loops, we must be careful to prevent infinite repetition when dealing with recursive procedures or functions. There are three requirements for successful recursion:

1. Every recursive subprogram must contain a control structure that prevents further recursion when the terminal state is reached.
2. The terminal state must necessarily be reached.
3. When the terminal state is reached, the subprogram must have completed the correct computation.

Successful use of recursion hinges on your attention to these three requirements. This is very similar to the way in which we learned to ensure correct loops in Chapter 11.

The concept of recursion comes from mathematics, where we often encounter **recurrence relations**. A recurrence relation is a relation between a desired mathematical result and a simpler result of exactly the same kind. For example, consider the problem of Section 11.2, where we were calculating an integer power, N, of a real number, X. Instead of performing the calculation iteratively, we can note that

$$X^N = X \cdot X^{N-1}$$

This expresses the result we seek, X^N, as a product involving a simpler result of the same kind, namely X^{N-1}, and is therefore a recurrence relation. Its value lies in the fact that the simpler calculation can be expressed in the same way in terms of a still simpler result:

$$X^N = X \cdot X^{N-1} = X \cdot X \cdot X^{N-2}$$

This in turn involves a factor, X^{N-2}, which can be expressed in terms of a still simpler factor, and so on.

The entire recursive process will necessarily terminate if $N > 0$ because eventually we will get down to a product involving X^0, which is nonrecursively defined to be 1. This is called the **base case** for the recurrence. Now we can see how the three requirements for successful recursion are satisfied:

Base case: The terminal state for a recursion.

1. We recur further if and only if the requested power of X is greater than 0; otherwise, we report the result to be 1.
2. The process will necessarily terminate because the power of X was initially greater than 0, and we subtract 1 from the power on each recursion.
3. The correct result is necessarily obtained because we multiply as many Xs as the original power.

As you can see, recursion is a process of breaking a computation down in a way that involves a simpler computation of the same kind, and continuing this decomposition until reaching a trivial base case. Throughout the rest of the chapter, we will consider how to apply this idea.

Questions

1. What is the definition of recursion?
2. What is the difference between recursion and iteration?

3. Why does every recursive subprogram need a nonrecursive base case?

4. Jackson P. Slipshod claims that recursion is useless because "If a procedure calls itself, which calls itself, then the same thing is done over and over, and nothing different is ever done." What is wrong with this argument?

5. The first version of `Strange` shown in Section 12.1, which echoes text backwards, is difficult to program iteratively. Why is this?

6. (From LeRoy Eide) What would the world be like if the sun set recursively?

Exercises

7. Suppose that the following procedure is given the input string

   `Now is the time<EOLn>for all good persons<EOLn><EOF>`

   Then what is displayed on the screen?

```
PROCEDURE Puzzle;
VAR
   Ch : Char;

BEGIN

   IF NOT EOF THEN
   BEGIN

      IF NOT EOLn THEN
      BEGIN
         Read( Ch );
         IF Ch <> ' ' THEN
            Write( Ch )
      END

      ELSE
         ReadLn;

      Puzzle

   END

END; { Puzzle }
```

8. In Exercise 7, suppose the recursive call to `Puzzle` is moved so that it appears immediately after the `Read( Ch )` call. Then what is displayed by the procedure?

12.3 ITERATION VERSUS RECURSION

Recursion sometimes leads to simpler code than iteration, and simpler code is often *clearer* code. Consider `IntPower`, the function we developed in Section 11.2 for calculating an integer power of a real number. We can use the mathematical recurrence relation described on the previous page to write a recursive version of `IntPower`. Here is the plan:

1. If `Power` is 0, $\texttt{Number}^{\texttt{Power}}$ is $\texttt{Number}^{0}$, which is 1.0. Thus no recursion is needed. This is called the *base case*.
2. If `Power` is positive, $\texttt{Number}^{\texttt{Power}}$ is $\texttt{Number} * (\texttt{Number}^{(\texttt{Power-1})})$, a recurrence relation that is used repeatedly until `( Power-1 )` reaches 0, at which point the recursion stops because the function value is $\texttt{Number}^{0}$, which is computed by step 1.
3. If `Power` is negative, $\texttt{Number}^{\texttt{Power}}$ is computed by taking the inverse of $\texttt{Number}^{(\texttt{-Power})}$, in which the exponent is positive.

It helps to have a picture of how the recursive process works. Figure 12.3.1 shows what happens when we calculate Number^2.

Figure 12.3.1 *The sequence of program states when calculating Number^2 recursively.*

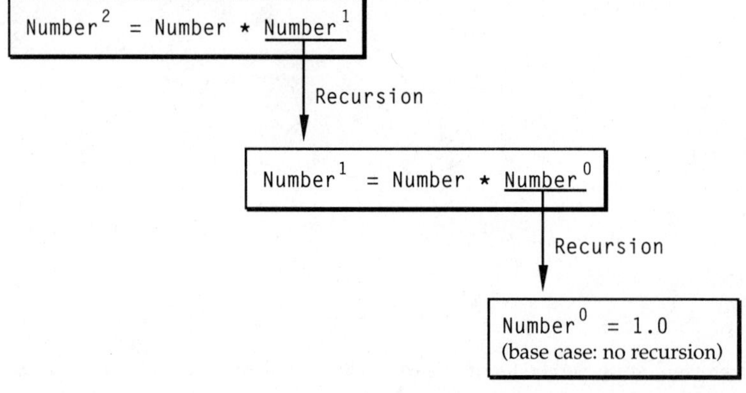

The recursive function is simply a literal representation of our outline:

```
FUNCTION IntPower( Number : Real;
                   Power  : Integer ) : Real;
{
  RECURSIVE VERSION

  PRECONDITIONS:
  Number and Power have been initialized.

  POSTCONDITION:
  IntPower = (Number ** Power ), where ** stands for exponentiation.
}

BEGIN

   IF Power = 0 THEN
      { -- Base case: no recursion. }
      IntPower := 1.0

   ELSE IF Power > 0 THEN
      {
        RECURSION INVARIANT:
        0 < Power
        and ( Number ** Power ) = Number * ( Number ** (Power-1) ).

        RECURSION CONDITION:
        Power <> 0.
      }
      IntPower := Number * IntPower( Number, Power - 1 )

   ELSE
      { -- Power is negative: invert the positive-power result. }
      IntPower := 1.0 / IntPower( Number, -Power )

END; { IntPower }
```

If `Power > 0`, the recursion

```
IntPower := Number * IntPower( Number, Power - 1 )
```

is applied. This is simply a Pascal-language translation of the recurrence relation, and states the **recursive invariant** property of the program states during recursion. During the recursive process, `Power` is greater than zero, but decreasing. When

```
IntPower( Number, Power-1 )
```

sends `Power-1 = 0` to the next copy of `IntPower`, we have the base case and there is no further recursion. Thus the condition for continuing the recursion is that `(Power <> 0)`; when `Power` becomes zero, recursion should terminate.

The sequence of execution

In order to be clear on how `IntPower` transmits parameters and returns the function values, let us trace its execution when computing 1.5^2. Some other program unit originally calls `IntPower(1.5, 2)`, and this `IntPower` executes down to the recursive call:

```
FUNCTION IntPower( Number : Real;                      Number:  [ 1.5 ]
                   Power : Integer ) : Real;           Power:   [  2  ]
BEGIN                                                  IntPower: [ ??? ]
      .
      .
      IntPower := Number * IntPower( Number, Power - 1 )
```

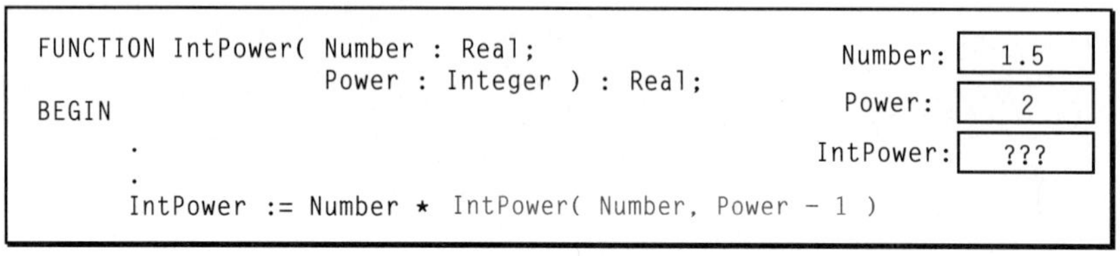

Then the first `IntPower` is suspended while a second `IntPower` function begins to run in its own area of memory with `Power` = 1:

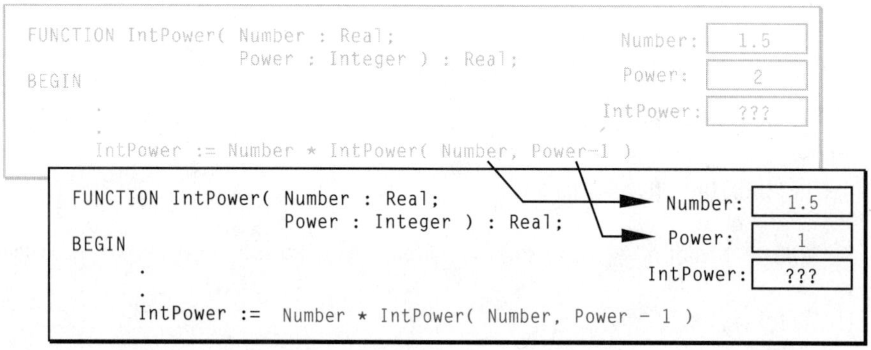

```
FUNCTION IntPower( Number : Real;                      Number:  [ 1.5 ]
                   Power : Integer ) : Real;           Power:   [  2  ]
BEGIN                                                  IntPower: [ ??? ]
      .
      .
      IntPower := Number * IntPower( Number, Power-1 )

   FUNCTION IntPower( Number : Real;                   Number:  [ 1.5 ]
                      Power : Integer ) : Real;        Power:   [  1  ]
   BEGIN                                               IntPower: [ ??? ]
         .
         .
         IntPower := Number * IntPower( Number, Power - 1 )
```

This second `IntPower` executes down to the recursive call, then is suspended while a third copy of `IntPower` begins to execute in its own area of memory with `Power` = 0:

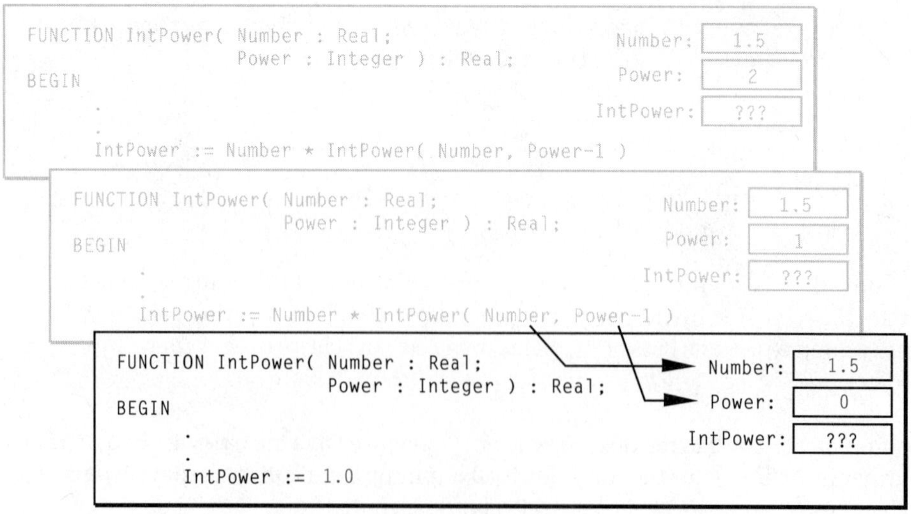

```
FUNCTION IntPower( Number : Real;                      Number:  [ 1.5 ]
                   Power : Integer ) : Real;           Power:   [  2  ]
BEGIN                                                  IntPower: [ ??? ]
      .
      .
      IntPower := Number * IntPower( Number, Power-1 )

   FUNCTION IntPower( Number : Real;                   Number:  [ 1.5 ]
                      Power : Integer ) : Real;        Power:   [  1  ]
   BEGIN                                               IntPower: [ ??? ]
         .
         .
         IntPower := Number * IntPower( Number, Power-1 )

      FUNCTION IntPower( Number : Real;                Number:  [ 1.5 ]
                         Power : Integer ) : Real;     Power:   [  0  ]
      BEGIN                                            IntPower: [ ??? ]
            .
            .
            IntPower := 1.0
```

The third `IntPower` executes the nonrecursive base case, assigning `1.0` to `IntPower`. This value is then returned to the second copy of `IntPower`:

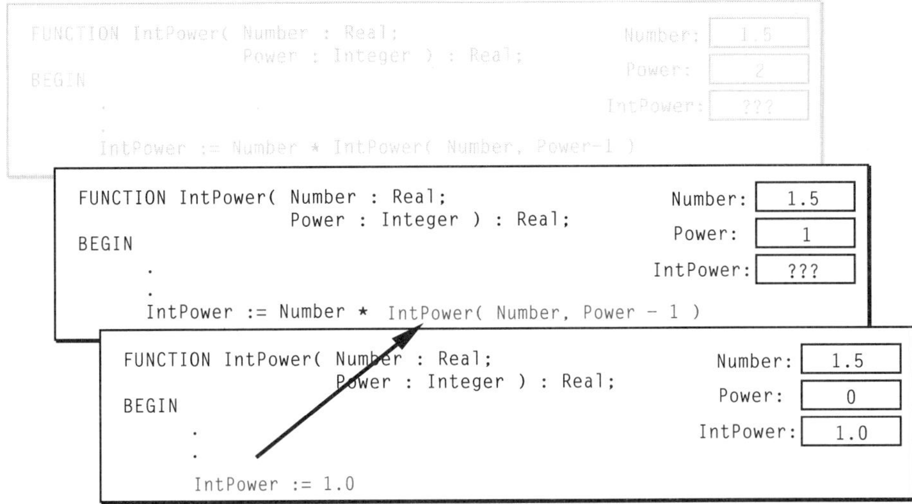

The second copy of `IntPower` then returns 1.5 x 1.0 = 1.5 to the first copy of `IntPower`:

```
FUNCTION IntPower( Number : Real;                    Number:   [ 1.5 ]
                   Power : Integer ) : Real;         Power:    [  2  ]
BEGIN                                                IntPower: [ ??? ]
    .
    .
    IntPower := Number * IntPower( Number, Power - 1 )

    FUNCTION IntPower( Number : Real;                    Number:   [ 1.5 ]
                       Power : Integer ) : Real;         Power:    [  1  ]
    BEGIN                                                IntPower: [ 1.5 ]
        .
        .
        IntPower := Number * 1.0
```

The first copy of `IntPower` then returns 1.5 x 1.5 = 2.25 to the calling program unit:

```
FUNCTION IntPower( Number : Real;                    Number:   [ 1.5  ]
                   Power : Integer ) : Real;         Power:    [  2   ]
BEGIN                                                IntPower: [ 2.25 ]
    .
    .
    IntPower := Number * 1.5
```

Understanding this sequence of execution is exactly the same as understanding the sequence of execution in *any* set of nested function calls. The only new feature here is that all functions called have the same name. *They do not all do the same thing,* however, because each time there is a call to `IntPower`, the second parameter value is slightly different. When we reach the point where `Power` is zero, we stop making recursive calls, and this stops the growth of the chain of nested function calls. We then return function values back up the chain to the beginning.

Table 12.3.1 *Running times of the iterative and recursive versions of IntPower, when computing 1.11^{111} on a typical microcomputer.*

Method	Time to execute function once (in seconds)
Iterative	0.032
Recursive	0.047

Disadvantages of the recursive IntPower

This version of the function is simpler than the iterative version, and easier to read, but is it as fast? To answer this question, both procedures were timed over 1,000 executions on a microcomputer, calculating 1.11^{111}. The running times per execution are shown in Table 12.3.1. From these data, it appears that the recursive version takes 50 percent longer to execute, but it is still fast enough that this isn't noticed in normal applications.

But what about the memory requirements? Each new copy of the `IntPower` function requires memory for the two parameters (eight bytes on a typical microcomputer), the returned value (four bytes), plus overhead for the function call and the return to the caller (roughly a couple of dozen bytes). As you may learn in later courses, the `IntPower` object code is actually reused, so multiple copies of it are not needed. Altogether, each copy of `IntPower` might consume about 40 bytes or so. It would be an exceptional calculation that would occupy more than a few thousand bytes of memory.

Exercises

9. In the `IntPower` algorithm, `Power` = 0 is a nonrecursive base case. However, `Power` = 1 is also a trivial case, and can be treated nonrecursively. Write and test a version of `IntPower` in which both of these cases are nonrecursive.

10. Design and write a recursive version of a function to add the first *N* positive integers, which was discussed iteratively in Section 11.1. Use a recursion invariant and recursion condition in your design.

11. Write an iterative version of the following recursive function. Test the two versions to confirm that they compute the same result.

```
FUNCTION NNP1D2( N : Integer ) : Integer;
BEGIN
   IF N > 1 THEN
      NNP1D2 := N + NNP1D2( N - 1 )
   ELSE
      NNP1D2 := 0
END; { NNP1D2 }
```

12. Write a program to prove that the NNP1D2 function in the previous exercise computes the value of N * (N + 1) DIV 2 for N = 1, 2, 3, . . ., 10. (Could this be the reason the function was called NNP1D2?)

13. Jackson P. Slipshod has written a version of the NNP1D2 function in which the decision structure is written IF N <>1 THEN rather than IF N > 1 THEN. What will happen if his program calls NNP1D2(-2)?

12.4 CASE STUDY: RECURSION FOR SQUARE ROOTS

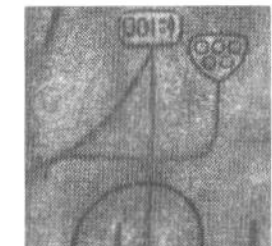

In Section 11.4, we worked out a relatively short function for estimating a square root by successive approximations. Now consider an alternative version, which requires both the number whose root is sought and a first estimate of the root:

```
FUNCTION SquareRoot( Number, OldEstimate : Real ) : Real;
{
  RECURSIVE SQUARE ROOT

  PRECONDITION:
  0 < Number and 0 < OldEstimate;
  OldEstimate is an estimate of the square root of Number.

  POSTCONDITION:
  Function value differs from the previous estimate by less than
  ConvergenceCriterion * NewEstimate.
}

CONST
   ConvergenceCriterion = 1.0e-8;  {Relative convergence criterion}

VAR
   NewEstimate, RelativeChange : Real;

BEGIN

      NewEstimate := ( OldEstimate + (Number / OldEstimate) ) / 2.0;
      RelativeChange :=
                     Abs((NewEstimate - OldEstimate) / NewEstimate);

      IF RelativeChange > ConvergenceCriterion THEN
         {
           RECURSION INVARIANT:
           0 <= Abs( NewEstimate - SqRt(Number) )
                <= Abs( OldEstimate - SqRt(Number) )

           RECURSION CONDITION:
           RelativeChange > ConvergenceCriterion
         }
         SquareRoot := SquareRoot( Number, NewEstimate )
```

```
      ELSE
         {
           Finished; quit with the current estimate.
           POSTCONDITION:
           0 <= RelativeChange <= ConvergenceCriterion.
         }
         SquareRoot := NewEstimate
END; { SquareRoot }
```

Instead of using a loop, this version says, "If the latest estimate differs significantly from the previous estimate, then call SquareRoot again to get a still better estimate." The function transmits NewEstimate to another copy of the same function, which treats the first function's NewEstimate as its OldEstimate. *Thus, every newly called copy of the function receives a different second parameter.* If the method started out with a reasonable estimate of the root, eventually some copy of SquareRoot will discover that its new estimate of the root differs very little from its OldEstimate parameter, and the ELSE clause will be executed, terminating the recursion.

Sequence of execution

Suppose that we are to find the square root of 4.0, and that our initial guess at the root is also 4.0. (As you recall, any positive first guess will work, and it is convenient to pick Number itself.) Then the main program calls SquareRoot(4.0, 4.0), and the function starts to execute. As it is activated, SquareRoot first sets up storage cells for its formal parameters, Number and OldEstimate, storing 4.0 in each. It sets up storage cells for its internal variables, NewEstimate and RelativeChange, and for its return value, Square-Root, all three of these initially containing garbage. Then the code begins to run. First NewEstimate is computed to be 2.5:

```
NewEstimate := 0.5 * ( 4.0 + (4.0 / 4.0) )
```

Then RelativeChange is computed to be 0.6:

```
RelativeChange := Abs((2.5 - 4.0) / 2.5)
```

RelativeChange is compared with ConvergenceCriterion:

```
IF RelativeChange > ConvergenceCriterion THEN
   {-- Not finished; get a better estimate }
   SquareRoot := SquareRoot( Number, NewEstimate )
ELSE
   {-- Finished; quit with the current estimate }
   SquareRoot := NewEstimate
```

Because RelativeChange is greater than ConvergenceCriterion, the THEN clause of the decision structure is executed:

```
IF 0.6 > 1.0e-8 THEN
   {-- Not finished; get a better estimate }
   SquareRoot := SquareRoot( 4.0, 2.5 )
```

This is a call to a function that happens to have the same name as the function doing the calling:

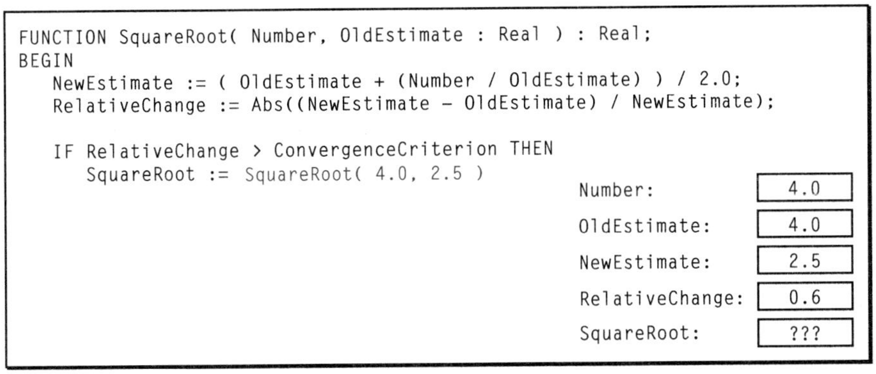

```
FUNCTION SquareRoot( Number, OldEstimate : Real ) : Real;
BEGIN
   NewEstimate := ( OldEstimate + (Number / OldEstimate) ) / 2.0;
   RelativeChange := Abs((NewEstimate - OldEstimate) / NewEstimate);

   IF RelativeChange > ConvergenceCriterion THEN
      SquareRoot := SquareRoot( 4.0, 2.5 )
                                           Number:          4.0
                                           OldEstimate:     4.0
                                           NewEstimate:     2.5
                                           RelativeChange:  0.6
                                           SquareRoot:      ???
```

At this point, the current copy of SquareRoot suspends execution as it calls for a new copy of SquareRoot to be activated. This is just like any other nested function call, with the sole difference that the second-activated function happens to have the same name as the first. Now the newly activated copy of SquareRoot sets up its own memory area containing its own formal parameters, storing 4.0 in its Number parameter and 2.5 in its OldEstimate parameter.

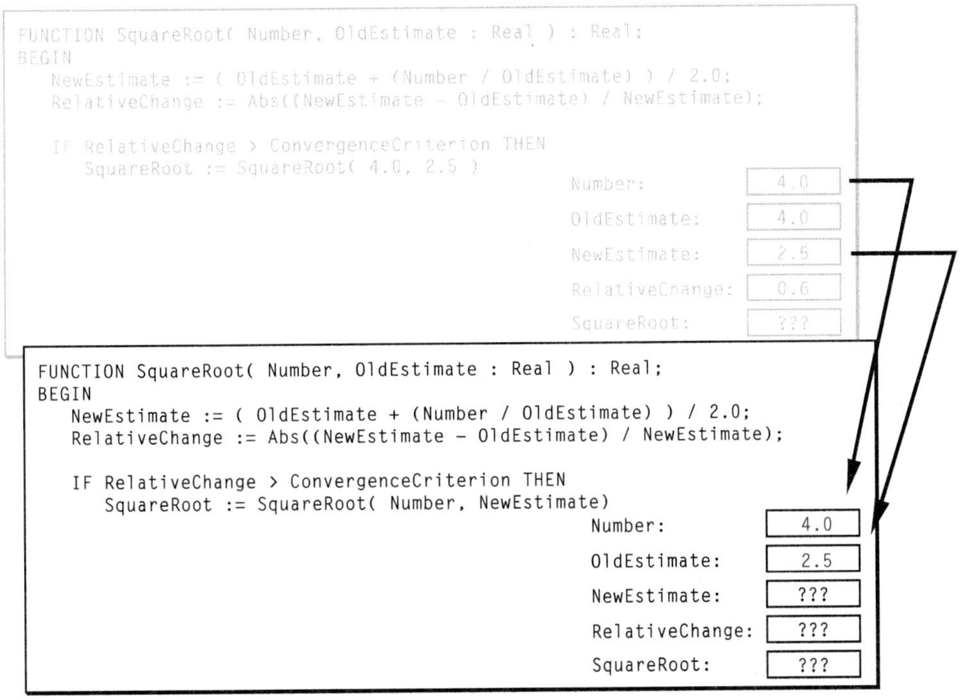

```
FUNCTION SquareRoot( Number, OldEstimate : Real ) : Real;
BEGIN
   NewEstimate := ( OldEstimate + (Number / OldEstimate) ) / 2.0;
   RelativeChange := Abs((NewEstimate - OldEstimate) / NewEstimate);

   IF RelativeChange > ConvergenceCriterion THEN
      SquareRoot := SquareRoot( 4.0, 2.5 )
                                           Number:          4.0
                                           OldEstimate:     4.0
                                           NewEstimate:     2.5
                                           RelativeChange:  0.6
                                           SquareRoot:      ???
```

```
FUNCTION SquareRoot( Number, OldEstimate : Real ) : Real;
BEGIN
   NewEstimate := ( OldEstimate + (Number / OldEstimate) ) / 2.0;
   RelativeChange := Abs((NewEstimate - OldEstimate) / NewEstimate);

   IF RelativeChange > ConvergenceCriterion THEN
      SquareRoot := SquareRoot( Number, NewEstimate)
                                           Number:          4.0
                                           OldEstimate:     2.5
                                           NewEstimate:     ???
                                           RelativeChange:  ???
                                           SquareRoot:      ???
```

Table 12.4.1 *Running times of the iterative and recursive versions of the SquareRoot function, as measured on a typical microcomputer.*

Method	Time to execute function once (in seconds)
Iterative	0.00494
Recursive	0.00565

Then this second function begins to execute its code. It first computes its `NewEstimate`, a local variable stored in its memory area, to be 2.05:

```
NewEstimate := 0.5 * ( 2.5 + (4.0 / 2.5) )
```

It goes on to compute `RelativeChange` to be 0.18, which is larger than `ConvergenceCriterion`, so it executes the `THEN` clause of its decision structure:

```
IF 0.18 > 1.0e-8 THEN
   {-- Not finished; get a better estimate }
   SquareRoot := SquareRoot( 4.0, 2.05 )
```

At this point, the second copy of `SquareRoot` joins the first copy in a state of suspension as it calls up a third copy of `SquareRoot`. The third copy begins to execute, and this continues until a copy of `SquareRoot` computes a value of `NewEstimate` differing by less than 1.0e–8 from its value of `OldEstimate`. When this happens, the value of `NewEstimate` will be 2.00000000 ± 0.00000001, and that function will execute the `ELSE` clause of its decision structure:

```
ELSE
   {-- Finished; quit with the current estimate }
   SquareRoot := 2.00000000
```

This copy of `SquareRoot` then terminates execution, returning the value 2.00000000 to the copy of `SquareRoot` that called it, which then returns the value 2.00000000 to the copy of `SquareRoot` that called it, and so on, all the way back to the original copy of `SquareRoot`, which then returns 2.00000000 to the main program.

Which would you use: recursion or iteration?

The recursive version of this function is simpler than the iterative version, and once recursion itself is understood, the recursive version of `SquareRoot` is easier to understand and debug than the iterative version.

As with `IntPower`, however, the recursion incurs a heavier cost in terms of execution speed and memory usage. Table 12.4.1 shows some timing results, obtained by timing 10,000 calculations of the square root of 3.0, using a typical microcomputer.

The difference between the iterative and recursive versions is less than it was with IntPower because the Gregory-Newton method for square roots converges so rapidly. For the same reason, the recursive version requires only slightly more memory.

It is worth getting comfortable with recursion despite its drawbacks. In addition to its elegance and simplicity, we will find that it allows easy solutions to problems that would be nearly impossible with iteration. Therefore, both methods should be in your mental tool kit.

Question

14. Why does the rapid convergence of the Gregory-Newton method imply that the recursive version of the algorithm will be almost as efficient as the iterative version?

Exercises

What do these recursive subprograms do if their parameters are positive?

15.
```
FUNCTION Mystery( Number : Integer ) : Integer;
BEGIN
   IF Number > 1 THEN
      Mystery := Number * Mystery( Number - 1 )
   ELSE
      Mystery := 1
END;
```

16.
```
FUNCTION Puzzle( Mumble, Fumble : Integer ) : Integer;
BEGIN
   IF Fumble > 0 THEN
     Puzzle := Mumble * Puzzle( Mumble, Fumble-1 )
   ELSE
      Puzzle := Mumble
END;
```

17.
```
PROCEDURE ToughNut( Number : Integer );
{ PRECONDITION: Number >= 0. }
BEGIN
   IF Number < 10 THEN
      Write( Number:1 )
   ELSE
   BEGIN
      ToughNut( Number DIV 10 );
      Write( (Number MOD 10):1 )
   END
END;
```

18. Write iterative versions of the subprograms in Exercises 15–17.

12.5 THE TOWERS OF HANOI

According to an old oriental legend, the monks in a remote mountain monastery could tell when the world would end. They had a set of three diamond needles. Stacked on the first diamond needle were 64 gold disks of decreasing size. The monks moved one disk to another needle each hour, subject to two rules:

1. Only one disk could be moved at a time.
2. A larger disk must never be stacked above a smaller disk.

The legend said that when all 64 disks had been transferred to the second needle according to these rules, the stars would be extinguished and the world would end.

In Victorian England, a parlor game called "The Towers of Hanoi" was based on this legend. The game is a good example of a problem that is relatively easy to solve recursively, but relatively difficult to solve in any other way. (But see Project 3 and the reference at the end of the chapter.)

Consider first some cases in which there are very few disks. Of course, if there is only one disk, there is no problem. We just move the disk from the needle A to needle B, and we are finished.

Moving two disks from A to B

If there are two disks, the problem is only slightly harder. Consider the diagram:

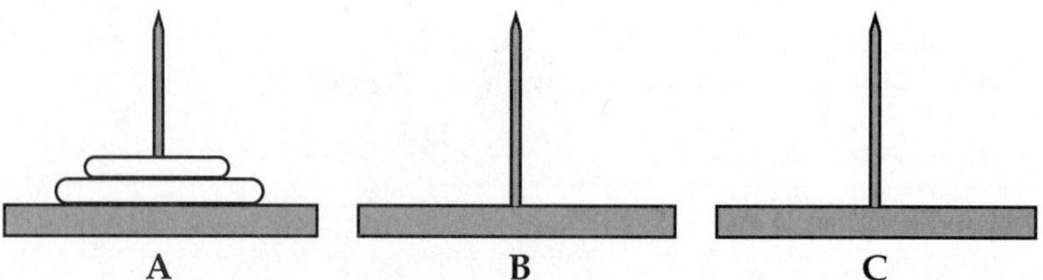

We simply move the top disk, the smaller one, from needle A to needle C, to get it out of the way. Then we move the larger disk to the needle B. Finally, we move the smaller disk from its temporary storage on needle C to its final position on needle B.

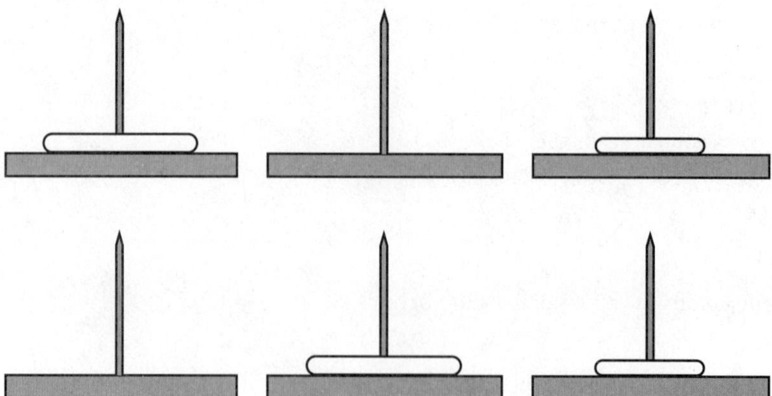

In shorthand notation, the two-disk process is

1. Move one disk from A to C.
2. Move one disk from A to B.
3. Move one disk from C to B.

Moving three disks from A to B

With three disks, the problem is more difficult.

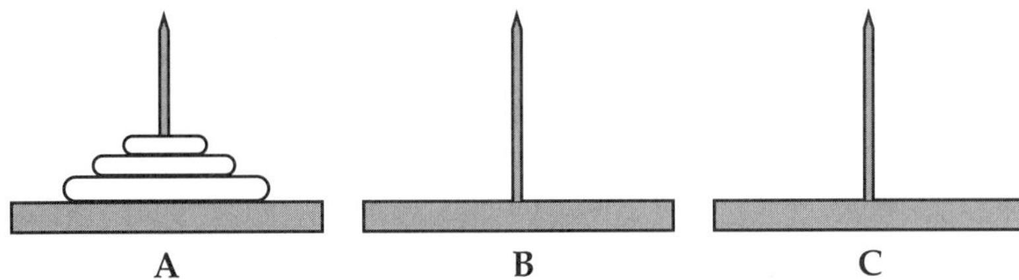

If you try out some moves, you will see that the first goal should be to get the largest disk moved to its final position on needle B. This can be done by first moving the top two disks to temporary storage on needle C. We already know how to move the top two disks because we worked out the two-disk process outlined above.

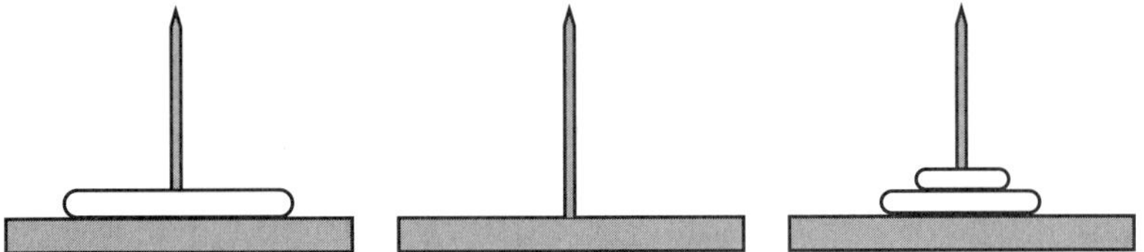

Once the top two disks are out of the way, we simply move the biggest disk directly to final storage on needle B:

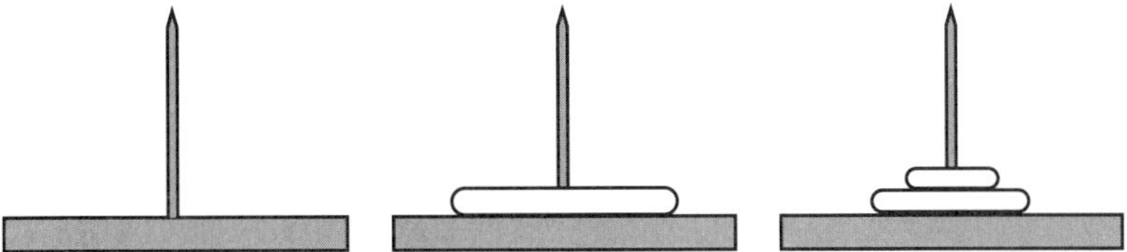

Finally, we move the two smaller disks from needle C to needle B. This again is done by the two-disk process outlined previously. The only thing new is that we are moving from C to B this time, using A for temporary storage along the way.

The whole three-disk process can now be outlined, building upon the two-disk process:

1. Move two disks from A to C, using B for temporary storage along the way.
2. Move one disk from A to B.
3. Move two disks from C to B, using A for temporary storage along the way.

As you can see by comparing this outline with the one for the two-disk process, a pattern is beginning to appear.

Moving four disks from A to B

The process is similar for the four-disk problem. You must first move the top three disks to temporary storage on needle C, which can be accomplished by the steps

Move disk 1 from A to C.
Move disk 2 from A to B.
Move disk 1 from C to B.
Move disk 3 from A to C.
Move disk 1 from B to A.
Move disk 2 from B to C.
Move disk 1 from A to C.

Then disk 4, the largest disk, is moved to its final position on needle B, after which the three disks on needle C are transferred to needle B by the steps

Move disk 1 from C to B.
Move disk 2 from C to A.
Move disk 1 from B to A.
Move disk 3 from C to B.
Move disk 1 from A to C.
Move disk 2 from A to B.
Move disk 1 from C to B.

The process is summarized below:

1. Move three disks from A to C, using B for temporary storage along the way.
2. Move one disk from A to B.
3. Move three disks from C to B, using A for temporary storage along the way.

By now, the pattern is apparent. The process for moving *N* disks, where $N \geq 1$, can be described easily in terms of the process for moving $N-1$ disks:

Process for moving *N* disks from A to B (where $N \geq 1$)

1. Move *N*–1 disks from A to C, using B for temporary storage along the way.
2. Move one disk from A to B.
3. Move *N*–1 disks from C to B, using A for temporary storage along the way.

This is the outline for a recursive procedure. The procedure for moving *N* disks is written in terms of two distinct calls to the same procedure, moving *N*–1 disks. The whole process must terminate when there are no more disks to be moved:

```
PROCEDURE MoveDisks ( Number : Integer;
                      Origin, Destination, TempStorage : Char );
BEGIN

   IF Number > 0 THEN
   BEGIN

      MoveDisks(Number - 1, Origin, TempStorage, Destination);

      WriteLn( 'Move disk ', Number : 2, ' from ', Origin, ' to ',
               Destination );

      MoveDisks(Number - 1, TempStorage, Destination, Origin)

  END

END; { MoveDisks }
```

It is much more difficult to invent an *iterative* Towers of Hanoi solution. It can be done; in fact, *any* recursive algorithm can be replaced by an iterative one, and vice versa. There is a simple iterative solution, but it is hard to invent. See Project 3 at the end of the chapter.

Question

19. Why isn't an `ELSE` clause needed in the `IF..THEN` structure of the `MoveDisks` procedure?

Exercise

20. Rewrite the `MoveDisks` procedure so that it displays a simplified picture at each stage of the disk-moving process. This can be done most easily by displaying the disk numbers at appropriate positions on the screen. For example, while solving a three-disk problem, the procedure could display

```
1
2
3
—       —       —
```

then

```
2               1
3
—       —       —
```

and so on, with one display during each recursive call.

12.6 TAIL RECURSION

You can see from the `Strange` procedure and the Towers of Hanoi problem that recursion possesses great power, and that it sometimes provides a simple solution for what seems to be a difficult problem. This might lead you to believe that recursion is more powerful than iteration, or that some problems yield to recursion but not to iteration. But *any problem that can be solved recursively can be solved iteratively, and vice versa.*

Some programs can be converted easily from one repetitive form to the other. The easiest case is that in which recursion occurs as the last action in a procedure. This is called **tail recursion**. Consider, for example, the second version of the `Strange` procedure, which echoes characters in the order in which they are entered at the keyboard:

```
PROCEDURE Strange;
VAR
   Ch : Char;

BEGIN

   IF NOT EOF THEN
   BEGIN
      Read( Ch );
      Write( Ch );
      Strange
   END

END; { Strange }
```

Here, the recursion is the very last action taken by the procedure, so the effect can be stated this way: "After doing the `Read` and the `Write`, repeat the whole process until we see the end-of-file signal." Obviously, this can be accomplished easily with a loop:

```
PROCEDURE Strange;
VAR
   Ch : Char;

BEGIN

   WHILE NOT EOF DO
   BEGIN
      Read( Ch );
      Write( Ch )
   END

END; { Strange }
```

When a tail-recursive procedure uses value parameters, the conversion to iteration is slightly more complicated. The second recursive call in the Towers of Hanoi procedure is of this type:

```
PROCEDURE MoveDisks ( Number : Integer;
          Origin, Destination, TempStorage : Char );
BEGIN

   IF Number > 0 THEN
   BEGIN

      MoveDisks( Number - 1, Origin, TempStorage, Destination );

      WriteLn( 'Move disk ', Number : 2, ' from ',
               Origin, ' to ', Destination );

      MoveDisks( Number - 1, TempStorage, Destination, Origin )

  END

END; { MoveDisks }
```

Because the tail recursion employs only value parameters, we can accomplish the repetition by looping *if we first make appropriate copies of the actual parameters for the procedure*:

```
PROCEDURE MoveDisks ( Number : Integer;
          Origin, Destination, TempStorage : Char );
BEGIN

   WHILE Number > 0 DO
   BEGIN

      MoveDisks( Number - 1, Origin, TempStorage, Destination );

      WriteLn( 'Move disk ', Number : 2, ' from ',
               Origin, ' to ', Destination );

      Number := Number - 1;
      SwapTwoChars( Origin, TempStorage )

  END

END; { MoveDisks }
```

(This assumes that there is a `SwapTwoChars` procedure. If you prefer, you can insert appropriate swapping code in the `MoveDisks` procedure itself.)

The partially iterative version is harder to understand. Let's trace the actions when there are two disks (next page).

`MoveDisks( 2, 'A', 'B', 'C' )` means to move two disks from `'A'` to `'B'`, using `'C'` for temporary storage. There are two trips through the loop:

First trip:

1A. `Origin = 'A'`, `Destination = 'B'`, `TempStorage = 'C'`, `Number = 2`.

2A. Call `MoveDisks( 1, 'A', 'C', 'B' )` to move one disk from `'A'` to `'C'`, using `'B'` for temporary storage (which isn't needed).

3A. Move disk number 2 from `'A'` to `'B'`.

4A. Decrement Number to 1.

5A. Swap the values of `Origin` and `TempStorage`. Now `Origin = 'C'` and `TempStorage = 'A'`.

Second trip:

1B. `Origin = 'C'`, `Destination = 'B'`, `TempStorage = 'A'`, `Number = 1`.

2B. Call `MoveDisks( 0, 'C', 'A', 'B' )` to move no disks from `'C'` to `'A'`, using `'B'` for temporary storage (which isn't needed).

3B. Move disk number 1 from `'C'` to `'B'`. (This is the final transfer of disk number 1 from the temporary storage to the final destination.)

4B. Decrement `Number` to 0.

5B. Swap the values of `Origin` and `TempStorage`. Now `Origin = 'A'` and `TempStorage = 'B'`.

(Because `Number` is now 0, there are no further trips.)

There were three single-disk moves in this process:

Move disk 1 from `'A'` to `'C'`.

Move disk 2 from `'A'` to `'B'`.

Move disk 1 from `'C'` to `'B'`.

This is exactly the same process as with the recursive procedure.

12.7 WHEN *NOT* TO USE RECURSION

Recursion should not be used

- When it makes the algorithm harder to understand.
- When it results in excessive demands on storage or takes inordinately long to run.

An example of the second situation occurs when the **factorial** function is written recursively. Recall that the factorial, $N!$, of an integer N is defined to be

$$N! = N(N-1)(N-2)\cdots 2\cdot 1$$

Examination of this formula reveals a recurrence relation:

$$N! = N\cdot(N-1)!$$

This means, for example, that 3! = 3 (2!), where 2! = 2 (1!). The recursive process is terminated by the base case, 1! = 1. It is very easy to write this as a recursive function in Pascal, using the recurrence relation directly:

```
FUNCTION Factorial( N : Integer ) : Integer;
{
  PRECONDITION:
  0 <= N.

  POSTCONDITION:
  Factorial = N!
}
BEGIN

   IF N < 2 THEN
      Factorial := 1
   ELSE
      Factorial := N * Factorial( N - 1 )

END; { Factorial }
```

This recursion is time-consuming, however. To compute 5!, the function must recursively call for 4!, which requires another call for 3!, which requires another for 2!, which requires another for 1!.

What about an iterative version of the function? The recursion shown above is not tail recursion because after the recursive call, the function performs a multiplication and an assignment. Nonetheless, it is easy to convert the function to a corresponding iterative form, using the original formula for N!:

```
FUNCTION Factorial( N : Integer ) : Integer;

VAR
   Product, Num : Integer;

BEGIN

   Product := 1;
   FOR Num := N DOWNTO 2 DO
      Product := Product * Num;

   Factorial := Product

END; { Factorial }
```

Because this version runs faster and is just as easy to understand, it is preferred over the recursive version.

LOOKING BACK

In this chapter, we compared the two techniques for repetition: iteration and recursion. Recursion is the process of having a subprogram invoke itself. We showed how recursion in programming is derived from the mathematical concept of recurrence relations.

We wrote recursive versions of the square root and integer power functions introduced in Chapter 11, and found that recursion gives simpler algorithms, but ones that run a little slower, with greater memory requirements. In such applications, iteration is often more desirable if it doesn't make the algorithms much harder to understand.

We also saw a recursive procedure that echoes its character inputs in reverse order. This procedure is simple and direct when designed recursively, but very difficult to write as an iterative algorithm. In this case, recursion was definitely the method of choice. Similarly, we developed a recursive procedure to solve the Towers of Hanoi puzzle. Again, this problem is easy to solve by recursion, but difficult to solve iteratively.

We wound up the chapter by giving some rules for deciding when recursion is not the method of choice.

Both recursion and iteration are powerful techniques for repetition. In later chapters, we will use whichever method seems most useful in a given case. With time and practice, they will become equally familiar to you.

TERMS EMPHASIZED IN THIS CHAPTER

PROJECTS

1. Write a program that allows you to time accurately the running times of the recursive and iterative versions of the factorial function. By what percentage is the iterative version faster on your Pascal system?

2. Leonardo of Pisa, who called himself Fibonacci, discovered an interesting sequence of numbers about 1200 AD. The sequence is 1, 1, 2, 3, 5, 8, 13, 21, 34, 55, ... These so-called **Fibonacci numbers** crop up in many places in science and mathematics. They have the interesting property that each Fibonacci number after the first two is the sum of the two preceding numbers.

   Fibonacci himself encountered these numbers while considering the patterns of animal reproduction. If, for example, a pair of adult rabbits produces a male/female pair of offspring every month, and if these children mature in two months, then produce a male/female pair of offspring every month, and so on, and if all rabbits survive throughout the experiment, the total number of rabbit pairs after month N is given by the Fibonacci number $F(N)$, where

   $$F(N) = F(N-1) + F(N-2)$$

There are two base cases for this recurrence relation:

$F(1) = F(2) = 1.$

Design and write both iterative and recursive functions to compute the Nth Fibonacci number. Are both versions easily implemented? Is the difference in running time significant? (Time them.) Explain the reasons for the difference in running time, if any.

3. The following iterative algorithm for the Towers of Hanoi problem was described by P. Buneman and L. Levy, in *Inf. Proc. Lett.* **10** (1980), pages 243–44. It assumes that the three needles are arranged in a circle:

```
Finished := False;
WHILE NOT Finished DO
BEGIN
   Move the smallest disk from its current needle to the next needle
      in clockwise order;
   IF all the disks are now stacked on one needle THEN
      Finished := True
   ELSE
      Make the only possible move that does not move the smallest disk
END
```

Write and test a program that uses this iterative algorithm. (Hint: As you move clockwise from needle to needle, increment a needle counter whose value is computed modulo 3. That is, use the `MOD` operator.)

4. Section 11.3 described an iterative function for computing the greatest common divisor (gcd) of two whole numbers. Write and test a recursive version of this function. (Hints: First determine the nonrecursive base case and how to handle it with a decision structure. Then design the recursion that should occur before the function reaches the base case.)

5. Write a recursive procedure that reads N integers from the keyboard, finally displaying the largest of the integers. N should be a parameter of the procedure.

6. An arithmetic expression can be written in what is called *prefix* notation, in which each binary operator is followed by its two operands. For example, the prefix expression `*AB` is equivalent to the normally written `A * B`. Similarly, `*A+BC` means that the `*` operates on `A` and the result of `+BC`, so the expression is equivalent to the normally written `A * (B + C)`.

Suppose we want to write a procedure that converts these prefix expressions to normal notation, and suppose for simplicity that the prefix expressions consist only of the binary operators +, –, *, and /, together with letters representing the operands. The procedure starts by looking at the first character in the expression. If the first character is a letter, the procedure merely displays the letter and is finished with its work. However, if the first character is an operator, the procedure postpones displaying the letter until it displays the first operand of the operator. To do that, it calls itself recursively. After displaying the first operand, the original procedure displays the original operator. Then it displays the second operand, for which the procedure again calls itself recursively.

Write such a procedure in Pascal and test it thoroughly.

REFERENCES

David Harel's book *Algorithmics: The Spirit of Computing* (Addison-Wesley Publishing, 1987) provides good discussions of recursion in general and the Towers of Hanoi in particular. There are also good books devoted entirely to recursion:

- Eric S. Roberts, *Thinking Recursively* (John Wiley & Sons, 1986).
- J. S. Rohl, *Recursion via Pascal* (Cambridge University Press, 1984).

The first of these is more nearly on the level of the current text.

Recursion in Everyday Life

One of the most common ways in which recursion appears in daily life is when you postpone completing a task in favor of a simpler task, often of the same type. Here is a good example. An executive has a fancy telephone and receives many calls on it. He is talking to A when B calls. To A he says, "Would you mind holding for a moment?" Of course he doesn't really care if A minds; he just pushes a button, and switches to B. Now C calls. The same deferment happens to B. This could go on indefinitely, but let us not get too bogged down in our enthusiasm. So let's say the call with C terminates. Then our executive "pops" back to B, and continues. Meanwhile, A is sitting at the other end of the line, drumming his fingernails against some table, and listening to some horrible Muzak piped through the phone lines to placate him. . . . Now the easiest case is if the call with B simply terminates, and the executive returns to A finally. But it could happen that after the conversation with B is resumed, a new caller—D—calls. B is once again pushed onto the stack of waiting callers, and D is taken care of. After D is done, back to B, then back to A. The executive is hopelessly mechanical, to be sure—but we are illustrating recursion in its most precise form.

—Douglas R. Hofstadter, *Godel, Escher, Bach: An Eternal Golden Braid* (Basic Books, 1979), page 127.

PART FOUR

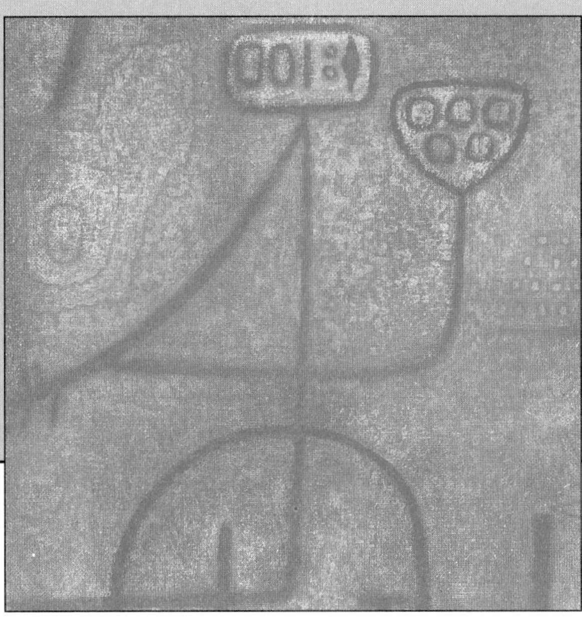

DATA STRUCTURES AND DATA ABSTRACTIONS

CHAPTER 13

Programmer-Defined Types

CHAPTER CONTENTS

INTRODUCTION

Up to this point, we have used only the four predefined simple data types: real, integer, character, and boolean. Each of these types is useful because of the unique set of operations it allows: integers and reals for their respective kinds of arithmetic, characters for their text-processing operations, and booleans for logic. In order to facilitate these four kinds of operations, each of these data types is stored in the computer in a different way. Thus, there are two important aspects to a data type: the set of operations it allows, and its storage representation. These two aspects together comprise what is called an **abstract data type (ADT)**.

The reason for pointing this out is that you are about to encounter data types invented by the programmer: the so-called **programmer-defined types**. This chapter describes the two simplest kinds of programmer-defined types, called **subrange** and **enumerated**. Such types are used to improve the self-documentation of programs and to help guarantee that they run correctly.

As we examine each new type of data, it is important to think about the two aspects of the data type: its operations and its storage representation. Think too about how it differs from and is related to other data types.

13.1 SUBRANGE TYPES

In Pascal, you can declare variables that are restricted to values in some predefined range within an ordinal type, from some low value through some high value. For example, if a variable `Count` should be allowed to contain only nonnegative integers, you can declare that `Count` is allowed to have values from zero through `MaxInt`:

```
VAR
   Count : 0..MaxInt;
```

With such a declaration, `Count` can be assigned only the integer values `0`, `1`, `2`, `3`, and so on, through `MaxInt`. It is illegal to attempt to store a negative value in `Count`, and any such attempt will generate a "range error" message. `Count`'s type is "`0..MaxInt`," which is said to be a "subrange of integers." The `Integer` type is said to be the **host type**, of which `Count` belongs to a subrange.

Host type or **base type**: The ordinal type in which we construct a subrange type.

Similarly, you can declare a variable called `CapitalLetter` that is allowed to contain only letters in the uppercase range, from capital `'A'` through capital `'Z'`:

```
VAR
   CapitalLetter : 'A'..'Z';
```

In this case, the host type of `CapitalLetter` is `Char`. With this declaration, a range violation will result if an attempt is made to store in `CapitalLetter` a character outside the stated subrange. (Note: The EBCDIC character code doesn't work as well for this because it has undefined gaps among the codes of the uppercase letters. Therefore, any character in the range of uppercase codes, including the interspersed undefined codes, can be stored if EBCDIC is being used.)

Pascal also allows you to give a name to a subrange type and then declare variables to be of that type. The following declarations are equivalent to those shown above but provide type names for use in parameter passing:

```
TYPE
   NonNegative = 0..MaxInt;
   UpperCase   = 'A'..'Z';

VAR
   Count         : NonNegative;
   CapitalLetter : UpperCase;
```

Of course, the identifiers `NonNegative` and `UpperCase` must be declared before they are used in the variable declarations. Besides, type declarations must always precede those of variables, as shown in Figure 3.2.4. Type declaration syntax was introduced in Section 8.9.

Subrange types aid self-documentation.

If we have a program that stores nonnegative numbers in variables, it is obviously clearer for the program to *declare* that those variables store nonnegative numbers. If the program merely uses integer variables for the same purpose, it will not be so easy to see that only nonnegative values are stored. In this way, subrange types help make the workings of a program clearer without excessive use of comments. This kind of **self-documentation** is an important element of good style, and it helps immensely when you (or another programmer) need to modify a program later.

Syntax for Subrange Declarations

A subrange type is a type of storage for values within a portion of the range of some ordinal type, from a stated low value to a stated high value, inclusive. The range is denoted by a specification of the form

LowValue .. *HighValue*

where *LowValue* is required to be less than or equal to *HighValue*.

A subrange variable can be declared directly in terms of the subrange specification. The type itself then has no name, and is therefore said to be **anonymous**:

Anonymous type: An unnamed type.

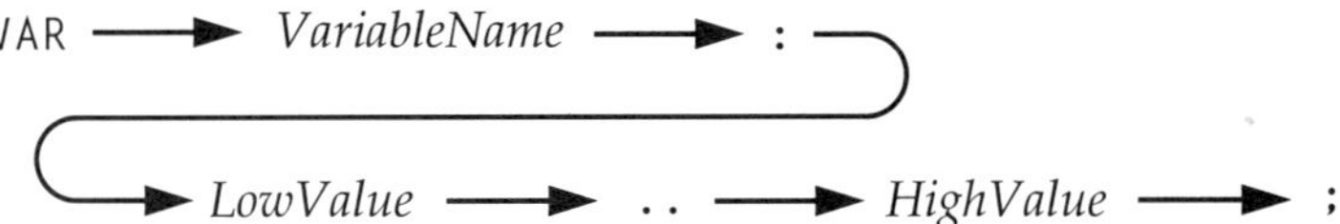

Alternatively, the type can be declared first, and then a variable can be declared to be of that type:

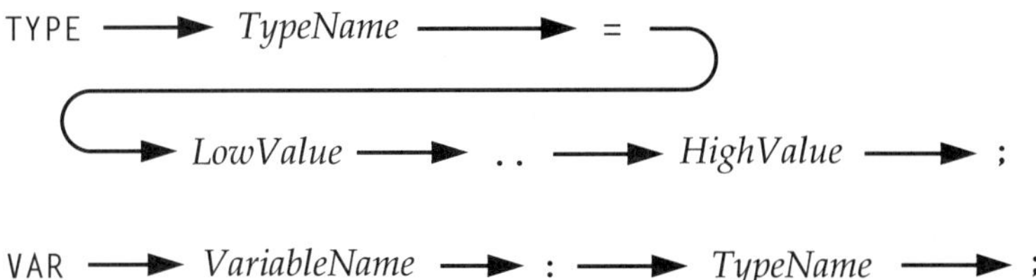

This method is generally preferred because type names are needed when declaring subprogram parameters, as explained below.

Compatibility of subrange types

In previous chapters, there were hardly any questions about the **compatibility** of data values and variables. We almost always stored values in variables of the same type: character data in character variables, boolean values in boolean variables, and numeric data in numeric variables. The only situation in which compatibility was questionable was when we wanted to store an integer value in a real variable, or vice versa. As you recall, an integer value is automatically type-converted to a real value before being stored in a real variable. On the other hand, a real value must be explicitly truncated or rounded to integer before being stored in an integer variable.

Now we have types that are subranges of ordinal types. Can a subrange value be stored in a variable of the host type? Can a host-type value be stored in a subrange variable? These are questions about **assignment compatibility**. The rules for assignment compatibility, as they pertain to types we have discussed so far, are shown on the next page.

Assignment Compatibility (Complete rules appear in Appendix E.)

A value of type T2 can be assigned to or read into a variable of type T1 if:

- T1 and T2 are the same type.
- T1 is a subrange of T2 or T2 is a subrange of T1 or they are both subranges of the same host type, and T2's value falls within the range of T1.
- T1 is real and T2 is integer.

These rules mean that with the declarations

```
TYPE
   NonNegative = 0..MaxInt;
   UpperCase   = 'A'..'Z';

VAR
   Count         : NonNegative;
   CapitalLetter : UpperCase;
   Int           : Integer;
   Ch            : Char;
```

it is legal to assign the value of `Count` to the `Int` variable or the value of `CapitalLetter` to the `Ch` variable. On the other hand, the value of `Int` can be assigned to `Count` only after confirming that it falls within the range `0..MaxInt`. Similarly, the value of `Ch` can be assigned to `CapitalLetter` only after confirming that it falls within the range `'A'..'Z'`. If an out-of-range assignment is made to a subrange variable while the Pascal system's range-checking feature is turned on, you should see a message saying `RANGE ERROR`.

Operations on a subrange type

A subrange type inherits the operations of its host. This means that a subrange of integers allows all integer arithmetic operations, with the constraint that it is an error for an operation to produce an out-of-range result. Similarly, a subrange of characters allows all character operations, as long as they don't go out of range. And all subranges are ordinal types, so they allow `Pred` and `Succ`.

Using a subrange type to protect the program from bad data

A value stored in a subrange variable is guaranteed to fall in the declared range, and therefore cannot be out of range. This in itself is partial verification of correctness in a program's execution, but when dealing with input data, we have no such guarantees. We need to check input data for correct range, and then store it in subrange variables.

We first store the input data in a variable of the host type, then check it for correct range, and finally store it in a subrange variable, making use of the assignment compatibility discussed above. For example, if we are asking for a capital letter from the keyboard, we would first read it into a `Char` variable and check it for correct range before storing it in a variable of type `UpperCase`. We prompt for the character repeatedly until we find it to be in the correct range:

```
REPEAT
   Write( 'Capital letter? ' );
   ReadLn( Ch )
UNTIL ( Ch >= 'A' ) AND ( Ch <= 'Z' );

{ POSTCONDITION: Ch is now in UpperCase subrange }
CapitalLetter := Ch;
```

Then, when processing data stored in `CapitalLetter`, we can be sure that it is in the expected range, as defined by the declarations of `CapitalLetter` and `UpperCase`.

13.2 ADVANTAGES OF SUBRANGE TYPES

As we have seen, subrange types are useful for a number of reasons:

- A subrange declaration states explicitly the range of values that are meaningful in a variable. Thus, a subrange declaration can be used to improve the documentation of a program.
- A subrange variable can be used to control the range of values stored, protecting the program from errors that might result if out-of-range values were encountered at runtime. Thus, a subrange declaration can be used to prevent execution errors caused by faulty data or by situations not anticipated by the programmer.

Let us apply these ideas to the decimal-to-binary program of Section 7.3. As you recall, the idea was to convert one-byte positive integers to binary, but we had no control over the user's input. Now we can remedy that problem.

We declare a type called `OneByteInteger`, and declare a variable of that type. Then we write a procedure to return a value of this type. We use the method described at the end of the last section: We prompt for a one-byte integer, read it into a variable of `Integer` type, test it for correct range, and keep doing this until we have a value that is in the correct range. Then, with a value belonging to the host type and known to be in the correct range, we can copy it into the subrange variable. Here is the complete program with the `GetOneByteInteger` procedure installed:

```
PROGRAM DecToBin (Input, Output);
{ Version 2, using subrange variable }

TYPE
   OneByteInteger = 0..255;

VAR
   Number: OneByteInteger;


PROCEDURE ShowPurpose;
{ From Section 7.3 }
BEGIN

   WriteLn('CONVERTING A ONE-BYTE DECIMAL INTEGER TO BINARY');
   WriteLn

END; { ShowPurpose }
```

```
PROCEDURE ShowOneBitAndGetNext ( PowerOfTwo : OneByteInteger;
                                 VAR Rem    : OneByteInteger );
{
  From Section 7.3.

  PRECONDITIONS:
  0 < PowerOfTwo <= 255;

  POSTCONDITIONS:
  Bit corresponding to PowerOfTwo has been displayed.
  Rem is now the remainder of division by PowerOfTwo.
}
BEGIN

   Write( ( Rem DIV PowerOfTwo ):1 );
   Rem := Rem MOD PowerOfTwo

END; { ShowOneBitAndGetNext }


PROCEDURE ShowBinaryOf ( Number : OneByteInteger );
{
  Based on Section 7.3, but using a loop this time.

  PRECONDITIONS:
  Number is in the range [ 0 .. 255 ];

  POSTCONDITIONS:
  The one-byte binary representation of Number
  has been displayed. Number is unchanged.
}
VAR
   Power, Remainder : OneByteInteger;

BEGIN

   WriteLn;
   Write( Number:3, ' is the same as ' );
   Remainder := Number;
   Power := 128;

   WHILE Power > 1 DO
   BEGIN

      ShowOneBitAndGetNext( Power, Remainder );
      Power := Power DIV 2

   END;

   WriteLn(Remainder:1, ' binary.')

END; { ShowBinaryOf }
```

```
PROCEDURE GetOneByteInteger ( VAR Number : OneByteInteger );
{
  POSTCONDITION:
  0 <= Number <= 255.
}
VAR
   Int : Integer;

BEGIN

   REPEAT

      Write('Integer between 0 and 255? ');
      ReadLn(Int)

   UNTIL ( Int >= 0 ) AND ( Int <= 255 );

   {
     Now that the value of the integer is known to be
     in the one-byte subrange, it can be copied
     into the Number variable.
   }
   Number := Int

END; { GetOneByteInteger }


BEGIN { main program }

   ShowPurpose;
   GetOneByteInteger(Number);
   ShowBinaryOf(Number)

END.
```

The main program now deals only with numbers in the correct range, so no out-of-range error can occur when the numbers are sent to `ShowBinaryOf`. Note also that `GetOneByteInteger`'s formal parameter is of type `OneByteInteger`. A formal `VAR` parameter and its corresponding actual parameter must be of the *same type*, so the main program's `Number` variable must also be of type `OneByteInteger`.

Parameter Compatibility Rules

- A *variable* (`VAR`) formal parameter must be associated with an actual parameter that is **strictly compatible**; that is, of *exactly the same type*.
- A *value* formal parameter must be associated with an actual parameter that is **assignment compatible**.

Test the program and you will see that it refuses integers outside the subrange. Here is a sample I/O:

```
CONVERTING A ONE-BYTE DECIMAL INTEGER TO BINARY

Integer between 0 and 255? -4
Integer between 0 and 255? 256
Integer between 0 and 255? 127

127 is the same as 01111111 binary.
```

Questions

1. What is the difference between a subrange type and its host type?
2. What are the advantages of using a subrange type instead of a host type?
3. What is the difference between assignment compatibility and strict compatibility?
4. What are the compatibility requirements when passing a `VAR` parameter? When using a value parameter?
5. What errors can occur when performing arithmetic on a subrange of integers? What can be done to prevent the error?
6. Why is a `REPEAT..UNTIL` loop used in `GetOneByteInteger` and not a `WHILE` loop?
7. In your Pascal system, is the subrange `0..255` stored in the same size storage cell as integers? If so, what about the subrange `0..127`?
8. How many values belong to each of the following subrange types? Does the answer depend upon the Pascal system?
   a. `-127..127`
   b. `0..127`
   c. `'a'..'z'`
   d. `'A'..'a'`
9. Suppose that `PosInt` is defined to be `1..127` and suppose that `Num` is of type `PosInt`. Then if `Num` has the value `127`, which of the following operations are illegal? Explain why.
   a. `Pred( Num )`
   b. `Succ( Num )`
   c. `Num := 0`
   d. `Num := 1.1`
10. Jackson P. Slipshod has invented the following subrange types. What is wrong with them?
    a. For the odd integers less than 10:
    ```
    TYPE
      OddLessThan10 = 1, 3, 5, 7, 9;
    ```
    b. The face value of playing cards:
    ```
    TYPE
      CardValues=2..10, 'A', 'J', 'Q', 'K';
    ```

c. Single-digit integers on either side of zero:

```
TYPE
   SingleDigitInt = -9..-1, 1..9;
```

Exercises

11. Write a loop invariant and loop bound for the `WHILE` loop shown in the `ShowBinaryOf` procedure.

12. Design and write a procedure called `GetCap` that prompts for and reads a capital letter, refusing all characters that are not capital letters. This procedure should return the received capital letter in a parameter of type `UpperCase`, which was defined in Section 13.1. Write a driver program and test your procedure.

13.3 ENUMERATED TYPES

An **enumerated type** is a type of storage for which all allowed values have been explicitly listed in order, or *enumerated*. For example, if I want to declare a type called `AdditivePrimaryColors`, for which the allowed values are `Red`, `Green`, and `Blue`, I can declare the type in this way:

```
TYPE
   AdditivePrimaryColors = ( Red, Green, Blue );
```

Then I can declare a variable of this type:

```
VAR
   Primary : AdditivePrimaryColors;
```

This is a variable that can be assigned the value `Red`, or the value `Green`, or the value `Blue`, but no other value. These three values are not the same as the strings `'Red'`, `'Green'`, and `'Blue'`; instead they are *identifiers* of the so-called **enumeration constants** of the type. Thus an enumerated type is a special kind of ordinal type, for which all the allowed values are listed explicitly, rather than being considered as a range of values. The allowed values are given names that you choose yourself to suit the data, and this helps to document the code.

Note that three things are accomplished by the declaration of an enumeration type:

1. The type is allowed to store only the listed values.
2. The allowed values are defined as named constants.
3. The enumeration constants are ordered; they are given ordinal values beginning with zero and increasing in the order of listing.

As with subrange types, a variable can be declared directly, without giving the type a name. The variable is then said to have an *anonymous type*:

```
VAR
   Primary : ( Red, Green, Blue );
```

This method is not recommended because type names are necessary when declaring parameters of subprograms.

Syntax for Enumerated Declarations

An enumerated type is a type of storage for values that have been explicitly listed in the declaration. The listing is of the form

Value1, *Value2*, *Value3*, ..., *ValueN*

The listed values are said to be the constants of the enumeration.

An enumerated variable can be declared directly in terms of the enumeration constants. The type itself then has no name, and is therefore said to be *anonymous*:

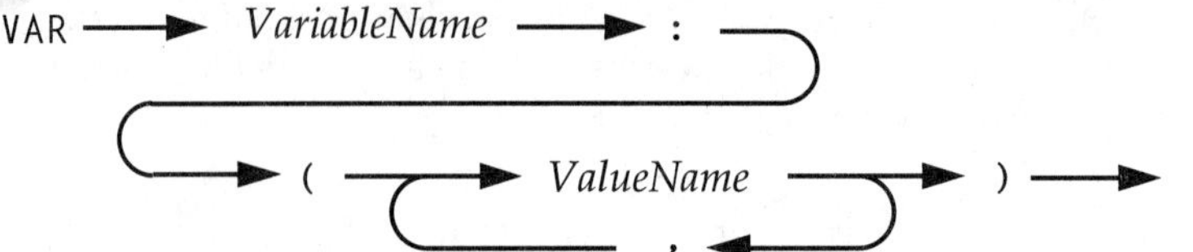

Alternatively, the type can be declared first, and then a variable can be declared to be of that type:

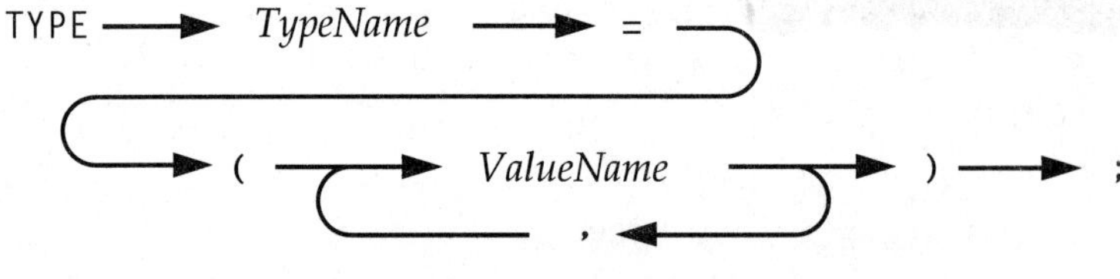

VAR → *VariableName* → : → *TypeName* → ;

This method of declaration is preferred because type names are needed when declaring subprogram parameters, as mentioned below.

Note:

- A *ValueName* must be unique and cannot be a reserved word.

Ordinal properties of enumerated values

The listed enumeration constants in a type declaration have the ordinal values 0, 1, 2, ... That is, the first-listed constant has ordinal value 0, the second has ordinal value 1, and so on. Thus, in the declarations

```
TYPE
   AdditivePrimaryColors = ( Red, Green, Blue );
VAR
   Primary : AdditivePrimaryColors;
```

the enumeration constant `Red` has ordinal value `0`; the next constant, `Green`, has ordinal value `1`, and `Blue` has ordinal value `2`. Thus the code

```
   Primary := Blue;
   WriteLn( 'Ord value is ', Ord( Primary ):1 );
```

will display the message

```
Ord value is 2
```

The ordinal operators apply.

The Pred and Succ functions can be used on an enumeration value to compute the value having the next-lower or next-higher ordinal value. (Of course, the first-enumerated value has no predecessor, and the last-enumerated value has no successor.) In the above example, where Red, Green, and Blue are declared in that order,

```
Primary := Pred( Green )
```

assigns the value Red to Primary, while

```
Primary := Succ( Green )
```

assigns the value Blue. (But Red has no predecessor, and Blue has no successor.)

Input and output of enumerated values

Enumerated values cannot be read by the Read or ReadLn procedures, nor can they be sent to Write or WriteLn. When output of such values is desired, it is necessary to use the values themselves to control the selection of corresponding strings of characters that can be written to an output device. Similarly, when you need to input enumerated values, you will actually input characters or strings of characters, and use these in the program to control the storage of enumerated values. The following CASE structure is an example of output:

```
CASE Primary OF

   Red   : WriteLn( 'Red' );
   Green : WriteLn( 'Green' );
   Blue  : WriteLn( 'Blue' )

END;
```

The method for input is similar:

```
REPEAT

   Write( 'Primary color? <R/G/B> ' );
   ReadLn( Ch );
   Ch := Upper( Ch )

UNTIL ( Ch = 'R' ) OR ( Ch = 'G' ) OR ( Ch = 'B' );

CASE Ch OF

   'R' : Primary := Red;
   'G' : Primary := Green;
   'B' : Primary := Blue

END;
```

Questions

13. What is the difference between the enumeration constant `Blue` and the string of characters `'Blue'`?
14. What is the difference between an enumeration type and a subrange type?
15. Why is the `REPEAT..UNTIL` loop needed in the code above, just before the `CASE` structure?
16. Is it legal to declare a subrange of an enumeration type? What about an enumeration of a subrange type?

13.4 CASE STUDY: A STATE VARIABLE IN PARSING

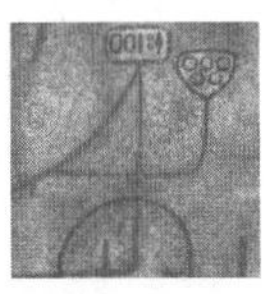

Parse (transitive verb): To analyze the syntax of text, determining the grammatical structure.

Enumerated types are often used to keep track of a complex process by indicating the state of the process. If there are only two possible states, a boolean variable can store it, but when there are more than two, we use an enumerated type.

A good example of such a process is the compilation of a Pascal program. There are several stages, of which the first is called *syntactic analysis* or **parsing**.

Parsing itself is a complex process with a number of states. A simple example of parsing is the checking for embedded comments in a program. The compiler must know which text is inside a comment and it must know when comments are nested, which is illegal in Pascal. To do this, the compiler keeps track of what we might call the `CommentState`. As compilation begins, no comment has started, so we can say that the `CommentState` is "noncomment."

This state continues until the parser encounters a left brace, `'{'`. (For the sake of simplicity, the following discussion ignores the fact that Pascal also allows comments to be delimited by parenthesis and star combinations.) Let's say that the program begins like this:

```
PROGRAM Foo ( Input, Output );
{
```

As the parser encounters the left brace, the `CommentState` changes to "comment." Then as parsing continues, the parser knows that it is inside a comment:

```
PROGRAM MyProg ( Input, Output );
{
  This program does nothing at all.
}
```

Now the parser encounters a right brace indicating the end of the comment, so the `CommentState` again becomes "noncomment," indicating that the parser is no longer inside a comment.

Toggle: To switch on and off, as with a toggle switch.

Normally, the parsing continues like this, with the comment state **toggling** on and off, but sometimes things get more complicated. One possibility is that one comment encloses another. In this case, the parser will encounter a second left brace before encountering the first right brace.

```
PROGRAM MyProg ( Input, Output );
{
  This program does nothing at all.
  {
```

This is illegal in Pascal because a comment is not allowed to include another comment. Therefore, the CommentState changes to "illegal nested comment."

Another possibility is that the programmer forgot to terminate a comment. If this is the case, the rest of the program following the unmatched left brace will be a comment, and the program will be incomplete:

```
PROGRAM MyProg ( Input, Output );
{
  This program does nothing at all.
BEGIN
  WriteLn( 'Nothing at all.' )
END.
```

The parser reaches the end of the program without finding a matching right brace, and the CommentState becomes "unmatched left brace."

As you can see from these examples, state changes depend on both the previous CommentState and the characters encountered. For example, if the CommentState is "noncomment" when the parser encounters a left brace, the state changes to "comment." On the other hand, if the CommentState is "comment" when the left brace is encountered, the state changes to "illegal nested comment." Table 13.4.1 lists all the possibilities if braces are the only comment delimiters considered:

Table 13.4.1 *State transitions in comment checking.*

Previous state	Character encountered	New state
Noncomment	{	Comment
Noncomment	}	Unmatched brace*
Comment	{	Illegal nested comment*
Comment	}	Noncomment
Comment	<EOF>	Program ends illegally*

*Each of these states indicates an error and should terminate parsing.

Figure 13.4.1 *State transitions when scanning for correctly constructed comments while compiling a Pascal program. The UnMatchedBrace and IllegalCommentNesting states are terminal, with no paths leading out of them. This is indicated by using a double circle for these states.*

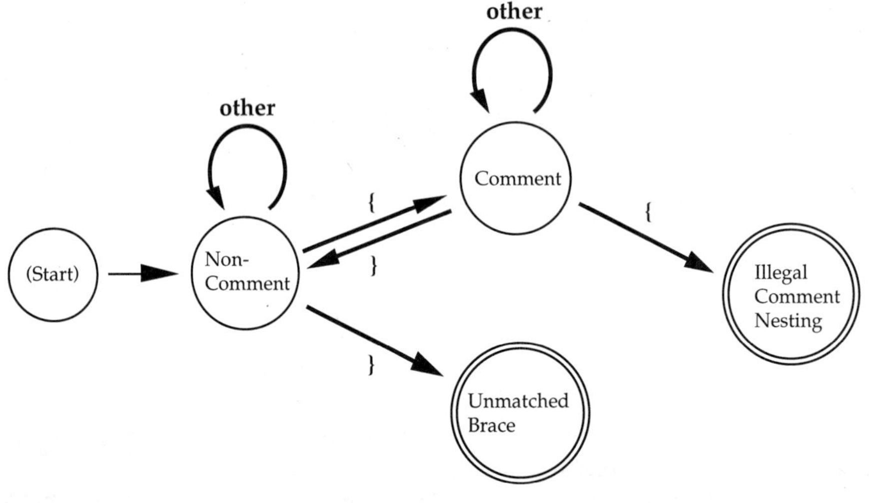

Another way to indicate the possible state changes is by means of a state transition diagram, such as we used in Section 5.4. The diagram corresponding to Table 13.4.1 is shown in Figure 13.4.1.

To build a procedure to check for correctly constructed comments, we consider all the paths in the state transition diagram, or all the state transitions listed in the table. When the procedure starts, it goes into the `NonComment` state. While in this state, encountering a left brace takes the procedure into the `Comment` state, while encountering a right brace takes it into the `UnmatchedBrace` state, which is an error condition. The `NonComment` state is unchanged if it encounters any other character.

Similarly, if the procedure is in the `Comment` state, encountering a left brace takes the procedure into the `IllegalCommentNesting` error state, while encountering a right brace takes it back to the `NonComment` state, and anything else leaves the `Comment` state unchanged.

These transitions are performed by the following procedure:

```
PROCEDURE CommentCheck( VAR InFile : Text );
{
  Checks a Pascal source code file for legal use of curly braces
  to enclose comments. This version does not allow for
  "star and parenthesis" comment delimiters. See Project 1.

  PRECONDITION:
  InFile has been reset for reading.

  POSTCONDITION:
  A message is displayed, telling whether comments were correct.
}
```

```
TYPE
   CommentState = ( NonComment, Comment,
                    IllegalNestingError, UnmatchedBraceError );
VAR
   State  : CommentState;
   Ch     : Char;

BEGIN

   State := NonComment;

   WHILE ( NOT EOF( InFile ) ) AND ( State <> IllegalNestingError )
           AND ( State <> UnmatchedBraceError ) DO
   BEGIN

      Read( InFile, Ch );

      IF ( Ch = '{' ) THEN

         CASE ( State ) OF

            NonComment:
               State := Comment;

            Comment:
               State := IllegalNestingError

         END

      ELSE IF ( Ch = '}' ) THEN

         CASE ( State ) OF

            Comment:
               State := NonComment;

            NonComment:
               State := UnmatchedBraceError

         END

   END; { WHILE }

   {--Show why we left the reading loop:}
   CASE ( State ) OF

      IllegalNestingError:
         WriteLn('Reading terminates with illegally nested comment.');

      UnmatchedBraceError:
         WriteLn('Reading terminates with unmatched ''}''.');

      Comment:
         WriteLn('Program ends erroneously inside a comment.');

      NonComment:
         WriteLn('Comments are structured correctly.')
   END { CASE }

END; { CommentCheck }
```

Questions

17. Which of the following types would be most suitable for storing the suit of a playing card? (Was that a pun?) Defend your answer.

a. `Integer`, with values `1, 2, 3, 4;`

b. `SuitRange = 1..4;`

c. `Suit = ('S', 'H', 'D', 'C');`

d. `Suit = ( Spades, Hearts, Diamonds, Clubs );`

18. Which of the following types would be most suitable for storing single-digit whole numbers for arithmetic? Defend your answer.

a. `Integer`, with values `0, 1, 2, 3, 4, 5, 6, 7, 8, 9;`

b. `OneDigitInt = 0..9;`

c. `OneDigitNumeral = '0'..'9';`

d.
```
OneDigitNum = ( One, Two, Three, Four, Five, Six,
                Seven, Eight, Nine );
```

19. Which of the following types would be most suitable for storing the gender of a job applicant? Defend your answer.

a.
```
VAR
    Female : Boolean;
```

b.
```
TYPE
    Sex = ( Male, Female );
```

c.
```
TYPE
    Sex = 1..2;
```

20. The `WHILE` structure in the `CommentCheck` procedure has no loop invariant. What *are* the invariant properties of this loop?

LOOKING BACK

Two programmer-defined types were introduced in this chapter: subranges and enumerations. These are both ordinal types.

A subrange type spans a subrange of some host type, from a specified low value to a specified high value. By specifying that all values of the type must belong to a specified subrange, the programmer guarantees that inappropriate values will never be stored, preventing out-of-range errors during computation. The use of a subrange declaration also helps to document the allowed range of values for anyone reading the source code. We saw two examples of subrange types in use: a positive integer subrange for counting, and a one-byte integer type for use in decimal-to-binary conversions. In the next chapter, you will learn to use subrange types for subscripts of arrays.

Enumerated types are used to store any of a specified list of values. One of the most important applications is for dealing with state variables; an example of this was presented in Section 13.4.

TERMS EMPHASIZED IN THIS CHAPTER

Abstract data type (ADT) 393
Anonymous type 395, 401
Assignment compatibility 395–396
Compatibility 395
Enumerated declaration 402
Enumerated types 401
Enumerated types,
 operations on 402–404
Enumeration constant 401
Host type (base type) 394
Parameter compatibility 399
Parse 404
Programmer-defined type 393
Self-documentation 394
State 405–406
State transition diagram 406
Strict compatibility 399
Subrange declaration 395
Subrange operations 396
Subrange types 394
Toggle 404

PROJECTS

1. Improve the CommentCheck procedure so that it correctly checks programs containing parenthesis and star comment delimiters as well as curly braces.

2. Revise the ShowBinaryOf procedure, replacing the repeated code by recursion.

3. Write a WordCount function that reads a stream of characters from the keyboard until encountering <EOF>, returning the number of words entered. For the purpose of this assignment, a word is considered to be any sequence of nonwhitespace characters terminated by whitespace. (Whitespace = Space, tab, end-of-line, or end-of-file.) Hint: Use a state variable having two states: InAWord and NotInAWord.

4. Design and write a program that reads dates in the form MM/DD/YY and echoes them in the form *MonthName Day, Year*. For example, if the program reads '11/20/91', it should echo 'November 20, 1991'. Use an enumerated type for storing the names of months, and make use of the ordinal values in this type.

5. Design and write a scanner program like that shown in Section 13.4, but scan for correctly matched parentheses in expressions. For the sake of simplicity in this assignment, assume that every statement containing parentheses ends with a semicolon. (If you want a real workout, don't make this simplifying assumption. How many different symbols can mark the end of a statement in Pascal?)

6. (Similar to 5.) Write a scanner that checks for correctly terminated strings of characters in expressions. Watch out for embedded apostrophes within strings.

REFERENCES

Bruce J. MacLennan, in Section 5.3 of his book, *Principles of Programming Languages*, second edition (Holt, Rinehart and Winston, 1987), explains how enumerated and subrange types can be used to prevent certain kinds of common programming errors.

An excellent discussion of clarity in programming is found in Henry Ledgard's *Professional Pascal: Essays on the Practice of Programming* (Addison-Wesley Publishing, 1986). Chapter 8, "Using Types," discusses enumerated types. This book is highly recommended.

CHAPTER 14
Arrays

CHAPTER CONTENTS

INTRODUCTION

Up to this point, we have used simple types of variables, in which only a single value can be stored. However, it is often convenient to group data values together in a **data structure.** A data structure is a collection of data values accessed under a single name and organized so that the individual values in the collection can be separately accessed. A data structure is also called a *structured data type* or **composite type**. The individual data values within the structure are called its *components, elements*, or *members*, depending on the type of structure.

Suppose you are writing a checkbook-balancing program. You want to store a list of all your deposits and a list of all your withdrawals. The word *list* implies that we think of an entire collection of numbers as a single composite data object. It is convenient to give the list a name and store it in a connected block of storage. So we will call the list of deposits `Credit`, and the list of withdrawals `Debit`. These are to be data structures appropriate to the concept of a **list**.

One of the issues in building such a data structure is to decide on the *representation;* that is, how it should be stored. We think of a list as a sequence of numbers stored one after another in an area of memory, so we seek a representation like this in the computer.

Another issue is how to perform operations on the data structure. Sometimes we will want to operate on the whole structure; for example, to copy the list of checking-account deposits. Sometimes we will want to operate on the individual values within the list; for example, to add a new withdrawal. So the way in which the list is accessed and the way in which it is stored must facilitate both whole-list and single-component operations. In the case of a list of numbers, we choose to store it as a sequence of real numbers in memory, stored one after another in a contiguous block of memory. We also need appropriate syntax for commanding both whole-list and single-component operations.

An important property of the `Credit` and `Debit` lists is that all of their components are the same type: these collections of data are **homogeneous data structures**. Pascal allows a collection of homogeneous data to be stored in one area of memory, under a single name, by regarding the storage area as a *subscripted variable* called an **array**. Within the array, **subscripts** are used to indicate the individual **elements**. In Pascal, the subscripts are written as integers within square brackets. Thus, `Credit[1]` would be the first deposit in the checking account, `Credit[2]` would be the second deposit, and so on. The following diagram shows a hypothetical `Credit` array in which `Credit[1] = 195.00` and `Credit[2] = 491.82`. Similarly, `Debit[1] = 14.79`, `Debit[2] = 52.25`, and so on.

Credit array:	195.00	491.82	299.95	320.27		
Debit array:	14.79	52.25	16.13	44.75	114.21	79.81

Some arrays, like the examples above, have a single subscript. These are called **one-dimensional arrays,** and are often thought of as lists. In mathematics, such arrays are often called vectors. We can also have arrays with two subscripts, called **two-dimensional arrays**. These can be thought of as two-dimensional **tables** in which the first subscript labels the rows, while the second subscript labels the columns. In mathematics, such arrays are often called matrices. Pascal arrays can have any number of dimensions; there is no limit on the number of subscripts. Thus, we can have **multidimensional arrays**, representing a many-dimensional table of data.

14.1 ONE-DIMENSIONAL ARRAYS

A one-dimensional array is an array having only one subscript. As with all arrays, the individual elements are all of the same type.

Suppose that we want to store the salaries of up to 50 employees of a business. We can use an array called `Salary`, in which `Salary[1]`, `Salary[2]`,`...`, `Salary[50]` are real variables that will store the salaries of the first employee, the second employee, ..., down to the 50th employee, respectively. The array thus contains `Real` elements, and the subscripts run over the integer subrange `[1..50]`. (Subranges were described in Chapter 13.)

Salary[1]	Salary[2]		...	Salary[50]

This array can be declared as follows:

```
TYPE
   FiftyReals = ARRAY [1..50] OF Real;

VAR
   Salary : FiftyReals;
```

The syntax for declaring a one-dimensional array is summarized in the syntax box on the next page.

Syntax for Declaring a One-Dimensional Array

Declaring an array as a variable:

→ VAR → *ArrayName* → : → *ArrayDefinition* →

Pseudocode:

```
VAR
    ArrayName : ArrayDefinition;
```

Declaring an array *type*, then an array of that type:

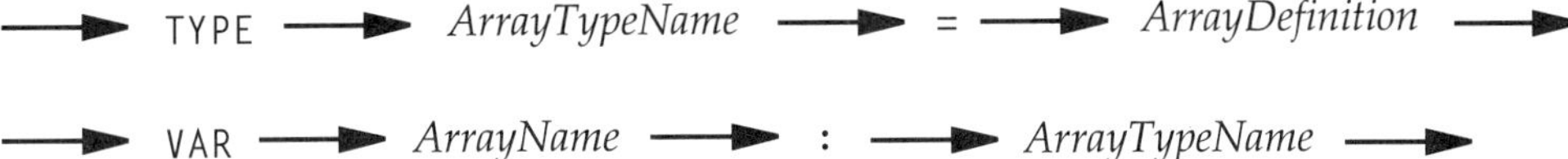

Pseudocode:

```
TYPE
    ArrayTypeName = ArrayDefinition;
VAR
    ArrayName : ArrayTypeName;
```

The *ArrayDefinition* itself:

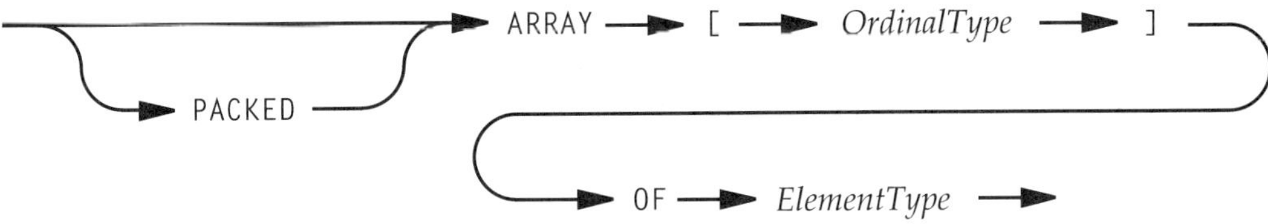

Pseudocode:

```
ARRAY [ OrdinalType ] OF ElementType;
```

Notes:

- The subscript range is specified as an *OrdinalType*; that is, the name of any ordinal type, or a subrange of an ordinal type.
- All the elements are of one *ElementType*, which can be any type at all, except the same array type that is being declared. That is, you cannot build a recursive array type. *ElementType* can be another array type, however, so you can build arrays in which the elements are themselves arrays. Such arrays are said to be multidimensional, and are discussed in Section 14.7.
- The reserved word PACKED can be prefixed to the declaration when you want the array elements to be packed into as little memory as possible. Such a declaration may or may not actually reduce the amount of storage needed, depending on the compiler and the type of array elements involved. A **packed array**, if it actually does economize on storage, is slower to access because of the packing and unpacking involved. String arrays are the most common examples of packed arrays and are discussed in Section 14.5.

A subscript can range over any ordinal type.

An array is declared to have some *ArrayDefinition*. For example, an array's definition could be `ARRAY [1..50] OF Real`. This says that we have an `ARRAY`, then declares the allowed range of subscript values, and finally declares the type of elements making up the array.

There are various ways of defining the subscript range. The most common is to do what we did in the example: to specify the lower and upper limits of a subrange (with the low limit less than or equal to the high limit, of course), enclosing the specification in square brackets, as in `[1..50]`.

But the subscripts can be of any ordinal type. (They *cannot* be `Real` because `Real` is not ordinal.) So the following declarations are legal:

```
TYPE
   CodeArray = ARRAY ['a'..'z'] OF Integer;

VAR
   Code : CodeArray;

BEGIN
   Code['a'] := 97;
   Code['b'] := 98;
       .
       .
```

In this example, the subscripts have character values in the subrange of lowercase letters, so the elements of the array are called `Code['a']`, `Code['b']`,..., `Code['z']`. These elements each store an integer value.

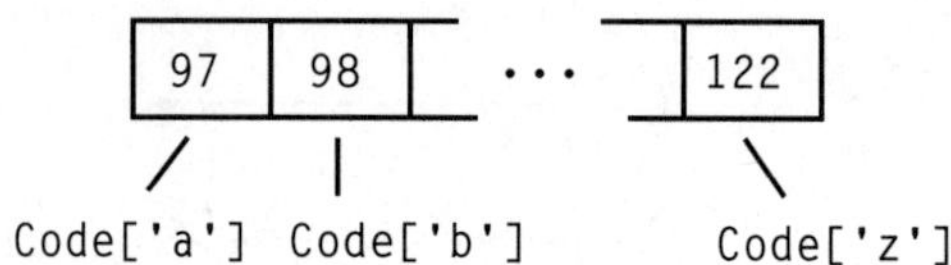

Pascal also allows a subscript to take on *all the values of any ordinal type*. Thus, the following declarations are legal:

```
TYPE
   BigCodeArray = ARRAY [ Char ] OF Integer;
   LotsOfReals  = ARRAY [ Integer ] OF Real;
   FiftyRange   = 1..50;
   LowerCase    = 'a'..'z';
   FiftyReals   = ARRAY [ FiftyRange ] OF Real;
   CodeArray    = ARRAY [ LowerCase ] OF Integer;

VAR
   MoreCode       : BigCodeArray;
   LotsOfSalaries : LotsOfReals;
   Salary         : FiftyReals;
   Code           : CodeArray;
```

With these declarations, `MoreCode` is an array containing as many elements as the ordinal size of the character set being used: 128 for ASCII code, or 256 for EBCDIC or extended ASCII. `LotsOfSalaries` is declared to have as many elements as there are integers, and is therefore an enormous array, often too big to fit in main memory. (Many Pascals will prohibit such a declaration as being too big.) `Salary` and `Code` are equivalent to arrays in previous declarations, even though declared differently.

Another possibility is to declare a subscript to take on a number of enumerated values. (See Section 13.3.) For example, you could declare

```
TYPE
   AdditivePrimaryColors = ( Red, Green, Blue );
   ColorArray = ARRAY [ AdditivePrimaryColors ] OF Integer;

VAR
   Frequency : ColorArray;

BEGIN
   Frequency[ Red ]   := 650;
   Frequency[ Green ] := 550;
   Frequency[ Blue ]  := 450;
```

With these declarations, `Frequency` is an array of three integer elements, in which the subscript takes on the values `Red`, `Green`, and `Blue`.

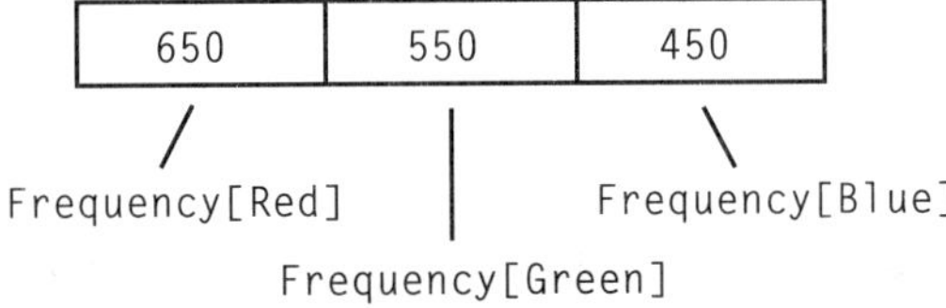

As all these examples have shown, an array subscript can range over any ordinal type or over a subrange of an ordinal type. This is summarized in the syntax box.

How Pascal stores arrays

When an array is declared, Pascal sets aside a block of memory large enough to store the elements of the array. The elements are stored contiguously, one after another. Suppose a `Salary` array is declared as

```
TYPE
   FiftyReals = ARRAY [1..50] OF Real;

VAR
   Salary : FiftyReals;
```

If our Pascal system is using the real-number storage scheme shown in Chapter 1 and Appendix K, this involves allocating four bytes of memory for each element, or a total of 200 bytes of main memory for the whole `Salary` array.

Pascal thinks of the array as being located at the memory address of the first element. To find later elements, it counts its way down the bytes of memory, four bytes per element. The element `Salary[3]` is located at the memory address eight bytes after the beginning of the array:

Byte 4106 | Byte 4107 | Byte 4108 | Byte 4109 | Byte 4110 | Byte 4111 | Byte 4112 | Byte 4113 | Byte 4114 | Byte 4115 | Byte 4116 | Byte 4117

Salary[1] — Salary[2] — Salary[3]

It is helpful to declare constants up front.

Useful programs are almost always modified later. For example, you may find the need to increase the size of your `Salary` array as your payroll grows. Such modifications are easier if the constants are named and defined at the beginning of the program, because the constants are then easier to find:

```
CONST
   Low  = 1;
   High = 50;

TYPE
   IndexRange = Low..High;
   FiftyReals = ARRAY [ IndexRange ] OF Real;

VAR
      Index  : IndexRange;
      Salary : FiftyReals;
```

This way, the numbers 1 and 50 appear only at the very beginning of the program, where they are quickly found and modified when necessary, without any chance that such changes will interfere with the operation of the rest of the program.

Expressions as subscript references

Expressions can be used as **subscript references**; that is, the value of a subscript can be written as an ordinal expression. The following code, for example, stores 97 in `Code['a']`, 98 in `Code['b']`, and 466.98 in `Salary[20]`:

```
TYPE
   FiftyReals = ARRAY [1..50] OF Real;
   CodeArray  = ARRAY ['a'..'z'] OF Integer;

VAR
   Salary : FiftyReals;
   Code   : CodeArray;
   Ch     : Char;
   Number : Integer;

BEGIN
   Ch := 'a';
   Number := 14;

   Code[ Ch ] := 97;
   Code[ Succ( Ch ) ] := 98;
   Salary[ Number + 6 ] := 466.98;
```

Notice how values are assigned to specific array elements, treating each element as a variable. The next section describes how this can be done systematically in order to fill a whole array or most of an array.

14.2 STORING VALUES IN AN ARRAY

Now that we have declared a `Salary` array of real numbers, it is time to consider how to **initialize** it. (Recall that Pascal never initializes variables automatically.) The simplest way to store values in the individual elements of the array is to **assign** them. For example, we can write a sequence of assignment statements, one for each element:

```
Salary[1] := 521.95;
Salary[2] := 497.46;
```

and so on. We can also use an assignment loop if all elements are to be initialized with the same value, or with the value of some expression:

```
FOR Index := Low TO High DO
   Salary[Index] := 499.95 + Index;
```

(Note that programmers often refer to a subscript as an **array index**.)

Filling an array from the keyboard

Arrays are often initialized with values read from the keyboard or a disk file. We can easily adapt our initialization loop to do this:

```
CONST
   Low  = 1;
   High = 50;

TYPE
   IndexRange = Low..High;
   FiftyReals = ARRAY [ IndexRange ] OF Real;

VAR
   Index  : IndexRange;
   Salary : FiftyReals;

BEGIN
   .
   .
   WriteLn( 'Enter employees'' salaries...' );
   WriteLn( '---------------------------------' );
   FOR Index := Low TO High DO
   BEGIN

      Write( 'Salary for employee #', Index:2, ': ' );
      ReadLn( Salary[ Index ] )

   END;
```

As you can see, a `ReadLn` can copy input values into an individual array element just as easily as into any other variable. But a `Read` or `ReadLn` cannot fill an entire array at once.

Assigning whole arrays

Whole arrays cannot be read or written, but whole arrays can be assigned. That is, a statement like `ReadLn(Salary)` is illegal and so is a statement like `WriteLn(Salary)`. This is why the code shown above initializes the array elements one by one. The only whole-array initialization allowed in Pascal is in an assignment statement, where you are allowed to assign the values of one array to another array of the same type. Here is an example:

```
CONST
   Low  = 1;
   High = 50;

TYPE
   IndexRange = Low..High;
   FiftyReals = ARRAY [ IndexRange ] OF Real;

VAR
   Index            : IndexRange;
   Salary, GrossPay : FiftyReals;

BEGIN
   .
   .
   WriteLn( 'Enter employees'' salaries...' );
   WriteLn( '------------------------------' );
   FOR Index := Low TO High DO
   BEGIN

      Write( 'Salary for employee #', Index:2, ': ' );
      ReadLn( Salary[Index] )

   END;

   {-- Copy the Salary array into the GrossPay array }
   GrossPay := Salary;
```

An assignment like this one is the only **whole-array operation** provided by Pascal.

Exercises

1. Which of the following type declarations are *illegal* on your Pascal system?
   a. `ManyReals = ARRAY [ Char ] OF Real;`
   b. `ManyChars = ARRAY [ Real ] OF Char;`
   c. `SomeReals = PACKED [ 1..500 ] OF Real;`
   d. `SomeSubR  = PACKED ARRAY [ 1..500 ] OF 1..500;`
   e. `SomeEnum  = ARRAY [ 1..2 ] OF (Bacon, Lettuce, Tomato );`
   f. `More Real = ARRAY [ Char ] OF ManyReals;`

2. List all syntax errors that would be reported by the compiler in the code fragment shown below. Explain the nature of each error.

```
TYPE
  YesNoReal = ARRAY [ Boolean ] OF Real;
```

```
VAR
   RealOrNot : YesNoReal;
BEGIN
   RealOrNot[ 1 ] := 1.23;
   RealOrNot[ 2 ] := 2.34;
  ...
```

3. List all syntax errors that would be reported by the compiler in the code shown below. Explain the nature of each error.

```
TYPE
   FeeFieFoFum  = ( Fee, Fie, Fo, Fum );
   LottsaStuff = ARRAY [ FeeFieFoFum ] OF Real;
VAR
   Stuff : ARRAY [ LottsaStuff ] OF LottsaStuff;
```

4. Write appropriate declarations for the arrays described below. Use good variable names and suitable choices for subscript and element types.

   a. An array of 100 characters in the range `'a'..'z'`, with integer subscripts ranging from 0 through 99. (Subscripts outside this range should be prevented.)

   b. An array with lowercase letter subscripts, in which each element stores a character.

   c. An array with integer subscripts, in which each element stores a traffic-light color.

   d. A list of 100 students, numbered 1 through 100, in which each element stores a real-number grade-point average.

5. Suppose that a `Salary` array is declared to be `ARRAY [1..10] OF Real`, and then the following statements are executed:

```
   Salary[ 1 ] := 100.0;
   FOR I := 2 TO 8 DO
      Salary[ I ] := ( 2.0 * Salary[ I - 1 ] ) - 50.0;
```

After all this, what values are stored in array elements `Salary[1]` through `Salary[8]`?

6. After the code of Exercise 5 is executed, and assuming that no other initialization code was executed, what values are in `Salary[9]` and `Salary[10]`?

7. Suppose we have these declarations:

```
CONST
   Low = 1;
   High = 10;
TYPE
   IndexRange = Low..High;
   RealArray  = ARRAY [ IndexRange ] OF Real;
VAR
   Index : IndexRange;
   Salary, Remuneration : RealArray;
```

Then what does the following code fragment display?

```
FOR Index := Low TO (High DIV 2) DO
   Salary[ 2 * Index ] := Index;

Index := High;
WHILE Index >= (Low+1) DO
BEGIN
   WriteLn( Salary[Index]:6:2 );
   Index := Index - 2
END;
```

8. Using the same declarations as in Exercise 7, what is printed by this code fragment?

```
Index := Low;
WHILE Index < High DO
BEGIN
   Salary[ Index ] := High - Index + 1;
   Index := Succ( Index )
END;

Remuneration := Salary;
FOR Index := High DOWNTO Low DO
   WriteLn( Remuneration[Index]:6:2 );
```

9. What does the following code fragment print?

```
TYPE
   CharArray = PACKED ARRAY [1..10] OF Char;

VAR
   Count : Integer;
   Name  : CharArray;

BEGIN
   FOR Count := 1 TO 10 DO
   BEGIN
      Name[Count] := Chr( Ord('A') + Count - 1 );
      Write( Name[Count] )
   END;
```

10. The following code fragment is supposed to determine whether the `Magnitude` array contains only positive elements. It does not work correctly. Locate the error, state what it is, and show how to correct it.

```
FOR Index := Low TO High DO
   FoundNegative := ( Magnitude[ Index ] < 0.0 );
```

11. Write appropriate declarations for the code in Exercise 10.

12. Suppose that the `Salary` array, declared as in Exercise 7, has been filled with values. Write a code fragment that displays the average salary stored in the array.

13. Similarly, write a code fragment that displays only any negative salaries stored in the array. (These are amounts owed to the company by employees.)

14. Similarly, write a code fragment that displays the maximum and minimum salaries stored in the array.

15. Suppose the `Word` array contains eight characters, initialized as shown below:

B	A	C	K	W	A	R	D

Write a code fragment that displays this array backwards, writing `DRAWKCAB` on the screen.

14.3 PITFALLS WITH ARRAYS

The most common problem in using an array is in keeping the subscript from going outside the declared range. Another problem occurs when using arrays as parameters of procedures or functions. We now examine these two pitfalls.

Range errors

The most common error in programming with arrays is to allow a subscript to reach a value outside its declared range. This is called a **range error**. Pascal will normally signal an error if you make such an attempt while running the program. However, some compilers allow you to disable the *range checking* used to detect such errors. This may allow your program to run faster, but your program may attempt to access nonexistent array elements, and in such a case, the results are unpredictable. The program will simply "walk off the end" of the array, accessing whatever bit patterns happen to be there. To prevent this, you should normally run with range checking turned on.

Range error: When a subscript's value goes outside the declared range.

Consider, for example, some code that writes array elements on the screen:

```
{ -- Example of a range error at runtime. }
CONST
   Low  = 1;
   High = 100;

TYPE
   ScoresArray = ARRAY [ Low..High ] OF Integer;

VAR
   Index : Integer;
   Score : ScoresArray;

BEGIN
   .
   .
   Index := 0;
   WHILE Index <= High DO
   BEGIN
      Index := Index + 1;
      WriteLn( 'Score #', Index:2, ' = ', Score[ Index ]:3 )
   END;
```

Here the programmer has allowed the loop to iterate as long as an array index called `Index` is no greater than `High`. Unfortunately, this means that another iteration is performed when `Index` is *equal* to `High`. In that event, `Index` is incremented to `101` and then the loop tries to write the value of the array element `Score[101]`, even though there is no such element. The program has walked off the end of the array, so to speak, generating a runtime error during the execution of the `WriteLn`. The program might print gibberish when it accesses the mythical `Score[101]`, and the true nature of the error might be hard to spot.

Subrange types can help to prevent range errors.

One way to make range errors less likely is to use a subrange type for any variable used to represent an array subscript. In the example above, we can write

```
CONST
   Low  = 1;
   High = 100;

TYPE
   IndexRange  = Low..High;
   ScoresArray = ARRAY [ IndexRange ] OF Integer;

VAR
   Index : IndexRange;
   Score : ScoresArray;
```

By so doing, you declare that your subscripts are allowed to take on only the values in the stated subrange, and not just any integer values whatsoever. This helps to clarify your intent, and that in turn makes it less likely that you or another programmer will misuse the `Index` variable.

If we simply place these declarations in the defective code shown previously, we have a new range error:

```
{ -- Another range error at runtime. }
CONST
   Low  = 1;
   High = 100;

TYPE
   IndexRange = Low..High;
   ScoresArray = ARRAY [ IndexRange ] OF Integer;

VAR
   Index : IndexRange;
   Score : ScoresArray;

BEGIN
   .
   .
   Index := 0;
   WHILE Index <= High DO
   BEGIN
      Index := Index + 1;
      WriteLn( 'Score #', Index:2, ' = ', Score[ Index ]:3 )
   END;
```

Now the range error occurs when we try to assign 0 to the `Index` variable. Using the subrange variable has not prevented all errors, but it has changed the place where it occurs, and made it easier to spot. With the nature of the error clear, it is easy to repair.

Just change the loop to read

```
FOR Index := 1 TO High DO
   WriteLn( 'Score #', Index:2, ' = ', Score[Index]:3 );
```

Because the FOR loop does not perform a final incrementation, the subscript will stay in the declared range.

A more subtle range error

Some range errors are more subtle. The following fragment of code is supposed to find the position within an array of the first instance of a given character or, if the character is not found, to set Position = 0. Unfortunately, a range error can occur if the searched-for character is not present:

```
CONST
   Limit = 100;

TYPE
   ArrayType  = ARRAY [ 1..Limit ] OF Char;

VAR
   Position, Index : Integer;
   ThisArray       : ArrayType;
   GivenChar       : Char;

BEGIN
   .
   .
   { ThisArray is filled with characters }
   .
   .
   Write( 'Character for which to search? ' );
   ReadLn( GivenChar );

   {
    PURPOSE:
    If GivenChar occurs in the array, find Position
    of first occurrence; otherwise, set Position = 0.
   }

   Index := 1;

   { -- A range error may occur at runtime: }
   WHILE ( Index <= Limit ) AND ( ThisArray[Index] <> GivenChar ) DO
      Index := Index + 1;

   IF ThisArray[Index] = GivenChar THEN
      Position := Index
   ELSE
      Position := 0;
```

If GivenChar is not found in the array, Index is eventually incremented to 101, after which the boolean expression

```
   ( Index <= Limit ) AND ( ThisArray[Index] <> GivenChar )
```

is evaluated. In this expression, the relational expression (`Index <= Limit`) is false, which in turn makes the entire compound boolean expression false, no matter what the value of the second relational expression. Since the second relational expression is then superfluous, you might expect that it will not be evaluated, *but this is not so.* In Pascal, there is no guarantee that the left-hand portion will be evaluated first, and no guarantee that the right-hand portion will be "short-circuited" if the left-hand clause is `False`. The result is that the boolean expression may try to access `ThisArray[101]`, generating a runtime range error. As mentioned previously, such errors may or may not result in an error message. If there is no message, this kind of error can be very hard to find.

As in the previous example, using a subrange type for `Index` will change the place where the error occurs, but won't prevent the error. (Where will the error occur then?) To avoid the error, the loop's relational expression (`Index <= Limit`) must be rewritten as (`Index < Limit`). This corrects the problem because it establishes the invariant shown below:

```
Index := 1;

WHILE ( Index < Limit ) AND ( ThisArray[Index] <> GivenChar ) DO
   {
     LOOP INVARIANT:
     1 <= Index <= Limit;
     GivenChar not contained in
        ThisArray[1], ThisArray[2], .. ThisArray[Index-1].
   }
   Index := Index + 1;

IF ThisArray[Index] = GivenChar THEN
   Position := Index
ELSE
   Position := 0;
.
.
```

Just before the loop begins, `Index` is 1 and we do not know whether `GivenChar` occurs in the array. In the language of the loop invariant, the empty set of array elements before `ThisArray[1]` is known not to contain the given character. The first iteration of the loop increments `Index`, which now becomes 2. At the end of the first iteration, the single-element set containing only `ThisArray[1]` is known not to contain the given character. This process continues, with the set of noncontaining elements growing at each iteration.

Eventually, one of two things happens:

1. We may find the given character in the array when we reach the top of the loop with a new value of `Index`. In this case, the loop terminates when `ThisArray[Index]` is the given character, and the set of elements `ThisArray[1], ThisArray[2], . . . , ThisArray[Index-1]` will not contain the given character, just as the loop invariant says.
2. The loop may terminate because `Index` becomes equal to `Limit`. In that case, we know that `ThisArray[1], ThisArray[2], . . . , ThisArray[Limit-1]` do not contain the given character, as the loop invariant says. We still don't know whether `ThisArray[Limit]` is the given character, but this question is answered by the decision structure following the loop.

Arrays as subprogram parameters

When an array is a formal parameter in a procedure or function, it is declared in the procedure or function header using a type name, just as we do with other parameters:

```
PROCEDURE Initialize( VAR Exam : ScoreArray );
PROCEDURE ShowArray( Exam : ScoreArray );
FUNCTION AllAlphabetic( FirstName : NameArray ) : Boolean;
```

In sending actual array parameters to procedures and functions, you must remember the two rules governing the type agreement between actual and formal parameters, previously mentioned in Section 13.1 but now applied to arrays:

1. A formal *variable* (VAR) parameter must be exactly the same type (must have the same type name) as the corresponding actual parameter.
2. A formal *value* parameter that is an array must be the same type (must have the same type name) as the corresponding actual parameter unless the array is a string array, in which case it is enough for the actual and formal parameters to be string arrays of the same length. (Strings are discussed in Section 14.5.)

In other words, actual and formal array parameters must generally agree in type name, the only exception being string arrays when used as value parameters. And always, an array's type must have been given a name before you can use that array as a formal parameter. You cannot define the array type in the formal parameter list. The following, for example, is *illegal*:

```
{-- This is illegal:}
PROCEDURE ShowArray( Exam : ARRAY [ 1..50 ] OF Integer );
```

Arrays and functions

An array cannot be the returned value of a function. Functions can only return a simple value; they cannot return any kind of composite value. (In order to return an array from a subprogram, we use a *procedure* and return the array as a VAR parameter.) This means that arrays and other composite types studied in the next few chapters are second-class data objects in Pascal, being accorded fewer privileges than simple types. We have already seen that arrays cannot be read or written in the usual way, and this too is a form of discrimination against them.

In order to give arrays fuller privileges in Pascal, we will need to equip them with a more complete set of **array operations**, including input and output operations. To do this, we will build array abstract data types in the next chapter. For now, we will put up with the shortcomings.

Partially filled arrays

In Pascal, the size of an array must be declared **statically**; that is, before compiling the program. This can cause trouble when the amount of data to be stored in the array varies from run to run. In some runs we may use only a few of the available array elements, while in others, we may use most of the elements. The only thing we can do is to give the array at least as many elements as we will ever need.

When the array is only partially filled, it is all too easy to accidentally use elements that have not been initialized. To prevent this common error, it is necessary to keep track of the ends of the filled portion. Here is an example, using a `FillLimit` variable to mark the upper end of the filled portion:

```
CONST
   Low  = 1;
   High = 50;

TYPE
   IndexRange = Low..High;
   DataArray  = ARRAY [ IndexRange ] OF Real;

VAR
   Index, FillLimit  : IndexRange;
   Salary            : DataArray;
   MoreData          : Boolean;
   Answer            : Char;

BEGIN
   .
   .
   WriteLn( 'Enter employees'' salaries...' );
   WriteLn( '--------------------------------' );

   MoreData := True;
   Index    := Low;
   WHILE ( Index < High ) AND ( MoreData ) DO
   BEGIN

      Write( 'Salary for employee #', Index:2, ': ' );
      ReadLn( Salary[ Index ] );
      FillLimit := Index;

      Write( 'More data? <Y/N> ' );
      ReadLn( Answer );
      Answer := Upper( Answer );

      IF ( Answer = 'Y' ) THEN
         Index := Index + 1

      ELSE
         MoreData := False

   END; { WHILE }
   .
   .
   { -- Display contents of array: }
   WriteLn;
   WriteLn( 'Employee #    Salary' );
   FOR Index := Low TO FillLimit DO
      WriteLn( ' ':3, Index:2, ' ':10, Salary[ Index ]:7:2 );
      .
      .
```

In this particular example, there was necessarily at least one filled element in the array, but other situations may allow an empty array, and the filled-portion code would have to be written to allow for such a case.

Sending a partially filled array to a subprogram

From the previous discussion, you can see that subprograms need to know the filled limits of an array if they are to use it. If, for example, we wanted a `ShowSalaries` procedure to display the `Salary` array, we would have to transmit both `FillLimit` and `Salary` to the procedure. The call would be `ShowSalaries( FillLimit, Salary )` if the procedure were declared as shown below:

```
PROCEDURE ShowSalaries( Limit  : IndexRange;
                        Salary : DataArray );
VAR
   Index : IndexRange;
BEGIN
   WriteLn;
   WriteLn( 'Employee #    Salary' );
   FOR Index := Low TO Limit DO
      WriteLn( ' ':3, Index:2, ' ':10, Salary[ Index ]:7:2 )
END; { ShowSalaries }
```

Exercises

Run-time errors occur, or can occur, in the following code fragments. State the nature of each error and show a corrected version of the code.

16. Check for the possibility that a subscript may go out of range:

```
CONST
  Low  = 1;
  High = 100;
TYPE
   IndexRange = Low..High;
   RealArray = ARRAY [ IndexRange ] OF Real;
VAR
   Salary : RealArray;
   Index  : IndexRange;
BEGIN
   .
   .
   OutOfOrder := False;
   FOR Index := Low TO High DO
      IF Salary[ Index-1 ] > Salary[ Index ] THEN
         OutOfOrder := True;
```

Rewrite the code to prevent the error.

17. Check for the possibility that a subscript may go out of range:

```
TYPE
   FiftyReals = ARRAY [1..50] OF Real;

VAR
   Count  : Integer;
   Number : FiftyReals;

BEGIN

   Count := 0;
   WriteLn( 'Enter your numbers,' );
   WriteLn( 'terminating with a zero:' );

   REPEAT
      Count := Succ( Count );
      ReadLn( Number[Count] )
   UNTIL Number[Count] = 0.0;
```

Rewrite the code to prevent the error.

18. An error occurs if the sought-for value is not in the array:

```
CONST
   Low  = 1;
   High = 50;

TYPE
   CharArray = PACKED ARRAY [ 1..50 ] OF Char;


FUNCTION FoundCh( Ch     : Char;
                  ChArry : CharArray ) : Boolean;
VAR
   Found : Boolean;
   Index : Integer;

BEGIN

   Index := Low;
   Found := False;
   WHILE ( NOT Found ) DO
      IF Ch = ChArry[ Index ] THEN
         Found := True
      ELSE
         Index := Index + 1

   FoundCh := Found

END; { FoundCh }
```

Rewrite the code to prevent the error.

19. What happens if the user enters `'Z'` at the menu prompt? What if the user enters `'L'`?

```
TYPE
   MenuSelection = 'K'..'M';
   ConstantArray = ARRAY [MenuSelection] OF Real;

PROCEDURE Initialize( VAR C : ConstantArray );
{ Initializes conversion constants }
BEGIN
   C['M'] := 1.609344; { Miles to kilometers }
   C['K'] := 0.6213712 { Kilometers to miles }
END; { Initialize }

PROCEDURE GetConversionConstant( C : ConstantArray;
                                 VAR ConvConst : Real );
{
  PRECONDITION :
  C [ 'M' ] and C [ 'K' ] initialized.

  POSTCONDITION :
  ConvConst contains conversion constant
  requested by the user .
}
VAR
   Choice : Char;

BEGIN
   WriteLn( 'You want to' );
   WriteLn( '  M: convert miles to kilometers' );
   WriteLn( '  K: convert kilometers to miles' );
   WriteLn;
   Write( 'Your choice? <M, K>  ' );
   ReadLn( Choice );

   ConvConst := C[ Choice ]
END; { GetConversionConstant }
```

Rewrite the procedure to prevent the error.

14.4 CASE STUDY: SORTING AN ARRAY

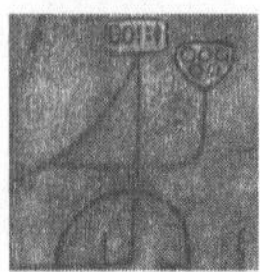

Sorting: The process of arranging the items in a list in a desired order.

Keys: The data items that are ordered by a sorting process.

As you have seen, arrays are used to store lists of similar data items—numbers, names, and so on. A long list of data is useful only if we can look up particular items and see how they are related to the other items in the list. To make it easier, we often arrange a list so that its contained data values are in a particular order. This is called **sorting the list**. The items that are sorted are called **keys**, to distinguish them from other data items that are not sorted, but may be related. For example, in later chapters, we will deal with employee records containing names, employee identification numbers, job descriptions, and salaries. If we sort such records in order to put the names in alphabetical order, the names are the keys for sorting, while the identification numbers, job descriptions, and salaries are the related data.

Computers often store extremely long lists, so array-sorting by computer can take up a significant percentage of total computer operation time unless we have well-designed sorting algorithms. The design of such algorithms turns out to be more subtle and difficult than it first appears. In this section, we present one of the simplest algorithms. In Chapter 19, we will develop and analyze more advanced methods.

One way to sort an array into nondecreasing order is to move the lowest-valued element to the first position in the array, then to move the second-lowest-valued element to the second position in the array, and so on. This is called **selection sort**. In more detail, the process works like this: First we select the lowest-valued element:

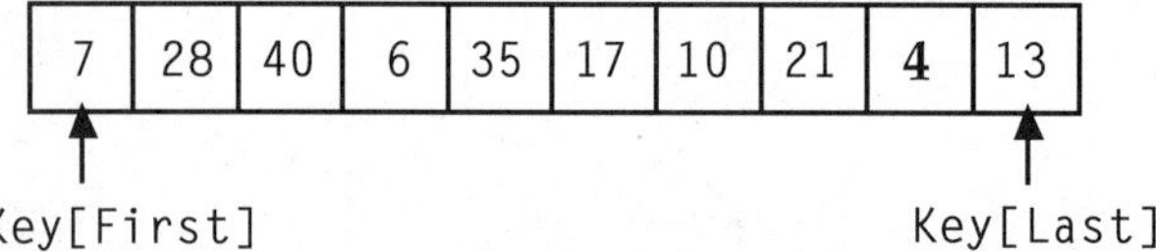

Then we swap this value with the first value in the array.

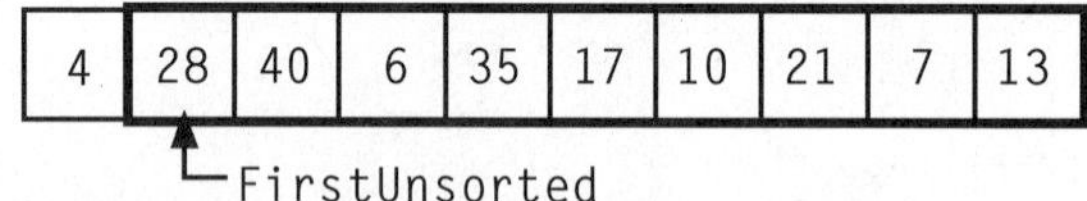

The lowest value is now in the correct position, so we needn't move it again. The remaining unsorted portion of the array consists of all elements after the first. We use a `FirstUnsorted` variable to keep track of where the unsorted portion begins:

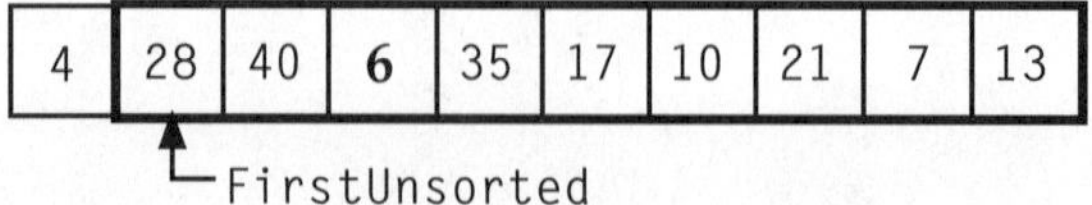

We search the remaining unsorted portion of the array for the second-lowest value, which turns out to be 6:

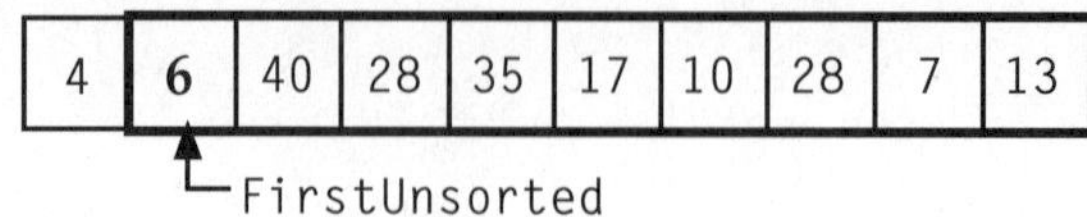

We swap this value with the value in the `FirstUnsorted` position:

4 | 6 | 40 | 28 | 35 | 17 | 10 | 28 | 7 | 13

`FirstUnsorted`

Now the two lowest values are in the correct positions, so we needn't move them again. We increment FirstUnsorted, indicating that the remaining unsorted portion of the array consists of all elements after the second:

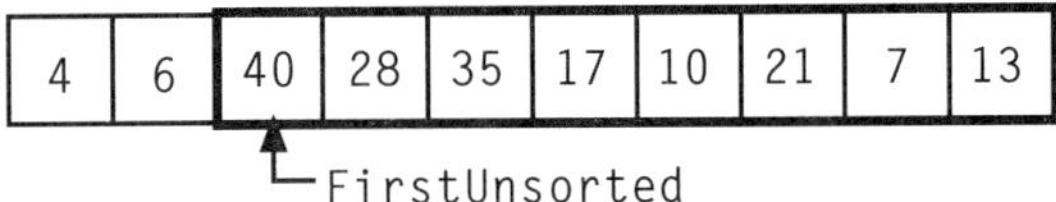

And we continue like this until the unsorted portion consists of only one element, in the last position. Because this element must be at least as large as the one preceding it, we are finished sorting:

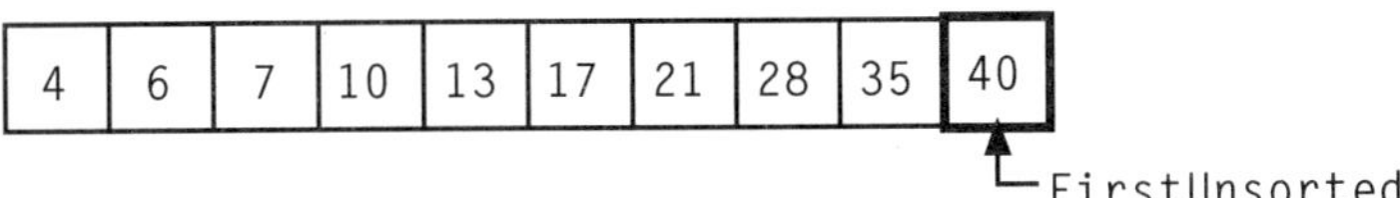

The algorithm requires an outer loop that sweeps FirstUnsorted from First to Last, as shown below. Note again that we use the shorthand Key[First..Last] for the elements Key[First],..., Key[Last].

Algorithm 14.4.1: Selection Sort

Purpose:
To sort the array Key[First..Last] into nondecreasing order.

Preconditions:
First, Last, and the elements Key[First..Last] are initialized.

Postconditions:
Key[First] ≤ Key[First+1] ≤..≤ Key[Last].

Steps:

1. Assign First to FirstUnsorted.
2. While FirstUnsorted < Last, do the following:
   a. Find the lowest value among the elements Key[FirstUnsorted..Last]
   b. Swap this lowest value with Key[FirstUnsorted] (A swap procedure was shown in Section 6.3.)
   c. Increment FirstUnsorted.

It takes another loop to perform step 2a. We tentatively assume that the first element encountered is the lowest-valued element, then walk through the rest of the elements looking for a lower one. If we find one, we remember where it is, then move on, looking for a still lower one, and so on. The code is shown on the next page:

```
FUNCTION PositionOfLowest( VAR Key : ArrayType;    { VAR for speed }
                               First   : SubscriptRange;
                               Last    : SubscriptRange ) : SubscriptRange;
{
  PRECONDITION:
  First <= Last;

  POSTCONDITIONS:
  Key[ PositionOfLowest ] <= Key[ First..Last ].
}
VAR
   LowestSoFar    : KeyType;
   LatestUnsorted : SubscriptRange;

BEGIN

   LowestSoFar      := Key[ First ];
   PositionOfLowest := First;

   FOR LatestUnsorted := First+1 TO Last DO
   {
     LOOP INVARIANT:
     First+1 <= LatestUnsorted <= Last+1;
     LowestSoFar <= Key[ First..LatestUnsorted-1 ].
   }
      IF Key[ LatestUnsorted ] < LowestSoFar THEN
      BEGIN

         PositionOfLowest := LatestUnsorted;
         LowestSoFar      := Key[ LatestUnsorted ]

      END

END; { PositionOfLowest }
```

Even though `LatestUnsorted` is of type `SubscriptRange`, it does not go out of range in the loop because the `FOR` structure leaves the variable undefined when the loop terminates.

Now it is easy to write down the main selection-sorting procedure:

```
PROCEDURE SelectionSort( VAR Key       : ArrayType;
                             First, Last : SubscriptRange );
{
  PRECONDITIONS:
  Key[ First..Last ] are initialized.

  POSTCONDITION:
  Key[ First ] <= Key[ First+1 ] <= ... <= Key[ Last ].
}
VAR
   FirstUnsorted : SubscriptRange;
```

```
BEGIN
   FOR FirstUnsorted := First TO Last-1 DO
   {
     LOOP INVARIANT:
     First <= FirstUnsorted <= Last;
     Key[First] <= Key[First+1] <= ... <= Key[FirstUnsorted-1];
     Key[ First..FirstUnsorted-1 ] <= Key[ FirstUnsorted..Last ].
   }
      Swap( Key[FirstUnsorted],
            Key[ PositionOfLowest( Key, FirstUnsorted, Last ) ] )
END; { SelectionSort }
```

An improvement?

You may have noticed that the procedure above always swaps `Key [FirstUnsorted]` with `Key[PositionOfLowest(...)]`, even when these are the same element, which occurs whenever part of the array is already in order. In other words, the procedure performs unnecessary swaps. When the array contains randomly ordered values, these unnecessary exchanges aren't common, but you may wonder why we don't prevent them with a decision structure:

```
LowPosition := PositionOfLowest( Key, FirstUnsorted, Last );

IF FirstUnsorted < LowPosition THEN
   Swap( Key[ FirstUnsorted ], Key[ LowPosition ] )
```

This would require the evaluation of a boolean expression on every trip through the outer loop of the procedure, in order to prevent an unnecessary swap that occurs only once in a while. Unless we are often dealing with nearly sorted arrays, in which the unnecessary swaps would be a frequent problem, it is just as well to leave the code as shown in the procedure. If the array elements themselves are large data structures, however, even a single swap might consume significant computer time. In such a case, it *would* be desirable to avoid unnecessary swaps.

The loop invariant

The loop in the `SelectionSort` procedure sweeps `FirstUnsorted` from `First` to `Last-1`, and then, just before terminating, increments `FirstUnsorted` to `Last`. At the

Swaps and key comparisons in selection sort. **Table 14.4.1**

N	Number of swaps proportional to N:	Number of comparisons proportional to N^2:
100	100	10,000
1,000	1,000	1,000,000
10,000	10,000	100,000,000
100,000	100,000	10,000,000,000

beginning of any given trip, the elements before `Key[ FirstUnsorted ]` have already been sorted, and all of these are less than or equal to the remaining unsorted elements, whose subscripts range from `FirstUnsorted` on up to `Last`. Thus the invariant properties of the loop are these:

1. The already-sorted portion of the array is `Key[First..FirstUnsorted-1]`.
2. The still-unsorted portion is `Key[FirstUnsorted..Last]`.
3. The already-sorted portion consists of elements all of which are less than or equal to the elements in the still-unsorted part:

```
Key[First..FirstUnsorted-1] <= Key[ FirstUnsorted..Last ].
```

Thus when the loop terminates, FirstUnsorted has been incremented to Last and

Sorted portion = `Key[ First..Last-1 ]`
Unsorted portion = `Key[ Last ]`

But the sorted portion consists of elements less than or equal to the elements in the unsorted portion, so the whole array is now sorted.

The running time is proportional to the number of swaps

The `SelectionSort` procedure swaps two elements of the array at the end of every trip through its loop, no matter what order the array elements were originally in. Thus, the procedure always performs $(N-1)$ swaps, where N is the number of elements in the array. If we introduce the decision structure discussed earlier, the number of swaps will be reduced in proportion to the degree of ordering in the original array. In fact, an already-sorted array would require no swaps at all with this modification. (Of course, we pay for this advantage by introducing additional code that is executed during every trip through the outer loop. In typical real-world sorting applications, this usually costs more time than it saves.)

Key comparison: A comparison between two keys, performed by a relational expression.

However, the number of **key comparisons** performed is always the same, even in the modified version of the procedure. The loop in `PositionOfLowest`, with its `IF` test, is executed $N-1$ times when `FirstUnsorted` is 1, $N-2$ times when `FirstUnsorted` is 2, and so on. The total number of comparisons is therefore

$$(N-1) + (N-2) + \ldots + 1 = N\,(N-1)\,/\,2$$

(The value of this sum is proven in Appendix G.)

Thus, the number of swaps increases like N, but the number of comparisons increases like N^2. This means that as N becomes very large, the amount of time consumed by comparisons increases much more rapidly than the time consumed by swaps. Thus, when the array is very large, the number of comparisons dominates the running time of selection sort, and this is proportional to N^2.

The advantages and disadvantages of selection sort

Selection sort is easy to understand because its method is intuitive. These factors make it easy to implement the algorithm correctly, which in turn makes selection sort easy to write when you suddenly find yourself in need of a sorting procedure. For this reason, it is popular among programmers. But there are at least three reasons why selection sort might not be chosen in a commercial application:

1. Selection sort performs roughly N^2 comparisons when N is large, and therefore is quite slow when sorting really big arrays—say 100,000 or more elements.
2. It is an *internal sorting* method; it requires the entire array to be in main memory. Commercial databases are often larger than main memory, and must be sorted in external storage.
3. Many commercial applications involve databases in which already sorted lists of data are updated and then resorted. In such situations, a typical sorting process involves an array that is already almost sorted. An ideal sorting method would quickly recognize the nearly sorted condition of the array, and work only on the unsorted elements. Selection sort does not do this.

In Chapter 19, we will examine insertion sort and quicksort, two methods that are more efficient than selection sort but more difficult to program correctly. These methods are more suitable for sorting very large arrays and already-sorted arrays. In the meantime, you should become thoroughly familiar with the selection sort algorithm.

Question

20. Cora Meltdown has written a shorter version of the `PositionOfLowest` function shown in this section:

```
FUNCTION PositionOfLowest( VAR Key       : ArrayType;
                           First, Last : SubscriptRange )
                           : SubscriptRange;

VAR
   LatestUnsorted : SubscriptRange;

BEGIN

   PositionOfLowest := First;

   FOR LatestUnsorted := First+1 TO Last DO
      IF Key[ LatestUnsorted ] < Key[ PositionOfLowest ] THEN
         PositionOfLowest := LatestUnsorted;

END; { PositionOfLowest }
```

Why won't Cora's function compile?

Exercises

21. Show how to modify `SelectionSort` to make it sort arrays into non*increasing* order.

22. If, in the code in the text, `KeyType` is `Char` and `Key` is the array

G	I	B	B	E	R	I	S	H

then what is the order of the `Key` elements at the beginning of the third trip through the loop of `SelectionSort`?

23. If `KeyType` is `Integer` and the `Key` array initially contains the list `12, 2, 1, 2, 7, 22, 9`, then what is the order of keys at the beginning of the fourth trip through the loop of the `SelectionSort` procedure?

24. If `KeyType` is `Integer` and the `Key` array initially contains the list `1, 3, 1, 2, 7, 13, 1`, then what is the order of keys at the beginning of the third trip through the loop of the `SelectionSort` procedure?

25. The following sorting procedure is popular with amateur programmers:

```
PROCEDURE BubbleSort ( VAR A        : ArrayType;
                       First, Last : SubscriptRange );

VAR
  I, LastUnsorted : SubscriptRange;
  Sorted          : Boolean;

  BEGIN

  IF Last > First THEN
  BEGIN

    LastUnsorted := Last;
    REPEAT

      Sorted := True;
      FOR I := First TO (LastUnsorted - 1) DO
        IF A[ I ] > A[ I + 1 ] THEN
        BEGIN
          Swap( A[ I ], A[ I + 1 ] );
          Sorted := False
        END;

      LastUnsorted := LastUnsorted - 1

    UNTIL (LastUnsorted = First) or Sorted

  END

END; { BubbleSort }
```

How many swaps are performed by this algorithm in the best and worst cases, as a function of the number of elements being sorted? How many comparisons are made by

```
IF A[ I ] > A[ I + 1 ] THEN
```

in the best and worst cases? In terms of swaps, how does this algorithm compare to `SelectionSort`?

26. State a loop invariant for the outer loop of the `BubbleSort` procedure of Exercise 25.

27. Show how to write a version of `SelectionSort` in which recursion replaces the loop.

14.5 STRING ARRAYS

A **string** is a list of characters, stored together as a single entity. Standard Pascal has no type called "String." (When such a type is predefined in a Pascal system, it is nonstandard.) There is, however, a special kind of array that is used to store strings, and this kind of array is accorded special privileges by the language. A **string array** must satisfy four requirements:

1. It must be an array of *characters*.
2. It must be a *packed* array, so that storage space can be economized.
3. The subscript range must begin with 1 (so that characters in the string are numbered from 1 upwards).
4. There must be at least two elements in the array. (Strings of length 0 or 1 are not allowed.)

We can have, for example, a string array called `FirstName`, in which `FirstName[1]` is the first character, `FirstName[2]` is the second character, and so on:

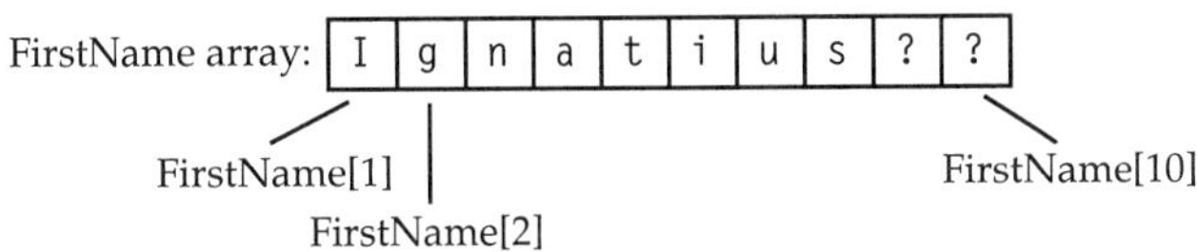

Thus, the arrays in the following declarations are string arrays:

```
TYPE
   String10 = PACKED ARRAY [1..10] OF Char;
   String2  = PACKED ARRAY [1..2] OF Char;

VAR
   FirstName : String10;
   Initials  : String2;
```

The following arrays are *not* string arrays, however, for the reasons shown:

```
TYPE
   NotAString40 = ARRAY [ 1..40 ] OF Char;         { Not packed }
   NotAString1  = PACKED ARRAY [ 1..1 ] OF Char;   { Too short }
   NotAString3  = PACKED ARRAY [ 0..2 ] OF Char;   { 0 subscript }
```

Special privileges accorded to string arrays

String arrays enjoy four privileges not accorded to ordinary arrays:

1. **String constants** are allowed. These are written as strings of at least two characters enclosed within apostrophes, as we have been using in output statements all along. For example, `'hello'` is a string constant, as is `'1234'`. But `'h'` is not a string constant, because it contains only one character. Similarly, the **empty string** constant `''` is not allowed.
2. String constants may be assigned to string arrays *of the same length*. For example, if `Salutation` is declared to be `PACKED ARRAY [1..5] OF Char`, we can assign to it the five-character strings `'hello'` or `'hi   '`, but not `'hi'` or `'greetings'`.

3. The `Write` and `WriteLn` procedures can receive string constants and string arrays as parameters. (But `Read` and `ReadLn` do *not* accept string parameters.) To input strings, we will have to write our own input procedures.
4. String constants and the values of string arrays may be compared (if the lengths are the same) by means of relational operators. Thus, the relational expression `'hello' > 'gdbye'` has the value `True`, but `'hello' > 'goodbye'` is illegal.

Assigning values to string arrays

A string array can be *assigned* a value of the same length. For example, a string constant of length 10 can be assigned to a string variable of length 10:

```
TYPE
   String10 = PACKED ARRAY [1..10] OF Char;

VAR
   Name1, Name2 : String10;

BEGIN
   Name1 := 'Hiram     ';
   Name2 := 'Heartthrob';
   .
   .
```

The first string constant is padded with spaces so that it is the same length as the variable. *A string constant cannot be assigned to a variable of a different length.*

As with all arrays, the value of one string array can be assigned to another. But in the case of string arrays, the two arrays need not be of exactly the same type, but only of the same length. The following assignment, for example, is legal:

```
TYPE
   String10 = PACKED ARRAY [1..10] OF Char;

VAR
   Name1 : String10;
   Name2 : PACKED ARRAY [1..10] OF Char;

BEGIN
   .
   .
   Name1 := 'Hiram     ';
   Name2 := Name1;        { This is legal! }
   .
   .
```

Comparing strings

Two strings can be compared if they have the same length, even if they are not of the same type. They are *equal* if and only if they have the same length and contain the same characters in the same order.

Two different strings of the same length have the relational order of the first character in which those strings differ. Thus, the following relational expressions are all `True`:

```
'One' < 'Two'
```

```
'Two  ' > 'Three'
'april' < 'may  '
```

However, the relational order of individual characters is their ordinal order according to the character code being used, so the relational order of some strings will depend on the character set being used. (See Appendix C.) For example, `'April'` differs from `'april'` in the first character position, so their relational order is the same as the ordinal order of `'A'` and `'a'`. That is, `'April' < 'april'` in the ASCII code, but `'April' > 'april'` in the EBCDIC code.

How string arrays are packed for storage

String arrays are always packed so that their characters, each of which needs only one byte for storage, will not occupy more than the minimum necessary space. For example, in a system using the ASCII character set, the code

```
TYPE
   String5 = PACKED ARRAY [1..5] OF Char;

VAR
   Name : String5;

BEGIN
   .
   .
   Name := 'Cecil';
```

might cause the `Name` array to be stored in a sequence of only five bytes, containing the codes for `'C'`, `'e'`, `'c'`, `'i'`, and `'l'`, in that order:

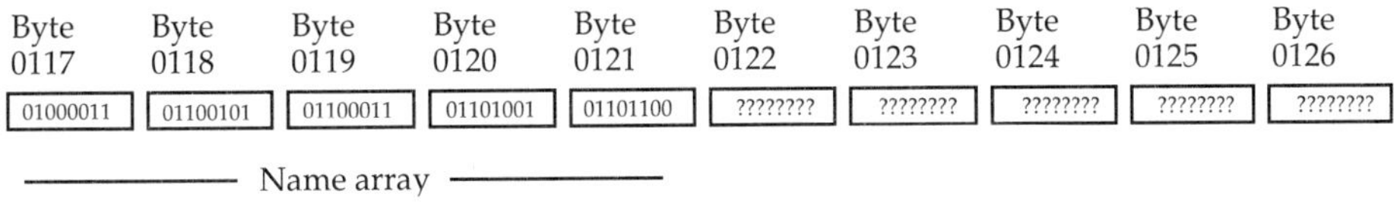

Byte 0117	Byte 0118	Byte 0119	Byte 0120	Byte 0121	Byte 0122	Byte 0123	Byte 0124	Byte 0125	Byte 0126
01000011	01100101	01100011	01101001	01101100	????????	????????	????????	????????	????????

——— Name array ———

On the other hand, if we had used the code

```
TYPE
   Char5Array = ARRAY [1..5] OF Char;

VAR
   Name : Char5Array;

BEGIN
   .
   .
   Name[1] := 'C';
   Name[2] := 'e';
   Name[3] := 'c';
   Name[4] := 'i';
   Name[5] := 'l';
```

the array would not have been packed. In a word-oriented machine with 16-bit words, each character might have been stored in a pair of bytes. This would have wasted half of the storage area:

Byte 0117	Byte 0118	Byte 0119	Byte 0120	Byte 0121	Byte 0122	Byte 0123	Byte 0124	Byte 0125	Byte 0126
01000011	00000000	01100101	00000000	01100011	00000000	01101001	00000000	01101100	00000000

Name array

A particular Pascal system may not actually compress the storage space when given a `PACKED` declaration. The only requirement of the Pascal Standard is that a `PACKED` array never occupy *more* storage than the corresponding unpacked array. However, most Pascal systems will store strings with each character occupying just one byte.

Exercises

28. Which of the following types are *not* string arrays? Explain your reasoning.

```
TYPE
   Gerald  = PACKED ARRAY [ 0..3 ] OF Char;
   Jimmy   = PACKED ARRAY [ 1..3 ] OF Char;
   Ronald  = PACKED ARRAY [ 1..1 ] OF Letters;
   George  = ARRAY [ 1..5 ] OF Char;
   Bill    = ARRAY [ 2..5 ] OF Char;
```

29. Suppose you have the declarations

```
TYPE
   Str8 = PACKED ARRAY [ 1..8 ] OF Char;

VAR
   S : Str8;
```

Then which of the following statements are *illegal* in Standard Pascal? Explain.

```
BEGIN
   S := 'Wirth';
   WriteLn( S );
   ReadLn( S );

   IF S <> 'Knuth' THEN
      WriteLn( 'NOT SAME NAME.' );
```

30. With the same declarations as in Exercise 29, which of the following statements are *illegal* in Standard Pascal? Explain.

```
   S[1] := 'BaldSpot';

   IF S = 'BaldSpot' THEN
      WriteLn( 'SAME' );

   ReadLn( S );
   WriteLn( S );
```

31. With the same declarations as in Exercise 29, which of the following statements are *illegal* in Standard Pascal? Explain.

```
   S := 'FlatSpot';

   IF S[1] <> 'Baldspot' THEN
      WriteLn( 'DIFFERENT' );

   WriteLn( S[8], S[7], S[6], S[5], S[4],  S[3], S[2],  S[1] );
```

14.6 CASE STUDY: STRING OPERATIONS

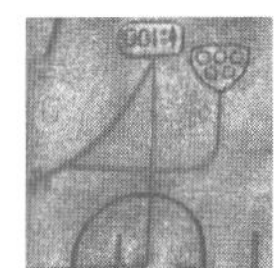

In Standard Pascal, the string array is a **second-class data type**, like other arrays. Although string arrays have special privileges, subprograms cannot return string values and hardly any operations are provided for dealing with string data—we can't even read them from the keyboard. Furthermore, we are not allowed to store empty strings in string arrays. These shortcomings make it difficult to use one of the most important data types in real-world applications. However, Pascal does provide tools for creating our own string operations, so in this section we will build a few subprograms we will need for later applications. (These operations are built into many commercial Pascal systems. If your system already provides them, you won't need to build them yourself. Still, the experience is definitely educational.)

Reading strings, even empty ones

In order to get strings for text processing, we often need to read them from the keyboard. Many commercial Pascal systems allow ReadLn to read data into string arrays, but Standard Pascal does not. So, for portability, one of our first needs is a homemade ReadLnStr procedure that works with string arrays. There are several considerations to make first.

We want to read a string of up to 80 characters, up to but not including any end-of-line or end-of-file signal (<EOLn> or <EOF>) that indicates the end of the string. This means that we want to read characters one by one until one of three things happens:

1. The user presses the RETURN key, signalling <EOLn>.
2. The user signals <EOF>.
3. The string reaches the maximum storable length.

It is possible that the user will enter the <EOLn> or <EOF> before any other characters. In this case, the string will be *conceptually empty*, and we should read no characters into the array. Therefore, the character-reading loop should be a WHILE rather than a REPEAT..UNTIL.

If the reading terminates before the array is full, the rest of the array should be filled with nondisplayable characters to mark the end of the conceptual string. This will facilitate the operation of other string procedures and *allows conceptually-empty strings*. Character codes provide a special **null character**—Chr(0)—for this purpose. Therefore, we will fill up unused character positions in a String80 variable with Chr(0) values.

If the array becomes full before the user presses RETURN, the procedure should discard any characters on the line, including the <EOLn> signal itself, so that a client program will be ready to read a fresh string if it needs to. On the other hand, if reading terminated because the user gave an <EOF> signal, the procedure should reset the Input file—the keyboard—so that further reading will be possible later. This is done in Pascal by calling Reset(Input). (Discussed further in Section 17.2.)

Finally, there is the troublesome fact that we cannot simply write the character-reading loop as

```
WHILE (NOT EOLn) AND (NOT EOF) AND (Count < MaxStrLength) DO
```

because Standard Pascal does not short-circuit the evaluation of AND expressions when the first clause is true. (Section 8.6.) Therefore, Pascal might try to evaluate (NOT EOLN) when EOF is true, which would be an error. This shortcoming of the Pascal language will force us to use a boolean variable in the loop and to split loop-termination testing into two parts.

After considering all these factors, we end up with a ReadLnStr procedure:

```
CONST
   MaxStrLength = 80;

TYPE
   PosRange     = 0..MaxStrLength;
   String80     = PACKED ARRAY [ 1..MaxStrLength ] OF Char;
.
.
PROCEDURE ReadLnStr( VAR Str : String80 );
{
  PRECONDITION:
  MaxStrLength > 0.

  POSTCONDITION:
  Str contains up to MaxStrLength chars read from keyboard,
  up to, but not including, the first <EOLn> or <EOF>.
  Unused elements of the array are filled with null chars.
}
VAR
   Count    : PosRange;
   Finished : Boolean;
   NullChar : Char;

BEGIN

   NullChar := Chr(0);
   Finished := False;
   Count := 0;

   WHILE ( NOT EOF ) AND ( NOT Finished ) DO

      { --Next char is either <EOLn> or char to be stored }
      IF ( NOT EOLn ) AND ( Count < MaxStrLength ) THEN
      BEGIN
         {
           ASSERTIONS:
           Next char is neither <EOF> not <EOLn>
           and array is not full.
         }
         Count := Count + 1;
         Read( Str[ Count ] )
      END

      ELSE
         { --Either EOLn or array is full }
         Finished := True;
```

```
   WHILE Count < MaxStrLength DO
   {
     LOOP INVARIANT:
     Count = number of filled elements in Str array.
   }
   BEGIN
      Count := Count + 1;
      Str[ Count ] := NullChar
   END;

   IF EOF THEN
      { --Discard end-of-file signal: }
      Reset( Input )
   ELSE
      { --Discard rest of line: }
      ReadLn

END; { ReadLnStr }
```

Finding the length of a string

We now write a function that will return the length of a String80, not including any trailing null characters. We can do this by checking the array elements one by one, keeping track of the last element containing a non-null character:

```
FUNCTION LengthOfStr( Str : String80 ) : PosRange;
VAR
   Index    : PosRange;
   Found    : Boolean;
   NullChar : Char;

BEGIN

   NullChar := Chr(0);
   Index    := MaxStrLength;
   Found    := False;

   WHILE ( Index > 0 ) AND ( NOT Found ) DO

      IF Str[ Index ] <> NullChar THEN
         Found := True

      ELSE
         Index := Index - 1;

   LengthOfStr := Index

END; { LengthOfStr }
```

Copying a substring

In later chapters, we will need to be able to copy part of one string into another String80 variable. In particular, we will want to be able to copy a given number of characters, starting at a given character position, from a source string to a destination string, afterwards padding out the destination string with null characters. The procedure uses ideas we developed in the last two examples:

```
PROCEDURE Copy( Source   : String80;
                StartPos : PosRange;
                NumChars : PosRange;
                VAR Dest : String80 );
VAR
   Index, Count : PosRange;
   NullChar     : Char;

BEGIN

   Count    := 0;
   NullChar := Chr(0);

   IF ( StartPos > 0 ) AND
        ( (StartPos + NumChars - 1) <= MaxStrLength ) THEN

      FOR Index := StartPos TO (StartPos + NumChars - 1) DO
      {
        LOOP INVARIANT:
        Count = Number of chars copied to Dest array.
      }
      BEGIN
          Count := Count + 1;
          Dest[ Count ] := Source[ Index ]
      END

   ELSE
      WriteLn( 'ILLEGAL RANGE IN COPY PROCEDURE.' );

   { --Fill rest of Dest with null chars: }
   FOR Index := (Count+1) TO MaxStrLength DO
      Dest[ Index ] := NullChar

END; { Copy }
```

Finding the integer value of a digit string

For our last example of string operations that will come in handy in later chapters, we consider how we might read a digit string like `'123'` or `'-43'` and convert it to its integer value. To do this, we have to look for an optional sign, then read digits one at a time, from left to right, building up the whole integer value by accumulating powers of ten. Since the subprogram will return an integer, it can be a function. Commercial Pascal systems often provide such a function and call it `Val` (for integer **val**ue), so we will do the same.

There are some exceptional cases to consider. If the given string does not properly represent an integer, we will have the function return 0. If the string is something like `'-123H42'`, which looks like a string up to a point, but then contains nondigit characters, we will have the function return the initial integer portion. Finally, we will need to consider the fact that a user can enter a string representing an integer magnitude too large to store in Pascal's Integer type. (Project 7.)

Note that the `Val` function calls the `IsDigit` function we wrote in Section 8.7:

```
FUNCTION Val( Str : String80 ) : Integer;
VAR
   Value, Sign          : Integer;
   Finished             : Boolean;
   Len, StartPos, Index : PosRange;

BEGIN

   Value    := 0;
   Sign     := 1;
   Finished := False;
   Len      := LengthOfStr( Str );
   StartPos := 1;

   IF Len > 0 THEN
   BEGIN

      IF Str[1] = '-' THEN
      BEGIN
         Sign := -1;
         StartPos := 2
      END

      ELSE IF Str[1] = '+' THEN
         StartPos := 2;

      Index := StartPos;
      WHILE ( NOT Finished ) AND ( Index <= Len ) DO
      BEGIN

         IF IsDigit( Str[Index] ) THEN
            Value := (10 * Value) + Ord( Str[Index] ) - Ord('0')

         ELSE
            { Str[Index] is not a digit }
             Finished := True;
         Index := Index + 1

      END { WHILE }

   END; { IF }

   Val := Sign * Value

END; { Val }
```

14.7 PARALLEL ARRAYS

As an application of one-dimensional arrays, including strings, we begin the construction of a payroll program to read and display employees' names and salaries for a small business. Over the next few chapters, we will improve this program as you learn more about Pascal's composite storage types.

Initially, we plan a simple program to read from the keyboard employee names and associated salaries. These are displayed in a neat table, along with the average salary. The I/O could look like this:

```
ENTER EMPLOYEES' ID NUMBERS AND SALARIES
------------------------------------------
Employee # 1
  Name:   Hoobert Heever
  Salary: $222.22

More data? <Y/N> Y

Employee # 2
  Name:   Grover Cincinnati
  Salary: $333.33

More data? <Y/N> Y

Employee # 3
  Name:   Millard Fulltime
  Salary: $444.44

More data? <Y/N> N

Employee                                    Salary
Hoobert Heever                            $ 222.22
Grover Cincinnati                         $ 333.33
Millard Fulltime                          $ 444.44

Average salary:                           $ 333.33
```

The program will need to store a two-part record for each employee, containing both the string that is the employee's name and the employee's real-number salary. An employee record is therefore heterogeneous, and cannot be stored entirely in one array. Instead, we will use a pair of arrays, called `Name` and `Salary`, which are said to be **parallel arrays** because their subscripts track together in the sense shown in Figure 14.7.1.

The program performs two major tasks: reading the data from the keyboard and displaying the table. These tasks will be carried out by separate procedures, for which we first write stubs:

```
PROGRAM Payroll0 ( Input, Output );
{ Skeleton of a payroll program, with stubs of procedures. }

CONST
   MaxEmployees = 50;  { Maximum number of employees }
```

Figure 14.7.1 *Salary and Name are said to be parallel because their subscripts track together. Salary[I] and ID[I] together make up the data record for the Ith employee.*

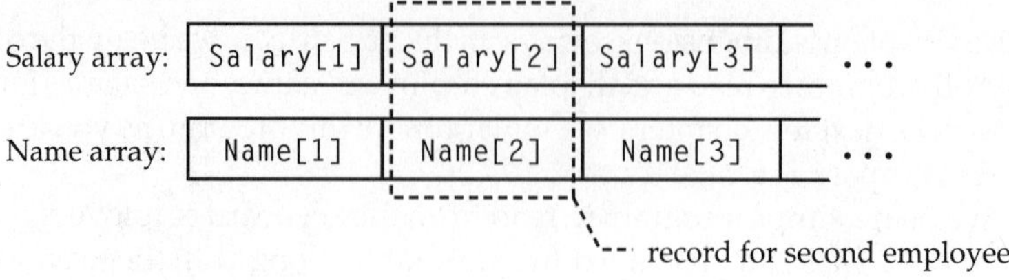

```
TYPE
   EmployeeRange = 0..MaxEmployees;
   NameString    = PACKED ARRAY[ 1..40 ] OF Char;
   NameArray     = ARRAY[ EmployeeRange ] OF NameString;
   SalaryArray   = ARRAY[ EmployeeRange ] OF Real;

VAR
   Name         : NameArray;      { Array of employee names    }
   Salary       : SalaryArray;    { Array of employee salaries }
   NumEmployees : EmployeeRange;  { Actual number of employees }


PROCEDURE GetPayData( VAR NumEmployees : EmployeeRange;
                      VAR Name         : NameArray;
                      VAR Salary       : SalaryArray );
{
  Reads from keyboard the actual number of employees
  and for each employee, a name and salary.
}
VAR
   Employee: EmployeeRange;

BEGIN

   WriteLn( 'GetPayData is a stub only.' );
   NumEmployees := 1;
   Name[1]      := 'Hoobert Heever                          ';
   Salary[1]    := 111.11

END; { GetPayData }


PROCEDURE ShowPay( NumEmployees : EmployeeRange;
                   Name         : NameArray;
                   Salary       : SalaryArray );
{ Displays a table of employee names and salaries. }
VAR
   Employee: EmployeeRange;

BEGIN

   WriteLn( 'ShowPay is a stub only.' )

END; { ShowPay }


BEGIN { main program }

   { --Get actual number of employees and data for arrays: }
   GetPayData( NumEmployees, Name, Salary );

   { --Display data for all employees: }
   ShowPay( NumEmployees, Name, Salary )

END.
```

In the GetPayData stub, notice that we assign dummy values to the VAR parameters so that the program will have data to display, even in the driver-and-stub stage. Note also that we must assign a 40-character string to Name[1] because Name was declared to be a string of 40 characters.

We compile and run the skeleton. So far, so good. Now we turn our attention to the manipulations of arrays. First we have to read in the values for the Name and Salary arrays. Since there will in general be fewer employees than elements in the arrays, and we don't know how many there are until we read the data, we will use a WHILE loop, as we did in Section 14.3. We read the Name elements by means of the ReadLnStr procedure we wrote in Section 14.6:

```
PROCEDURE GetPayData( VAR NumEmployees : EmployeeRange;
                      VAR Name         : NameArray;
                      VAR Salary       : SalaryArray );
{
  POSTCONDITIONS:
  NumEmployees < 0;
  Name[1 .. NumEmployees] and Salary[1 .. NumEmployees] initialized.
}
VAR
   Employee : EmployeeRange;
   MoreData : Boolean;
   Answer   : Char;

BEGIN

   WriteLn( 'Enter employees'' names and salaries:' );
   WriteLn;

   MoreData := True;
   Employee := 1;
   NumEmployees := 0;
   WHILE ( Employee <= MaxEmployees ) AND MoreData DO
   {
     LOOP INVARIANT:
     1 <= Employee <= MaxEmployees;
     0 <= NumEmployees <= MaxEmployees;
     Name[1..NumEmployees] and Salary[1..NumEmployees] initialized.
   }
   BEGIN

      WriteLn( 'Employee #', Employee:2 );
      Write( 'Name:   ' );
      ReadLnString( Name[Employee] );
      Write( 'Salary: ' );
      ReadLn( Salary[Employee] );
      WriteLn;
      NumEmployees := Employee;

      Write( 'More data? <Y/N> ' );
      ReadLn( Answer );
      WriteLn;
      Answer := Upper( Answer );
```

```
      IF ( Answer = 'Y' ) AND ( Employee < MaxEmployees ) THEN
         Employee := Employee + 1
      ELSE
         MoreData := False

   END; { WHILE }

END; { GetPayData }
```

Note the call to a ReadLnString procedure. Although many real-world Pascal systems can use ReadLn to read a string, Standard Pascal cannot do this. If your Pascal system needs one, you will have to write your own ReadLnString procedure. (See Project 7 at the end of the chapter.) The GetPayData procedure also calls an Upper function of the kind we defined in Chapter 8.

In the ShowData procedure, we can display a table of employees' names and salaries by means of a FOR loop, because at that point, we know how many records there are. Using a declared constant, ColumnWidth, to specify the width of a column in the table, the code might be

```
FOR Employee := 1 TO NumEmployees DO
   WriteLn( Name[ Employee ], ' ':ColumnWidth-40,
            '$', Salary[ Employee ]:7:2 );
```

Of course, if NumEmployees = 0, the FOR loop makes no trips and no employee records are printed. The employees' names are printed in fields up to 40 characters wide. Assuming that salaries are in the hundreds of dollars, we print them in fields seven columns wide. In between, we print enough spaces to make the first column of the table the desired width. To allow the width to be easily adjustable, we print the space character, ' ', in a field of width (ColumnWidth - 40). This trick gives us an automatically adjusted number of spaces between the name and the dollar sign, and also adjusts the table header automatically.

We also need to display the average of salaries, so we should add up the salaries as we display them:

```
SumOfSalaries := 0.0;
FOR Employee := 1 TO NumEmployees DO
BEGIN

   WriteLn( Name[Employee], ' ':ColumnWidth-40,
            '$', Salary[Employee]:7:2 );
   SumOfSalaries := SumOfSalaries + Salary[Employee]

END; {FOR}
```

With these insertions, we end up with the following version of the ShowPay procedure:

```
PROCEDURE ShowPay( NumEmployees : EmployeeRange;
                   Name     : NameArray;
                   Salary : SalaryArray );
{
  PRECONDITIONS:
  Name [1..NumEmployees] and Salary [1..NumEmployees] initialized.

  POSTCONDITIONS :
  Name [1..NumEmployees] and Salary [1..NumEmployees] displayed.
}
VAR
   Employee       : EmployeeRange;
   SumOfSalaries : Real;

BEGIN

   WriteLn( 'SUMMARY' );
   WriteLn( '-------' );
   WriteLn;
   WriteLn( 'Employee', ' ' : ColumnWidth - 7, 'Salary' );

   SumOfSalaries := 0.0;
   FOR Employee := 1 TO NumEmployees DO
   BEGIN
      WriteLn( Name[Employee], ' ' : ColumnWidth-40,
               '$', Salary[Employee]:7:2 );
      SumOfSalaries := SumOfSalaries + Salary[Employee]
   END; {FOR}

   WriteLn;
   IF NumEmployees > 0 THEN
      WriteLn( 'Average salary:  $',
               ( SumOfSalaries / NumEmployees ):7:2 )

END;  { ShowPay }
```

In this example, the `Name` and `Salary` arrays were passed to and from the `GetPayData` procedure as variable parameters, but were passed to the `ShowPay` procedure as value parameters. This is appropriate because only the `GetPayData` procedure modifies the values in the arrays.

> However, passing arrays as value parameters requires copying all their elements, and for large arrays, this can be time- and memory-consuming. Therefore, programmers often choose to pass arrays as variable parameters even when the subprogram will not modify them. We will follow this practice in later examples.

Exercises

32. Prove that the loop invariant in the `Payroll1` program is valid.

33. The following boolean function is supposed to indicate whether the first *N* elements of an array are in increasing order; that is, whether $A_1 \le A_2 \le \ldots \le AN$. Unfortunately, the function doesn't always run correctly.

```
TYPE
   PosInt     = 1..MaxInt;
   RealVector = ARRAY [ 1..Limit ] OF Real;

FUNCTION InIncreasingOrder( N     : PosInt;
                            VAR A : RealVector ) : Boolean;

VAR
   Index : PosInt;

BEGIN

   InIncreasingOrder := True;
   FOR Index := 1 TO N DO
     IF A[ Index ] > A[ Index + 1 ] THEN
         InIncreasingOrder := False

END; { InIncreasingOrder }
```

Explain what is wrong with the function and show how to fix it.

34. In the following code fragment, something bad might happen after the user enters numbers like –2 or –123. Explain what is wrong and show how to fix it.

```
CONST
   Low  = 1;
   High = 10;

TYPE
   IndexRange  = Low..High;
   NonNegInt   = 0..MaxInt;
   LotsOfStuff = ARRAY [ IndexRange ] OF NonNegInt;

VAR
   Index   : IndexRange;
   Numbers : LotsOfStuff;
   Value   : Integer;

BEGIN
   { Fill array }
   FOR Index := Low TO High DO
   BEGIN
      Write( 'Integer value? ' );
      ReadLn( Value );
      Numbers[ Index ] := Value
   END;
   .
   .
```

35. In the following code fragment, something bad might happen even if the user enters numbers like 23 or 123. Explain what is wrong and show how to fix it.

```
CONST
   Low  = 1;
   High = 10;

TYPE
   IndexRange  = Low..High;
   NonNegInt   = 0..MaxInt;
   LotsOfStuff = ARRAY [ IndexRange ] OF NonNegInt;
```

```
VAR
   Index   : IndexRange;
   Numbers : LotsOfStuff;
   Value   : Integer;

BEGIN
   { Fill array }
   FOR Index := Low TO High DO
   BEGIN
      Write( 'Positive integer value? ' );
      ReadLn( Value );
      Numbers[ Index ] := 10 - Value
   END;
   .
   .
```

14.8 MULTIDIMENSIONAL ARRAYS

As you have seen, an array contains a sequence of elements, all of the same *ElementType*. The element type, we said, can be any type, even an array (but not the same array). Thus we can have an array of arrays. For example, we can have

```
CONST
   NumExams    = 6;
   NumStudents = 25;

TYPE
   ExamScores = ARRAY [ 1..NumExams ] OF Integer;
   Student    = ARRAY [ 1..NumStudents ] OF ExamScores;
```

`Student` can be thought of as an array of 25 elements, each of which corresponds to a particular student. Each element is itself an array of six exam scores for the corresponding student. In other words, we have an array of students, each of whom is represented by an array of scores. This can be pictured as a two-dimensional table in which each row represents a student and each column represents a particular exam score (Figure 14.8.1).

Figure 14.8.1 *A two-dimensional array in which each row corresponds to a student and each column corresponds to an exam. Thus, each element of the array contains a particular exam score for a particular student.*

	Exam 1					Exam 6
Student 1	98	77	71	85	0	84
Student 2	91	94	89	90	85	91
Student 3	84	82	79	70	65	59
	⋮	⋮	⋮	⋮	⋮	⋮
Student 25	99	95	91	92	89	96

Pascal thinks of this as a doubly subscripted array, in which the first subscript specifies a student (a row of the table) and the second subscript specifies an exam (a column of the table). Thus the score on the fourth exam for student 7 would be stored in the array element `Student[7][4]`. Pascal also allows this to be written in the shorthand notation `Student[7, 4]`. Either notation indicates that we are talking about the element on row 7 and column 4 of the array. Arrays like this one, with two subscripts, are called **two-dimensional arrays**. The first subscript always specifies the row, and the second subscript always specifies the column.

We can also have arrays of arrays of arrays of . . . , to whatever complexity you want, with as many subscripts as needed. The general syntax is shown below.

More examples of two-dimensional arrays

Consider the declarations

```
TYPE
   PayArray = ARRAY [1..50, 1..26] OF Real;

VAR
   Pay : PayArray;
```

or, better yet,

```
CONST
   LowEmployee  = 1;
   HighEmployee = 50;
   LowPeriod    = 1;
   HighPeriod   = 26;

TYPE
   EmployeeRange  = LowEmployee..HighEmployee;
   PayPeriodRange = LowPeriod..HighPeriod;
   PayArray = ARRAY [EmployeeRange, PayPeriodRange] OF Real;
```

Syntax for Declaring a Multidimensional ArrayType

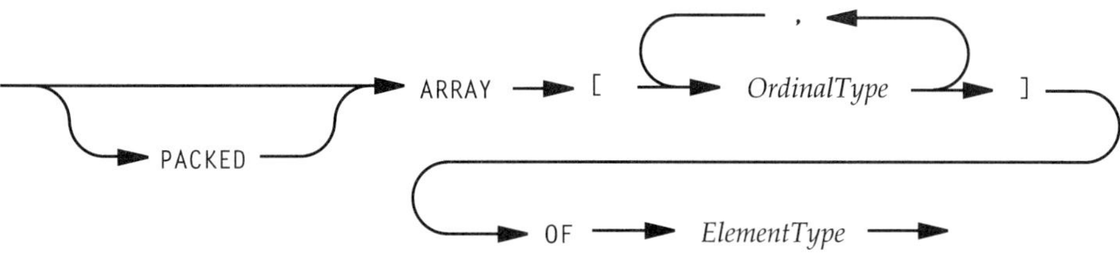

Pseudocode:

`ARRAY [` *OrdinalType1*`,` *OrdinalType2*`, . . . ,` *OrdinalTypeN* `] OF` *ElementType*

Notes:

- The subscript ranges are declared as *OrdinalTypes*; that is, the name of any ordinal type or a subrange of an ordinal type.
- The reserved word `PACKED` can be prefixed. See the discussion of singly dimensioned arrays in Section 14.1.

```
VAR
   Pay : PayArray;
```

These define a `Pay` array containing 50 rows, with 26 real elements on each row. Conceptually, the array can be imagined as the two-dimensional table shown below, where each row represents an employee and each column a pay period.

```
Pay[1,1]    Pay[1,2]    Pay[1,3]    ...   Pay[1,26]
Pay[2,1]    Pay[2,2]    Pay[2,3]    ...   Pay[2,26]
Pay[3,1]    Pay[3,2]    Pay[3,3]    ...   Pay[3,26]
   .           .           .                  .
   .           .           .                  .
   .           .           .                  .
Pay[50,1]   Pay[50,2]   Pay[50,3]   ...   Pay[50,26]
```

Order of storage of array elements

We imagine it this way, but the actual **array order of storage** is different. *The elements of a two-dimensional Pascal array are stored row-wise.* That is, the elements of the first row are stored one after another in memory, followed by the elements of the second row, and so on. Thus, the elements of an array, even a multidimensional array, are stored *linearly* in memory. In the example shown above, the `Pay[2,1]` element would be the 27th element in memory after the beginning of the array. If each real number occupies four bytes of storage, the `[2,1]` element would be stored in the four bytes beginning at a point 26 x 4 = 104 bytes after the beginning of the array.

An array of arrays

The array type declared by

```
TYPE
   .
   .
   PayArray = ARRAY [EmployeeRange, PayPeriodRange] OF Real;
```

is really a shorthand for the longer declaration

```
TYPE
   .
   .
   PayArray = ARRAY [EmployeeRange]
                 OF ARRAY [PayPeriodRange] OF Real;
```

The longer form of the declaration makes it clearer that `PayArray` is an array of rows, each of which is an array of columns containing real numbers.

Filling a two-dimensional array

As mentioned in Section 14.1, arrays must be filled element by element. To fill a two-dimensional array from a file, we would use a pair of nested `FOR` loops. With the same declarations shown above, we might have

```
VAR
   Employee  : EmployeeRange;
   PayPeriod : PayPeriodRange;
   InFile    : Text;
   .
   .
   FOR Employee := LowEmployee TO HighEmployee DO
   BEGIN

      FOR PayPeriod := LowPeriod TO HighPeriod DO
         Read( InFile, Pay[ Employee, PayPeriod ] )

   END; { FOR Employee }
```

Arrays with more than two dimensions

As mentioned previously, a multidimensional array is really a shorthand notation for an array of arrays. For example, if we have

```
TYPE
   AdditivePrimaryColors = ( Red, Green, Blue );
```

then all of the following declarations are equivalent:

```
   ARRAY [ 1..50 ] OF ARRAY [ AdditivePrimaryColors ]
        OF ARRAY [ 1..4 ] OF Integer;

   ARRAY [ 1..50 ] OF ARRAY [ AdditivePrimaryColors, 1..4 ]
        OF Integer;

   ARRAY [ 1..50, AdditivePrimaryColors, 1..4 ] OF Integer;
```

When an array is packed, the equivalency is more complicated. For example,

```
   PACKED ARRAY [ 1..3, 1..26 ] OF Char;
```

is a shorthand notation for

```
   PACKED ARRAY [ 1..3 ] OF PACKED ARRAY [ 1..26 ] OF Char;
```

On the other hand, there is no shorthand for declarations of the form

```
   ARRAY [ 1..3 ] OF PACKED ARRAY [ 1..26 ] OF Char;
```

or

```
   PACKED ARRAY [ 1..3 ] OF ARRAY [ 1..26 ] OF Char;
```

Questions

36. In what order are the elements of a two-dimensional array stored in memory?

37. Using the two-dimensional array as a model, in what order do you suppose the elements of a three-dimensional array would be stored?

Exercises

38. Which of the following multidimensional array type declarations are syntactically *illegal*? Explain why.

```
CONST
   Low  = 1;
   High = 50;

TYPE
   Scores = ARRAY [ 1..High; 1..High ] OF Integer;
   Salary = ARRAY [ 1..High ] [ 1..High ] OF Real;
   Points = ARRAY [ Low..High ] OF ARRAY [ Low..High ] OF Real;
   Strike = ARRAY [ High..Low, High..Low ] OF Char;
   Beaver = ARRAY [ Char, Char ] OF Integer;
```

39. Which of the following multidimensional array type declarations are syntactically *illegal*? Explain why.

```
CONST
   Low  = 1;
   High = 50;

TYPE
   Rows = Low..High;
   Cols = Low..High;
   FoodGroups = ( Sugar, Coffee, Burgers );
   Goodies = ARRAY [ Rows ] OF ARRAY [ Cols ] OF FoodGroups;
   Foodies = ARRAY [FoodGroups] OF ARRAY [FoodGroups] OF FoodGroups;
   Poodies = ARRAY [ FoodGroups ] [ FoodGroups ] OF Rows;
   Woodies = ARRAY [ FoodGroups, FoodGroups ] OF Cols;
   Zoodies = ARRAY [ FoodGroups, FoodGroups ] OF Foodies;
```

40. Suppose you are given these declarations:

```
CONST
   Low  = 1;
   High = 50;

TYPE
   Rows = Low..High;
   Cols = Low..High;
   Sins = ( Drinking, Cussing, Carousing );
   Troubles = ARRAY [ Cols ] OF Sins;
   Inmates = ARRAY [ Rows ] OF Troubles;

VAR
   Convict : Inmates;
   Evil    : ARRAY [ Sins ] OF Rows;
```

Then state the type of each of the following items:

```
Convict
Convict[ 2 ]
Convict[ 3 ] [ 2 ]
Evil
Evil[ Cussing ]
```

37. Given the declarations

```
TYPE
   Rows     = 1..5;
   Cols     = 2..3;
   SalArray = ARRAY [ Rows, Cols ] OF Real;

VAR
   Salary, Monies : SalArray;
   R              : Rows;
   C              : Cols;
```

which of these statements are syntactically illegal? Why?

```
Salary[ 3, 2 ] := 111.95;
Salary := 0.0;
Salary [3][2] := 999.15;
Salary[5,1] := 123.45;
```

14.9 CASE STUDY: THE PAYROLL PROGRAM REVISITED

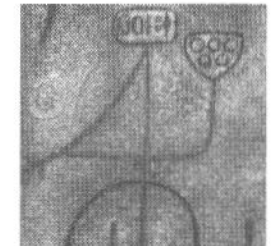

As an example of using a two-dimensional array, we modify the payroll program of Section 14.7 so that it handles a payroll involving up to 50 employees who are paid varying amounts during each of four weekly pay periods. The first employee will be paid, over the four-period month, the amounts stored in row 1 of the array:

```
Pay[1,1],  Pay[1,2],  Pay[1,3],  Pay[1,4].
```

Suppose that we want the program to display the total monthly pay for each employee, as well as the average total pay for the month. To accomplish this, we keep a running sum of the current employee's pay and, once we have the total, we add it to the combined total for all employees. After we have the grand total, we divide it by the number of employees to get the average total pay per employee:

```
TotalOfTotals := 0.0;
FOR Employee := 1 TO NumEmployees DO
BEGIN

   Write( Name[Employee], '    ' );

   TotalPay := 0.0;
   FOR PayPeriod := 1 TO NumOfPayPeriods DO
   BEGIN

      ThisPay  := Pay[Employee, PayPeriod];
      TotalPay := TotalPay + ThisPay;
      Write( '$', ThisPay:6:2, '    ' )

   END; {FOR PayPeriod}

   {-- Display this employee's total pay }
   WriteLn( '$', TotalPay:7:2 );
```

```
      {
       -- Add this employee's total pay to the total
          for all employees
      }
      TotalOfTotals := TotalOfTotals + TotalPay

   END; {FOR Employee}

   WriteLn;
   WriteLn( 'Average total pay = $',
           (TotalOfTotals / NumEmployees):7:2 );
```

With these additions, we have the program shown on the following pages. In this version, `ShowPay` uses `VAR` parameters to avoid having to copy the arrays. This issue was discussed at the end of Section 14.7.

```
PROGRAM Payroll2 (Input, Output);
{
  Reads list of employee names and for each employee, the
  amount of pay for each of four pay periods. Displays a chart
  of these data plus total pay for each employee and average
  total pay for all employees.
}
CONST
   MaxEmployees = 50;  { Maximum number of employees }
   MaxPeriods   = 4;   { Maximum number of pay periods }
   ColumnWidth  = 43;  { Width of column in displayed table }

TYPE
   EmployeeRange  = 1..MaxEmployees;
   PayPeriodRange = 1..MaxPeriods;
   NameString     = PACKED ARRAY[ 1..40 ] OF Char;
   NameArray      = ARRAY[ EmployeeRange ] OF NameString;
   PayArray       = ARRAY[ EmployeeRange, PayPeriodRange ] OF Real;

VAR
   Name         : NameArray;      { Array of employee names }
   Pay          : PayArray;       { Array of employee pay amounts }
   NumEmployees : EmployeeRange;  { Actual number of employees }
   NumPeriods   : PayPeriodRange; { Actual number of pay periods }


PROCEDURE ReadLnStr( VAR Str : NameString );
BEGIN
   {
      A simple ReadLn will work in many real-world Pascals.
      Standard Pascal, however, requires that you read
      strings character-by-character. See Section 14.6.
   }
   ReadLn( Str )

END; { ReadLnStr }
```

```
{------------------------------------------------------}
{ Read payroll data from the keyboard.                  }
{------------------------------------------------------}
PROCEDURE GetPayData( VAR NumEmployees : EmployeeRange;
                      VAR NumPeriods   : PayPeriodRange;
                      VAR Name : NameArray;
                      VAR Pay  : PayArray );
VAR
   Employee  : EmployeeRange;
   PayPeriod : PayPeriodRange;
   IntNumber : Integer;

BEGIN

   REPEAT
      Write( 'Number of employees? <1 TO 50> ' );
      ReadLn( IntNumber )
   UNTIL ( IntNumber >= 1 ) AND ( IntNumber <= MaxEmployees );
   NumEmployees := IntNumber;
   WriteLn;

   REPEAT
      Write( 'Number pay periods? <1 TO 4> ' );
      ReadLn( IntNumber )
   UNTIL ( IntNumber >= 1 ) AND ( IntNumber <= MaxPeriods );
   NumPeriods := IntNumber;
   WriteLn;
   WriteLn;

   WriteLn( 'Enter names of employees:' );
   FOR Employee := 1 TO NumEmployees DO
      ReadLnStr( Name[Employee] );

   {-- Get pay for each period for each employee }
   FOR PayPeriod := 1 TO NumPeriods DO
   BEGIN
      WriteLn;
      WriteLn( 'Enter amounts of pay for pay period #', PayPeriod:1, ':' );

      FOR Employee := 1 TO NumEmployees DO
      BEGIN
         Write( 'Pay for ', Name[Employee], ':  ' );
         ReadLn( Pay[Employee, PayPeriod] )
      END; { FOR Employee }

   END { FOR PayPeriod }

END; { GetPayData }
```

```
{-----------------------------------------------------------------}
{ Show list of employees and their pay, with total pay for each   }
{ and average pay for all.                                         }
{-----------------------------------------------------------------}
PROCEDURE ShowPay( NumEmployees    : EmployeeRange;
                   NumOfPayPeriods : PayPeriodRange;
                   VAR Name        : NameArray;
                   VAR Pay         : PayArray );
VAR
   PayPeriod : PayPeriodRange;
   Employee  : EmployeeRange;
   TotalPay, ThisPay, TotalOfTotals : Real;

BEGIN

   WriteLn;
   WriteLn( 'SUMMARY' );
   WriteLn( '-------' );
   WriteLn;
   Write( 'Employee', ' ':ColumnWidth-10 );

   FOR PayPeriod := 1 TO NumOfPayPeriods DO
      Write( 'PayPeriod ', PayPeriod:1, '    ' );

   WriteLn( '  Total Pay' );
   WriteLn;

   {
     Write each employee's name, followed on same line
     by pay amounts and then total pay
   }
   TotalOfTotals := 0.0;
   FOR Employee := 1 TO NumEmployees DO
   BEGIN

      { --Write an employee's name: }
      Write( Name[Employee], ' ':ColumnWidth-40 );

      {--List employee's pay on same line and compute total pay: }
      TotalPay := 0.0;
      FOR PayPeriod := 1 TO NumOfPayPeriods DO
      BEGIN
         ThisPay := Pay[ Employee, PayPeriod ];
         TotalPay := TotalPay + ThisPay;
         Write( '$', ThisPay:6:2, '      ' )
      END; { FOR PayPeriod }

      {--Write that employee's total pay on same line }
      WriteLn( '  $', TotalPay:7:2 );

      {-- Add this employee's total pay to the grand total }
      TotalOfTotals := TotalOfTotals + TotalPay

   END; { FOR Employee }
```

```
   WriteLn;
   WriteLn( 'Average total pay = $',
            (TotalOfTotals / NumEmployees):7:2 );
   WriteLn

END;  { ShowPay }


BEGIN { main program }

   GetPayData( NumEmployees, NumPeriods, Name, Pay );
   { GetPayData returns values of NumEmployees and NumPeriods > 0 }

   ShowPay( NumEmployees, NumPeriods, Name, Pay )

END.
```

LOOKING BACK

This chapter has introduced the concept of a *data structure*: a collection of data values accessed under a single name and organized so that each value can be accessed individually. In this chapter, we have examined the homogeneous data structures called *arrays*. In an array, we use subscripts to access the individual elements. Arrays have both advantages and disadvantages:

- The subscripts used to access the individual elements in an array can be calculated by the program, so the process of accessing elements can be automated easily. This is an advantage.
- The range of subscripts in an array must be declared before the program is compiled. All elements must have the same type, which also must be declared. Thus, the size of an array is statically declared; that is, it cannot be changed while the program is running. The program must therefore declare its arrays to be at least as large as will ever be needed. When fewer array elements are used during a run, the program wastes memory. This is a disadvantage.
- There is only one whole-array operation; the values in one array can be assigned to another array of the same type. Other desirable operations, like reading an array, are not provided by Standard Pascal. This is another disadvantage.

We discussed both singly and multiply dimensioned arrays:

- A one-dimensional array has only one subscript, and is imagined as a list or vector. The elements are stored in sequence in memory, beginning with the address of the lowest-subscripted element.
- A two-dimensional array has two subscripts, and is imagined as a table with rows and columns. The first subscript is considered to be the row label, while the second subscript is considered to be the column label. Such an array is stored row-wise in memory.
- An array can have more than two subscripts, in which case it is imagined as a multidimensioned table.

Subscripts in arrays can be of any ordinal type:

- A subscript normally ranges over a declared subrange of an ordinal type, from a low constant value to a higher constant value.
- If the constants are declared up front, the program will be more easily checked and maintained. If the array size must be changed later, the programmer can simply change the appropriate constants at the front of the program.

Loops are usually used to access a number of array elements in sequence:

- `FOR` loops are particularly suitable.
- The program can compute the sequence of subscripts corresponding to the elements to be accessed.
- The program can use loops to sweep through an entire array or part of it.

The most common errors in dealing with arrays are subscript errors:

- The programmer must design the program so that subscripts cannot go outside their declared ranges.
- It is all too easy for a loop to carry a subscript slightly too far, or to start or stop just short of the correct value. Watch out for fencepost errors.

Arrays pose special problems when sent to subprograms:

- When sending large array parameters to subprograms, it is often desirable to make them `VAR` parameters, so that duplicates of the large array will not be stored.
- When using a subprogram to operate on only a *part* of an array, the subscript values marking the boundaries of that part must also be sent to the subprogram.

We had a first look at an algorithm for sorting arrays, an algorithm called *selection sort*. When an array contains N elements, this algorithm requires roughly N^2 comparisons between array elements to perform the sort, no matter whether the array is in random order or partially sorted to begin with. N^2 comparisons consume enough computer time for large arrays that we will find it necessary to investigate more advanced sorting algorithms in Chapter 19.

In Section 14.5, we studied special string arrays, which are used to store text. In Standard Pascal, string arrays are characterized by several special properties:

- They are arrays of `Char`.
- They are `PACKED`.
- They have elements numbered `1..`L, where $L \geq 2$.

In Standard Pascal, string arrays are accorded special privileges not shared by other arrays. In particular, their values can be assigned, they can be written by `Write` and `WriteLn`, and strings of equal length can be compared by relational operators. However, Standard Pascal does not allow `Read` and `ReadLn` to read strings from the keyboard or other text files and does not provide most of the other useful string operations. Therefore, we designed some of our own string procedures and functions in Section 14.6.

TERMS EMPHASIZED IN THIS CHAPTER

PROJECTS

1. A vector **A** is a one-dimensional array of numbers whose length is given by

$$\text{Length}(A) = \sqrt{\sum_{i=1}^{n} A_i^2} = \sqrt{A_1^2 + A_2^2 + \cdots + A_n^2}$$

Write a `Length` function that computes the length of a given vector having a given number of real elements. Allow for the possibility that the array may be only partially filled, or may even be empty.

2. The standard deviation of a set of numbers is a statistical measure of the probable deviation from average. The larger the standard deviation, the more the numbers are scattered away from the average; the smaller the standard deviation, the more tightly the numbers are clustered around the average. There are two kinds of standard deviation: *population* standard deviation and *sample* standard deviation. The latter is more suitable for small sets, and is defined to be the root-mean square deviation; that is, it is defined as the square root of the average of the squares of the deviations from average. Mathematically, if the numbers in the set are called A_1, A_2, ..., AN, the sample standard deviation is defined as

$$\sigma = \sqrt{\frac{\sum_{i=1}^{N}\left(A_i - \overline{A}\right)^2}{N-1}}$$

where A with an overbar indicates the average of all the A_i. A little algebra yields the relation

$$\sigma^2 = \frac{\sum_{i=1}^{N} A_i^2}{N-1} - \frac{\left(\sum_{i=1}^{N} A_i\right)^2}{N(N-1)}$$

where the quantity σ^2 is called the *sample variance*. This formula is used in many hand-held calculators. It facilitates calculating the variance, and therefore the standard deviation, from a list of numbers as they are entered at the keyboard. Using this formula, write a function that returns the sample standard deviation of a one-dimensional array of real numbers. Allow for the possibility that the array may be only partially filled or even empty.

Note: Although this formula is correct, the approximate nature of real-number calculations in a computer sometimes causes it to fail. If the array elements are very close together, the two terms in the formula may be relatively large and almost equal. In such a case, subtracting one term from the other will cause cancellation error—a situation in which many, perhaps even all, of the significant digits are lost. Try, for example, giving your function the array elements

1.0000000, 1.0000001, and 1.0000002

Your function may find no standard deviation among these values. Your hand-held calculator may do just as badly. However, Project 3 describes a better algorithm.

3. Write a function that computes the sample standard deviation of a one-dimensional array containing the elements $X_1, X_2, \ldots, XN$. Standard deviation should be calculated by means of the *recurrence relation*

$$\sigma_N^2 = \left(\frac{N-2}{N-1}\right)\sigma_{N-1}^2 + \left[\frac{N}{(N-1)^2}\right](X_N - A_N)^2$$

for the sample standard deviation σN of N data items. Here AN is the average of the first N elements of the array, and σ_0 and σ_1 are defined to be zero. Allow for the possibility that the array may be only partially filled or even empty.

4. Suppose the `Word` array contains up to five characters:

```
VAR
   Word : ARRAY [ 1..5 ] OF Char;
```

Write a procedure that displays all possible permutations of the characters in `Word`, allowing for the possibility that the array is not full.

5. Write a boolean function that reports whether a given singly dimensioned array is ordered—that is, whether each element is no greater than the next element. Allow for the possibility that the array may be only partially filled or even empty.

6. Write a procedure that deletes from a one-dimensional character array all characters that have already appeared in the array. The deletion process should push all non-deleted characters down toward the front of the array. Afterward, any unused elements at the end of the array should be filled with spaces. Example: If the array initially contains `abcadbbecf`, it should wind up containing `abcdefΔΔΔΔ`, where Δ indicates a space. Allow for the possibility that the array may be only partially filled or may even be empty.

7. The `Val` function of Section 14.6 is not protected from the possibility that a user will enter a string representing an integer magnitude too large for `Integer` storage. For example, when running under Turbo Pascal, where the `Integer` type stores a maximum value of 32767, `Val` returns the following values:

   `Val( '32766' )` returns `32766`
   `Val( '32767' )` returns `32767`
   `Val( '32768' )` returns `-32768`
   `Val( '32769' )` returns `-32767`

Improve the Val function so that it returns 0 if it is sent a number larger than the maximum storable integer.

8. The following function uses the declaration of `Pay` given in Section 14.7. The function is supposed to return the average annual salary received by employees, but it does not give the correct result. Show how to correct the error.

```
FUNCTION AverageAnnualPay( P : PayArray ) : Real;
VAR
   Empl   : LowEmployee..HighEmployee;
   Per    : LowPeriod..HighPeriod;
   Num    : Integer;
   TotPay : Real;

BEGIN

   Num := ( HighEmployee - LowEmployee + 1 )
            * ( HighPeriod - LowPeriod + 1 );

   TotPay := 0.0;
   FOR Empl := LowEmployee TO HighEmployee DO
      FOR Per := LowPeriod TO HighPeriod DO
         TotPay := TotPay + P[ Empl, Per ];

   AverageAnnualPay := TotPay / Num

END; { AverageAnnualPay }
```

10. Write a procedure that *transposes* a two-dimensional square array. That is, given an array with equal numbers of rows and columns, the procedure should swap rows and columns. For example,

1 2 3		1 4 7
4 5 6	should be changed to	2 5 8
7 8 9		3 6 9

11. A *histogram* is a graph showing the frequency with which a given array contains values in specified intervals of its range. For example, if a one-dimensional integer array has elements of type `0..9` and happens to contain the 15 values

```
6, 4, 4, 1, 9, 7, 5, 6, 4, 2, 3, 9, 5, 6, 4
```

then its histogram would be

This indicates that 0 and 8 do not appear in the array, while 1, 2, 3, and 7 appear once; that 5 and 9 appear twice; that 6 appears three times; and that 4 appears four times. Write a procedure that displays a histogram of the above form for any given array having elements belonging to the integer subrange `0..9`. Allow for the possibility that the array may be only partially filled or even empty. (Hint: Plot the histogram rotated 90 degrees clockwise, so that the value intervals go down the screen instead of to the right. Then each bar of the histogram will be plotted to the right across a row of the screen.)

12. Write a boolean function that reports whether a given square, two-dimensional array A is symmetric; that is, whether $Aij = Aji$ for all i and j.

13. A maze can be represented by a square array containing characters representing walls and passages. If we use asterisks to symbolize walls and spaces to symbolize passages, a typical 20 x 20 maze might look like this:

Write a modularized program that

- Initializes such an array.
- Asks the user for a starting point.
- Automatically finds a path through the maze.
- Displays the path to the user.

(Hints: Whenever the algorithm comes to a fork in the path, it should always try the same side of the fork first. If this side leads to a dead end, the algorithm should backtrack to the fork and try the other side. Properly used recursion can make the algorithm simpler.)

14. The Game of Life—a survival simulation game—was invented by John H. Conway, a Cambridge mathematician, and first reported in print by Martin Gardner in the October 1970 issue of *Scientific American* magazine. (Look it up.) It has become one of the legendary pastimes among programmers. The game runs on a square, two-dimensional array, representing a flat surface that can contain "creatures." Initially, the surface is sprinkled randomly with creatures; that is, each cell in the two-dimensional grid is randomly either empty or occupied by a creature. Then the program goes into a loop, each trip through which represents a "tick" of the environmental clock. At each tick, creatures propagate or die according to two immutable laws:

a. An empty cell contains a "birth" if at least three neighboring cells contain creatures.

b. In an occupied cell, the creature continues to live for another tick if and only if neighboring cells contain at least two but not more than three creatures.

Thus the game simulates in a crude way the effects of congregation, loneliness, and overcrowding. Write a modular program that plays the Game of Life, using the following declarations:

```
CONST
   Size = 20;

TYPE
   IndexRange = 1..Size;
   Cells      = ( Empty, Occupied );
   GridArray  = ARRAY [ IndexRange, IndexRange ] OF Cells;
```

Fill your array by "flipping a coin" for each cell, using a random-number generator provided by your Pascal system or like the one described in Appendix I. Notice that each cell has eight neighbors—up, down, right, left, and diagonally—except for the cells on the edge of the grid. Keep your algorithm from walking off the edge of the grid.

15. Write a version of the Game of Life in which the grid "wraps around" both horizontally and vertically. That is, the next cell to the "right" of the last cell on a row is the cell at the beginning of the row; the next cell "below" the cell at the bottom of a column is the cell at the top of the column. This is the effect you would get if you wrapped your grid horizontally and vertically to form a doughnut. (Hint: use `MOD` arithmetic.)

16. The planet of Wa-tor is doughnut-shaped and entirely covered by water. In the water live two species: sharks and fish. The fish always have enough food, but sharks can live only if they have enough nearby fish to eat. On the other hand, if the sharks eat too many fish, the sharks will start to die off. When lots of fishes or sharks get together with members of their own species, the species propagates. These observations imply that the populations of fishes and sharks might fluctuate. As the fish population grows, the sharks will propagate. Then the more-numerous sharks will eat up a lot of fishes, which in turn will lead to starvation of sharks. Then the fishes will be able to recover, and so on. Write a modular program that simulates life conditions on Wa-tor, using the ideas described in Projects 12 and 13. The game of Wa-tor was described in detail in the December 1984 issue of *Scientific American* magazine, on pages 14–22. It would be very helpful to read this material.

17. Pascal's Triangle is the array of integers shown below:

```
          1
       1     1
     1    2    1
  1    3    3    1
1    4    6    4    1
1    5  10  10  5    1
```

and so on, where each number except the first and last on a row is the sum of the two most nearly above it. The numbers in Pascal's Triangle are the binomial coefficients. Write a procedure that generates and displays Pascal's Triangle.

18. After 2, all the prime integers are odd. A scheme for finding the primes among the 1000 odd integers from 3 to 2001 goes like this: The first 1000 odd integers after 1 are given by $2i + 1$, where i ranges from 1 to 1000. We set up a 1000-element boolean array called `Prime`, where `Prime[ I ]` is used to indicate whether `2I + 1` is a prime number. We initialize the array to `True`, indicating that, as far as we know to begin with, all odd integers could be prime numbers. Then we progressively rule out many of the numbers as follows:

- Three is a prime number, so its multiples cannot be primes. To indicate this, we set the array elements corresponding to multiples of 3 to `False`. The multiples of 3 are $2(2 \cdot 1 + 1), 3(2 \cdot 1 + 1), 4(2 \cdot 1 + 1), \ldots$, but the only ones of these that concern us are the odd multiples of the form $(2K + 1)(2 \cdot 1 + 1)$, where $K = 1, 2, 3, \ldots$. Therefore, set to `False` the corresponding array elements.

- Five was not ruled out in the first step because it is not a multiple of 3. Therefore, it must be a prime. Rule out all of its odd multiples, which are of the form $(2K + 1)(2 \cdot 2 + 1)$. Therefore, set to `False` the corresponding array elements.

- Seven has not been ruled out, so it must be a prime. Rule out its odd multiples, which are of the form $(2K + 1)(2 \cdot 3 + 1)$. Therefore, set to `False` the corresponding array elements.

- Nine has been ruled out because it is an odd multiple of a previously considered prime.

- Eleven has not been ruled out, so it must be a prime.

And so on. Each step has the following form:

> If $(2I + 1)$ has not yet been ruled out, it is a prime, so rule out its odd multiples by setting to `False` the array elements corresponding to numbers of the form $(2K + 1)(2I + 1)$.

In order to perform the ruling out, notice that $(2K + 1)(2I + 1)$ is $4KI + 2(K + I) + 1$. This is an odd number, and therefore of the form $2J + 1$. Solving for J, we find that $J = 2KI + K + I$. Therefore, we set to `False` all elements `Prime[2*K*I + K + I]`, where `K` takes on the values 1, 2, 3, . . . , as long as `2*K*I + K + I` does not go beyond the end of the array. This algorithm was first recorded by the Greek mathematician Eratosthenes about 450 BC. Of course, he didn't have a computer or arrays. Write a procedure that uses this algorithm to display all primes among the first 1,000 odd numbers after 1.

18. The book *Intelligent Life in the Universe*, by I. S. Shklovskii and Carl Sagan (Delta, 1966, page 423), reports the following problem, suggested by Frank Drake. You are a radio astronomer and you have received this transmission from the depths of interstellar space:

```
11110000010100100001100100000000100000010100
10000001100101100111100000110000110100000
0010000001000010000100010101000010000000000
00000000001000100000000000010110000000000000
000000010001110110101101010000000000000000
00001001000011101010101000000000101010101
000000000111010101011101011000000001000000
000000000001000000000000010001001111111000
00111010000010110000001110000000010000000000
10000000001000000001111110000000101100010111 0
10000000110010111110101111100010011111001
000000000001111110000000101100011111100000
10000011000001100001000011000000001100010 1
001000111100101111
```

This message was repeated many times, so there is no question of its being radio noise rather than a significant pattern. But is it a deliberate communication from another civilization? You notice that there are 551 bits, that 551 factors uniquely as the product of 19 and 29, and that 19 and 29 are both prime numbers. This seems too unique to be an accident. You therefore surmise that this message might actually be a 19 x 29 or 29 x 19 array of booleans. You further surmise that the array of booleans might actually represent an image made up of dots. Test your hypothesis by displaying a visual representation of the array. If you discover an image that appears to be an intelligent communication, try to interpret what it means.

REFERENCES

The following books describe how array elements are stored in memory, and how the CPU locates a given element in an array by computing its address from the subscripts:

- Daniel D. McCracken, *A Second Course in Computer Science with Pascal* (John Wiley & Sons, 1987).
- Daniel F. Stubbs and Neil W. Webre, *Data Structures with Abstract Data Types and Pascal*, second edition (Brooks/Cole, 1989).

Many useful array procedures are developed in R. G. Dromey's *How to Solve It by Computer* (Prentice Hall, 1982).

Minds, Brains, and Programs

[A reply to those who interpret the Turing Test as indicating the nature of human intelligence. See "The Turing Test," at the end of Chapter 1.]

One way to test any theory of the mind is to ask oneself what it would be like if my mind actually worked on the principles that the theory says all minds work on. Let us apply this test . . . with the following *Gedankenexperiment*. Suppose that I am locked in a room and given a large batch of Chinese writing. Suppose furthermore (as is indeed the case) that I know no Chinese, either written or spoken, and that I'm not even confident that I could recognize Chinese writing as Chinese writing distinct from, say, Japanese writing or meaningless squiggles. . . . Now suppose further that after this first batch of Chinese writing I am given a second batch of Chinese script together with a set of rules for correlating the second batch with the first batch. The rules are in English, and I understand these rules as well as any other native speaker of English. They enable me to correlate one set of formal symbols with another set of formal symbols, and all that "formal" means here is that I can identify the symbols entirely by their shapes. Now suppose also that I am given a third batch of Chinese symbols together with some instructions, again in English, that enable me to correlate elements of this third batch with the first two batches, and these rules instruct me how to give back certain Chinese symbols with certain sorts of shapes in response to certain sorts of shapes given me in the third batch. Unknown to me, the people who are giving me all of these symbols call the first batch a "script," they call the second batch a "story," and they call the third batch "questions." Furthermore, they call the symbols I give them back in response to the third batch "answers to the questions," and the set of rules in English that they gave me, they call the "program." Now just to complicate the story a little, imagine that these people also give me stories in English, which I understand, and they then ask me questions in English about these stories, and I give them back answers in English. Suppose also that after a while I get so good at following the instructions for manipulating the Chinese symbols and the programmers get so good at writing the programs that from the external point of view—that is, from the point of view of somebody outside the room in which I am locked—my answers to the questions are absolutely indistinguishable from those of native Chinese speakers. Nobody just looking at my answers can tell that I don't speak a word of Chinese. Let us also suppose that my answers to the English questions are, as they no doubt would be, indistinguishable from those of other native English speakers, for the simple reason that I am a native English speaker. From the external point of view . . . the answers to the Chinese questions and the English questions are equally good. But in the Chinese case, unlike the English case, I produce the answers by manipulating uninterpreted symbols. As far as the Chinese is concerned, I behave like a computer. . . . I am simply an instantiation of a computer program.

Gedankenexperiment: German for "thought experiment"—an experiment performed in the imagination.

Now the claims made by [some proponents of artificial intelligence] are that the programmed computer understands the stories and that the program in some sense explains human understanding.

–John R. Searle, "Minds, Brains, and Programs," from *The Behavioral and Brain Sciences*, volume 3 (Cambridge University Press, 1980). Reprinted in Douglas R. Hofstadter and Daniel C. Dennett, *The Mind's I: Fantasies and Reflections on Self and Soul* (Basic Books, 1981), pages 353-56.

CHAPTER

15

Records

CHAPTER CONTENTS

INTRODUCTION

In an array, all of the elements must be of the same type; different types of data cannot share the same array. But there are many situations in everyday programming that demand data of several different types, grouped together. Consider a program that maintains employee records. For each employee, we want to list the employee's name, his or her Social Security number, and salary. A typical record of this type might be

Name:	Leopold Bloom
Social Security number:	987-65-4321
Salary:	$1234.56

As you saw in Section 14.7, we can store such records in a set of three parallel arrays, so that if Mr. Bloom is the first employee in the list, his name will be stored in `Name[1]`, his Social Security number in `SS[1]`, and his salary in `Salary[1]`. The arrays could be declared as follows:

```
TYPE
   EmployeeRange = 1..50;
   String40      = PACKED ARRAY [ 1..40 ] OF Char;
   String40Array = ARRAY [ EmployeeRange ] OF String40;
   RealArray     = ARRAY [ EmployeeRange ] OF Real;

VAR
   Name, SS : String40Array;
   Salary   : RealArray;
```

Unfortunately, the data record for a particular employee is never available as a unit; it is scattered over three arrays. For example, when passing employee data to a subprogram, we would have to pass three arrays as parameters. For this reason, Pascal also provides **record types** in which heterogeneous data can be grouped together into one data object called a **record**. A record is therefore a **heterogeneous data structure**.

15.1 RECORD TYPES

As our first example of a record type, consider storing the bibliographic data for a computer science journal article. We want to store authors' names, the title of the paper, the name of the journal, the volume number (an integer), the initial page number (integer), and the year (integer). Thus, there are three strings to be stored together with three integers. In Pascal, we might write declarations like these:

```
TYPE
   String40 = PACKED ARRAY [1..40] OF Char;
   JournalArticle =
        RECORD
           Author  : String40;
           Title   : String40;
           Journal : String40;
           Volume  : Integer;
           Page    : Integer;
           Year    : Integer
        END;

VAR
   Paper : JournalArticle;
```

(Notice the `END` with no `BEGIN`.) This record contains three `String40` objects, which are arrays. This is an example of the fact that a record can contain other composite types.

Identifying the record fields

According to these declarations, we have a `Paper` variable, which is a single record. It consists of six **record fields**, each of which has a **record field name** or **identifier** formed from the record name, followed by a period and then the field name:

- `Paper.Author` is the name of the first field, which is a string of 40 characters.
- `Paper.Title` is the name of the second field, which is a string of 40 characters.
- `Paper.Journal` is the name of the third field, which is a string of 40 characters.
- `Paper.Volume` is the name of the fourth field, which is an integer.
- `Paper.Page` is the name of the fifth field, which is also an integer.
- `Paper.Year` is the name of the sixth field, which is again an integer.

The record and its fields can be pictured as shown in Figure 15.1.1.

Initializing a record variable

As with all other composite data types except string arrays, there is no record constant, so a constant value cannot be assigned to a record variable. Instead, the various fields of the record must be assigned values individually. In our example, we can use the following code:

```
Paper.Author  := 'Dijkstra, E.                            ';
Paper.Title   := 'Go To Statement Considered Harmful      ';
Paper.Journal := 'Communications of the ACM               ';
```

A record of type JournalArticle and the fields within the record. **Figure 15.1.1**

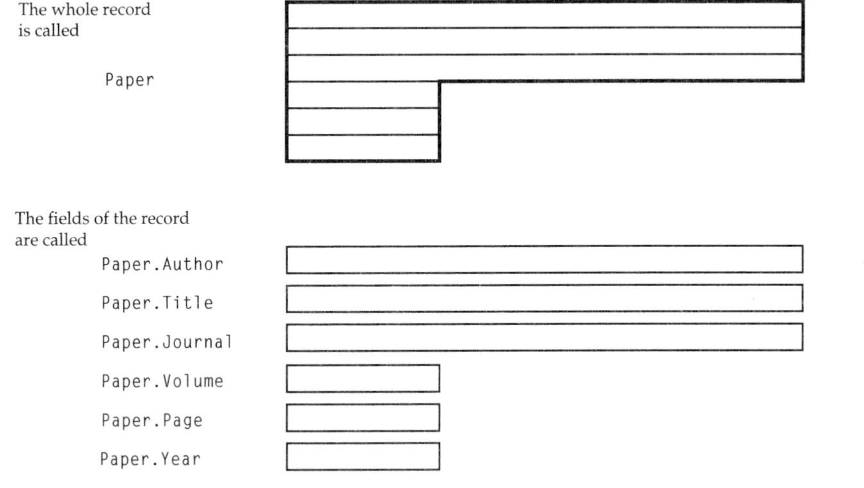

Syntax for a Record Type

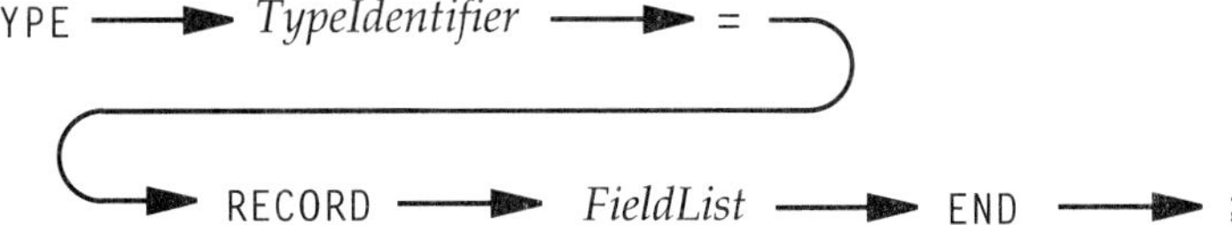

Pseudocode:

```
TYPE
   TypeIdentifier = RECORD
                       FieldList
                    END;
```

Notes:

- This syntax diagram does not allow for the less common variant records, which will be discussed in a later section.
- A *FieldList* is a list of field declarations, separated by semicolons.

Each *FieldDeclaration* takes the form

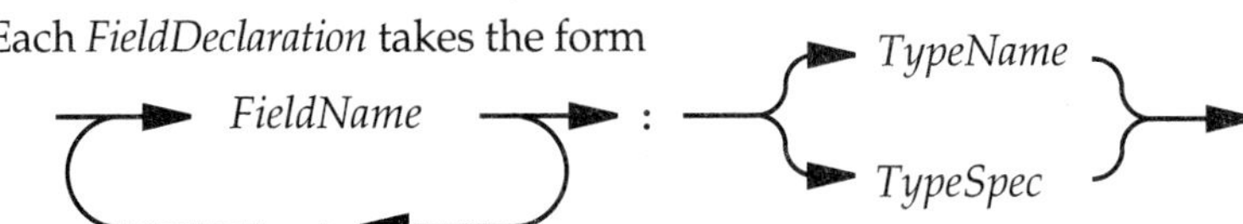

Here the term *TypeSpec* is a type specification. There is no limitation on the types of fields in a record, except that they cannot be the same type as the record itself. That is, a record type declaration cannot be recursive.

```
Paper.Volume  := 11;
Paper.Page    := 147;
Paper.Year    := 1968;
```

A whole record can be assigned.

The only whole-record operation provided by Pascal is the assignment statement. If `Paper1` and `Paper2` are two records of *exactly the same type* (in this example, type `JournalArticle`), then the value of one can be assigned to the other:

```
Paper1 := Paper2;
```

This accomplishes the same thing as if we copied all the fields separately:

```
Paper1.Author  := Paper2.Author;
Paper1.Title   := Paper2.Title;
Paper1.Journal := Paper2.Journal;
Paper1.Volume  := Paper2.Volume;
Paper1.Page    := Paper2.Page;
Paper1.Year    := Paper2.Year;
```

Reading data into a record

As with other composite types except strings, we cannot read an entire record at once from the keyboard or other text files; instead, the `Read` and `ReadLn` procedures must read the fields one by one. As we have done in the past, we will want to write our own procedure for reading a record.

```
{----------------------------------------------------------}
{ Reads bibliographic data for journal article from the    }
{ keyboard. Six fields are read:                           }
{   1. Authors' name(s)                                    }
{   2. Title of paper                                      }
{   3. Name of journal                                     }
{   4. Journal volume number                               }
{   5. Page number                                         }
{   6. Year                                                }
{                                                          }
{ OTHER PROCEDURES REQUIRED:                               }
{   ReadLnStr  (reads a String40 value)                    }
{----------------------------------------------------------}
PROCEDURE ReadJournalArticle( VAR Paper : JournalArticle );
BEGIN

   WriteLn( 'Author or authors: (40-character maximum)' );
   ReadLnStr( Paper.Author );

   WriteLn( 'Title of paper: (40-character maximum)' );
   ReadLnStr( Paper.Title );

   WriteLn( 'Name of journal: (40-character maximum)' );
   ReadLnStr( Paper.Journal );
```

```
   WriteLn( 'Volume number: (integer)' );
   ReadLn( Paper.Volume );

   WriteLn( 'Starting page number: (integer)' );
   ReadLn( Paper.Page );

   WriteLn( 'Year: (4-digit integer)' );
   ReadLn( Paper.Year );
   WriteLn

END; { ReadJournalArticle }
```

As the documentation says, this procedure assumes that we have a `ReadLnString` procedure that reads values into a `String40` variable. Such a procedure can be built as part of a `String40` ADT similar to the one shown in Section 14.6.

Writing a record

To write a record to the screen or other text files, we write the fields separately. If we assume that a record has already received a value by assignment or by means of `ReadJournalArticle`, then we can display its contents with the help of a procedure like the one shown below. We assume that we already have a `WriteStr` procedure that can display `String40`s.

```
{----------------------------------------------------------}
{ Displays bibliographic data for journal article.         }
{                                                          }
{ OTHER PROCEDURES REQUIRED:                               }
{   WriteStr  (writes a String40 value)                    }
{----------------------------------------------------------}
PROCEDURE WriteJournalArticle( Paper : JournalArticle );
BEGIN

   Write( 'Author(s):  ' );
   WriteStr( Paper.Author );
   WriteLn;

   Write( 'Title    :  ' );
   WriteStr( Paper.Title );
   WriteLn;

   Write( 'Journal  :  ' );
   WriteStr( Paper.Journal );
   WriteLn;

   Write( 'Volume   :  ' );
   WriteLn( Paper.Volume:4 );

   Write( 'Page     :  ' );
   WriteLn( Paper.Page:4 );

   Write( 'Year     :  ' );
   WriteLn( Paper.Year:4 );
   WriteLn

END; { WriteJournalArticle }
```

Sample output from the `WriteJournalArticle` procedure looks like this:

```
Author(s):  Shaw, M.
Title    :  Abstraction Techniques in Mod Prog Langs
Journal  :  IEEE Software
Volume   :     1
Page     :    10
Year     :  1984
```

Questions

1. What is the conceptual difference between arrays and records?
2. Is it possible to reuse the same identifier in a record, as shown in the following example? (Try it and see what your compiler says.) If not, can any two of the identifiers be the same?

```
TYPE
   Redundant = RECORD
                  Redundant : Integer;
                  Redundant : Real
               END;
```

3. An array is said to be a *homogeneous* data structure, while a record is said to be a *heterogeneous* data structure. What does this mean?
4. A program contains the declarations

```
TYPE
   SignalColor  = ( Red, Yellow, Green );
   TrafficLight = RECORD
                     Color    : SignalColor;
                     Duration : Real
                  END;

VAR
   ThisLight : TrafficLight;
```

State the *type* of each of the following identifiers:

```
ThisLight
ThisLight.Color
ThisLight.Duration
```

5. What operations does Pascal provide to act on a record type? What other operations might be desirable?
6. Suppose you have the declarations

```
TYPE
   Science = RECORD
                Physical   : Char;
                Biological : Char
             END;

VAR
   SciA, SciB : Science;
```

and the initializations

```
SciA.Physical   := 'P';
SciB.Physical   := 'C';
SciA.Biological := 'B';
SciB.Biological := 'H';
```

Then what is displayed by the statements

```
WriteLn( SciA.Physical, SciA.Biological );
WriteLn( SciB.Physical, SciB.Biological );
```

7. In Question 6, if the initializations were

```
SciA.Physical   := 'P';
SciB.Physical   := 'C';
SciA.Biological := 'B';
SciB.Biological := 'H';
SciA := SciB;
SciA.Physical   := 'S';
SciB := SciA;
```

then what would be displayed?

8. Suppose we have the declarations

```
TYPE
   Str3 = PACKED ARRAY [ 1..3 ] OF Char;
   MonthDays = 1..31;

   Month = RECORD
              Abbrev   : Str3;
              NumDays  : MonthDays
           END;

VAR
   M, Mnth : Month;
   Mon   : RECORD
              Abbrev   : Str3;
              NumDays  : MonthDays
           END;
```

Then which of the following assignments are syntactically legal? Explain.

a. `Abbrev  := 'Jan';`

b. `NumDays := 31;`

c. `Mnth.Abbrev  := 'Feb';`

d. `Mnth.NumDays := 28;`

e. `M    := Mnth;`

f. `Mon := Mnth;`

Exercises

9. Write declarations for a record type and variable for storing registration data for an automobile. The following data must be stored in the record:

   a. Manufacturer's name, as a four-letter abbreviation.

   b. Model, as a 20-character string.

c. Year, as an integer.
d. Number of cylinders in engine, as an integer.
e. Liter displacement of engine, as a real number.
f. Annual registration fee (property tax), as a real number.

10. Write declarations for a record type and variable for storing the following information about a chemical element:
    a. The one- or two-letter symbol for the element. (For example, the symbol for carbon is `'C'`, while the symbol for silicon is `'Si'`.)
    b. The atomic number of the element, as an integer.
    c. The average atomic mass of the element, as a real number.

11. Write declarations for a record type and variable for storing a student's performance in class. The following data must be stored in the record:
    a. Student's last name, as a 40-character string.
    b. Student's first name and initial, as a 40-character string.
    c. Student's Social Security number, as a 40-character string.
    d. An array of up to four exam scores (integers).
    e. An array of up to six quiz scores (integers).
    f. The final cumulative score, as a percentage of the maximum possible score (a real number).

12. Write procedures that input and output record data of the kind described in Exercise 9.

13. Write procedures that input and output record data of the kind described in Exercise 10.

14. Write procedures that input and output record data of the kind described in Exercise 11.

15.2 ARRAYS OF RECORDS

In the previous section, we saw that a record can contain arrays. Conversely, it is often useful to build arrays in which the elements are records. Consider building a bibliographic array containing journal references of the type we used in the last section:

```
CONST
   BiblioSize = 100;

TYPE
   String40 = PACKED ARRAY [1..40] OF Char;

   JournalArticle =
        RECORD
           Author  : String40;
           Title   : String40;
           Journal : String40;
           Volume  : Integer;
           Page    : Integer;
           Year    : Integer
        END;

   Bibliography = ARRAY [ 1..BiblioSize ] OF JournalArticle;

VAR
   Biblio : Bibliography;
```

Identifying the record fields in an array of records

These declarations describe a `Biblio` array containing 100 records of `JournalArticle` type. This is a hierarchical declaration because the array contains records, each of which contains arrays and integers. The names of these objects reflect the hierarchy:

`Biblio` is the name of the whole array of records.

`Biblio[1]` is the name of the first record in the `Biblio` array.

`Biblio[1].Author` is the name of the first field of the first record. It is a string of 40 characters.

`Biblio[1].Title` is the name of the second field of the first record. It is a string of 40 characters.

`Biblio[1].Journal` is the name of the third field of the first record. It is a string of 40 characters.

`Biblio[1].Volume` is the name of the fourth field of the first record. It is an integer.

`Biblio[1].Page` is the name of the fifth field of the first record. It is an integer.

`Biblio[1].Year` is the name of the sixth field of the first record. It is an integer.

Figure 15.2.1 shows these relationships for the first two elements of the array.

Initializing an array of records

Of course, to fill an array of records, we must fill each record individually, which in turn requires filling each field of each record individually. Building on our previous work, it is easy to write a top-level procedure to fill a `Bibliography` array, calling the `ReadJournalArticle` procedure to fill each record. Note how the following procedure prevents the user from entering more records than the array will hold:

The first two elements of the Biblio array, an array of records. **Figure 15.2.1**

Biblio[1]	Biblio[2]
Biblio[1].Author:	Biblio[2].Author:
Biblio[1].Title:	Biblio[2].Title:
Biblio[1].Journal:	Biblio[2].Journal:
Biblio[1].Volume:	Biblio[2].Volume:
Biblio[1].Page:	Biblio[2].Page:
Biblio[1].Year:	Biblio[2].Year:

```
{-----------------------------------------------------------}
{ Reads journal articles for the entire bibliography.       }
{                                                           }
{ OTHER PROCEDURES REQUIRED:                                }
{   ReadJournalArticle  (reads record for one article)      }
{                                                           }
{ FUNCTIONS REQUIRED:                                       }
{   Upper  (from Chapter 8 or 9)                            }
{-----------------------------------------------------------}
PROCEDURE ReadBibliography( VAR Biblio   : Bibliography;
                            VAR NumRecs : NonNegInt );
VAR
   Answer     : Char;
   NoneToRead : Boolean;

BEGIN

   NoneToRead  := False;
   NumRecs     := 1;
   REPEAT

      ReadJournalArticle( Biblio[ NumRecs ] );
      WriteLn;

      IF NumRecs < BiblioSize THEN
      BEGIN
         Write( 'Another? <Y/N> ' );
         ReadLn( Answer );
         Answer := Upper( Answer );

         IF Answer = 'Y' THEN
            NumRecs := NumRecs + 1
         ELSE
            NoneToRead := True
      END

      ELSE
         NoneToRead := True;

      WriteLn

   UNTIL NoneToRead

END; { ReadBibliography }
```

Displaying an array of records

Similarly, it is trivial to display an array of records because we can call on our previous `WriteJournalArticle` procedure. We use a `VAR` parameter to minimize memory usage, as explained in Section 14.7.

```
{-----------------------------------------------------------}
{ Writes entire bibliography to the screen.                 }
{ The bibliography contains records for NumRecs articles.   }
{                                                           }
{ OTHER PROCEDURES REQUIRED:                                }
{   WriteJournalArticle  (writes record for one article)    }
{-----------------------------------------------------------}
PROCEDURE WriteBibliography( VAR Biblio  : Bibliography;
                             NumRecs     : NonNegInt );
VAR
   Index  : NonNegInt;

BEGIN

   FOR Index := 1 TO NumRecs DO
   BEGIN

      WriteJournalArticle( Biblio[ Index ] );
      WriteLn

   END

END; { WriteBibliography }
```

A sample display of an array of three records is shown below:

```
Author(s):  Parnas, D. L.
Title    :  Decomposing Systems into Modules
Journal  :  Communications of the ACM
Volume   :     5
Page     :  1053
Year     :  1972

Author(s):  Wirth, N.
Title    :  Composition of Well-Structured Programs
Journal  :  Computing Surveys
Volume   :     6
Page     :   247
Year     :  1974

Author(s):  Bastani, F. B., and Iyengar, S. S.
Title    :  Effct of Data Strucs on Logical Complxty
Journal  :  Communications of the ACM
Volume   :    30
Page     :   250
Year     :  1987
```

Other composites involving records

This section has shown an example of an array of records. Previously we saw an example of a record containing arrays of characters. Pascal allows all sorts of such compositions: We can have records containing other records, arrays of records of arrays, or just about anything we need. The only limitation is that a record cannot contain records of the same type as itself, because such a recursive type would never terminate.

Questions

15. What is the difference between an array of records and a record containing arrays?

16. What are the advantages of using an array of records instead of a set of parallel arrays?

17. Suppose you have a program in which parallel arrays are used to store structured data of some kind. If you change the program to use an array of records instead, will the new program require more storage space? Discuss.

18. Suppose that a program contains the declarations

```
CONST
   NumStudents = 25;
   NumExams    = 4;

TYPE
   String40 = PACKED ARRAY [ 1..40 ] OF Char;
   ExamList = ARRAY [ 1..NumExams ] OF Integer;

   StudentRec = RECORD
                   Name : String40;
                   Exam : ExamList;
                   Cum  : Real
                END;

   StudentList = ARRAY [ 1..NumStudents ]
                    OF StudentRec;

VAR
   Student : StudentList;
```

Then what is the *type* of each of the following identifiers?

a. `Student[2].Name`
b. `Student[2].Name[3]`
c. `Student[3].Exam`
d. `Student[3].Exam[1]`
e. `Student[1]`
f. `Student`

19. A program contains the declarations

```
CONST
   NumLights = 100;

TYPE
   SignalColor = ( Red, Yellow, Green );
   TrafficLight = RECORD
                     Color    : SignalColor;
                     Duration : Real
                  END;
   LightArray = ARRAY [ 1..NumLights ] OF TrafficLight;

VAR
   Light : LightArray;
```

Then what is the *type* of each of the following identifiers?

a. `Light`
b. `Light[22]`

c. `Light[22].Duration`

d. `Light[22].Color`

Exercises

20. Imagine that you are writing a program to control the airline departure and arrival video displays at an airport. One of the arrays you need to store will contain information on arriving flights. Each element of the array will represent one arriving airplane, using a record in which the fields are

  a. Name of airline, stored as a four-character abbreviation.

  b. City from which the plane is arriving (another four-character abbreviation).

  c. Gate at which the plane will arrive (an integer).

  d. Time of arrival (a five-character string like '21:34'). Write declarations for such an array.

21. Write declarations for an array representing a deck of playing cards, where each card is represented by a record containing the face value of the card and its suit. It's up to you to choose appropriate declarations.

22. The text mentions that a record can contain fields that are themselves records (though not records of the same type as the parent record). This is useful when dealing with hierarchies of data. For example, suppose you are storing an array of census data on families. Each family is represented by a record of the following structure:

  a. Family name, stored as a 40-character string.

  b. Street address, stored as a 40-character string.

  c. City, state, and zip code, stored as a 40-character string.

  d. Number of minors (under 18) in the family (a non-negative integer).

  e. Record for the father (see below).

  f. Record for the mother (see below). Records (e) and (f) store these data:

    1. Boolean indicating whether this parent is living in the home.

    2. Age (a non-negative integer; zero if deceased). Write type declarations for an array of 1,000 records of this kind.

23. Bruce Partington plans to write a procedure that swaps two records in an array of `Bibliography` type, but he can't figure out how to do it. Help him out by writing a procedure that receives the array and the indices of the two records as parameters.

24. Write a boolean function that reports whether the records in a `Bibliography` array are in ascending order according to their `Author` fields.

25. A program contains the declarations

```
TYPE
   Kind = ( Valencia, Dwarf );
   Orange = RECORD
               Variety : Kind;
               Weight  : Real
            END;

   PipArray = ARRAY [ 1..5 ] OF Orange;

VAR
   Pip : PipArray;
```

Make procedures to read and write the five elements of the `Pip` array. Write a driver program and test your procedures.

15.3 USING THE *WITH* STATEMENT

When writing code that refers frequently to the various fields of a given record such as `Paper.Author`, and `Paper.Title`, the long identifiers become tedious, so Pascal offers an alternative. A `WITH` statement can be used to enclose the statements referencing the same record, allowing those statements to use the field names alone. In other words, the following two samples of code are equivalent:

```
{ First version, using WITH }
WITH Paper DO
BEGIN

   WriteLn( 'Author or authors: (40-character maximum)' );
   ReadLnString( Author );

   WriteLn( 'Title of paper: (40-character maximum)' );
   ReadLnString( Title );
   .
   .
END; { WITH }

{ Second version, without WITH }
WriteLn( 'Author or authors: (40-character maximum)' );
ReadLnString( Paper.Author );

WriteLn( 'Title of paper: (40-character maximum)' );
ReadLnString( Paper.Title );
.
.
```

The field identifier can be used without its record identifier only within the `WITH` structure. The general syntax is shown on the next page.

Example of precedence with nested WITHs

Consider this pair of nested `WITH` structures:

```
WITH Biblio[ M ] DO
BEGIN

   Write( 'Author:  ' );
   ReadLnString( Author );

   WITH Biblio[ N ] DO
   BEGIN

      Write( 'Title of article:  ' );
      ReadLnString( Title )

   END; { WITH Biblio[ N ] }

   Write( 'Journal:  ' );
   ReadLnString( Journal )

END; { WITH Biblio[ M ] }
```

The outer `WITH` encompasses all three `ReadLnString` statements, but the inner `WITH` encompasses only the second, and this overrides the outer `WITH`'s scope in the second `ReadLnString`. Therefore, the code initializes the `Title` field of the `Biblio[ N ]` record, not the `Biblio[ M ]` record. Of course, ambiguous code like this is hard to read and check, and is therefore poor style.

Syntax for WITH Structure

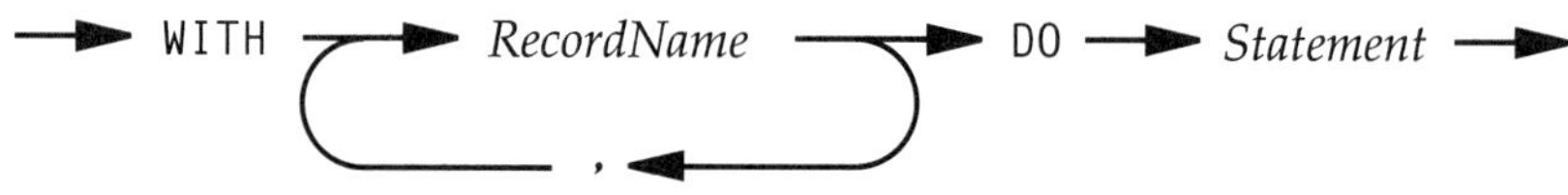

Pseudocode:

```
WITH RecordName DO
   Statement
```

Compound form:

```
WITH RecordName1, RecordName2,..., RecordNameN DO
   Statement
```

Note:

- The compound form is equivalent to the nested `WITH` statements

```
WITH RecordName1 DO
   WITH RecordName2 DO
       .
       .
       WITH RecordNameN DO
          Statement
```

The outer `WITH` statements have scope extending through *Statement* and thus including the scope of the inner `WITH` statements. This means that if two or more of the *RecordNames* refer to records with identically named fields, there is a question as to which record's field is referred to. As always in Pascal, the innermost scope has precedence. An example is shown in the text.

Questions

26. PUZZLE: The following awful code fragment contains syntax errors. What are they and where are they? (Use your compiler to test it.)

```
TYPE
   First = RECORD
              First, Last : Integer
           END;
VAR
   Last : First;
BEGIN
   First       := 1;
   First.First := 2;
   Last        := 3;
   Last.First  := 4;
   Last.Last   := 5;
   .
   .
```

27. What is displayed by the following code fragment?

```
TYPE
   GearType = RECORD
                 Num   : Integer;
                 Ratio : Real
              END;
VAR
   Gear1, Gear2 : GearType;
BEGIN
   Gear1.Num   := 1;
   Gear1.Ratio := 1.23;
   Gear2.Num   := 2;
   Gear2.Ratio := 4.32;
   WITH Gear1 DO
   BEGIN
      WITH Gear2 DO
         WriteLn( Num:1 );
      WriteLn( Ratio:4:2 );
      WriteLn( Num:1 )
   END;
   WriteLn( Gear2.Ratio:4:2 )
   .
   .
```

Exercises

28. The nested WITH structures

```
WITH Rec1 DO
   WITH Rec2 DO
      Statement
```

can be written more succinctly by using two arguments in a single WITH structure. Show how to do this.

29. Rewrite the WriteJournalArticle procedure of Section 15.1, using a WITH structure to simplify the syntax of the record accesses.

30. Using a WITH structure, write a ReadCensusRecord procedure that reads from the keyboard a census record of the form described in Exercise 22, Section 15.2.

15.4 CASE STUDY: BUILDING A BIBLIOGRAPHIC DATABASE

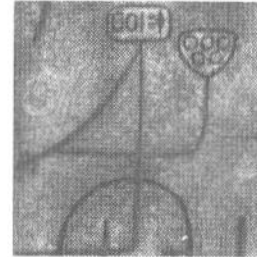

It might be helpful at this point to pull together several of the ideas presented in this chapter and the last, combining them in a single programming project. So let's design a program that reads a bibliographic list of journal article citations from the keyboard, sorts them by author, and displays the resulting alphabetized list on the screen.

First plan the I/O.

As usual, we begin by imagining how the program should run. Let's say that the I/O in a typical short run should look like this:

```
Author(s):  Parnas, D. L.
Title    :  Decomposing Systems into Modules
Journal  :  Communications of the ACM
Volume   :  5
Page     :  1053
Year     :  1972

Another? <Y/N> y

Author(s):  Wirth, N.
Title    :  Composition of Well-Structured Programs
Journal  :  Computing Surveys
Volume   :  6
Page     :  247
Year     :  1974

Another? <Y/N> y

Author(s):  Bastani, F. B., and Iyengar, S. S.
Title    :  Effect of Data Structures on Logical Complexity
Journal  :  Communications of the ACM
Volume   :  30
Page     :  250
Year     :  1987

Another? <Y/N> n
```

```
Sorting. Please wait a moment...

BIBLIOGRAPHY:

Bastani, F. B., and Iyengar, S. S.
Effect of Data Structures on Logical Complexity
Communications of the ACM  30, 250 (1987)

Parnas, D. L.
Decomposing Systems into Modules
Communications of the ACM   5, 1053 (1972)

Wirth, N.
Composition of Well-Structured Programs
Computing Surveys   6, 247 (1974)
```

Draw on previous work.

We have already written many of the pieces needed for such a program. At the beginning of Section 15.2, we described a suitable record structure for the bibliography itself. Furthermore, if you look carefully at the I/O sketched above, you will see that the sequence of events can be carried out by the following sequence of calls to procedures we've already (mostly) written:

```
{ Get Biblio array and number of records }
ReadBibliography( Biblio, NumRecs );

{ Sort the array if it contains more than one record }
IF NumRecs > 1 THEN
   SelectionSort( Biblio, 1, NumRecs );

{ Display the records in the sorted Biblio array }
WriteBibliography( Biblio, NumRecs )
```

Of course, we'll have to rework the `SelectionSort` procedure to work with `Biblio` records, we'll have to tinker with `ReadBibliography` and `WriteBibliography` to get them to display in our new I/O format, and we'll have to use whatever procedure you developed in the last chapter for reading strings from the keyboard, but these are minor jobs. Here, then, is the complete program. To keep it from consuming too many pages of the book, its comments have been mostly deleted:

```
PROGRAM BiblioDataBase( Input, Output );
{
  Reads bibliography from keyboard, then sorts it by author
  and displays it.
}
CONST
   BiblioSize = 50;  { Must be > 1 }

TYPE
   String80 = PACKED ARRAY [ 1..80 ] OF Char;
   {
     In Turbo and other extended Pascals, this can be changed to
     String80 = String[80];
   }
```

```
   JournalArticle =
        RECORD
           Author  : String80;
           Title   : String80;
           Journal : String80;
           Volume  : Integer;
           Page    : Integer;
           Year    : Integer
        END;

   SubscriptRange = 1..BiblioSize;
   Bibliography   = ARRAY [ SubscriptRange ] OF JournalArticle;

VAR
   Biblio  : Bibliography;
   NumRecs : SubscriptRange;


{-------------------------------------------------------------}
{ Reads into Str until 80 chars have been read or the end-of- }
{ line has been reached, whichever occurs first. The end-of-  }
{ line signal is discarded.                                   }
{-------------------------------------------------------------}
PROCEDURE ReadLnString( VAR Str : String80 );
BEGIN
   {
     The following works in many extended Pascals, but in
     Standard Pascal you will have to write your own
     implementation, as discussed in Section 14.6.
   }
   ReadLn( Str )

END; { ReadLnString }


{-------------------------------------------------------------}
{ Returns the uppercase version of Ch, if Ch is a letter;     }
{ otherwise, returns Ch unchanged.                            }
{-------------------------------------------------------------}
FUNCTION Upper( Ch : Char ) : Char;
BEGIN

   IF ( (Ch >= 'a') AND (Ch <= 'z') ) THEN
      Upper := Chr( Ord( Ch ) + Ord( 'A' ) - Ord( 'a' ) )
   ELSE
      Upper := Ch

END; { Upper }
```

```
{--------------------------------------------------------------}
{ Writes one journal article citation to the screen.           }
{--------------------------------------------------------------}
PROCEDURE WriteJournalArticle( Paper : JournalArticle );
BEGIN

   WriteLn( Paper.Author );
   WriteLn( Paper.Title );
   Write( Paper.Journal, ' ' );
   Write( Paper.Volume:3, ', ' );
   Write( Paper.Page:4 );
   WriteLn( ' (', Paper.Year:4, ')' )

END; { WriteJournalArticle }


{--------------------------------------------------------------}
{ Reads one journal article citation from the keyboard.        }
{ (Calls ReadLnString)                                         }
{--------------------------------------------------------------}
PROCEDURE ReadJournalArticle( VAR Paper : JournalArticle );
BEGIN

   Write( 'Author(s): ' );
   ReadLnString( Paper.Author );

   Write( 'Title    : ' );
   ReadLnString( Paper.Title );

   Write( 'Journal  : ' );
   ReadLnString( Paper.Journal );

   Write( 'Volume   : ' );
   ReadLn( Paper.Volume );

   Write( 'Page     : ' );
   ReadLn( Paper.Page );

   Write( 'Year     : ' );
   ReadLn( Paper.Year )

END; { ReadJournalArticle }


{--------------------------------------------------------------}
{ Reads article citations from the keyboard until user says    }
{ there are no more or until the array is filled, whichever    }
{ occurs first.                                                }
{ (Calls ReadJournalArticle and Upper)                         }
{--------------------------------------------------------------}
PROCEDURE ReadBibliography( VAR Biblio  : Bibliography;
                            VAR NumRecs : SubscriptRange );
VAR
   Answer     : Char;
   NoneToRead : Boolean;
```

```
BEGIN

   WriteLn( 'Enter bibliographic data for all articles--' );
   WriteLn;

   NoneToRead  := False;
   NumRecs     := 1;
   REPEAT

      ReadJournalArticle( Biblio[ NumRecs ] );
      WriteLn;

      IF NumRecs < BiblioSize THEN
      BEGIN
         Write( 'Another? <Y/N> ' );
         ReadLn( Answer );
         Answer := Upper( Answer );

         IF Answer = 'Y' THEN
            NumRecs := NumRecs + 1
         ELSE
            NoneToRead := True
      END

      ELSE
         NoneToRead := True;

      WriteLn

   UNTIL NoneToRead

END; { ReadBibliography }


{------------------------------------------------------------}
{ Writes all article citations to the screen.                }
{ (Calls WriteJournalArticle)                                }
{------------------------------------------------------------}
PROCEDURE WriteBibliography( VAR Biblio   : Bibliography;
                                 NumRecs  : SubscriptRange );
VAR
   Index  : SubscriptRange;

BEGIN

   WriteLn( '------------' );
   WriteLn( 'BIBLIOGRAPHY' );
   WriteLn( '------------' );
   WriteLn;

   FOR Index := 1 TO NumRecs DO
   BEGIN
      WriteJournalArticle( Biblio[ Index ] );
      WriteLn
   END

END; { WriteBibliography }
```

```
{-------------------------------------------------------------}
{ Returns array subscript for record containing the author    }
{ with lowest alphabetic ranking among the elements           }
{ Biblio[ First..Last ].                                      }
{-------------------------------------------------------------}
FUNCTION PositionOfLowest( VAR Biblio : Bibliography;
                           First      : SubscriptRange;
                           Last       : SubscriptRange )
                         : SubscriptRange;
VAR
   LowestSoFar    : String80;
   LatestUnsorted : SubscriptRange;

BEGIN

   LowestSoFar      := Biblio[First].Author;
   PositionOfLowest := First;

   FOR LatestUnsorted := First + 1 TO Last DO
      IF Biblio[LatestUnsorted].Author < LowestSoFar THEN
      BEGIN
         PositionOfLowest := LatestUnsorted;
         LowestSoFar      := Biblio[LatestUnsorted].Author
      END

END; { PositionOfLowest }


{-------------------------------------------------------------}
{ Swaps two records of type JournalArticle.                   }
{-------------------------------------------------------------}
PROCEDURE SwapJAs( VAR JA1, JA2 : JournalArticle );
VAR
   Temp : JournalArticle;

BEGIN

   Temp := JA1;
   JA1  := JA2;
   JA2  := Temp

END; { SwapJAs }


{-------------------------------------------------------------}
{ Sorts the Biblio array to nondecreasing order.              }
{ (Calls PositionOfLowest and SwapJAs)                        }
{-------------------------------------------------------------}
PROCEDURE SelectionSort( VAR Biblio  : Bibliography;
                         First, Last : SubscriptRange );
VAR
   FirstUnsorted : SubscriptRange;
```

```
BEGIN

   WriteLn( 'Sorting. Please wait a moment...' );
   WriteLn;

   FOR FirstUnsorted := First TO Last - 1 DO
      SwapJAs( Biblio[FirstUnsorted],
          Biblio[ PositionOfLowest(Biblio, FirstUnsorted, Last) ] )

END; { SelectionSort }


BEGIN { main program }

   { Get Biblio array and number of records }
   ReadBibliography( Biblio, NumRecs );

   { Sort the array if it contains more than one record }
   IF NumRecs > 1 THEN
      SelectionSort( Biblio, 1, NumRecs );

   { Display the records in the sorted Biblio array }
   WriteBibliography( Biblio, NumRecs )

END.
```

Questions

31. What runtime error can occur if the line `IF NumRecs > 1 THEN` is deleted from the main program?

32. Jackson P. Slipshod proposes the following version of the `ReadBibliography` procedure. Compare his version to the one shown in the text and criticise its performance.

```
PROCEDURE ReadBibliography( VAR Biblio  : Bibliography;
                            VAR NumRecs : SubscriptRange );
VAR
   Answer     : Char;
BEGIN
   NumRecs     := 1;
   REPEAT
      ReadJournalArticle( Biblio[ NumRecs ] );
      Write( 'Another? <Y/N> ' );
      ReadLn( Answer );
      Answer := UpperCase( Answer );
      IF Answer = 'Y' THEN
            NumRecs := NumRecs + 1
   UNTIL NoneToRead
END; { ReadBibliography }
```

33. Does your Pascal system require a homebrewed version of the `ReadLnString` procedure? If so, what implementation will work?

15.5 CASE STUDY: STRINGS WITH A LENGTH FIELD

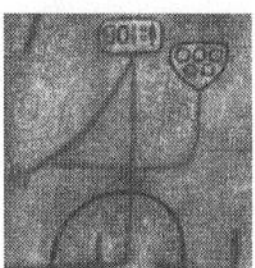

When we consider the operations that are commonly used in text processing, we find that many of them are inefficient to implement if a string is defined to be a `PACKED ARRAY [ 1..MaxStrLength ] OF Char`. For example, consider what is involved if you ask me to find the position of the substring `'ei'` within the string `'receipt'`. I have to search through the given string from the beginning, character by character, looking for an `'e'`. If I find one, I have to look to see if there is a following `'i'`. In doing this, I have to be careful not to walk off the end of the given string, so I have to know how long the string is. Furthermore, if I know the length of the `'receipt'` string to begin with, and you ask me to find the substring `'disestablishmentarianism'` in it, I can tell you right away that it's not to be found in `'receipt'` because `'receipt'` is too short to contain it. So in performing a substring search, it is useful to know the lengths of the strings to begin with.

Or suppose you ask me to concatenate ("glue together") the strings `'fruit'` and `'cake'` to make a longer string `'fruitcake'`. In order for me know where to start appending the characters of `'cake'` to the end of `'fruit'`, I have to know how long 'fruit' is. Again, it is helpful to know the lengths of the strings we process.

In fact, we find that many of the procedures and functions that are needed to make strings useful require knowing the lengths of the strings. If we define a string to be simply `PACKED ARRAY [ 1..MaxStrLength ] OF Char`, many of our string-processing procedures will spend a significant amount of their running times traversing strings, looking for the position of the last character.

However, we can avoid this problem by representing a string as a record. We declare

```
CONST
   MaxStrLength = 80;
TYPE
   PosRange = 1..MaxStrLength;
   String80 = RECORD
                 Len   : 0..MaxStrLength;
                 Chars : PACKED ARRAY [ PosRange ] OF Char
              END;
```

With this change, each string carries a storage cell called a *length header*, which contains the current length of the string stored in the `Chars` field. Not only does this enable procedures to be simpler and run faster, it also makes it unnecessary to pad the strings with trailing null characters or perform other tricks to help a procedure find the end of a string by testing it.

Implementing string procedures

Let's design a few procedures to see how this reduces the amount of work that needs to be done. Suppose we declare

```
VAR
   Str : String80;
```

and then call `MakeEmptyStr( Str )`, to initialize an empty string (something that isn't allowed in simple string array). To make the string empty, the procedure needs only to set `Str.Len` equal to zero:

```
PROCEDURE MakeEmptyStr( VAR Str : String80 );
BEGIN

   Str.Len := 0

END; { MakeEmptyStr }
```

(With this representation for strings, the character array of an empty string can contain garbage; it doesn't matter. The fact that the length field is zero is enough to mark the string as empty.)

Similarly, when reading a string from the keyboard, we store the count of characters in the string's `Len` field. The resulting `ReadLnStr` procedure is a little simpler than it was in Chapter 14:

```
PROCEDURE ReadLnStr( VAR Str : String80 );
VAR
   Count    : Integer;
   Finished : Boolean;

BEGIN

   { ASSERTION: MaxStrLength > 0 }

   Finished := False;
   Count    := 0;

   WHILE NOT Finished DO
   BEGIN

      { Next char is either <EOLn> or char to be stored }
      IF ( NOT EOLN ) AND ( Count < MaxStrLength ) THEN
      BEGIN
         {
           ASSERTIONS:
           Next char is not <EOLn> and array is not full.
         }
         Count := Count + 1;
         Read( Str.Chars[ Count ] )

      END

      ELSE
         { ASSERTION: Either <EOLn> or array is full }
         Finished := True

   END; { WHILE NOT Finished }

   Str.Len := Count;

   { Discard the rest of the line }
   ReadLn

END; { ReadLnStr }
```

All string procedures that change the number of characters must also update the `Len` field. This makes all such procedures slightly more complicated than in our simpler array representation. However, the advantage is that the current string length is immediately available, making other procedures simpler.

```
FUNCTION LengthOfStr( Str : String80 ) : Integer;
BEGIN

   LengthOfStr := Str.Len

END; { LengthOfStr }
```

Furthermore, the many calls to `LengthOfStr` in other string procedures can be replaced by references to the `Str.Len` field. For example,

```
PROCEDURE WriteLnStr( Str : String80 );
VAR
   Index : PosRange;

BEGIN

   FOR Index := 1 TO Str.Len DO
      Write( Str.Chars[ Index ] );

   WriteLn;

END; { WriteLnStr }
```

Other procedures are simplified in a similar way. (Several are left as exercises.)

Should users access the Len field directly?

It is obviously useful to have the length of the string readily available in `Str.Len`. In fact, it is so useful that other programmers who use your procedures might prefer to access `Str.Len` directly rather than call your `LengthOfStr` procedure. But a client programmer who does this might start tinkering around with the fields in the record or with your procedures, causing some of your carefully built code to fail. It is safer to keep clients from doing this. What we need is a way to post a sign on the whole string's implementation, saying "NO USER-SERVICEABLE PARTS INSIDE." Standard Pascal provides no way to do this, but many large Pascal systems do. This issue is so important that it is the subject of the next chapter.

Questions

34. Why do we need a `LengthOfStr` function? That is, why would a user of strings call `LengthOfStr( Str )` for the length of string `Str` instead of simply referring to `Str.Len`?

35. If `String80` is a length-header string, which of the following operations can be made to run faster than if `String80` were simply an array of characters?

- **a.** Writing a string to the screen.
- **b.** Reading a string from the keyboard.
- **c.** Finding the length of a string.
- **d.** Adding a character to the end of a string.
- **e.** Adding a character to the beginning of a string.

Exercises

36. Write an `AppendChar` procedure that appends a given character to the end of a given string.

37. Write a `Concatenate` procedure as defined in the text.

38. Write a `CompareStrings` function that returns the characters `'<'`, `'='`, or `'>'` to indicate whether `Str1` is lexically "less than," "equal to," or "greater than" `Str2`.

15.6 VARIANT RECORDS

The trouble with the `Biblio` records in Section 15.2 is that they are suitable only for journal articles. Suppose that we want a bibliography to list both journal articles and books. Then we might want entries of the following two kinds:

```
Author(s):  Wirth, N.
Year     :  1971
Title    :  The Programming Language Pascal
Journal  :  Acta Informatica
Volume   :     1
Page     :    35

Author(s):  Wirth, N.
Year     :  1976
Title    :  Algorithms + Data Structures = Programs
Publisher:  Prentice Hall
```

These records differ in their field structures. To build a bibliography, we need an array containing both of these kinds of records, but an array must be homogeneous.

To get around this problem, Pascal allows a record to contain not only fixed fields but **variant fields**. A variant field is one that depends upon the value of a **variant-selector variable**, also called a **tag field**. The selector value is chosen by a `CASE`-selection structure. Here is an example:

```
TYPE
   Publication = ( Book, Journal );
   String40    = PACKED ARRAY [1..40] OF Char;

   Reference =
        RECORD
           Author  : String40;
           Year    : Integer;
           Title   : String40;

           CASE BookJournal : Publication OF

              Book    : ( Publisher : String40 );

              Journal : ( JournalName : String40;
                          Volume      : Integer;
                          Page        : Integer )

        END;
```

In this example, `Reference` is a record consisting of three parts:

1. A *tag field*, `BookJournal`, which determines whether the rest of the record refers to a book or to a journal.
2. A *fixed part*, consisting of the fields

```
Author  : String40;
Year    : Integer;
Title   : String40;
```

   These are said to be fixed because they are the first three fields of every record of type `Reference`.

3. A *variant part* whose structure depends upon the value of the `BookJournal` variable, which is called the *selector* or *tag*:
   a. If `BookJournal = Book`, the remainder of the record consists of the one field

```
Publisher : String40
```

   b. If `BookJournal = Journal`, the remainder of the record consists of the three fields

```
JournalName : String40;
Volume      : Integer;
Page        : Integer
```

Thus, a `Reference` record has either the first or the second structure shown below, depending on whether `BookJournal` is `Book` or `Journal`, respectively:

```
RECORD                            RECORD
   Author    : String40;             Author  : String40;
   Year      : Integer;              Year    : Integer;
   Title     : String40;             Title   : String40;
   Publisher : String40              Journal : String40;
                                     Volume  : Integer;
                                     Page    : Integer
END;                              END;
```

This solves our problem. We can have an array of `Reference` records, with `Reference` a sort of "chameleon type." The syntax for this kind of variant record, in which a selector variable is used to discriminate between structures, is shown in the following syntax box.

Syntax for Variant Records,
with Variant Fields Discriminated by a Selector Variable
(also called a discriminated union)

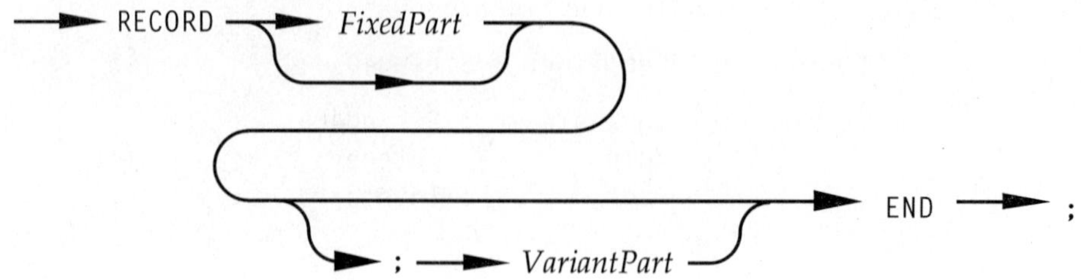

Syntax of fixed part, which is just a field list:

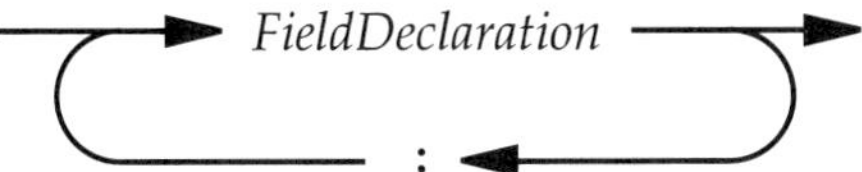

Syntax of variant part:

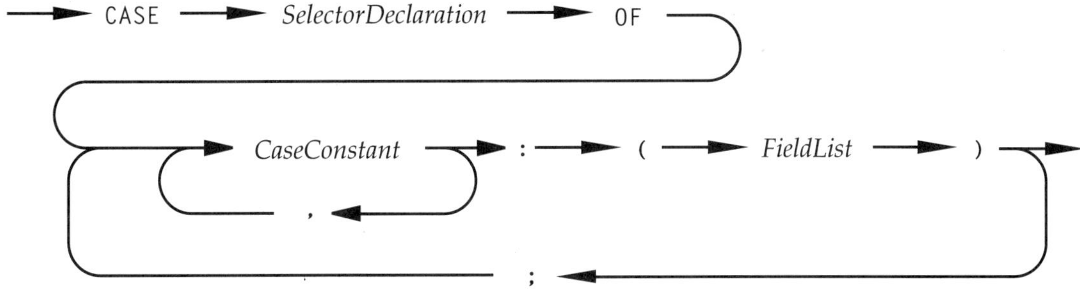

Pseudocode:

```
RecordTypeName = RECORD
                     FixedFieldList;
                     CASE Selector : SelectorType OF
                        CaseConstantList1 : ( FieldList );
                        CaseConstantList2 : ( FieldList );
                        .
                        .
                        CaseConstantListN : ( FieldList )
                 END;
```

Notes:

- The fixed part is optional. If not present, we have an entirely variant record.
- The variant part, consisting of the `CASE` structure, is optional. If not present, we have a record of the fixed type shown in Section 15.1.
- The variant part, if present, must be the last part of the record.
- There can be only one variant part.
- The *SelectorType* must be ordinal, and must be the name of a standard type or a previously declared type.
- It is an error if any value of *SelectorType* does not appear in one (and only one) of the *CaseConstantList*s. (This makes it impractical to use `Integer`, and tedious to use `Char`, as the *SelectorType*. An enumerated type is often chosen.)
- The *FieldList* associated with a *CaseConstantList* may be empty, but the parentheses are still required.
- There is only one `END`, marking the end of the record declaration. The `CASE` does not have another `END`.
- Once a value has been assigned to the *Selector* variable, the corresponding *FieldList* is said to be *active*. Only one *FieldList* can be active at a time.
- It is an error to reference a field in an inactive *FieldList*.
- It is an error to pass the selector of a variant part as a variable (`VAR`) parameter.

A more complicated example should make these rules clearer. Suppose we have

```
TYPE
   Publication = ( Book, Journal, Report, UnpublishedCommun );
   String40    = PACKED ARRAY [1..40] OF Char;

   Reference =
        RECORD
           Author  : String40;
           Title   : String40;
           Year    : Integer;

           CASE Pub : Publication OF

              Book, Report        : ( Publisher   : String40 );

              Journal             : ( JournalName : String40;
                                      Volume      : Integer;
                                      Page        : Integer );

              UnpublishedCommun   : ()

       END;
```

With these declarations, if `Pub = UnpublishedCommun`, the record consists only of the three fields in the fixed part, plus the `Pub` selector itself. If `Pub = Book` or `Report`, the record contains the fixed part plus the `Publisher` field, plus `Pub`. If `Pub = Journal`, the record consists of the fixed part plus the `Journal`, `Volume`, and `Page` fields, plus `Pub`.

Use of memory in a variant record

The compiler must reserve a fixed amount of memory for the whole record before the program runs, so *it reserves enough memory for the largest possible version of the record*: the fixed part, plus the selector, plus the largest declared variant. During execution, the variant portion of the memory area is used as specified by the current value of the selector variable. It is as though we have overlaid all of the alternate record structures on the same area of memory, as shown in Figure 15.6.1.

Figure 15.6.1 *The same area of memory is apportioned according to the current value of the selector variable (tag field).*

If `Ref.Pub = UnpublishedCommun`,

Ref.Author	Ref.Title	Ref.Year	Ref.Pub	(unused)	

If `Ref.Pub = Book` or `Ref.Pub = Report`,

Ref.Author	Ref.Title	Ref.Year	Ref.Pub	Ref.Publisher	(unused)

If `Ref.Pub = Journal`,

Ref.Author	Ref.Title	Ref.Year	Ref.Pub	Ref.JournalName	Ref.Volume	Ref.Page

Example of writing variant records

In our example, the following procedure could be used to display records of `Reference` type:

```
PROCEDURE WriteLnReference( Ref : Reference );
BEGIN

   CASE Ref.Pub OF

      Book, Report       : BEGIN
                              IF Ref.Pub = Book THEN
                                 WriteLn( 'BOOK' )
                              ELSE
                                 WriteLn( 'REPORT' );

                              WriteLnFixedPart( Ref );
                              WriteLn( 'Publisher: ', Ref.Publisher )
                           END;

      Journal            : BEGIN
                              WriteLn( 'JOURNAL ARTICLE' );
                              WriteLnFixedPart( Ref );
                              WriteLn( 'Journal  : ', Ref.JournalName );
                              WriteLn( 'Volume   : ', Ref.Volume );
                              WriteLn( 'Page     : ', Ref.Page )
                           END;

      UnPublishedCommun : BEGIN
                              WriteLn( 'UNPUBLISHED COMMUNICATION' );
                              WriteLnFixedPart( Ref )
                           END

   END; { CASE }

   WriteLn

END; { WriteLnReference }
```

Accompanied by an appropriate `WriteLnFixedPart` procedure, the output would look like this:

```
BOOK
Author(s): Goldstine, H. H.
Title    : The Computer, from Pascal to von Neumann
Year     : 1972
Publisher: Princeton U. Press

REPORT
Author(s): Dijkstra, E. W.
Title    : Cooperating Sequential Processes EWD-123
Year     : 1965
Publisher: Technological Univ., Eindhoven
```

```
JOURNAL ARTICLE
Author(s): Wirth, N.
Title    : Prog Development by Stepwise Refinement
Year     : 1971
Journal  : Communications of the ACM
Volume   : 14
Page     : 221

UNPUBLISHED COMMUNICATION
Author(s): Mills, H. D.
Title    : none
Year     : 1990
```

Subverted types

Because a variant record allows alternate fields to occupy the same area of memory, it provides a way to store a datum as one type, then to retrieve it as another type. This is the only chink in Pascal's armor protecting the sanctity of types, and is called **type subversion**. This is not a method for type conversion, but a method for reinterpreting a value as though it were a type different from the one used when storing the value.

If you do this inadvertently, it is an error, and can in fact be a difficult error to track down. On the other hand, it can be used to advantage under a few unusual circumstances. For example, it can be used to inspect the value of a file pointer variable. Pascal does not ordinarily allow the display of pointer values. However, with the help of a variant record, it is possible to store a file pointer value and then retrieve it as though it were an integer. (File pointers are discussed in Chapter 17.)

Undiscriminated unions

When using variant records, there is nothing that forces a program to retrieve a variant field value using the same selection value that was used when the field was stored. Thus, there is no protection from type subversion. Making things even more dangerous, Pascal does not even require that a selection variable be used. The syntax box below shows another form of variant records in which there is no selection (tag) variable. This usage is not recommended, however; it is shown here only for the sake of completeness.

Questions

39. The text says that "a variant record uses a structure superficially resembling a `CASE` structure." Why is the resemblance between `CASE` in a variant record and a `CASE` control structure only superficial, both syntactically and semantically?

40. What does it mean to say that alternate variant fields are overlaid on the same area of memory?

**Syntax for Variant Records,
with Undiscriminated Variant Fields
(also called an undiscriminated union or free type union)**

Same as syntax for discriminated variant record, except for syntax of variant part:

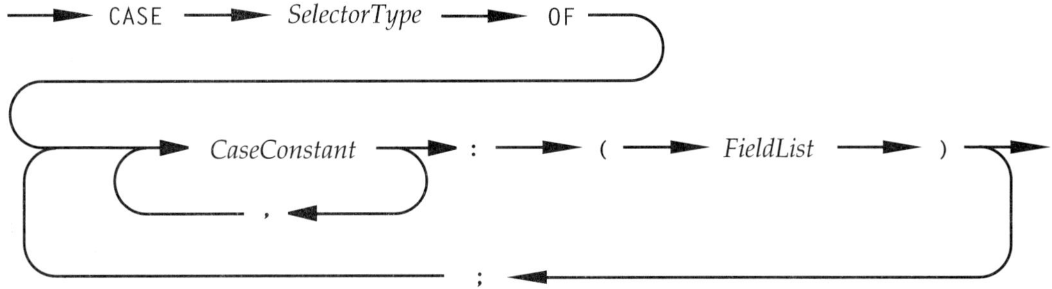

Note:

- *SelectorType* must be the name of a previously declared ordinal type. It specifies the type of the *CaseConstants*.

Exercises

41. Rewrite the `WriteLnReference` procedure so that a `WITH` structure is used to specify the record.

42. PUZZLE: What is displayed by the following code fragment?

```
TYPE
   Thing = ( This, That, TheOther );
   What  = RECORD
              A : Char;
              CASE It : Thing OF
                 This     : ( B, C : Char );
                 That     : ( D, E : Char );
                 TheOther : ()
           END;
VAR
   Wazzit : What;

BEGIN
   WITH Wazzit DO
   BEGIN
      It := That;
      A  := 'a';
      D  := 'd';
      E  := 'e';

      CASE It OF
         This     : WriteLn( A, B, C );
         That     : WriteLn( A, D, E );
         TheOther : WriteLn( A )
      END
   END;
```

43. PUZZLE: What is displayed by the following code fragment?

```
TYPE
   Thing = ( This, That );
   What  = RECORD
              One : Integer;
               CASE It : Thing OF
                  This : ( Two, Three : Integer );
                  That : ( Four, Five : Integer )
            END;
VAR
   Wazzit : What;
BEGIN
   Wazzit.It    := This;
   Wazzit.One   := 1;
   Wazzit.Two   := 2;
   Wazzit.Three := 3;
   Wazzit.It    := That;
   WriteLn( Wazzit.One );
   WriteLn( Wazzit.Four );
   WriteLn( Wazzit.Five  );
```

15.7 TESTING AND DEBUGGING

When referencing a field of a record, the full field name must be specified unambiguously. The reference may be of the form

RecordVariableName.FieldName

or of the form *FieldName*, within the scope of a `WITH` structure specifying the record name:

```
WITH RecordVariableName DO
BEGIN
    . . . FieldName . . .
END;
```

Unfortunately, it is all too easy to make an ambiguous reference. One possibility is that the field name is (Heaven forbid!) identical to the name of a simple variable whose scope extends over this part of the program. Another possibility is that two record variables with the same field structure are being referenced in the same `WITH` structure. The result is hard to read. In the following example, does the assignment statement initialize the `Salary` field of `Employee[ 1 ]`, `Employee[ 2 ]`, or both?

```
TYPE
   String9  = PACKED ARRAY[ 1..9 ] OF Char;
   String60 = PACKED ARRAY[ 1..60 ] OF Char;
```

```
   EmployeeRec = RECORD
                   Name   : String60;
                   SS     : String9;
                   Salary : Real
                 END;

  EmployeeArray = ARRAY[ 1..50 ] OF EmployeeRec;

VAR
   Employee : EmployeeArray;
   Salary   : Real;

BEGIN
   WITH Employee[ 1 ], Employee[ 2 ] DO
      Salary := 999.99;

   WriteLn( Employee[ 1 ].Salary : 7 : 2 );
   WriteLn( Employee[ 2 ].Salary : 7 : 2 );
   WriteLn( Salary:7:2 );
```

In fact, the last-named record in the `WITH` statement takes precedence, so the highlighted code initializes `Employee[2].Salary`, not `Employee[1].Salary` or the simple variable called `Salary`. This is far from clear, however, so it is terrible style.

Ambiguities of this kind are especially easy when using `WITH` structures; often, it is better to avoid using `WITH`. To understand code of this kind, it is essential to understand the naming of arrays, records, and arrays of records. In this example, we have identifiers

`Employee`	(the name of an array of records)
`Employee[ 1 ]`	(the name of a record that is an element in the array)
`Employee[ 1 ].Salary`	(the name of a field within the record that is an element in the array)

Figure 15.7.1

An error message resulting from the use of a record type name in place of a record variable name.

```
Variable name expected

TYPE
   Employee = RECORD
                 Name   : String40;
                 Salary : Real
              END;

VAR
   Empl : Employee;

BEGIN
   .
   .
   Employee.Salary := 999.99;
```

Figure 15.7.2

Confusing error message resulting from missing END in the record type declaration. The compiler apparently thinks that VAR is intended as a field in the record.

```
Identifier expected

TYPE
   Employee = RECORD
                 Name   : String40;
                 Salary : Real;

VAR
   Empl : Employee;

BEGIN
   .
   .
   Employee.Salary := 999.99;
```

Another common error is to accidentally use the name of a record *type* in place of the name of a record *variable*. This is a syntax error, resulting in an error message like the one shown in Figure 15.7.1. If you use names that clearly distinguish between variables and types, you will be less likely to make such errors.

The third common error is to omit the `END` from a record type declaration. This can sometimes lead to confusing syntax error messages. An example is shown in Figure 15.7.2.

LOOKING BACK

This chapter has introduced the data structure called the record. Records are heterogeneous data structures, while arrays are homogeneous. This makes records especially convenient for grouping together related data of various types. In this chapter, the case studies included employee records, strings with length headers, and bibliographies.

We saw that records, like other built-in data structures, are not fully equipped with operations. (The only whole-record operation provided is assignment.) In particular, whole records cannot be read or written with Pascal's standard I/O procedures. I/O, like other operations, must be performed on the individual fields within the record. This involves specifying the full field name by using a period or with the help of a `WITH` structure.

All of this is an incentive to build our own abstract data types, in which we provide our own procedures and functions for whatever operations are needed. We started two in this chapter:

- A bibliographic database, provided with procedures for reading, writing, and sorting bibliographic citations.
- An improved representation for strings, in which a string has a length header, making it unnecessary to measure the length frequently. This representation allows most operations to run faster than the representation shown in Chapter 14.

TERMS EMPHASIZED IN THIS CHAPTER

PROJECTS

1. Write a modular program that maintains a database of bibliographic references of the form shown in Section 15.2. Your program should allow users to enter a list of references, view the list, search for a desired reference by author or title, delete references, and save the list as a text file.

2. Complete the implementation of the `String80` data type, using length-header strings. Finish writing the procedures and functions mentioned in Exercises 35 and 36.

3. Write an abstract data type for rational numbers, in which a rational number is represented by a record containing the numerator and denominator. The numerator can be any integer, but the denominator must be a *positive* integer. Write procedures to implement the four operations of addition, subtraction, multiplication, and division, producing rational-number results in reduced form. Also write procedures for reading and writing rational numbers. Finally, write a driver program and test all of your procedures. The program should produce output like this:

```
First fraction:            2 / 3
Second fraction:           1 / 12
Operation <+ - * />:       +

Result:                    2 / 3  +  1 / 12  =  3 / 4
```

4. Write a menu-driven program to read data about circles, equilateral triangles, squares, and rectangles. Use a variant record to store the data about the geometric shape. If the shape is a circle, store the radius; if an equilateral triangle or a square, store the length of a side; if a rectangle, store the two side lengths. In each case, have your program compute and display the area.

5. (Variation on Project 4) Write a program that interactively reads the coordinates of up to four points in the *xy*-plane, automatically calculating the enclosed area.

6. In the game of Hangman, the purpose is to guess a secret word of up to 15 letters. The player is shown a sequence of blanks representing the letter positions in the word, and then guesses at the letters one at a time. Each time that a correct letter is guessed, all instances of that letter are shown in their correct positions. For example, if the secret

word is "RAPTOR" and the player has made one guess at the letter "R," the display shows

```
R _ _ _ _ R
```

Each time the player guesses a letter not present in the word, one piece is added to a stick figure of a hanging person. When eight incorrect guesses have been made, the picture is complete as shown below, and the player loses the game.

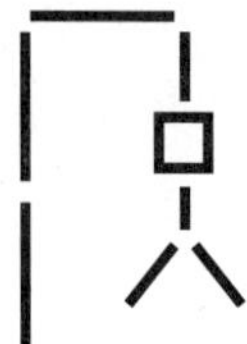

Write a program that plays Hangman with a human player. The program should select secret words from a predetermined list, which may be a text file. During the game, the letters in the word should each be represented by a record of the form

```
LetterRec = RECORD
               Letter  : Char;
               Visible : Boolean
            END;
```

The hanged man diagram can be displayed as a two-dimensional array of characters such as are used in the turtle graphics of Section 16.3.

7. (Uses a random-number generator. See Appendix I.) The Wumpus is a dangerous beast who lives in an imaginary cave. But being the brave person you are, you enter the cave, armed only with a bow and five arrows. The cave contains 20 rooms, each connected by three tunnels to other rooms. You don't know the interconnection pattern of the rooms at first, and you don't know what room the Wumpus is in. But when you enter the cave, you can see, with the help of your flashlight, that the rooms are numbered. By shining your light into the connecting rooms, you can see the room numbers of rooms adjacent to your room. At any given moment, you have the choice of moving to one of the adjacent rooms or shooting an arrow, but you can't do both at once. You can move to any of the three rooms connected to your present room. However, if you enter the room occupied by the Wumpus, he will eat you and the game will be over. There are two other hazards. Two of the rooms—you don't know which—contain bottomless pits. If you enter one of those rooms, you will fall in a pit and the game will be over. Also, two of the rooms contain very large bats. If you enter those rooms, the bats will snatch you away and deposit you in some random room which may or may not contain a pit or the Wumpus, and then the bats will fly off to some random room. You have some help in avoiding the hazards, though. When you are in a room adjacent to one containing a pit, you will feel a draft. When you are in a room adjacent to one containing bats, you will hear their wings fluttering. Also, the Wumpus suffers from terrific body odor. When you are within two rooms of the Wumpus, you will smell him. When you shoot an arrow, you can aim it at any of the three adjacent rooms. The arrow will travel through the room you are in, through the aimed-at room, and through a total of N interconnected rooms, where N is a random integer from 2 through 6. If the arrow passes through the room containing the Wumpus, the Wumpus is killed and you win the game. On the other hand, if the arrow does not pass through the Wumpus's room (forgive the pun), the Wumpus will move to another room chosen at random. Furthermore, if the arrow passes a second time through your room—it can curve around corners—you will be killed and will therefore lose the game. Write a modular program that presents the "Hunt the Wumpus" game to a human player. Use an array of records to represent the rooms in the cave. Each record in the array corresponds to a room, and should contain the numbers of the three rooms connected to that room, as well as saying whether the Wumpus, bats, or a pit are in the room. Assume that the rooms and their interconnections form a dodecahedron, with a room at each vertex.

8. A substitution cipher can be generated by representing the alphabet by an array of records of the form

```
TYPE
   LetterRec = RECORD
                  PlainText : Char;
                  Cipher    : Char
               END;

   LetterArray = ARRAY [ 1..26 ] OF LetterRec;

VAR
   Letter : LetterArray;
```

To encipher the letter `'A'`, you would look up `Letter[1]`, in which `Letter[1].PlainText = 'A'`, and print out `Letter[1].Cipher`, which is the enciphered version of `'A'`. To decipher a message, you would search through the `Cipher` fields in the array for a given letter, then print out the corresponding `PlainText` field. Write a program that enciphers and deciphers messages by this method.

9. This project demonstrates the surprising ways in which beautiful patterns can arise from chaos. It uses a pseudorandom number generator, as described in Appendix I. Define three vertices of an equilateral triangle, and start at any vertex. Then repeatedly choose a vertex *at random* and move halfway there from the current point. Each time you arrive at a new point, plot it on the screen. Store each point as a record of the form

```
TYPE
   PointXY = RECORD
                X, Y : Integer
             END;
```

Your results will depend very much on the resolution you can attain in your plot, and on the quality of your pseudorandom generator. In high resolution, with a good generator, your results should look like this:

REFERENCES

Further discussion of the use of Pascal's record types and their manner of storage can be found in Niklaus Wirth's *Algorithms + Data Structures = Programs* (Prentice Hall, 1976), and in Allen B. Tucker, Jr.'s *Programming Languages*, second edition (McGraw-Hill, 1986). Variant records and their dangers are discussed in Terrence W. Pratt's *Programming Languages*, second edition (Prentice Hall, 1984).

CHAPTER 16

Data Abstraction

CHAPTER CONTENTS

INTRODUCTION

As you saw in the last two chapters, Pascal's support for arrays and records is not as complete as its support for simple data types. Arrays and records cannot be returned by functions, assignment is the only whole-array or whole-record operation, and whole arrays or records cannot be read by `Read` and `ReadLn`.

As our applications become more ambitious, we will increasingly use data structures, and therefore come under increasing pressure to seek ways around these shortcomings, which are shared by other programming languages. In response, we will *extend the Pascal language*, using its built-in tools for constructing new data types and new procedures and functions. We will learn to *encapsulate* with our own data types our own sets of operations, so that we have our own *abstract data types* (ADTs) that will better meet our needs. The techniques are illustrated in this chapter as we construct a fraction ADT and then a turtle ADT. The latter is a graphics "animal" that draws pictures.

So this chapter sees us entering a new country. We will no longer rely on Pascal's built-in data types; instead, we will begin to package our own data types together with our own operations to build new data abstractions. In many extended Pascal systems, we can package these in such a way that they will seem almost as natural as if they had been built into Pascal in the first place. From here on, we are no longer at the mercy of the language.

16.1 ABSTRACT DATA TYPES

In Section 2.2, we introduced the concept of *data abstraction*, also called an *abstract data type*. An abstract data type, (ADT) is a data declaration, encapsulated with declarations for all the operations that are meaningful on the data type. The simplicity of this idea conceals some important advantages for programming.

Extending the language

We want to build new data types that are, as nearly as possible, like those built into the language in the first place. In other words, we want to *extend the language* by adding new types, along with their operators. To accomplish this, we need to copy three advantages possessed by built-in types:

Opaque type or **opaque operation**: A data type or operation whose implementation details are hidden from the user.

- *The types themselves are* **opaque**. That is, we can use them without knowing how they are stored in the hardware.
- *The operations have a natural syntax*, so we can invoke them easily and naturally.
- *The operations are opaque*. We can use them without knowing how they are accomplished. In other words, we can know *what* they do without having to know *how* they do it.

Information hiding

Note the distinction between *using* a built-in data type and knowing how to *build* it. Pascal enforces this distinction by not telling us how the built-in types are stored, or how their operations are implemented. It tells us only what we need to know in order to use the built-in types and operations. This strategy of hiding from users the implementation details they don't need to know is called **information hiding**. It is an important factor in high-level programming, because it frees us to think more abstractly about the data types.

Information hiding: The policy of showing to client programmers only what they need to know to use a data type, and not revealing to them the details of the implementation.

The interface

Compare this to the way an automobile is designed. A driver (as opposed to a mechanic) considers a car as an opaque object; it is just a *car*, and never mind how it works internally. From the driver's point of view, *car* is an abstraction, a thing that transports, and not a particular assemblage of 5,000 parts. The driver's abstraction also involves the operations in using the car, like accelerating, steering, braking, and so on. As you can see, a driver's perception of a car is in terms of the **interface** between driver and machine.

The driver's perception of *car* as an abstraction is made possible by good design and the smooth integration of car parts that results in easy, natural-seeming operation. This is the interface between car and driver (Figure 16.1.1).

Figure 16.1.1

The car as an abstraction of the driver. The driver sees only the interface.

The implementation

On the other hand, a mechanic or automotive engineer (or a driver with a broken-down car) must deal with the inner construction of the car. These people perceive the car in a completely different way. They must think in terms of the hierarchy of subassemblies in the car, rather than the car as a whole. They can be said to have gone *under the abstraction*, delving into the **implementation** (Figure 16.1.2).

The car as an ADT

Now think of the car as an abstract data type. Viewed from the user's point of view, a car is a concept, taken together with a set of operations that are meaningful when using that concept: a car to be *driven*. That image is called the **interface** of the abstract data type. On the other hand, the **implementation** of the abstract data type consists of all the parts that make the interface work: the code for the procedures and functions. By separating

Figure 16.1.2

The car as a hierarchy of parts, as pictured by a mechanic. The mechanic sees the implementation of the car.

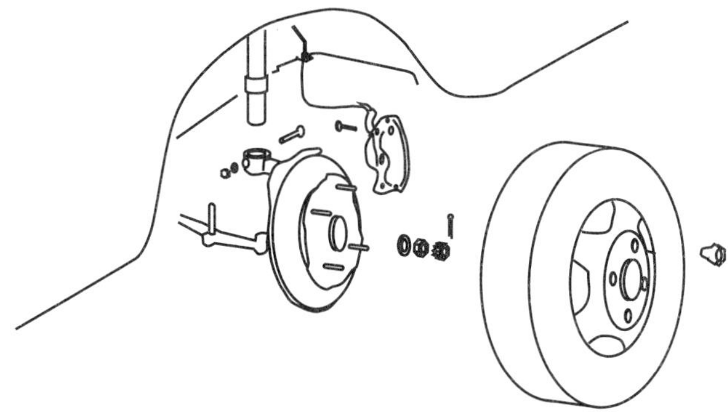

Figure 16.1.3 *The car as a hierarchy of functions.*

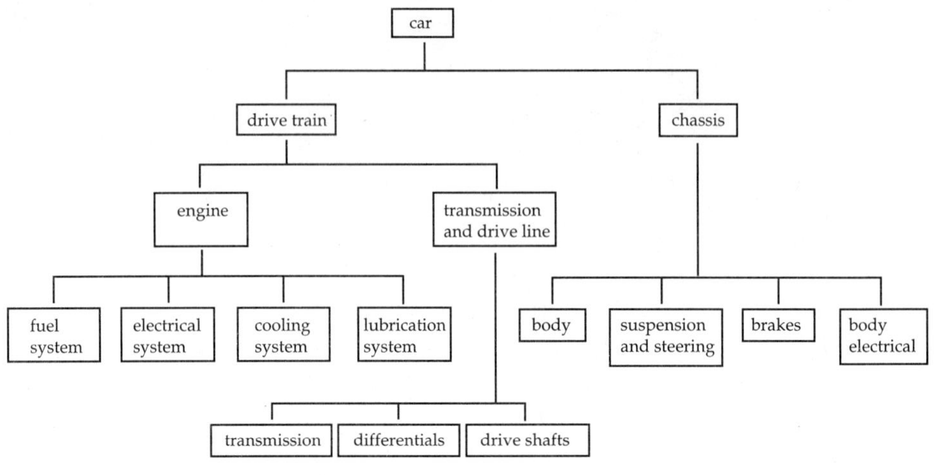

the implementation from the interface, we draw an important distinction between using a concept and the inner mechanics of the concept.

There is another reason for making the distinction: *A particular interface may be achieved by more than one implementation.* For example, an automotive engineer may design the car as a hierarchy of functions. The parts are the same as in the previous hierarchy diagram, but they are now visualized in terms of a different organization, as shown in Figure 16.1.3.

This organization may seem more natural to an engineer than to a mechanic. Drivers, however, don't usually care about either of the hierarchical points of view; drivers care how the completed car looks and feels and handles.

This has been an analogy to get you used to the difference between an abstract system's interface and its implementation. Now let's see how the distinction affects the construction of an abstract data type in Pascal.

ADT = Interface + Implementation

Client program: A program that uses an ADT.

A program that uses an abstract data type is called a **client program**. The client program must be provided with all information needed to use the ADT, but the inner workings of the ADT—the storage representation and the implementations of procedures and functions—are normally hidden from the client. Thus an abstract data type is built in two parts: an **interface part**, which includes all **public information** needed by client programs, and the **implementation part**, which includes **private information** to be hidden from client programs.

The interface part of an ADT

The interface part of the ADT normally contains the following:

- The data type that is being abstracted.

- Supporting constants and data types used to define the main data type. These would include, for example, subranges or enumerations used to specify array subscripts.
- Headers for all procedures and functions associated with the ADT.

Thus the interface part lists all public declarations of constants, types, variables, procedures, and functions needed by client programs. It is provided separately to client programmers as part of the documentation for the ADT.

The implementation part of an ADT

The implementation part of the ADT contains the proprietary details of the ADT's representation and implementation:

- Any declarations required by the implementation but not needed by client programs.
- The implementations (code bodies) of the procedures and functions listed in the interface, plus any procedures and functions called by these.

The implementation part contains details not needed by client programs, and therefore not made available to them. The code in the implementation part is not usually provided to users of the ADT. (This is an example of *information hiding*.)

The interface should be independent of the implementation.

Ideally, a client programmer should be able to use the ADT solely in terms of information provided by the interface, and without knowing anything about the underlying implementation. In fact, it should be possible for the ADT designer to change the underlying representation without affecting client programs in any way. Modern industrial-strength languages have features that make this possible. Standard Pascal does not, but as you will see, many real-world Pascal systems provide nonstandard features that help us accomplish this.

Exercises

1. In your own words, explain how an abstract data type differs from the arrays and records we studied in the last two chapters.

2. As in the analogy of the automobile discussed on page 512, explain the difference between a user's perception of the abstraction called "a computer" and a computer manufacturer's point of view about this device.

3. Again as in the analogy of the automobile discussed above, describe the abstract data type called "Boolean," both from the client programmer's point of view and from the implementer's point of view.

4. Again as in the analogy of the automobile discussed above, describe the abstract data type called "array," both from the client programmer's point of view and from the implementer's point of view.

5. In your own words, explain the concept of information hiding as it applies to ADTs.

16.2 BUILDING A FRACTION ADT

To illustrate how an abstract data type can be used to extend the Pascal language, we will build an ADT for fractional numbers, complete with the usual operations for fractional arithmetic. First, we will need a data representation for a `Fraction`. Since a fraction consists of two parts called the numerator and denominator, it seems natural to define `Fraction` to be a record:

```
TYPE
   Fraction = RECORD
                 Numerator   : Integer
                 Denominator : Integer
              END;
```

To make such a data type useful, we must encapsulate with it a set of appropriate arithmetic operations, plus some I/O operations and a function that converts a fraction to a decimal number:

Write a fraction to the screen.	(A procedure)
Read a fraction from the keyboard.	(A procedure)
Reduce a fraction.	(A procedure)
Add two fractions.	(A procedure)
Subtract one fraction from another.	(A procedure)
Multiply two fractions.	(A procedure)
Divide one fraction by another.	(A procedure)
Calculate the real-number value of a fraction.	(A function)

The first of these is a procedure because it does not return a value. The rest, except for the last, are procedures because a Pascal function cannot return a composite data type. The last is a function because it returns only a real number—a simple data type.

Refining the plan for reading a fraction

We should stop after carrying the plan this far and try to anticipate any difficulties and special cases. For example, when we read a fraction from the keyboard, we want to allow inputs in any notation commonly used for fractions. For one thing, the procedure should accept inputs of the form *Numerator*<space>/<space>*Denominator*, as in the following I/O example:

```
Fraction: -3 / 5
```

On the other hand, it should also accept inputs without the spaces around the slash:

```
Fraction: 7/9
```

This is an important consideration because, as you will see later, Pascal makes the latter form fairly difficult to handle.

Then there is a special case to worry about. What should the read-fraction procedure do if the user attempts to enter a fraction with a zero denominator? Surely, the procedure should issue an error message and prompt again for the input:

```
Fraction: 3/0
ZERO DENOMINATOR NOT ALLOWED; PLEASE RE-ENTER: _
```

If the read-fraction procedure is the only way a user can store a value of type `Fraction`, the other procedures in the ADT can be assured that they will never encounter zero-valued denominators. This simplifies the work of the other procedures. (Of course, we will have to do what we can to prevent users from storing fractions by any means other than calling the read-fraction procedure.)

Refining the plan for writing a fraction

When we write a fraction to the screen, we want it to look normal even if it is negative or if the numerator or denominator is very small or large. We do not, for example, want to write the numerator and denominator in such a way that they display in default fields wide enough to show all integers, because that would look bad when the numerator or denominator is very small:

```
Looks bad:    -3 /     2
```

Furthermore, if the user has entered a fraction with a negative denominator, we want the minus sign to be stored with the numerator so that output will look normal:

```
Fraction: 3 / -2
You entered -3 / 2
```

Similarly, if the user enters both a negative numerator and a negative denominator, we want the fraction stored positively so that it will display normally:

```
Fraction: -3 / -2
You entered  3 / 2
```

Refining the plan for reducing a fraction

To reduce a fraction, we divide both the numerator and denominator by the *greatest common (nonnegative) divisor*. (Euclid's algorithm for finding the *gcd* was described in Sections 1.1 and 11.3.) Of course, reduction isn't possible if the denominator is 0, so we must be guaranteed to begin with that the denominator is nonzero.

Also, there is no need to reduce the fraction if the denominator is 1.

Refining the plan for arithmetic procedures

The arithmetic procedures—addition, subtraction, multiplication, and division—are binary operations. These only make sense if both fractions have nonzero denominators.

Writing a specification

We start by writing a specification for the ADT, in which we give a description of the data type itself, as an abstraction, along with a very specific list of the operations to be allowed on that data type. By starting with a clear and specific specification, we will be less likely to forget any of the details as we design code for the ADT's implementation. (See the specification on the next page.)

Fraction ADT Specification

Data structure:
A `Fraction` is a record with two fields: a `Numerator` and a `Denominator`.

Operations allowed on fractions:

- A procedure that writes a fraction in the form *Numerator / Denominator*, leaving the cursor on the same line.
- A procedure that reads a line of data into a `Fraction` variable; that is, it reads a numerator, then a space-slash-and-space combination, then a denominator, and then an end-of-line signal.
- A procedure that reduces a fraction so that the numerator and denominator have no common divisors with magnitude greater than 1.
- A procedure that adds two given fractions, returning the sum.
- A procedure that subtracts one fraction from another, returning the difference.
- A procedure that multiplies two given fractions, returning the product.
- A procedure that divides one fraction by another, returning the quotient.
- A function that returns the decimal value of a given fraction.

The ADT interface

Having planned this much, we can write an interface for the ADT. These are the public declarations we want to supply to client programmers:

```
{ FractionADT interface }

TYPE
   NonNegInt = 0..MaxInt;

   Fraction = RECORD
                 Numerator   : Integer;
                 Denominator : Integer
              END;

{---------------------------------------------------}
{ Writes a fraction to the screen.                  }
{---------------------------------------------------}
PROCEDURE WriteFr( VAR Fr : Fraction );
{
  PRECONDITION:  Fr has a nonzero denominator.

  POSTCONDITION: Fr has been displayed on the screen.
}
```

```
{----------------------------------------------------}
{ Reads a fraction from the keyboard.                }
{----------------------------------------------------}
PROCEDURE ReadLnFr( VAR Fr : Fraction );
{
  POSTCONDITION: Fr contains a fraction with nonzero denominator.
}

{----------------------------------------------------}
{ Reduces the fraction Fr.                           }
{----------------------------------------------------}
PROCEDURE Reduce( VAR Fr : Fraction );
{
  PRECONDITION:  Fr has a nonzero denominator.

  POSTCONDITION: The numerator and denominator of Fr have no
                 common factors with magnitude greater than 1.
}

{----------------------------------------------------}
{ Adds the fractions Fr1 and Fr2.                    }
{----------------------------------------------------}
PROCEDURE AddFr( Fr1, Fr2 : Fraction;
                 VAR Sum  : Fraction );
{
  PRECONDITION:   Fr has a nonzero denominator.

  POSTCONDITIONS: Sum contains (Fr1 + Fr2).
}

{----------------------------------------------------}
{ Subtracts Fr2 from Fr1.                            }
{----------------------------------------------------}
PROCEDURE SubtractFr( Fr1, Fr2 : Fraction;
                      VAR Diff : Fraction );
{
  PRECONDITION:   Fr has a nonzero denominator.

  POSTCONDITIONS: Diff contains (Fr1 - Fr2).
}

{----------------------------------------------------}
{ Multiplies the fractions Fr1 and Fr2.              }
{----------------------------------------------------}
PROCEDURE MultiplyFr( Fr1, Fr2    : Fraction;
                      VAR Product : Fraction );
{
  PRECONDITION:   Fr has a nonzero denominator.

  POSTCONDITIONS: Product contains (Fr1 * Fr2).
}
```

```
{-----------------------------------------------------}
{ Divides the Fr1 by Fr2.                             }
{-----------------------------------------------------}
PROCEDURE DivideFr( Fr1, Fr2     : Fraction;
                    VAR Quotient : Fraction );
{
  PRECONDITION:   Fr has a nonzero denominator.

  POSTCONDITIONS: Quotient contains (Fr1 / Fr2).
}

{-----------------------------------------------------}
{ Returns the real-number value of Fr.                }
{-----------------------------------------------------}
FUNCTION RealValOf( Fr : Fraction ) : Real;
{
  PRECONDITION:   Fr has a nonzero denominator.

  POSTCONDITIONS: Returns real-number value of Fr.
}
```

> This interface is saved as a separate source code file, to be supplied as documentation to client programmers. The interface tells a client programmer what operations can be performed on the ADT, and the syntax to use for each operation.

Actually, the interface is more than just documentation: Many Pascal systems automatically check th e implementation code and client programs against the interface to ensure that they are consistent. (This is not a feature of ISO Standard Pascal, however.)

Implementing the I/O operations (rough draft)

After we write the interface, we can write the ADT's implementation, which contains definitions of the various procedures and the one function, together with any constants or data types needed by these, but not needed by client programmers who will use the unit. Client programmers need to know only how to use the ADT, not how it is constructed internally.

> The central idea of data abstraction is to separate the use of the ADT (its interface) from its construction (its implementation). In this vein, we hide the implementation code from client programmers by placing it in a different file from the one used to store the interface.

The subprogram definitions in the implementation part of the unit do not *have* to be in the same order as their headers were listed in the interface part, but we *will* list them in that order for convenience in reading. We don't write many comments in the implementation part because the purpose and pre- and postconditions were already listed in the interface. The `WriteFr` procedure is the first one in the implementation part of the ADT:

```
{ FractionADT implementation }

TYPE
   String80  = PACKED ARRAY [1..80] OF Char;


PROCEDURE WriteFr( VAR Fr : Fraction );
BEGIN

   Write( Fr.Numerator );
   Write( ' / ' );
   Write( Fr.Denominator )

END; { WriteFr }
```

The ReadLnFr procedure is more difficult, because it must read a numerator, then scan for a slash and discard it, and finally read a denominator. It's a three-part process that is trickier than it looks. Here is a rough draft, but it won't be our final version:

```
PROCEDURE ReadLnFr( VAR Fr : Fraction );
VAR
   Ch : Char;

BEGIN

   REPEAT

      Read( Fr.Numerator );

      REPEAT
         Read( Ch )
      UNTIL Ch = '/';

      ReadLn( Fr.Denominator );

      IF Fr.Denominator = 0 THEN
         Write( 'ERROR IN INPUT. Try again: ' )

   UNTIL Fr.Denominator <> 0;

   { --Put any negative sign with the numerator: }
   IF Fr.Denominator < 0 THEN
   BEGIN
      Fr.Denominator := -Fr.Denominator;
      Fr.Numerator   := -Fr.Numerator
   END

END; { ReadLnFr }
```

This implementation works correctly if there are spaces around the slash, it will not work without the spaces. We will come back to this problem shortly, but first let's sketch the rest of the implementation's rough draft.

Implementing Reduce

To reduce a fraction, we divide the numerator and denominator by their greatest common divisor. A *gcd* algorithm was described in Section 1.1, so we use that, writing the `Reduce` procedure to allow for 0 or 1 in the denominator:

```
FUNCTION GCD( PosInt1, PosInt2 : NonNegInt ) : NonNegInt;
{
  POSTCONDITION:
  Returns the greatest common divisor of nonnegative
  integers PosInt1 and PosInt2.
}
VAR
   Remainder : NonNegInt;

BEGIN

   REPEAT
      Remainder := PosInt1 MOD PosInt2;
      PosInt1   := PosInt2;
      PosInt2   := Remainder
   UNTIL PosInt2 = 0;

   GCD := PosInt1

END; { GCD }


PROCEDURE Reduce( VAR Fr : Fraction );
VAR
   Divisor : NonNegInt;

BEGIN

   Divisor        := GCD( Abs(Fr.Numerator), Abs(Fr.Denominator) );
   Fr.Numerator   := Fr.Numerator DIV Divisor;
   Fr.Denominator := Fr.Denominator DIV Divisor

END; { Reduce }
```

Implementing arithmetic

Addition is simple, if we assume that denominators cannot be zero:

```
PROCEDURE AddFr( Fr1, Fr2 : Fraction;
                 VAR Sum  : Fraction );
BEGIN

   Sum.Numerator   := (Fr2.Denominator) * (Fr1.Numerator)
                    + (Fr1.Denominator) * (Fr2.Numerator);
   Sum.Denominator := (Fr1.Denominator) * (Fr2.Denominator)

END; { AddFr }
```

The procedures for subtraction, multiplication, and division are similar and are left as exercises for the reader. Here are the skeletons, finishing up the implementation part of the ADT's rough draft:

```
PROCEDURE SubtractFr( Fr1, Fr2 : Fraction;
                      VAR Diff : Fraction );
BEGIN
   { Stub }
END; { SubtractFr }

PROCEDURE MultiplyFr( Fr1, Fr2     : Fraction;
                      VAR Product : Fraction );
BEGIN
   { Stub }
END; { MultiplyFr }

PROCEDURE DivideFr( Fr1, Fr2      : Fraction;
                    VAR Quotient : Fraction );
BEGIN
   { Stub }
END; { DivideFr }

FUNCTION RealValOf( Fr : Fraction ) : Real;
BEGIN
   { Stub }
END; { RealValOf }

END. { of the unit }
```

Saving and using the Fraction ADT

The Pascal Standard does not describe a way to use ADTs, but there are three methods in common use among today's commercial Pascal systems. The simplest is to save the implementation source code in its own text file and then to **copy and paste** it into the source code for any program that needs to use it.

However, there are three drawbacks to the copy-and-paste approach. The fact that the ADT source code is literally copied into the client program before compilation means that the source code of every client program is made longer. It also means that any programmer using the ADT can read the implementation source code, and this is a drawback if your ADT contains proprietary secrets. The third drawback is that client programmers can modify your ADT and perhaps cause it to malfunction. The second and third reasons are why we wanted to hide the implementation in the first place, and with the copy-and-paste method, we have failed to hide anything.

An alternative but nonstandard method provided by some Pascal systems is to save the ADT's declarations and implementation code in a separate file that is automatically copied into client programs during compilation. Such a file is called an **include file**, and the automatic copying is done by the compiler, in response to an `INCLUDE` statement incorporated into the client program. Check your system's reference manual to see if this method is allowed; examples are discussed in Appendix H. The `INCLUDE` method is slightly better than copy-and-paste, because the source code of the client program is not lengthened; only the object code is lengthened. But the implementation source code is still available to anyone wanting to look at it, so proprietary information cannot be restricted and there is no way to prevent subversion and perversion of the ADT.

Unit or **compilation unit**: A special source code file that can be separately compiled and used by client programs, but which cannot be run by itself.

A more modern and professional method is allowed by some commercial Pascal systems. It involves putting both the interface and implementation code in a special source code file called a **unit**, which can be **separately compiled** but not separately run. Once compiled, a unit can be called on by any client program containing an appropriate statement declaring that the program uses the ADT. Again, check your reference manual to see if this is possible with your system. Examples are discussed in Appendix H. Separately compiled units have the advantage that their code is kept as secret as you want: you sell your customers the object code for the whole ADT and a copy of the interface text, *but not the implementation source code*. With this approach, your customers can't see how you implemented your procedures and functions and cannot subvert the operation of your ADT.

Write a driver for testing the ADT.

Then we need a driver for testing the ADT. Here's a simple one that tests `ReadLnFr`, `WriteFr`, `Reduce`, and `AddFr`:

```
PROGRAM TestFractions( Input, Output );
{
  Tell the program to use FractionADT, however you do this
  in your Pascal system.
}

VAR
   Fr1, Fr2, Sum : Fraction;

BEGIN

   Write( 'First fraction: ' );
   ReadLnFr( Fr1 );
   Reduce( Fr1 );
   Write( 'Reduces to ' );
   WriteFr( Fr1 );
   WriteLn;
   WriteLn;

   Write( 'Second fraction: ' );
   ReadLnFr( Fr2 );
   Reduce( Fr2 );
   Write( 'Reduces to ' );
   WriteFr( Fr2 );
   WriteLn;
   WriteLn;

   AddFr( Fr1, Fr2, Sum );
   Reduce( Fr2 );
   Write( 'Sum is ' );
   WriteFr( Sum );
   WriteLn;
   WriteLn

END.
```

> Don't forget to tell the program to use `FractionADT`; if you don't do this, you will get `Unknown identifier` syntax errors wherever the driver refers to names declared in the ADT.

The first test

When we run the driver, we see that part of the ADT is working as it should:

```
First fraction: 2 / 3
Reduces to 2 / 3

Second fraction: -3 / 9
Reduces to -1 / 3

Sum is  1 / 3
```

Unfortunately, the input doesn't work correctly if the user enters a fraction without a space in front of the slash:

```
Fraction: 2/3
```

This gives an error message when `Read( Fr.Numerator )` is executed. In Turbo Pascal, the message looks like this:

```
Error 106: Invalid numeric format.
```

The problem lies in the way a `Read(` *Integer* `)` or `ReadLn(` *Integer* `)` determines the end of the integer it is reading. According to Section 8.2, the procedure will "read the longest unbroken string of characters interpretable as an integer number. Once a character is encountered that cannot be part of an integer number, the string up to that point is converted to an integer value." In other words, the characters are read one by one until a noninteger character has been read. If this character is not whitespace, some Pascal systems generate an error message and remove the troublesome character from the input buffer so that it will not be available to be read by the `REPEAT` loop that was intended to deal with it.

Rethinking the ReadLnFr procedure

We will have to design a better `ReadLnFr` implementation, because we can't count on users following a particular format when entering input data.

> Programmers have no control over the people who will use their programs. Therefore, programs must be designed to behave reasonably, no matter what the users may do.

Therefore, we redesign the procedure from the top down. This time, we use some of our homemade string operations from Section 14.6 to find the slash in the input, and we use the slash's position to split the fraction string into numerator and denominator. The code is shown on the next page, with calls to our homemade operations highlighted in color:

```
PROCEDURE ReadLnFr( VAR Fr : Fraction );
VAR
   FrStr, NumerStr, DenomStr : String80;
   SlashPos, ErrorPos : NonNegInt;

BEGIN

   REPEAT

      { Make sure the fraction contains a slash. Find the slash. }
      REPEAT

         ReadLnStr( FrStr );
         SlashPos := Pos( '/', FrStr );

         { A numerator should occupy at least 1 char before slash: }
         IF SlashPos < 2 THEN
            Write( 'NOT A FRACTION. Re-enter: ' )

      UNTIL SlashPos > 1;

      { ASSERT: The input string contains a numerator and slash. }

      { Extract the numerator: }
      NumerStr := Copy( FrStr, 1, (SlashPos-1) );
      TrimTrailingSpaces( NumerStr );
      Val( NumerStr, Fr.Numerator, ErrorPos );

      IF ErrorPos > 0 THEN
         WriteLn( 'ERROR IN NUMERATOR AT POSITION ',
                  ErrorPos:2, ' Re-enter:' );

      { Extract the denominator: }
      DenomStr :=
            Copy( FrStr, (SlashPos+1), (Length(FrStr)-SlashPos) );
      TrimTrailingSpaces( DenomStr );
      Val( DenomStr, Fr.Denominator, ErrorPos );

      IF ErrorPos > 0 THEN
         WriteLn( 'ERROR IN DENOMINATOR AT POSITION ',
                  ErrorPos:2, ' Re-enter:' )
      ELSE IF Fr.Denominator = 0 THEN
         WriteLn( 'IMPROPER FRACTION; ZERO DENOMINATOR.',
                   'Re-enter:' )

   UNTIL Fr.Denominator <> 0

END; { ReadLnFr }
```

Some Pascal systems provide a `ReadLn` procedure that functions like our homemade `ReadLnStr`, plus `Pos`, `Copy`, and `Val` operations—all built-in. Other commercial Pascal systems often provide something similar.

As you can see, this procedure requires the two data types, `String80` and `NonNegInt`, that we defined at the top of the implementation part of the unit. These were not declared at the top of the interface part because clients do not need to know about them.

Also, the `ReadLnFr` procedure calls a `TrimTrailingSpaces` procedure, which is used to remove any trailing spaces from the numerator string and denominator strings.

`TrimTrailingSpaces` is relatively simple:

```
PROCEDURE TrimTrailingSpaces( VAR Str : String80 );
VAR
   Index, LastNonspacePos : NonNegInt;

BEGIN

   FOR Index := 1 TO Length( Str ) DO
      IF Str[ Index ] <> ' ' THEN
         LastNonspacePos := Index;

   Str := Copy( Str, 1, LastNonspacePos )

END; { TrimTrailingSpaces }
```

Try it out!

Recompile and relink the ADT code and your driver. The driver should be compatible with the revised implementation because we didn't change the interface. When you run the driver with the new ADT implementation, you will find that it reads fractions with or without spaces around the slash:

```
First fraction: 2/3
Reduces to 2 / 3

Second fraction: -3 / 9
Reduces to -1 / 3

Sum is  1 / 3
```

Questions

6. In what sense is the implementation of an ADT independent of the interface? In what sense does it depend on the interface?

7. Why does a modification of an ADT's implementation require the programmer to check the interface for possible modification?

8. Why does a modification of an ADT's interface imply that the implementation may need to be modified?

9. Can an ADT implementation be revised without any change in the interface? If so, under what circumstances?

Exercises

10. Complete the implementations of `SubtractFr`, `MultiplyFr`, and `DivideFr` in the same style we used for `AddFr`. Recompile the unit. Then modify the driver to exercise your new procedures and run a test of them.

11. Write an implementation for the `RealValOf` function. Modify the driver to exercise your new function and test it.

12. Add to your `FractionADT` unit an interface and implementation for an `InvertFr` procedure, which inverts a given fraction. For example, if given the fraction 3/2, it should return the fraction 3/2. Modify the driver and test your new procedure.

13. Add to your `FractionADT` unit an interface and implementation for a `WholeAndFr` procedure, which converts a fraction greater than 1 to a whole number and reduced fraction. For example, if given the fraction 14/4, it should return the whole number 3 and the fraction 1/2, indicating that 14/4 = 3 1/2. Modify the driver and test your new procedure.

16.3 BUILDING A TURTLE ADT

Pixel: A "dot" on the screen. (Stands for "picture element.")

In most computer systems, the graphics screen is made up of dots called picture elements, or **pixels** for short. The pixels are arranged in rows, so *the screen is actually a two-dimensional array of pixels.* With such a screen, we draw a line by turning on the pixels that lie along the line. Then with the appropriate arrangement of lines, we can draw shapes. By building up an appropriate hierarchy of drawing procedures, we can draw increasingly complicated shapes.

One of the simplest standard approaches to such drawing is called **turtle graphics**. This was invented by Seymour Papert and colleagues at the Massachusetts Institute of Technology for teaching geometry and algorithmic thinking to children. Turtle graphics became an integral part of the LOGO programming language (actually a dialect of LISP), and was made available on many home computers. (See Papert's important book *Mindstorms,* listed in the references at the end of this chapter.) The version of turtle graphics described below is adapted from the LOGO language, but here *we think of the turtle as an abstract data type.*

The turtle as an ADT

Imagine that the two-dimensional computer screen, thought of as a drawing plane, is inhabited by a pen-equipped turtle that is a navigator. The turtle's position on the screen at any moment is specified by its x- and y-coordinates and by the direction it is pointed, called its *heading*. A heading is a counterclockwise angle relative to the positive x-axis, as shown in Figure 16.3.1. The turtle, then, is an abstraction with five attributes:

1. The turtle has a position on the screen, specified by x- and y-coordinates.
2. The turtle has a direction, called its heading.
3. The turtle has a pen with an eraser on its other end. If the turtle is using the pen as it moves, it will draw lines. If it is using the eraser, it will erase lines where it passes over them.
4. At any given moment, the turtle's pen is either in contact with the drawing surface or lifted up from the surface. If the pen is lifted up, it can neither draw nor erase.
5. The turtle's pen can have various kinds of "ink" in it, leaving various patterns of trails.

This tells us what the turtle itself *is*, but to make the abstraction complete, we need to know what the turtle can *do*.

The turtle's heading is its direction relative to the positive x-axis, measured in degrees. **Figure 16.3.1**

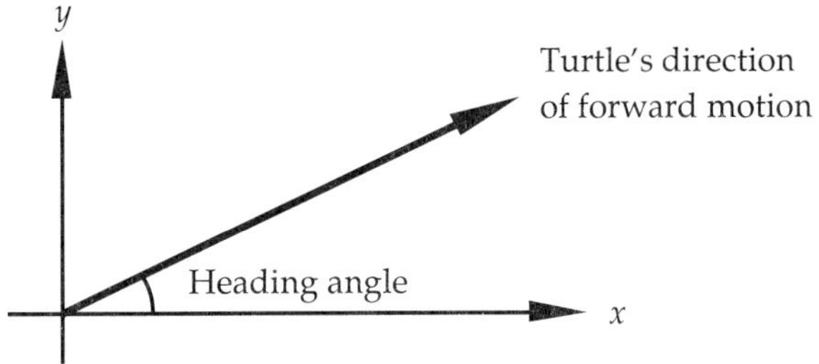

Basic turtle commands for turning and moving

The turtle's heading is initially 0°, but can be changed at any time by issuing a command to turn left or right relative to the current heading. Thus, we have our first two operations that can be performed on the turtle abstract data type:

`Right( Degrees )` makes the turtle turn to its right (i.e., clockwise) by the specified number of degrees, relative to its current heading.

`Left( Degrees )` makes the turtle turn to its left (that is, counterclockwise) by the specified number of degrees, relative to its current heading.

These two commands make the turtle pivot to its right or left while remaining on the same spot on the screen. They do not make the turtle move. To make the turtle move, there are two more commands:

`MoveForward( Steps )` makes the turtle take the specified number of "turtle steps" (arbitrary units) in the direction of its heading. If the turtle's pen is down, it will leave a trail as it moves.

`MoveBack( Steps )` makes the turtle take the specified number of turtle steps in the direction *opposite* to its heading. If the pen is down, the turtle will leave a trail as it moves.

Initially, the turtle is in the center of the screen, which is called the *home* position, with a heading of 0°. At any time, the turtle can be returned to this condition by giving the `Home` command:

`Home` returns the turtle to the center of the screen ($x = 0, y = 0$), giving it a heading of 0°. Note that the `Home` command does *not* clear or otherwise change the screen.

Drawing with the turtle

All this is useful because the turtle can be used for drawing. If the turtle is using its pen, it will leave a trail when it waddles across the screen. There is an eraser on the pen, with which the turtle can erase marks that it travels over. By giving appropriate commands to use the pen or eraser, and to move, we can make the turtle draw all sorts of patterns on the screen.

There are three basic pen and eraser commands:

`DropPen` commands the turtle to lower its pen, so that it will leave a trail when it moves.

`DropEraser` commands the turtle to lower its eraser, so that it will erase any "ink" it passes over.

`LiftPen` commands the turtle to raise its pen and eraser, so that it will not leave a trail or erase.

We also have a command for erasing the whole screen:

`ClearScreen` erases all marks from the screen.

The interface for the turtle ADT

Thinking of the turtle as an abstraction to be packaged as a unit as we did with the fraction ADT, we write an interface part telling clients what a turtle is, and what operations can be performed on a turtle. Clients do not need to know how we represent a turtle in computer memory or about the mathematics involved in making the turtle turn or move. Here is the interface:

```
{
  TURTLE ADT INTERFACE

  A turtle is an invisible creature that lives on the screen.
  At any given moment, it has a position and a heading.
  It can be made to turn or move.

  The turtle is equipped with a pen that has an eraser.
  The turtle can be commanded to lower the pen onto the drawing
  surface or to lift it away from the surface, and it can be
  commanded to use the eraser end or the pen.
}

TYPE
   NonNegInt = 0..MaxInt;

{---------------------------------------------------------------}
{ Make turtle turn right by TurnAngle,                          }
{ relative to its current heading.                              }
{---------------------------------------------------------------}
PROCEDURE Right( TurnAngle : Integer );
{
  PRECONDITION:
  TurnAngle and Heading have been initialized.

  POSTCONDITION:
  Heading has decreased by the number of degrees given in TurnAngle.
}
```

```
{----------------------------------------------------------}
{ Make turtle turn left by TurnAngle,                      }
{ relative to its current heading.                         }
{----------------------------------------------------------}
PROCEDURE Left( TurnAngle : Integer );
{
  PRECONDITION:
  TurnAngle and Heading have been initialized.

  POSTCONDITION:
  Heading has increased by the number of degrees given in TurnAngle.
}

{----------------------------------------------------------}
{ Make turtle take a specified number of steps forward     }
{ from its current position.                               }
{----------------------------------------------------------}
PROCEDURE MoveForward( NumSteps : NonNegInt );
{
  PRECONDITION:
  Heading, position, and NumSteps have been initialized.

  POSTCONDITION:
  Turtle has moved along direction of Heading from
  previous position by number of pixels specified in NumSteps.
}

{----------------------------------------------------------}
{ Make turtle take a specified number of steps backward    }
{ from its current position.                               }
{----------------------------------------------------------}
PROCEDURE MoveBack( NumSteps : NonNegInt );
{
  PRECONDITION:
  Heading, position, and NumSteps have been initialized.

  POSTCONDITION:
  Turtle has moved along direction opposite to Heading from
  previous position by number of pixels specified in NumSteps.
}

{----------------------------------------------------------}
{ Lower the turtle's pen for drawing.                      }
{----------------------------------------------------------}
PROCEDURE DropPen;
{
  POSTCONDITION:
  Pen is lowered to the drawing surface.
}
```

```
{----------------------------------------------------------}
{ Lower the turtle's eraser.                               }
{----------------------------------------------------------}
PROCEDURE DropEraser;
{
  POSTCONDITION:
  Eraser is down on the drawing surface.
}

{----------------------------------------------------------}
{ Lift the turtle's pen/eraser,                            }
{ so that it will neither draw nor erase.                  }
{----------------------------------------------------------}
PROCEDURE LiftPen;
{
  POSTCONDITION:
  Pen has been raised from the drawing surface.
}

{----------------------------------------------------------}
{ Return the turtle to the center of the screen, pointed   }
{ to the right, without otherwise changing the screen.     }
{----------------------------------------------------------}
PROCEDURE Home;
{
  POSTCONDITION:
  Turtle is at center of screen with Heading = 0 degrees.
}
```

A portable implementation

To draw using the pixels in the computer screen, we will have to use system-dependent code that will run on one kind of computer system but not another. Instead, for the purposes of this section, we will use *portable code* that will work on any system running Standard Pascal, and not just systems with graphics hardware. We will model the screen as a two-dimensional array of characters. The screen array will initially be full of blanks, representing a cleared screen. Then when we draw a line, we will represent the ink as a trail of some visible character—for example, an asterisk (*).

There are two big problems with this plan, though. If we represent the screen as a two-dimensional array of characters, we will typically have only 80 x 25 points to work with. This means that our drawings will be fairly crude. This is the best we can do if we want our Pascal code to be portable, however. To do better, we would have to access the individual dots on the computer screen in a system-dependent way. (See Project 6 at the end of the chapter.) Another problem is that to show each turtle step as it occurs, we have to redraw the entire screen after every step, making the animation unacceptably slow on many computers. To avoid this, we will show the "screen array" only on demand. This is the reason for the last procedure shown in the interface:

`ShowScreen` displays the current contents of the two-dimensional array of characters representing the drawing screen.

The turtle after the Home command is executed. In practice, the turtle is invisible. **Figure 16.3.2**

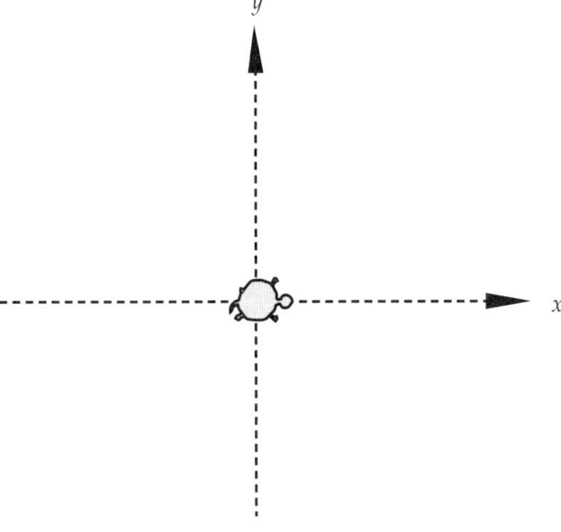

Example: Drawing a square

Leaving aside for a moment how we are going to write the fundamental graphics procedures listed above, imagine how they might work when we have them. (Again, we are thinking top-down.) Suppose that we want to draw a 10x10 square on the screen. We start out by erasing the screen with the `ClearScreen` command, lowering the turtle's pen, and initializing the turtle's position and heading with the `Home` command (Figure 16.3.2). Then we make the turtle walk 10 steps forward and turn 90° to the right, as shown in Figure 16.3.3. We repeat this four times, after which the turtle is back at its starting point, pointed to the original heading, as shown in Figure 16.3.4.

The imaginary turtle after moving forward 10 turtle steps and turning 90 degrees to the right. **Figure 16.3.3**

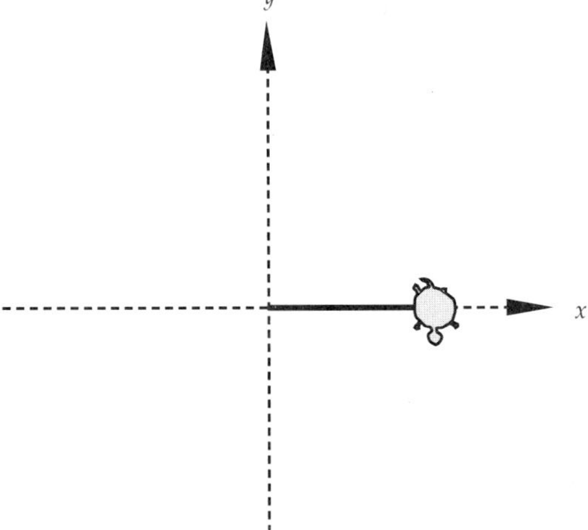

Figure 16.3.4 *The turtle after drawing a square.*

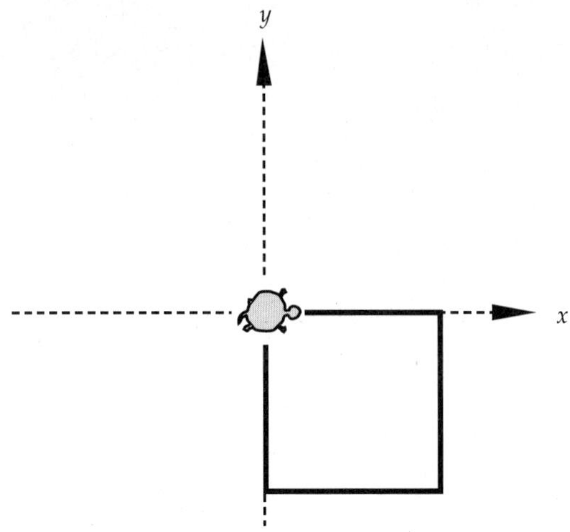

A program to draw the square might therefore look like this:

```
PROGRAM Square( Output );

USES TurtleADT;

VAR
   Count : NonNegInt;

BEGIN

   { Initialize screen and turtle }
   ClearScreen;
   Home;
   DropPen;

   { Draw four sides of a square }
   FOR Count := 1 TO 4 DO
   BEGIN

      MoveForward( 10 );
      Right( 90 )

   END

END.
```

To make it more convenient to draw squares in the future, we might build the loop into a `DrawSquare` procedure, with the size of the square as a parameter:

```
PROCEDURE DrawSquare( Size : NonNegInt );
{
  PRECONDITION:
  0 <= Size <= MaxInt.

  POSTCONDITION:
  A right-turning square has been drawn using the
  current pen condition, ending up at the starting
  point with the original heading.
}
VAR
   Count : NonNegInt;

BEGIN

   FOR Count := 1 TO 4 DO
   BEGIN
      MoveForward( Size );
      Right( 90 )
   END

END; { Square }
```

But what happens if the square is so big that the turtle waddles off the screen? Should it just disappear, or should it "wrap around" to the other side of the screen? We will address this question when we design the `MoveForward` and `Backward` procedures later. For now, just assume that the issue will be handled somehow. Let's continue to examine how shapes can be drawn.

Example: Drawing a circle

The turtle can be made to walk in a quasi circle to the left by taking a step and turning a little, taking a step and turning a little, and so on. For example, the loop

```
FOR Count := 1 TO 120 DO
BEGIN
   MoveForward( 1 );
   Left( 3 )
END
```

turns 120 times, 3° at each turn, for a total of 360°. Before each turn, the turtle takes one step, so the circumference of the "circle," which is actually a 120-sided polygon, is 120 turtle steps. The diameter is therefore $120/\pi$, or about 38 steps. This is too big to fit on the screen, which we assume is only 25 lines tall (Figure 16.3.5).

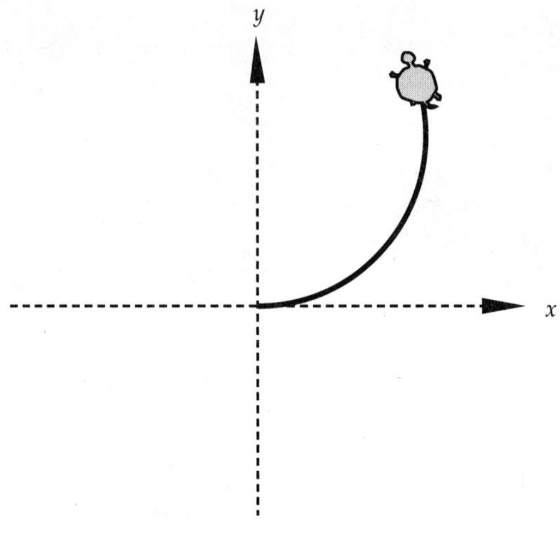

Figure 16.3.5 *Starting a big circle, turning to the left.*

A smaller circle can be drawn by increasing the angle of each turn. For example, the loop

```
FOR Count := 1 TO 60 DO
BEGIN
   MoveForward( 1 );
   Left( 6 )
END
```

draws a circle with half the diameter of the previous circle (Figure 16.3.6).

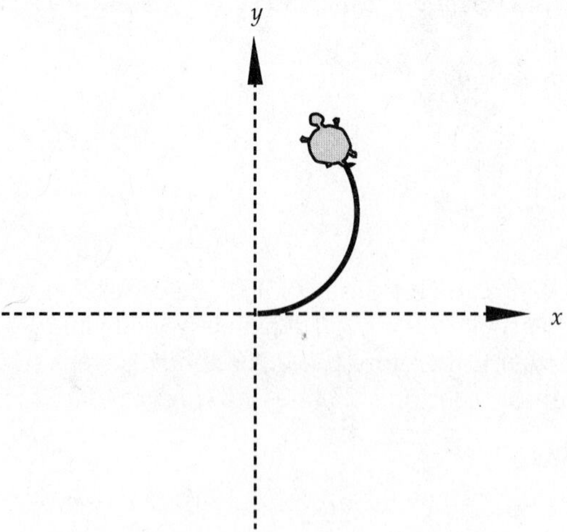

Figure 16.3.6 *Starting a half-sized circle, turning to the left.*

Thus, we have the basis for a `DrawCircle` procedure, in which the steps per turn and the angle per turn can be computed from a radius specified as a parameter. We use the fact that

(Number of turns)(Steps per turn) = Circumference = $2\pi r$.

If the turtle takes only one step per turn, then the number of turns required is $2\pi r$, which we round off to the nearest integer:

```
PROCEDURE DrawCircle( Radius : NonNegInt );
{
  PRECONDITION:
  0 <= Radius <= MaxInt.

  POSTCONDITION:
  A left-turning circle has been drawn using the
  current pen condition. The turtle finishes at
  approximately the starting point with
  approximately the original heading.
}
CONST
   TwoPi = 6.2832;

VAR
   Count, NumTurns, AnglePerTurn : NonNegInt;
   RealNumTurns : Real;

BEGIN

   RealNumTurns := TwoPi * Radius;
   NumTurns     := Round( RealNumTurns );
   AnglePerTurn := Round( 360.0 / RealNumTurns );

   FOR Count := 1 TO NumTurns DO
   BEGIN
      MoveForward( 1 );
      Left( AnglePerTurn )
   END

END; { DrawCircle }
```

Of course, the radius ends up being only very approximate in this procedure, and in fact, the procedure may draw slightly less or slightly more than a full circle. As an exercise, you should try to improve the algorithm.

Example: Drawing flower petals

Surprisingly interesting patterns can be drawn even with such crude graphics. Consider what happens if you call `HexPetals` in the following code:

```
PROCEDURE Hexagon;
{ Draws a hexagon with sides of length 10 }
VAR
  Count : NonNegInt;

BEGIN

   FOR Count := 1 TO 6 DO
   BEGIN
      MoveForward( 10 );
      Left( 60 )
   END

END; { Hexagon }


PROCEDURE HexPetals;
VAR
   Count : NonNegInt;

BEGIN

   FOR Count := 1 TO 8 DO
   BEGIN
      Hexagon;
      Left( 45 )
   END

END; { HexPetals }
```

When HexPetals is called, it produces the pattern shown in Figure 16.3.7.

Figure 16.3.7 *The pattern drawn by HexPetals when a high-resolution implementation is used. In low-resolution graphics, the pattern looks as shown in Figure 16.3.12.*

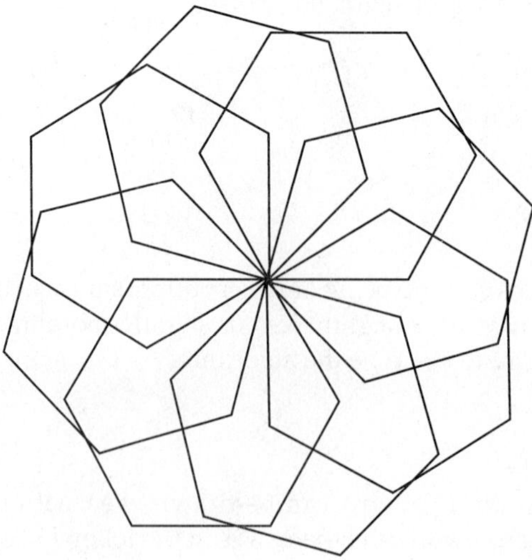

The turtle ADT implementation

The turtle actually moves in a two-dimensional array of characters, and has the five attributes listed at the beginning of this section. We hide all that in the implementation part of the ADT because client programmers don't need to know about it and therefore *shouldn't* know about it. In other words, we deliberately hide from the user the current heading, the x- and y-coordinates of the turtle's position, the character being used as the pen's "ink," and the state of the turtle's pen. These properties of the turtle are actually stored in variables, but none of these variables appear as parameters of the procedures because we do not want the user to know about them, think about them, or, worst of all, to modify them by any means other than those we provide in the ADT. Because of this, the `Heading` variable is made *global*, and the `Right` and `Left` procedures modify this global variable. Similarly, the `MoveForward` and `MoveBack` procedures modify global `X` and `Y` variables in which the current x- and y-coordinates of the turtle are stored. And again, the `DropPen`, `DropEraser`, and `LiftPen` procedures modify a global `PenDown` variable. Altogether, we end up with six global variables in the ADT implementation:

```
{
  TURTLE ADT IMPLEMENTATION

  This version uses a 79x25 grid of characters to represent the
  screen. The center of the screen is the point (0, 0), called
  "home". Directions are expressed as headings, in degrees.
  A heading of zero degrees points "to the right," as in
  trigonometry.
}

CONST
   TwoPi = 6.2831853;      { Used to convert degrees to radians }
   MaxX  = 39;             { X limits of screen are +/- 39      }
   MaxY  = 12;             { Y limits of screen are +/- 12      }

TYPE
   XRange    = -MaxX..MaxX;   { Range of allowed x-positions       }
   YRange    = -MaxY..MaxY;   { Range of allowed y-positions       }

   Grid      = ARRAY [ XRange, YRange ] OF Char;
                           { Array type for storing "screen"    }

VAR
   Heading : Integer; { Current heading in degrees
                        (zero degrees points to the "right")    }
   X, Y    : Real;    { Current position; [Home position is
                        (0, 0), in center of screen]            }
   PenChar : Char;    { Current drawing char; either '*' or ' ' }
   PenDown : Boolean; { Indicates whether "pen" touches screen  }
   Screen  : Grid;    { Array for storing "screen" characters   }
```

Saving and using the Turtle ADT

As explained in connection with the `FractionADT`, Standard Pascal provides no way to keep these declarations hidden from the user, but commercial Pascal systems featuring **compilation units** allow us to hide the implementation. We place the interface text in its own file, which we provide to clients. We place the implementation code in another file, which we do *not* provide to clients. Then we compile the implementation, and provide its object code to clients. See Appendix H for details.

Implementing the procedures

Because of the global variables, the turtle procedures risk a danger that we have not faced before. Unless we are careful to prevent it, one procedure's effect on a global variable may interfere with another procedure using the same variable. (This is called a *side effect.*) To help avoid this danger, we will keep careful track of the globals affected by each procedure.

Several of the procedures have trivial implementations:

```
PROCEDURE DropPen;
{
  GLOBALS AFFECTED: PenDown and PenChar.
}
BEGIN

   PenDown := True;
   PenChar := '*'

END; { DropPen }


PROCEDURE DropEraser;
{
  GLOBALS AFFECTED: PenDown and PenChar.
}
BEGIN

   PenDown := True;
   PenChar := ' '

END; { DropEraser }


PROCEDURE LiftPen;
{
  GLOBAL AFFECTED: PenDown.
}
BEGIN

   PenDown := False

END; { LiftPen }
```

```
PROCEDURE Home;
{
  GLOBALS AFFECTED: X, Y, Heading.
}
BEGIN

   Heading := 0;
   X       := 0.0;
   Y       := 0.0

END; { Home }


PROCEDURE ClearScreen;
{
  GLOBAL AFFECTED: Screen.
}
VAR
   Row, Col : Integer;

BEGIN

   FOR Row := -MaxY TO MaxY DO
      FOR Col := -MaxX TO MaxX DO
         Screen[Col, Row] := ' '

END; { ClearScreen }


PROCEDURE ShowScreen;
{
  GLOBALS AFFECTED: None.
}
VAR
   Row, Col : Integer;

BEGIN

   FOR Row := MaxY DOWNTO -MaxY DO
   BEGIN

      FOR Col := -MaxX TO MaxX DO
         Write( Screen[ Col, Row ] );

      WriteLn

   END

END; { ShowScreen }
```

The turning procedures

The turning procedures, `Right` and `Left`, merely increase or decrease `Heading` by a specified amount. But we want $0 \le$ `Heading` ≤ 360, so we compute the new heading modulo 360:

```
PROCEDURE Right( TurnAngle : Integer );
{
  GLOBAL AFFECTED: Heading.
}
BEGIN

   Heading := ( Heading - TurnAngle ) MOD 360

END; { Right }
```

This gives the correct result when `(Heading - TurnAngle)` is negative if `MOD` is a true modulus operator, as required by the Pascal Standard. If your Pascal system implements `MOD` as a simple remainder, you will have to write

```
Heading := ( Heading - TurnAngle ) MOD 360;
IF Heading < 0 THEN
   Heading := Heading + 360
```

The `Left` procedure is similar, except that `TurnAngle` is *added* to `Heading`.

The moving procedures

Now we come to the difficult procedures. To travel along a given `Heading` from the point `(X, Y)` to the new point `(NewX, NewY)`, we need the change in x and the change in y, computed with the help of trigonometry (Figure 16.3.8). Since the cosine and sine functions require radian arguments, we will have to convert the heading from degrees to radians. This is done by multiplying by 2π and dividing by 360. Once we know the destination point, we will draw a line from the current position to that point. To do this, we will use a `DrawLineTo` procedure. Don't worry for the moment about how we will do this; just concentrate on the `MoveForward` procedure itself. Here it is:

```
PROCEDURE MoveForward( NumSteps : NonNegInt );
{
  GLOBALS AFFECTED: X, Y, and Screen.
}
VAR
   NewX, NewY, Rads : Real;
```

Figure 16.3.8 *Computing the change in x and y.*

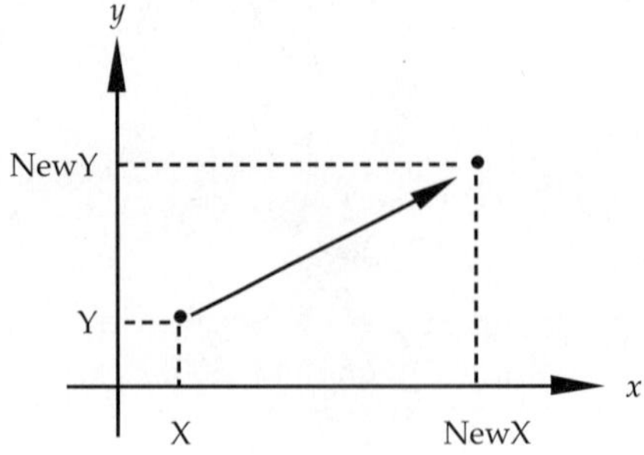

```
BEGIN

   { -- Calculate coordinates of destination. }
   Rads := ( TwoPi / 360.0 ) * Heading;
   NewX := X + ( NumSteps * Cos( Rads ) );
   NewY := Y + ( NumSteps * Sin( Rads ) );

   IF PenDown THEN
      { -- Draw a straight line to the destination. }
      DrawLineTo( NewX, NewY );

   { -- Destination is now the current position. }
   X := NewX;
   Y := NewY

END; { MoveForward }
```

You can see from this code that the computation of `NewX` and `NewY` will often produce noninteger values. That is, the new position may lie in between pixels. Because of this, the turtle's position is always stored as a real number. In order to display the position, the nearest integer pixel position is found by rounding, as you will see in the `SetPixel` procedure below.

Next, we discuss how to draw the line from the current position to the new position.

A heuristic line-drawing algorithm

We can imagine drawing a line from one point to another as a process of progressively incrementing x, and, for each value of x, computing the corresponding value of y from the slope, and marking the incremented point. For example, suppose we are drawing a line from the point (x_1, y_1) to the point (x_2, y_2), as shown in Figure 16.3.9.

All points (x, y) along this line obey the equation

$$\frac{y - y_1}{x - x_1} = \frac{y_2 - y_1}{x_2 - x_1}$$

which rearranges to

$$y(x) = y_1 + s(x - x_1), \quad \text{where } s = \text{slope} = (y_2 - y_1) / (x_2 - x_1).$$

The line from one point to another, and its slope. **Figure 16.3.9**

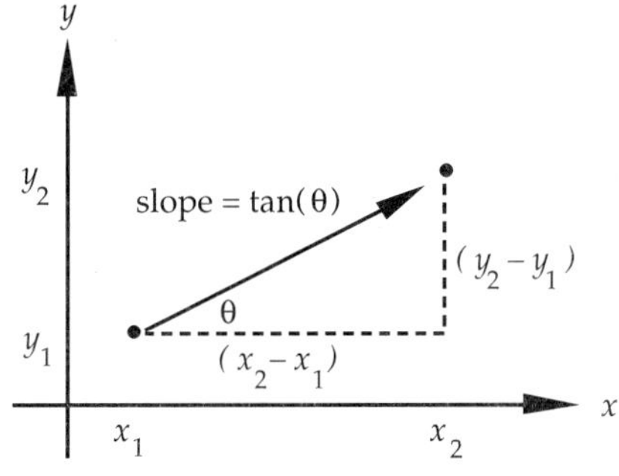

Figure 16.3.10 *Points along the line.*

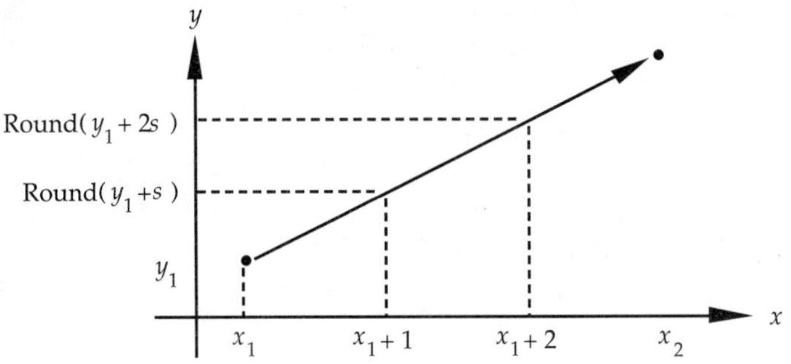

In plotting the line on a computer screen, x and y can take on only the integer values corresponding to pixel coordinates, so our line must be plotted as a sequence of incremented x-values, starting with x_1 and continuing to x_2. The sequence is

$$x_1,\ (x_1 + 1),\ (x_1 + 2),\ (x_1 + 3),\ \ldots,\ x_2$$

For a given value of x, the corresponding value of y is equal to sx, which is a real number. We round off this value to the nearest integer so we can plot it on the computer screen. As shown in Figure 16.3.10, the sequence of pixels that will represent the straight line is then

$$(x_1, y_1),\ (x_1 + 1,\ \text{Round}(y_1 + s)),\ (x_1 + 2,\ \text{Round}(y_1 + 2s)),$$
$$(x_1 + 3,\ \text{Round}(y_1 + 3s)), \ldots,\ (x_2, y_2)$$

Preventing gaps in the line

There is one last issue to be dealt with. If points are plotted along the line as just described, the plotted line will look fine if the slope is less than 45°, but will have gaps if the slope is greater than 45°. This is shown in Figure 16.3.11. The solution is to plot y

Figure 16.3.11 *Steep lines will have some gaps if plotted as described above.*

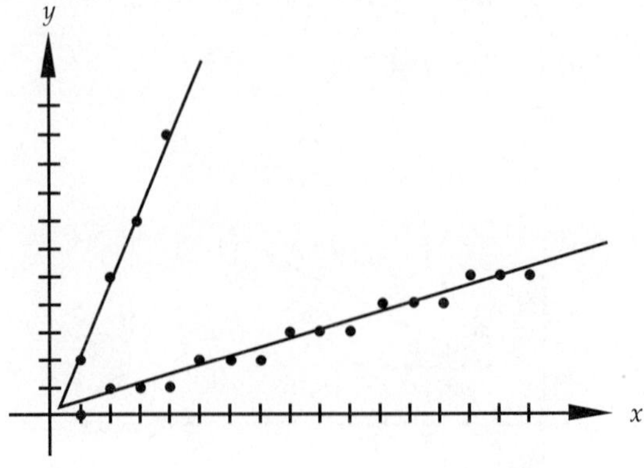

as a function of x if the slope is less than 45°, but to plot x as a function of y if the slope is steeper than this.

Putting it all together

Here are the two procedures that compute the sequence of points and set the pixels along our approximation to the line:

```
{-------------------------------------------------------------------}
{ Mark the pixel at position (IX, IY), using the current pen       }
{ character. Points outside the screen area are not plotted.       }
{-------------------------------------------------------------------}
PROCEDURE SetPixel( IX, IY : Integer );
{
  PRECONDITION:
  Global PenChar has a value.

  POSTCONDITION:
  Turns on pixel (IX, IY) in the global Screen array.

  GLOBAL AFFECTED: Screen.
}
BEGIN

   { -- If coordinates are in grid, set the appropriate pixel. }
   IF ( IX >= -MaxX ) AND ( IX <= MaxX )
      AND ( IY >= -MaxY ) AND ( IY <= MaxY ) THEN
         Screen[ IX, IY ] := PenChar

END; { SetPixel }


{-------------------------------------------------------------------}
{ Mark pixels along the straight line from the current position    }
{ to the point (NewX, NewY). Then make that point the new current }
{ position.                                                         }
{-------------------------------------------------------------------}
PROCEDURE DrawLineTo( NewX, NewY : Real );
{
  PRECONDITION: Globals X, Y and params NewX, NewY have values.

  POSTCONDITION: Pixels have been set along the straight line
  from (X, Y) to (NewX, NewY), in the global Screen array.

  GLOBALS AFFECTED: X and Y.
}
VAR
   NumSteps, Step               : Integer;
   DeltaX, DeltaY, XStep, YStep : Real;

BEGIN

   { --Get number of steps needed in x- and y-directions }
   DeltaX := Abs(NewX - X);
   DeltaY := Abs(NewY - Y);
```

```
{ --Take enough steps so there are no gaps }
IF DeltaX > DeltaY THEN
   NumSteps := Round( DeltaX )
ELSE
   NumSteps := Round( DeltaY );

{ --Set pixel at starting point }
SetPixel( Round(X), Round(Y) );

IF NumSteps > 0 THEN
BEGIN
   { --Get Real size of X- and Y-steps }
   XStep := ( NewX - X ) / NumSteps;
   YStep := ( NewY - Y ) / NumSteps;

   { --Sweep running point (X, Y) over the line segment }
   FOR Step := 1 TO NumSteps DO
   BEGIN
      X := X + XStep;
      Y := Y + YStep;

      { -- Set pixel nearest to latest point }
      SetPixel( Round(X), Round(Y) )
   END

 END { IF NumSteps > 0 }
END; { DrawLineTo }
```

Note that these two procedures are not documented in the ADT interface. They are to be used only by the `MoveForward` and `MoveBack` procedures, so they should be hidden from the user, tucked away in the implementation part.

Question

14. The discussion of the line-drawing algorithm involved the slope, which does not appear explicitly in the `DrawLineTo` procedure. How does slope play an implicit role in this procedure?

Exercises

15. Write a `DrawRect` procedure that makes the turtle draw a rectangle with sides of given lengths. That is, `Rect( 10, 20 )` should make the turtle draw a 10 x 20 rectangle. Your procedure should make good use of the turtle ADT procedures.

16. Write a `DrawStar` procedure that makes the turtle draw a five-pointed star, as shown below. The length of the straight lines should be a parameter of the procedure. (Hint: In figuring the turning angle, note that the turtle makes five equal turns while turning completely around twice.) Your procedure should make good use of the turtle ADT procedures.

Figure 16.3.12

Figure drawn by HexPetals procedure, using the portable low-resolution implementation presented in this section. The distortion is caused by the printed line spacing, which is greater than the horizontal character spacing. A high-resolution version is shown in Figure 16.3.7.

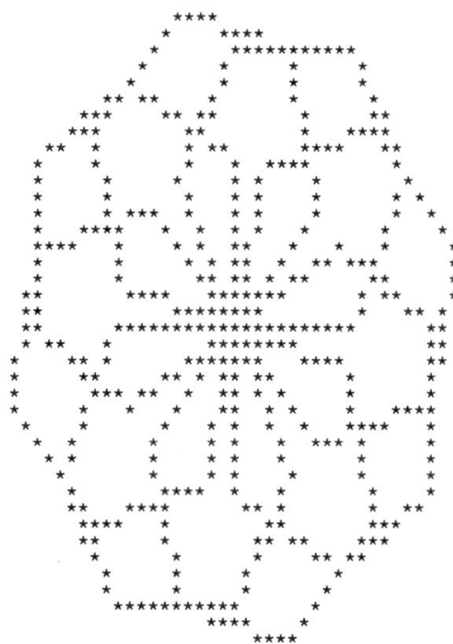

17. Embellish the `DrawStar` procedure from Exercise 16 so that the number of points is specified as a parameter. Consider only an odd number of points; if the number of points is even, the problem is much harder.

18. Write a `DrawPoly` procedure that makes the turtle draw a regular polygon with a given number of sides and given side length. That is, `Poly( 6, 20 )` should draw a regular hexagon with 20 turtle steps on each side. Your procedure should make good use of the turtle ADT procedures.

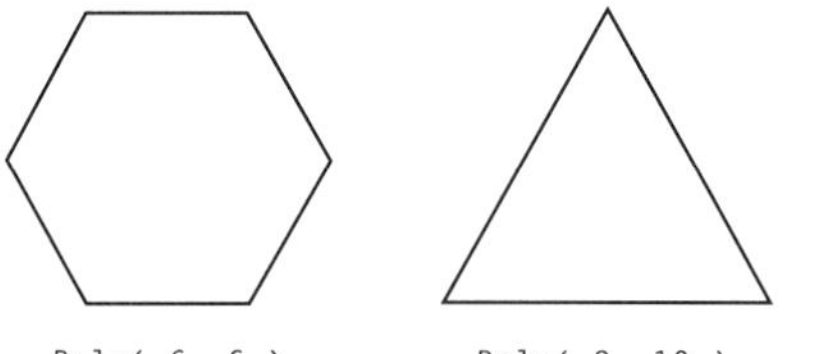

19. Write a `PolyTurn` procedure that draws a `Poly` (see Exercise 19), turns through a given angle to the right, halves the polygon side length, then calls `Poly` again, and so on, until the side length becomes less than two turtle steps. Some examples are shown below. Your procedure should make good use of the turtle ADT procedures.

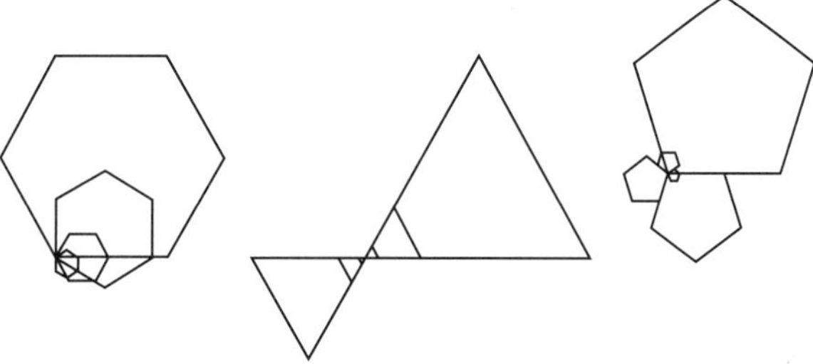

20. What does the following recursive procedure do? Run the procedure with regular angles like 90 and 120, then with irregular angles like 99 or 110. Print your outputs and explain what you see.

```
PROCEDURE MysteryPattern( Side, Angle : Integer );
BEGIN
   IF ( Side > 1 ) THEN
   BEGIN
      MoveForward( Side );
      Right( Angle );
      MysteryPattern( Side - 1, Angle )
   END
END; { MysteryPattern }
```

21. What does the following recursive procedure do?

```
PROCEDURE AnotherMystery( Side, Angle,
                          Incr : Integer );
BEGIN
   IF ( Angle < 360 ) THEN
   BEGIN
      MoveForward( Side );
      Right( Angle );
      AnotherMystery( Side, Angle + Incr, Incr )
   END
END; { AnotherMystery }
```

Run the procedure with small `Side` and varying values of `Angle` and `Incr`. Print your outputs and explain what you see.

LOOKING BACK

This chapter has shown how we build and use *abstract data types* (*ADTs*) in Pascal. An abstract data type is the data type itself, together with declarations of the operations that are allowed to act on that data type. Ideally, these are packaged together, or *encapsulated*, in such a way that users of the data type cannot act on the data type except by means of the operations provided by the ADT. This prevents users from subverting or misusing the data type. The ideal is to build the ADT in two parts: an *interface part*, containing all declarations needed by users of the ADT, and an *implementation part*, containing the code for the procedures and functions and all declarations that are to be hidden from users.

Standard Pascal does not provide adequate tools for such encapsulations, but many real-world Pascal systems provide such tools. The textbook describes ADTs in such a way that they can be built in Pascal either as files to be incorporated directly in client programs, or indirectly as *include files*, or as *compilation units*. The latter two methods, which are nonstandard, are explained in Appendix H for those who can use them.

Fractions provided our first real example of an ADT. There is no fraction type in Pascal, so we built our own. Our homemade `Fraction` type was represented in memory as a record with `Numerator` and `Denominator` fields. We then encapsulated with the type a set of operations to use with it.

We explained why client programmers are given source code for the interface part of the ADT's unit, but not the source code for the implementation part. We want client programmers to use the ADT only by means of the operations we have encapsulated in it.

We also showed how the implementation part of a unit can be modified without affecting the interface part, and therefore without affecting client programs.

We finished the chapter by building a less conventional sort of abstract data type: an invisible turtle that lives in the two-dimensional world of the computer screen, and which can be commanded to draw pictures. The turtle ADT contains procedures for turning and moving the turtle, for lowering and raising the turtle's pen or eraser, for changing the pen's ink, and for clearing the screen. With these few commands, we are able to build up a hierarchy of drawing procedures that allow us to easily draw more complicated shapes. Examples included squares, circles, regular polygons, stars, and other shapes based on these.

TERMS EMPHASIZED IN THIS CHAPTER

PROJECTS

1. Write a program that uses the `Fraction` ADT to add a series of fractions entered at the keyboard, displaying the sum in whole-number-and-fraction reduced form. For example, given the inputs 13/16, 5/8, 1/2, –2/3, and 7/8, the program should display the sum as `2   7/48`.

2. Write a program that uses the `Fraction` ADT to convert any given decimal number representing an inch measurement to the nearest 32d of an inch. For example, given the number 0.22, the program should display the fraction `7 / 32`.

3. Add to the `Fraction` ADT the following two encapsulated operations:

   a. A `CompareFr` function that takes two fractions as its parameters, returning the character `'<'`, `'='`, or `'>'` to indicate whether the first fraction is less than, equal to, or greater than the second fraction.

   b. A `ComplementFr` procedure that takes a fraction less than 1 and returns the complement of the fraction; that is, the fraction equal to 1 minus the given fraction.

4. In analogy to the `Fraction` ADT developed in Section 16.2, design and write a `Calendar` ADT in which a date is represented as a record with three fields called `Month`, `Day`, and `Year`, respectively. For the purposes of this project, the ADT should provide only two operations, shown in the interface below. Write a driver and test your ADT. (Hint: The algorithm for leap years is not as simple as many people think. It is described in Project 5, Chapter 8.)

```
UNIT CalendarADT;

INTERFACE

TYPE
   MonthRange = 1..12;
   DayRange   = 1..31;
   YearRange  = 1901..2099;

   Date = RECORD
             Month : MonthRange;
             Day   : DayRange;
             Year  : YearRange
          END;

{----------------------------------------------}
{ Reports whether a given year is a leap year }
{----------------------------------------------}
FUNCTION IsLeapYear( Yr : YearRange ) : Boolean;

{----------------------------------------------}
{ Reports number of days between two days     }
{----------------------------------------------}
FUNCTION NumDaysBetween( Date1, Date2 : DateRange ) : Integer;
```

5. Design and write a `String80` ADT that represents the type `String80` as a record and implements the operations shown in Section 15.5, including the `AppendChar` and `CompareStrings` operations described in the exercises in that section. Use your new ADT in writing a program that enciphers a given plaintext string according to the following cipher:

   a. Translate the entire message to uppercase and remove whitespace and punctuation.

   b. Reverse the whole message.

   c. Shift each letter upward two places alphabetically, wrapping the alphabet around, so that `'A'` becomes `'C'`, `'X'` becomes `'Z'`, `'Z'` becomes `'B'`, and so on.

   Example: The plaintext message "Fire when ready, Gridley" becomes the enciphered "AGNFKTIAFCGTPGJYGTKH". Also write a procedure that deciphers the enciphered text, producing (except for the whitespace, punctuation, and capitalization) the original plaintext. Use the `String80` ADT operations wherever possible.

6. Many interactive computer systems provide a way to directly control pixels on the screen, and thus can be made to produce much higher graphics resolution than is possible with the Standard Pascal code shown in the text. In particular, such systems often provide procedures like `DrawLineTo` and `ClearScreen`. Check your system's reference manual to see if such things are possible with your system. If so, modify the implementation of the `Turtle` ADT so that it produces high-resolution graphics.

7. Modify the `MysteryPattern` procedure from Exercise 20 so that it marks on the screen only the vertices of the polygons. Then test the modified procedure with a variety of parameter values. You will find that you get patterns with radiating arms, sometimes curving. Can you explain this? (See the reference to the book by Abelson and diSessa.)

8. (From Abelson and diSessa book cited at end of chapter) Design a procedure that will draw both of the following patterns, which differ only in their parameter values.

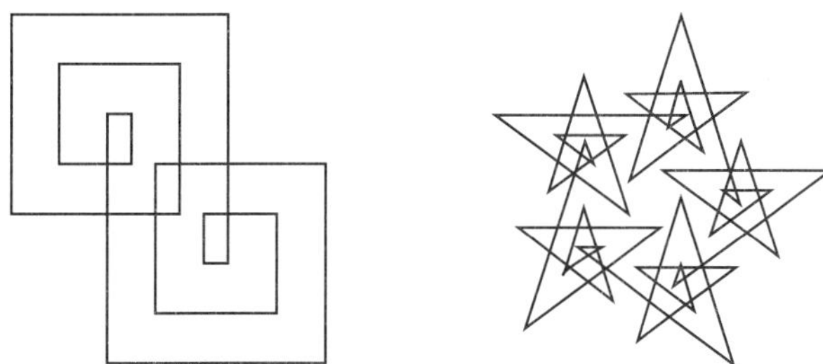

9. Write a procedure that can plot a graph of the values stored in a given array. Your procedure should make good use of the `Turtle` ADT.

10. Imagine measuring the coastline of an island. First, you get a map of the ocean, find the island, and measure the length of the coastline according to the map. Then, in order to gain more accuracy, you get a larger-scale map, on which the island looks much larger. On this map, the coastline looks much more ragged than it did on the first map, and your measured coastline turns out to be correspondingly longer. But suppose that you measure the coastline directly, by walking all of it, being careful to walk very close to the edge of the water at all times. This makes the coastline seem much more ragged than before, and therefore much longer. But suppose you were a tiny insect, walking along the same coastline, again staying as close as you could to the edge of the water. In that case, the coastline would seem more ragged still, and even longer. Clearly, we can continue this progression, measuring the coastline on a smaller and smaller scale. If we do so, it appears that the measured coastline will seem longer and longer without bounds, even though it is the circumference of a finite area. There seems to be a paradox here . . . or is there? What do you think?

    A similar problem arises in connection with certain curves in mathematics. Consider first an equilateral triangle. Then consider replacing each side of the triangle with a straight line in which the middle third is replaced by two sides of a small equilateral triangle. Then consider replacing each straight line in this figure by a straight line in which the middle third is replaced by a still smaller equilateral triangle, and so on. We get the following progression of figures:

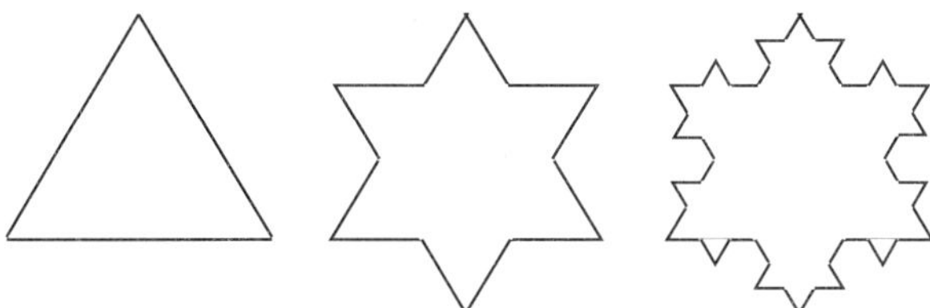

    This progression leads to what is called a **Koch curve** or **snowflake curve**. It appears that an infinite progression of this kind would lead to a curve of infinite length surrounding a finite area. Is this a paradox? (For an interesting discussion of this subject, see the book by Rucker cited in the chapter references.) Write a procedure that uses recursion to draw a snowflake curve. Design the procedure so that the recursion is automatically terminated when the length of straight-line segments becomes less than some preset amount. Your procedure should do its drawing by calling procedures in the `Turtle` ADT.

11. The following algorithm for drawing a straight line from integer position (X1, Y1) to integer position (X2, Y2) was first described by J. E. Bresenham in *IBM Systems Journal* **4, no. 1**, page 25 (1965). It is the fastest method for drawing a line, using only integer arithmetic and requiring no multiplications or divisions. (Multiplication by 2 requires only a left shift by one bit position.)

```
PROCEDURE DrawLineTo( X1, Y1, X2, Y2 : Integer );
{ Bresenham's algorithm }
VAR
  Sum, RunningX, RunningY, Dx, Dy, Index : Integer;

BEGIN

   Sum := X1 - X2;
   Dx  := 2 * ( X2 - X1 );
   DY  := 2 * ( Y2 - Y1 );

   RunningX := X1;
   RunningY := Y1;

   FOR Index := 0 TO (-Sum) DO
   BEGIN

      SetPixel( RunningX, RunningY );

      RunningX := RunningX + 1;
      Sum := Sum + Dy;

      IF Sum >= 0 THEN
      BEGIN

         RunningY := RunningY + 1;
         Sum := Sum - Dx

      END { IF }

   END { FOR }

END; { DrawLineTo }
```

The code shown works only for lines in the first quadrant. Generalize the algorithm so that it will work for all straight lines, regardless of quadrant.

REFERENCES

A readable discussion of the history and concepts of data abstraction can be found in J. Craig Cleaveland's book, *An Introduction to Data Types* (Addison-Wesley Publishing, 1986). Two of the original papers are Edsger Dijkstra's "Notes on Structured Programming" and C. A. R. Hoare's "Notes on Data Structuring," both of which are reprinted in Dahl, Dijkstra, and Hoare's famous book, *Structured Programming* (Academic Press, 1972). Fuller discussions of this subject are found in textbooks on programming languages and their design. See, for example, Chapter 5 of Terrence Pratt's *Programming Languages, Design and Implementation*, second edition (Prentice Hall, 1984).

The rationale behind turtle graphics was explained eloquently in Seymour Papert's book, *Mindstorms: Children, Computers, and Powerful Ideas* (Basic Books, 1980). Many interesting examples of the use of turtle graphics are given in Harold Abelson and Andrea diSessa's *Turtle Geometry* (MIT Press, 1980) and in Brian Harvey's three-volume *Computer Science, Logo Style* (MIT Press, 1985). An unusually lucid explanation of Koch curves and other fractals (Project 10) can be found in Rudy Rucker's *Mind Tools* (Houghton Mifflin, 1987). J. E. Bresenham's line-drawing algorithm (Project 11) is discussed in Cornel K. Pokorny and Curtis F. Gerald's *Computer Graphics* (Franklin, Beedle & Associates, 1989), and in J. D. Foley, A. van Dam, S. K. Feiner, and J. F. Hughes's *Computer Graphics*, second edition (Addison-Wesley Publishing, 1990).

Software Design Is a Communications Craft

A writer makes an initial draft and then begins to revise and rewrite. Hemingway, for example, rewrote the ending of *A Farewell to Arms* thirty-nine times. He had trouble "getting the words right." James Michener has protested that he is "not a great writer" but he is "one of the world's great rewriters."

Filmmaking involves constant revision. Scriptwriters spend months rewriting before a film script is acceptable. Even after the script is ready, Neil Simon will bring the actors together to read it. "Why," he says, "should I wait until the very first day of rehearsal to find out I'm going to be in trouble?"

With *The Goodbye Girl*, Simon brought the actors together for readings three times before he was satisfied that the script was finished. He said that if he had started shooting with the original script, he could not have saved the film. He did "a month's rewriting before shooting began."

Shooting begins, rewriting continues. It continues on the set when problems are discovered; writers will spend all night rewriting a scene so it can be reshot the next day. After shooting ends, editing begins. This can take six (or more) months.

. . . In other arts, revision is the rule. Beethoven's draft manuscripts survive today, and from them we know that those great, simple, wonderful melodies were the result of many revisions. Picasso typically painted one or two pictures a day. Yet, his most powerful painting—*Guernica*—was the result of six weeks of constant revision.

If you accept the premises that designing friendly software is a communications craft and that we can learn from the experiences of other communications craftsmen, you must accept the necessity of constantly revising your programs to get them to be easy to use. We cannot expect success the first or second time. If our program is at all innovative, we can't expect it to be right even on the third or fourth time.

—Paul Heckel, *The Elements of Friendly Software Design: The New Edition* (SYBEX, Inc., 1991), pages 112–13.

CHAPTER

17

Files

CHAPTER CONTENTS

INTRODUCTION

Chapters 14 and 15 presented two of Pascal's data structures: arrays and records. In addition, we have used a third data structure all along, though we didn't mention it. *Files* are data structures too, but they differ from arrays and records in a number of ways:

- Files created during execution of a program can be saved on an external storage medium and can continue to exist after the program terminates. They can be reused by the same program in another run or by another program, either in the same computing session or in a later one. Such files are said to be *nonvolatile*.
- A file is limited in size only by the storage medium in which it is recorded. It can, in fact, be much larger than main memory. The size is not declared in advance, as it is with other data structures; a file can grow or shrink during execution of a program. We say that the file's storage is **dynamically allocated**. By contrast, arrays and records are *statically allocated*; Their sizes are declared at compile time.
- A text file can be accessed for reading or it can be accessed for writing, but it cannot be accessed for both reading and writing at the same time.
- Files must be **accessed sequentially**. When writing to a file, the data must be written in order; the program cannot skip around in the file. Similarly, when reading data from a file, the items in the file must be read in order, starting with the first item.
- Like arrays, files are *homogeneous* in that they can contain only one type of data values. The items in a file, called its **components**, can be of any type except one that contains a file.

(These properties are required by Standard Pascal. Some Pascal systems provide extensions to the Standard, allowing random access to files and files that can be accessed for simultaneous reading and writing.)

Dynamically allocated: Having memory set aside for storage during the execution of the program.

Sequential access: Having the data written or read only in sequence, not in random order. In Standard Pascal, unlike some commercial Pascal systems, all files are sequential-access data structures.

17.1 CREATING A TEXT FILE

(This section can be read after Section 4.3, if desired.)

Text file: A sequence of characters, divided by end-of-line signals into lines of text.

Stream of characters: A sequence of characters written or read in order, one after another.

In our previous examples, we have used Pascal's standard output procedures, `Write` and `WriteLn`, to send output to the screen. Such output consists of a stream of characters divided into lines, and is called a **text file**. There is nothing difficult about the concept of a text file in Pascal. The **stream of characters** is just one character followed by another, until all characters have been sent. And it is not hard to imagine that sometimes we might want to send the stream of characters to a storage device instead of to the screen. In the next few sections, we will explore the techniques for doing this.

It is easy to make `Write` or `WriteLn` send its output to a mass storage device such as a floppy disk, hard disk, or optical disk. We specify a file variable associated with the name of the disk file to which we want to send the output. Then we open the file so that data can be written to the file. Then we write the data. Finally, we close the file.

Suppose you want to open a new text file on your default disk drive, and you want to send a Fahrenheit temperature and the corresponding Celsius temperature to the file, on a single line:

```
32.00    0.00
```

There are four steps in doing this:

1. Invent a file variable for the output file—call it `OutFile`, for example. Include this variable in the list of program parameters in the `PROGRAM` header.
2. Declare this variable to be of type `Text`, so that Pascal will know that the file will contain a stream of characters, divided into lines.
3. Open the new file by calling Pascal's `Rewrite` procedure, telling it the name of the file variable:

   ```
   Rewrite( OutFile );
   ```

   The `Rewrite` procedure makes the file available for output only; you can write to the file, but not read from it. (The file is said to be **write-only**.) If the file existed previously, writing to it will replace the old data with the new data; all of the old data will be lost.

   Write-only file: A file that can —for the moment, at least—be written but not read.

   Many Pascal systems provide a nonstandard extension to `Rewrite`, which not only opens the file for writing, but also associates a file name with the file. These Pascal systems would use the call

   ```
   Rewrite( OutFile, FileName );
   ```

   Turbo Pascal requires a call to a special `Assign` procedure to associate an external file name with the file variable. This is done before calling `Rewrite`. The Turbo calls would look like this:

   ```
   Assign( OutFile, FileName );
   Rewrite( OutFile );
   ```

4. Write to the file by means of `Write` or `WriteLn` calls, specifying the file variable as the first parameter in the call. In our example, we use a single call to `WriteLn`:

   ```
   WriteLn( OutFile, Fahrenheit:8:2,
           ((5.0/9.0) * (Fahrenheit - 32.0)):8:2 );
   ```

A text file consists of lines of text.

At the beginning of this section, we defined a text file as a stream of characters, *divided into lines*. In other words, you can think of a text file as being a sequence of characters that could be displayed as lines of text on the screen. On the screen, of course, text is displayed in lines. The computer must be told where one line of text ends and the next begins. For this purpose, computer systems recognize an *end-of-line signal*, which we abbreviate `<EOLn>`, wherever it appears in a stream of characters. In some computer systems, the `<EOLn>` signal is a single character, usually the carriage return character, transmitted by the RETURN or ENTER key, and stored as ASCII code 13. In MS-DOS systems, however, `<EOLn>` is a sequence of two characters: a carriage return (ASCII 13) followed by a line feed (ASCII 10). The carriage return sends the screen cursor back to the left edge of the screen, while the line feed moves the cursor down to the next line.

According to the definition, a Pascal text file consists of *whole lines* of text. This means that a proper text file has the following structure:

Characters`<EOLn>`*Characters*`<EOLn>` . . . *Characters*`<EOLn><EOF>`

where `<EOF>` indicates a terminating signal marking the end of the file. This means that the last character(s) written to the text file should be written by a `WriteLn` rather than a `Write`. This may seem to be an unimportant point, but *text files that don't conform to the proper structure may not read back correctly.*

An example program

In order to show how the various pieces hook up, the next page shows a complete (but artificially simple) program that carries out the essential steps: The file variable is listed as a program parameter, the file variable is declared to have type `Text`, the file is opened for writing only, and data are written to the file.

Syntax for opening a write-only file

Pseudocode:

`Rewrite(` *FileVariable* `)`

Notes:

- `Rewrite` opens the file for writing only; the file can't be read.
- If the associated external file existed previously, writing to it will replace the old data with the new data; all of the old data will be lost. If the file did not exist previously, the `Rewrite` command will create the file.
- Some Pascal systems allow `Rewrite` to associate an external filename with the file variable. Check your reference manual.

```
PROGRAM TextFileTest1( Input, Output, OutFile );

PROCEDURE WriteFCFile;
VAR
   Fahrenheit : Real;
   OutFile    : Text;

BEGIN

   {--Get temperature: }
   Write( 'Fahrenheit temperature: ' );
   ReadLn( Fahrenheit );
   WriteLn;
   WriteLn( 'Writing Fahrenheit and Celsius to file...' );

   {--Open OutFile for writing only: }
   Rewrite( OutFile );

   {--Write Fahrenheit and Celsius to the file: }
   WriteLn( OutFile, Fahrenheit:8:2,
            ((5.0/9.0) * (Fahrenheit - 32.0)):8:2 );

   WriteLn( 'Finished.' )

END; { WriteFCFile }

BEGIN

   WriteFCFile

END.
```

The source and destination of I/O

Notice that the first `Write`, the following two `WriteLn`s, and the last `WriteLn` do not have an `OutFile` parameter. Therefore, they send output to the screen, not to the external file. Similarly, the `ReadLn` gets input from the keyboard because it does not specify a different file as its source. In fact, Pascal allows us to specify explicitly that these calls deal with the screen and keyboard. The following code is fully equivalent to that shown in the program:

```
Write( Output, 'Fahrenheit temperature: ' );
ReadLn( Input, Fahrenheit );
WriteLn( Output );
WriteLn( Output, 'Writing Fahrenheit and Celsius to file...' );
```

On the other hand, the call to `Rewrite` and the following three `WriteLns` send output to the external file because they specify `OutFile` as a parameter.

The program header

This program receives input from the standard `Input` text file (the keyboard) and sends output to the standard `Output` text file (the screen) and to our `OutFile` text file (which is on a mass storage device). For the sake of portability to other Pascal systems, we declare all three text files in the `PROGRAM` header, even though some Pascal systems do not require it.

Syntax for Calling Write and WriteLn

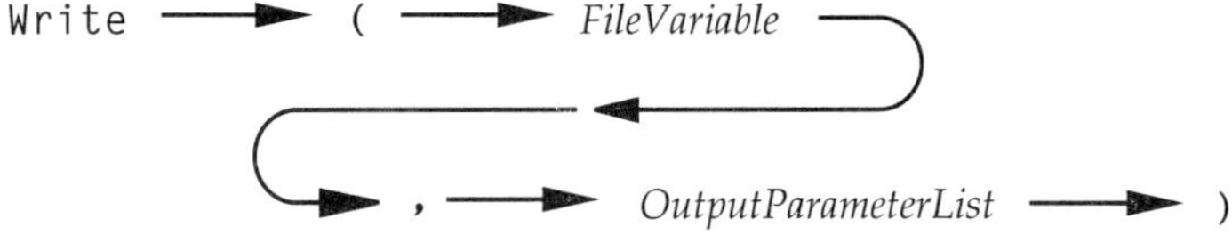

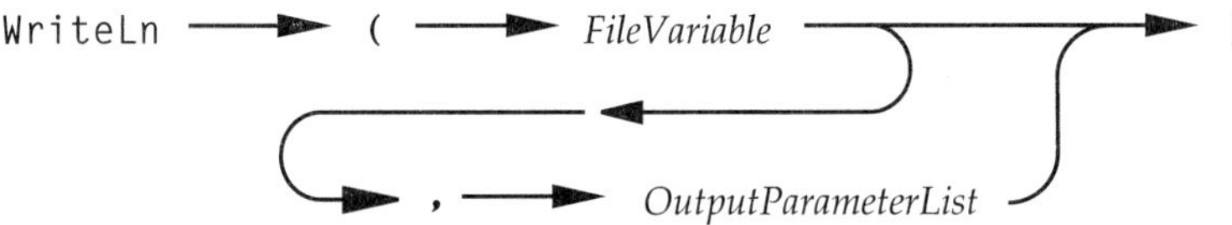

Pseudocode:

```
Write( FileVariable, OutputParameterList )
WriteLn( FileVariable, OutputParameterList )
WriteLn( FileVariable )
```

Notes:

- The *FileVariable* is optional. If it is omitted, output is sent to the standard `Output` file. If it is included, it must be the first parameter in the `Write` or `WriteLn` call, and must be associated with a file. (It can, in fact, be `Output`, in which case the output will be sent to the screen.)
- `Write` transmits the *OutputParameterList* values in the order listed.
- `WriteLn` transmits the *OutputParameterList* values in the order listed, and then transmits an `<EOLn>`.
- If *OutputParameterList* is omitted from a call to `WriteLn`, a blank line is sent to the file. (The *OutputParameterList* cannot be omitted from a call to `Write`.)
- The appearence of output values can be specified in the `Write` or `WriteLn` call. This is called *formatting* and was described in Section 4.3.
- `Write` and `WriteLn` can be used only with files that have been opened for writing by means of a call to `Rewrite`, or with the standard `Output` file, which is automatically opened for writing.

Closing the file

In Standard Pascal, a file is automatically closed when the program terminates. There is no other way to close a file. However, many commercial Pascal systems provide a nonstandard `Close(` *FileVariable* `)` instruction so that files can be closed manually. As you will see later, this comes in handy when you want to close a write-only file in order to reopen it for reading in the same program.

Run it!

When you run the program, you should see something like this on the screen:

```
Fahrenheit temperature: 32.0

Writing Fahrenheit and Celsius to file...
Finished.
_
```

After the program terminates, you will find a new file on your disk in the default directory. If you look in the new file with a "viewer" program or a text editor, you should see these characters:

```
   32.00    0.00
```

That is, the file contains the following stream of characters: (with the Δ symbols representing spaces):

```
ΔΔΔ32.00ΔΔΔΔ0.00<EOLn><EOF>
```

Letting the user specify the filename (nonstandard)

Unfortunately, Standard Pascal provides no way to associate an external filename with a file variable, so our program provides no control over where the file will be stored. In the real world, we prefer the program to be more user-friendly than this. In most commercial Pascal systems, we can have the program read the filename (as a string of characters) from the keyboard, storing the name in a string-array variable, or even in a `String` variable if the system provides such a type. Then the contents of the string variable can be used to associate a filename with the file variable, usually in a nonstandard version of the `Rewrite` call. (In Turbo Pascal, a special `Assign` procedure is used.) If you are reading this section immediately after Section 4.3, you don't have any previous experience with string variables, but the idea is simple. In many Pascal systems, the new code might look like this:

```
PROCEDURE WriteFCFile;
VAR
   Fahrenheit : Real;
   OutFile    : Text;
   FileName   : String; { Nonstandard }

BEGIN

   Write( 'Name of file to be written? ' );
   ReadLn( FileName );
```

```
{--Get temperature: }
Write( 'Fahrenheit temperature: ' );
ReadLn( Fahrenheit );
WriteLn;
WriteLn( 'Writing Fahrenheit and Celsius to file...' );

{--Give OutFile a name and open it for writing only: }
Rewrite( OutFile, Filename );
.
.
.
```

Questions

1. The text says that a text file consists of a stream of characters, divided into lines. What is meant by a "stream of characters"? What is a "line"?

2. What is the difference between writing the variable `Two` to a text file and writing the string `'Two'` to the file?

3. When the `Write` or `WriteLn` procedure writes real numbers to a text file, it writes *characters* to the file. For example, when 1.1 is written to a text file, what gets written is the string `'Δ1.1000000000E+00'`, for example, and not the real number 1.1. What distinction is being made here?

4. In the call `WriteLn( Output, One, Two )`, the first parameter serves a different function than the other two parameters. What is the difference?

Exercises

5. Make the change shown in the text, so that the `TextFileTest1` program reads not only the data, but also the filename, from the keyboard. Compile and run the program.

6. What is written to the external file by the following procedure? (Show *exactly* what will be written by your system.)

```
PROCEDURE WriteIt;
CONST
   Pi = 3.14159265;
VAR
   OutFile        : Text;
   Radius, Height : Real;

BEGIN

   Radius := 1.5;
   Height := 2.0;
   Rewrite( OutFile );
   WriteLn( OutFile, 'VOLUME OF A CONE' );
   WriteLn( OutFile );
   WriteLn( OutFile, 'Radius = ', Radius:4:1 );
   WriteLn( OutFile, 'Height = ', Height:4:1 );
   WriteLn( OutFile, 'Volume = ',
         ((Height * Pi * Radius * Radius) / 3.0):8:2 );

END; { WriteIt }
```

7. What is written to the external file by the following program? (Show *exactly* what will be written by your system.)

```
PROCEDURE WriteEnergy;
CONST
   PlancksConstant = 6.626176e-34; { Joule-sec }
VAR
   DataFile : Text;
   Frequency, Energy : Real;
BEGIN
   Frequency := 5.43e+12;
   Energy    := PlancksConstant * Frequency;
   Rewrite( DataFile );
   WriteLn( DataFile, 'FREQUENCY-ENERGY RELATION' );
   WriteLn( DataFile );
   Write( DataFile, 'Frequency ', Frequency:10, '/sec,' );
   WriteLn( DataFile, ' is equiv to ', Energy:10, ' Joules' )
END; { WriteEnergy }
```

8. What is written to the external file by the following procedure? (Show *exactly* what will be written by your system.)

```
PROCEDURE WriteMasses;
VAR
   FileA        : Text;
   Mass1, Mass2 : Real;
BEGIN
   WriteLn( 'AVERAGE OF TWO MASSES' );
   WriteLn;
   Mass1 := 1.23;
   Mass2 := 2.659;
   Rewrite( FileA );
   WriteLn( FileA, 'Average of masses ', Mass1:5:2,
            ' and ', Mass2:5:2 );
   WriteLn( FileA, 'is ',
            ( 0.5 * (Mass1 + Mass2) ):5:2 )
END; { WriteMasses }
```

9. What is written to the external file by the following procedure? (Show *exactly* what will be written by your system.)

```
PROCEDURE WriteFNums;
VAR
   Photo : Text;
   FocalLength, Diameter, FNumber : Real;
BEGIN
   Rewrite( Photo );
   WriteLn( Photo, 'F-NUMBER' );
   FocalLength := 135.0;
```

```
   Diameter    := 48.2;
   FNumber     := FocalLength / Diameter;
   WriteLn( Photo, 'f = ', FocalLength:8:2 );
   WriteLn( Photo, 'd = ', Diameter:8:2 );
   WriteLn( Photo, 'gives f/', FNumber:4:1 )
END; { WriteFNums }
```

10. Write a small program that writes the message

```
The magic number<EOLn>7.0,<EOLn>plus or minus 2.0<EOLn>
```

to the screen. Then write another version that writes this message to a disk file. Write the two numbers as formatted real output.

17.2 READING FROM A TEXT FILE *(Can be read after Section 4.4)*

The `Read` and `ReadLn` procedures read data from the `Input` file (the keyboard) unless you say otherwise. In fact, the usual forms of the calls to these procedures are shorthand for more explicit versions in which the `Input` file is specified explicitly, as in these examples:

`Read( X, Y, Z )`	is shorthand for	`Read( Input, X, Y, Z );`
`ReadLn( X, Y, Z )`	is shorthand for	`ReadLn( Input, X, Y, Z );`
`ReadLn`	is shorthand for	`ReadLn( Input ).`

As you can imagine from the previous section, reading data from a disk file is hardly more complicated than reading it from the keyboard. Only four steps are required:

1. Invent a new file variable for the input, and include this variable in the list of program parameters in the `PROGRAM` header.

2. Declare the new file variable to be of type `Text`. (This declares that the file will be a stream of characters, organized into lines.)

3. Open the file with a call to the `Reset` procedure, with the new file variable as a parameter. `Reset` makes the file available for *input only*. That is, you will be able to read from the file, but not write to it. (The file is said to be **read-only**.) After `Reset` opens a file, the first `Read` or `ReadLn` will read the data at the beginning of the file.

Many commercial Pascal systems provide a nonstandard extension to `Reset`, which not only opens the file for reading, but associates a file name with the file. These Pascal systems would use the call

`Reset( OutFile, ` *FileName* ` );`

Turbo Pascal requires a call to a special `Assign` procedure to associate an external file name with the file variable. This is done before calling `Reset`. The Turbo calls would look like this:

`Assign( OutFile, ` *FileName* ` );`
`Reset( OutFile );`

Read-only file: A file that can—for the moment, at least—be read but not written.

4. Read from the file by means of explicit-form `Read` or `ReadLn` calls, using your declared file variable as the first parameter, in place of the standard `Input` variable.

Syntax for opening a file for reading

Pseudocode:

`Reset(` *FileVariable* `)`

Notes:

- `Reset` opens the file for reading only; the file can't be written.
- The file must already exist. `Reset` will not create a new file.
- The file is "reset" so that reading will commence at the beginning of the file.
- Many Pascal systems allow `Reset` to associate an external filename with the file variable. Check your reference manual.

For example, here is a little program that reads the temperature data written by the corresponding program of Section 17.1:

```
PROGRAM TextFileTest2( Input, Output, InFile );

PROCEDURE ReadFCFile;
VAR
   InFile               : Text;
   Fahrenheit, Celsius : Real;
   FileName             : String;  { Nonstandard }
BEGIN
   { -- Get filename: }
   Write( 'Name of file to read: ' );
   ReadLn( FileName );

   { -- Open file for reading only: }
   Reset( InFile, FileName );      { Nonstandard }

   { -- Read two real numbers from the file: }
   ReadLn( InFile, Fahrenheit, Celsius );

   { -- Display the temperatures on the screen: }
   WriteLn( Fahrenheit:8:2, ' F.' );
   WriteLn( Celsius:8:2, ' C.' )
END; { ReadFCFile }

BEGIN
   ReadFCFile
END.
```

When this program is used to read back the data from the file created by TextFileTest1, the dialog on the screen looks like this:

```
Name of file to read: FC.TXT
   32.00 F.
    0.00 C.
```

Syntax for Calling Read and ReadLn

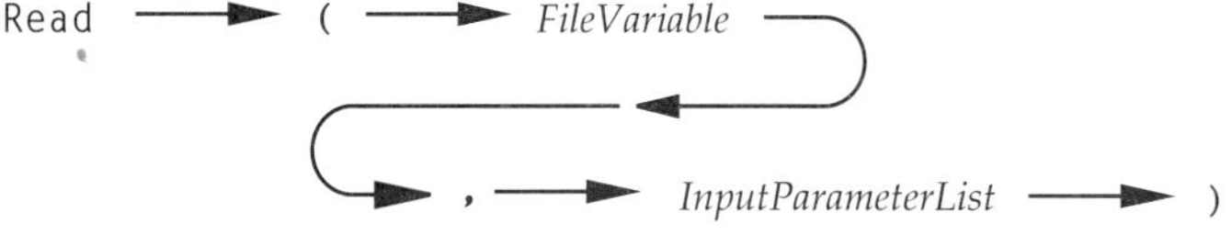

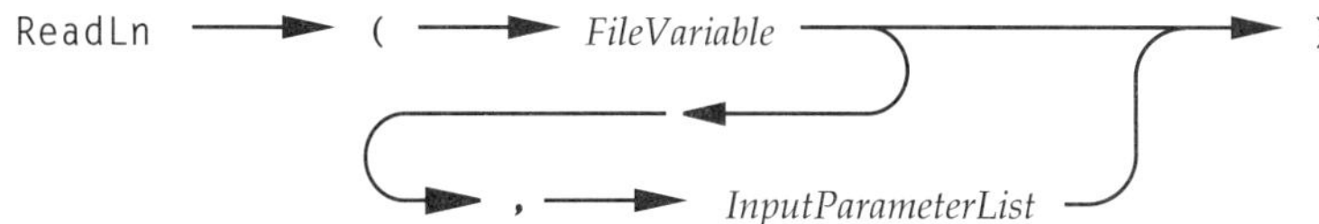

Pseudocode:

```
Read( FileVariable, InputParameterList )
ReadLn( FileVariable, InputParameterList )
ReadLn( FileVariable )
```

Here *FileVariable* is the variable associated with the input text file and *InputParameterList* is a list of the names of the variables to receive input value, separated by commas.

Notes:

- The `Read` and `ReadLn` parameters after the optional file variable are the variables in which input values are to be stored. Therefore these parameters must be variables, not constants or expressions. For example, `Read(` *FileVariable*, *Variable1*, *Variable2* `)` or `ReadLn(` *FileVariable*, *Variable1*, *Variable2* `)` will copy the first input value into *Variable1* and the second input value into *Variable2*.
- The `Read` procedure gets input values for each of its parameters in the order in which these parameters are listed. If not enough input values are provided, `Read` will wait for the rest, and the program will not continue until those values are provided. If more values are provided than there are parameters in which to store them, `Read` will leave the remaining values in the input stream, to be read by later calls to `Read` or `ReadLn`.

Reading numbers from a text file

When `Read` and `ReadLn` read data from a text file (including the `Input` file), they are reading characters. This means that input data to be stored in noncharacter variables will have to be translated as part of the input process. For example, the process of reading a real number from a text file involves four stages:

1. Leading whitespace characters (blanks, tabs, end-of-line characters) are skipped.
2. The input procedure reads the string of numeric characters, terminating input when it encounters a character that cannot be part of the real number. Such a character is called a **delimiter**. The normal delimiters are whitespace characters.
3. The received string of characters is translated into a real-number value.
4. The resulting real number is stored in the corresponding parameter variable.

Delimiter: A character that marks the end or beginning of a datum.

More complicated write/read combinations

The steps we've just described, which are involved when Pascal reads a number from a text file, determine what happens when a program is reading a mixture of numeric and nonnumeric data. For example, suppose that our previous `WriteFCFile` procedure is changed so that it writes labels into the file, as well as numbers:

```
PROCEDURE WriteFCFile;
VAR
   Fahrenheit : Real;
   OutFile    : Text;
   FileName   : String;  { Nonstandard }

BEGIN

   {--Get temperature: }
   Write( 'Fahrenheit temperature: ' );
   ReadLn( Fahrenheit );
   WriteLn;

   { -- Get filename: }
   Write( 'Name of file to write: ' );
   ReadLn( FileName );

   { -- Open file for writing only: }
   Rewrite( OutFile, FileName );  { Nonstandard }
   WriteLn( 'Writing Fahrenheit and Celsius to file...' );

   {--Write Fahrenheit and Celsius to the file: }
   WriteLn( OutFile, Fahrenheit:8:2, ' F.' );
   WriteLn( OutFile, ((5.0/9.0) * (Fahrenheit - 32.0)):8:2, ' C.' );

   WriteLn( 'Finished.' )

END; { WriteFCFile }
```

Then if the user specifies a Fahrenheit temperature of 32.0, as before, the new version of the procedure writes a mixture of numeric and nonnumeric data to the file:

```
ΔΔΔ32.00ΔF.<EOLn>ΔΔΔΔ0.00ΔC.<EOLn><EOF>
```

The data file now has a different structure than before, so the `ReadFCFile` procedure has to be changed accordingly:

```
PROCEDURE ReadFCFile;
VAR
   InFile               : Text;
   Fahrenheit, Celsius  : Real;
   FileName             : String;  { Nonstandard }

BEGIN

   { -- Get filename: }
   Write( 'Name of file to read: ' );
   ReadLn( FileName );

   { -- Open file for reading only: }
   Reset( InFile, FileName );  { Nonstandard }
```

```
    { -- Read two real numbers from the file: }
    ReadLn( InFile, Fahrenheit );
    ReadLn( InFile, Celsius );

    { -- Display the temperatures on the screen: }
    WriteLn( Fahrenheit:8:2, ' F.' );
    WriteLn( Celsius:8:2, ' C.' )

END; { ReadFCFile }
```

The first `ReadLn` reads, for example, ΔΔΔ`32.00` from the file, reading no more when it encounters the space after the number. Because it is a `ReadLn` and there are no more variables into which it is to read values, it discards the rest of the line of text—the `' F.'`. The second `ReadLn` works similarly while reading a value for `Celsius`. Because of the structure of the data in the file, we cannot use the single statement we had in the earlier version,

```
ReadLn( InFile, Fahrenheit, Celsius );
```

This would read the `32.00` successfully, and then encounter the string `' F.'` while trying to read a value for `Celsius`. The `'F'` and the `'.'`, not being whitespace, would cause a read error and the program would halt.

Questions

11. When you enter a real number at the keyboard, you are pressing keys that send character codes to your Pascal program. How, then, does your program know that your keystrokes are supposed to symbolize a real number?

12. How do the `Read` and `ReadLn` procedures differ from the `Write` and `WriteLn` procedures in the way they use their parameters?

13. Would the statements

```
    ReadLn( InFile, Fahrenheit );
    ReadLn( InFile, Celsius );
```

read correctly the data written by the following procedure? Why or why not?

```
PROCEDURE WriteIt;
VAR
    OutFile : Text;
    F, C    : Real;

BEGIN
    Rewrite( OutFile );
    WriteLn( OutFile, 'Fahrenheit = ', 32.0 );
    WriteLn( OutFile, 'Celsius    = ', 0.0 )

END; { WriteIt }
```

Exercises

14. Jackson P. Slipshod has been trying to compile this procedure for the past five hours. (He's not bright, but he's determined.) Find all of his syntax errors.

```
PROCEDURE SlipshodWrite;
VAR
   Millimeters = Real;

BEGIN
   Rewrite( OutFile );
   Write( Output, 'Number of millimeters? ' );
   ReadLn( Input, Millimeters:6:2 );
   WriteLn( OutFile, 'mm = ', Millimeters:6.2 )
END;
```

15. Cora Meltdown has written this procedure, intending it to write and then read back two numbers. Why won't this procedure work?

```
PROCEDURE Meltdown1;
VAR
   Num1, Num2 : Real;
   NumFile    : Text;

BEGIN
   Write( 'Your two Numbers: ' );
   ReadLn( Num1, Num2 );

   Rewrite( NumFile );
   WriteLn( NumFile, Num1, Num2 );

   ReadLn( Num1, Num2 );
   WriteLn( 'File contains ', Num1, Num2 )
END;
```

16. If the user enters the characters 33<EOLn>3.21<EOLn>, then what will be written to the external file by this procedure? (Show *exactly* what will be written on your system.)

```
PROCEDURE Exer16;
VAR
   FCFile : Text;
   Fahrenheit, Celsius : Real;

BEGIN
   Write( 'Fahrenheit and Celsius temperatures? ' );
   ReadLn( Fahrenheit, Celsius );

   Rewrite( FCFile );
   WriteLn( FCFile, Fahrenheit:6:2, ' F.' );
   WriteLn( FCFile, Celsius:6:2, ' C.' )
END;
```

17. Write a procedure that reads a text file written by the `WriteIt` procedure shown in Question 13, displaying the contents of the file on the screen.

17.3 FILE POINTERS AND FILE WINDOWS *(Can be read after Section 10.3)*

Text files in Pascal are always *sequential*. This means that after a text file is opened for writing, characters are written to the file in order, from beginning to end. Similarly, after a file is opened for reading, the characters in the file are read in order, from beginning to end. There is no way to "hop around" in a text file.

Whether reading or writing the file, Pascal must keep track of the position of the next character to be read or written in the file. For this, Pascal uses a **file pointer**, which is, in fact, the `Text` variable associated with the file. As you know, this is also called the *file variable*, but more precisely, it is a variable containing the memory address of the next character position to be written or read in the file buffer, and is more precisely called a *file pointer*. This can be made clearer by an example.

File pointer or **file variable**: A special variable for storing the address of the next character to be accessed in the file buffer.

Suppose that a program is opening an external text file for reading. The file pointer is declared in the program header and in the variable declaration, and then the file is opened with a call to `Reset`:

```
PROGRAM ReadExample( InFile );
VAR
   InFile : Text;

BEGIN
   .
   .
   Reset( InFile );
```

Now suppose the external file contains the two lines

```
Here<EOLn>and now<EOLn><EOF>
```

After executing `Reset( InFile )`, the file pointer contains the address of the first character in the file buffer. We say that the file pointer "points to" the first character, and we indicate this by an arrow in the following diagram. (The "bent arrow" symbol represents an <EOLn>, while a black square represents an <EOF>.)

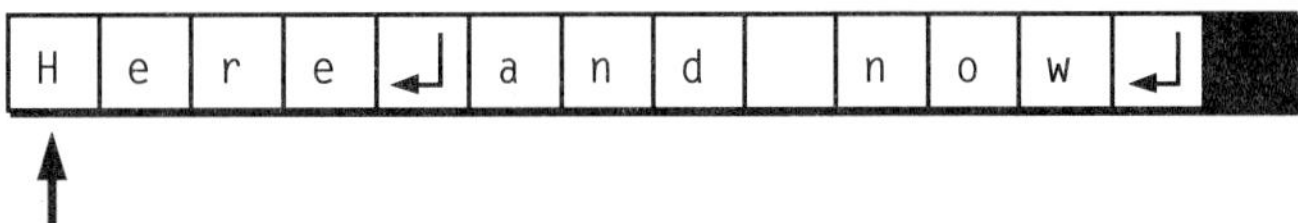

Then the file can be read sequentially, character by character. The process of reading the first character automatically increments the value of `InFile` to the address of the second character, which is one byte farther along in memory:

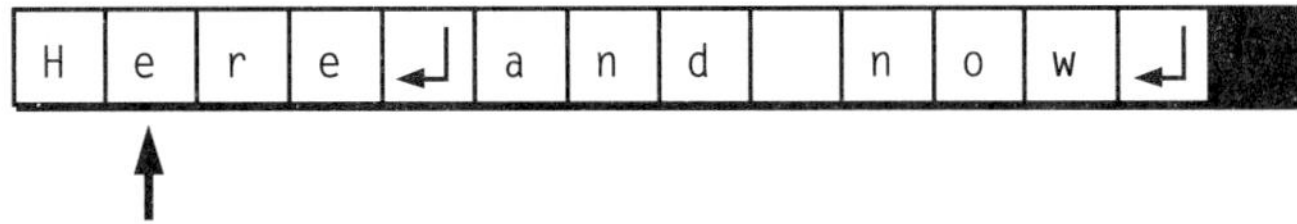

Then we read the second, third, and fourth characters, after which the file pointer points to the fifth character, which happens to be <EOLn>:

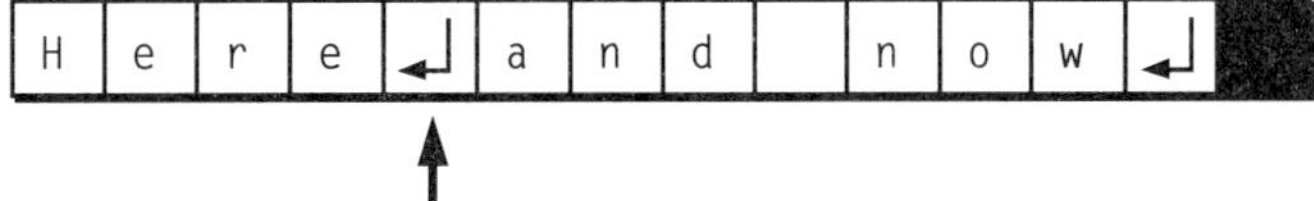

Usually, a program will read the characters on a line by means of a `ReadLn` or a loop. (The loops are described in Section 17.4.) With loops, Pascal needs to detect the end-of-line signal, to know where the line ends. For this, there is a standard `EOLn` function, as described in the accompanying syntax box. `EOLn` is a boolean function, returning `True` when the file pointer currently points to an `<EOLn>` character, or `False` if the pointer points to anything else.

Thus, in our example, calling `EOLn( InFile )` will return `True` only when the file pointer is in one of the two positions shown below:

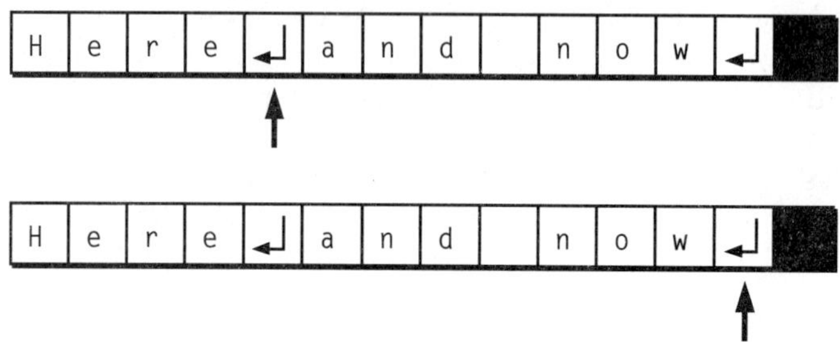

With the help of the `EOLn` function, we can set up a loop that reads a line automatically. Then, to read the whole file, we will use an outer loop that reads lines until reaching the end of the file. To detect `<EOF>`, Pascal provides a standard `EOF` function, as described in the second syntax box.

The EOLn function

Pseudocode:

`FUNCTION EOLn(` *FilePtr* `:` *FileType* `) : Boolean;`

Notes:

- Returns `True` if *FilePtr* points to `<EOLn>`, or `False` otherwise.
- The function tests the value of the character pointed to, but does not read the character or advance the file pointer.
- `EOLn(` *FilePtr* `)` is undefined if *FilePtr* has not been associated with a file by means of `Rewrite` or `Reset`, or if `EOF(` *FilePtr* `)` is True. (See the discussion of `EOF` that follows.) It is an error to call `EOLn(` *FilePtr* `)` under these circumstances.
- When reading from the `Input` file, `EOLn` may have to wait for a character to test. That is, if no characters are currently in the input buffer, or if your system does not buffer input, `EOLn` will wait for a key to be pressed to see whether this is the end-of-line signal.
- The keyboard end-of-line signal is sent by the RETURN or ENTER key.

The EOF function

Pseudocode:

```
FUNCTION EOF( FilePtr : FileType ) : Boolean;
```

Notes:

- Returns `True` if *FilePtr* points to `<EOF>`, or `False` otherwise.
- The function tests the value of the character pointed to, but does not read the character or advance the file pointer.
- `EOF ( ` *FilePtr* ` )` is undefined if *FilePtr* has not been associated with a file by means of `Rewrite` or `Reset`, or if `EOLn( ` *FilePtr* ` )` is `True`. It is an error to call `EOF(`*FilePtr*`)` under these circumstances.
- When reading from the `Input` file, `EOF` may have to wait for a character to test. That is, if no characters are currently in the input buffer, or if your system does not buffer input, `EOF` will wait for a key to be pressed, to see whether this is the end-of-file signal.
- The keyboard end-of-file signal in Turbo Pascal is Control-Z. In THINK Pascal, it is Command-Period. For other Pascal systems, see your reference manual.

Preventing catastrophe

It is an error to attempt to read data from a file when the file pointer points to the end-of-file character. To prevent this, always check the value returned by the `EOF` function before attempting to read. The correct form is

```
IF NOT EOF( FilePointer ) THEN
...
   Read( FilePointer, ... )
```

Complete examples of reading text files by means of loops are shown in the next section.

Questions

18. What is the value of the `EOLn` function when the file pointer is pointing to the end of file? Why?

19. What is the value of the `EOF` function when the file pointer is pointing to the end of a line? Why?

20. Is it possible for `EOLn` and `EOF` to be `True` simultaneously? Why?

17.4 LOOPS FOR PROCESSING TEXT FILES *(Can be read after Section 10.3)*

We can now apply the techniques described in Sections 17.1–3 to the problem of reading a sizable text file. The problem breaks down into two stages:

1. Read the lines of text until encountering the end-of-file signal.
2. To read a line of text, read the characters until encountering the end-of-line signal.

In deciding what structures to use for these two tasks, note that a file might be empty and therefore contain no lines, and that a line may be empty and therefore contain no characters. Thus, the loops needed for both stages might have nothing to do, so we should use `WHILE` structures. Furthermore, the two stages comprise a hierarchy, with stage 1 containing stage 2. Therefore, we will need *nested* `WHILE` structures. Inside the inner loop, we can read characters one by one or in groups as integers, reals, or whatever.

Suppose, in particular, that we want a procedure to count the characters in an already-opened text file. (Opening the file is a task distinct from reading it, so we will separate these two tasks in the code.) We send the file's already-reset pointer to the procedure, and then use two nested `WHILE` loops to perform the counting. There is one important restriction:

File pointers, when used as parameters, must be `VAR` parameters.

```
PROCEDURE CountChars( VAR InFile : Text;
                      VAR Count  : Integer );
{
   PRECONDITION:
   InFile is associated with an already-reset text file
   and is pointing to the beginning of the file.

   POSTCONDITION:
   0 <= Count and
   Count = number of characters in the file,
   not including <EOLn>s and <EOF>.
}
VAR
   Ch : Char;        { To hold the latest character read }

BEGIN

   Count := 0;

   {
     LOOP PRECONDITIONS:
     Count = 0
     and InFile has been reset.
   }
```

```
WHILE NOT EOF( InFile ) DO
{
  LOOP INVARIANT:
  0 <= Count;
  Count = number of characters read,
  not including <EOLn>s or <EOF>.
}
BEGIN

   WHILE NOT EOLn( InFile ) DO
   {
     LOOP INVARIANT:
     Next character is not <EOF>;
     0 <= Count;
     Count = number of characters read,
     not including <EOLn>s or <EOF>.
   }
   BEGIN
      Read( InFile, Ch );
      Count := Count + 1
   END; { WHILE NOT EOLn }

   { -- Discard the end-of-line signal }
   ReadLn( InFile )

END { WHILE NOT EOF }
{
  POSTCONDITIONS:
  InFile points to <EOF>;
  0 <= Count;
  Count = number of characters in file,
  not including <EOLn>s and <EOF>.
}

END; { CountChars }
```

Here is the sequence of events. After the initialization of `Count`, the outer loop begins. First the boolean expression is evaluated:

```
Count := 0;
WHILE NOT EOF( InFile ) DO
.
.
```

In order to determine whether the `InFile` pointer is at the end of the file, `EOF` must look ahead to see whether the next character in the file buffer is the end-of-file signal. Suppose that the file contains

```
Here<EOLn>and now<EOLn><EOF>
```

Then InFile is initially pointing to the letter 'H'; EOF returns False, so NOT EOF is True, and the outer loop's body is executed:

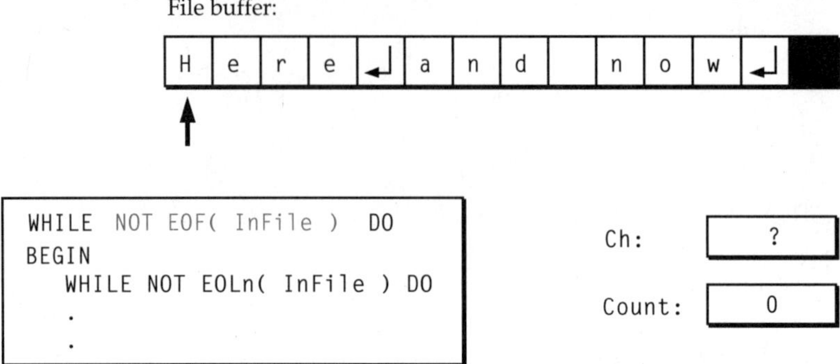

Here, as in a previous example, the bent arrow in the file buffer indicates <EOLn> and the black square indicates <EOF>.

The first statement in the body of the outer loop is WHILE NOT EOLn(InFile) DO, so EOLn must now look ahead to see whether the next character in the file is the end-of-line signal. The next character in the file is still 'H' — we still haven't read any characters — so EOLn returns False, NOT EOLn is True, and the inner loop's body is executed.

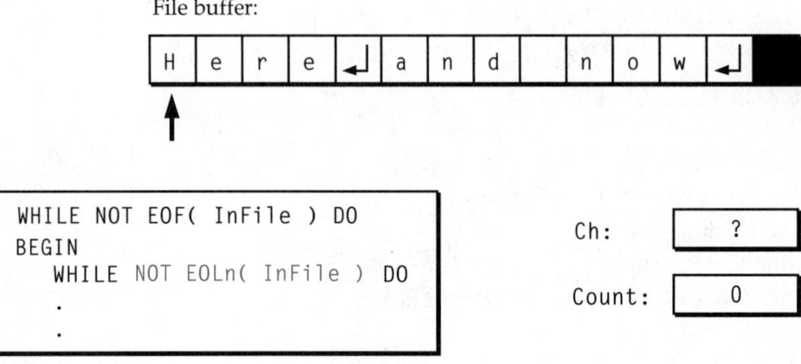

A character is read, the file pointer is advanced, and Count is incremented. The file pointer now points to 'e':

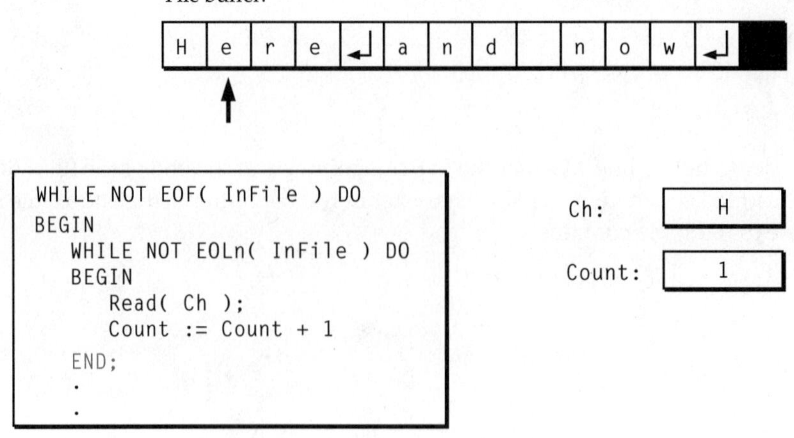

The process is repeated for 'e', then 'r', and then 'e', after which the file pointer points to <EOLn> and Count contains 4:

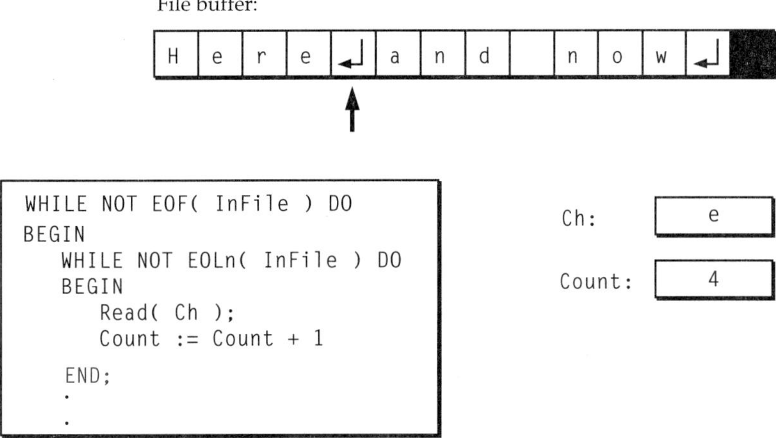

Returning to the top of the inner loop, EOLn is called again. Now EOLn returns True, causing the inner loop to terminate. Execution passes to the ReadLn beyond the inner loop:

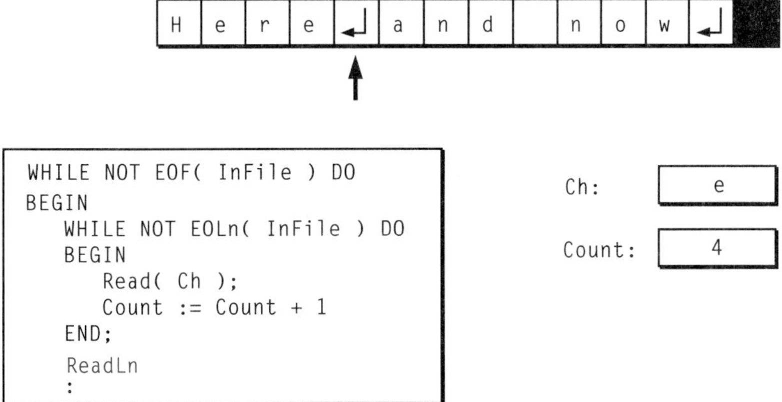

ReadLn discards the end-of-line signal without storing it, by advancing the file pointer past it. Then execution loops back to the top of the outer loop, where EOF is called for the second time:

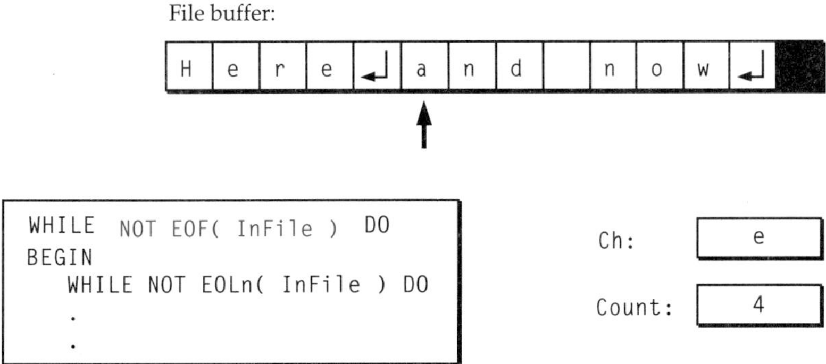

The next character is `'a'`, so `EOF` returns `False`, and the body of the outer loop is executed for the second time. During this trip through the outer loop, the inner loop reads the entire second line of text from the file, incrementing `Count` to 11. Finally, the outer loop's `ReadLn` discards the remaining <EOLn> by advancing the file pointer past it. The `InFile` pointer points to the end-of-file signal as execution returns to the top of the outer loop:

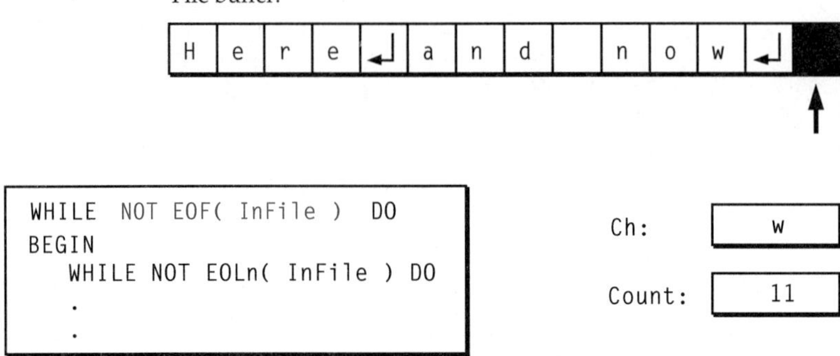

The `EOF` function returns `True`, terminating the outer loop. The procedure returns the final value of `Count`, which is 11. It also returns the final value of `InFile`, which is the memory address of the <EOF> in the file buffer.

Reading from the Input file

If the `CountChars` procedure is used with `InFile = Input`, neither the `EOF` nor the `EOLn` function will be able to return a value until a character has entered the `Input` buffer. This will cause the program to halt at the beginning of the outer `WHILE` loop, waiting for the first key to be struck. You must be aware of this when using such loops to read from the keyboard, or the screen display might be confusing. The following variant of the procedure produces strange-looking output on some systems:

```
PROCEDURE CountCharsKeyed( VAR Count   : Integer );
{
   POSTCONDITION:
   0 <= Count and
   Count = number of characters keyed, not counting
   <EOLn>s and <EOF>.
}
VAR
   Ch : Char;        { To hold the latest character read }

BEGIN

   Count := 0;

   WriteLn( 'Enter text now, terminated by <EOF>.' );
   WriteLn( 'Program will count characters,' );
   WriteLn( 'not including <EOLn>s and <EOF>.' );
   WriteLn;
```

```
   WHILE NOT EOF DO
   BEGIN

      WHILE NOT EOLn DO
      BEGIN

         Write( Count:2, ': ' );
         Read( Ch );
         WriteLn;
         Count := Count + 1

      END; { WHILE NOT EOLn }

      ReadLn

   END { WHILE NOT EOF }

END; { CountCharsKeyed }
```

The idea is that if the user enters `Wow!<EOLn><EOF>`, the interaction should look like this:

```
Enter text now, terminated by <EOF>.
Program will count characters,
not including <EOLn>s and <EOF>.

0: W
1: o
2: w
3: !
4: <EOLn><EOF>
```

Because of the way the `EOF` and `EOLn` functions work, however, and because in some systems the input buffer is flushed by an `<EOLn>`, you may see this:

```
Enter text now, terminated by <EOF>.
Program will count characters,
not including <EOLn>s and <EOF>.

Wow!<EOLn>
0:
1:
2:
3:
<EOF>
```

Try this out on your computer system. (You will need to know the `<EOF>` signal for your Pascal system.)

Writing text files

Writing text files is not very different from reading them. Suppose, for example, a program needs to read text from the keyboard and copy it to a disk file that is already open. Reading the characters from the keyboard has already been explained, and all we do now is add `Write` statements to echo the keyed characters to the already-opened file. Here is the completed procedure, complete with driver program:

```
PROGRAM TestEchoFile( Input, Output, OutFile );

VAR
   OutFile : Text;


PROCEDURE WriteEchoFile;
VAR
   Ch : Char;        {The latest character keyed}

BEGIN

   WriteLn( 'Enter text now, as a sequence of lines,' );
   WriteLn( 'terminated by <EOF>.' );
   WriteLn;
   WHILE NOT EOF DO
   BEGIN

      WHILE NOT EOLn DO
      BEGIN
         Read( Ch );
         Write( OutFile, Ch )
      END;

      ReadLn;
      WriteLn( OutFile )

   END

END; { WriteEchoFile }


BEGIN { main program }

   { -- Open external file for writing }
   Rewrite( OutFile );

   { -- Echo keyed characters to the external file }
   WriteEchoFile;

   WriteLn;
   WriteLn( 'File written.' )

END.
```

In Standard Pascal, the file buffer is flushed automatically when the program terminates. Therefore, even the last data remaining in the output buffer end up in the external file. In Turbo Pascal, this is not automatic, and a call to the nonstandard `Close` procedure must be used in order to ensure that all data reach the file.

Questions

21. Why was `CountChars` written as a procedure instead of as a function? (Review Section 7.3 if you need to.)

22. Jackson P. Slipshod claims that the CountChars procedure contains an error. "The loop invariant says that the next character in the file is not <EOF>. Therefore, when the loop terminates, the next character is not <EOF>. But the postcondition asserts that InFile points to <EOF>. These assertions are inconsistent." Is Jackson right? Why or why not?

23. Cora Meltdown has written her own version of the CountChars procedure, claiming that it is shorter and therefore more efficient. Explain to her why it won't work correctly.

```
PROCEDURE CountChars( VAR InFile : Text;
                      VAR Count  : Integer );

VAR
   Ch : Char;

BEGIN

   Count := 0;

   REPEAT

      Read( Ch );
      IF ( NOT EOLn( InFile ) ) AND ( NOT EOF( InFile ) ) THEN
         Count := Count + 1

      END;

   UNTIL EOF( InFile );

END; { CountChars }
```

Exercise

24. Standard Pascal requires that a file can be open for reading or open for writing, but not for both at the same time. Furthermore, it provides no way for a program to close a file and then reopen it for the opposite mode of I/O. Check with your instructor or reference manual to see if your Pascal system allows this. If it does, write a test program to try it out. Have your program write a text file, then close it, reopen it for reading, and read the data back, showing it on the screen.

17.5 THE FILE BUFFER VARIABLE

Suppose we have an output text file pointer called OutFile:

```
VAR
   OutFile : Text;
```

Then OutFile is a pointer to a text file buffer that can hold characters. Suppose Rewrite is used to connect the pointer to the buffer and the buffer to the file, positioning the pointer at the beginning of the buffer. Then we start to write the file, character by character, with OutFile always pointing to the next byte to be written in the file buffer.

Standard Pascal's file buffer variable

File window or **file buffer variable**: The file buffer storage cell to which the file pointer points. That is, the next item to be accessed in the file buffer.

Standard Pascal allows us to refer to the memory cell to which `OutFile` points; the cell is called `OutFile↑`. This is pronounced "`OutFile`-up-arrow." Because standard keyboards have no up-arrow key, most systems require a circumflex (^) or @ instead; we will use the circumflex. Then `OutFile^` is the next buffer storage cell to be accessed—the cell to which `OutFile` points—and is called the **file window** or **file buffer variable**. See Figure 17.5.1.

Dereferencing the file pointer

Dereference: To refer to a storage cell in terms of a pointer that points to the cell, instead of using the cell's own identifier.

The process of referring to the file buffer variable in terms of its pointer, by attaching an up-arrow to the pointer name, is called **dereferencing** the pointer. Dereferencing is the only way to access the file buffer variable, which has no name of its own. (Because it has no name of its own, it is sometimes said to be an **anonymous variable**.)

Using the file buffer variable

The file buffer variable is useful because it contains the next file component to be read from the file or the location of the next component to be written. By accessing this variable, we can look ahead in the file buffer without moving the file buffer pointer. We will have need of this ability in later algorithms—in the next section, for example.

Standard Pascal also provides two procedures, called `Put` and `Get`, for manipulating the contents of the file buffer variable. The `Put` procedure appends the contents of the file buffer variable to the end of the file by copying *FilePointer^* to the end of the file, then advancing the buffer pointer. The `Get` procedure does the reverse: It first advances the buffer pointer, then copies the next file component into *FilePointer^*. These are described in the accompanying syntax boxes.

`Put` and `Get` are fundamental file I/O procedures. In fact, the procedures `Write` and `WriteLn` actually make calls to `Put`, while `Read` and `ReadLn` make calls to `Get`. For example, `Write( OutFile, Ch )` is equivalent to

```
OutFile^ := Ch;   { Copy Ch into file buffer variable.       }
Put( OutFile );   { Copy file buffer variable to end of file }
                  {  and then advance the buffer pointer.    }
```

Figure 17.5.1 *(Standard Pascal only) After 't' is written, the file buffer pointer OutFile points to the buffer cell called OutFile^.*

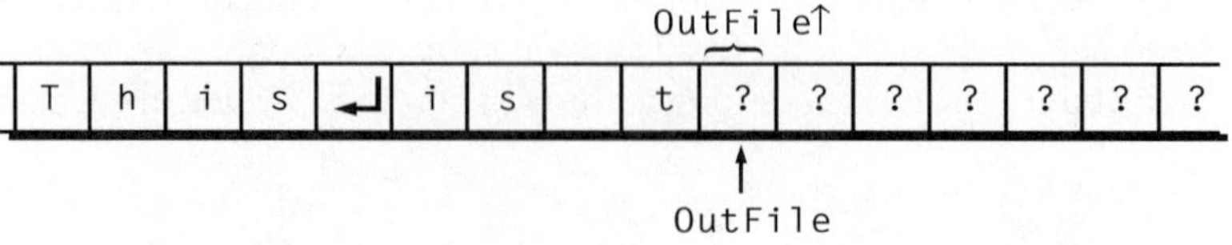

Syntax for Calling the Get Procedure

Pseudocode:

`Get(` *FilePointer* `)`

This advances the file buffer pointer and then copies the next component of the file into *FilePointer*^; that is, into the file buffer storage cell pointed to by the already-advanced *FilePointer*.

Notes:

- It is an error to call `Get` when the file is not open for reading.
- It is an error to call `Get` when *FilePointer* is pointing at `<EOF>`. In this case, `Get` will leave an unpredictable value in *FilePointer*^.

Similarly, `Read( InFile, Ch )` is equivalent to

```
Ch := InFile^;    { Copy file buffer variable into Ch.       }
Get( InFile );    { Advance the InFile pointer and then copy }
                  {  the next file component to the file     }
                  {  buffer variable.                        }
```

The `Read` and `Write` procedures have great advantages over `Get` and `Put`, however, because they accept varying numbers of parameters and they hide the inner workings of the file buffer, making I/O seem conceptually simpler.

In Turbo Pascal, the file buffer variable must be simulated.

Unfortunately, Turbo Pascal does not allow dereferencing the file pointer in order to check the value of the file buffer variable. In the same vein, it doesn't implement the `Get` and `Put` procedures. This is a serious impediment to the design of some algorithms, so we will need a *simulated file buffer variable*. The following procedure provides one.

Syntax for Calling the Put Procedure

Pseudocode:

`Put(` *FilePointer* `)`

This appends the contents of *FilePointer*^ to the end of the file; that is, it copies the contents of the file buffer storage cell pointed to by *FilePointer* to the end of the file. Then it advances the file buffer pointer.

Notes:

- It is an error to call `Put` when the file is not open for writing.
- It is an error if a file error prevents the appending process from being completed.

```
PROCEDURE GetValue( VAR FileBufferVar : Char;
                    VAR InFile        : Text;
                    VAR Value         : Char;
                    VAR EndOfBuffer   : Boolean );
{
  Used in Turbo Pascal to simulate
  Standard Pascal's file buffer variable.

  PRECONDITION:
  EndOfBuffer is False; FileBufferVar has a value.

  POSTCONDITION:
  Value has been assigned the value in FileBufferVar.
  Also, either
     EndOfBuffer = True
  or
     EndOfBuffer = False and FileBufferVar contains
                   the next value from the file.
}
BEGIN

   Value := FileBufferVar;

   IF EOF( InFile ) THEN
      EndOfBuffer := True

   ELSE
   BEGIN
      EndOfBuffer := False
      Read( InFile, FileBufferVar )
   END

END; { GetValue }
```

Exercises

25. Assume that the state of an *input* text file is as shown below, with `InFile` pointing to the character cell containing `'t'`.

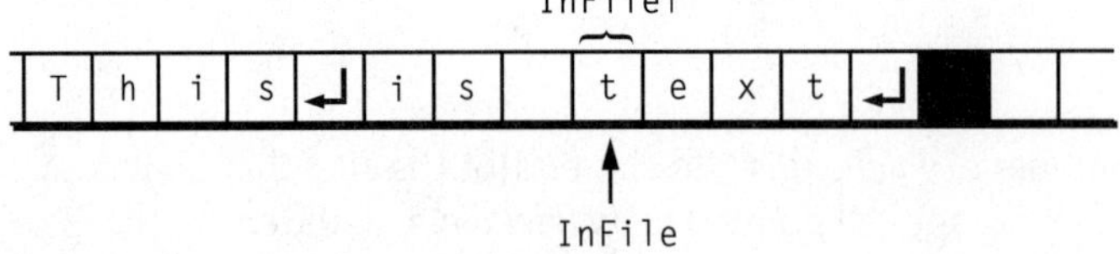

Assume also that the file was originally opened by a call to `Reset`. Then draw a diagram to show the state after executing the following instructions:

```
Get( InFile );
Get( InFile );
```

26. Assume that the state of a text file is as shown in Figure 17.5.1, with `OutFile` pointing to the character cell after the `'t'`. Assume also that the file was opened by a call to `Rewrite`. Then draw a diagram to show the state after executing the following instructions:

```
OutFile^ := 'o';
Put( OutFile );
OutFile^ := 'd';
Put( OutFile );
Put( OutFile );
```

27. If you are using Turbo Pascal, write a procedure `PutValue` that acts as a companion to `GetValue`. Your procedure should copy the contents of `Value` to the simulated file buffer variable and, if `<EOF>` has not been signaled from the keyboard, should get the next value for the `Value` variable.

17.6 CASE STUDIES: COPYING, DELETING, AND APPENDING

The previous sections explained how to write a new text file or read an existing one. Now we describe some more complicated common operations: **copying a file, deleting data from a file,** and **appending data to a file.** We start with copying because it is the simplest.

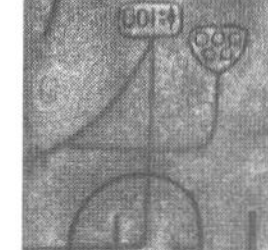

Copying a text file

Files, unlike arrays and records, cannot be copied by means of assignment statements. Instead, an existing file is read component by component, with each component copied individually to the copy file. This means that we open the existing file for reading, open a copy file for writing, and then use a loop to read components from the old file and write them to the copy file, individually:

```
{ Code fragment 17.6.1: Copying a text file }
VAR
   OldFile, CopyFile          : Text;
   Ch                         : Char;

BEGIN

   { -- Open existing file for reading }
   Reset( OldFile );

   { -- Open new file for writing }
   Rewrite( CopyFile );

   WHILE NOT EOF( OldFile ) DO
   BEGIN

      WHILE NOT EOLn( OldFile ) DO
      BEGIN
         Read( OldFile, Ch );
         Write( CopyFile, Ch )
      END; { WHILE NOT EOLn }

      {-- Skip end-of-line signal in OldFile }
      ReadLn( OldFile );
      {-- Copy <EOLn> to copy file }
      WriteLn( CopyFile )

   END; { WHILE NOT EOF( OldFile ) }
```

Deleting a component from an existing text file

In Standard Pascal, a file can be opened for reading or for writing, but not for both. This makes it difficult to perform some common file-maintenance tasks like deleting data from, or appending data to, an existing file. Although many Pascal systems provide nonstandard extensions to the language to help with such tasks, it is instructive to see how to perform them while conforming to the Standard.

To delete a component from a file, the file must be open for reading so that we can look for the target component. This automatically means that the file itself cannot be changed, so we write all of its components, except the one to be deleted, to a new file. The new file is then considered to be the replacement for the old one. The resulting code is only a slight variation on that used for copying. Let's assume that the goal is to delete only the first instance of the target component:

```
{ Code fragment 17.6.2: Deleting first instance of a character. }
VAR
   OldFile, NewFile          : Text;
   ChToDelete, Ch            : Char;
   Deleted                   : Boolean;

BEGIN

   GetDeletionCharacter( ChToDelete );

   { -- Open existing file for reading }
   Reset( OldFile );

   { -- Open new file for writing }
   Rewrite( NewFile );

   Deleted := False;

   WHILE NOT EOF( OldFile ) DO
   BEGIN

      WHILE NOT EOLn( OldFile ) DO
      BEGIN

         Read( OldFile, Ch );

         IF ( NOT Deleted ) AND ( Ch = ChToDelete ) THEN
            Deleted := True
         ELSE
            { ASSERTION: Deleted OR ( Ch <> ChToDelete ) }
            Write( NewFile, Ch )

      END; { WHILE NOT EOLn }

      { -- Skip end-of-line signal in OldFile }
      ReadLn( OldFile );
      { -- Copy <EOLn> to copy file }
      WriteLn( NewFile )

   END; { WHILE NOT EOF }
```

Appending data to an existing text file

Adding new data to the end of an existing file is just a small step from the code we just wrote. The appending process (Is that the opposite of an appendectomy?) consists of three major tasks:

1. Read the old data from an existing file that is open for reading.
2. Write the old data to a new file that is open for writing.
3. Write the new data to the new file.

With the basic operations worked out in the previous code fragments, we can easily write a complete program this time. Note that the file pointers are initialized by the main program and sent to the procedures as parameters. As previously mentioned in Section 17.4, *Pascal requires file-pointer parameters to be* `VAR` *parameters.*

```
PROGRAM AppendText ( Input, Output, OldFile, NewFile );
{ Copies the contents of OldFile to NewFile,  }
{ then appends new data to NewFile.           }

VAR
   OldFile, NewFile : Text;

PROCEDURE CopyOldData( VAR File1, File2 : Text );
{
  PRECONDITIONS:
  File1 is open for reading; File2 is open for writing.

  POSTCONDITIONS:
  The characters of File1 have been copied to File2.
}
VAR
   Ch : Char;

BEGIN

   WHILE NOT EOF( File1 ) DO
   BEGIN

      WHILE NOT EOLn( File1 ) DO
      BEGIN
         Read( File1, Ch );
         Write( File2, Ch );

         { -- Echo character to screen }
         Write( Output, Ch )
      END; { WHILE NOT EOLn }

      {-- Discard <EOLn> from old file }
      ReadLn( File1 );
      {-- Echo <EOLn> to the new file and to the screen }
      WriteLn( File2 );
      WriteLn( Output )

   END { WHILE NOT EOF }

END; { CopyOldData }
```

```
PROCEDURE AppendNewData( VAR File2 : Text );
{
  PRECONDITIONS:
  File2 is open for writing;
  the pointer lies after the last character.

  POSTCONDITIONS:
  New data from the keyboard have been appended to
  the data originally in File2.

  NOTE: Code assumes that Read and ReadLn automatically
  echo to the screen.
}
VAR
   Ch : Char;

BEGIN

   WriteLn( 'Enter new text:' );

   WHILE NOT EOF( Input ) DO
   BEGIN

      WHILE NOT EOLn( Input ) DO
      BEGIN

         Read( Input, Ch );
         Write( File2, Ch )

      END; { WHILE NOT EOLn }

      ReadLn( Input );
      WriteLn( File2 )

   END; { WHILE NOT EOF }

END; { AppendNewData }

BEGIN { main program }

   { Open old disk file for reading only and new disk file for     }
   { writing only. Many Pascal systems will require you to         }
   { associate filenames with the file variables at this point.    }
   Reset( OldFile );
   Rewrite( NewFile );

   CopyOldData( OldFile, NewFile );
   AppendNewData( NewFile )

END.
```

Question

28. Why can't files be copied by means of an assignment statement?

Exercises

29. Write a version of code fragment 17.6.2 that deletes *all* instances of a given character from the text file. Use only features of Standard Pascal, as shown in this book.

30. Write a version of code fragment 17.6.2 that deletes the first instance of a given string from the text file. Assume that there is no `<EOLn>` in the string.

31. Consult your Pascal system's reference manual to find out if you can open a file for both reading and writing. If so, write a simplified version of `AppendText`, using this feature.

32. Write a version of `AppendNewData` that appends a string, provided as a parameter, to the end of an existing text file.

17.7 NONTEXT FILES

The text files we've considered so far are files of characters, divided into lines. That is, they contain the bit patterns for characters that symbolize the data, and, every once in a while, an `<EOLn>` character or characters are embedded. In order to write such files, Pascal must first translate all data into characters. Later, when reading them back, Pascal must translate the characters into internal data of appropriate types. These translations take time, so text files are relatively slow to read and write when noncharacter data are involved.

Pascal can also write files containing all kinds of data encoded into the same data representations used in main memory. Such files usually contain mostly noncharacter data and therefore cannot be displayed directly on the screen or manipulated in the usual editors. On the other hand, these files can be written and read more quickly by Pascal programs because the data representations do not need translation. We can have files of real numbers, files of any ordinal type, files of arrays, files of records—in fact, we can have files of any type that does not in turn contain files. Here are two simple examples:

Nontext file or **binary file**: A file whose components, of whatever type, are stored as the same bit patterns used in main memory. The file is not organized into lines.

```
TYPE
   AgeFile       = FILE OF Integer;
   EmployeeRec   = RECORD
                      ID     : Integer;
                      Salary : Real
                   END;
   EmployeeFile  = FILE OF EmployeeRec;

VAR
  SaveAges : AgeFile;
  OutFile  : EmployeeFile;
```

This example uses two files. The first is associated with file pointer `SaveAges`, and is a file of integers; that is, it contains binary bit patterns for integers. The second file is associated with file pointer `OutFile`, and is a file of `EmployeeRecs`. This file contains bit patterns representing employee records, each with an integer `ID` field followed by a real `Salary` field. These are shown in Figure 17.7.1.

Figure 17.7.1 *(a) The first component of a FILE OF Integer, containing the four-byte integer 515, stored as a binary bit pattern. (b) The first component of a FILE OF EmployeeRec, where an EmployeeRec contains a four-byte Integer followed by a four-byte Real.*

(a)
```
0000 0000  0000 0000  0000 0010  0000 0011 | ...
```

(b)
```
0000 0000  0000 0000  0000 0001  1010 0010 ¦ 0000 0001  0000 0000  0000 0000  1110 0001 | ...
```

Writing a nontext file

To write a nontext file, simply open the file with `Rewrite`, then write the components to the file in sequence. Suppose, for example, that we have the declarations

```
CONST
   Limit = 50;

TYPE
   RealArray = ARRAY [ 1..Limit ] OF Real;
```

Syntax for Nontext Files

A nontext file is declared to be a `FILE OF` *BaseType*, where *BaseType* is the type of component to be stored in the file:

```
TYPE
   FileType = FILE OF BaseType;

VAR
   FilePointer : FileType;
```

Alternately, the file pointer can be declared without naming the file type, but the lack of a type name prevents *FilePointer* from being used as a parameter:

```
VAR
   FilePointer : FILE OF BaseType;
```

Notes:

- The procedures `Rewrite`, `Reset`, `Read`, and `Write`, and the `EOF` function, work the same with nontext files as they do with text files.
- The procedures `ReadLn` and `WriteLn` and the `EOLn` function cannot be used with nontext files because such files do not contain lines.
- In Turbo Pascal, though not in Standard Pascal, a nontext file is open for reading and writing, regardless of whether it was opened with `Reset` or `Rewrite`.

Then the following procedure can be used to write *N* elements of a real array to a file. If *N* is greater than or equal to the number of elements in the array, the whole array is written to the file:

```
PROCEDURE WriteRealFile( A          : RealArray;
                         N          : Integer );
{
  PRECONDITIONS:
  Array elements A[1], A[2], ..., A[m] have been initialized,
  where m = minimum of ( N, Limit ).

  POSTCONDITIONS:
  m elements of the A array have been written to a real file,
  overwriting any previous contents.

  FUNCTION REQUIRED: Minimum.
}
VAR
   I       : Integer;
   OutFile : FILE OF Real;

BEGIN

   {--Open file for writing }
   Rewrite( OutFile );

   { -- Write as many elements as possible to the file }
   FOR I := 1 TO Minimum( N, Limit ) DO
      Write( OutFile, A[ I ] )

END; { WriteRealFile }
```

That's all there is to it. The output buffer is flushed and the file is marked with an end-of-file character when closed. If the same program that writes the file also needs to read it back, the file can be reopened for reading by means of a call to `Reset`.

Reading a nontext file

On the next page is an example of reading the same file that was written above, under the assumption that we know how many elements to read.

```
PROCEDURE ReadRealFile( VAR A      : RealArray;
                            N      : Integer );
{
  PRECONDITIONS:
  The file to be opened exists.

  POSTCONDITIONS:
  Reads m real numbers from a real file into the A array,
  where m = minimum of ( N, Limit ).

  FUNCTION REQUIRED: Minimum.
}
VAR
   I      : Integer;
   InFile : FILE OF Real;

BEGIN

   { -- Open file for reading }
   Reset( InFile );

   { -- Read up to N values into the array, if they will fit }
   FOR I := 1 TO Minimum( N, Limit ) DO
      Read( InFile, A[ I ] )

END; { ReadRealFile }
```

On the other hand, if we don't know how many elements are in the file, the program can loop until it detects the end-of-file marker. There are no end-of-line signals because this is not a text file:

```
PROCEDURE ReadRealFile( VAR A      : RealArray;
                        VAR N      : Integer );
{
  PRECONDITIONS:
  The file exists.

  POSTCONDITIONS:
  Reads N Real numbers from a Real file into the A array,
  where N <= Limit.
}
VAR
   InFile : FILE OF Real;

BEGIN

   { -- Open file for reading }
   Reset( InFile );

   N := 0;
```

```
    WHILE ( N < Limit ) AND ( NOT EOF( InFile ) ) DO
    {
      LOOP INVARIANT:
      0 <= N <= Limit
      and A[1], A[2], ..., A[N] initialized.
    }
    BEGIN
       N := N + 1;
       Read( InFile, A[ N ] )
    END;

    { ASSERTION: A[1], A[2], ..., A[N] initialized from file. }

END; { ReadRealFile }
```

Exercises

33. A nontext file does not, in general, contain characters. Try displaying such a file on the screen by opening it with a text editor. What do you see?

34. Write declarations for a file in which the components are student records, each containing a student's name, Social Security number, a list of up to four exam scores (integers from 0 to 100), and a list of up to 10 assignment scores (integers from 0 to 25).

35. Write declarations for a file in which the components are of type `String80`, as defined in Section 15.5.

36. Rewrite code fragment 17.6.1 so that it copies a file of `Real` to another file of `Real`.

37. Rewrite the `AppendText` program of Section 17.6 so it appends a `Real` value to a file of `Real`.

17.8 CASE STUDY: MERGING FILES

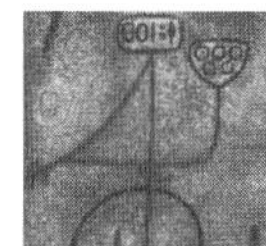

As an example of using nontext files, let's consider the problem of merging two ordered files of integers. Given two files of integers, each of which has already been arranged in nondecreasing order, the problem is to **merge** these files into one file, with the integers still in nondecreasing order. This is shown in Figure 17.8.1.

Why merge?

The merging algorithm is a standard problem in computer science because it is the basis for one of the better methods for sorting values. Suppose we are given a file in random order:

```
File1:  13  4  2  7  15  12  15  5  10
```

We can group the values into imaginary successive pairs, and sort each pair by itself. The `10` at the end is left over and placed in a group by itself:

```
File1:  (4  13)  (2  7)  (12  15)  (5  15)  (10  )
```

Now we begin a repetitive process called **distributing** and merging. First we *distribute* successive pairs to alternate files:

Figure 17.8.1 *The problem is to merge two ordered files of integers into one file, with the numbers still ordered.*

```
File1:          2   5   11  12  16  <EOF>

File2:          7   9   10  15  <EOF>
_____________________________________________

Merged file:  2   5   7   9   10   11   12   15   16   <EOF>
```

```
File2:  (4   13)  (12   15)  (10   )

File3:  (2   7)    (5   15)
```

Now we *merge* the first ordered group in file 2 with the first ordered group of file 3, the second group of file 2 with the second group of file 3, . . . , placing the results back into the original file. This gives us ordered groups *twice as big* as before:

```
File1:  (2   4   7   13)  (5   12   15   15)  (10)
```

Then we repeat the whole distribute-and-merge process. We distribute the groups into alternating files:

```
File2:  (2   4   7   13)   (10   )

File3:  (5   12   15   15)
```

Now we merge the first groups of these two files, followed by the second groups, and so on, all into file 1:

```
File1:  (2   4   5   7   12   13   15   15)  (10)
```

You can see how this is going: The already-sorted groups get longer and longer, until the whole file is one big sorted group. After one more distribute-and-merge process, the whole file will be sorted. This is *merge sort*, an important method in computing, to be discussed further in Chapter 19.

How to merge

Now that you know what it means to merge files and why we might want to merge them, let's go back to Figure 17.8.1 and see how to do it. Suppose we are given the following two files of ordered integers:

```
File1:  2   5   11   12   16   <EOF>

File2:  7   9   10   15   <EOF>
```

We want to merge these two files into one file called `MergedFile`. We first mark starting positions in both files, using file pointers called `File1` and `File2`. `MergedFile` is initially empty.

```
 2  5  11  12  16  <EOF>
 ↑
File1

 7  9  10  15  <EOF>
 ↑
File2

 (empty)
 ↑
MergedFile
```

The 2 is less than 7, so we copy 2 to the `MergedFile` and advance the `File1` and `MergedFile` pointers:

```
 2  5  11  12  16
    ↑
   File1

 7  9  10  15
 ↑
File2

 2
    ↑
   MergedFile
```

The 5 is less than 7, so we copy 5 to the `MergedFile` and advance the `File1` and `MergedFile` pointers:

```
 2  5  11  12  16  <EOF>
        ↑
        File1

 7  9  10  15  <EOF>
 ↑
File2

 2  5
        ↑
      MergedFile
```

So far, we have executed an action that can be described as

```
WHILE ( NOT EOF(File1) ) AND ( NOT EOF(File2) ) DO
   IF File1^ < File2^ THEN
   BEGIN
      Copy File1^ to MergedFile^;
      Advance File1;
      Advance MergedFile
   END;
```

Now 11 > 7, so we copy the 7 to `MergedFile`, and then advance the `File2` and `MergedFile` pointers:

```
2   5   11   12   16   <EOF>
        ↑
      File1

7   9   10   15   <EOF>
    ↑
  File2

2   5   7
          ↑
        MergedFile
```

We are now in the midst of a process that can be described as

```
WHILE ( NOT EOF(File1) ) AND ( NOT EOF(File2) ) DO
   IF File2^ < File1^ THEN
   BEGIN
      Copy File2^ to MergedFile^;
      Advance File2;
      Advance MergedFile
   END;
```

The two processes continue until we reach the following state:

```
2   5   11   12   16   <EOF>
                  ↑
                File1

7   9   10   15   <EOF>
                   ↑
                 File2

2   5   7   9   10   11   12   15
                                  ↑
                                MergedFile
```

Now `File2` has been used up, and all that remains is to copy the rest of the first file into `MergedFile`:

```
WHILE NOT EOF( File1 ) DO
BEGIN
   Copy File1^ to MergedFile^;
   Advance File1;
   Advance MergedFile
END;
```

We now have the core of the procedure. The whole thing is shown on the next page.

```
TYPE
  Component = Integer;
  CompFile  = FILE OF Component;


PROCEDURE MergeFiles( VAR File1, File2, MergedFile : CompFile );
{
  PRECONDITIONS:
  File1 and File2 exist
  and their components are in nondecreasing order.

  POSTCONDITIONS:
  File1 and File2 are unchanged.
  MergedFile is in nondecreasing order
  and contains all components of both File1 and File2.
  Duplicate components are preserved.
}
VAR
   Value : Component;

BEGIN

   { -- Open the three files }
   Reset(File1);
   Reset(File2);
   Rewrite(MergedFile);

   { -- Perform the comparative merge }
   WHILE (NOT EOF(File1)) AND (NOT EOF(File2)) DO

      IF File1^ < File2^ THEN
      BEGIN
         Read(File1, Value);
         Write(MergedFile, Value)
      END

      ELSE { File2^ <= File1^ }
      BEGIN
         Read(File2, Value);
         Write(MergedFile, Value)
      END;

  { -- One file used up; copy remainder of other into MergedFile }
  WHILE NOT EOF(File1) DO BEGIN
     Read(File1, Value);
     Write(MergedFile, Value)
  END;

  WHILE NOT EOF(File2) DO BEGIN
     Read(File2, Value);
     Write(MergedFile, Value)
  END

END; { MergeFiles }
```

Exercises

38. The `MergeFiles` algorithm can be shortened by ending the two original files with a sentinel that is the largest allowed value of type `Component`. Then the first loop can do the whole job, and we can delete both of the "copy the remainder" loops. Rewrite the procedure along these lines and test it.

39. Jackson P. Slipshod claims that by changing the "AND" into an "OR" in the first `WHILE` header, the one loop can be made to perform the entire merge, and the other two loops can be removed. What is wrong with this proposal?

By placing at the end of each input file a sentinel value greater than any meaningful value in either file, Jackson's proposal can be made to work. But then we find that, under some conditions, the algorithm runs slower than the version shown in the text. Why does this happen?

17.9 TESTING AND DEBUGGING

Never, *never* read a component from a file until you have determined that `EOF(`*FilePointer*`)` is `False`. Failure to do this is the most common file error. The result is shown in Figure 17.9.1.

Another common reason for the `Attempt to read past end of file` message is that a text file is being read, but is lacking its last `<EOLn>`. Every text file must be divided into lines, so there must be an `<EOLn>` just before the `<EOF>`. If this is missing, a program is likely to attempt to read the `<EOF>`, which is illegal.

Failure to consider the `<EOLn>`s causes other troubles with text files. For example, it can cause an interactive program to seem to need extra RETURNs from the keyboard. When this happens, check to see if the program properly discards ends of lines; the control structures are likely to contain an error.

Sometimes a programmer will forget that a text file that is open for reading cannot be written to, and that a file open for writing cannot be read. Figure 17.9.2 shows an example.

Figure 17.9.1 *This program attempts to read from a file before checking the value of EOF. Unfortunately, the file pointer is at <EOF>.*

```
Attempt to read past end of file

ReadLn( InFile, Index );
WHILE NOT EOF( InFile ) DO
BEGIN

    Count := Count + 1;
    ReadLn( InFile, Index )

END;
```

This file is open for reading, not writing.

Figure 17.9.2

```
File not open for output

VAR
   ProjFile : Text;
   Ch : Char;

BEGIN

   Reset( ProjFile );
   .
   .
   Write( ProjFile, Ch );
```

LOOKING BACK

Files are data structures. They differ from arrays and records in two ways:

- A file is usually stored on a mass storage device. That is, most files are stored external to main memory, in a nonvolatile medium. An external file can therefore be larger than main memory.
- Files in Standard Pascal must be accessed sequentially, while arrays, records, and nontext files can be accessed randomly. (Some Pascal systems support random-access files.)

There are three common methods for classifying files in Standard Pascal, according to where they are stored, what they contain, and their mode of access:

- Internal files are stored in main memory, while external files are stored on mass storage devices like floppy or hard disks, tapes, or optical disks. (Internal files are not discussed in this book.)
- Text files are files of characters, divided into lines separated by end-of-line signals. Nontext files are files of some type of component, in which the component values are represented by the same bit patterns used in main memory.
- In Standard Pascal, a file is either open for reading or open for writing, but not for both. (Some Pascal systems relax this rule.)

A file pointer is a variable that stores the next address to be accessed in a file buffer. The pointer is associated with the buffer, and the buffer with an actual file, by opening the file with a call to `Reset` or `Rewrite`:

- `Reset(` *FilePointer* `)` associates the file and its buffer with *FilePointer*, opens the file for reading only, and initializes the file pointer with the address of the first storage cell in the input buffer.
- `Rewrite(` *FilePointer* `)` associates the file and its buffer with *FilePointer*, opens the file for writing only, and initializes the file pointer with the address of the first storage cell in the output buffer.

The storage cell to which the file pointer points at a given moment is called the *file window* or *file buffer variable*. As the components of the file are sequentially read or written, the file pointer advances through the file. It always points to the next component to be accessed, which is "in the file window."

There are two standard procedures for transferring values between the file buffer variable and the file itself:

- `Get(` *FilePointer* `)` advances the file buffer pointer and then copies the next file component into the file buffer variable.
- `Put(` *FilePointer* `)` appends a copy of the contents of the file buffer variable to the end of the file, then advances the file buffer pointer.

While discussing these subjects, we developed useful algorithms for copying a file, deleting the first occurrence of a given file component, appending a component to the end of an existing file, merging two ordered files, and random access.

TERMS EMPHASIZED IN THIS CHAPTER

PROJECTS

1. Write a rudimentary line-editor program that performs the following simple tasks:
   a. The program should first ask for a text file in which to save the user's text. It should then open the file for reading and place the user in text-entry mode.
   b. The user enters text in the usual way, pressing RETURN at the end of each line. Each time the user presses RETURN, the program should write the just-completed line to the text file.
   c. The user should be able to modify lines while keying them in, but not after hitting RETURN. This can be accomplished by reading each line as an 80-character string and afterwards writing the string to the file.
   d. The user should signal the end of the text by entering some sentinel, which might be, but needn't be, `<EOF>`.
2. Write a program that formats text read from the keyboard. That is, every time the user presses RETURN, the program should add blanks (spaces) between sentences and words to fill the line out to a given width, without splitting any words at line breaks. The formatted version of each line should be stored in a file, so that when the file is later displayed on the screen, the right and left margins will be flush and smooth.
3. Word-processing programs embed many invisible control characters in their files, indicating formatting, typeface, characteristics like italic or boldface letters, and many other things. These embedded control codes can interfere with proper display when another program like an editor or "view" program is used to examine the file. Write a program that strips all invisible characters from a text file with the following exceptions:
   a. Carriage returns and line feeds should be unaffected.
   b. Tabs should be converted to a sequence of spaces; let the user specify how many.
4. Write a program that counts the words in a user-specified text file. For the sake of this assignment, a word is defined as a sequence of letters delimited by whitespace.
5. Write a program that counts the real numbers in a user-specified `FILE OF Real`.
6. Operating-system programmers, or *systems programmers* as they are usually called, often use a software tool that lets them examine the bit patterns in a file by displaying a hexadecimal representation of the file contents, byte by byte. Write a rudimentary program that does this. Here are some tips:
   a. Let the user specify the file to be read. Assume that the file is `FILE OF Integer`.
   b. Read the integers from the file into an array of records, in which each record is of the variant form (assuming four-byte integers)

```
TYPE
   Modes = ( Decimal, Character );
   IntRec = RECORD
               CASE DisplayMode : Modes OF
                  Decimal   : ( Int : Integer );
                  Character : ( Ch1, Ch2, Ch3, Ch4 : Char )
               END;
```

   In other words, if your system stores integers in N bytes, declare N character variables in the variant record.

c. With the integers read into the array records as integers, you can then examine them in one-byte chunks by switching the variant record to `Character` mode, and looking at `Ord( Ch1 ),Ord( Ch2 ), . . . .` This is a down-and-dirty way of examining one type as though it were another type.

d. Display the four (or whatever) `Ord` values from step **c** in hexadecimal, side-by-side with the actual decimal integers. Organize your display for convenient reading, so that the user can easily see the correspondence between the bytewise hexadecimal printout and the whole-integer decimal values.

REFERENCES

There are whole books on the subject of file I/O. A good one is Nancy E. Miller's *File Structures Using Pascal* (Benjamin/Cummings, 1987). See also the chapter on files in Kathleen Jensen and Niklaus Wirth's *Pascal User Manual and Report*, third edition (Springer-Verlag, 1985).

A more advanced book, not using Pascal, is Owen Hanson's *Design of Computer Data Files* (Computer Science Press, 1982).

Control Leads to Obligations.

Once the automatic computer was there, it was not only a new tool, it was also a challenge and, if the tool was without precedent, so was the challenge. The challenge was—and still is—a two-fold one.

Firstly we are faced with the challenge of discovering new (desirable) applications, and this is not easy, because the applications could be as revolutionary as the tool itself. Ask the average computing scientist: "If I were to put a ten-megabuck machine at your disposal, to be installed for the benefit of mankind, how and to what problem would you apply it?", and you will discover that it will take him a long time to come up with a sensible answer. This is a serious problem that puts great demands on our fantasy and on our powers of imagination. . . .

Secondly, once an (hopefully desirable!) application has been discovered, we are faced with the programming task, i.e. with the problem of bending the general tool to our specific purpose. For the relatively small and slow machines of the earlier days the programming problem was not too serious, but when machines at least a thousand times as powerful became generally available, society's ambition in applying them grew in proportion and the programming task emerged as an intellectual challenge without precedent. . . .

On the one hand the mathematical basis of programming is very simple. Only a finite number of zeros and ones are to be subjected to a finite number of simple operations, and in a certain sense programming should be trivial. On the other hand, stores [memories] with a capacity of many millions of bits are so unimaginably huge and processing these bits can now occur at so unimaginably high speeds that the computational processes that may take place and that, therefore, we are invited to invent—have outgrown the level of triviality by several orders of magnitude. It is the unique combination of basic simplicity and ultimate sophistication which is characteristic for the programming task.

We realize what this combination implies when we compare the programmer with, say, a surgeon who does an advanced operation. Both should exercise the utmost care, but the surgeon has fulfilled his obligations in this respect when he has taken the known precautions and is then allowed to hope that circumstances outside his control will not ruin his work. Nor is the surgeon blamed for the incompleteness of his control: the unfathomed complexity of the human body is an accepted fact of life. But the programmer can hardly exonerate himself by appealing to the unfathomed complexity of his program, for the latter is his own construction! With the possibility of complete control, he also gets the obligation: it is the consequence of the basic simplicity.

—Edsger W. Dijkstra, *A Discipline of Programming* (Prentice Hall, 1976), pages 209–10.

CHAPTER 18

Sets

CHAPTER CONTENTS

INTRODUCTION

As our last example of Pascal's built-in data structures, we consider **sets**. A set is simply a collection of objects of the same kind. For example, we can have the set of positive odd integers less than 10, or the set of lowercase vowels, or the set of additive primary colors. Sets are useful in programming when the data are grouped in classes and we want to know whether a given data value belongs to a certain class. Perhaps the simplest useful examples are in text processing, where we often need to know whether a given character is a lowercase letter, an uppercase letter, a numeral, or whatever. We handled such problems by crude means in Chapter 8, but now we can show a better way. In this chapter, you will first learn about sets, then about the syntax for set manipulations in Pascal, and then how to build a set abstract data type (ADT). Finally, we will examine a typical computer science application.

18.1 SETS IN MATHEMATICS

A **set** is a collection of items of the same type. These items are called the *elements* or **members** of the set, and are said to *belong to the set*. In mathematics, a set is often specified by listing its members inside curly braces. For example, the set of planets in our solar system inside the orbit of the Earth contains the two planets, Mercury and Venus, and we can specify that set as { Mercury, Venus }. Similarly, the set of traffic-light colors is { Red, Yellow, Green }.

Sets are **unordered** collections; that is, the set { 1, 2, 3 } is the same as { 2, 1, 3 } or { 2, 3, 1 }. Duplication of members is not significant, so the set { 2, 1, 3, 1 } is the same as the set { 2, 1, 3 }.

The number of (distinct) members in a set is called the **cardinality** of the set. So the set { 2, 1, 3 } has cardinality 3, as does the identical set { 2, 1, 3, 1 }.

Empty and infinite sets

Empty set or **null set**: A set with no members.

A set with no members is called an **empty set** or **null set**, and has cardinality zero. Such a set is denoted by a pair of empty braces: { }. For example, the set of planets in our solar system inside the orbit of Mercury is empty, and is written in this way. Similarly, the set of integers between 0 and 1 is empty.

Sets can also be **infinite**; that is, they can contain infinitely many members. Examples include the set of real numbers between 0 and 1, the set of all integers, and the set of all Pascal programs. (However, huge sets and of course infinite sets cannot be represented in computer memory, which is limited.)

The universal set

Universal set: The set with all possible members of the type under consideration.

Complement of *S*: The set of all possible members except those contained in *S*.

The collection of all possible items of the type under consideration is called our **domain of discourse**, or the **universe of discourse**, or the **universal set**. Any set containing some of these items is part of the universal set, and can be represented by a **Venn diagram** (after the British mathematician John Venn [1834–1923]). The Venn diagram in Figure 18.1.1 is intended to suggest that a set S is contained within its universal set, and that the universal set has two classes of members: those belonging to S, and those that do not belong to S. The part of the universal set lying outside S is called the **complement** of S, and is written $U - S$. For example, if the universal set happens to be the nine major planets in our solar system, the complement of the set {Mercury, Venus} is the set containing the rest of the planets:

U – {Mercury, Venus} = {Earth, Mars, Jupiter, Saturn, Uranus, Neptune, Pluto}.

Figure 18.1.1 *A set S is part of the universal set, U. The rest of U is called the complement of S.*

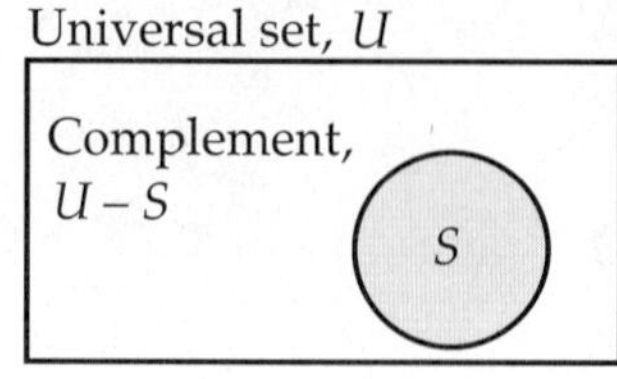

The set of all vowels except "y." **Figure 18.1.2**

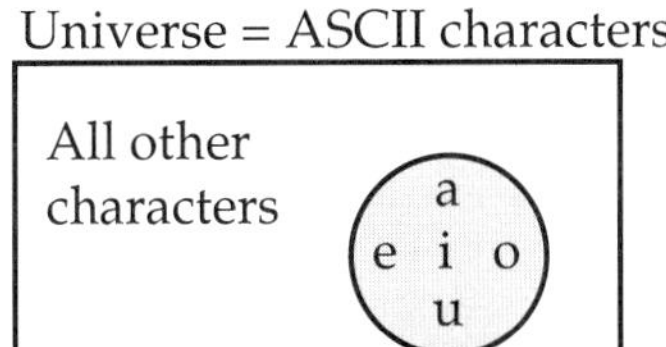

A set of characters

If, for example, we are interested in sets of characters, then the universal set is the computer system's entire character set. Our universal set might, for example, consist of the 128 characters comprising the ASCII code. (These are listed in Appendix C.) Suppose we want to consider within this universal set a set L of lowercase vowels, not including "y." Then the Venn diagram for L within the ASCII code would be as shown in Figure 18.1.2.

As mentioned previously, the order of elements in a set is immaterial. Figure 18.1.2 is equivalent to Figure 18.1.3.

There are various ways to describe this set:

1. By listing (enumerating) the set members:

L = { "a", "e", "i", "o", "u" };

2. By giving a rule in English for choosing the set members:

L = { All lowercase vowels other than "y" }

or

L = { All c such that c is a lowercase vowel other than "y" }

3. By giving a rule in mathematical shorthand:

L = { c | c is a lowercase vowel other than "y" }

Comparing sets

A set S_1 is said to be a **subset** of S_2 if all the members of S_1 are also members of S_2. To indicate that S_1 is a subset of S_2, we write $S_1 \subseteq S_2$. If S_1 is not a subset of S_2, we write $S_1 \not\subseteq S_2$.

Because the order of the members does not matter, this set is the same as the one shown in Figure 18.1.2. **Figure 18.1.3**

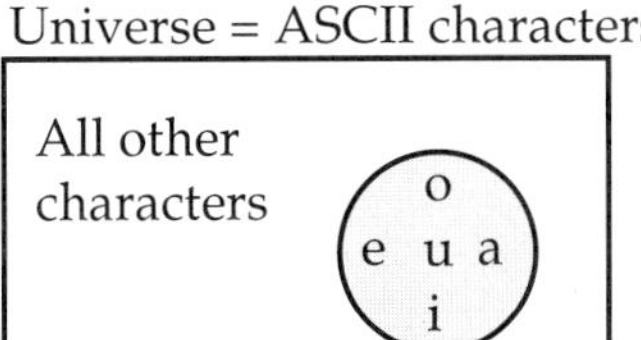

Figure 18.1.4 *A subset may consist of part of the parent set, or all of it.*

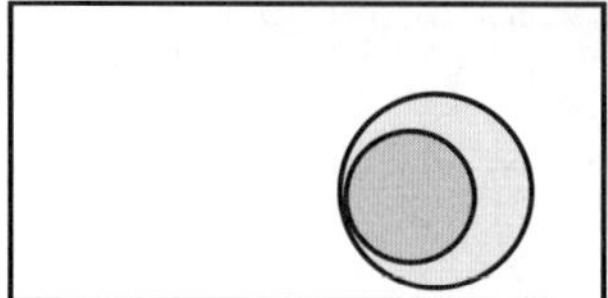

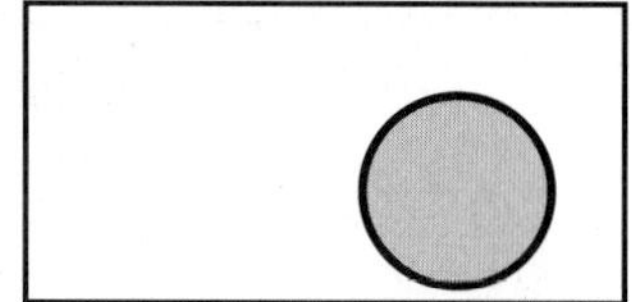

Examples:

$\{1\} \subseteq \{1,2,4\}$ $\{5,3,7\} \subseteq \{3,5,7\}$

$\{2,1\} \subseteq \{1,2,4\}$ $\{1,3\} \not\subseteq \{3,5,7\}$

$\{\} \subseteq \{1,2,4\}$

If a set S_1 is a subset of S_2 and S_2 is also a subset of S_1, it must be that S_1 and S_2 contain exactly the same members. In such a case, the sets are said to be **equal**, and we write $S_1 = S_2$. On the other hand, if S_1 is not the same as S_2, we write $S_1 \neq S_2$.

Examples:

$\{2,1\} = \{1,2\}$ $\{2,1\} \neq \{1,2,3\}$

If S_1 is a subset of S_2 but is not equal to S_2, we say that S_1 is a **proper subset** of S_2, and write $S_1 \subset S_2$.

Examples:

$\{1,2\} \subset \{1,2,4\}$ $\{\} \subset \{1,2,4\}$

Note that the empty set { } is a proper subset of all nonempty sets.

Set membership

The fundamental set operation is a boolean test to determine whether a given member is contained within a set. In mathematics, if an item I belongs to a set S, we write

Figure 18.1.5 *The set S_1 is a proper subset of S_2.*

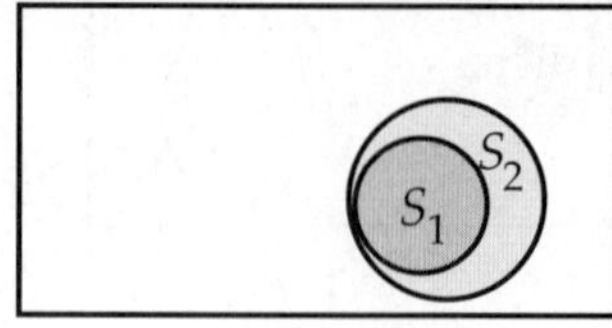

The union $S_1 \cup S_2$ is the set containing all members of S_1 and all members of S_2. **Figure 18.1.6**

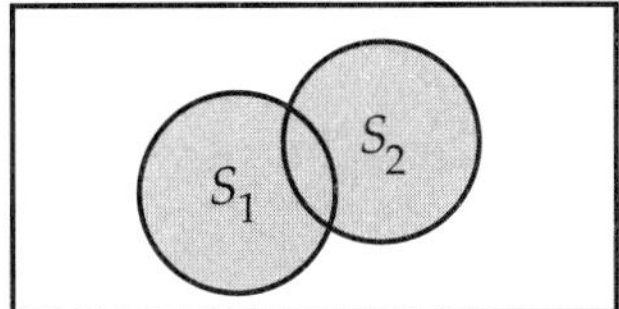

$I \in S$. If I belongs to S, the boolean expression $I \in S$ is true; otherwise, it is false. Similarly, if I does not belong to S, we write $I \notin S$.

Note the distinction between the set { M } containing only the single member M, and the member M itself. For example, 2 is an integer, but { 2 } is a *set* containing one integer. A set of integers like { 1, 3, 5 } can contain multiple integers simultaneously, while an integer itself can have only one value at a time.

Union of sets

There are various ways to combine sets to make new sets. Given two sets, S_1 and S_2, we can make a new set containing all values that are members of either S_1 or S_2 or both. This is called the **union** of the two sets, symbolized by $\cup$. The union $S_1 \cup S_2$ is the set containing all members of S_1 and all members of S_2 (Figure 18.1.6).

Example:

$$\{1,2,4\} \cup \{2,3\} = \{1,2,3,4\}$$

Set union provides a way to add members to a given set. If we have a set of characters containing "a" and "b" and we want to add "c" to the set, we can take the union of { "a", "b" } and { "c" }:

{ "a", "b", "c" } = { "a", "b" } ∪ { "c" }

Intersection of sets

Another way to combine two sets is to build an **intersection**, denoted by the symbol $\cap$. The intersection of S_1 and S_2 is defined to be the set of all items that belong to both S_1 and S_2 (Figure 18.1.7).

Example:

$$\{1,2,4\} \cap \{2,3\} = \{2\}$$

Thus intersection is a way of finding the set of elements that are common to two sets.

Figure 18.1.7

The intersection $S_1 \cap S_2$ is the set consisting of all members of S_1 that are also members of S_2.

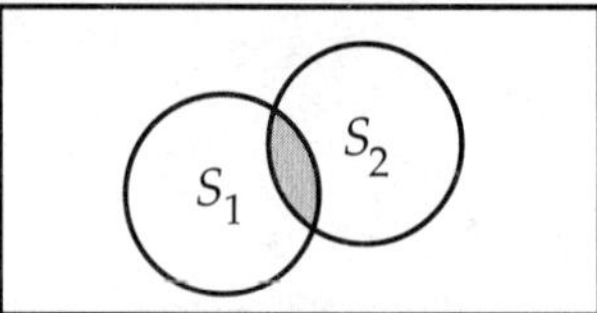

Difference of sets

Another way of combining sets is to take their **difference**. The difference $S_1 - S_2$ is the set of all members of S_1 that are not also members of S_2 (Figure 18.1.8).

Example:

$$\{1, 2, 4\} - \{2, 3\} = \{1, 4\}$$

The difference operation can be used to delete elements from a set. For example, to delete all even positive integers less than or equal to 10 from the set $\{1, 2, 3, 5, 7, 8\}$, we take the difference with respect to $\{2, 4, 6, 8, 10\}$:

Example:

$$\{1, 2, 3, 5, 7, 8\} - \{2, 4, 6, 8, 10\} = \{1, 3, 5, 7\}$$

Questions

1. In your own words, define a mathematical set.

2. Is a herd of cows a set? Are there any collections of real objects in the physical world that are *not* sets? According to quantum mechanics, the electrons in an atom are, in principle, not distinguishable. Assuming this to be true, is the collection of electrons in an atom a set?

3. Which of the following sets are finite? Which are infinite?

- **a.** The set of all automobiles being driven at a given moment.
- **b.** The set of all Pascal programs with fewer than 1,000 statements.
- **c.** The set of all legal Pascal programs.

Figure 18.1.8

The difference $S_1 - S_2$ is the set consisting of all members of S_1 that are not *members of S_2.*

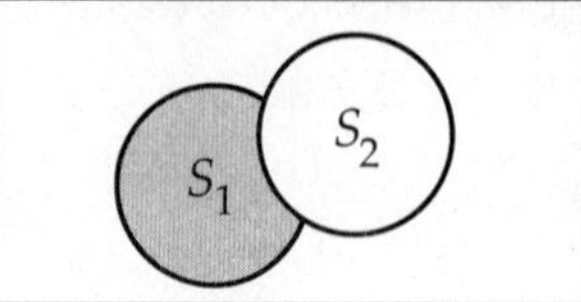

   d. The set of all true statements about living musicians.

   e. The set of all sets.

4. What is the difference between the union and intersection of two sets?

5. What is the value of the set difference { } – *S*, where *S* is a nonempty set?

6. Give three mathematical notations for the infinite set of odd integers.

7. What is the cardinality of the set of all standard ASCII characters? (Hint: See Appendix C.)

8. Which of the following sets are proper subsets of the set of American presidents?

   a. The set of American politicians.

   b. The set of deceased American presidents.

   c. { Harrison, Garfield }

   d. { }

9. If *S* is the set of titles of novels currently in print in the United States, which of the following assertions is true?

   a. *War and Peace* $\in$ *S*

   b. { *War and Peace* } $\subset$ *S*

   c. { *War and Peace* } = *S*

   d. { *War and Peace* } $\subseteq$ *S*

   e. Cardinality(*S*) > 1,000

   f. *S* is an infinite set

   g. { } $\subset$ *S*

10. Are the following statements true or false?

    a. The intersection of the set of lowercase letters and the set of uppercase letters is empty.

    b. The union of the set of lowercase letters and the set of uppercase letters is empty.

    c. The union of the empty set with the set of odd positive integers less than 10 has cardinality 6.

    d. The intersection of the empty set with the set containing only 0 has cardinality 1.

    e. The intersection of any set with itself is empty.

Exercises

11. Describe each of the following sets in two different notations. (Examples of notation were given on page 605.)

    a. The set of odd integers between –10 and +10.

    b. The set of even integers between –10 and +10, inclusive.

    c. The set of ASCII characters with ordinal values 32 through 38.

    d. The set of signs of the zodiac.

    e. The set of all nonnegative integers.

12. Tell whether each of the following assertions is true or false:

a. $\{1,2,4\} \subseteq \{4,2,1\}$
b. $\{1,2,4\} \subset \{4,2,1\}$
c. $\{1,2\} \subseteq \{1,2\}$
d. $\{1,2,4\} = \{4,2,1\}$
e. $\{1\} \subset \{1,2\}$
f. $\{1,2,4\} \subseteq \{1,2\}$
g. $\{2,2\} \neq \{2\}$
h. $\{2,1\} = \{1,2\}$
i. $\{1,2,3\} \cap \{2,3\} = \{3,2\}$
j. $\{1,2,3\} \cup \{2,3\} = \{3,2\}$
k. $\{1,2,4,3\} \cup \{2,3\} = \{1,2,3,4\}$
l. $\{1,2,4,3\} \cap \{2,3\} = \{3,2\}$
m. $\{3,2\} - \{2,3\} = \{\}$
n. $\{1,2,3,4\} - \{2\} = \{1,3,4\}$
o. $\{\} - \{2,3\} = \{\}$

13. Evaluate the following expressions. Some have set values and some are boolean.

a. $\{2,4,6\} \cap \{1,2,3\}$
b. $\{2,3,6\} \cup \{1,2,3\}$
c. $\{2,4,6\} - \{1,2,3\}$
d. $\{1,2\} \cap \{\}$
e. $\{\} \cup \{\}$
f. $\{\} - \{1,2,3\}$
g. $\{1,2,3\} - \{\}$
h. $\{4,9\} \subseteq \{9,4\}$
i. $(\{2,4,6\} \cap \{5,1,2\}) \subset \{4,2,1\}$
j. $((\{2,4,6\} \cup \{5,1,2\}) \cap \{4,2,1\}$
k. $(\{2,4,1\} - \{5,4,2\}) \subseteq \{4,2,1\}$
l. $2 \in (\{2,4,6\} \cap \{5,1,2\})$
m. $2 \in (\{2,4,6\} \cap \{1,3,5\})$
n. $2 \in (\{2,4,6\} \cup \{1,3,5\})$

18.2 SET TYPES IN PASCAL

Base type: The type of members in a set.

In Pascal, a set type can store a collection of values of *any single ordinal type*. So we can have sets of integers, sets of characters, sets of booleans, or sets of subranges or enumerations, but these types cannot be mixed within a set. The type of values that can belong to a given set is called the **base type** of that set. Note that while simple variables can store only one value at a time, *a set variable can store multiple values simultaneously.*

Here is an example in which we declare a variable for storing a set of lowercase letters:

```
TYPE
   LowerCaseSet = SET OF 'a'..'z';

VAR
   LowerCase : LowerCaseSet;
```

You can also declare `SET OF Char`, which is the type for sets of characters, and many other kinds of sets. Here are a few examples:

```
TYPE
   PrimaryColorSet = SET OF ( Red, Green, Blue );
   CharSet         = SET OF Char;
   DigitSet        = SET OF 0..9;

VAR
   Digits     : DigitSet;
   Characters : CharSet;
   Primaries  : PrimaryColorSet;
```

As always in Pascal, these variables are not initialized by their declarations, so initializations must be performed by assignment statements as described in the following syntax box.

Cardinality

Each Pascal system places some limitation on the maximum cardinality of sets. There was a time when many Pascal systems limited sets to as many members as there are bits in a machine word (often 16), but today many systems allow as many set members as will fit in memory. Check your reference manual for the limitations of your system. In this book, we assume that sets as large as `SET OF Char` can be declared. Note that extremely large sets and, of course, infinite sets cannot be implemented in the computer.

Set operations

Pascal has more built-in operations for sets than for other composite types:

- A base type value `B` can be tested for membership in the set `S` by evaluating the Boolean expression `B IN S`.
- A set constant value can be assigned to a set variable, or the value of one set variable can be assigned to another of a compatible type. In Pascal, a set constant is enclosed in square brackets:

```
Set1 := [ 1, 3, 5 ];
Set2 := Set1;
```

- A set union is constructed with the + operator. The value of `Set1 + Set2` is the set of all members belonging to `Set1` or `Set2` or both.

Syntax for Set Declaration

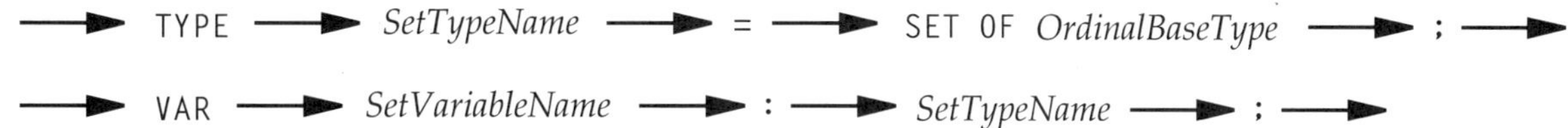

Pseudocode:

```
TYPE
    SetType = SET OF OrdinalBaseType;

VAR
    SetVariableName : SetType;
```

Notes:

- The *OrdinalBaseType* of a set can be any ordinal type, though some Pascal systems place a limit on the cardinality of the set, and may not allow declarations of sets as large as `SET OF Integer` or even `SET OF Char`.
- A set can be `PACKED` for the most efficient storage. As with packed arrays and records, packed sets may or may not be stored more efficiently; it depends on your system. Packed sets, if stored more efficiently, will be slower to access.

- A set intersection is constructed with the * operator. The value of `Set1 * Set2` is the set of all members of `Set1` that are also members of `Set2`.
- A set difference is constructed with the – operator. The value of `Set1 - Set2` is the set of members of `Set1` that are not members of `Set2`.
- Compatible sets can be compared for equality or inequality with the relational operators, = and <>. Two sets are equal if they have identical members; otherwise, they are unequal.
- Compatible sets can be compared with the relational operators, <= and >=. The expression `Set1 <= Set2` is true if and only if `Set1` is a subset of `Set2`. The expression `Set1 >= Set2` is true if and only if `Set2` is a subset of `Set1`. (There is, however, no operation for determining *proper* subsets.)

Set I/O

Like most other composite types, sets cannot be read from or written to text files. In order to read a set from a text file or write one to a text file, its members must be read or written individually. (Set values *can*, however, be read from or written to nontext files declared as `FILE OF` the appropriate kind of set.) Examples of how sets can be displayed on the screen are shown later in the chapter.

Next we will examine Pascal's built-in set operations in more detail. But first we should mention that Pascal's set notation differs a little from that of mathematics.

Set constants

In Pascal, we cannot enclose set constants in curly braces as in mathematics, because curly braces are used for comments. Instead, Pascal encloses set constants in *square brackets*. Here are some examples:

A set of integers, containing 1 and 3:	`[ 1, 3 ]`
A set of characters, containing `'a'` and `'A'`:	`[ 'a', 'A' ]`
The empty set:	`[ ]`

Initialization of set variables

Set variables are not initialized by their declarations, so you must assign values to them. For example,

```
TYPE
   DigitSet = SET OF 0..9;
   CharSet  = SET OF Char;
   PrimaryColorSet = SET OF (Red, Green, Blue);

VAR
   Digits     : DigitSet;
   Characters : CharSet;
   Primaries  : PrimaryColorSet;
```

```
BEGIN
   Digits     := [ 3, 7, 8 ];
   Characters := [ 'H', 'r' ];
   Primaries  := [ ];
   .
   .
```

With these assignments, the `Digits` set contains the three integers 3, 7, and 8; the `Characters` set contains the two characters `'H'` and `'r'`; and the `Primaries` set is empty.

Adding to a set by union

To add elements to an initialized set, we simply take the union of the set with the set of members we want to add. For example, if `Primaries` contains `Red`, then `Primaries + [ Blue ]` is the set containing both `Red` and `Blue`. Hence, the pair of assignments

```
Primaries := [ Red ];
Primaries := Primaries + [ Blue ];
```

has the same effect as

```
Primaries := [ Red, Blue ];
```

or

```
Primaries := [ ];
Primaries := Primaries + [ Red, Blue ];
```

These all result in `Primaries` containing both `Red` and `Blue`.

Selecting common members by intersection

The set intersection `S1 * S2` is a set containing those elements found in both set `S1` and set `S2`. For example, in the code

```
TYPE
   DigitSet = SET OF 0..9;

VAR
   S1, S2, S3 : DigitSet;

BEGIN
   S1 := [ 1, 2, 3, 5 ];
   S2 := [ 2, 4, 5 ];
   S3 := S1 * S2;
```

`S3` receives the elements common to `[1, 2, 3, 5]` and `[2, 4, 5]`. Thus, `S3` is given the value `[2, 5]`. On the other hand, the code

```
   S1 := [ 1, 3, 5 ];
   S2 := [ 2, 4, 6 ];
   S3 := S1 * S2;
```

makes `S3` the empty set, since `S1` and `S2` have no elements in common.

Finding the elements in one set but not another

The set difference S1 - S2 is the set containing those members of set S1 that are not members of set S2. If S1 is [1, 2, 3, 5] and S2 is [1, 3, 5], then the assignment

```
S3 := S1 - S2;
```

gives S3 the value [2]. On the other hand, if S1 is [1, 2, 3, 5] and S2 is [4], the same operation leaves S3 unchanged.

Checking for set equality and for subsets

Two compatible sets S1 and S2 can be compared by means of the relational operators =, <>, <=, and >=. The results are shown in Table 18.2.1.

For example, the code

```
S1 := [ 1, 5 ];
S2 := [ 1, 2, 3, 4, 5 ];
WriteLn( S1 = S2 );
WriteLn( S1 <> S2 );
WriteLn( S1 <= S2 );
WriteLn( S1 >= S2 );
```

would print

```
False
True
True
False
```

Note again that Pascal has no built-in test for *proper* subset.

Questions

14. **a.** What types of data can be members of Pascal sets?

b. How does a Pascal set differ from simple data types?

c. How does a Pascal set differ from other composite types?

15. Discuss the ways in which Pascal sets differ from mathematical sets.

Table 18.2.1 *Relational expressions involving sets.*

Relational expression	True if and only if
S1 = S2	S1 and S2 contain identical members.
S1 <> S2	S1 differs from S2 in at least one member.
S1 <= S2	S1 is a subset of S2.
S1 >= S2	S2 is a subset of S1.

16. Suppose that a program contains the following declarations and initializations:

```
TYPE
   NumeralSet = SET OF [ '0'..'9' ];

VAR
   S0, S1, S2, S3, S4 : NumeralSet;
BEGIN
   S0 := [ ];
   S1 := [ '0', '3', '6', '9' ];
   S2 := [ '1' ];
   S3 := [ '1', '3', '7', '2', '4' ];
   S4 := S2 + S3;
```

Then which of the following statements are syntactically illegal? Why? What values are assigned in the legal statements?

a. `S0 := S4 + { 'a' };`

b. `S1 := S1 * S1;`

c. `S2 := S4 + [ 3 ];`

d. `S3 := S0 - 3;`

e. `S4 := S1 <= S2;`

Exercises

17. Suppose that a program contains the following declarations and initializations:

```
TYPE
   OneByteSet = SET OF [ 0..255 ];

VAR
   S0, S1, S2, S3, S4 : OneByteSet;

BEGIN
   S0 := [ ];
   S1 := [ 0 ];
   S2 := [ 2, 4, 8, 16, 32, 64, 128 ];
   S3 := [ 1, 3, 7, 15, 63, 127, 255 ];
   S4 := S2 + S3;
```

Then write Pascal code to display the values of the following mathematical expressions:

a. $S_0 \subseteq S_2$

b. $5 \in S_3$

c. $(S_2 \cap S_4) - \{32, 64, 128\}$

d. $(S_2 \cap S_3) \cup \{32, 64, 128\}$

e. $S_1 \subset S_2$

18. Suppose that a program contains the following declarations and initializations:

```
TYPE
   NumeralSet = SET OF [ '0'..'9' ];

VAR
   S0, S1, S2, S3, S4 : NumeralSet;

BEGIN
   S0 := [ ];
   S1 := [ '0', '3', '6', '9' ];
```

```
S2 := [ '1' ];
S3 := [ '1', '3', '7' ];
S4 := S2 + S3;
```

Then what are the values of the following Pascal expressions?

a. `( S1 * S2 ) <= S0`

b. `S2 <= ( S3 + S4 )`

c. `( S3 * S2 ) >= [ '1' ]`

d. `( (S1 + S3) * S2 ) = [ ]`

e. `'3' IN ( S1 * S3 )`

19. What is printed by the following procedure if it is called by `Numbers( 1, 3, 5 )` ?

```
PROCEDURE Numbers( Item1, Item2, Item3 : Integer );

TYPE
   DigitRange = 0..9;
   DigitSet   = SET OF DigitRange;

VAR
   S   : DigitSet;
   Num : DigitRange;

BEGIN

   S := [ Item1+1, Item2-1, Item3 ];

   Write( '[' );
      FOR Num := 0 TO 9 DO
         IF Num IN S THEN
            Write( Num:2 );
   WriteLn( ' ]' )

END; { Numbers }
```

20. (More difficult) Improve the procedure of Exercise 19 so that commas are printed appropriately, making the output look nicer. This is tricky because there should be no comma after the last member of the set.

21. If we have the declarations

```
TYPE
   AdditivePrimaries = ( Red, Green, Blue );
   ColorSet = SET OF AdditivePrimaries;
```

then what is printed by the call `Mix( Red, Green, Blue )` ?

```
PROCEDURE Mix( Color1, Color2, Color3 : AdditivePrimaries );
VAR
   S1, S2, S3 : ColorSet;

BEGIN

   S1 := [ Color1 ];
   S2 := [ Color2 ];
   S3 := [ Color1, Color3 ];

   S1 := S1 + S2;
   S3 := S1 * S2;
   S2 := S3 - S1;
   WriteLn( 'Color    in S1   in S2   in S3' );
   WriteLn( '------------------------------' );
```

```
      WriteLn( 'Red     ', (Red IN S1):5,
               (Red IN S2):8, (Red IN S3):8 );
      WriteLn( 'Green   ', (Green IN S1):5,
               (Green IN S2):8, (Green IN S3):8 );
      WriteLn( 'Blue    ', (Blue IN S1):5,
               (Blue IN S2):8, (Blue IN S3):8 )
   END; { Mix }
```

22. Explain how to determine whether two Pascal sets are identical without using the built-in = or <> operators.
23. Explain how to determine whether one Pascal set is a *proper* subset of another. (There is no built-in operator for this.)
24. Show how to determine whether one Pascal set is a subset of another without using the built-in <= and >= operators.

18.3 SIMPLE USES FOR SETS

One of the common uses of sets is in processing text. For example, in Section 8.7, we wrote the `Boolean` functions `IsLowerCase`, `IsUpperCase`, `IsDigit`, `IsLetter`, and `IsAlphanumeric` to report on the properties of characters. At that time, we wrote code that depended on the ASCII character set. Now we can write these functions with more generality, using sets.

Using set variables

Suppose that the `SetOfMembers` type is declared as follows:

```
TYPE
   Member        = Char;
   SetOfMember   = SET OF Member;
```

Also suppose that we have three set variables:

```
VAR
   LowerCaseSet, UpperCaseSet, DigitsSet : SetOfMember;
```

All three of these variables are now sets of `Char`. (This assumes that your Pascal system will allow sets this large.) We initialize the set variables:

```
BEGIN
   { -- Initialize the set variables }
   LowerCaseSet := [ 'a'..'z' ];
   UpperCaseSet := [ 'A'..'Z' ];
   DigitsSet    := [ '0'..'9' ];
```

This is the simple way to initialize the variables, but it doesn't allow for the fact that some character codes, like EBCDIC, have gaps among the letters. To avoid this, we can resort to the foolproof method, although it is tedious:

```
   LowerCaseSet := [ 'a', 'b', 'c', 'd', 'e', 'f', 'g', 'h', 'i',
                     'j', 'k', 'l', 'm', 'n', 'o', 'p', 'q', 'r',
                     's', 't', 'u', 'v', 'w', 'x', 'y', 'z' ];
```

Then we can write the functions. In place of `IsLowerCase`, `IsUpperCase`, and `IsDigit`, we can just write the in-line code

```
Ch IN LowerCaseSet
Ch IN UpperCaseSet
Ch IN DigitsSet
```

The `IsLetter` and `IsAlphanumeric` functions are still needed, but they are simple to write. *Because the three sets are not conceptual arguments of the functions, we make the sets global.* Note that although global variables are seldom good style and are always dangerous, this application is an example of the kind of situation in which they are desirable.

```
FUNCTION IsLetter( Ch : Char ) : Boolean;
{ GLOBALS USED: LowerCaseSet, UpperCaseSet. }
BEGIN

   IsLetter := ( Ch IN LowerCaseSet ) OR ( Ch IN UpperCaseSet )

END; { IsLetter }


FUNCTION IsAlphanumeric( Ch : Char ) : Boolean;
{ GLOBAL USED: DigitsSet. }
BEGIN

   IsAlphanumeric := IsLetter( Ch ) OR ( Ch IN DigitsSet )

END; { IsAlphanumeric }
```

If the set variables were parameters of these functions, the function calls would look unnatural, and the sets would appear to have variable contents. For example, `IsLetter` might be called in an `IF` structure:

```
IF IsLetter( Ch, LowerCaseSet, UpperCaseSet ) THEN
   ..
```

Such syntax would obscure the fact that `IsLetter` merely reports whether `Ch` contains a letter. Therefore, it seems better to use global sets, even with the disadvantages and dangers of global variables.

Using set constants

In the example above, it is actually simpler to use set constants instead of variables. If we make the global declarations

```
CONST
   LowerCaseSet := [ 'a'..'z' ];
   UpperCaseSet := [ 'A'..'Z' ];
   DigitsSet    := [ '0'..'9' ];
```

we can write the `IsLetter` and `IsAlphanumeric` just as before, but with less syntax and no chance that a program will accidentally change the contents of `LowerCaseSet`, `UpperCaseSet`, or `DigitsSet`. This is better style.

Case study: Checking an identifier

As a simple application of these functions, consider checking a word to see if it is a legal Pascal identifier. We check the first character to see if it is a letter, then check the rest to see if they are either letters or digits:

```
PROGRAM SimpleSetExample( Input, Output );
{
  String80, ReadString, and LengthOfString are declared
  in the String80 ADT of Section 15.5.

  Include the ADT, however you do this with your Pascal
  system. Two methods are explained in Appendix H.
}
CONST
   LowerCaseSet = [ 'a'..'z' ];
   UpperCaseSet = [ 'A'..'Z' ];
   DigitsSet    = [ '0'..'9' ];

VAR
   Ident : String80;


FUNCTION IsLetter( Ch: Char ): Boolean;
BEGIN

   IsLetter := ( Ch IN LowerCaseSet ) OR ( Ch IN UpperCaseSet )

END; { IsLetter }


FUNCTION IsAlphanumeric( Ch: Char ): Boolean;
BEGIN

   IsAlphanumeric := IsLetter( Ch ) OR ( Ch in DigitsSet )

END; { IsAlphanumeric }


PROCEDURE CheckIdentifier( Identifier : String80 );
TYPE
   NonNegInt = 0..MaxInt;

VAR
   StrLength, Index : NonNegInt;
   NoError          : Boolean;

BEGIN

   StrLength := LengthOfStr( Identifier );
   {
     Check for legal identifier: first char must be a letter;
     the rest must be letters or digits.
   }
   Index := 1;
   NoError :=  IsLetter( Identifier.Chars[ Index ] );
```

```
   WHILE ( Index < StrLength ) AND NoError DO
   {
     LOOP INVARIANT:
     1 <= Index <= StrLength
     and
     NoError = (identifier legal in char positions 1, 2,..., Index).
   }
   BEGIN
      Index := Index + 1;
      NoError := IsAlphanumeric( Identifier.Chars[ Index ] )
   END;
   { ASSERTION: NoError = ( identifier is legal ) }

   IF NoError THEN
      WriteLn( 'Legal identifier' )

   ELSE
      WriteLn( 'ILLEGAL IDENTIFIER' )

END;  { CheckIdentifier }


BEGIN { main program }

   Write( 'Identifier? ' );
   ReadString( Ident );
   WriteLn;

   CheckIdentifier( Ident )

END.
```

Reading and writing sets

Pascal lacks procedures for reading and writing sets, although it allows us to read or write individual set members. Therefore, we can easily design our own set I/O procedures.

Reading a set from a text file

Suppose that we are given a text file pointer corresponding to an already-`Reset` file. Suppose that this file contains a list of set members, delimited as necessary for the set's member type. Then to fill a given set `S` with these members, overwriting any previous set members, we must carry out two steps:

1. Make `S` empty.

2. Repeat until the file is empty:

   a. Read a member.

   b. Add this member to `S` by taking the union.

To allow for the lines in the text file, the program must watch for end-of-line signals. Other than this, the code follows immediately from the outline:

```
PROCEDURE ReadSet( VAR FilePointer : Text;
                   VAR S           : SetType );
{
  PRECONDITIONS:
  FilePointer is associated with a text file that has been Reset.

  POSTCONDITIONS:
  Set members have been read from the FilePointer file into S,
  overwriting any previous members. Reading is terminated by <EOF>.
}
VAR
   M : Member;

BEGIN

   { -- Set is initially empty }
   S := [ ];

   { -- Copy file into set }
   WHILE NOT EOF( FilePointer ) DO
   BEGIN

      WHILE NOT EOLn( FilePointer ) DO
      BEGIN
         Read( FilePointer, M );
         S := S + [ M ];
      END;

      ReadLn( FilePointer )

   END

END; { ReadSet }
```

This implementation has a limitation: It cannot read members of sets of enumerated types, since the `Read` procedure cannot handle enumerated values. Project 8 asks you to improve the implementation to allow for this possibility.

Writing a set to a text file

To write a set's members to a file, the program needs to sweep through all possible members, writing each member that is present to the file. This requires a loop that sweeps out all possible set members, from the lowest allowed ordinal value to the highest allowed ordinal value. Therefore, let us add declarations for `Low` and `High` constants. When dealing with sets of uppercase letters, the declarations would be

```
CONST
   Low  = 'A'; { Set member with lowest allowed ordinal value  }
   High = 'Z'; { Set member with highest allowed ordinal value }
```

Now we can copy the set members to a file as shown in the procedure below:

```
PROCEDURE WriteLnSet( VAR FilePointer : Text;
                          S           : SetType );
{
  PRECONDITIONS:
  FilePointer corresponds to a file already opened
  with Rewrite; the set S is initialized.

  POSTCONDITIONS:
  All members of set S have been written to the text
  file associated with FilePointer.
}
VAR
   M : Member;

BEGIN

   FOR M := Low TO High DO

      IF M IN S THEN
         Write( FilePointer, M );

   WriteLn( FilePointer )

END; { WriteLnSet }
```

Of course, this assumes that `Member` is a type that can be sent to the `Write` procedure.

18.4 A SET ADT

Many programming languages, like BASIC, Fortran, and C, have no built-in provision for set types. It is instructive to see how sets can be implemented in such languages. Learning to build our own set types also helps to appreciate what Pascal does for us. This section briefly sketches a simple ADT for sets, using the techniques developed in Chapter 16.

The *set abstract data type* consists of an abstract definition of the type itself, together with the operations to be allowed on that type. The specification is shown in the following box.

Set ADT Specification

Data structure:
A set is a collection of members of a declared type.

Operations:

- Determine the cardinality of a set.
- Determine if a given value belongs to a set.
- Determine whether a set is empty.
- Determine whether a set is the universal set; that is, whether it contains all possible members.

- Determine whether two sets are equal.
- Determine whether one set is a subset of another.
- Determine whether one set is a *proper* subset of another.
- Add a given member to a set.
- Delete a given member from a set.
- Find the complement of a given set, relative to the universal set.
- Make a set empty.
- Make a set the universal set, overwriting any previous members.
- Read a set's members from a file, replacing any previous members.
- Write a set to a file.

An interface for a set abstract data type

First we determine from the specifications how to declare types and appropriate procedures and functions, so that the ADT will be versatile and easy to use. We do not reveal to users how a `SetType` is actually implemented: the `SetType` should be *opaque* to users, with its declaration appearing only in the implementation. Here are the declarations we will make available to users, in the interface file:

```
CONST
   Low  = 'A';  { or whatever }
   High = 'z';  { or whatever }

TYPE
   NonNegInt = 0..MaxInt;
   Member    = Low..High;

  { SetType is an opaque type }

{-----------------------------------------------------}
{ Returns the cardinality of S.                       }
{-----------------------------------------------------}
FUNCTION Cardinality( S : SetType ) : NonNegInt;
{
  PRECONDITIONS:
  S has been initialized.

  POSTCONDITIONS:
  Returns the number of members of S.
}
```

```
{-------------------------------------------------------}
{  Indicates whether M is a member of S.                }
{-------------------------------------------------------}
FUNCTION BelongsToSet( M : Member;
                       S : SetType ) : Boolean;
{
  PRECONDITIONS:
  M and S have been initialized.

  POSTCONDITIONS:
  Returns True if M is in S; otherwise, returns False.
}

{-------------------------------------------------------}
{ Indicates whether S is empty.                         }
{-------------------------------------------------------}
FUNCTION SetIsEmpty(S : SetType ) : Boolean;
{
  PRECONDITIONS:
  S has been initialized.

  POSTCONDITIONS:
  Returns True if S is the empty set;
  otherwise, returns False.
}

{-------------------------------------------------------}
{ Indicates whether S is full: whether it contains      }
{ all possible members.                                 }
{-------------------------------------------------------}
FUNCTION SetIsFull( S : SetType ) : Boolean;
{
  PRECONDITIONS:
  S has been initialized.

  POSTCONDITIONS:
  Returns True if S contains all possible members;
  otherwise, returns False.
}

{-------------------------------------------------------}
{ Indicates whether S1 and S2 are identical sets.       }
{-------------------------------------------------------}
FUNCTION SetsAreEqual( S1, S2 : SetType ) : Boolean;
{
  PRECONDITIONS:
  S1 and S2 have been initialized.

  POSTCONDITIONS:
  Returns True if S1 and S2 contain the same members;
  otherwise, returns False.
}
```

```
{-----------------------------------------------------}
{ Indicates whether S1 is a subset of S2.             }
{-----------------------------------------------------}
FUNCTION IsSubset( S1, S2 : SetType ) : Boolean;
{
  PRECONDITIONS:
  S1 and S2 have been initialized.

  POSTCONDITIONS:
  Returns True if all members of S1 are members of S2;
  otherwise, returns False.
}

{-----------------------------------------------------}
{ Indicates whether S1 is a proper subset of S2.      }
{-----------------------------------------------------}
FUNCTION IsProperSubset( S1, S2 : SetType ) : Boolean;
{
  PRECONDITIONS:
  S1 and S2 have been initialized.

  POSTCONDITIONS:
  Returns True if all members of S1 are members of S2,
  but the sets are not identical; otherwise, returns False.
}

{-----------------------------------------------------}
{ Adds member M to set S.                             }
{-----------------------------------------------------}
PROCEDURE AddMemberToSet( M     : Member;
                          VAR S : SetType );
{
  PRECONDITIONS:
  M and S have been initialized.

  POSTCONDITIONS:
  S contains M.
}

{-----------------------------------------------------}
{ Deletes member M from set S.                        }
{-----------------------------------------------------}
PROCEDURE DeleteMemberFromSet( M     : Member;
                               VAR S : SetType );
{
  PRECONDITIONS:
  M and S have been initialized.

  POSTCONDITIONS:
  S does not contain M.
}
```

```
{-----------------------------------------------------}
{ Find the complement of set S.                       }
{-----------------------------------------------------}
PROCEDURE Complement( S         : SetType;
                      VAR Compl : SetType );
{
  PRECONDITIONS:
  S has been initialized.

  POSTCONDITIONS:
  Compl contains all possible set members
  not contained in S.
}

{-----------------------------------------------------}
{ Makes S empty.                                      }
{-----------------------------------------------------}
PROCEDURE MakeEmptySet( VAR S : SetType );
{
  POSTCONDITIONS:
  S contains no members.
}

{-----------------------------------------------------}
{ Makes S contain all possible members.               }
{-----------------------------------------------------}
PROCEDURE MakeUniversalSet( VAR S : SetType );
{
  POSTCONDITIONS:
  S contains every possible member.
}
```

This interface is saved as a text file, to be provided to the user as documentation. These declarations can be imported by a program in various ways that depend on the Pascal system. See Appendix H for details.

An implementation for the set ADT

With the declarations in front of us, we see in detail how the ADT specifications translate into Pascal. Only the declaration of `SetType` is missing. We want an implementation of the data structure that will work in a variety of computer languages. A simple choice is to build the structure as an array of booleans:

```
TYPE
   SetType = PACKED ARRAY[ Low..High ] OF Boolean;
```

With this implementation, a character set `S`, containing the members `'a'`, `'A'`, and `'G'`, would be represented by setting

```
   S[ 'a' ] := True;
   S[ 'A' ] := True;
   S[ 'G' ] := True;
```

and setting all other elements `False`. In other words, each element of the array acts as a yes/no signal, indicating whether the set contains the member appearing in the subscript.

Now we can write code to implement the procedures and functions, one by one. Some of them are trivial; for example, we can write

```
PROCEDURE AddMemberToSet( M     : Member;
                          VAR S : SetType );
BEGIN

   S[ M ] := True

END; { AddMemberToSet }


FUNCTION SetIsEmpty( S : SetType ) : Boolean;
BEGIN

    SetIsEmpty := ( Cardinality( S ) = 0 )

END; { SetIsEmpty }
```

Then there are several subprograms that require sweeping through all possible members in `SetType`. The `Cardinality` function is typical:

```
FUNCTION Cardinality( S : SetType ) : NonNegInt;
VAR
   M     : Member;
   Count : NonNegInt;

BEGIN

   Count := 0;
   FOR M := Low TO High DO
      IF S[ M ] THEN
         Count := Count + 1;

   Cardinality := Count

END; { Cardinality }
```

Finally, we come to the implementations of the text file I/O procedures. We have to allow for the fact that some sets—sets of enumerated values, for example—cannot receive or transmit their members by means of the standard I/O procedures. Therefore, we write our own I/O procedures for set members as well as for whole sets. We use a *local procedure* to write a set member within the procedure that writes a set:

```
PROCEDURE WriteLnSet( VAR FilePointer : Text;
                      S               : SetType );
VAR
   M : Member;


   PROCEDURE WriteMember( VAR FilePtr : Text;
                          M           : Member );
   { If Member type cannot be written by standard    }
   { Write procedure, this will have to be changed. }
   BEGIN

      Write( FilePtr, M )

   END; { WriteMember }


BEGIN { WriteLnSet }

   FOR M := Low TO High DO
      IF S[ M ] THEN
         WriteMember( FilePointer, M );

   WriteLn( FilePointer )

END; { WriteLnSet }
```

The remainder of the implementations are—you guessed it—left as exercises.

Advantages of the ADT

The ADT shown above has gained us several advantages:

- The abstract data type can provide as many set operations as we desire, all prebuilt and ready for use. This makes the set type fully functional, rather than a partial implementation, as in Standard Pascal. In essence, we have *extended the language.*
- The implementation details of the more complex operations, such as reading or writing a set, are hidden within the corresponding ADT procedures. Users of the ADT needn't worry about how these operations are accomplished; instead, they can concentrate on the applications in which they are interested. Hiding the details in this way is called *information hiding*, and is a fundamental principle of good software engineering.
- To the extent that we can not only hide the inner workings of set operations but also prevent users from applying operations other than the ones we provide in the ADT, we can protect sets from misuse. This is called *making the type opaque.*
- Writing the set implementation in terms of arrays is a good example of building a more abstract data structure from a less abstract one.
- Building a set ADT in this way shows how sets can be added to languages that would otherwise lack them.

Disadvantages of the array implementation

The array implementation of sets requires a `Boolean` variable, typically one byte, for each possible set member. Large sets will therefore occupy considerable memory. It is not hard to see that a single *bit* would suffice for each set member. With such an implementation, a set would be stored as a sequence of bits, called a **bit vector**. This is, in fact, how Pascal and several other programming languages implement sets. For further discussion of how this works, see the references by McCracken and Pratt listed at the end of the chapter.

Exercises

25. If the `ReadSet` procedure is implemented as shown below, it does not automatically stop when the set is full. Instead, it reads one more set member or one more end-of-line signal. Why?

```
FullSet := SetIsFull( S );
WHILE ( NOT EOF( FilePointer ) )
      AND ( NOT FullSet ) DO
BEGIN
   WHILE ( NOT EOLn( FilePointer ) )
         AND ( NOT FullSet ) DO
   BEGIN
      Read( FilePointer, M );
      IF NOT SetIsFull( S ) THEN
         S := S + [ M ]
      ELSE
         FullSet := True
   END;
   IF EOLn( FilePointer ) THEN
      ReadLn( FilePointer )
END;
```

26. Write an implementation for the `BelongsToSet` function.

27. Write an implementation for the `SetsAreEqual` function.

28. Write an implementation for the `IsSubset` function.

29. Write an implementation for the `IsProperSubset` function.

30. Write an implementation for the `Complement` procedure.

31. Jackson P. Slipshod suggests implementing the `SetIsFull` function as follows. (See next page.) What is wrong with his suggestion? Show how to fix the error.

```
FUNCTION SetIsFull( S : SetType ) : Boolean;
{
   Returns True if S contains all possible members;
   otherwise returns False.
}
VAR
   M    : Member;
   Full : Boolean;

    BEGIN

       Full := True;
       M    := Low;
       WHILE ( M <= High ) AND Full DO
       BEGIN

          Full := S[ M ];
          M := Succ( M )

       END;

       SetIsFull := Full

    END; { SetIsFull }
```

18.5 CASE STUDY: SCANNING INTEGER EXPRESSIONS

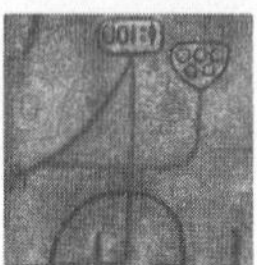

As a more advanced example of the use of sets, we write a part of a compiler called a **parser** or **lexical scanner**. A scanner reads characters from a text file, looking for recognizable structures. For simplicity, we will consider a scanner that determines the values of expressions involving integer constants.

Scanning integer constants

First we design a scanner that can recognize a literal integer constant alone; that is, it can read a string representing an integer constant and compute from the string the integer value. The scanner must be able to recognize constants like these:

```
1
-47
+56338791
ΔΔΔ-152ΔΔ
```

(The symbol Δ is used to represent a space.)

When told to read such a constant, the scanning process goes through the following steps, in the order listed:

1a. The scanner discards leading whitespace, if any.

1b. The next character must be a sign or a digit; anything else is an error.

2a. The scanner interprets the sign, if any, as indicating a factor of +1 or −1 in the resulting integer value. If there is no sign, the sign factor is implicitly +1.

2b. If there is a sign, the next character must be a digit; anything else is an error.

3a. The scanner reads the digit characters of the integer, translating them into an integer value. For example, the digit characters `'1'`, `'5'`, `'2'`, in that order, must be translated to the integer value

$1 \times 100 + 5 \times 10 + 2 \times 1 = 152$

(There is no limit to the number of digits, but too many will cause overflow.)

3b. After the first digit, the constant is terminated by any character other than a digit. Thus algebraic expressions like `-X` are not recognized; just literal integer constants.

4. The final integer value is the product of the sign factor from step **2a** and the numeric magnitude from step **3a**.

Suppose that the scanner encounters the following string of characters, where the symbol Δ is used to indicate spaces and color highlighting is used to indicate the present position of the scanner as it reads the characters:

`ΔΔΔ-1234ΔΔ`

The scanner must take the following actions. Sets play an important part in the process:

1. The first character in the string is a member of *the set of whitespace characters*. Leading whitespace of any kind—spaces, tabs, end-of-line signals—should be discarded. This process stops when the program reads a nonwhitespace character.
2. The first nonwhitespace character is found to be a member of *the set of sign characters*:

   `-1234ΔΔ`

   This sign is stored as a multiplicative factor of −1, called the *sign factor*. The next character is read.
3. The next character is found to be a member of *the set of digits*, indicating that the numeric magnitude of the integer is beginning:

   `1234ΔΔ`
4. The digit characters are read one by one, and the numeric magnitude is accumulated:

   $1 \times 1000 + 2 \times 100 + 3 \times 10 + 4 = 1234$

   The next character is a space, terminating the scanning of the integer:

   `ΔΔ`
5. The net integer value is the product of the sign factor, −1, and the magnitude of the number, 1234. The result is −1234. The termination character—the space after the digits—remains as the last character read.

As you can see, the program must maintain at all times a character variable containing the next character to be processed. The first action of the program is to read the first character from the input string, to see whether this character is whitespace, a sign, or a digit. Then, after processing each character, the program reads the next character into the character variable, "priming the pump" for the next step. A state transition diagram of the general process is shown in Figure 18.5.1.

Figure 18.5.1 *State transitions in scanning a literal integer constant. A character variable Ch is used to store the next character to be processed.*

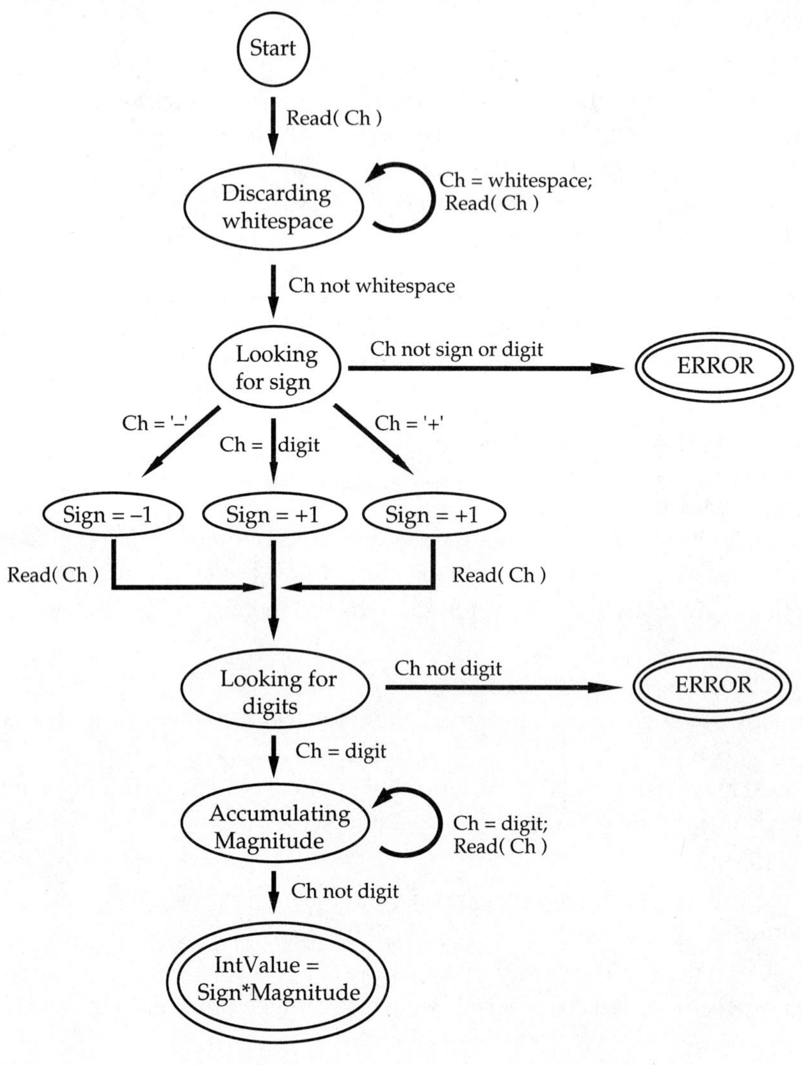

Here is Pascal code for the whole process:

```
PROGRAM Scanner1( InFile, Output );

CONST
   TabCode      = 9;                    { ASCII code }
   LineFeedCode = 10;                   { ASCII code }
   ReturnCode   = 13;                   { ASCII code }

CONST
   Signs  = [ '-', '+' ];
   Digits = [ '0'..'9' ];
```

```
   Whitespace = [ Chr( TabCode ), Chr( LineFeedCode ),
                  Chr( ReturnCode ), ' ' ];  { See Project 4 }

TYPE
   NonNegInt = 0..MaxInt;

VAR
   InFile   : Text;
   IntValue : Integer;
   Ch       : Char;
   NoError  : Boolean;


{----------------------------------------------------}
{ Reads characters from input string until a         }
{ nonwhitespace character is encountered.            }
{----------------------------------------------------}
PROCEDURE DiscardWhiteSpace( VAR InFile : Text;
                             VAR Ch     : Char );
{
  PRECONDITION:
  Ch is initialized.

  POSTCONDITION:
  Ch is not a whitespace character.
}
BEGIN

   WHILE ( NOT EOF( InFile ) ) AND ( Ch IN WhiteSpace ) DO
      Read( InFile, Ch )

END; { DiscardWhiteSpace }

{---------------------------------------------------------------}
{ Determines from current char whether the sign of the number is }
{ + or -, representing the sign by a multiplicative sign factor.  }
{ If current char is neither sign nor digit, an error is reported.}
{---------------------------------------------------------------}
PROCEDURE GetSign( VAR InFile     : Text;
                   VAR SignFactor : Integer;
                   VAR Ch         : Char;
                   VAR NoError    : Boolean );
{
  PRECONDITIONS:
  Ch is initialized.

  POSTCONDITIONS:
  SignFactor is either +1 or -1; either (Ch is a digit and
  NoError = True) or (Ch is not a digit and NoError = False).
}
```

```
BEGIN

   IF Ch IN Signs THEN
   BEGIN

      IF Ch = '-' THEN
         SignFactor := -1
      ELSE
         SignFactor := +1;

      IF NOT EOF(InFile) THEN
      BEGIN

         Read(InFile, Ch);

         IF Ch IN Digits THEN
            NoError := True
         ELSE
            NoError := False

      END

      ELSE { EOF }
         NoError := False

   END

   ELSE { NOT ( Ch IN Signs ) }
   BEGIN

      SignFactor := +1;

      IF Ch IN Digits THEN
         NoError := True
      ELSE
         NoError := False

   END

 END; { GetSign }


{-------------------------------------------------------------------}
{ Computes absolute value corresponding to the digits of the        }
{ number being read. The reading is terminated by the first         }
{ nondigit character, which is returned in Ch.                      }
{-------------------------------------------------------------------}
PROCEDURE GetMagnitude( VAR InFile : Text;
                        VAR Mag    : NonNegInt;
                        VAR Ch     : Char );
{
  PRECONDITION:
  Ch is a digit.
```

```
  POSTCONDITION:
  Mag contains the accumulated integer value of the digits,
  which are terminated by any nondigit character. Ch contains
  the first nondigit character unless EOF was encountered.
}
BEGIN

   Mag := 0;
   WHILE ( NOT EOF( InFile ) ) AND ( Ch IN Digits ) DO
   BEGIN

      Mag := 10 * Mag + Ord( Ch ) - Ord( '0' );
      Read( InFile, Ch )

   END

 END; { GetMagnitude }


{-----------------------------------------------------------------}
{ Returns                                                         }
{  1. Integer value corresponding to the string.                  }
{  2. Next character to be processed.                             }
{  3. Signal indicating whether an error occurred.                }
{-----------------------------------------------------------------}
 PROCEDURE GetIntConst( VAR InFile   : Text;
                        VAR IntValue : Integer;
                        VAR Ch       : Char;
                        VAR NoError  : Boolean );
{
  POSTCONDITION:
  IntValue contains the integer value corresponding to the
  longest string of characters consisting of an optional sign
  followed by integer digits. Translation is terminated by any
  nondigit character occurring after at least one digit.
  Ch contains the character that terminated the digit string.
  NoError indicates whether an error was encountered while
  reading the integer string; if so, IntValue = 0.
}
VAR
   SignFactor : Integer;
   Magnitude  : NonNegInt;

BEGIN

   IF NOT EOF(InFile) THEN
   BEGIN

      Read( InFile, Ch );
      DiscardWhitespace( InFile, Ch );
      { ASSERTION: Ch is not a whitespace character. }

      GetSign( InFile, SignFactor, Ch, NoError );
```

```
      IF NoError THEN
      BEGIN
         { ASSERTION: Ch is a digit character. }
         GetMagnitude( InFile, Magnitude, Ch );
         IntValue := SignFactor * Magnitude
      END

      ELSE
      BEGIN
         WriteLn( '++ ERROR IN INT CONSTANT ++' );
         IntValue := 0
      END

   END

END; { GetIntConst }


BEGIN { main program }

   { -- Open the input file }
   Reset( InFile );

   { -- Compute integer value of input string }
   GetIntConst( Input, IntValue, Ch, NoError );

   IF NoError THEN
      WriteLn( 'Value is ', IntValue )
   ELSE
      WriteLn( 'MAIN PROGRAM RECEIVES ERROR FROM GetIntConst.' )

END.
```

Allowing for binary operators

Constant expressions can also involve binary operators of equal precedence. In such a case, the structure of the expression takes the form shown in Figure 18.5.2.

Allowing for whitespace between constants and operators, the process of reading and computing the value of a constant integer expression is fairly simple, now that we have a procedure for scanning a constant:

1. Call `GetIntConst` to compute the first integer constant, discarding any leading whitespace.
2. While the first nonwhitespace character is a member of the set of allowed operators, repeatedly execute the following:
   a. Store the operator and get the next character.
   b. Call `GetIntConst` to compute the first integer constant, discarding any leading whitespace.
   c. Accumulate the value of the integer expression up to this point.

If we assume for simplicity that the only operators are + and –, the following code can be used for scanning the expressions. (Project 5 asks you to use the `*` and `DIV` operators as well.)

An integer expression containing only constants and operators of equal precedence. Whitespace is allowed between the items shown.

Figure 18.5.2

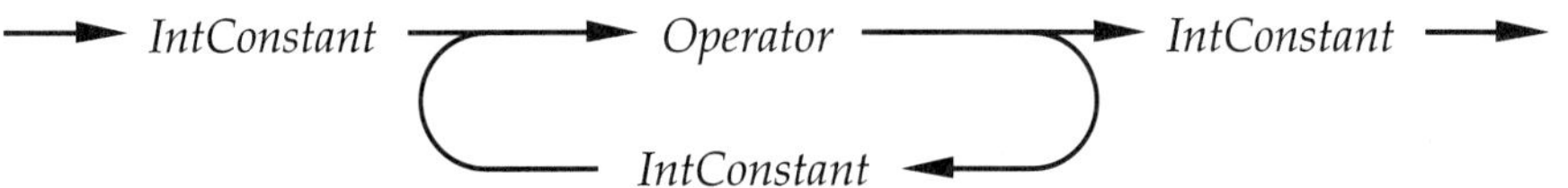


```
CONST
   Operators = [ '+', '-' ];
.
.
{---------------------------------------------------}
{ Returns                                           }
{  1. Integer value of expression.                  }
{  2. Next character to be processed.               }
{  3. Signal indicating whether an error occurred.  }
{                                                   }
{ THIS VERSION ALLOWS ONLY + AND - OPERATIONS,      }
{ which have equal precedence.                      }
{---------------------------------------------------}
PROCEDURE GetExpression( VAR InFile   : Text;
                         VAR IntValue : Integer;
                         VAR Ch       : Char;
                         VAR NoError  : Boolean );
{
  POSTCONDITIONS:
  IntValue contains the value of the expression read, up to the
  first nondigit following the first digit. Ch contains the
  next unprocessed character: that is, the character that caused
  termination of reading. A signal is returned indicating whether
  an error occurred.
}
VAR
   NewIntValue : Integer;
   OperatorCh  : Char;

BEGIN

   GetIntConst(InFile, IntValue, Ch, NoError);
   {
     ASSERTIONS:
     IntValue contains value of first constant;
     Ch contains next unprocessed character;
     NoError indicates whether error occurred .
   }

   DiscardWhitespace(InFile, Ch);
```

```
   WHILE (Ch IN Operators) AND NoError DO
   BEGIN

      OperatorCh := Ch;

      IF NOT EOF(InFile) THEN
      BEGIN

         {-- Constant must follow operator }
         GetIntConst(InFile, NewIntValue, Ch, NoError);

         IF NoError THEN
         BEGIN

            CASE OperatorCh OF

               '+':
                    IntValue := IntValue + NewIntValue;

               '-':
                    IntValue := IntValue - NewIntValue;

            END; { CASE }

            DiscardWhitespace(InFile, Ch)

         END

         ELSE
            WriteLn('ERROR IN OPERAND')

      END { IF NOT EOF( InFile ) THEN }

      ELSE { EOF after operator }
      BEGIN

         WriteLn('MISSING OPERAND');
         NoError := False

      END { ELSE }

   END { WHILE }

END; { GetExpression }
```

LOOKING BACK

A *set* is an unordered collection of *members* of one type. A set S is specified by listing its members either implicitly or explicitly. A set is considered within a context called the *universal set*, U. The universal set is the set of all possible members of the type under discussion.

There are several important operations involving mathematical sets S, S_1, and S_2 within a universal set U:

- The *complement* of S is $U - S$, the set of all members of U that are not members of S.
- The *union* $S_1 \cup S_2$ is the set containing all members of S_1 and all members of S_2.
- The *intersection* $S_1 \cap S_2$ is the set of all members of S_1 that are also members of S_2.
- The *difference* $S_1 - S_2$ is the set of all members of S_1 that are *not* also members of S_2.

Pascal provides types of the form `SET OF` *BaseType*, where *BaseType* can be any ordinal type. The set can be `PACKED` if desired. Pascal has more built-in operations for sets than for other composite types:

- Set membership is tested in an expression of the form `M IN S`.
- A set constant value can be assigned to a set variable, or the value of one set variable can be assigned to another of a compatible type.
- A set union is constructed with the + operator.
- A set intersection is constructed with the * operator.
- A set difference is constructed with the - operator.
- Compatible sets can be compared for equality or inequality with the relational operators = and <>.
- Subset relations are tested with the <= and >= operators.

There is, however, no built-in test for a proper subset, and there are no built-in I/O procedures for sets.

We used Pascal's set types for simple applications involving characters and we developed I/O procedures for sets. In order to compensate for Pascal's lack of set operations and to show how set types can be added to languages lacking them, we worked out the beginnings of a set ADT. Finally, we showed a more complicated application, in which sets were used in parsing and evaluating integer expressions.

TERMS EMPHASIZED IN THIS CHAPTER

Adding to a set 607, 613
ADT, advantages of 628
Base type 610
Binary operator 636
Bit vector 629
Cardinality 604, 611
Character sets 605, 610
Complement of a set 604
Deleting from a set 608
Difference of sets 608, 612, 614
Domain of discourse 604
Empty set 604
Equality of sets 606, 612, 614
Extending the language 628
Global variable 618
Implementation 626–28
`IN` (operator) 611
Infinite set 604
Information hiding 628
Interface 623–26
Intersection of sets 607, 612–13
Lexical scanner 630
Local procedure 627–28
Member 604, 606, 611
Null set 604
Opaque type 628
Parser 630
Proper subset 606, 612, 614
Reading a set 620–21
Relational expressions 612, 614
Scanner 630
Scanning integer expressions 630–38
Set 604
Set ADT 622–28
Set assignment 611
Set constant 611–12, 618
Set declaration 611
Set I/O 612, 620, 627
Set membership 611
Set notation 604, 611
Set operations 611–12
Set variables 612–13, 617
State transition diagram 632
Subset 605
Union of sets 607, 611, 613
Universal set 604
Universe 604
Unordered 604
Venn diagram 604
Writing a set 621–22

PROJECTS

1. Write a program that reports the number of times that each digit character—`'0'`, `'1'`, `'2'`,..., `'9'`—appears in a given integer number. Use Pascal's built-in set types, as were used in the examples in the text.
2. Same as Project 1, but use the `SetADT` from Section 18.4, with `Low = '0'` and `High = '9'`.
3. Rewrite the program in Project 1 without using sets. Which method is easiest? Which method yields the clearest program?
4. Standard Pascal does not allow function calls in the definition of a `CONST`. Therefore, values like `Chr( TabCode )` are not allowed in the definition of the `Whitespace` set constant of Section 18.5 under Standard Pascal, even though many commercial Pascal systems allow it. Rewrite the `Scanner1` program to get around this shortcoming of Standard Pascal, using global set variables instead of constants.
5. Design and write a version of `GetExpression` that allows for * and / operators representing integer multiplication and division. These operators are equal in precedence, but both are higher in precedence than + and –.
6. Write a program that reports the frequency with which each letter of the alphabet appears in the text read from a given text file. `Frequency` is defined as the number of appearances of the letter, divided by the total number of letters in the file. Your program should make no distinction between the upper- and lowercase versions of a letter.

7. A *prime number* is defined to be an integer greater than 1, having no exact integer divisors but itself and 1. Thus 2, 3, 5, 7, 11, 13, . . . are primes. (Note that 2 is the only even prime.)

   Prime numbers up to a number `High` can be found by a method called the *Sieve of Eratosthenes*, which dates back to 300 BC. The method is this:

   Initialize set to contain all integers from 2 to `High`;

   REPEAT

   Print next number in set (it is a prime);

   Delete that number and all its multiples from the set

   UNTIL set is empty

   Write a Pascal program that implements this algorithm, using the `SetADT` of Section 18.4. Warning: In some Pascal systems, `High` may have to be as small as 127.
8. Improve the implementation of the `ReadSet` procedure shown in Section 18.3 so that it can handle enumerated types in a reasonably convenient way.
9. Determine the best way to build a set abstract data type (ADT) in your Pascal system. This may involve *include files* or *units*, both of which are discussed in Appendix H. Then build the set ADT shown in the text, so that you can use it in the following projects.
10. Write a small test program that empties a set, then adds each possible member in order, displaying the set resulting after each additional member, until the set is full. Use the procedures and functions provided by the text's set ADT wherever possible.
11. Write a small test program that builds a full set, then deletes each member in order, displaying the set resulting after each member deletion, until the set is empty. Use the procedures and functions provided by the text's set ADT wherever possible.
12. Add to the set ADT a procedure that constructs the complement of one set relative to another. For example, the complement of `[ 0, 2, 4 ]` relative to `[ 0, 1, 2, 3, 4, 5, 6 ]` is `[ 1, 3, 5, 6 ]`.
13. Add to the set ADT a boolean function that reports whether one set is a *proper subset* of another. Use the procedures and functions provided by the text's set ADT wherever possible in the construction of this new function.

REFERENCES

A good discussion of mathematical sets, with applications to computer science, can be found in Susanna S. Epp's *Discrete Mathematics with Applications* (Wadsworth Publishing, 1990). Daniel D. McCracken explains clearly how sets are implemented in programming languages in Chapter 3 of *A Second Course in Computer Science with Pascal* (John Wiley & Sons, 1987). Also see Terrence W. Pratt's *Programming Languages*, second edition (Prentice Hall, 1984).

The Artichoke Theory

In the beginning, we were the gigafreaks, nerds, and dweebs. We thought Pascal was a romance language, and we all had girlfriends named Ada. We read BYTE and loved those intricate line drawings, which we discussed at Homebrew [Computer Club] and the Boston Computer Society. We spawned the PC revolution, and we began it by meeting and selling products to each other. But we didn't get rich until we figured out how to sell the stuff to the "others."

The others were not computer champs. They were people who wore white socks only with running shoes. They were people with "real" jobs who used PCs not for the sheer joy of it, but for solving problems at work. They hated user's manuals thicker than unabridged dictionaries. They found the dot prompt user-hostile. Nevertheless, they were willing to climb that steep learning curve for the productivity benefits offered by products like dBase and VisiCalc. Times have changed.

Twenty years ago, I created a computer interface that was so easy to use that people understood how to operate my program within 15 seconds. The interface was so compelling that people were willing to pay 25 cents every few minutes for the excitement of using it. It was called Pong, and it started Atari.

My contribution to the PC revolution was in trying to make computers easy to use and compel millions of people to play. To some degree, that has happened. But it has not gone nearly as far as I had hoped.

The PC cannot be mastered in 15 seconds. It still isn't as easy to use as a toaster or TV. And when I think of all the aspects of new technology—networking, voice-mail, E-mail, fax, and video—I fear that things may be getting more difficult. . . .

The problem goes beyond simply providing an easy-to-use product. Different people—from the receptionist to the MIS manager to the CEO—have different needs to know the many aspects of integrated or unified systems. And they each have different desires to understand it. Yet we force them all to use the same interface.

Why can't we technologists assemble multidimensional interface systems? Why not let those who have the greatest fear and the least time to learn deal with just the outer level of a complex system? Let the technologists in an organization have access to the depth and complexity. I call this configuration the artichoke approach. . . .

How do we take this incredible complexity and present it so that everyone is empowered to use it? With games, we tell the machine our level of expertise. Why not with networked office systems?

The interface can best be described as a great electronic artichoke. At its heart is a complex mass of technology in which the systems integrator can feast. At the outer leaf is a system so easy to use that even a CEO will partake.

The CEO can learn the outer leaf of this electronic artichoke in 30 seconds. Once the user learns and digests the first leaf, the next leaf can be taken, digested and understood, and so on, until he or she readily understands all the capabilities at its heart.

The key to ease of use is to make the front end enjoyable, easy, nonintimidating, and intuitive. The value of the system should be apparent. Everyone should want to take the next bite.

— Nolan Bushnell in BYTE, September 1992, page 378.

PART FIVE

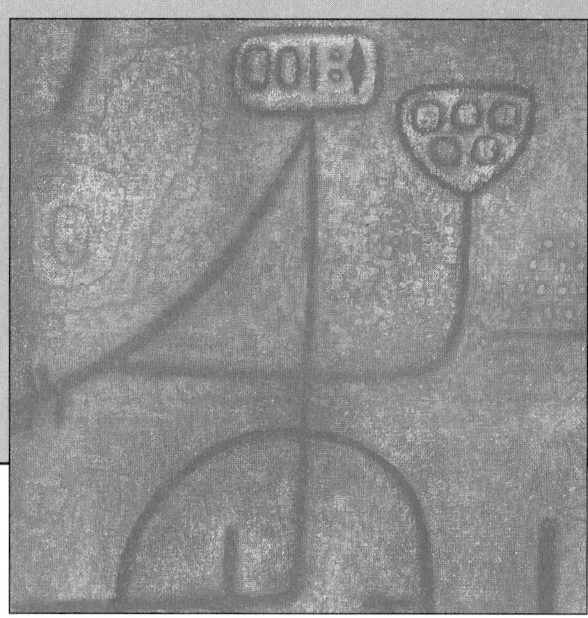

ADVANCED TOPICS

CHAPTER

19

Algorithms for Searching and Sorting

CHAPTER CONTENTS

INTRODUCTION

It has been said that more than a quarter of all actual computation time expended by CPUs is spent in sorting data or searching for data. It matters very much which algorithms we use for these processes because some are much slower than others, especially when dealing with large collections of data. In this chapter, we study some of the best-known algorithms for searching and sorting arrays. We will also analyze how their running times depend on the number of data values in the arrays and the order of the data before the sorting process begins.

Suppose we are **searching** for a given data value in an array of records. For example, we might be searching the `Biblio` array of Section 15.2:

```
CONST
   BiblioSize = 100;

TYPE
   String40 = PACKED ARRAY [1..40] OF Char;

   JournalArticle =
        RECORD
           Author  : String40;
           Title   : String40;
           Journal : String40;
           Volume  : Integer;
           Page    : Integer;
           Year    : Integer
        END;

   Bibliography = ARRAY [ 1..BiblioSize ] OF JournalArticle;

VAR
   Biblio : Bibliography;
```

On one occasion, we might be searching for a particular author; on another, we might be searching for a title. Whichever it is, the fields that we are searching through are called the **search keys** of the array. In the example above, if we are searching for a particular author, the keys in the array are the fields named `Biblio[1].Author,Biblio[2].Author,...,Biblio[100].Author`.

Keys: The data values being searched or sorted.

It is possible that the searched-for key is not in the array. It is also possible that keys are duplicated in the array. In the latter situation, the search algorithm may be designed to find *any one* occurrence of the key, or the *first* occurrence of the key, or *all* occurrences of the key, or the *last* occurrence. In this chapter, it doesn't matter which occurrence of the key is found, although some projects at the end of the chapter ask for searches to find a particular instance of a key.

Sorting is the process of arranging a list of keys in some desired order. If we are sorting a `Key` array containing the elements `Key[First], Key[First + 1],..., Key[Last]`, there are four common orders:

Increasing order:
`Key[ First ] < Key[ First + 1 ] <... < Key[ Last ]`
(applicable only if all keys are distinct)

Nondecreasing order:
`Key[ First ] ≤ Key[ First + 1 ] ≤...≤ Key[ Last ]`

Decreasing order:
`Key[ First ] > Key[ First + 1 ] >...> Key[ Last ]`
(applicable only if all keys are distinct)

Nonincreasing order:
`Key[ First ] ≥ Key[ First + 1 ] ≥... ≥ Key[ Last ]`

In this chapter, we will sort keys into nondecreasing order, although some exercises will ask for other orders.

As with searching, the most obvious sorting algorithm is seldom the best. Enormous effort has been made to discover efficient sorting algorithms, and some of the standard methods are truly ingenious. In addition to the desire for speed, we sometimes need a sorting algorithm that can sort arrays too large to fit in main memory. In such a case, we want an **external sorting algorithm** that sorts an external file, producing a new, sorted, external file without ever bringing the whole file into main memory at once. Such algorithms are relatively complex, though one is described briefly in Section 17.8 and in the lab manual. This chapter will deal primarily with **internal sorting algorithms**, in which an array is sorted in main memory. We will find that the best algorithm for sorting random data is not the best algorithm for sorting nearly-ordered data.

External sort: A sorting process in which the data reside mostly outside main memory, in mass storage devices.

Internal sort: A sorting process in which all of the data reside in main memory.

We begin with searching. We will examine the sequential search algorithm and the binary search algorithm, finding that the latter is far more efficient, though harder to program correctly. Then we will examine the insertion sort algorithm and quicksort algorithm, finding that the latter is more efficient for sorting random data but trickier to write.

19.1 SEQUENTIAL SEARCH

The most obvious and primitive way to search through an array for a given key is to start at the beginning of the array, looking at each element in sequence. This is called **sequential search** or **linear search**. The algorithm is simple:

Algorithm 19.1.1: Sequential Search

Purpose:
To find the first array element containing a given `SearchKey` in a specified portion of an array of keys, beginning with `Key[First]` and ending with `Key[Last]`. This sequence of keys is denoted by the shorthand `Key[First..Last]`.

Preconditions:
`Key[ First..Last ]` are initialized.

Postconditions:
Reports whether the search key was found and, if found, the subscript of an array element containing the search key. If the search key was not found, reports the location `Last + 1`.

Steps:

1. Set the boolean variable `Found` to `False` and initialize `Location` to `First`.
2. While `Location` is no greater than `Last` and `Found` is still `False`,

   If `Key[ Location ]` is the key we seek, then we are finished, so
   record the location and set `Found` to `True`;

   otherwise,
   increment `Location`.
3. Return the values of `Found` and `Location`.

For example, suppose that `First = 1` and `Last = 10`, that the array is as shown in the diagram below, and that the algorithm is searching for `17`:

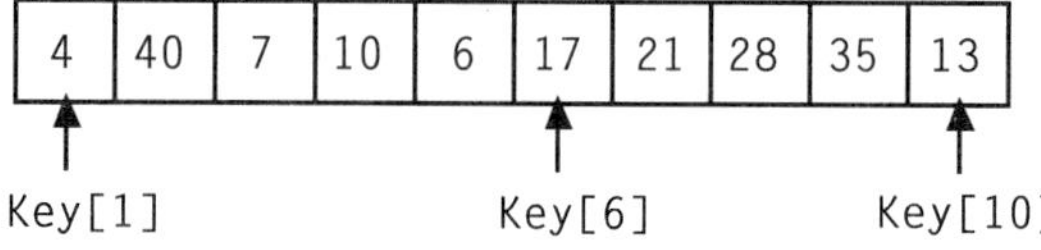

Then the algorithm should report a subscript of 6 for the location of the first-encountered occurrence of the searched-for key, 17.

The translation into Pascal is fairly straightforward. For illustrative purposes, we use a simple array, in which both the keys and the subscripts are integers:

```
CONST
   First     = 1;     { Or whatever }
   Last      = 10;    { Or whatever  }
   LastPlus1 = 11;    { (Last+1), reported if SearchKey not found }
```

```
TYPE
   KeyType        = Integer;  { or whatever }
   SubscriptRange = First..Last;
   AugmentedRange = First..LastPlus1;
   ArrayType      = ARRAY [ SubscriptRange ] OF KeyType;
```

Since we want to avoid unnecessary duplication of the array, which may be very large, we make it a `VAR` parameter of the search procedure. (See Section 14.7.) This, of course, carries the danger of undesired *side effects*, so we will have to be careful not to modify the array in the search procedure.

In implementing the search procedure, we might have the parameters

```
VAR Key      : ArrayType;       { The array being searched          }
SearchKey    : KeyType;         { The key for which we search       }
First, Last  : SubscriptRange;  { The range of subscripts in array }
VAR Location : AugmentedRange;  { Subscript at which key is found   }
```

With these declarations, we might be tempted to implement the algorithm's second step as a `WHILE` structure:

```
   Location := First;
   WHILE (Location <= Last) AND ( Key[ Location ] <> SearchKey ) DO
      Location := Location + 1;
```

However, there is an error here. If `SearchKey` is not found in the array, `Location` is incremented to a final value of `Last + 1`. This is okay in itself because we declared `Location` to be of type `AugmentedRange`, which extends to `Last + 1`. However, after the last trip, the `WHILE` structure will try to evaluate the boolean expression

```
   ( Location <= Last ) AND ( Key[ Location ] <> SearchKey )
```

with `Location = Last + 1`:

```
   ( (Last + 1) <= Last ) AND ( Key[ Last + 1 ] <> SearchKey )
```

Recall from Chapter 8 that Pascal cannot be counted on to shortcircuit compound boolean expressions, so `Key[ Last + 1 ]` will be accessed by many Pascal systems, even though the first clause of the expression is false. Since `Key[ Last + 1 ]` is outside the range of initialized array elements and perhaps outside the whole array, strange things will happen when the program is run.

Another problem is that the proposed loop structure does not report a failure to find `SearchKey` in the array except to report `Location = Last + 1`. To get around these shortcomings, we design the loop as shown below:

```
{-----------------------------------------------------------------}
{ Searches Key[ First ] through Key[ Last ]                       }
{ for the first occurrence of SearchKey.                          }
{-----------------------------------------------------------------}
PROCEDURE SequentialSearch( VAR Key      : ArrayType;
                            SearchKey    : KeyType;
                            First, Last  : SubscriptRange;
                            VAR Location : AugmentedRange;
                            VAR Found    : Boolean );
```

```
{
  PRECONDITIONS:
  First, Last, SearchKey, and Key[ First ]..Key[ Last ]
  have been initialized.

  POSTCONDITIONS:
  If SearchKey was found in the array,
     Found = True and Key[ Location ] = SearchKey.
  If SearchKey was not found,
     Found = False and Location = Maximum( First, Last + 1 ).
}
BEGIN

   Found    := False;
   Location := First;

   WHILE ( Location <= Last ) AND ( NOT Found ) DO
      {
        LOOP INVARIANT:
        First <= Location <= Last + 1;
        SearchKey not found in Key[ First..Location - 1 ].
      }
      IF Key[ Location ] = SearchKey THEN
         Found := True
      ELSE
         Location := Location + 1

   {
     ASSERTION:
     Either
        Found = True and Key[ Location ] = SearchKey
     or
        Found = False and Location = Maximum( First, Last + 1 ).
   }

END; { SequentialSearch }
```

The loop invariant

The algorithm successively eliminates `Key[First]`, `Key[First+1]`, ... as possible locations for `SearchKey`. If eventually the whole array is eliminated, the procedure reports failure. On the other hand, if the procedure encounters a copy of `SearchKey`, searching quits and success is reported immediately, by setting `Found` to `True`. The **loop invariant** captures the progressive elimination of the portion of the array not containing `SearchKey`.

At the beginning of the first trip through the loop, `Location = First` and `SearchKey` is known to be absent from the set

```
Key[ First..First - 1 ]
```

But this is an empty set. In other words, we know nothing about where `SearchKey` does not occur, because we haven't checked any array elements yet.

At the end of the first trip and the beginning of the second, `Location = First + 1` and `SearchKey` is known not to be in the set

```
Key[ First..First ]
```

This is the set containing the single element `Key[ First ]`, so the invariant is saying that `SearchKey` is not found in the first element of the array.

At the end of the second trip and the beginning of the third, `Location = First + 2` and `SearchKey` is known not to be in the two-member set

```
Key[ First..First + 1 ]
```

If the procedure fails to find `SearchKey`, this process continues until the final trip with `Location = Last`. If `SearchKey` is not found on this last trip, `Location` is incremented to `Last + 1` and the final trip ends with the invariant saying that `SearchKey` is not found in

```
Key[ First..Last ]
```

This confirms that `SearchKey` is not in the array at all.

The running time

The sequential search algorithm quits as soon as it finds a copy of `SearchKey` in the array. If we are extremely lucky, the very first key examined may be the one we are looking for, in which case the algorithm reports success after only one **key comparison**. This is the best possible case.

In the worst case, the algorithm may search the entire search area, from `Key[First]` to `Key[Last]`, before finding the search value in the last element or finding that it isn't present. In either of these cases, there are as many comparisons of keys as there are elements in the search area of the array.

In general, the running time will be between these two extremes. If all possible arrangements of keys are equally likely in the array, then an average search will go halfway through the array, and the average running time of sequential search will be proportional to $N/2$, where N is the number of keys in the search area of the array.

Exercises

1. Explain why it may be advantageous to increment `Index` by `Index := Succ(Index);` instead of adding 1 to `Index`.

2. Cora Meltdown has written the following version of the sequential search procedure, but it gives a subrange error. Explain to Cora why this happens.

```
PROCEDURE SequentialSearch( VAR Key      : ArrayType;
                            SearchKey    : KeyType;
                            First, Last  : SubscriptRange;
                            VAR Location : SubscriptRange;
                            VAR Found    : Boolean );

BEGIN

   Found    := False;
   Location := First;
```

```
    WHILE ( Location <= Last ) AND ( NOT Found ) DO
    BEGIN
       IF Key[ Location ] = SearchKey THEN
          Found := True;
       Location := Succ( Location )
    END
 END; { SequentialSearch }
```

3. Explain how the best-case and worst-case running times depend on the number of elements in the array if the code in `SequentialSearch` is rewritten as follows, with `Index` declared to be of type `AugmentedRange`:

```
Found    := False;
Location := First;

FOR Index := First TO Last DO
   IF Key[ Index ] = SearchKey THEN
   BEGIN
      Found    := True;
      Location := Index
   END
```

Also state what is returned in `Location` when the loop terminates.

19.2 BINARY SEARCH

Imagine that you are looking up Elwood P. Dowd's telephone number in the phone book. You certainly won't use sequential search, because it will take too long and because the phone book has *names listed in order*, so a more efficient approach is possible. Instead, you open the book to about where you expect "Dowd" to appear. Then you determine whether "Dowd" actually appears on, before, or after the opened page. Depending on what you see, you ignore part of the book and repeat the same process on the part of the book now known to contain the name. This part is called the **search area**. Every time you repeat the process, the search area in the book is reduced, until eventually you locate the correct page and then the correct place on the page. Basically, the process proceeds by dividing the search area until you find Elwood's name or discover that he isn't listed in the book.

Binary search is a process very much like the phone book example, for searching any **ordered list**. It repeatedly divides an ordered list until it homes in on the spot where the searched-for item should be found, if present. For example, suppose we are searching for any occurrence of the number 17 in the following sorted array containing elements `Key[ 1 ]`, `Key[ 2 ]`, ..., `Key[ 10 ]`, which we will hereafter denote by the shorthand notation `Key[ 1..10 ]`:

Ordered list: A sorted list; that is, a list in which the keys are arranged in some order.

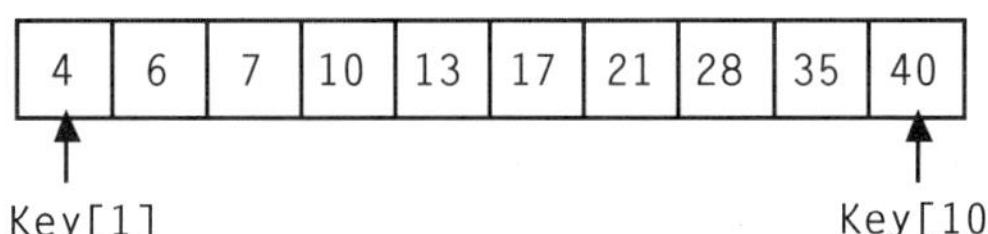

The middlemost element of the array is the one with subscript (1 + 10) DIV 2, or 5. We compare Key[5] = 13 with the searched-for key, 17, and because Key[5] is less than 17, we realize that elements 1 through 5 can be ignored in future searches. Now the search area has been reduced to elements 6 through 10:

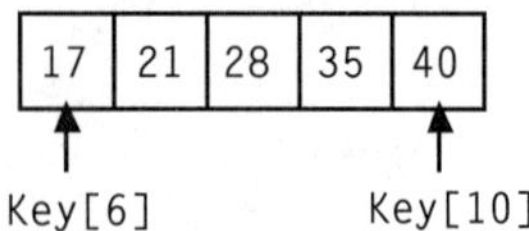

We repeat the process on the remaining portion of the array. The middlemost element of the remaining elements is the one with subscript (6 + 10) DIV 2, or 8. We compare Key[8] = 28 with the searched-for key, 17, and realize that because Key[8] is greater than 17, we can ignore elements 8 through 10 in future searches. Now the search area consists only of elements 6 through 7:

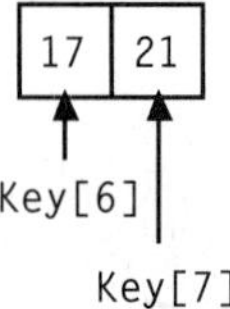

The middlemost of the remaining elements is the one with subscript (6 + 7) DIV 2, or 6. We compare Key[6] = 17 with the searched-for key, 17, and discover that element 6 contains the searched-for value. We report a subscript of 6 and the algorithm terminates.

Here is an outline of the algorithm when searching an already-sorted array of keys for a given SearchKey. It uses variables First and Last to store the first and last subscripts in the search area of the array, and uses a variable Location to store the midpoint of the search area.

Algorithm 19.2.1: Binary Search

Purpose:
To find any array element containing a given SearchKey in a specified portion of a given ordered array of keys, Key[First], Key[First+1],...,Key[Last]. This sequence of keys is denoted by the shorthand Key[First..Last].

Preconditions:
Key[First] ≤ Key[First+1] ≤...≤ Key[Last].

Postconditions:
Reports whether the search key was found and, if found, reports its Location; that is, the subscript of an array element containing the search key. If the search key was not found, Location is meaningless.

Steps:

1. If `First ≤ Last`, do the following:

   a. Calculate the middlemost subscript in the search area:
   `Location =( ( First + Last ) DIV 2 ).`

   b. If `SearchKey = Key[ Location ]`,
   then we have found the searched-for item:
   Report that `SearchKey` was found at the current `Location` and terminate the search.

   Otherwise, we have not yet finished:

   If `Key[ Location ] < SearchKey`, then `SearchKey`, if present in the array at all, must be among the elements `Key[ Location + 1..Last ]`. Therefore, ignore the lower-numbered elements by redefining `First` to be `Location + 1`. *Then repeat step 1, using the new value of* `First` *but the old value of* `Last`. This narrows the search area.

   Otherwise `SearchKey < Key[ Location ]`, in which case `SearchKey`, if present in the array at all, must be among the elements `Key[ First..Location - 1 ]`. Therefore, ignore the higher-numbered elements by redefining `Last` to be `Location - 1`. *Then repeat step 1, using the new value of* `Last` *but the old value of* `First`. This narrows the search area.

2. If `First > Last`, then the search area of the array is empty and `SearchKey` cannot be present. Report that the search key was not found.

The sentences in italics call for repetition of step 1, but with updated parameters. This can be accomplished by iteration or recursion. Suppose that the keys and subscripts of the array happen to be integers and that we have the following declarations:

```
TYPE
   SubscriptRange = 1..1000; { or whatever }
   KeyType        = Integer; { or whatever }
   ArrayType      = ARRAY [ SubscriptRange ] OF KeyType;
```

Then the following procedure is an iterative implementation of the algorithm:

```
{---------------------------------------------------------------}
{ Iteratively finds the subscript of an occurrence of          }
{ SearchKey in an ordered array Key[ First..Last ].             }
{---------------------------------------------------------------}
PROCEDURE BinarySearch( VAR Key      : ArrayType; { VAR for speed }
                        SearchKey    : KeyType;
                        First, Last  : Integer;
                        VAR Location : Integer;
                        VAR Found    : Boolean );
{
  PRECONDITIONS:
  Key[ First ] <= Key[ First+1 ] <= .. <= Key[ Last ].

  POSTCONDITIONS:
  If SearchKey is in the specified portion of the array,
     Found = True and Location = subscript where found;
  otherwise,
     Found = False and Location may be uninitialized.
}
BEGIN

   Found := False;

   WHILE ( First <= Last ) AND ( NOT Found ) DO
   {
     LOOP INVARIANT:
     SearchKey, if present, is in Key[ First..Last ].
   }
   BEGIN

      Location := ( First + Last ) DIV 2;
      { ASSERTION: First <= Location <= Last }

      IF Key[ Location ] = SearchKey THEN
         Found := True

      ELSE IF Key[ Location ] < SearchKey THEN
         {
           ASSERTION:
           SearchKey, if present, is in Key[ (Location+1)..Last ].
         }
         First := Location + 1

   END { WHILE }

END; { BinarySearch }
```

Notice that the Key array is passed to the procedure as a VAR parameter, even though the procedure does not modify the array. This is done for the sake of speed; if the array is large, merely copying the array into a value parameter could take much more time than running the search! You will see why this is so when we analyze the running time a little later.

A sample search

With this procedure, a search for 17 in a 10-element array involves a call of the form

```
BinarySearch( Key, 17, 1, 10, Location, Found );
```

Here is a play-by-play description of execution:

SearchKey is 17.

First trip through the loop:
First = 1 and Last = 10;
Location = (1 + 10) DIV 2 = 5;
Key[5] = 13;
Since 13 < SearchKey, assign Location+1 = 6
to First. (Now the search area is Key[6..10].)

Second trip:
First = 6 and Last = 10.
Location = (6 + 10) DIV 2 = 8;
Key[8] = 28;
Since SearchKey < 28, assign Location-1 = 7
to Last. (Now the search area is Key[6..7].)

Third trip:
First = 6 and Last = 7;
Location = (6 + 7) DIV 2 = 6.
Key[6] = 17;
Since Key[6] = SearchKey,
Found is set to True and Location is reported as 6.

Observe that a trip through the loop can require up to two comparisons between keys. We will make use of this observation when we analyze the worst-case running times.

Improving the algorithm

The algorithm as stated is simple and clean, but it leaves Location uninitialized when the search area of the array is empty; that is, when First > Last as the procedure begins to run. Furthermore, when the search area is not empty but SearchKey is not found, the procedure homes in on a location that is only approximately where SearchKey *would have been if it had been in the array*. Suppose we are searching for 8 in the following search area:

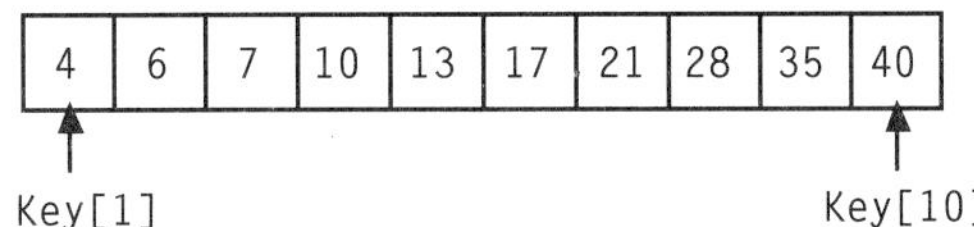

Then the procedure returns Found = False and Location = 3. (Work through it.) In this case, Key[3] is the element *before* the one where 8 would be found if it were added to the array. On the other hand, if we search for 15, we obtain Found = False and Location = 6. Key[6], however, is the element *after* the one where 15 would be found if it were added to the array. Thus, when Found = False, Location is only within ±1 of the subscript where the unfound SearchKey would fit in the ordered array.

If SearchKey is not present, it would be nice if the procedure would report the position where SearchKey should be inserted in the array, maintaining the nondecreasing order. This is left as a project for the reader. (See Project 2.)

A simpler and more common way to keep Location defined when the search fails is to arbitrarily define it to be the subscript before the beginning of the original search area. Thus if First is initially 1, Location = 0 if Found = False. This is accomplished by a simple modification:

```
VAR
   BeforeFirst : Integer;

BEGIN

   BeforeFirst := First - 1;
   Found       := False;

   WHILE ( First <= Last ) AND ( NOT Found ) DO
   BEGIN
      .
      .
   END;

   IF NOT Found THEN
      Location := BeforeFirst;
```

Recursive version of binary search

Recursion requires about the same amount of machinery as iteration, but in a different arrangement. Here is recursive Pascal code for Algorithm 19.2.1:

```
{-------------------------------------------------------------------}
{ Recursively finds the subscript of an occurrence of               }
{ SearchKey in an ordered array Key[ First..Last ].                 }
{-------------------------------------------------------------------}
PROCEDURE BinarySearch( VAR Key      : ArrayType; { VAR for speed }
                        SearchKey    : KeyType;
                        First, Last  : Integer;
                        VAR Location : Integer;
                        VAR Found    : Boolean );
{
  PRECONDITIONS:
  Key[ First ] <= Key[ First + 1 ] <= .. <= Key[ Last ].

  POSTCONDITIONS:
  If SearchKey is in the specified portion of the array,
     Found = True and Location = subscript where found;
  otherwise,
     Found = False and Location may be uninitialized.
}
```

```
BEGIN

   IF First > Last THEN { search area is empty }
      Found := False

   ELSE { First <= Last }
   BEGIN

      Location := ( First + Last ) DIV 2;
      {
        ASSERTION:
        First <= Location <= Last;
        SearchKey, if present, is in Key[ First..Last ].
      }

      IF Key[ Location ] = SearchKey THEN
         Found := True

      ELSE IF Key[ Location ] < SearchKey THEN
         {
           ASSERTION:
           SearchKey, if present, is in Key[ Location + 1..Last ].
         }
         BinarySearch( Key, SearchKey,
                       Location + 1, Last, Location, Found )

      ELSE { SearchKey < Key[ Location ] }
         {
           ASSERTION:
           SearchKey, if present, is in Key[ First..Location - 1 ].
         }
         BinarySearch( Key, SearchKey,
                       First, Location - 1, Location, Found )

   END { ELSE First <= Last }

END;  { BinarySearch }
```

To search the elements `Key[ 1..10 ]` for `SearchKey`, the procedure is called by

```
BinarySearch(Key, SearchKey, 1, 10, Location, Found);
```

Suppose that the `Key` array is as shown in previous diagrams and `SearchKey` is 17. Then the chain of recursive calls works as shown in Figure 19.2.1, returning `Found = True` and `Location = 6`.

Figure 19.2.1 *The recursion during a binary search for SearchKey = 17 in the array shown at the beginning of the section.*

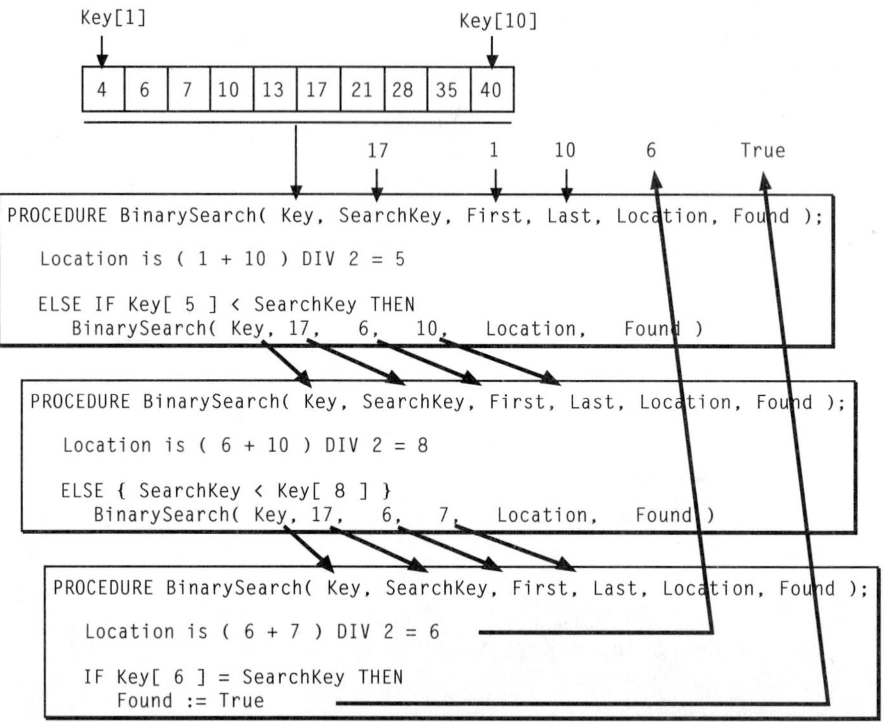

When SearchKey is not present

When `SearchKey` is not in the specified portion of the array, the algorithm reports `Found = False`. If the array is empty, `Location` will remain uninitialized. If the array is nonempty, the resulting location will be within ±1 of the position where `SearchKey` would belong if added to the **ordered array**. Figure 19.2.2 shows what happens when the procedure searches for 5 in the example array.

When SearchKey lies outside the range of values in the array

If `First` ≤ `Last` and `SearchKey < Key[ First ]`, the algorithm homes in on position `Location = First`. Similarly, if `Key[ Last ] < SearchKey`, the algorithm homes in on `Location = Last`. The procedure reports this value of `Location`, together with `Found = False`. Exercise 11 asks you to diagram the process.

The recursion during an unsuccessful binary search for SearchKey = 5 in the array shown at the beginning of the section. **Figure 19.2.2**

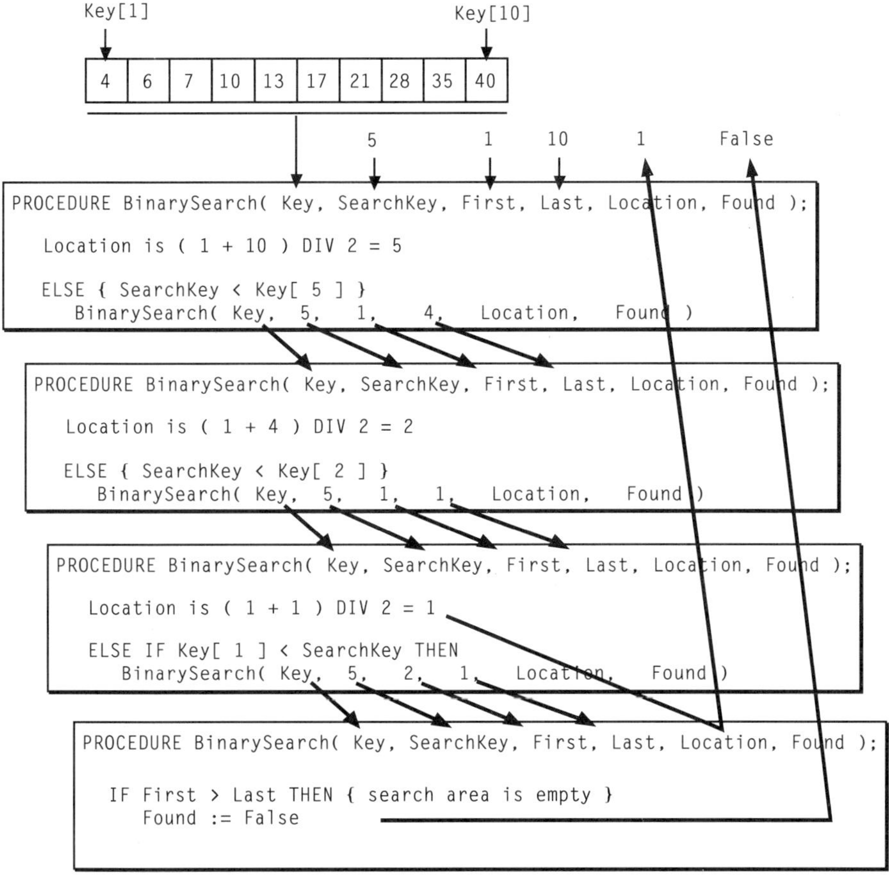

The repetition always terminates.

There are three cases during the iterative or recursive process:

1. If `First < Last`, `Location` will be computed to be in the range `First ≤ Location < Last`, so if `Key[ Location ] <> SearchKey`, the search area shrinks before the next repetition, either by decreasing `Last` or by increasing `First`. Eventually, the search area shrinks until `First = Last`.
2. When `First = Last`, there is only one element in the search area, and the procedure computes `First = Location = Last`. If `Key[ Location ] <> SearchKey`, either `First` is incremented or `Last` is decremented; in either of these cases, the next repetition has `First > Last`.
3. If `First > Last`, the search area is empty and the process terminates immediately, returning `Found = False` and the latest value of `Location`.

Therefore, the process terminates in all possible cases.

Recursion versus iteration

Every recursive call consumes memory and requires time to copy the `First`, `Last`, and `SearchKey` variables into the newly called procedure, so the recursive version of binary search consumes more memory and runs slower than the iterative version. However, it turns out that binary search is so fast that the slight difference in speed between the two versions hardly matters. Let's see why this is.

Estimating the running time of binary search

Whether recursive or iterative, binary search halves the search area until only one array element is left. This array element either is, or is not, the value for which we are searching. Whichever is the case, we are then finished searching.

The running time is measured by the number of repetitions required; that is, the number of trips through the loop or the number of recursions. This is the same as the number of times that we can halve the number of array elements in the original search area until we have only one element left.

Let N be the number of array elements and let C be the number of times N can be halved until we have one element left. Then C is the largest integer such that

$$\frac{N}{2^C} \geq 1$$

This is the same as saying that C is the largest integer such that

$$N \geq 2^C$$

In other words, C is the largest integer such that 2^C is no greater than N. But when $2^L = N$, L is called the **base 2 logarithm** of N, or $\log_2 N$. Thus C is the integer part of $\log_2 N$, which we can write $\text{Trunc}(\log_2 N)$.

From this, we see that the number of repetitions required by binary search in the worst case is $\text{Trunc}(\log_2 N) + 1$. Because there are up to two key comparisons in every trip but the last, the total number of key comparisons is $2 \cdot \text{Trunc}(\log_2 N)$.

In the best case, binary search might stumble onto the search key at the first midpoint, requiring only one comparison of keys. This is the same as the best-case performance of sequential search. But in the worst case, binary search is much faster for large N. Consider the examples shown in Table 19.2.1.

Table 19.2.1

Worst cases of binary search and sequential search (searching for a key larger than any in the array).

N = Size of array	Number of key comparisons	
	Binary search ($2 \cdot \text{Trunc}(\log_2 N)$)	Sequential search $N+1$
100	12	101
1,000	18	1,001
10,000	26	10,001
100,000	32	100,001

Table 19.2.2

Worst-case running times, in milliseconds, on a typical microcomputer.

N = Size of array	Binary search Recursive	Binary search Iterative	Sequential search Iterative
100	1.6	0.5	2.4
1,000	2.2	0.8	24.
10,000	2.9	1.0	240.

There is obviously an enormous difference between the worst-case running times of these two algorithms. Table 19.2.2 shows some actual times on a typical microcomputer, when searching an array of character keys for a key larger than any in the array. (When an array of 100,000 elements was used, all three methods had insufficient memory to run.)

Questions

4. In the two versions of the `BinarySearch` procedure, `First`, `Last`, and `Location` are declared to be `Integer`. Explain why a range error might occur if they were declared to be of type `SubscriptRange`.
5. When `BinarySearch` is asked to find `SearchKey = 40` in the array

   7, 28, 40, 6, 35, 17, 10, 21, 4, 13

   it fails to find it. Why is that? Hint: What preconditions are required by `BinarySearch`?
6. `BinarySearch` asserts that `First ≤ Location ≤ Last`, but `Location = ( First + Last ) DIV 2`. How, then, can `Location` ever be equal to `Last`?

Exercises

7. Show that in searching for a given name in a 250,000-name phone book, binary search will never require more than 34 comparisons between the given name and the listed names.
8. In the situation in Exercise 7, how many comparisons would be required by sequential search in the worst case? Explain your thinking.
9. It has been suggested that `BinarySearch` could simply report `Location = 0` or `-1` if the search key was not found, and then it wouldn't have to report a separate `Found` value as well. Discuss the merits (and demerits) of this suggestion.
10. In `BinarySearch`, it has been suggested that if `SearchKey` is not found, `Location` be reported as the subscript where `SearchKey` would be inserted if the array were to be kept in sorted order with `SearchKey` present. Give an example of how this might be useful.
11. Diagram the process when recursive `BinarySearch` is asked to find `49` in the array shown in the text in this section.
12. Prove that `BinarySearch` does not require that `Location` be assigned the value `( First + Last ) DIV 2`, but only that `Location` be given a value such that `First ≤ Location ≤ Last`. Also show that setting `Location = ( First + Last ) DIV 2` makes binary search as fast as possible in the worst case.

13. Show that `BinarySearch` can be speeded up, on the average, by replacing the decision structure with one of the form

```
IF Key[ Location ] < SearchKey THEN
        .
        .
ELSE IF Key[ Location ] > SearchKey THEN
        .
        .
ELSE { Key[ Location ] = SearchKey }
        .
        .
```

14. Show that `BinarySearch` can be implemented by the following code, and that this code is faster than the code given in the text, on the average. Assume that `First ≤ Last` initially.

```
WHILE First < Last DO
BEGIN
   Location := ( First + Last ) DIV 2;
   IF Key[ Location ] < SearchKey THEN
      First := Location + 1
   ELSE
      Last := Location
END;
Found := (Key[ Location ] = SearchKey );
```

15. In Table 19.2.1, the entries for sequential search differ by multiplicative factors of 10. Explain why the entries for binary search differ by *additive* increments of about 6.

19.3 BIG-OH NOTATION

As we found when comparing sequential and binary search, different algorithms for the same task can differ enormously in the amount of computation required. In fact, the difference can be whole orders of magnitude when many data items are involved. Such huge differences between algorithms are much more important than the improvements that can be made by optimizing the code for a given algorithm, so it is important that we be able to predict mathematically the running times of such algorithms even before we use them in programs. In this section, we introduce the most common notation for describing running times as functions of the amount of data to be processed.

The idea

Table 19.2.2 showed worst-case running times for an iterative sequential search program, running on a typical microcomputer. The running time turned out to be $0.000024N$ seconds, where N is the number of elements in the array to be searched. Although it isn't shown in the table, the same program ran on a faster microcomputer in $0.000008\,N$ seconds. In both cases, the running times are proportional to the number of elements in the array. The only effect of a faster computer system is to change the constant in the running-time function, which is a linear function of time.

The important point here is that the worst-case running time of sequential search is a *linear function of time*. The exact value of the constant in the running-time function depends on such incidentals as the computer and compiler being used. When searching big arrays, these factors are not nearly as important as the nature of the algorithm being used to perform the search. Consider the worst-case running times of the recursive and iterative binary search programs shown in Table 19.2.2. These programs ran in approximately $0.0008 \log_{10} N$ and $0.00025 \log_{10} N$ seconds, respectively. Again, the exact multiplicative constants don't matter nearly as much as the fact that, in the worst case, binary search programs run in times that are proportional to $\log N$ rather than N itself. As you can see from Table 19.2.2, this makes binary searches enormously faster than sequential searches when N is large.

In order to make rapid theoretical comparisons between different algorithms, we use a notation that measures how fast a function grows with N, the number of data values being processed, *while ignoring all multiplicative and additive constants*. This is called "big-oh" notation, and is written as a function called O.

For example, the functions $2N + 3$, $N + 7$, and $0.5N$ differ only in multiplicative and additive constants. They all grow in proportion to N, and we therefore say that they are all linear functions of N. In big-oh notation, we indicate this by saying that all three functions are $O(N)$. As you saw in the previous section, sequential search runs in $O(N)$ time, where N is the number of elements in the array to be searched.

Similarly, the functions $N^2 + 2N + 3$, $2N^2 + 7$, and $7N^2 + 0.5N - 4$ differ only in multiplicative and additive constants. As N becomes very large, the N^2 terms grow much faster than the linear and constant terms, so the functions are approximately proportional to N^2 as N becomes extremely large. In big-oh notation, we indicate this by saying that all three functions are $O(N^2)$. Clearly, $O(N^2)$ functions increase with N much faster than $O(N)$ functions, and this is the significant point about them. You will encounter some $O(N^2)$ running times later in this chapter.

Functions like $2\log_{10} N + 1$ and $7\ln N$ increase with N much more slowly than linear functions, and are said to be $O(\lg N)$. Since the logarithm of N to one base is proportional to the logarithm of N to another base, we often use the symbol "$\lg N$" to indicate a generic logarithm with unspecified base. As you saw in the previous section, binary search—whether recursive or iterative—runs in $O(\lg N)$ time in the worst case, where N is the number of elements in the array to be searched.

Now we examine the exact mathematical definition of big-oh. Readers who feel this is more than they need to know may skip to the subsection called "More examples."

Conceptual mathematical definition

If, for large values of a variable x, a real function $f(x)$ is always closer to the x-axis than some multiple of another function, $g(x)$, we say that $f(x)$ is of order $g(x)$ and we write $f(x) = O(g(x))$. This is sometimes pronounced "$f(x)$ is **big-oh** of $g(x)$."

Precise mathematical definition

Specifically, the notation $f(x) = O(g(x))$ means that there exist constants C and x_0 such that $-C\,g(x) \le f(x) \le C\,g(x)$ for all $x \ge x_0$. In other words,

$$f(x) = O(g(x)) \qquad \text{means} \qquad |f(x)| \le C\,|g(x)| \text{ for } x \ge x_0$$

Thus $|g(x)|$ is an **upper bound** for $|f(x)|$, as illustrated in Figure 19.3.1.

Figure 19.3.1 *$f(x) = O(g(x))$ if there exist numbers C and x_0 such that $|f(x)| \le C\,|g(x)|$ for all $x \ge x_0$.*

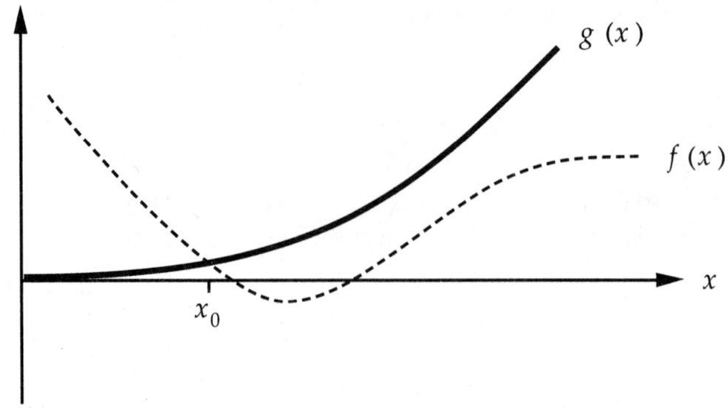

An example

Suppose that $f(x) = 2x^2 + 3x - 1$. Then

$$\begin{aligned}
& f(x) \le 3.5x^2 && \text{for } x \ge 1.6; \\
& f(x) \le 2x^3 && \text{for } x \ge 1.8; \\
\text{and } \quad & f(x) \le x^4 && \text{for } x \ge 1.9.
\end{aligned}$$

Therefore, $f(x) = O(x^2)$, $f(x) = O(x^3)$, and $f(x) = O(x^4)$, and of course, we could continue through all higher powers. Multiples of all of these powers can act as upper bounds on $f(x)$ if x is sufficiently large. However, we are primarily interested in the *lowest power* that can act as an upper bound, so we usually are most interested in the fact that $f(x) = 2x^2 + 3x - 1 = O(x^2)$. See Figure 19.3.2.

Comparing monomial orders

Suppose that $1 < x$. Then, by repeatedly multiplying both sides of the inequality by the positive x, we also have

$$x < x^2, \quad x^2 < x^3, \quad x^3 < x^4, \ldots$$

By induction, it is clear that $1 = x^0 < x^1 < x^2 < x^3 < \ldots$ when $1 < x$. In other words,

$xn < xn^{+1}$ for all $x > 1, n \ge 0$

Therefore,

$$xn = O(xn) = O(xn^{+1}) = O(xn^{+2}) = \ldots$$

Because we are almost always interested in the lowest upper bound for a given function, we usually say that for any constant k,

$$k = O(1)$$
$$kx = O(x)$$
$$kx^2 = O(x^2) \ldots$$

Figure 19.3.2

The functions $3.5x^2$, $2x^3$, and x^4 all lie above the curve $f(x) = 2x^2 + 3x - 1$ when x is large enough.

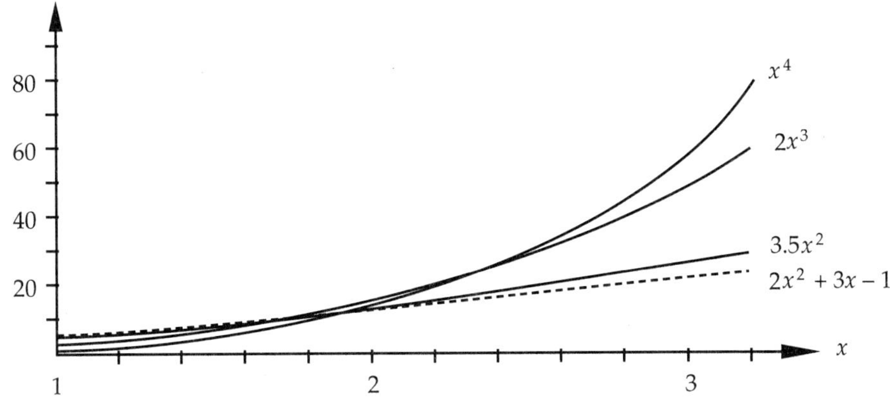

Orders of polynomial functions

Consider a quadratic function, $ax^2 + bx + c$. If $x > 1$, we have

$$ax^2 + bx + c \;<\; ax^2 + bx^2 + cx^2 \;=\; (a + b + c)\,x^2$$

so $ax^2 + bx + c = O(x^2)$

In the general case, we have

$$\begin{aligned} &axn + bxn^{-1} + \cdots + gx + h \\ &\qquad < axn + bxn + \cdots + gxn + hxn \\ &\qquad = (a + b + \cdots + g + h)\,xn \end{aligned}$$

so $axn + bxn^{-1} + \cdots + gx + h = O(xn)$

Thus a degree-n polynomial function of x is $O(xn)$ for $x > 1$, $n \geq 0$.

Logarithmic and exponential orders

It is proven in calculus that the function e^x can be expressed as an infinite series of powers of x:

$$e^x = 1 + x + \frac{x^2}{2!} + \frac{x^3}{3!} + \frac{x^4}{4!} + \cdots$$

From this, it is easy to see that an exponential function has an order greater than any monomial order:

$$ke^x = O(e^x) > O(x^n) \text{ for any } n.$$

Similarly, it is possible to prove that a logarithmic function has an order less than any positive monomial order:

$$k \log_b x = O(\log_b x) < O(x^n) \text{ for } b > 1 \text{ and any integer } n \geq 1.$$

The proof lies beyond the scope of this book, but the graph in Figure 19.3.3 gives visual confirmation.

Figure 19.3.3 *For large x, the graph of e^x lies above the graph of any power of x. Similarly, for large x, the graph of ln x lies below the graph of any power of x.*

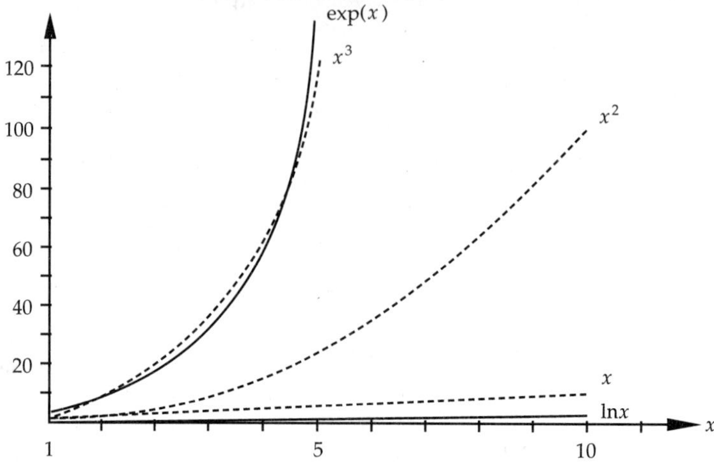

Logarithms differing only in base are proportional.

Before leaving the subject of logarithms, it is worth recalling that different-base logarithms of the same number are proportional. Suppose b and B are different bases, so that the logarithms of a number x in these bases are defined by the equations

$$x = b^{\log_b x} \quad \text{and} \quad x = B^{\log_B x}$$

Taking the base-B logarithm of the first equation, we have

$$\log_B x = \log_B\left(b^{\log_b x}\right) = \left(\log_b x\right)\left(\log_B b\right)$$

Taking the base-B logarithm of the second equation, we have

$$\log_B x = \log_B\left(B^{\log_B x}\right) = \left(\log_B x\right)\left(\log_B B\right) = \log_B x$$

Equating these two results, we have

$$\log_b x = \frac{\log_B x}{\log_B b}$$

Common examples in computer science are

$$\log_2 x = \frac{\log_{10} x}{\log_{10} 2} = 3.3219281 \ \log_{10} x$$

and

$$\log_2 x = \frac{\ln x}{\ln 2} = 1.4426950 \ \ln x$$

We learn from this that logarithmic functions of all bases have the same order:

$$O(\log_{10} x) = O(\ln x) = O(\log_2 x) = O(\lg x)$$

The notation **lg** x is often used to indicate a logarithm in which the base does not matter; it's a sort of "generic" log function.

More examples

The big-oh measure of a function's dependence on its independent variable is the order of its *fastest-growing term*. Here are some examples:

$2n^3 - 7n + 3 = O(n^3)$

$(r^2 - 2r + 1) / (r - 1) = O(r)$

$14 = O(1)$

$\log_{10} N + 4N = O(N)$

$\log_2 D + (4 / D) = O(\lg D)$

Big-oh arithmetic

From the definition of big-oh notation, it is possible to derive the following useful rules of big-oh arithmetic:

$O(f(x)) + k = O(f(x))$, where k is a constant

$O(kf(x)) = O(f(x))$, where k is a constant

$O(f(x)) + O(g(x)) = O(g(x)) + O(f(x))$

$O(f(x)) + O(g(x)) = O(g(x))$ if $O(f(x)) \leq O(g(x))$

The proofs are left as exercises.

Using big-oh for running times

Our interest in big-oh notation is in estimating rough upper bounds for the dependence of running times on the amount of data involved. If an algorithm runs in $0.0035N^2 - 0.00042N + 0.017$ seconds, where N is the number of elements in an array being manipulated, we say that the algorithm is $O(N^2)$. On the other hand, if other algorithms for the same task run in $O(N)$ time and $O(\lg N)$ time, respectively, we know that these algorithms will be faster than the first when N is large.

Consider the searching algorithms described earlier. In their best cases, both sequential and binary searches require only one comparison between keys. This means that their best-case running times do not depend on the amount of data; they are constants, which is to say they are proportional to 1. We say that the best-case running times of these algorithms are order 1, or $O(1)$.

On the other hand, in their worst cases, sequential search and binary search do depend on N in extremely different ways. Sequential search runs all the way through the array, requiring $O(N)$ time. Binary search divides the array, requiring only $O(\lg N)$ time, which is enormously less than $O(N)$ when N is large.

Exercises

16. Prove the following statements by using the definition of big-oh notation.

- **a.** $n^2 + 2n + 1$ is $O(n^2)$
- **b.** $n^2(n + 1)$ is $O(n^3)$
- **c.** $x^2 + (1 / x)$ is $O(x^2)$
- **d.** $x^2 + \ln x$ is $O(x^2)$
- **e.** $r + r \log r$ is $O(r \lg r)$

17. Express the order of the following functions in big-oh notation. Explain your answers.

a. $n(n+1)/2$

b. $(1/n)-n(n+1)$

c. $e^{-2r}-r(r+1)$

d. $x^2+3x\ln x$

e. $x\ln x+\ln x-6x$

f. $x^2\ln x+e^x-6x^8$

g. $n^2\ln n+e^{-n}-6n^8$

h. $x\ln x+e^{-x}-6x^{-8}$

i. $(r-2)(r+1)/(r+3)$

j. $x^4(x^2-1)$

18. Prove the four rules of big-oh arithmetic given in the text.

19. Estimate the running times of the following code fragments, showing your estimate in big-oh notation.

a.
```
FOR Row := 1 TO N-1 DO
   FOR Col := 1 TO N-1 DO
      Statement;
```

b.
```
FOR Row := 1 TO N-1 DO
   FOR Col := 1 TO Row DO
      Statement;
```

c.
```
FOR Row := 1 TO 10 DO
   FOR Col := 1 TO 10 DO
      Statement;
```

d.
```
WHILE Num > 1 DO
BEGIN
   Statement;
   Num := Num DIV 10
END;
```

e.
```
FOR Count := N DOWNTO 2 DO
   Statement;
```

19.4 INSERTION SORT

In Section 14.4, we described an intuitive method for sorting the elements (called *keys*) in an array. The method was called *selection sort*, and the idea was to search the array for the smallest key and swap it into the first position in the array, then search for the second-lowest key and swap it into the second position in the array, and so on. It was an easy algorithm to design correctly and was easy to code into Pascal.

Now we consider another intuitive algorithm for sorting, called **insertion sort**. This too is easy to describe and understand, but not so easy to program correctly. In coding it, we will encounter an important shortcoming in the Pascal language.

Insertion sort works the way most people sort a hand of playing cards: Pick up a card and hold it in the hand. Then add a second card to the hand, inserting it in the correct position relative to the first card. Then each successive card picked up is inserted in the correct position among the already-sorted cards. The process is one of moving cards one by one from a pile of unsorted cards into a hand that is kept sorted at all times.

Let's apply the same idea to insertion sorting an array consisting of the elements `Key[First]`, `Key[First + 1]`,..., `Key[Last]`. The array is partitioned into an already-sorted part and an as-yet-unsorted part. Initially, the already-sorted part contains just

Key[First], while the unsorted part contains Key[First + 1], . . ., Key[Last], as shown below:

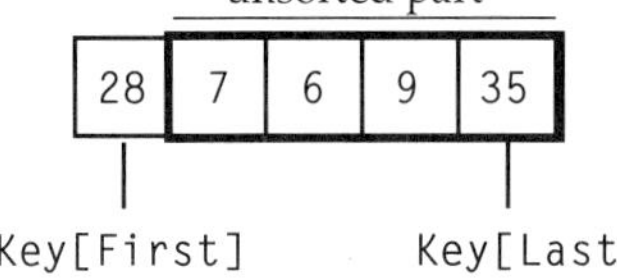

Then we move the Key[First + 1] value downward in the array to its sorted position relative to Key[First]. If the value of Key[First] is greater than the value of Key[First + 1], the Key[First] value will have to be moved upward to make room:

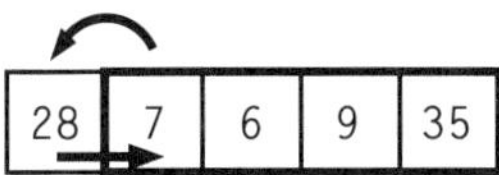

As the process continues, the pattern becomes clear. When the sorted part of the array consists of Key[First], Key[First + 1], . . ., Key[I-1], the next task is to place the value of Key[I] in its correct place among the already-sorted elements by moving it downward to its correct position. Here's the shifting that occurs when I = 4:

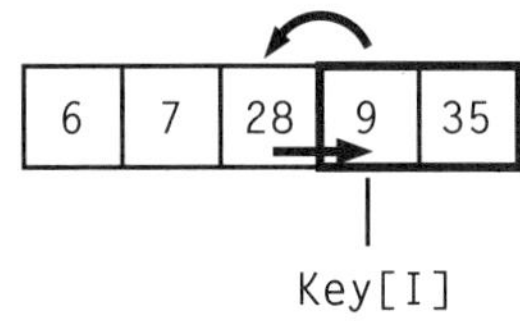

Algorithm 19.4.1: Insertion Sort

Purpose:
To sort the array Key[First..Last] into nondecreasing order.

Preconditions:
First, Last, and the elements Key[First..Last] are initialized.

Postconditions:
Key[First] ≤ Key[First+1] ≤..≤ Key[Last].

Steps:

1. Assign (First + 1) to I.
2. While I ≤ Last, do the following:
   a. Assign Key[I] to MovedValue.
   b. Insert MovedValue into its correct position among the elements Key[First..(I-1)].
   c. Increment I.

The bulk of the algorithm therefore consists of a loop:

```
FOR I := (First + 1) TO Last DO
BEGIN
   MovedValue := Key[I];
   Insert MovedValue into correct position in the sorted part of array,
    which is Key[ First..(I-1) ].
END
```

The "insertion" step is performed by hunting backwards from `Key[I]` until we find an element that is ≤ `MovedValue`. As we search backwards, we shift each element that is greater than `MovedValue` upward one place:

```
J := I;
WHILE MovedValue < Key[J-1] DO
BEGIN
   Key[J] := Key[J-1];
   J := J-1
END;
Key[J] := MovedValue
```

There is a problem here, however. If `MovedValue` happens to be less than all of the elements `Key[First]`, `Key[First + 1]`,…, `Key[I-1]`, the `WHILE` loop will eventually try to evaluate `Key[First - 1]`, which is out of range. The natural way to try to prevent this is to rewrite the loop condition:

```
J := I;
WHILE ( First < J ) AND ( MovedValue < Key[J-1] ) DO
BEGIN
   Key[J] := Key[J-1];
   J := J-1
END;
Key[J] := MovedValue
```

However, as we mentioned in Section 8.6, Standard Pascal will not shortcircuit an `AND` expression when the first clause becomes false, so the new version of the loop may try to evaluate `Key[First - 1]` when `J = First`. This is just as bad as the first version of the loop.

One way to solve the problem is to add to the array an additional "phantom" element, `Key[First - 1]`, containing a value less than any that could be in the elements to be sorted. This phantom element would then act as a sentinel and keep the loop from walking off the bottom end of the array.

But adding a phantom element, with a value "less than any that could be in the array," is a **kludge**—a shoddy way to patch up the algorithm. Why clutter up the array with an extra element that isn't normally used? What sentinel value would we pick to store in this element?

Kludge: A Rube Goldberg device in hardware or software. See the Hackers's Dictionary sidebar at the end of Chapter 20.

We can make insertion sort work correctly without a sentinel. We simply prepare the array for sorting by first finding the lowest value in the array and swapping it into `Key[First]`. This guarantees that `MovedValue` will always be greater than `Key[First]`. Then, whatever is in `Key[First + 1]`, it will be greater than `Key[First]`, so the first two elements of the array will be already sorted. Therefore, we can start the insertion sort itself with `I = (First + 2)`. Here's the whole procedure:

```
PROCEDURE InsertionSort( First, Last : SubscriptRange;
                         VAR Key     : ArrayType );
VAR
   LowestValue, MovedValue : KeyType;
   LowestIndex, I, J       : SubscriptRange;

BEGIN

   { First put lowest key into position 1 }
   LowestValue := Key[First];
   LowestIndex := First;
   FOR I := (First + 1) TO Last DO
      IF Key[I] < LowestValue THEN
      BEGIN
         LowestValue := Key[I];
         LowestIndex := I
      END;

   Key[LowestIndex] := Key[First];
   Key[First] := LowestValue;

   { Now comes the insertion sort: }
   FOR I := (First + 2) TO Last DO
   BEGIN
      {
        INVARIANT:
        Key[First]..Key[I - 1] are sorted and
        Key[I]..Key[Last] are unsorted and
        Key[First] <= (Key[I]..Key[Last]).
      }
      MovedValue := Key[I];
      J := I;

      WHILE MovedValue < Key[J - 1] DO
      BEGIN
         {
           INVARIANT:
           MovedValue <= (Key[J]..Key[I]).
         }
         Key[J] := Key[J - 1];
         J := J - 1
      END;

      Key[J] := MovedValue

   END { FOR }

END; { InsertionSort }
```

When it's good, it's very, very good.

Insertion sort doesn't do much work if it is given an already-sorted array. In this case, each trip through the outer loop takes only one comparison to discover that `MovedValue > Key[I - 1]` and, therefore, that `MovedValue` does not need to be moved. The total number of comparisons performed is therefore equal to the number of trips through the `FOR` loop, which is `Last - (First + 2) + 1`, or `Last - First - 1`. Since this number is proportional to the number of elements in the array, the running time of insertion sort is also proportional to N in the best case. Using big-oh language, we say that *insertion sort is $O(N)$ in the best case.*

The best-case performance of insertion sort is a significant advantage over selection sort. It often happens that we need to add a few data values to an already sorted list and then re-sort. In such situations, insertion sort works well because it takes advantage of the nearly sorted condition of the augmented list.

But when it's bad . . .

When insertion sort is given a reverse-sorted list, it shows its worst-case behavior. The third element of the array, `Key[First+2]`, is moved downward one position (two comparisons), then `Key[First+3]` is moved downward two positions (three comparisons), and so on, until finally, `Key[Last-1]` is moved downward `(Last-First-2)` positions (`(Last-First-1)` = $(N-2)$ comparisons, where N = `Last - First + 1` = number of elements to be sorted). Finally, the `Last` element is not moved at all (one comparison). The total number of comparisons is therefore (See Appendix G.)

$$1+2+3+\cdots+(N-2) = \frac{(N-2)(N-1)}{2}$$

As you can see, the *worst-case running time of insertion sort is $O(N^2)$*, like selection sort. This means that insertion sort can be very slow when sorting large arrays.

The advantages and disadvantages of insertion sort

Insertion sort is intuitive and as easy to understand as selection sort. Unfortunately, it is not as easy to program correctly in Pascal. (The fault is Pascal's, not the algorithm's.) Insertion sort is $O(N)$ when the array is already sorted or nearly sorted. In this, its best case, insertion sort is as fast as any sorting algorithm. However, there are two drawbacks:

1. When data are in random order or reverse-sorted, insertion sort performs roughly N^2 comparisons when N is large, and therefore is quite slow when sorting really big random arrays—say 100,000 or more elements. In the next section, we will examine *quicksort*, which is much faster at sorting randomly ordered arrays.
2. It is an *internal sorting* method; it requires the entire array to be in main memory. Commercial databases are often larger than main memory, and must be sorted in external storage. In Section 17.8, we mentioned *merge sort*, an external sorting method for dealing with arrays stored in mass storage.

Exercises

20. Time 100 repetitions of the insertion sort process when sorting randomly ordered arrays of 100, 1,000, and 10,000 elements. Compare your results to those in Table 19.2.2. Confirm that insertion sort is $O(N^2)$ in this situation.

21. Time 100 repetitions of the insertion sort process when sorting reverse-sorted arrays of 100, 1,000, and 10,000 elements. Compare your results to those in Table 19.2.2. Confirm that insertion sort is $O(N)$ in this situation.

22. Modify the `InsertionSort` procedure so that it sorts the array into *nonincreasing* order.

23. Suppose that `KeyType = Char` and that the `Key` array initially contains the nine letters `HEFFALUMP`, in that order. If we call `InsertionSort( 1, 9, Key )`, then what will be the order of letters in the `Key` array after the fourth trip through the `FOR I` loop?

24. Suppose that `KeyType = Char` and that the `Key` array initially contains the eight letters `BOGOSITY`, in that order. If we call `InsertionSort( 1, 5, Key )`, then what will be the order of letters in the `Key` array after the fourth trip through the `FOR I` loop?

25. Write a recursive version of the `InsertionSort` procedure. (The subscript bounds were specified as `First` and `Last` in this section in order to make this easier.) Test your procedure by timing 100 or more repetitions when sorting 100, 1,000, and 10,000 array elements.

26. Jackson P. Slipshod has written his own "turbocharged" version of the insertion sort procedure, as shown below. What are the shortcomings of his version? Will it work? Will it really run faster than the version shown in the text?

```
CONST
   Maximum = 100;

TYPE
   IArray = ARRAY [ 1..Maximum ] OF Integer;


PROCEDURE InsertionSort( A : IArray; Limit : Integer );
VAR
   I, J : Integer;
BEGIN
   FOR I := 2 TO Limit DO
      FOR J := (I - 1) DOWNTO 1 DO
         IF A[J] > A[I] THEN
            A[J + 1] := A[J]
         ELSE
            A[J] := A[I]
END;
```

19.5 QUICKSORT

In contrast to selection sort and insertion sort, we now present a sorting method that is simple but nonetheless harder to understand and even harder to program correctly. It is called **quicksort** (spelled as one word), and was invented in 1960 by C. A. R. Hoare. When carefully tuned and used to sort randomly ordered arrays, it is the fastest-sorting method yet invented that actually compares keys. The idea behind this method is to split the array into a subarray of smaller elements and a subarray of larger elements, then to split those into subsubarrays, and so on. Thus, like binary search, it is a divide-and-conquer algorithm.

Suppose we are given the array

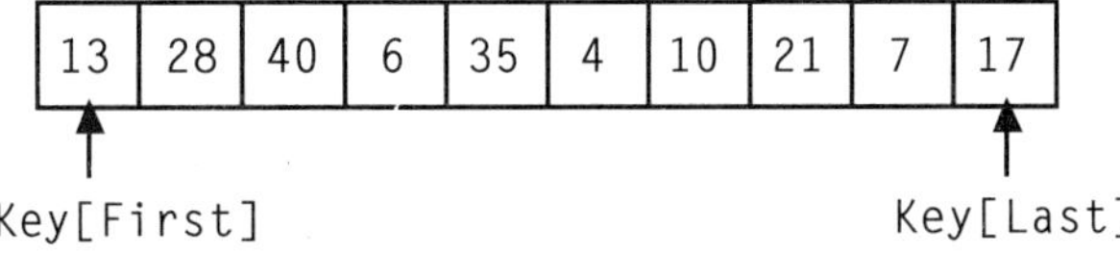

We select at random a value from the array and refer to it as the **partitioning value** or **pivot**. Suppose in the example that we pick as our pivot the first value, 13. Then we **partition** the array by rearranging its values so that all values smaller than the pivot are listed before the pivot, while all values greater than or equal to the pivot are listed after the pivot:

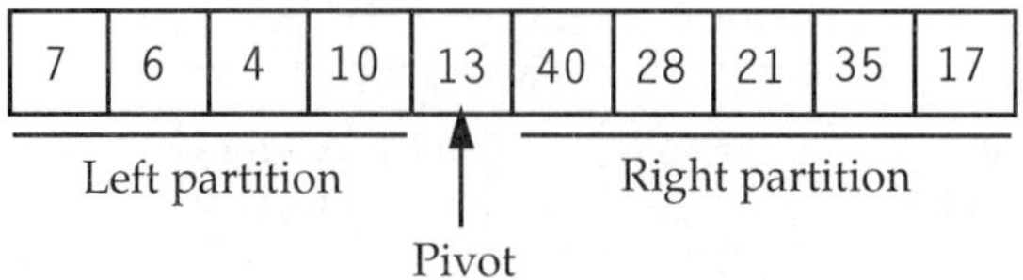

At this point, the array is said to have been partitioned. (Later, we will examine an algorithm for partitioning.) There is a *left partition* of elements smaller than the pivot and a *right partition* of elements at least as large as the pivot, and, in between, there is the pivot value itself. The pivot value is now located in its correct position relative to the elements in the left and right partitions, and *need never be moved again*. This is an important point.

Now we are faced with two smaller sorting problems: We need to sort the left partition internally, and we need to sort the right partition internally. Each of these partitions is (in this example) about half the size of the original array, so we have succeeded in breaking the original sorting problem down into a pair of half-sized sorting problems. Taking the left partition alone, we partition it as we did the entire array:

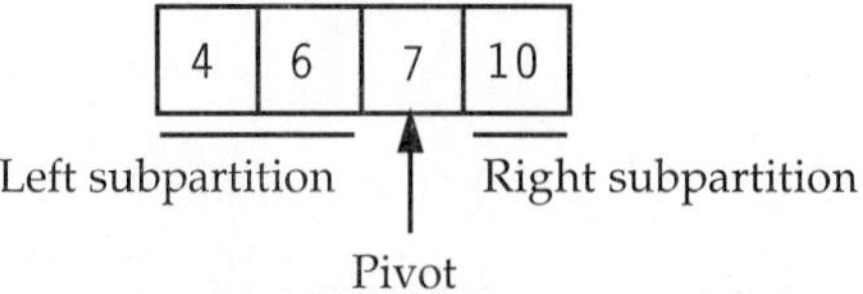

Now we have moved the partitioning element of the left partition (7, let's say) to its correct position, and split the old left partition into two subpartitions, each of which we will sort by partitioning. This continues until we eventually get down to subsubsub-partitions that are either empty or contain a single element. These require no further partitioning. At that point, the entire original left partition has been sorted.

Next we go on to sort the right partition in the same way, by partitioning it again and again. The whole algorithm is recursive and simply stated. Again we use the shorthand `Key[ First..Last ]` to stand for `Key[ First ],...,Key[ Last ]`.

Algorithm 19.5.1: QuickSort

Purpose:
To sort the array elements `Key[ First..Last ]` into nondecreasing order.

Preconditions:
`First`, `Last`, and the elements `Key[ First..Last ]` have been initialized.

Postconditions:
`Key[ First ] ≤ Key[ First+1 ] ≤...≤ Key[ Last ]`.

Steps:

If `First < Last` then

1. Select a pivot value `Pivot` and rearrange the elements in the array so that

a. `Pivot` is stored in element `Key[ PivotPos ]`, which is its final position in the to-be-sorted array.

b. The elements `Key[ First..PivotPos-1 ]` are all less than `Pivot`, which is `Key[ PivotPos ]`.

c. The elements `Key[ PivotPos+1..Last ]` are all ≥ `Pivot`, which is `Key[ PivotPos ]`.

(How we accomplish step 1 will be explained later.)

2. Recursively perform quicksort on the left partition alone.

3. Recursively perform quicksort on the right partition alone.

(The algorithm lends itself naturally to recursion; it can be implemented iteratively, but with considerably more complication.)

All of step 1 should be performed by a separate `Partition` procedure, which we describe later. With such a procedure, the `QuickSort` procedure is easy to write:

```
PROCEDURE QuickSort( VAR Key     : ArrayType;
                     First, Last : Integer );
{
  PRECONDITIONS:
  First, Last, and the elements Key[ First..Last ]
  have been initialized.

  POSTCONDITIONS:
  Key[ First ] <= Key[ First+1 ] <= . . . <= Key[ Last ].
}
VAR
   PivotPos : SubscriptRange;

BEGIN

   IF First < Last THEN
   BEGIN
      {-- Partition the array and find pivot position }
      Partition( Key, First, Last, PivotPos );
      {
        ASSERTIONS:
        First <= PivotPos <= Last;
        Key[ First..PivotPos-1 ] < Key[ PivotPos ];
        Key[ PivotPos ] <= Key[ PivotPos+1..Last ].
      }

      {-- Sort the left partition alone }
      QuickSort( Key, First, PivotPos-1 );

      {-- Sort the right partition alone }
      QuickSort( Key, PivotPos+1, Last )

   END

END; { QuickSort }
```

Of course, all the hard work has been concealed in the `Partition` procedure, which we will discuss next.

Selecting a partitioning element

As we will show later, `QuickSort` runs fastest when the partitioning process divides the array into two approximately equal partitions. This means that the pivot value should be approximately the *median value*.

Median value: That value chosen from a set such that the number of values higher than the chosen value equals the number of values lower than the chosen value. (The median is not in general the same as the mean. The mean is the arithmetic average.)

But how can we choose the median? We could write an algorithm that walks through the entire array, determining the median by counting. But this consumes considerable computing effort. (See Exercises 31 and 32 following.) At the other extreme of effort, we can simply choose any element at random; if the array is randomly ordered, each element is just as likely as any other to be the median value. This simple method is used in the following code to choose the partitioning value. On the average, it works reasonably well, only failing badly when the array is partially sorted or partially reverse-sorted. In these special cases, as we will see later, `QuickSort` will be slowed by the poor choice of the pivot.

There is, in fact, a better way. We can select any three elements at random, and then choose *the median of these three* as our pivot value. This method of choice will almost always provide us with good partitioning, and is computationally simple. It has not been used in the sample code for the sake of simplicity, but Exercise 33 mentions it.

A partitioning algorithm

The hard part of the quicksort algorithm is the partitioning, which must accomplish goals 1a, 1b, and 1c of Algorithm 19.5.1. Various algorithms have been proposed for the partitioning, but perhaps the easiest to understand is that described by Jon Bentley and ascribed by him to Nico Lomuto. (See the Bentley reference at the end of the chapter.) It is described in Algorithm 19.5.2.

Let's trace the algorithm during partitioning of the example array shown previously. If 13 is chosen as the partitioning value, then the situation as step 3 begins to look like this:

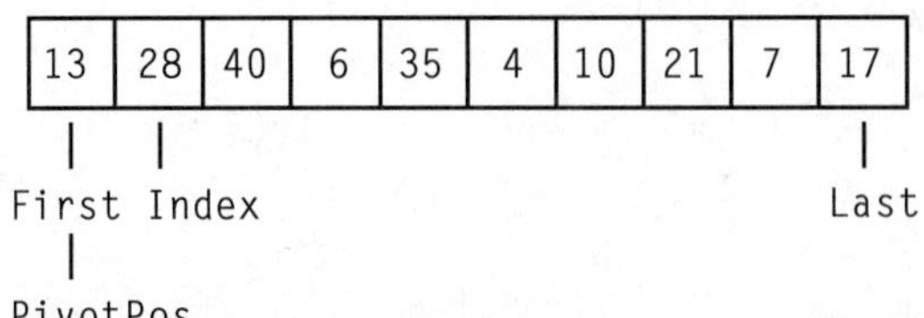

`Index` is swept through the array until it is the subscript of an element smaller than the partitioning value:

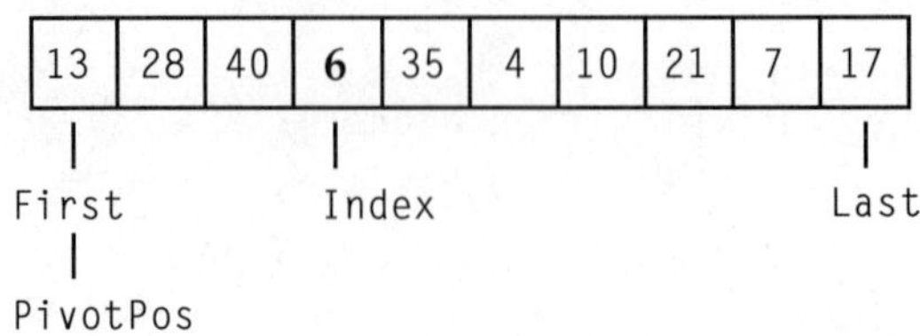

Algorithm 19.5.2: Lomuto's Method for Partitioning an Array

Purpose:
To partition `Key[ First..Last ]` so that
`Key[ First..PivotPos-1 ] < Key[ PivotPos ]`
and `Key[ PivotPos ] ≤ Key[ PivotPos+1..Last ]`.

Preconditions:
`Key[ First..Last ]` have been initialized.

Postconditions:
`Key[ First..PivotPos-1 ] < Key[ PivotPos ]`
and `Key[ PivotPos ] ≤ Key[ PivotPos+1..Last ]`.

Steps:

1. Select a suitable partitioning value and swap it into `Key[ First ]`.
2. Use an index called `PivotPos` to mark the eventual proper position of the pivot value. Initially, `PivotPos` equals `First`.
3. For all values of a running `Index` from `First + 1` to `Last`:

   If `Key[ Index ]` is less than the partitioning value,

   a. Increment `PivotPos` by `1`.

   b. Swap `Key[ Index ]` with `Key[ PivotPos ]`.
4. `PivotPos` is now at the end of the entire left partition, where the partitioning value should be. Therefore, swap `Key[First]`, which is the pivot value, with `Key[PivotPos]`.

Having found a value < 13, `PivotPos` is incremented:

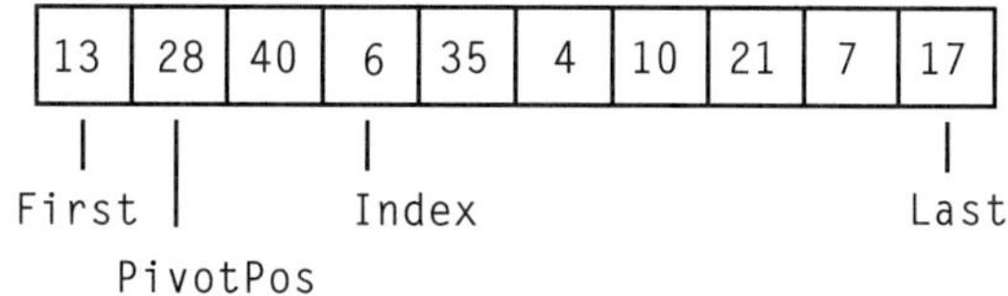

Then `Key[ Index ]` is swapped with `Key[ PivotPos ]`. Afterwards, `Index` moves on until it finds an element smaller than the pivot value:

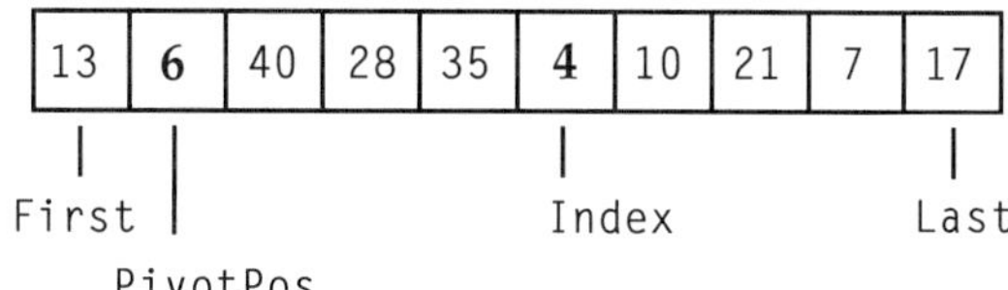

Then PivotPos is incremented again,

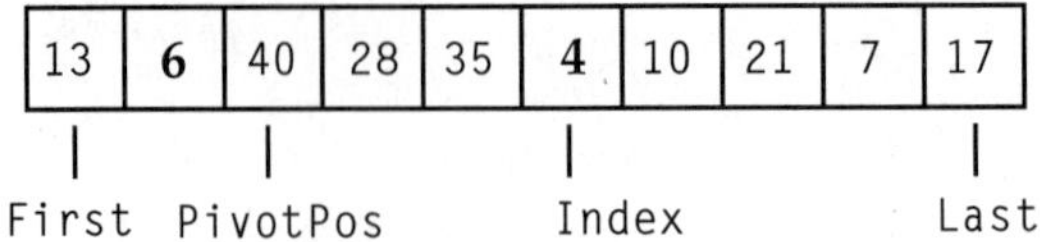

and Key[Index] is swapped with Key[PivotPos]:

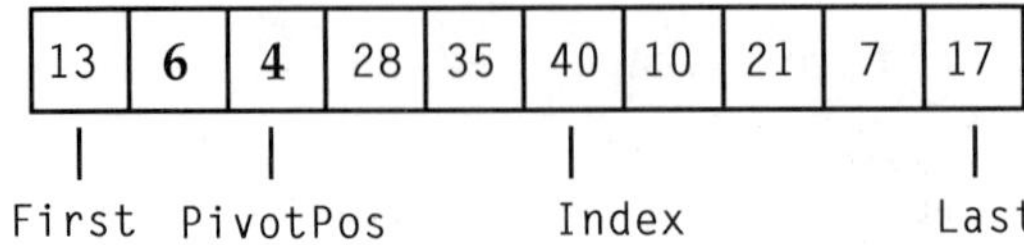

This process continues as Index moves all the way to the end of the array, after which the situation looks like this:

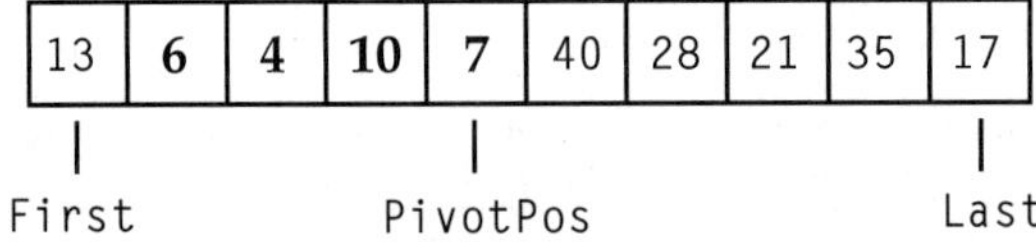

PivotPos now marks the correct position of the partitioning value, relative to the lower values on the left and the higher values on the right. So we swap the partitioning value, which is stored in Key[First], with Key[PivotPos]:

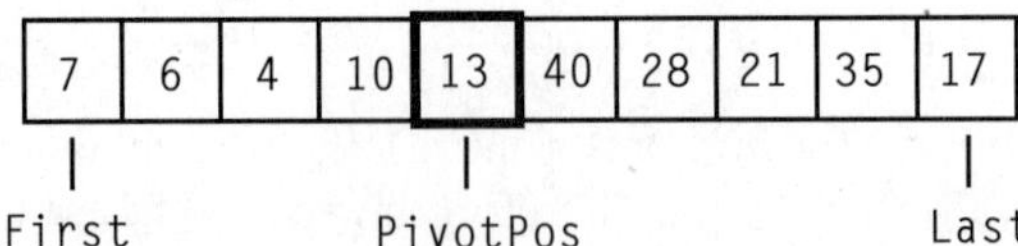

Now the array is correctly partitioned according to the three criteria listed in Algorithm 19.5.1, step 1.

A loop invariant

The significance of the loop in step 3 of Algorithm 18.5.2 is that the elements

```
Key[ First + 1..PivotPos ]
```

at that point comprise the left partition, which is gradually discovered as the loop runs. Initially, First+1 is greater than PivotPos, so none of the left partition is known. Then, each time a value smaller than the partitioning value is discovered, PivotPos is incremented and the small value is swapped into Key[PivotPos]. Thus PivotPos marks the right end of the left partition throughout the running of the loop. This fact is captured in the loop invariant

```
{
  LOOP INVARIANT:
  First <= PivotPos <= Last;
  Key[ First + 1..PivotPos ] < Pivot.
}
```

The partitioning code

The partitioning algorithm is encapsulated in its own procedure:

```
PROCEDURE Partition( VAR Key      : ArrayType;
                     First, Last  : SubscriptRange;
                     VAR PivotPos : SubscriptRange );
{
  PRECONDITIONS:
  Key[ First..Last ] have been initialized.

  POSTCONDITIONS:
  Key[ First..PivotPos-1 ] < Key[ PivotPos ]
  and Key[ PivotPos ] <= Key[ PivotPos+1..Last ].
}
VAR
   Pivot : KeyType;
   Index : SubscriptRange;

BEGIN

   {-- Choose first element as partitioning value }
   PivotPos := First;
   Pivot    := Key[ First ];

   {-- Swap all values < Pivot down to beginning of array }
   FOR Index := First+1 TO Last DO
   {
     LOOP INVARIANT:
     First <= PivotPos <= Last;
     Key[ First+1..PivotPos ] < Pivot.
   }
      IF ( Key[ Index ] < Pivot ) THEN
      BEGIN
         PivotPos := PivotPos + 1;
         Swap( Key[ PivotPos ], Key[ Index ] )
      END;
   {
     ASSERTION:
     PivotPos is now at the last position in the left partition
     or, if the left partition is empty, is the position
     of the partition value.
   }
   Swap( Key[ First ], Key[ PivotPos ] )

END; { Partition }
```

Estimating the running time of quicksort

The process of quicksorting an array is shown in Figure 19.5.1. In the diagram, the steps are numbered in the order in which they are performed, and marked with "p" for partitioning or "r" for recursion.

Figure 19.5.1 *The quicksort algorithm as described in the text, as it progressively partitions an array, recursively applying quicksort to the resulting partitions. The steps are numbered in the order of execution and marked "p" for a partitioning step or "r" for a recursion step.*

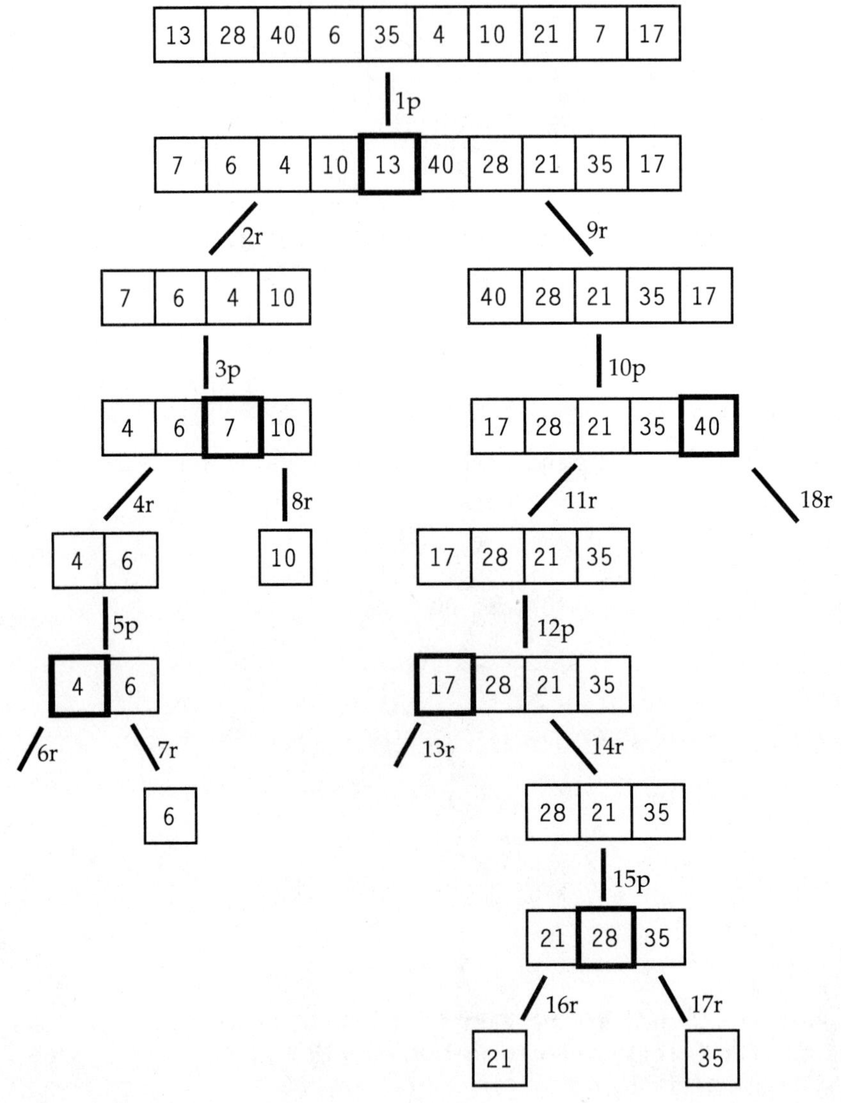

As the diagram shows in steps 10p and 12p, our choice of the first element as pivot may result in the left or right partition being empty, making the next step relatively inefficient. But with the median-of-three choice of pivot, the process partitions the array nearly in half virtually every time.

When quicksort is working at its best, the partitioning divides the current array segment roughly in half. The partitioning sweeps `Index` from `First + 1` to `Last`, requiring $N-1$ comparisons between keys. If the number of key comparisons required to sort N keys is $C(N)$, then $C(N)$ is $N-1$ plus the number of key comparisons required to sort the two half-length partitions:

$$C(N) = (N-1) + 2C(N/2)$$

This equation expresses the number of key comparisons required to sort N keys, which is $C(N)$, in terms of the number of key comparisons required to sort $N/2$ keys, which is $C(N/2)$. In other words, *it expresses the result we seek in terms of a smaller result of the same kind*. This kind of equation is called a **recurrence relation**: it plays a role in mathematics similar to the role played in computer science by recursion.

The above equation is meaningless unless $N/2$ is an integer. For algebraic simplicity, let us assume that N is not only even, but that it happens to be a power of 2. (The general problem turns out to give a similar result, but requires considerably more work.) Then there exists an integer L such that $N = 2^L$ or $L = \log_2 N$. In this case, the recurrence relation can be rewritten

$$\begin{aligned} C(2^L) &= (2^L - 1) + 2C(2^L/2) \\ &= (2^L - 1) + 2C(2^{L-1}) \end{aligned}$$

Here we pull a trick, dividing both sides by 2^L:

$$\begin{aligned} \frac{C(2^L)}{2^L} &= 1 - 2^{-L} + \frac{2}{2^L}C(2^{L-1}) \\ &= 1 - 2^{-L} + \frac{C(2^{L-1})}{2^{L-1}} \end{aligned}$$

Substituting the similar recurrence relation for $C(2^{L-1})$, we obtain

$$\frac{C(2^L)}{2^L} = (1+1) - \left[2^{-L} + 2^{1-L}\right] + \frac{C(2^{L-2})}{2^{L-2}}$$

We continue in this way by repeated recurrence until we reach the term containing $C(2^{L-L}) = C(2^0) = C(1)$:

$$\frac{C(2^L)}{2^L} = (1 + 1 + \cdots + 1) - \left(2^{-L} + 2^{1-L} + \cdots + 2^{L-1-L}\right) + C(1)$$

There are L terms in the first sum, which is therefore equal to L. The last term is $C(1)$, which is the number of key comparisons required to sort one key, or zero. Thus

$$\frac{C(2^L)}{2^L} = L - \left(\frac{1}{2^L} + \frac{1}{2^{L-1}} + \frac{1}{2^{L-2}} + \cdots + \frac{1}{2}\right)$$

The sum in parentheses is $(1/2 + 1/4 + 1/8 + \cdots + 1/N)$. When N is very large, this sum is approximately unity. This give us our final result:

$$\begin{aligned} C(N) &= C(2^L) \approx 2^L(L-1) = N(\log_2 N - 1) \\ &= N\log_2 N - N = O(N \lg N) \end{aligned}$$

We have shown, under a simplifying assumption, that the number of key comparisons required in the best case is $O(N \lg N)$, which is considerably faster than the $O(N^2)$ best performance of selection sort. The comparison is shown in Table 19.5.1.

This advantage is lost to the extent that partitioning splits the array into very unequal parts. The worst cases are when the array is initially in order or in reverse order. In these

Table 19.5.1 *Number of key comparisons required in the best cases.*

N	Quicksort, $O(N \log_2 N)$:	Selection Sort, $O(N^2)$:
100	664	10,000
1,000	9,966	1,000,000
10,000	132,877	100,000,000
100,000	1,660,964	10,000,000,000

cases, either the left or right partition is empty at every stage, and partitioning therefore serves only to remove the pivot value from the one nonempty partition. This means that every recursive call to the `QuickSort` procedure reduces the size of the problem by only a single element. Then there are $O(N)$ recursive calls, each of which requires an $O(N)$ partitioning process. The whole sorting process is therefore $O(N^2)$, on the same order as selection sort or insertion sort.

Table 19.5.2 shows actual running times of the three sorting methods when sorting arrays of random integers on a typical microcomputer. As you can see, the theoretical advantage of quicksort in such a situation is borne out in practice.

When to use quicksort

As mentioned previously, quicksort is not the method of choice when the array is nearly ordered; in such a case, insertion sort is preferred.

Quicksort is, however, faster than any other known general-purpose method when dealing with randomly ordered arrays. For this reason, it often is the method of choice for sorting large arrays that fit in main memory. Even then, quicksort should call insertion sort on partitions of less than about 25 keys.

But what about sorting arrays too large to fit in main memory? For such situations, there are *external sorting methods*, in which most of the array is kept at any given moment in an external file. The most common external method is called *merge sort*; it was explained briefly in Section 17.8 and is discussed in the lab manual. See the references at the end of this chapter.

Table 19.5.2 *Running times for sorting arrays of random integers, in seconds, on a microcomputer.*

N	Quicksort	Selection Sort	Insertion Sort
250	0.08	0.18	0.18
500	0.17	0.68	0.68
1,000	0.46	2.60	2.65
2,000	0.88	10.3	11.0
4,000	1.93	40.4	43.6

Questions

27. Why can't `First` and `Last` be of type `SubscriptType` in the `QuickSort` procedure?

28. In the `Partition` procedure, why can't `PivotPos` go out of range?

29. In Table 19.5.2, the times for selection sort and insertion sort roughly *quadruple*, and the times for quicksort more than *double*, when N doubles. Explain these observations.

Exercises

30. Show how to modify the `Partition` procedure so that `QuickSort` sorts arrays into non*increasing* order.

31. Describe an algorithm to find the *median value* in an array of N values by locating the mth-lowest value, where $m = (N + 1)$ DIV 2. Such an algorithm could be used to provide more dependable partitioning values for quicksort. (But read Exercise 32!)

32. Estimate the dependence of the running time of your algorithm in Exercise 31 on N, using big-oh notation. What does this say about the advisability of using a median-finding technique when choosing the partitioning value in quicksort?

33. What is the probability that the median of three values, chosen as described in the text, will yield an improvement over simply selecting a partitioning value at random?

34. Show that, in an already-sorted array or a reverse-sorted array, the partitioning algorithm described in the text will leave either the left or right partition empty every time, and that quicksort will therefore merely reduce the size of the array by one element during each partitioning, instead of halving it.

35. As you saw in Section 19.2, searching can be faster in an already-sorted array. For example, binary search is $O(\lg N)$, while sequential search is $O(N)$. But sorting an array takes at least $O(N \lg N)$ time, so which is faster: sequential search in an unsorted array, or quicksort followed by binary search? Explain your answer.

36. Modify `QuickSort` so that it will correctly sort into nondecreasing order, according to customer name, arrays in which the elements are of type

```
Customer = RECORD
             Name : String40;
             SSN  : String40;
             ID   : Integer
           END;
```

37. If, in the `QuickSort` procedure, `KeyType` is `Char` and `Key` is the array

G	I	B	B	E	R	I	S	H

then what is the order of the `Key` elements the third time a `QuickSort` procedure is invoked? (Careful: Notice the order of the recursive calls!)

38. The text states, in estimating the running time of `QuickSort`, that the inner loop of the `Partition` procedure sweeps `Index` from `First+1` to `Last`, and that this is an $O(N)$ process. But `QuickSort` repeatedly splits the array in half. Therefore, after the first split, partitioning is an $O(N/2)$ process; after the second split it is $O(N/4)$; and so on. So how can we say that partitioning is an $O(N)$ process?

LOOKING BACK

In this chapter, we examined some algorithms for searching and sorting arrays. We also used big-oh notation to state rough upper-bound estimates of running times as functions of the number of data values.

- Sequential search checks the N elements one by one, in sequence. This algorithm is $O(N)$.
- Binary search requires that the array is ordered. This algorithm eliminates half of the search area after each repetition, and is $O(\lg N)$. We implemented the code both recursively and iteratively.
- Selection sort (Section 14.4), when sorting into nondecreasing order, selects the lowest key in the array and swaps it into the first position. Then it selects the second-lowest key and swaps it into the second position, and so on. The algorithm is intuitive and easily coded. On the other hand, selection sort is $O(N^2)$, even in the best case. It does not benefit from existing order in the array.
- Insertion sort starts with a single key, then inserts a second key in the correct position relative to the first. Then it continues by inserting the remaining keys, one by one, in the correct positions. The algorithm is intuitive but slightly tricky to code correctly in Pascal. Insertion sort is $O(N^2)$ in the worst case, but benefits from existing order in the array. If the array is already sorted or almost sorted, insertion sort is $O(N)$. This makes it particularly well suited to sorting nearly ordered arrays.
- Quicksort operates by partitioning the array into a portion containing keys lower than the pivot key, and a portion containing keys at least as large as the pivot. When the pivot key is well-chosen, quicksort divides the array roughly in half, reducing the original sorting problem to a pair of half-sized problems. If this occurs upon every partitioning, quicksort is $O(N \lg N)$. This makes quicksort, in its best case, as fast as any known sorting method that operates by comparing keys. But quicksort does not benefit from existing order in the array; if the array is already sorted or reverse-sorted, the running time is $O(N^2)$.

All of these are *internal methods* since they process the entire array in main memory.

TERMS EMPHASIZED IN THIS CHAPTER

PROJECTS

1. Rewrite the recursive `BinarySearch` procedure so that it will work with any ordinal subscripts, not just integer subscripts.

2. Add code to the iterative version of the `BinarySearch` procedure so that if `SearchKey` is not found, the procedure returns the `Location` where `SearchKey` could be inserted in the array, maintaining the nondecreasing order. Note that the present version of the procedure nearly does this; you need only add an additional decision structure at the end of the procedure. Test your modified procedure.

3. Similarly modify the recursive version of the `BinarySearch` procedure. Test your modified procedure.

4. The sequential search algorithm could be made to benefit from an already-sorted array of the type used in binary search. If the searched array were in nondecreasing order, sequential search could be made to stop and report failure as soon as it encountered an element larger than `SearchKey`. Design, code, and test such an improvement. Also estimate the best- and worst-case behaviors of such an algorithm, using big-oh notation. Is the order-of-magnitude behavior improved?

5. Write a recursive version of the sequential search algorithm.

6. Write a `SequentialSearch` procedure that finds either the first or last occurrence of a given `SearchKey`, depending upon the value of a suitable parameter. It's up to you to design the parameter so that your procedure is easy and natural to use.

7. Redesign the recursive binary search procedure so that it outputs a list of *all* occurrences of a given search value in the array.

8. Many Pascal systems provide a way to measure the running time of a procedure. Determine how to do this on your system and then time both sequential search and binary search when searching for a key at the ends of some rather large arrays. Try this with large arrays increasing in size by factors of 2, then compile a table of your times as functions of the sizes of the arrays. Do your data confirm the running time estimates given in the text?

9. Write a program that reads a positive integer from the keyboard, then writes that many pseudorandom numbers to an external file. Then time the `InsertionSort` and `QuickSort` procedures as they sort the random numbers from this file. (Be careful not to include the time it takes the program to read the numbers from the file.) Time your programs when sorting 500, 1,000, 2,000, and 4,000 numbers, and plot all your results on a graph. Also time both methods when sorting 500, 1,000, 2,000, and 4,000 already-sorted numbers. Plot the results. Do your results confirm the predictions in this chapter?

10. Arrays often contain composite elements like records. If we are keeping employee records for some company, we might have these declarations:

```
CONST
   First     = 1;     { First array subscript }
   Last      = 5000;  { Last array subscript  }
   StrLength = 40;

TYPE
   EmployeeRange = First..Last;
   FixedString   = PACKED ARRAY [1..StrLength] OF Char;
   EmployeeRec   =
        RECORD
           Name   : FixedString;
           SSN    : FixedString;
           Title  : FixedString;
           Months : Integer;
           Salary : Real
        END;
   EmployeeArray = ARRAY [EmployeeRange]
                      OF EmployeeRec;

VAR
   Employee : EmployeeArray;
```

Write a program that searches an `EmployeeArray` for a given Social Security number, using the declarations above and a recursive binary search procedure.

11. Write a procedure that reports the position and value of the median value of three elements, as described in the text. Integrate your procedure with the `QuickSort` code shown in the text, and test your modified sorting program.

12. Implement an external merge sort, as discussed in Section 17.8. Use the `Merge` procedure that appears there.

REFERENCES

The classic reference on searching and sorting is Donald E. Knuth's *The Art of Computer Programming: Volume 3 / Sorting and Searching* (Addison-Wesley Publishing, 1973). Every professional programmer should study this encyclopedic reference.

Two more recent algorithms texts are also helpful. Robert Sedgewick's *Algorithms,* second edition (Addison-Wesley Publishing, 1988), is a standard reference. Sedgewick has done important research on quicksorting and gives a full treatment in his book, along with good comparisons of various sorting methods. The second edition also benefits from innovative illustrations created with the help of Marc Brown. Sara Baase's *Computer Algorithms,* second edition (Addison-Wesley Publishing, 1988), provides a very complete and cogent analysis of running times.

Jon Bentley's engaging little book *Programming Pearls* (Addison-Wesley Publishing, 1986) contains two very clear and very interesting discussions of binary search. The first, called "Writing Correct Programs" (pages 35–45), discusses the difficulty of getting subtle algorithms like this one to work correctly in all cases. The second, on pages 85–88, describes tuning it for maximum speed. In Chapter 10, Bentley gives one of the more lucid treatments of quicksort. Our treatment of Lomuto's partitioning algorithm was based on this source.

An especially clear introduction to big-oh notation appears in Susanna S. Epp's *Discrete Mathematics with Applications* (Wadsworth Publishing, 1990). A more advanced treatment can be found in Ronald L. Graham, Donald E. Knuth, and Oren Patashnik's *Concrete Mathematics: A Foundation for Computer Science* (Addison-Wesley Publishing, 1989).

Technology Is Burning the Social Fabric.

[A] workman I know, employed in Paris by a friend of mine, . . . frequently repairs the machines that abound in my friend's laboratory. When a particularly complicated piece of American equipment broke down, this old workman, skilled in mechanics, offered to fix the broken part or make a new one. When he came back the next day there were tears in the old man's eyes. "This is the first time in my life I have to admit I cannot manufacture something. This part, sir, was not made by a human being!" The device he held in his hand had been cut by a computer-guided tool, where the angle of the blade had to change as a function of the cutting. More than the fear of seeing his skill become obsolete, this workman had experienced the terror of realizing that man could not even duplicate the perfection created by the computer.

The machines, I thought that day . . ., were moving too fast for our language, and were creating too many new concepts for the cultures that hosted them. It was the kind of acceleration that America might be able to tolerate and absorb, but the kind that older cultures would be able to integrate only at the price of their social structures and their modes of thought. What the white man did to the Native American, the computer was doing to the cultures of Europe: the technology was accelerating, and in the process was burning the social fabric that supported it.

—Jacques Vallee, *The Network Revolution: Confessions of a Computer Scientist* (AND/OR Press, 1982), pages 84–85.

CHAPTER

20

Pointers and Dynamic Data Structures

CHAPTER CONTENTS

INTRODUCTION

In this chapter, we introduce a fundamentally different kind of variable, one that is used to store the memory address of another variable. Variables used to store addresses rather than conventional values are called **pointer variables**, or **pointers** for short. Pascal has special ways of declaring, initializing, and manipulating pointers, as we will see.

Pointer (**pointer variable**): A storage cell used to store the address of another storage cell.

We use a pointer to find the storage cell whose address is stored in the pointer. In other words, the pointer is not usually what we are interested in; we are usually interested in the cell pointed to. The distinction between the pointer variable and the variable pointed to is an important one, but one that is easily confused. We will emphasize this distinction throughout the chapter.

The reason for using pointers is that they make possible data structures that come into existence, grow, shrink, and even disappear while the program is running. These are called **dynamic data structures**, and we will be discussing them here and in Chapter 21.

20.1 POINTERS AND THINGS POINTED TO

A **pointer variable** is used to store the memory address of another variable. For example, Figure 20.1.1 shows a diagram of a pointer called `CharPtr` that is used to store the address of a character variable, which in turn stores the letter `'A'`.

A pointer variable is said to **point to** another variable. We indicate this by drawing an arrow, as shown in Figure 20.1.2. The arrow is merely shorthand for the address storage shown in the first diagram.

Declaring pointers

The pointer shown in these diagrams is for storing the address of a character variable. *When a pointer variable is declared, the type of storage to which it points must be declared.* For example, we can declare a pointer to a character variable, a pointer to an array of integers, a pointer to a record, or whatever. We can even declare pointer variables that point to other pointers. To declare a pointer, we use a special notation in which the symbol ^ means "points to." Here are some examples:

```
TYPE
   IntArray    = ARRAY [ 1..50 ] OF Integer;
   EmployeeRec = RECORD
                    Name : String40;
                    SSN  : String40;
                    Salary : Real
                 END;

   CharacterPointer   = ^Char;
   IntArrayPointer    = ^IntArray;
   EmployeeRecPointer = ^EmployeeRec;

VAR
   CharPtr : CharacterPointer;
   IAPtr   : IntArrayPointer;
   ERPtr   : EmployeeRecPointer;
```

As mentioned in Section 17.5, the symbol ^ is the usual character representing the standard Pascal ↑, pronounced "up-arrow." The notation `^Char` means "pointer to

Figure 20.1.1 *A pointer stores the address of a storage cell. Here, a character pointer is storing the address of a character variable.*

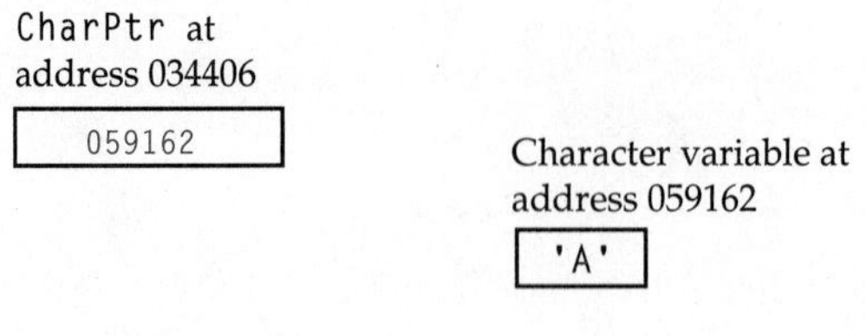

Figure 20.1.2

A pointer is said to "point to" another variable when it contains that variable's address. This is indicated by an arrow.

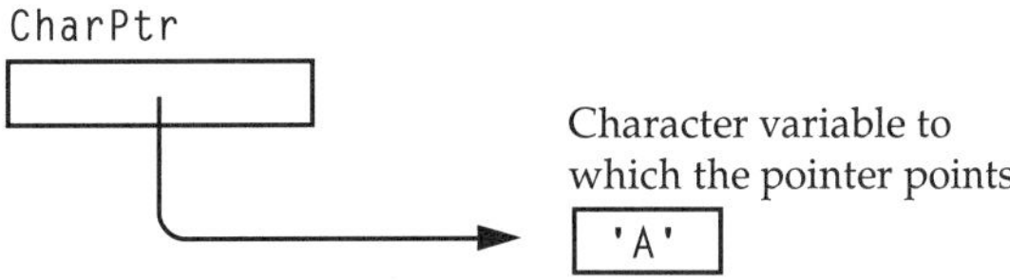

Char." According to these declarations, CharPtr is a pointer to a character variable, IAPtr is a pointer to an IntArray, and ERPtr is a pointer to an EmployeeRec.

However, if CharPtr contains the address of a character variable, *what is the name of the character variable whose address it contains?* In the declarations above, there is no direct declaration of a character variable. The answer is that CharPtr points to a character variable whose name is given only as "character variable to which CharPtr points." In Pascal, this is written CharPtr^. In other words,

- CharPtr^ is the name of the variable whose address is stored in CharPtr;
- IAPtr^ is the name of the variable whose address is stored in IAPtr;
- ERPtr^ is the name of the variable whose address is stored in ERPtr.

The variables to which the pointers point are said to be **anonymous**, because they have no declared names of their own. They can be accessed or **referenced** only through the pointers that point to them. To refer to a variable by putting a ^ after the name of the corresponding pointer name is called **dereferencing** the pointer. For example, we can refer to the variable pointed to by CharPtr only by dereferencing CharPtr, which means that we write CharPtr^ as the name of the variable pointed to.

Reference: (verb) To refer to; to access by name. (noun) A name or symbol for an entity that is accessed.

Dereference: To derive from the name of a pointer a reference to the variable pointed to, by writing a circumflex (^) after the name of the pointer.

Syntax for Pointer Declaration

→ TYPE → *PointerType* → = → ^ → *TypeName* → ;

Pseudocode:

TYPE
    PointerType = ^*TypeName*;

VAR
    PointerVariable : *PointerType*;

or (short form)

VAR
    PointerVariable : ^*TypeName*;

These declarations create *PointerVariable*, a variable that can store the address of a storage cell of the type called *TypeName*. The declaration of *PointerVariable* creates only the pointer itself; it does not create a storage cell for *PointerVariable* to point to.

What exists, and when does it exist?

Static: Existing throughout the execution of the declaring block.

When a pointer variable is declared in a block, it exists—its memory is allocated—as soon as the block begins executing, and it continues to exist throughout the execution of the block. In this sense, a pointer is like the other variables you studied previously. Its memory allocation is said to be **static** because it exists throughout the execution of the declaring block, unlike the variable to which the pointer points. This is an important point:

> The declaration of a pointer creates the pointer, but not the variable pointed to.

Furthermore, a declared pointer variable is not initialized automatically; in Standard Pascal, it contains garbage until we initialize it deliberately.

Initializing pointers

One of the peculiar things about pointers is that only one pointer constant is predefined: The constant `NIL`, a reserved word, means "pointer to nothing." `NIL` is defined to be a constant of any pointer type: pointer to `Char`, pointer to `IntArray`, or whatever. So we can initialize our example variables by writing

```
BEGIN
   CharPtr := NIL;
   IAPtr   := NIL;
   ERPtr   := NIL;
```

Having initialized the pointers this way, we can diagram the fact that they point to nothing by drawing a slash through the box, as shown in Figure 20.1.3. (Some books instead use an electrical ground symbol to indicate a `NIL` pointer value.)

The New procedure

A pointer can be made to point to a variable or data structure in only one way: by using Pascal's standard `New` procedure to create such a variable or data structure. For example, the statement

```
   New( CharPtr );
```

calls the `New` procedure to operate on `CharPtr`, and this accomplishes two things:

- It allocates a new variable of the type that `CharPtr` can point to (in this case, a `Char` variable).
- It loads the address of that new variable into `CharPtr`.

Figure 20.1.3 *Pointers initialized to NIL.*

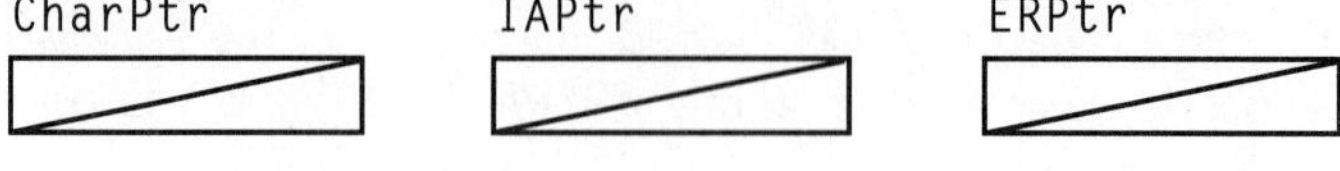

Figure 20.1.4

The New procedure creates an anonymous variable and makes the specified pointer point to it, but the newly created variable is not initialized by the New procedure.

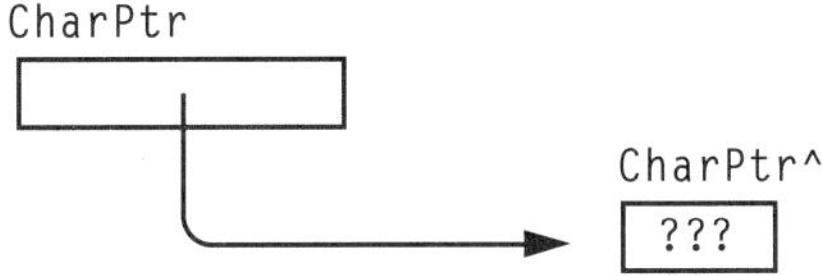

Running `New` does not initialize the new variable created, however: that variable still contains garbage. After executing `New(CharPtr)`, `CharPtr` contains the address of the new, uninitialized variable—that is, it "points to" that new variable. The name of the new variable created by `New` is `CharPtr^`, meaning "the variable pointed to by `CharPtr`." This is shown in Figure 20.1.4.

Disposing of a variable that is pointed to

Pascal also provides a matching procedure that de-allocates a pointed-to variable, freeing up its storage area for other use. This procedure is called `Dispose`. For example, the statement

```
Dispose( CharPtr );
```

de-allocates the memory being used by the character variable to which `CharPtr` points, *leaving the value of the pointer undefined,* as shown in Figure 20.1.5. (In some Pascal systems, the de-allocation may not happen immediately or even at all. Check your reference manual.)

Afterwards, if the pointer is not to be reinitialized with `New`, we should assign `NIL` to it to indicate that it points to nothing. After executing

```
CharPtr := NIL;
```

the situation can be diagrammed as shown in Figure 20.1.6.

Assigning a value to a pointed-to variable

Once a pointed-to variable has been created with the `New` procedure, we can assign a value to it. Here is an example in which we create a variable for `CharPtr1` to point to, and then assign a value to the pointed-to variable, `CharPtr1^`:

Figure 20.1.5

After Dispose discards a variable that was pointed to, the pointer has an undefined value.

CharPtr

?????

Figure 20.1.6 *After calling Dispose to de-allocate the storage cell to which CharPtr points, and then assigning NIL to CharPtr.*

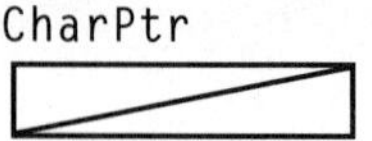


```
TYPE
   CharacterPointer = ^Char;

VAR
   CharPtr1, CharPtr2 : CharacterPointer;

BEGIN
   New( CharPtr1 );     { Creates CharPtr1^ }
   CharPtr1^ := 'A';    { Assigns 'A' to CharPtr1^ }
```

The resulting situation is shown in Figure 20.1.7.

Copying one pointer into another

The value of one pointer may be copied into another *of the same type* by assigning it. If, in our example, we execute

```
CharPtr2 := CharPtr1;
```

we have both `CharPtr2` and `CharPtr1` containing the address of `CharPtr1^`. This is shown in Figure 20.1.8. Since both `CharPtr2` and `CharPtr1` now point to the variable containing `'A'`, this variable can be referred to either as `CharPtr1^` or `CharPtr2^`.

Figure 20.1.7 *Now CharPtr1 points to CharPtr1^, which has been assigned the value 'A'.*

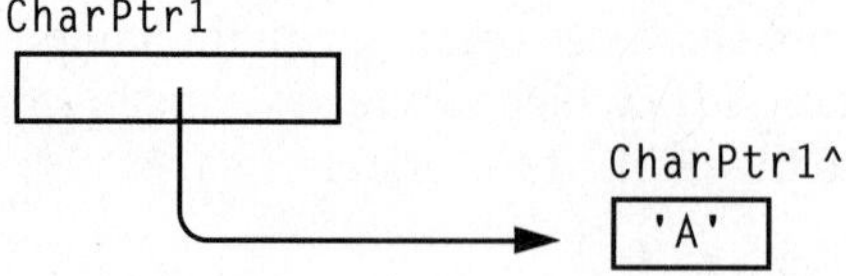

Figure 20.1.8

After CharPtr1 is copied into CharPtr2, both pointers point to the same variable.

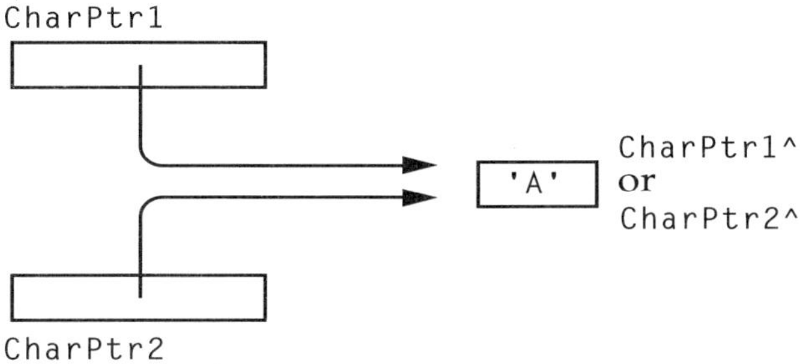

"Losing" a pointed-to variable

One of the dangers with pointed-to variables is the ease with which we can accidentally misplace the variable and not be able to find it again. For example, suppose that the code above is followed by

```
CharPtr1 := NIL;
CharPtr2 := CharPtr1;
```

Now neither of the pointers contains the address of the character variable, and we no longer have a way to find the variable or to access it. For all practical purposes, the variable has been lost, although memory is still allocated for it. The situation is shown in Figure 20.1.9.

Static versus dynamic allocation

In earlier chapters, we dealt only with storage cells that were allocated as the declaring block started running. Such cells are said to be **statically allocated**, because they exist throughout the lifetime of the block. Pointer variables, like the variables we've studied earlier, are statically allocated.

Figure 20.1.9

After NIL has been assigned to CharPtr1 and CharPtr2, these pointers no longer point to anything. The character variable still exits, but cannot be accessed because there is no way to reference it.

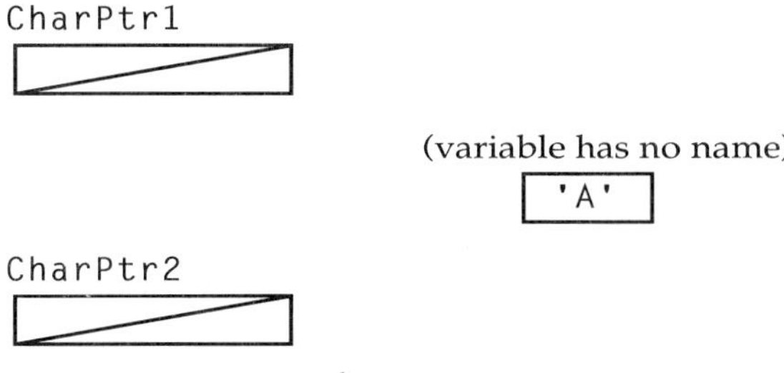

Variables to which pointers can point are created by the `New` procedure, and disposed of by the `Dispose` procedure, while the block is executing. Such variables are said to be **dynamically allocated and de-allocated**. With these new abilities, we will be able to use exciting new data types that come into existence and grow, shrink, and even disappear under program control.

Exercises

1. Suppose that we have the declarations

```
TYPE
    Index = 0..9;
    IndexPointer = ^Index;

VAR
   I    : Index;
   IPtr : IndexPointer;
```

a. Then what does `IPtr` contain?

b. If we then execute the code

```
New( IPtr );
IPtr^ := 2;
I := 4;
```

then what does `IPtr` contain? What does `IPtr^` contain?

2. After executing the code fragment

```
TYPE
   Thing = Integer;
   ThingPointer = ^Thing;

VAR
   T, TT : Thing;
   TPtr, TTPtr : ThingPointer;

BEGIN
   TPtr := NIL;
   New( TTPtr );
```

which of the following variables contain garbage?

a. `TPtr`

b. `TTPtr`

c. `T`

d. `TT`

e. `TPtr^`

f. `TTPtr^`

3. Draw a pointer diagram showing the initialization situation after executing the code fragment in Exercise 2.

4. If, after executing the code in Exercise 2, the program also executes the code TTPtr^ := 3; then what is the initialization situation? Draw a pointer diagram.

5. Suppose that

```
VAR
   It : ^Char;
```

Then is it legal to call `New( It^ )`? What about `New( It )`? Explain.

6. Suppose that

```
TYPE
   Puzzle = Real;
   PuzP   = ^Puzzle;

VAR
   P1, P2 : PuzP;
```

Then which of the following statements are legal?

a. `P1 := 1.1;`

b. `P1 := 1.1^;`

c. `New( P1 );`

d. `P1 := NIL;`

e. `P1^ := 1.1;`

f. `New( P1^ );`

g. `P1^ := 1.1;`

h. `P2 := P1;`

i. `P2 := ^1.1;`

j. `P2 := ^P1;`

k. `WriteLn( P1 );`

l. `WriteLn( P1^ );`

7. What does the following program print?

```
PROGRAM Whazzup( Output );
TYPE
   CPointer = ^Char;

VAR
   P1, P2 : CPointer;

BEGIN
   New( P1 );
   New( P2 );
   P1^ := 'A';
   P2^ := 'B';
   P1 := P2;
   WriteLn( P1^ );
   WriteLn( P2^ )

END.
```

20.2 A LIST ADT INTERFACE

One of the most important applications of pointers is in implementing a data structure called a **list**. A list is an ordered sequence of items, structured in such a way that each item but the first has a unique predecessor and each item but the last has a unique successor. The beginning and end of the list are called the **head** and **tail**, respectively.

List operations are shown in the specification below. This is intended only as a minimal subset of useful list operations; many others are desirable in applications.

List Abstract Data Type Specification

Data structure:
A linear sequence of items in which each item except the first has a unique predecessor, and each item except the last has a unique successor.

Operations:
- Create an empty list.
- Insert a new item at the head of a list.
- Insert a new item at the tail of a list.
- Delete the head item from a list.
- Delete the tail item from a list.
- Append a list at the end of another list.
- Check for an empty list.
- Check for a full list.
- Count the number of items in a list.
- Retrieve the *n*th item in a list.
- Find the first instance of a given item in a list, if present.
- Display the items in a list, in sequence.
- Replace a list with a list containing all but the first item of the original list.

Picturing lists

The list is such an important and fundamental data structure that in some programming languages like LISP(LISt-Processing language), it is *the* data structure. It is, in fact, so fundamental that other needed data structures can be built from it.

Conceptually, a list can be thought of as a sequence in which each item carries information about where the next item is. For example, the alphabetized list containing the names "Edsger Dijkstra," "Donald Knuth," and "Alan Turing" can be pictured as

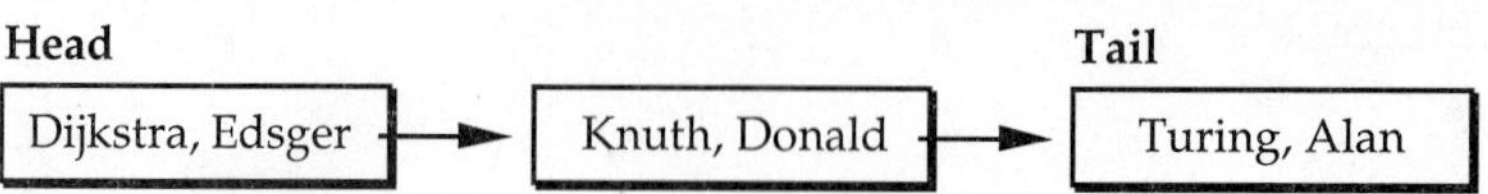

Here the arrows are meant to indicate only that each item carries some kind of information telling where to find the next item. No specific representation for doing this has been presented at this point; the list might actually be stored in a singly dimensioned array, as we did in Chapters 14 and 15, or it may use pointers in some way. *Our goal is to define a list ADT interface that is independent of the implementation that is used.*

Note that a list, defined in this way, is a *one-way sequence* of items. From a given item in the list, we can travel to the **successor item**, but not to the **predecessor item**. This will cause a few problems that we will address later.

The main defect of lists represented as arrays is, as we saw in Chapters 14–16, that operations like insertion and deletion of items are relatively difficult. One of our goals is to find a list implementation that facilitates such operations.

Another drawback of arrays is that they are *statically allocated*: Their memory cells must be allocated before the program runs and before the program determines how much memory will really be needed during the run. As a result, the programmer must always design the array to hold the maximum number of items that will ever be needed, even if most runs require much less. We can avoid this by proper use of pointers and dynamic allocation, which will allow us to allocate memory as it is needed while the program is executing.

Writing the interface

Before we consider an improved implementation for lists, we first write the ADT's interface, since this acts as a set of detailed specifications for the implementation—blueprints, so to speak. Here is the interface, as it translates into Pascal from the initial rough specifications:

```
{************************************************}
{ TYPE                                           }
{    DataType : Type of data stored in a list,   }
{               perhaps structured.              }
{    List     : A sequence of DataType.          }
{************************************************}
TYPE
   DataType  = String40;  { or whatever }
   NonNegInt = 0..MaxInt;

   { List = opaque type }

{************************************************}
{ Makes Head an empty list.                      }
{************************************************}
PROCEDURE CreateEmptyList( VAR Head : List );
{
  POSTCONDITION:
  Head is an empty list.
}
```

```
{************************************************}
{ Copies the Nth datum of Head list into D.      }
{************************************************}
PROCEDURE RetrieveNth( Head  : List;
                       N     : NonNegInt;
                       VAR D : DataType;
                       VAR Found : Boolean );
{
  PRECONDITIONS:
  Head and N have been initialized.

  POSTCONDITIONS:
  If N <= ListLength( Head ),
     Found = True and D contains a copy of
     Nth datum of Head list;
  otherwise,
     Found = False and D is unchanged.
}


{************************************************}
{ Reports position of Target in Head list;       }
{ if Target not present, reports zero.           }
{************************************************}
FUNCTION Position( Head   : List;
                   Target : DataType ) : NonNegInt;
{
  PRECONDITIONS:
  Head and Target have been initialized.

  POSTCONDITIONS:
  If Target is present in Head list,
     returns cardinal position of Target;
  otherwise,
     returns 0.
}


{************************************************}
{ Adds NewData at the front of the Head list.    }
{ The length of the list increases by one.       }
{************************************************}
PROCEDURE InsertAtHead( VAR Head : List;
                        NewData  : DataType );
{
  PRECONDITIONS:
  Head and NewData have been initialized.

  POSTCONDITIONS:
  NewData has been appended to front of Head list.
}
```

```
{***********************************************}
{ Adds NewData at the end of the Head list.     }
{ The length of the list increases by one.      }
{***********************************************}
PROCEDURE InsertAtTail( VAR Head : List;
                        NewData  : DataType );
{
  PRECONDITIONS:
  Head and NewData have been initialized.

  POSTCONDITIONS:
  NewData has been appended to end of Head list.
}


{***********************************************}
{ Deletes the first item of the Head list if the }
{ list is not empty. If list empty, does nothing. }
{ The length of the list decreases by 1 unless  }
{ the list was already empty.                   }
{***********************************************}
PROCEDURE DeleteHead( VAR Head : List );
{
  PRECONDITION:
  Head has been initialized.

  POSTCONDITIONS:
  Previous first item of list, if any, has been deleted.
}

{***********************************************}
{ Deletes the last item of the Head list if the }
{ list is not empty. If list empty, does nothing. }
{ The length of the list decreases by 1 unless  }
{ the list was already empty.                   }
{***********************************************}
PROCEDURE DeleteTail( VAR Head : List );
{
  PRECONDITION:
  Head has been initialized.

  POSTCONDITIONS:
  Previous last item of list, if any, has been deleted.
}
```

```
{************************************************}
{ Adds List2 to the end of the Head list.        }
{************************************************}
PROCEDURE AppendList( VAR Head : List;
                      List2    : List );
{
  PRECONDITION:
  Head and List2 have been initialized.

  POSTCONDITIONS:
  List2 list has been added to end of Head list.
}

{************************************************}
{ Reports whether Head is empty.                 }
{************************************************}
FUNCTION ListIsEmpty( Head : List ) : Boolean;
{
  PRECONDITION:
  Head has been initialized.

  POSTCONDITIONS:
  Returns True if Head list contains no items;
  otherwise, returns False.
}

{************************************************}
{ Reports whether Head is full: that is, whether }
{ it is unable to accept more items.             }
{************************************************}
FUNCTION ListIsFull( Head : List ) : Boolean;
{
  PRECONDITION:
  Head has been initialized.

  POSTCONDITIONS:
  Returns True if Head cannot add more items;
  otherwise, returns False.
}

{************************************************}
{ Reports the number of items in Head list.      }
{************************************************}
FUNCTION ListLength( Head : List ) : NonNegInt;
{
  PRECONDITIONS:
  Head has been initialized.

  POSTCONDITIONS:
  Returns number of items in Head list.
}
```

```
{************************************************}
{ Displays items of list in sequence on screen.  }
{************************************************}
PROCEDURE DisplayList( Head : List );
{
  PRECONDITION:
  Head has been initialized.

  POSTCONDITIONS:
  All items in Head list have been displayed
  in sequence on the screen.
}

{************************************************}
{ Returns list containing all but first item of  }
{ original list.                                 }
{************************************************}
PROCEDURE ButFirst( VAR Head : List );
{
  PRECONDITION:
  Head has been initialized.

  POSTCONDITIONS:
  Head is now the list containing all but the first item
  of the original list.
}
```

These procedures and functions all refer to a list in terms of its `Head`. There may actually be other items in front of the `Head` item, but looking at the list from the `Head` item, these subprograms can only see "downstream," toward the tail item.

Note too that `Retrieve` and `RetrieveNth` are written as procedures rather than functions because they return `DataType`, which may be composite. Composite types cannot be returned by Pascal functions.

It is also worth mentioning that a parameter of type `List` is shown as a `VAR` parameter only when the procedure modifies it. As far as you can see from the ADT's interface, lists can be sent to or from procedures without concern about the speed of transfer. We will, in fact, be able to find an ADT implementation that justifies this.

20.3 CASE STUDY: LINKED LIST ADT

We seek a list implementation that allows easy insertion and deletion in lists, and memory allocation for list components only as needed at runtime. We can achieve all this by using a dynamically allocated data structure in which each list component contains a pointer to the next. In such an implementation, the items are called **nodes**, the nodes are said to be **linked**, and they hook up to form a **linked list**. Here is a sample declaration for a list storing people's names:

Node: A component of a linked data structure. A node contains a data item plus one or more links to other nodes.

```
TYPE
   DataType = RECORD
                 LastName  : String20;
                 FirstName : String20
              END;

   List = ^Node;
   Node = RECORD
             Data : DataType;
             Link : List;
          END;

VAR
   Name : List;
```

Note the *mutually recursive* nature of `List`: a `List` points to a `Node`, which points to another `List`. (This is the sense in which nodes are *linked*: Each node points to the next.) The form of the `List` declaration is interesting, too, because it refers to `Node`, which is declared afterwards. Pascal allows a pointer to be declared to point to an object declared later in the same group of type declarations, so that we can build linked structures like this one.

The declarations allocate memory only for a pointer variable called `Name`, *not* for a `Node`. The pointer initially contains garbage and must be initialized deliberately. After the variable declaration, here's what we have:

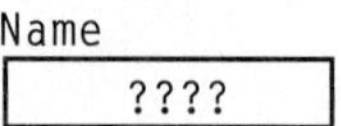

Creating an empty list

To create a new empty list, we assign `NIL` to the list pointer, so that the pointer points to nothing. This is the job of the `CreateEmptyList` procedure:

```
PROCEDURE CreateEmptyList( VAR Head : List );
{
  POSTCONDITION:
  Head is an empty list.
}
BEGIN

   Head := NIL

END; { CreateEmptyList }
```

After executing `CreateEmptyList( Name )`, the list really *is* empty since no nodes have been allocated in memory:

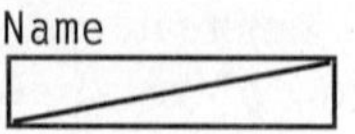

Inserting a node at the head of an empty list

Suppose we want a name list containing only the name "Alan Turing." To get it, we call `InsertAtHead`, sending to the procedure an empty list and the name to be inserted. The procedure adds a node to the empty list in three steps:

1. Call `New( Head )` to allocate a node's worth of memory and make `Head` point to it. The new node is called `Head^`, or "the thing that `Head` points to."

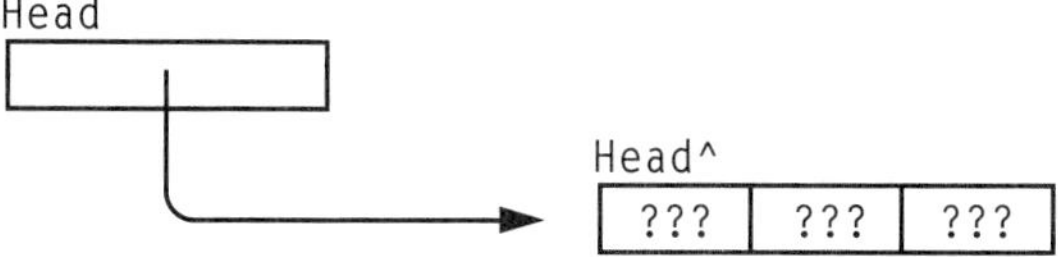

2. Copy `'Alan'` into `Head^.FirstName` and `'Turing'` into `Head^.LastName`.

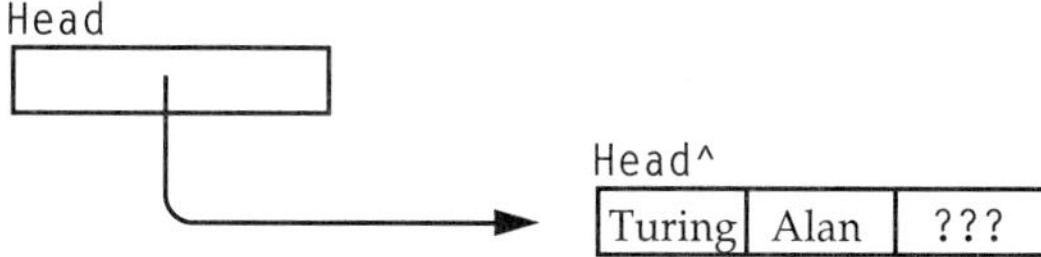

3. Set `Head^.Link`, the `Link` field of the new node, to `NIL` so that it points to nothing.

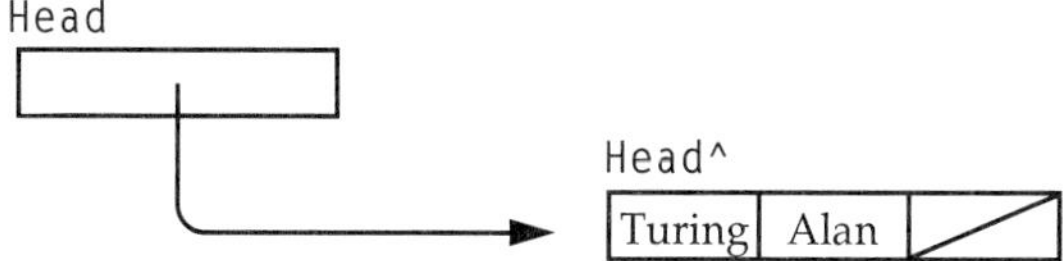

Inserting another node at the head of the list

To add a second node in front of the node shown above, we carry out four steps similar to those in the previous process. Suppose that the new node is to contain the name "Edsger Dijkstra":

1. Copy `Head` into a local variable called `ExistingList`. Now `Head` and `ExistingList` point to the one existing node.

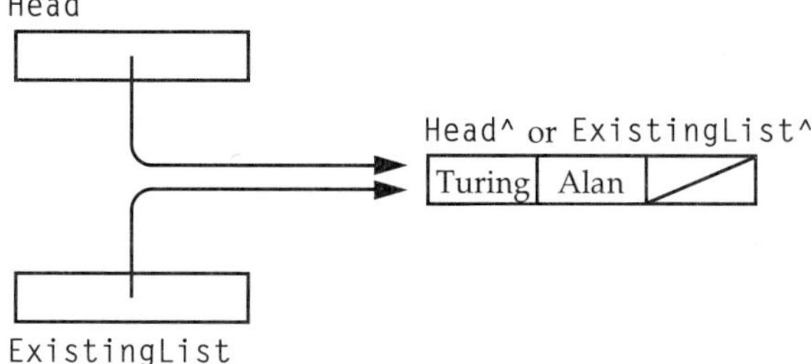

2. By calling `New( Head )`, allocate a node's worth of memory and make `Head` point to it.

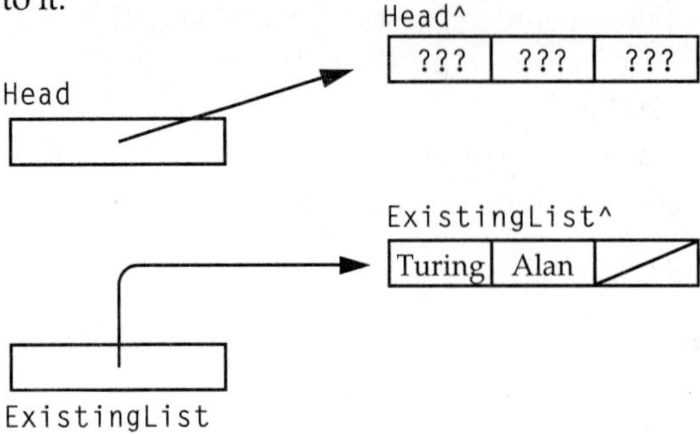

3. Copy "Edsger Dijkstra" into the new node's `Data` fields:

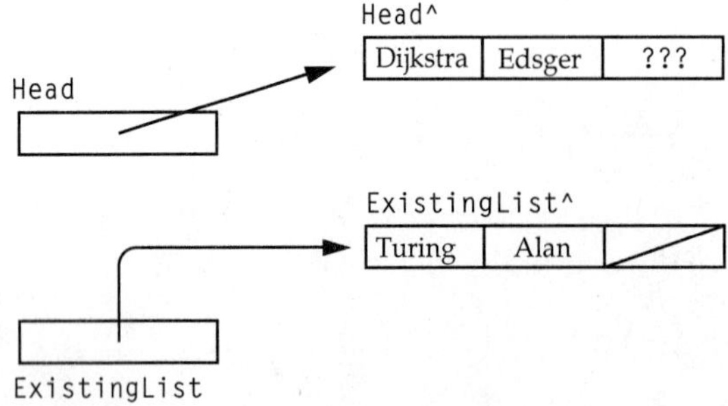

4. Copy the `ExistingList` pointer into the `Link` field of the new node.

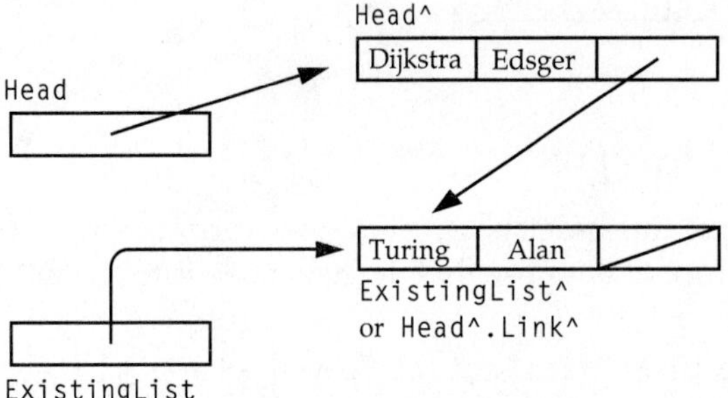

The resulting diagram can be redrawn to make it easier to read:

Noticing the similarity between the steps for inserting before an empty list and those for inserting before a nonempty list, we discover that the latter code works for both cases:

```
PROCEDURE InsertAtHead( VARHead : List;
                        NewData  : DataType );
{
  PRECONDITION:
  Head and NewData have been initialized.

  POSTCONDITIONS:
  A new node containing a copy of NewData has been
  added at the head of the list, before previously
  existing nodes.
}
VAR
   ExistingList : List;

BEGIN

   {-- Copy the Head pointer }
   ExistingList := Head;

   {-- Allocate new node, make Head point to it }
   New( Head );
   { ASSERTION: Head^ is the just-created node. }

   {-- Copy new data into new node }
   Head^.Data := NewData;

   {-- Make new node point to old list }
   Head^.Link := ExistingList
   {
    ASSERTION:
    Head^.Link now points to first previously
    existing node, if any.
   }

END; { InsertAtHead }
```

Deleting the node at the tail of the list

For a change of pace, consider deleting the node at the tail of a list when we are given only a pointer to the head. There are three cases:

1. If `Head = NIL`, the list is empty and there is nothing to delete.
2. If `Head <> NIL` but `Head^.Link = NIL`, there is only one node in the list:

Call `Dispose( Head )` to de-allocate the node; then assign `NIL` to `Head`.

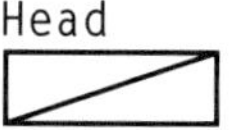

3. If `Head^.Link <>NIL`, there is more than one node and the procedure must traverse the list to find the tail.

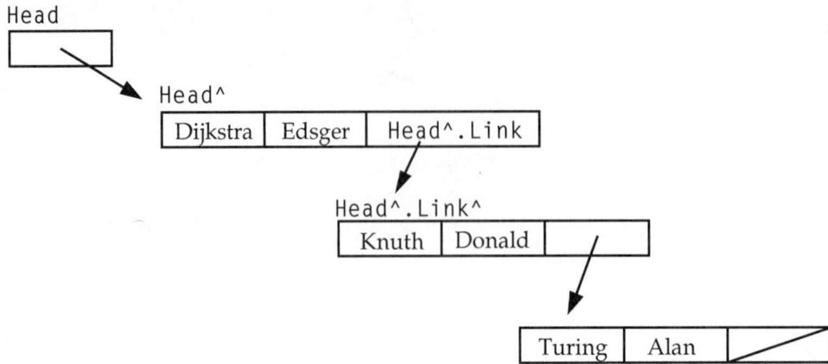

To deal with the traversal in the third case, we simply "walk" down the list, moving to the next `Link` pointer until we find ourselves pointing to the last node. In other words, *while the next* `Link` *pointer is not* `NIL`*, repeatedly replace the current pointer to the next node with the* `Link` *pointer found in that node.* Proceed in this way until the next `Link` is `NIL`, at which point the current pointer points to the last node:

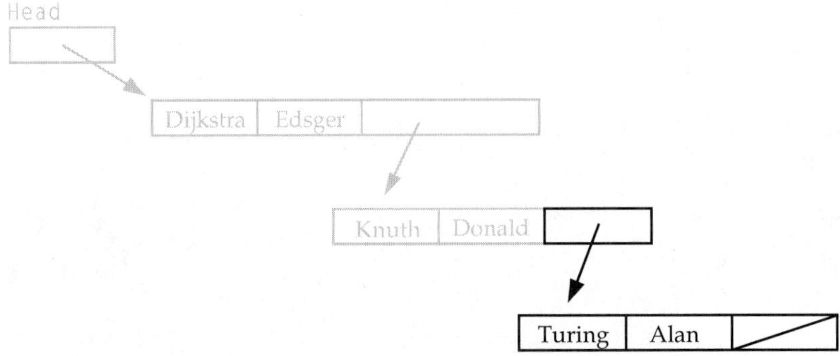

Execute `Dispose` to de-allocate the currently pointed-to node. This leaves the tail pointer undefined.

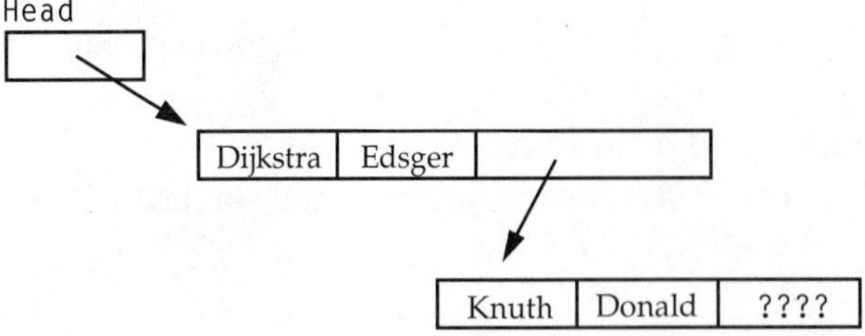

Finally, set the tail pointer to `NIL`, indicating that there are no more nodes in the list after that one. The resulting `Head` list contains "Edsger Dijkstra," followed by "Donald Knuth." The name "Alan Turing" is no longer in the list, and its node has been de-allocated. The diagram can be redrawn for simplicity and clarity:

Implementing DeleteTail recursively

The code for deleting the tail node can be written directly from the diagrams, using recursion. We send a copy of Head to the procedure and use a running pointer as the formal parameter:

```
PROCEDURE DeleteTail( VAR Head : List );
BEGIN

   IF Head <> NIL THEN
   BEGIN

      IFHead^.Link = NIL THEN
      {-- Head points to tail node }
      BEGIN
         Dispose( Head );
         Head := NIL
      END

      ELSE
         {-- Move on down the line...}
         DeleteTail( Head^.Link )

   END

END; { DeleteTail }
```

The operation of this procedure when deleting the tail node of a list of characters is illustrated in the following figure:

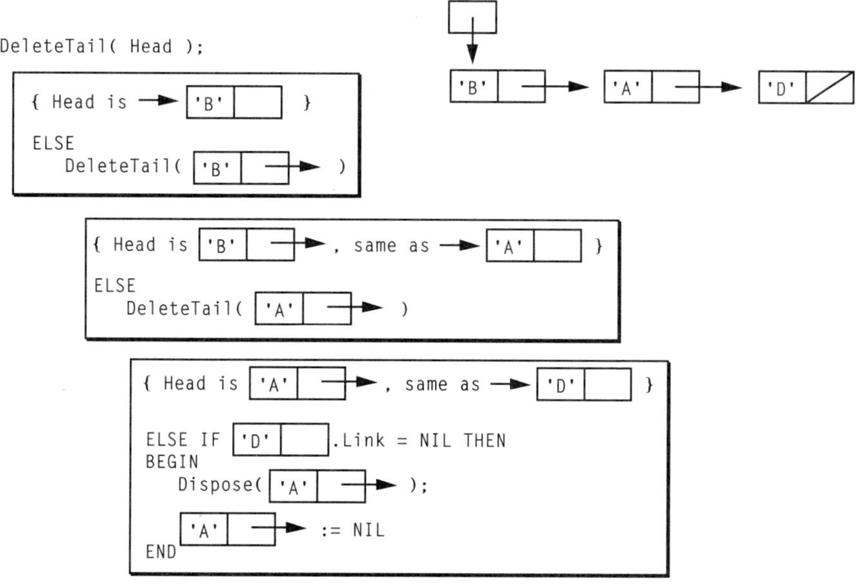

Here, the symbol →['B' |]

means "pointer to the B-node," while ['B' |]→

means "`Link` pointer coming from the B-node."

Implementing ButFirst

The `ButFirst` procedure is trivial. It simply replaces the previous value of `Head` with the previous value of `Head^.Link`:

```
PROCEDURE ButFirst( VAR Head : List );
BEGIN

   IF Head <> NIL THEN
      Head := Head^.Link

END; { ButFirst }
```

Implementing ListLength iteratively

Some of the simpler procedures in the ADT require traversal of the list. It is sometimes convenient to handle the traversal with an auxiliary pointer that points to the current position as we travel down the list. `ListLength` is a typical example; the rest are left as exercises.

```
FUNCTION ListLength( Head : List ) : NonNegInt;
{
  PRECONDITIONS:
  Head exists and is initialized.

  POSTCONDITION:
  Returns the number of nodes in the list, after the Head pointer.
}
VAR
   Count   : NonNegInt;
   Current : List;

BEGIN

   Current := Head;
   Count   := 0;

   WHILE Current <> NIL DO
   {
     LOOP INVARIANT:
     0 <= Count = no. of nodes before Current^.
   }
   BEGIN

      Count   := Count + 1;
      Current := Current^.Link

   END;
```

```
   {
     ASSERTION:
     0 <= Count = no. nodes before NIL.
   }

   ListLength := Count

END; { ListLength }
```

Implementing ListLength recursively

The same function can be written more succinctly with the help of recursion. It is not surprising that a recursive data structure lends itself to recursive processing.

```
FUNCTION ListLength( Head : List ) : NonNegInt;
{
  PRECONDITIONS:
  Head exists and is initialized.

  POSTCONDITION:
  Returns the number of nodes in the list, after the Head pointer.
}
BEGIN

   IF Head = NIL THEN
      {-- Head points to nothing }
      ListLength := 0

   ELSE {-- Head points to a node }
      ListLength := 1 + ListLength( Head^.Link )

END; { ListLength }
```

In imagining how this works, it is essential to use pictures. If, for example, `Head` is the list of characters

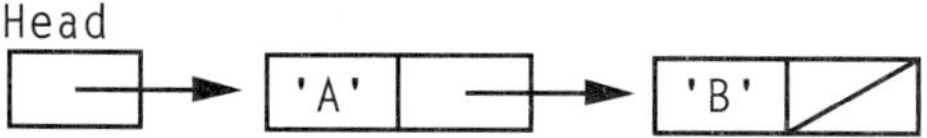

then the nest of recursive function calls can be imagined with the help of a notation that uses pictures for "pointer to the A-node," "pointer to the B-node,"and so on. When `ListLength` is originally called with `Head` being a pointer to the A-node, the situation is

```
FUNCTION ListLength( ——► [A] )

   ELSE
      ListLength := 1 + ListLength( [A].Link )
```

At this point, ListLength calls another copy of ListLength, sending to it the Link pointer from the A-node, which is a pointer to the B-node:

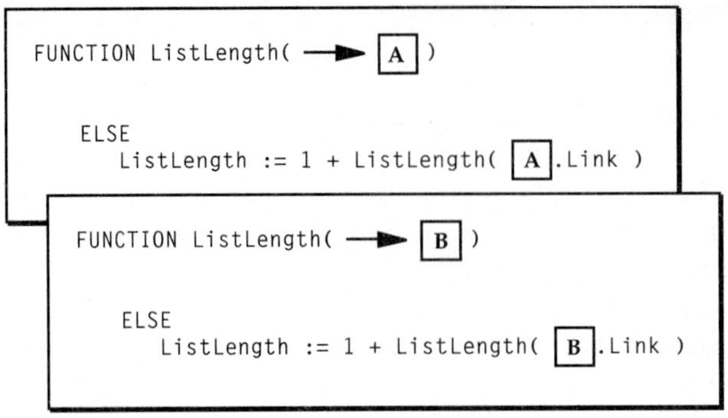

```
FUNCTION ListLength( ──► [A] )

  ELSE
     ListLength := 1 + ListLength( [A].Link )

    FUNCTION ListLength( ──► [B] )

      ELSE
         ListLength := 1 + ListLength( [B].Link )
```

This function calls yet another ListLength, sending to it the Link pointer from the B- node, which is a NIL pointer:

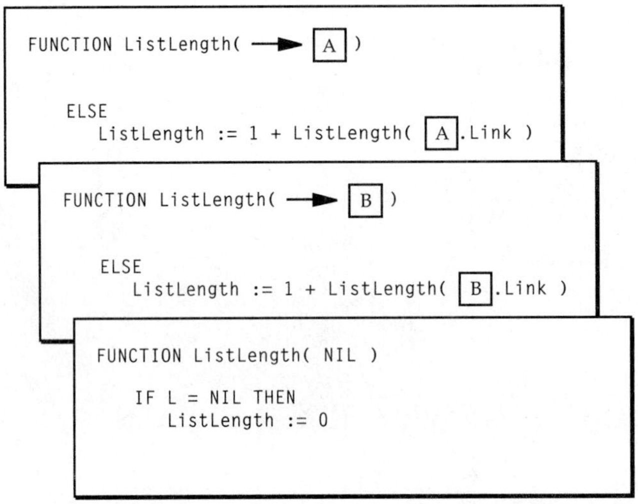

```
FUNCTION ListLength( ──► [A] )

  ELSE
     ListLength := 1 + ListLength( [A].Link )

    FUNCTION ListLength( ──► [B] )

      ELSE
         ListLength := 1 + ListLength( [B].Link )

        FUNCTION ListLength( NIL )

          IF L = NIL THEN
             ListLength := 0
```

The third function returns 0 to the second function, which adds it to 1, giving 1. The second function then returns this 1 to the first function, which adds it to 1, giving a final result of 2. Thus, the length of the list is computed recursively to be 2.

With one exception, the other procedures and functions in the ADT are similar to those that have been worked out here, and they are left as exercises. The exception is the ListIsFull function. In the linked-list implementation, the only reason why a list could not accept a new node would be if all memory had been allocated. There is no way in Standard Pascal to determine whether more memory is available, but many Pascal systems provide a nonstandard way to do this, often with a MemAvail or similar function. Check your reference manual for information about your system.

Exercises

8. Suppose that we have the declarations

```
TYPE
   String40 = PACKED ARRAY [ 1..40 ] OF Char;

   DataType = RECORD
                 LastName  : String40;
                 FirstName : String40;
                 SSN       : String40;
                 Salary    : Real
              END;

   List     = ^Node;
   Node     = RECORD
                 Data : DataType;
                 Link : List;
              END;
```

Write an appropriate `DisplayList` procedure for such a list and test it. Have your procedure call a `DisplayData` procedure for display of a `DataType` record.

9. Jackson P. Slipshod has written this recursive function to return a pointer to the tail node in a list:

```
FUNCTION Tail( L : List ) : List;
{
  THIS IS A SLIPSHOD FUNCTION.
  POSTCONDITION: Returns NIL if L is empty;
  otherwise, returns pointer to last node.
}
BEGIN

   IF L = NIL THEN
      Tail := NIL
   ELSE
      Tail := Tail( L^.Link )

END; { Tail }
```

Explain to Jackson what is wrong with his procedure.

10. Write a procedure that deletes a node from the head of a given list. If the list is initially empty, the procedure should, of course, leave the list empty.

11. Write an `AddNodeAfterPosition` procedure that inserts a new node, containing a given datum, after a given position in a given list. For example, if `Head` is initially

the call `AddNodeAfterPosition( Head, 2, 'R' )` should give

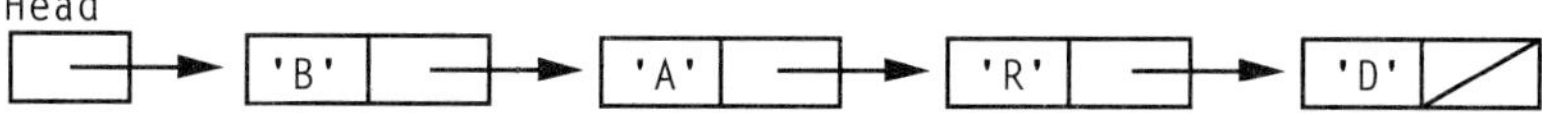

But if the given position is negative or if the position is greater than the length of the list, the procedure should do nothing.

12. Write an iterative version of a `DiscardList` procedure, which de-allocates the nodes in a list and sets the list pointer to `NIL`.
13. Write a recursive version of the procedure in Exercise 12.
14. Write a procedure that displays a list *backward*.
15. The following version of `InsertAtTail` has been proposed. Explain why it doesn't work correctly.

```
FUNCTION Tail( L : List ) : List;
{
  POSTCONDITION:
  Returns pointer to tail node of L if L has nodes;
  otherwise, returns NIL.
}
BEGIN

   IF L = NIL THEN
      Tail := NIL

   ELSE { L points to a node }
      IF L^.Link = NIL THEN
         { L points to the last node }
         Tail := L

      ELSE
         { Move on down the line... }
         Tail := Tail( L^.Link )

END; { Tail }


PROCEDURE InsertAtTail( VAR L    : List;
                        NewData : DataType );
{
  PRECONDITION:
  L has been initialized.

  POSTCONDITION:
  New node, containing NewData, has been added after
  last previous node in L.
}
VAR
   LTail : List;
BEGIN
   {
     Get pointer to last node in list;
     if list is empty, get NIL list pointer.
   }
   LTail := Tail(L);

   IF LTail = NIL THEN
      { Insert new node at head of empty list }
      InsertAtHead( LTail, NewData )
```

```
   ELSE
      { Insert new node after tail node }
      InsertAtHead( LTail^.Link, NewData )
END; { InsertAtTail }
```

16. Write an `InsertAfter` procedure that inserts a new node, containing a given data field, after the first node that contains a given data field in a given list. For example, calling `InsertAfter( L, 'A', 'R' )` on the list

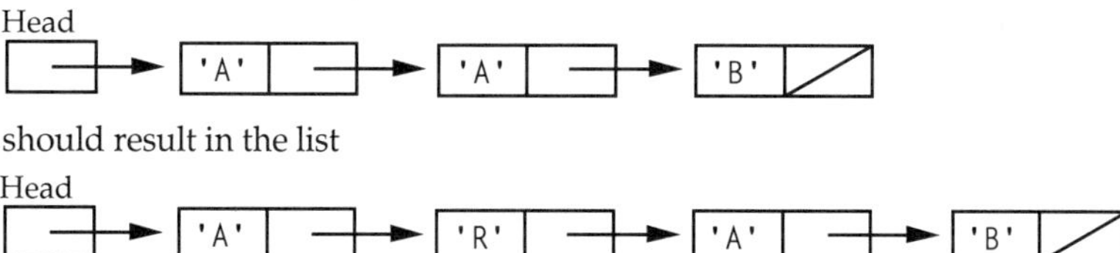

should result in the list

If `L` is empty or the target node is not in the list, the procedure should do nothing.

17. Jackson P. Slipshod is having trouble debugging this program. When he runs this program, he sees gibberish on the screen but sometimes gets a `NIL DEREFERENCE` error message. Explain where and why he gets this error, and show the best way to fix it.

```
PROGRAM Bug1;
TYPE
   DataType = Char;

   List = ^Node;
   Node = RECORD
            Data : DataType;
            Link : List
         END;
VAR
   L : List;

PROCEDURE ShowList( Lst : List );
BEGIN

   REPEAT
      WriteLn( Lst^.Data );
      Lst := Lst^.Link
   UNTIL Lst = NIL

END;

PROCEDURE CreateList( VAR Lst : List );
BEGIN

   Lst := NIL

END;
```

```
BEGIN
   New( L );
   WITH L^ DO
   BEGIN
      Data := 'B';
      Link := NIL
   END;
   ShowList( L );
   CreateList( L );
   ShowList( L )
END.
```

18. Cora Meltdown is having trouble debugging this little program, which is supposed to create a list containing the first four letters of the alphabet, print the list, and then dispose of it. Correct the errors.

```
PROGRAM Bug2;
TYPE
   DataType = Char;
   List = ^Node;
   Node = RECORD
             Data : DataType;
             Link : List
          END;
VAR
   L, Old : List;
   Ch     : Char;

PROCEDURE ShowList( Lst : List );
BEGIN
   REPEAT
      WriteLn( Lst^.Data );
      Lst := Lst^.Link
   UNTIL Lst = NIL
END;

PROCEDURE CreateList( VAR Lst : List );
BEGIN
   Lst := NIL
END;

BEGIN
   CreateList(L);
   Ch := 'A';
```

```
   WHILE Ch < 'D' DO
   BEGIN
      Old := L;
      New(Old);
      Old^.Data := Ch;
      Old^.Link := L;
      Ch := Succ(Ch);
      L := Old
   END;

   ShowList(L);
   WHILE L <> NIL DO
   BEGIN
      Dispose(L);
      ShowList(L)
   END

END.
```

19. Ephraim Ishkabibble sees a `NIL DEREFERENCE` error message when he tries to run this program. What's the problem, and how should Ephraim repair it?

```
PROGRAM Bug3;
TYPE
   DataType = Char;

   List = ^Node;
   Node = RECORD
             Data : DataType;
             Link : List
          END;
VAR
   L, Old : List;
   Ch     : Char;

PROCEDURE ShowList( Lst : List );
BEGIN

   IF Lst <> NIL THEN
   BEGIN
      WriteLn( Lst^.Data );
      ShowList( Lst^.Link )
   END

END;

PROCEDURE CreateList( VAR Lst : List );
BEGIN

   Lst := NIL

END;
```

```
PROCEDURE RemoveStuff( VAR L : List );
VAR
   Old : List;
BEGIN
   IF L <> NIL THEN
   BEGIN
      RemoveStuff(L^.Link);
      Dispose(L);
      L := NIL
   END
END;

PROCEDURE InsertStuff( VAR L : List;
                       VAR It : DataType );
VAR
   Old : List;
BEGIN
   IF L^.Link <> NIL THEN
      InsertStuff(L^.Link, It)
   ELSE
   BEGIN
      Old := L;
      New(L);
      L^.Data := It;
      It := Succ(It);
      L^.Link := Old
   END
END;

BEGIN
   CreateList( L );
   Ch := 'A';
   InsertStuff( L, Ch );
   ShowList( L );
   RemoveStuff( L );
   ShowList( L )
END.
```

20.4 CASE STUDY: DYNAMIC STRING ADT

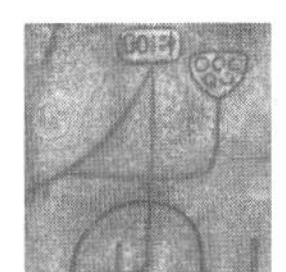

The nice thing about ADTs is that they extend the programming language, making it easier to tackle more complex problems. Each well-designed ADT acts as a tool kit for building other ADTs, and the building process becomes progressively easier.

Consider our problem in Chapters 14 and 15 when we built our own string types. We used arrays or records containing arrays, which forced us to build fixed-length strings in which most of the memory was wasted most of the time. But now we have an ADT for dynamically allocated lists, and we can easily build strings as lists of characters. We will use the `List` ADT to build a dynamic string ADT. Here's the specification:

Dynamic String ADT Specification

Data structure:
A dynamically allocated string, considered as a list of characters.

Operations:

- Create an empty string.
- Append a given character to a given string.
- Read a string from the keyboard as a line of text.
- Write a string to the screen as a line of text.
- Concatenate two given strings to make a longer string.
- Find the length of a given string.
- Compare two strings, reporting their lexical relationship (equal, less than, greater than).

Of course, other string operations are desirable, but this is enough for illustration.

Declaring dynamic strings

The declaration of the ADT is trivial because we now define a string to be simply a dynamically allocated list of characters. In other words, we declare `DynString` to be a synonym for `List`, where `List` was previously defined in its own ADT.

```
{
  Uses declarations from the ListADT of Sec. 20.3.
}
TYPE
   DynString = List { of Char };
```

```
{**********************************************}
{ Create a null string.                        }
{**********************************************}
PROCEDURE CreateEmptyStr( VAR Str : DynString );
{
  POSTCONDITION:
  Str is a string of length zero.
}

{**********************************************}
{ Add a given character at the end of          }
{ a given string.                              }
{**********************************************}
PROCEDURE AppendCh( VAR Str : DynString;
                        Ch  : Char );
{
  PRECONDITIONS:
  Str and Ch have been initialized.

  POSTCONDITIONS:
  A copy of Ch has been added to the end of Str.
}

{**********************************************}
{ Read first line of keyboard text into Str.   }
{**********************************************}
PROCEDURE ReadLnStr( VAR Str : DynString );
{
  POSTCONDITION:
  The first line of text from the keyboard
  has overwritten previous contents of Str.
}

{**********************************************}
{ Display Str as a line of text on the screen. }
{**********************************************}
PROCEDURE WriteLnStr( Str : DynString );
{
  PRECONDITION:
  Str has been initialized.

  POSTCONDITION:
  Str has been written on a line of the screen.
  Cursor is on the next line.
}
```

```
{************************************************}
{ Copy Str1 and then Str2 into ConcatStr,        }
{ making one long string.                        }
{************************************************}

PROCEDURE Concatenate( Str1, Str2    : DynString;
                       VAR ConcatStr : DynString );
{
  PRECONDITIONS:
  Str1 and Str2 have been initialized.

  POSTCONDITIONS:
  Previous contents of ConcatStr have been overwritten by the
  characters of Str1, followed by the characters of Str2.
}

{************************************************}
{ Return the number of characters in Str.        }
{************************************************}
FUNCTION StrLength( Str : DynString ) : NonNegInt;

{
  PRECONDITION:
  Str has been initialized.

  POSTCONDITION:
  Returns the number of characters in Str.
}

{************************************************}
{ Lexically compare Str1 and Str2, indicating    }
{ their relation by returning '=', '<', or '>'.  }
{************************************************}
FUNCTION StrCompare( Str1, Str2 : DynString ) : Char;
{
  PRECONDITION:
  Str1 and Str2 have been initialized.

  POSTCONDITIONS:
  If Str1 < Str2, returns '<';
  if Str1 = Str2, returns '=';
  if Str1 > Str2, returns '>'.
}
```

Using the ADT

The declarations in the interface say that a `DynString` is a `List`, but say nothing about how a `List` is constructed. Similarly, the interface says nothing about the implementations of its procedures and functions. This is because a user of the ADT doesn't need to know these details. As far as the user is concerned, an ADT is defined by the way it is *used*, not by how it is implemented. Here is an example of the `DynString` ADT in use:

```
PROGRAM StringTest( Input, Output );
{ Uses DynStringADT }
VAR
   Str1, Str2, Str3 : DynString;

BEGIN

   CreateEmptyStr( Str1 );
   WriteLn( 'Length of Str1 = ', StrLength(Str1):2 );
   WriteLn( 'Add an ''s''...' );
   AppendCh( Str1, 's' );
   WriteLn( 'Now length of Str1 = ', StrLength(Str1):2 );

   CreateEmptyStr( Str2 );
   WriteLn;
   WriteLn( 'Length of Str2 = ', StrLength(Str2):2 );
   Write( 'Str2?  ' );
   ReadLnStr( Str2 );
   WriteLn( 'Now length of Str2 = ', StrLength(Str2):2 );

   WriteLn;
   WriteLn( 'Concatenating Str1 after Str2...' );
   Concatenate( Str2, Str1, Str3 );
   WriteLn( 'Length of concat string = ', StrLength(Str3):2 );
   Write( 'Concatenated string = ' );
   WriteLnStr( Str3 );

   WriteLn( 'Comparisons:' );
   WriteLn( 'Str1 ', StrCompare( Str1, Str2 ), ' Str2' );
   WriteLn( 'Str2 ', StrCompare( Str2, Str1 ), ' Str1' );
   WriteLn( 'Str1 ', StrCompare( Str1, Str3 ), ' ConcatStr' );
   WriteLn( 'ConcatStr ', StrCompare( Str3, Str1 ), ' Str1' );
   WriteLn( 'Str1 ', StrCompare( Str1, Str1 ), ' Str1' );
   WriteLn( 'Str2 ', StrCompare( Str2, Str2 ), ' Str2' );
   WriteLn( 'ConcatStr ', StrCompare( Str3, Str3 ), ' ConcatStr' )
END.
```

A typical run with this program should look like this:

```
Length of Str1 =  0
Add an 's'...
Now length of Str1 =  1

Length of Str2 =  0
Str2?  bat
Now length of Str2 =  3
Concatenating Str1 after Str2...
Length of concat string =  4
Concatenated string = bats
Comparisons:
Str1 > Str2
Str2 < Str1
```

```
Str1 > ConcatStr
ConcatStr < Str1
Str1 = Str1
Str2 = Str2
ConcatStr = ConcatStr
```

Implementing the ADT

There is almost nothing to the implementation of this ADT, if we call on `ListADT`. `CreateEmptyStr` requires only a call to `CreateEmptyList`, `AppendCh` requires only a call to `InsertAtTail`, and `StrLength` requires only a call to `ListLength`. Even `Concatenate` requires only three calls to the `ListADT`:

```
PROCEDURE CreateEmptyStr( VAR Str : DynString );
BEGIN

   CreateEmptyList( Str )

END; { CreateEmptyStr }


PROCEDURE AppendCh( VAR Str : DynString;
                    Ch      : Char );
BEGIN

   InsertAtTail( Str, Ch )

END; { AppendCh }


FUNCTION StrLength( Str : DynString ) : NonNegInt;
BEGIN

  StrLength := ListLength( Str )

END; { StrLength }


PROCEDURE Concatenate( Str1, Str2    : DynString;
                       VAR ConcatStr : DynString );
BEGIN

   CreateEmptyList( ConcatStr );
   AppendList( ConcatStr, Str1 );
   AppendList( ConcatStr, Str2 )

END; { Concatenate }
```

Why bother to write string routines that do nothing but call the corresponding list routines? So that the user will be insulated from the nature of the implementation. We don't want users to worry about how strings are represented in memory, and we certainly don't want users to tinker with the underlying list structures. The best way to prevent this is to hide the way strings are implemented.

Reading a dynamic string from the keyboard as a line of text

Now we come to the few string operations that require much work. The `ReadLnStr` procedure reads characters from the keyboard into a given string until the input is terminated by `<EOLn>` or `<EOF>`:

```
PROCEDURE ReadLnStr( VAR Str : DynString );
VAR
   Ch: Char;

BEGIN

   CreateEmptyList( Str );

   WHILE ( NOT EOLn ) AND ( NOT EOF ) DO
   BEGIN
      Read( Ch );
      InsertAtTail( Str, Ch )
   END;

   IF EOLn THEN
      ReadLn

END; { ReadLnStr }
```

Comparing two strings for alphabetic order

Comparing two strings is the most difficult implementation in the ADT. The basis for the algorithm comes from the definition of string relations: `Str1` is said to be less than `Str2` if, in the first differing character position, the character in `Str1` is lexically less than the corresponding character in `Str2`. If, on searching through both strings, we find them to be the same in every character position and to have the same number of characters, we say that the strings are equal.

The algorithm for comparing strings can therefore be outlined as follows:

1. Initially, we are looking at the first character position in each string.
2. As long we haven't run beyond the end of either string, and as long as the characters in the current position are the same, advance to the next character position in both strings.
3. Having completed step 2, there are three possible conditions:
   a. If we ran beyond the ends of both strings, it was because the strings are identical.
   b. If we ran beyond the end of one string but not the other, the longer string is lexically greater than the shorter one.
   c. Otherwise, the loop in step 2 stopped because the strings differ in the last character position considered. The strings are related in the same way as the characters in the latest character position.

The Pascal procedure follows. It uses `ListIsEmpty` and `ButFirst` from `List` ADT and also a `FirstChar` function, which returns the first character in a string.

```
FUNCTION StrCompare( Str1, Str2 : DynString ) : Char;

{ SUBPROGRAMS REQUIRED: ListIsEmpty, FirstChar, ButFirst }

VAR
   Finished : Boolean;

BEGIN

   Finished := False;

   WHILE ( NOT ListIsEmpty(Str1) ) AND ( NOT ListIsEmpty(Str2) )
         AND ( NOT Finished ) DO

      IF FirstChar( Str1 ) = FirstChar( Str2 ) THEN
      BEGIN
         ButFirst( Str1 );
         ButFirst( Str2 )
      END

      ELSE { characters differ }
         Finished := True;

   {-- Why did the loop terminate? }
   IF ListIsEmpty( Str1 ) AND ListIsEmpty( Str2 ) THEN
      StrCompare := '='

   ELSE IF ListIsEmpty( Str1 ) THEN
      StrCompare := '<'

   ELSE IF ListIsEmpty( Str2 ) THEN
      StrCompare := '>'

   ELSE { characters differ }
      IF FirstChar( Str1 ) > FirstChar( Str2 ) THEN
         StrCompare := '>'
      ELSE
         StrCompare := '<'

 END; { StrCompare }
```

Exercises

20. Jackson P. Slipshod has written the following `StrCompare` function. Help him figure out why it doesn't work correctly.

```
FUNCTION StrCompare( Str1, Str2 : DynString ) : Char;
BEGIN
   WHILE ( NOTListIsEmpty( Str1 ) )
      AND ( NOT ListIsEmpty( Str2 ) )
         AND FirstChar( Str1 )
             = FirstChar( Str2 ) DO
   BEGIN
      Advance( Str1 );
      Advance( Str2 )
   END;

   IF FirstChar( Str1 ) = FirstChar( Str2 ) THEN
      StrCompare := '='
   ELSE IF FirstChar( Str1 )
                  < FirstChar( Str2 ) THEN
      StrCompare := '<'
   ELSE
      StrCompare := '>'
END; { StrCompare }
```

21. Write an implementation for the `WriteLnStr` procedure.

20.5 OTHER LIST IMPLEMENTATIONS

When inserting or deleting nodes, there is an occasional need to **traverse** the list, looking for the tail end. In some applications, this can be a frequent process. Consider, for example, a business mailing list in which duplicate entries are undesirable. We want a procedure that will remove nodes containing duplicate data.

Here's how we can build one. Suppose that a `Head` pointer points to the first node in the list and that we have a `ListIsEmpty` function as defined in the ADT interface. Suppose also that we have a `Tail` function, which returns a pointer to the last node in a list, and a boolean function `Duplicate( Pointer1, Pointer2 )`, which reports whether two nodes contain duplicate customer records. The plan uses two local variables, `Current` and `LookAhead`, to keep track of addresses as we traverse the list:

1. Set `Current = Head`.
2. If `ListIsEmpty( Current )`, there is nothing to do; otherwise, go to step 3.
3. While `Current <> Tail( Head )`, do the following:
   a. Initialize a `LookAhead` pointer to point to the node beyond `Current` by setting `LookAhead = Current^.Link`.
   b. While `NOT ListIsEmpty( LookAhead )` do the following:
      i. If `Duplicate( Current, LookAhead )`, then delete the node to which `LookAhead` points.
      ii. Advance `LookAhead` by copying `LookAhead^.Link` into `LookAhead`.

The outer loop checks to see whether `Current` points to the tail node. Since the inner loop may delete the existing tail node, the position of the tail node may change during a trip through the outer loop. Therefore the outer loop must call `Tail` at the beginning of every trip.

`Tail` returns a pointer to the last node in the list, which is found by traversing the list:

```
FUNCTION Tail ( Head : List ) : List;
{
  PRECONDITIONS:
  Head is not an empty list.

  POSTCONDITIONS:
  Returns pointer to the tail node of the
  Head list.
}
VAR
   Current : List;

BEGIN

   { ASSERTION: Head <> NIL. }
   Current := Head;

   WHILE Current^.Link <>NIL DO
      Current := Current^.Link;

   { ASSERTION: Current^.Link = NIL. }
   Tail := Current

END; { Tail }
```

This procedure is $O(N)$, where N is the number of nodes in the list. If it is called frequently, mailing-list programs will spend a lot of time traversing the list again and again.

As another example, suppose we are writing a program to keep track of orders in a fast-food restaurant. We maintain a list of current food orders, which are to be processed in first-come, first-served order. (Such lists are called *queues*, and are discussed at length in the next chapter.) New orders are inserted at the head of the list, and processed orders are deleted from the tail of the list as customers pick up their food. This too involves repeatedly traversing the list. Many other processes involving ordered lists are like this.

Because situations like these are fairly common in applications, it is desirable to redesign the `List` data structure so that traversals are minimized. This can be accomplished by equipping each list with a `Tail` pointer as well as a `Head` pointer:

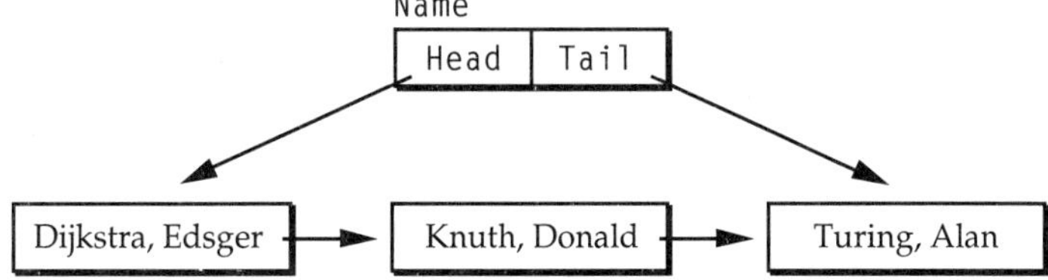

Such a data structure can be declared as a record containing both head and tail pointers:

```
TYPE
   DataType = RECORD
                 LastName  : String20;
                 FirstName : String20
              END;

   NodePointer = ^Node;
   Node = RECORD
             Data : DataType;
             Link : NodePointer;
          END;

   List = RECORD
             Head : NodePointer;
             Tail : NodePointer
          END;

VAR
   Name : List;
```

With this implementation of the list abstraction, the `Head` and `Tail` pointers must be updated by any operation that affects the location of the head or tail nodes, but it saves considerable work in operations like those we have just discussed. The trade-off is often advantageous.

Implementing a list as a singly dimensioned array

In Chapters 14–16, we implemented lists as singly-dimensioned arrays, using the single subscript to keep track of the ordering of data in the list. If we declare, for example,

```
CONST
   High = 50;  { or whatever }

TYPE
   SubscriptRange = 1..High;
   List = ARRAY [ SubscriptRange ] OF String40;

VAR
   Name : List;
```

then the items in the list are stored one after another in 50 contiguous memory cells, labeled by the subscripts:

Name[1]	Name[2]	Name[3]	•••	Name[48]	Name[49]	Name[50]

If we intend to store items in a certain order in the list—alphabetical order, for example—there are three major problems with such an implementation:

1. We must declare ahead of time the maximum length of the list, so that Pascal can statically allocate the array's storage. Even if we don't actually use all of the array elements, we must allocate memory for the largest number that might be needed. This is often wasteful.

2. In order to insert a new item in its proper place in the list, all later items must be moved up one position, to make room for it. This is an awkward, time-consuming process.
3. In order to delete items from the list, we must move all the later items down one position. This, too, is an awkward, time-consuming process.

Implementing an ordered list as a linked array

If we have to use statically allocated arrays, a better implementation for ordered lists is to have each array element store the subscript of its successor in the list, or a 0 if there is no successor. This can be done if an array element is a record containing not only data but also the successor's subscript. This is called linking the element to its successor, by analogy to the linking we can do with pointers. For example, we might declare

```
CONST
   High = 50; { or whatever }

TYPE
   SubscriptRange = 1..High;
   FullRange      = 0..High;
   Element    = RECORD
                 LastName  : String20;
                 FirstName : String20;
                 Link      : FullRange
                END;

   List = ARRAY [ SubscriptRange ] OF Element;

VAR
   Name : List;
   Head : FullRange;
```

An example will make this clearer. Suppose we have a list containing the names of two famous computer scientists, Edsger Dijkstra and Alan Turing, listed alphabetically according to last name. The list might be diagrammed like this:

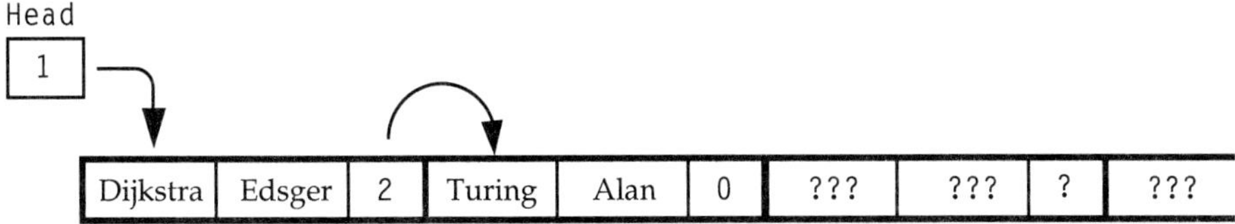

The diagram shows that we have a variable named `Head`, storing the subscript of the first member of the list. Since `Head` contains 1, the list begins with `Name[1]`, containing the name Edsger Dijkstra. This element also contains the `Link` value 2, indicating that the second member of the list is `Name[2]`. This second element contains the name Alan Turing, and also the `Link` value 0, indicating that there are no more members in the list.

The advantage of this implementation for lists is that it makes addition and deletion much easier. For example, to add the name Donald Knuth to the list, we insert it in the first unused array element, which is `Name[3]`, then redefine the `Link` values so that Knuth will be listed between Dijkstra and Turing, as shown at the top of the next page.

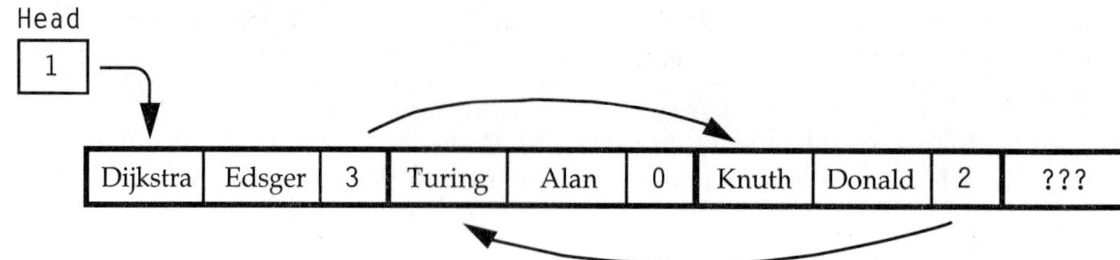

Knuth is now listed *physically* after Turing, but *logically* between Dijkstra and Turing.

To delete the last member of the list, we simply set the preceding `Link` value to 0, indicating that there are no more members after Knuth:

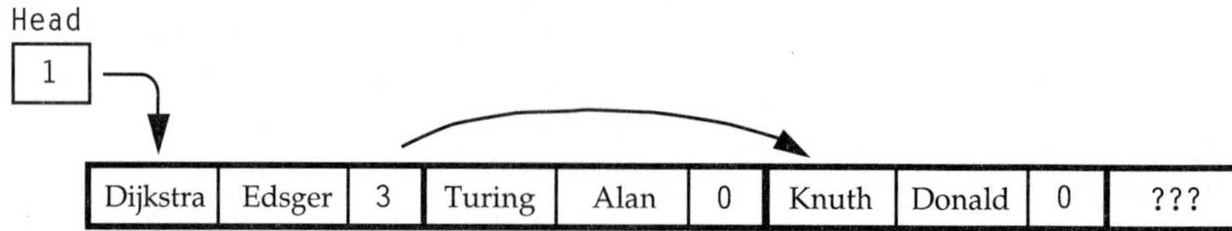

Turing is still stored physically in the array, but is no longer a member of the list.

Finally, to delete the first member of the list, we simply set the value of `Head` to the value of the `Link` field in the next member:

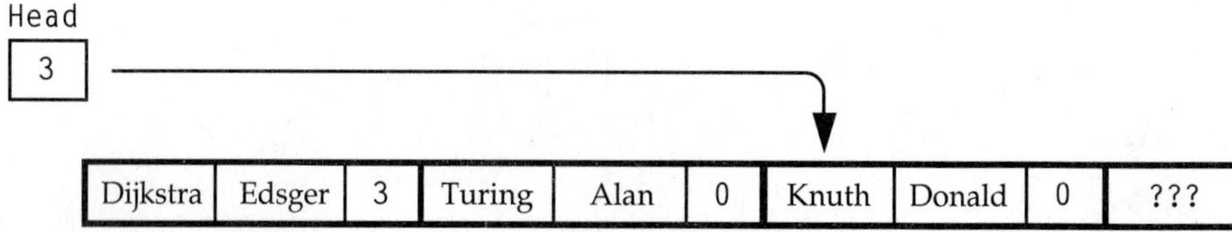

Dijkstra and Turing are still stored physically in the array, but are no longer members of the list.

Doubly linked lists

There is another shortcoming in all of the list implementations examined so far: *They are all one-way sequential*. That is, we can traverse down the list from the head to the tail, but there is no way to work backwards. In the `DeleteTail` procedure, this forced us to look two nodes ahead while seeking the tail node, so that we wouldn't need to back up to find the new tail node after deletion. This kind of problem arises frequently. The solution is to implement a list in which each node contains pointers to both its predecessor and its successor. Such a list is said to be **doubly linked**. An example is shown below:

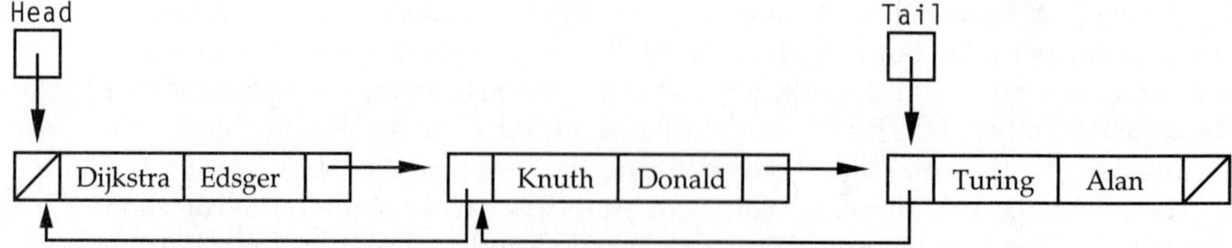

A doubly linked list is declared like a singly linked list, but with two link fields, which we can call `LLink` and `RLink`. Here is a declaration that uses double linking as well as head and tail pointers:

```
TYPE
   DataType = RECORD
                 LastName  : String20;
                 FirstName : String20
              END;

   NodePointer = ^Node;
   Node = RECORD
             LLink : NodePointer;
             Data  : DataType;
             RLink : NodePointer
          END;

   List = RECORD
             Head : NodePointer;
             Tail : NodePointer
          END;

VAR
   Name : List;
```

Further discussion of this topic is beyond the scope of this book. The sequel to this book, *Abstractions and Analysis*, provides more details.

Exercises

22. Draw diagrams of a `Name` list as declared on page 728, showing its contents after each of the following operations, which are performed in sequence:

   a. The list is initially empty.

   b. The names "Hoobert Heever" and "Walter Mitty" are added to the end of the list, in that order.

   c. The first record is deleted from the list.

   d. The name "James Kirk" is added to the end of the list.

23. Write declarations for a list of records, each of which contains a 20-character city name; a two-letter state abbreviation; a five-digit ZIP code stored as a string; and a link to the next record. This list is to be implemented as a linked array, as described in this section. Draw diagrams showing the contents of the array after each operation in the following sequence:

   a. The list is initially empty.

   b. Add Why, AZ 86445 to the list.

   c. Add Filbert, WV 24835 and then Eek, AK 99578 to the list.

   d. Delete Filbert from the list.

   e. Delete the remaining first record and then the last record.

24. Write declarations for a linked array list in which both `Head` and `Tail` variables are used to mark the subscripts of the array elements representing the first and last list members.

20.6 CASE STUDY: BINARY TREES

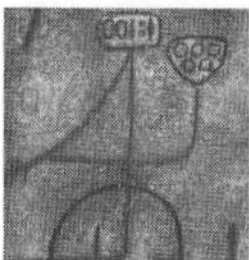

Linked data structures often use more than one link per node. In a **binary tree**, each node is linked to two other nodes. In particular, a binary tree is a set of nodes that is either the empty set or a set consisting of a **root node** linked to two disjoint binary trees called the **left subtree** and the **right subtree**. Each of these subtrees is in turn a binary tree. Figure 20.6.1 shows some examples in which the nodes store characters.

Tree nomenclature

A strange jargon has grown up around tree structures. Consider the binary tree shown in Figure 20.6.2. In this tree, the G-node is the *root* of the tree. (The tree is conventionally drawn upside down, with the root at the top.) Mixing the metaphor, the D-node and K-node are said to be the *children* of the G-node, the D- and K-nodes are said to be *siblings*, and the G-node is said to be their *parent*. Naturally, then, the G-node is the *grandparent* of the B-, E-, H-, and M-nodes. Similarly, the *ancestors* of the C-node are the B-, D-, and G-nodes, while the *descendants* of the K-node are the H-, I-, J-, L-, and M-nodes. This much of the jargon is genealogical.

Returning to the botany metaphor, nodes having no descendants, like the A-, C-, F-, I-, and L-nodes, are called **leaves** of the tree. On the other hand, nodes with descendants are called **interior nodes**. It's a totally confused nomenclature.

A **full binary tree** is a binary tree in which every node has either two children or no children; that is, all interior nodes have two children.

The **level** of a node is defined to be one more than the number of its ancestors. In the example tree, the G-node is alone at level one, the D- and K-nodes are at level two, the B-, E-, H-, and M-nodes are at level three, and the rest are at levels four and five. The **height** of a tree is the number of distinct levels. The example tree, therefore, has a height of five.

Figure 20.6.1 *Examples of binary trees containing characters. The upper diagrams are a shorthand for the lower diagrams, in which the link fields are shown explicitly.*

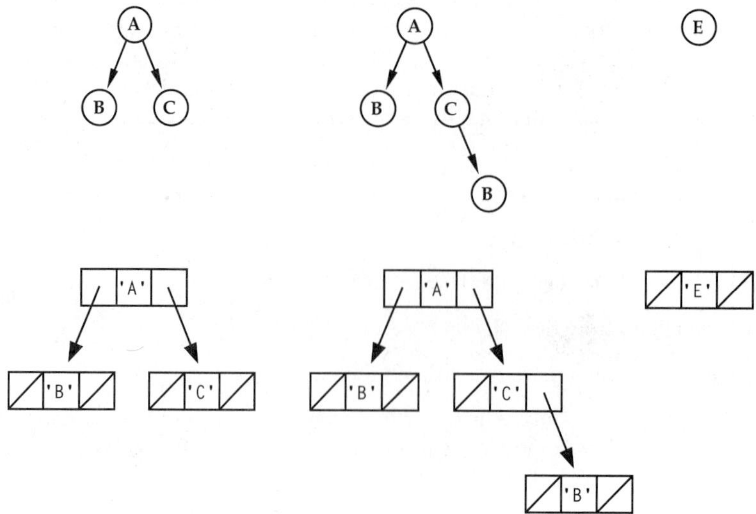

Sample binary tree for discussing tree nomenclature. **Figure 20.6.2**

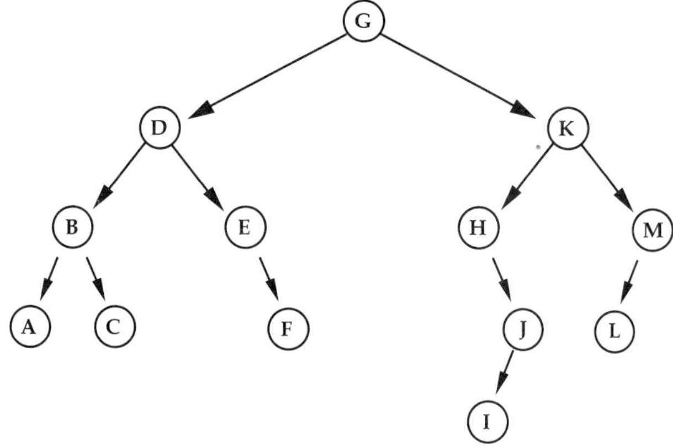

Binary tree traversal

Moving around in a tree, accessing the data in the nodes, is called **traversing** the tree. The tree can be traversed in various orders. The three most common traversals are categorized according to when a root is visited, relative to visiting its subtrees:

Preorder traversal	Inorder traversal	Postorder traversal
1. Visit the root.	1. Traverse left subtree.	1. Traverse left subtree.
2. Traverse left subtree.	2. Visit the root.	2. Traverse right subtree.
3. Traverse right subtree.	3. Traverse right subtree.	3. Visit the root.

In the example tree of Figure 20.6.2,

- Preorder traversal visits nodes in the order GDBACEFKHJIML.
- Inorder traversal visits nodes in the order ABCDEFGHIJKLM.
- Postorder traversal visits nodes in the order ACBFEDIJHLMKG.

Case study: expression trees

Binary trees are used in programming-language compilers to represent binary expressions. Figure 20.6.3 shows an expression tree for the expression $(A + B) * C$.

Binary expression tree representing $(A + B) * C$. **Figure 20.6.3**

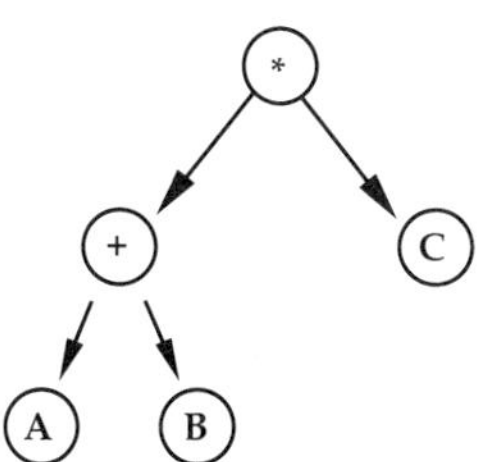

The standard traversals of this tree yield prefix, infix, and postfix versions of the expression:

- Preorder traversal yields `*+ABC`, the prefix version of the expression. Using the rule that a binary operator applies to the two operands immediately following it, the expression is unambiguous without the need for parentheses or precedence rules.
- Inorder traversal yields `A+B*C`, the infix version of the expression. This is the ordinary algebraic notation in which the expression is evaluated left-to-right, but the precedence of operators must be used to resolve the ambiguous meaning of the expression, or parentheses must be added.
- Postorder traversal yields `AB+C*`, the postfix version of the expression. Using the rule that a binary operator applies to the two operands immediately preceding it, the expression is unambiguous without the need for parentheses or precedence rules.

Both the postfix and prefix versions have the advantage that they are completely unambiguous without the need for parentheses or precedence rules. The output from a compiler's expression scanner is in one of these forms.

Application: game trees

Trees are often used to help resolve strategy issues in programs. As an example, consider the game tree in Figure 20.6.4 for considering moves in a tic-tac-toe game. Similar trees are used in chess-playing programs and in artificial-intelligence programs that simulate strategies for more serious purposes such as medical diagnosis or warfare.

Figure 20.6.4 *A game tree for a tic-tac-toe game. This is not a binary tree because more than two moves are possible in a typical state.*

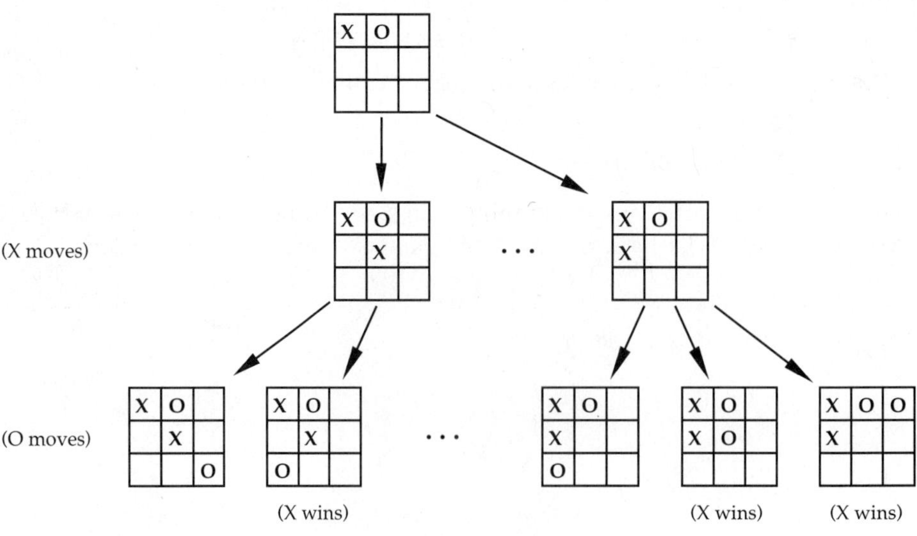

After inserting in a BST the integers 3, 1, 5, 4, in that order. **Figure 20.6.5**

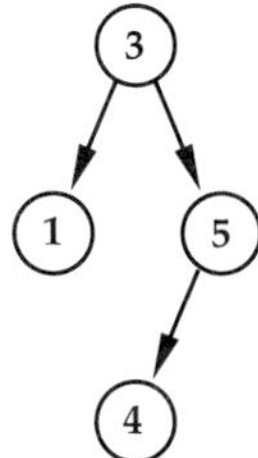

Binary search trees

A **binary search tree** (**BST**) is a binary tree in which, for every root, the nodes in the left subtree contain data less in value (in some sense) than that in the root, while all nodes in the right subtree contain data greater in value than that in the root. It follows that a binary search tree contains no duplicate nodes. The tree in Figure 20.6.2 is a binary search tree. In Figure 20.6.1, only the rightmost tree is a binary search tree.

The structure of a BST depends on the order in which nodes were inserted into the tree. For example, if the integers 3, 1, 5, 4 are inserted into an integer BST in that order, we get the BST shown in Figure 20.6.5. However, if the nodes are inserted in the order 1, 3, 4, 5, we get the BST shown in Figure 20.6.6.

The most obvious application of binary search trees is to facilitate searching for data. Once a set of data has been inserted into a BST, any datum can be found quickly by looking at a root node; if it isn't equal to the desired value, then descend to the left or right subtree, according to whether the desired value is less than or greater than the root node value. This, of course, is the binary search we discussed in Section 19.2.

Binary search trees also facilitate sorting. *Once the data have been inserted into a BST, a simple inorder traversal of the tree produces a sorted list.* This process of BST insertion, followed by inorder traversal, is called **tree sort**. It is $O(N \lg N)$, though not quite as fast as quicksort's best performance. It has the same Achilles' heel as quicksort: When the data are already in sorted or reverse-sorted order, tree sort degenerates to an $O(N^2)$ process.

After inserting in a BST the integers 1, 3, 4, 5, in that order. **Figure 20.6.6**

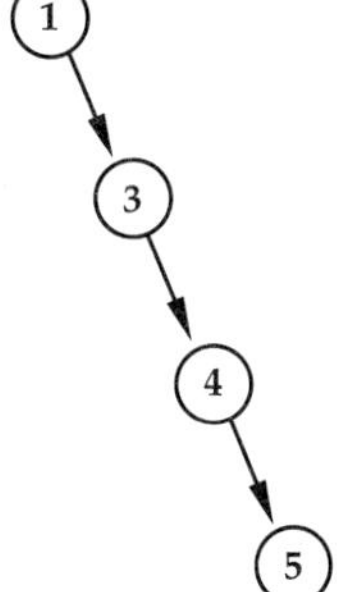

A binary search tree ADT

The binary tree, as an abstract data type, can be defined as shown in the following box. Here we show only a minimal subset of the operations that might be desired in real-world applications.

Binary Search Tree ADT Specification

Data structure:
A binary search tree (BST) is defined to be a set of nodes obeying the following three rules:

1. The tree is either empty or contains at least one node.
2. If the tree contains at least one node, then that node is linked to two disjoint subtrees, called the left and right subtrees of the node. Each of these subtrees is, in turn, a binary search tree.
3. The nodes in a left subtree contain data keys that are less in value than the root key. The nodes in a right subtree contain data keys that are greater in value than the root key.

Operations:

- Create a new binary search tree.
- Insert new data into a BST by adding a new node that preserves the BST properties.
- Delete the node containing a given data key, preserving the BST properties of the remaining tree.
- Traverse a tree in preorder, processing the data in some predefined way.
- Traverse a tree in inorder, processing the data in some predefined way.
- Traverse a tree in postorder, processing the data in some predefined way.
- Report whether a given tree is empty.
- Retrieve the data from the current node.
- Find the location of a given datum in the tree—that is, return the subtree of which the given datum is the root. However, if the datum is absent from the tree, report this.

A binary search tree interface

The rough specification translates into the following interface:

```
TYPE
   DataType = Char; { Or whatever; it might be composite. }
   {
     Tree   = binary search tree, an opaque type
              declared in the implementation.
   }
```

```
{*************************************************}
{ Create a new binary search tree.                }
{*************************************************}
PROCEDURE CreateEmptyBST( VAR Root : Tree );
{
  POSTCONDITION:
  Root is an empty tree.
}

{*************************************************}
{ Insert new data into a BST by adding a new node }
{ that preserves the BST properties of the tree.  }
{ If Root specifies a BST already containing      }
{ NewData, the tree is unchanged.                 }
{*************************************************}
PROCEDURE InsertBSTNode( VAR Root : Tree;
                         NewData  : DataType );
{
  PRECONDITIONS:
  Root and NewData have been initialized;
  Root is a BST.

  POSTCONDITIONS:
  Root is a BST containing NewData.
}

{*************************************************}
{ Delete the node containing a given data key,    }
{ preserving the BST properties of the remaining  }
{ tree. If Root specifies a BST that does not     }
{ contain TargetData, the tree is not changed.    }
{*************************************************}
PROCEDURE DeleteBSTNode( VAR Root   : Tree;
                         TargetData : DataType );
{
  PRECONDITIONS:
  Root and TargetData have been initialized;
  Root is a BST.

  POSTCONDITIONS:
  Root is a BST that does not contain TargetData.
}
```

```
{**************************************************}
{ Preorder traversal of a tree, processing the     }
{ data in some predefined way.                      }
{**************************************************}
PROCEDURE PreorderTraversal( Root : Tree );
{
  PRECONDITION:
  Root has been initialized as a BST.

  POSTCONDITION:
  All data in Root have been processed
  by preorder traversal.
}

{**************************************************}
{ Inorder traversal of a tree, processing the      }
{ data in some predefined way.                      }
{**************************************************}
PROCEDURE InorderTraversal( Root : Tree );
{
  PRECONDITION:
  Root has been initialized as a BST.

  POSTCONDITION:
  All data in Root have been processed
  by inorder traversal.
}
{**************************************************}
{ Postorder traversal of a tree, processing the    }
{ data in some predefined way.                      }
{**************************************************}
PROCEDURE PostorderTraversal( Root : Tree );
{
  PRECONDITION:
  Root has been initialized as a BST.

  POSTCONDITION:
  All data in Root have been processed by
  postorder traversal.
}
```

```
{************************************************}
{ Report whether a given tree is empty.          }
{************************************************}
FUNCTION BSTIsEmpty( Root : Tree ) : Boolean;
{
  PRECONDITION:
  Root has been initialized as a BST.

  POSTCONDITION:
  Returns True if Root is empty;
  otherwise returns False.
}

{************************************************}
{ Retrieve data from the root node.              }
{************************************************}
PROCEDURE RetrieveRoot( Root         : Tree;
                        VAR RootData : DataType );
{
  PRECONDITION:
  Root is a nonempty subtree.

  POSTCONDITION:
  Returns in RootData the data in the root node.
}

{************************************************}
{ Report whether TargetData is contained in a    }
{ given tree. If so, report the location by      }
{ returning the subtree of which TargetData is   }
{ the root.                                      }
{************************************************}
PROCEDURE FindInBST( Root         : Tree;
                     TargetData   : DataType;
                     VAR Location : Tree;
                     VAR Found    : Boolean );
{
  PRECONDITION:
  Root and TargetData have been initialized;
  Root is a BST.

  POSTCONDITION:
  If TargetData is in the Root tree,
     returns Found = True
     and the Location of TargetData;
  otherwise,
     returns Found = False and Location undefined.
}
```

A binary search tree implementation

The usual way to implement a BST is to dynamically allocate the nodes, each of which contains pointers to its two subtrees, either of which can be NIL. Thus, we can declare

```
TYPE
   Tree     = ^TreeNode;
   TreeNode = RECORD
                 Data        : DataType;
                 Left, Right : Tree
              END;
```

This declaration corresponds to the structure shown in Figure 20.6.1.

As usual, some of the procedures are trivial to implement:

```
PROCEDURE CreateEmptyBST( VAR Root : Tree );
BEGIN

   Root := NIL

END; { CreateEmptyBST }


FUNCTION BSTIsEmpty( Root : Tree ) : Boolean;
BEGIN

   BSTISEmpty := ( Root = NIL )

END; { BSTIsEmpty }


PROCEDURE RetrieveRoot( Root         : Tree;
                        VAR RootData : DataType );
BEGIN

   RootData := Root^.Data

END; { RetrieveRoot }


PROCEDURE Process( T : Tree );
{ Used by traversal procedures }
BEGIN

   {-- Insert the appropriate processing here }
   WriteLn( T^.Data )

END; { Process }
```

```
PROCEDURE InorderTraversal( Root : Tree );
{
  Procedure required: Process.
}
BEGIN

   IF Root <> NIL THEN
   BEGIN

      InorderTraversal( Root^.Left );
      Process( Root );
      InorderTraversal( Root^.Right )

   END

END; { InorderTraversal }
```

Of course, the preorder and postorder traversals are implemented similarly. The idea is to recursively traverse each subtree, and to process the root node at the correct time relative to the subtree traversals. Recursion terminates when `Root` is `NIL`, which indicates an empty subtree. The only remaining question is what it means to `Process` a node. The processing can be as simple as displaying the data, as we have done in the example, or it may be something else, depending on the task at hand. Whatever the processing to be done, it is performed by a separate `Process` procedure. Note that `WriteLn` cannot be used to display composite data.

Finding a target datum within the binary search tree is a simple process of recursion. If `TargetData` equals the value in the current root node, we have found the target: We simply report `Found = True` and a pointer to the current root node. Otherwise, we search down the current left subtree if the target datum is smaller, or down the current right subtree if the datum is greater. Recursion terminates when we either find the target datum or find ourselves at the root of an empty subtree. Note that `Same` and `LessThan` functions are required for comparing data that might be composite:

```
FUNCTION Same( D1, D2 : DataType ) : Boolean;
{ Used by FindInBST and InsertBSTNode }
BEGIN

   { -- Insert here a comparison appropriate to the DataType }
   Same := ( D1 = D2 )

END; { Same }


FUNCTION LessThan( D1, D2 : DataType ) : Boolean;
{ Used by FindInBST and InsertBSTNode }
BEGIN

   { -- Insert here a comparison appropriate to the DataType }
   LessThan := ( D1 < D2 )

END; { LessThan }
```

```
PROCEDURE FindInBST( Root         : Tree;
                     TargetData   : DataType;
                     VAR Location : Tree;
                     VAR Found    : Boolean );
{
  FUNCTIONS REQUIRED: Same, LessThan.
}
BEGIN

   IF Root = NIL THEN
      Found := False

   ELSE IF Same( TargetData, Root^.Data ) THEN
   BEGIN
      Location := Root;
      Found    := True
   END

   ELSE IF LessThan( TargetData, Root^.Data ) THEN
      FindInBST( Root^.Left, TargetData, Location, Found )

   ELSE { TargetData greater than Root^.Data }
      FindInBST( Root^.Right, TargetData, Location, Found )

END; { FindInBST }
```

The `FindInBST` process is shown in Figure 20.6.7.

Figure 20.6.7 *Finding the character 'C' in the tree.*

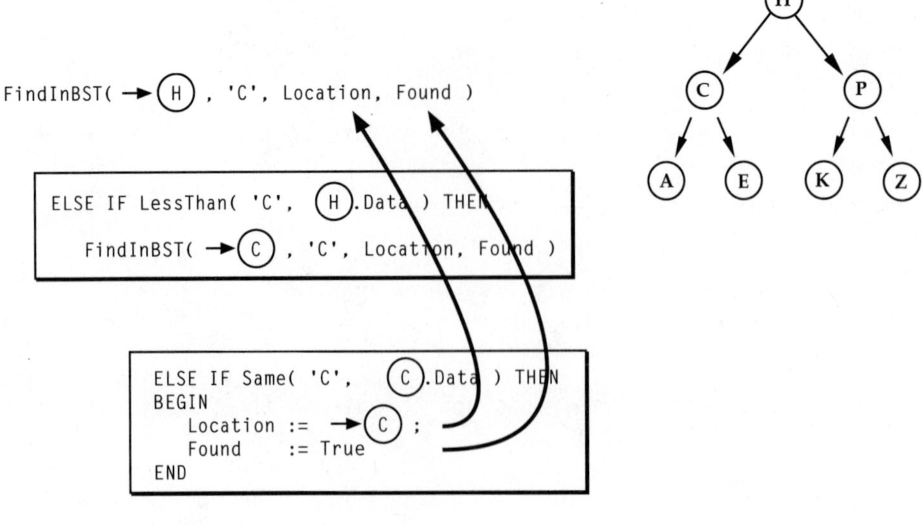

After inserting 'B' in the tree of Figure 20.6.7. **Figure 20.6.8**

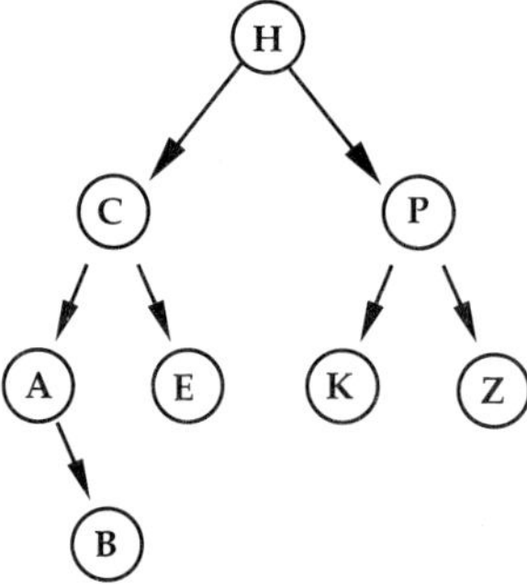

Last but certainly not least, we discuss insertion and deletion. Consider inserting data into a binary search tree, maintaining the tree's BST properties. If the tree is as shown in Figure 20.6.7 and we insert `'B'`, we should end up with the tree shown in Figure 20.6.8.

On the other hand, if we insert `'D'` into the same tree, we should end up with the tree shown in Figure 20.6.9.

No matter what we insert, it ends up in a leaf node. (But remember that we can't insert duplicates.) The process is implemented by the procedure shown on the next page.

After inserting 'D' in the tree of Figure 20.6.7. **Figure 20.6.9**

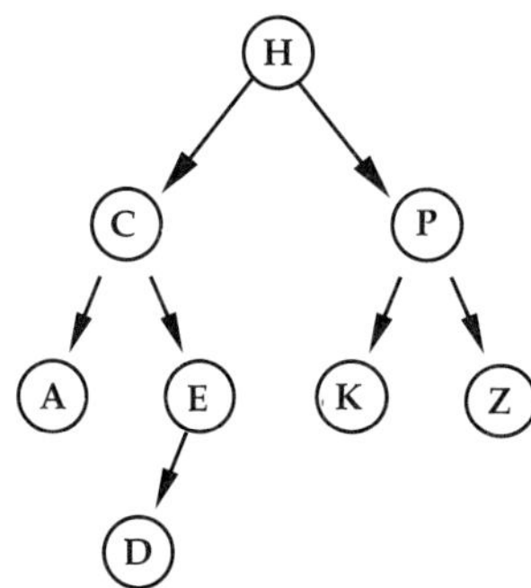

```
PROCEDURE InsertBSTNode( VAR Root : Tree;
                         NewData  : DataType );
VAR
   Loc            : Tree;
   IsInBSTAlready : Boolean;

   PROCEDURE AddLeaf( VAR Root : Tree;
                      NewData  : DataType);
   {
     PRECONDITION:
     Root is NIL.

     POSTCONDITION:
     Root points to a new leaf node containing NewData.
   }
   BEGIN
      New( Root );
      Root^.Data  := NewData;
      Root^.Left  := NIL;
      Root^.Right := NIL
   END; { AddLeaf }

   PROCEDURE DoInsertion( VAR Root : Tree;
                          NewData  : DataType );
   {
     PRECONDITION:
     Root points to a BST that does not contain NewData.

     POSTCONDITION:
     Root points to a BST containing NewData.
   }
   BEGIN

      IF Root = NIL THEN
         AddLeaf( Root, NewData )

      ELSE IF LessThan( NewData, Root^.Data ) THEN
         DoInsertion( Root^.Left, NewData )

      ELSE { NewData is greater than Root^.Data }
         DoInsertion( Root^.Right, NewData )

   END; { DoInsertion }

BEGIN { InsertBSTNode }

   FindInBST( Root, NewData, Loc, IsInBSTAlready );

   IF IsInBSTAlready THEN
      WriteLn( 'ATTEMPT TO INSERT DUPLICATE DATA' )
   ELSE
      DoInsertion( Root, NewData )

END; { InsertBSTNode }
```

Insertion of 'E' into the BST. **Figure 20.6.10**

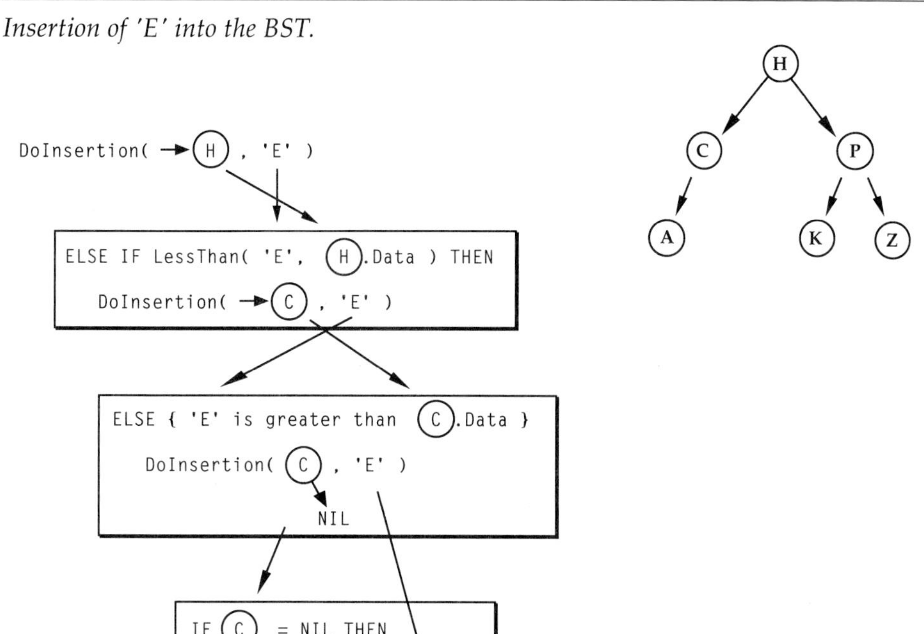

This process is illustrated in Figure 20.6.10.

Deleting a node from a binary search tree

Deleting nodes is rather tricky. The first step is to find a pointer to the node that should be deleted. Once we have the pointer, there are three possible cases:

1. The node might be a leaf node, like the E-node in the BST below:

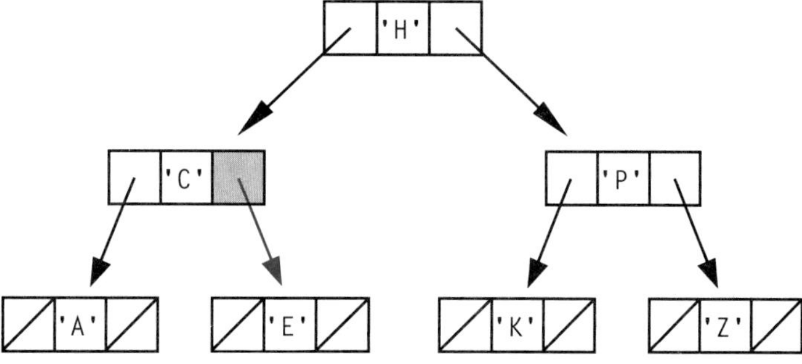

In this case, we simply `Dispose` the pointer to the node in question, then set the pointer to `NIL`:

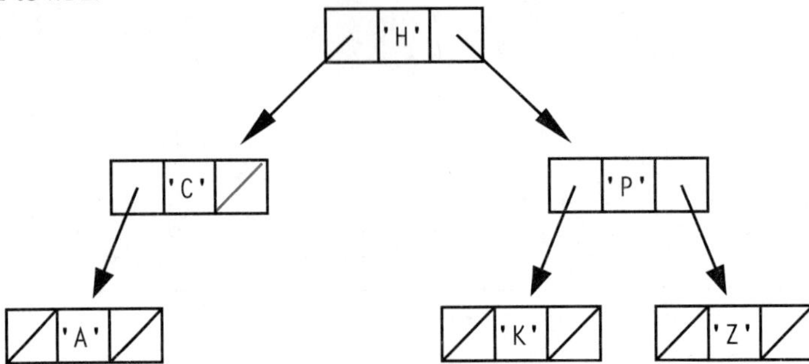

2. The node to be deleted might have only one child, like the C-node above. In this case, we simply copy the pointer to the child into the pointer to the deletion node, and dispose of the deletion node:

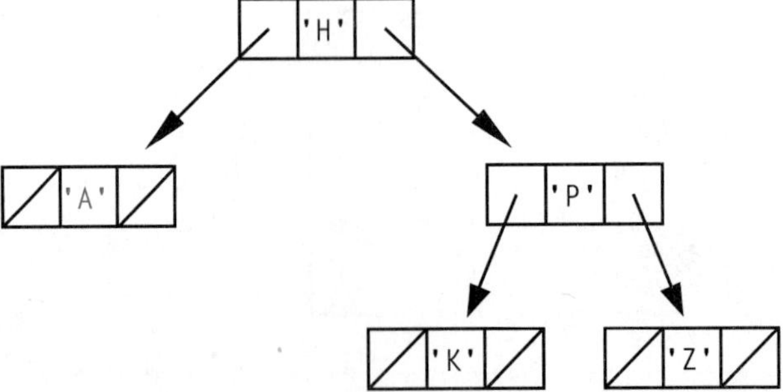

3. The node to be deleted might be an interior node, like the C-node shown in the following diagram:

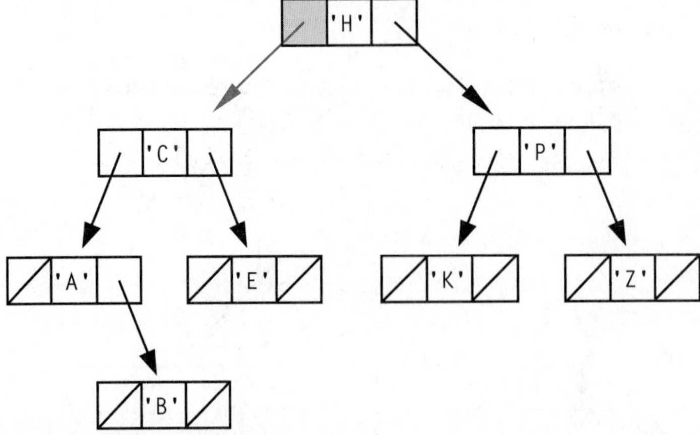

In this case, we find the node in the left subtree containing the largest value that is smaller than the value we intend to delete. This node is said to be the **predecessor** of the deletion node:

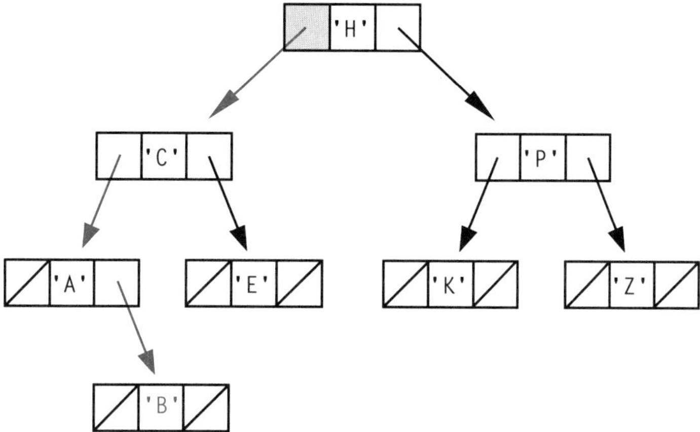

We copy the predecessor node's data into the target node, overwriting the target node's data, then delete the predecessor node:

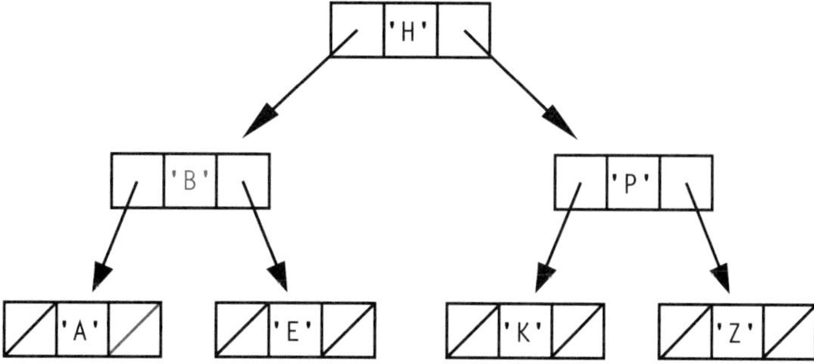

The implementation of this algorithm is—you guessed it—left as an exercise.

Exercises

25. Searching for a datum in a *full* binary search tree is an $O(\lg N)$ process, but searching for a datum in a binary search tree can take as long as $O(N)$. Explain.

26. Explain the remark on page 735 that tree sort can be as fast as $O(N \lg N)$, but also can be as slow as $O(N^2)$.

27. Implement the preorder and postorder traversal procedures and test them on the BST shown in Figure 20.6.2.

28. Explain why `RetrieveRoot` should not be written as a function.

29. Implement the `DeleteBSTNode` procedure outlined above, using a `Predecessor` function.

30. In the `DeleteBSTNode` procedure, a successor datum will work just as well as a predecessor, if we define the successor to be the smallest value that is larger than the value to be deleted. Implement the procedure in this way.

LOOKING BACK

A pointer is a variable used to store the address of another variable. We can have pointers to characters, pointers to integers, pointers to arrays—pointers to any type. A pointer's type depends on what it points to. A pointer to one type cannot be used as a pointer to any other type.

The declaration of a pointer creates only the pointer itself, not the variable pointed to. To create a variable to which a pointer points, we use the `New` procedure. For example, to create a variable to which `P` points, we call `New( P )`. This creates a storage cell to which `P` points, but it does not initialize the cell, or give the cell a name. The created cell is simply called "the cell to which `P` points," and is referred to as `P↑` or "`P`-up-arrow," which is usually entered as `P^`.

Pointed-to cells are de-allocated by means of the standard `Dispose` procedure. The call `Dispose( P )` de-allocates the storage used for `P^`, leaving the `P` pointer undefined. Some Pascal systems, however, do not actually recycle the memory de-allocated by `Dispose`.

Pascal uses the reserved word `NIL` for the standard value of a pointer that does not point to anything. `NIL` is the points-to-nothing value for all pointers in Pascal, no matter what type of storage they point to. The `NIL` value can be assigned to any pointer.

The importance of pointers lies in their use to reference dynamically allocated storage cells. In this chapter, we used pointers to build three dynamic data structures—structures that can grow and shrink while the program runs.

1. We built a linked-list abstract data type.
2. We used linked lists to build a dynamic string ADT.
3. We built a binary search tree ADT.

These data structures provided further examples of the advantages of building abstract data types. We built the list ADT in such a way that its implementation could be changed without altering the interface. We looked at an array implementation as well as the pointer implementation.

We also found that the pointer implementations of linked lists and binary trees were intrinsically recursive data structures, and found that such data structures lend themselves to recursive implementations of their operations.

TERMS EMPHASIZED IN THIS CHAPTER

Allocation 692–93
Assigning a pointer 694
Ancestor node 732
Anonymous variable 691, 693
Binary search tree (BST) ADT 735–47
Binary tree 732
Child node 732
Copying a pointer 694
Deallocation 693
Declaring pointers 690–91
Deleting a node 745–47
Dereference 691
Descendant node 732
`Dispose` (standard procedure) 693
Doubly-linked list 730–31
Dynamic allocation 696
Dynamic data structure 689, 696
Dynamic string ADT 719–25
Expression tree 733–34
Full binary tree 732
Game tree 734
Grandparent node 732
Head of list 704, 726
Height 732
Implementation 704, 723, 725, 740
Initializing pointers 692–94
Inorder traversal 733, 734
Inserting a node 743–45
Interface 699, 719, 736
Interior node 732
Leaf node 732
Level of node 732
Linked-array list 729–30
Linked list ADT 698–704, 725–31
List 698
Mutually recursive 704
`New` (standard procedure) 692–93
`NIL` 692–93
Node 703
Parent node 732
Point to 690
Pointer variable 690
Postorder traversal 733
Predecessor node 699, 746
Preorder traversal 733
Queue 727
Recursion 711
Reference 691
Root node 732
Sibling node 732
Static allocation 692, 695, 699
String 719
Subtree 732
Successor node 699
Tail of list 726
Traversing a list 726
Traversing a tree 733
Tree 732
Tree sort 735
Up-arrow 690

PROJECTS

1. Modify the `SelectionSort` procedure of Section 14.4 so that it will work correctly with the linked lists implemented in Section 20.3.

2. Devise a program to test experimentally whether `Dispose` actually frees up memory for reuse by your Pascal system. Run your program and report your findings.

3. Write a program that reads employee records from a data file, stores them in an ordered linked list, allows the data to be edited, and finally stores the resulting list in another text file.

4. The `Concatenate` procedure of Section 20.4 behaves strangely when `Str1` and `Str2` happen to be the same dynamic string. In this situation, `ConcatStr` becomes a string linked list whose tail points to its own head! What will happen if such a string is sent to the `WriteLnStr` procedure? Modify `Concatenate` to prevent this behavior and test your new procedure.

5. Write a recursive version of `Concatenate`.

6. Write a procedure that finds and reports the positions of all instances of a given data value in a linked list.

7. A major drawback of the linked lists of Section 20.3 is that the links point only from the head toward the tail. As a result, list operations must always begin at the head and then work their way down the list. This makes it relatively time-consuming to perform operations at the tail. Correct this problem by rewriting the `ListADT` for doubly linked lists in which there are both `Head` and `Tail` pointers, and in which each node contains pointers to both its successor and predecessor. Such lists were described in Section 20.5.

8. Write a procedure that reverses a linked list. (Hint: This can be done without moving any data.)

9. A sublist is a portion of a list. Write a boolean function that reports whether a given list is a sublist of another given list.

10. Write a procedure that swaps two given data items in a linked list.

11. Write a procedure that deletes all duplicate nodes in a linked list. A helpful algorithm was described in Section 20.5

12. Design and write both an interface and an implementation for an ordered list ADT. An ordered list is one in which the items are arranged in order: Item1 ≤ Item2 ≤. . . . Your ADT should include procedures to create an ordered list, insert an item while maintaining the order, delete an item, and search a list for an item.

REFERENCES

The list is such an important data type that some programming languages treat it as the fundamental data structure. The primary example is the LISP ("LISt Processing") language, invented in 1956 by John McCarthy. LISP has recently surged in importance with the introduction of a standardized version called Common LISP. Excellent introductions to LISP programming include Harold Abelson, Gerald Jay Sussman, and Julie Sussman, *Structure and Interpretation of Computer Programs* (MIT Press/McGraw-Hill, 1985); Daniel P. Friedman and Matthias Felleisen, *The Little LISPer*, second edition (SRA, 1986); and John Anderson, Albert Corbett, and Brian Reiser, *Essential LISP* (Addison-Wesley Publishing, 1986).

Binary search trees are discussed in data structures texts. Some of the clearest are Dan McCracken, *A Second Course in Computer Science with Pascal* (John Wiley & Sons, 1987); Paul Helman, Robert Veroff, and Frank R. Carrano, *Intermediate Problem Solving and Data Structures: Walls and Mirrors*, second edition (Benjamin/Cummings, 1991); and Daniel F. Stubbs and Neil W. Webre: *Data Structures with Abstract Data Types and Pascal*, second edition (Brooks/Cole, 1989).

Excerpts from *The Hacker's Dictionary*

CREEPING FEATURISM *(kreep'eeng feetch':r-iz':m) noun.*
The tendency for anything complicated to become even more complicated because people keep saying, "Gee, it would be even better if it had this feature too." (See FEATURE.) The result is usually a patchwork, because it grew one *ad hoc* step at a time, rather than being planned. Planning is a lot of work, but it's easy to add just one extra little feature to help someone . . . then another . . . and another. . . .

FEATURE *noun.*

1. An intended property or behavior (as of a program). Whether it is good is immaterial.
2. A good property or behavior (as of a program). Whether it was intended is immaterial.
3. A surprising property or behavior; in particular, one that is purposely inconsistent because it works better that way. . . . The inconsistency is therefore a feature and not a BUG.

HACK

1. *noun.* A quick bit of work that produces what is needed, but not well.
2. The result of that work: a CROCK. (Occasionally the connotation is affectionate.)
3. An incredibly good, and perhaps very time-consuming, piece of work that produces exactly what is needed.
4. The result of that work.
5. A clever technique.
6. A brilliant practical joke. The value of the hack varies in proportion to its cleverness, harmlessness, surprise value, fame, and appropriate use of technology.
7. *verb.* With "together," to throw something together so it will work. See KLUDGE.

CROCK *noun.*

1. Something, especially a program, that works but does so in an unbelievably ugly or awkward manner; more specifically, something that works acceptably but which is quite prone to failure if disturbed in the least.
2. A tightly woven, almost completely unmodifiable structure; something very complicated that ought to be simple.

Computer programs seldom stay the same forever. They tend to evolve, and are constantly changed as BUGS are fixed or new FEATURES added. Crocks make this difficult because, although they work, they are very difficult to make small changes to. Synonym: KLUDGE.

KLUGE, KLUDGE *(klooj) noun.*

1. A Rube Goldberg device in hardware or software.
2. A clever programming trick intended to solve a particularly nasty case in an efficient, if not clear, manner. Often used to repair BUGS. Often verges on being a CROCK.
3. Something that works for the wrong reason.

—From *The Hacker's Dictionary*, by Guy L. Steele, Jr., Donald R. Woods, Raphael A. Finkel, Mark A. Crispin, Richard M. Stallman, and Geoffrey S. Goodfellow (Harper & Row, 1983). Based on the "jargon file" evolved at a number of universities.

Rube Goldberg: American cartoonist (1883–1970) who satirized the modern infatuation with technology by drawing cartoons of outlandishly complex machines.

CHAPTER

21

Stacks and Queues

CHAPTER CONTENTS

INTRODUCTION

The lists that we have examined so far can be accessed more or less randomly. Data values can be inserted, examined, or deleted at the head, at the tail, or in the middle. Sometimes, however, an application demands a list with "controlled access." We examine two common types of controlled access in this chapter, stack and queue access, along with typical applications.

For example, if we are simulating the operation of an airport ticket counter, the line of customers can be represented as a list in which nodes (customers) are added to the list at the tail, but are removed from it at the head as they are served by the ticket agent. Such a list is called a **queue** (pronounced "kyoo"). The first customer in the queue is served first; this is called **first-in, first-out (FIFO)** processing.

FIFO: First-in, first-out.

On the other hand, to compute the taxes on business inventory, we might prefer to model the inventory as a list in which the last item to be added to the list (purchased) is the first item to be removed from the list (sold). Assuming that prices tend upward over time, later-produced goods cost more, so our **last-in, first out (LIFO)** inventory model would minimize profits and therefore taxes. Our model makes both insertions and deletions at the head of the list. A list processed in this way is called a **stack**.

LIFO: Last-in, first-out.

Stacks and queues are both important special cases of lists, and can be easily built as ADTs, using the list ADT of Chapter 20.

21.1 STACKS

Stack: A list in which items are inserted and retrieved from the same end. In other words, a last-in, first-out list.

A **stack** is treated as a single-ended list, in which insertions, inspections, and deletions occur only at the head, which is called the **top** of the stack. Adding a node to the top of the stack is called **pushing** it onto the stack. Removing a node from the top is called **popping** it from the stack. This terminology is based on the operation of a spring-loaded plate dispenser in a cafeteria (Figure 21.1.1).

A stack ADT

A stack, considered as an abstract data type, can be described as follows:

Stack ADT Specification

Data structure:

A stack is a list in which all insertions and deletions occur at the head end, called the top.

Operations:

- Create an empty stack.
- Check for an empty stack.
- Check for a full stack.
- *Push* a given item onto the top of the stack.
- *Pop* an item from the top of the stack.

Declaring the stack ADT

A stack can be declared like a list, and the stack operations can be implemented in terms of the list operations we wrote in Section 20.3. Thus, to `Push` is the same as to `InsertAtHead`, and to `Pop` is the same as to copy the top item, and then `DeleteHead`. This is shown in Figures 21.1.2 and 21.1.3.

Figure 21.1.1 *Stack terminology is derived from the operation of a cafeteria plate dispenser.*

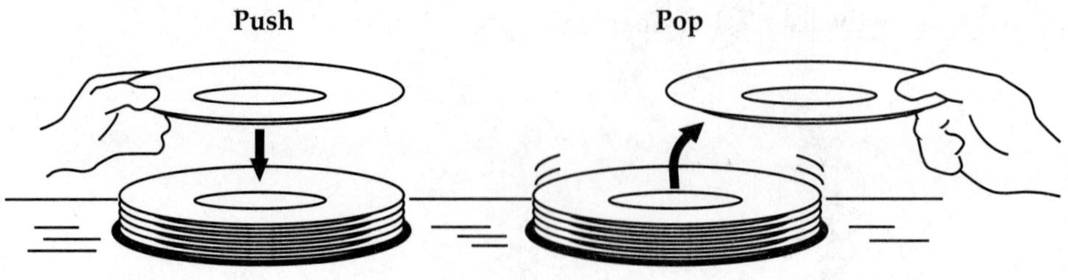

Pushing the value 'T' onto a stack of characters. **Figure 21.1.2**

Before the push:

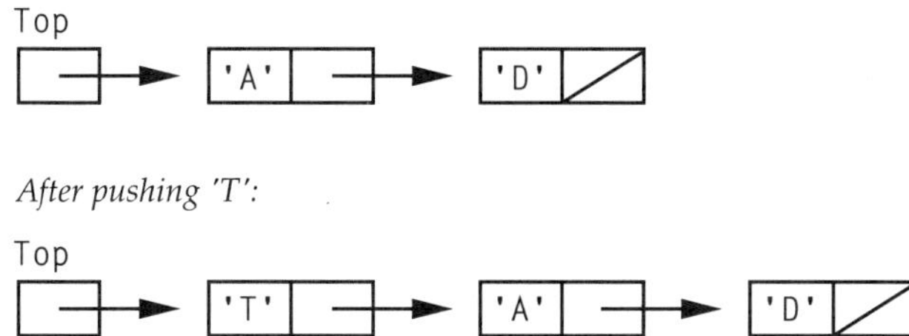

The stack ADT interface

Because we've already built the useful list operations in Chapter 20, the stack implementation is trivial:

```
TYPE
   { Uses ListADT from Sections 20.2 and 20.3. }

   Stack = List;

{***************************************************}
{ Creates an empty stack.                           }
{***************************************************}
PROCEDURE CreateEmptyStack( VAR Top : Stack );
{
  POSTCONDITION:
  Top is an empty stack.
}
```

Popping a value from a stack of characters. **Figure 21.1.3**

Before popping:

Top

After popping:

Top

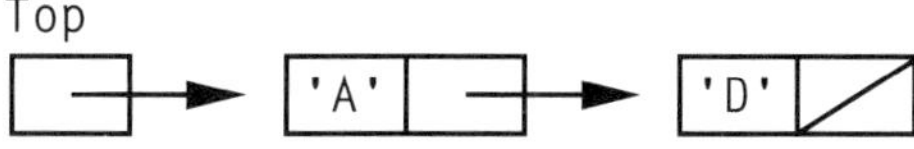

and the 'T' has been copied into a variable.

```
{************************************************}
{ Reports whether the given stack is empty.      }
{************************************************}
FUNCTION StackIsEmpty( Top : Stack ) : Boolean;
{
  PRECONDITION:
  Top has been initialized.

  POSTCONDITION:
  Returns True if Top is an empty stack;
  otherwise, returns False.
}

{************************************************}
{ Reports whether the given stack is full;       }
{ that is, if it is unable to accept a Push.     }
{************************************************}
FUNCTION StackIsFull( Top : Stack ) : Boolean;
{
  PRECONDITION:
  Top has been initialized.

  POSTCONDITION:
  Returns True if Top cannot accept more data;
  otherwise, returns False.
}

{************************************************}
{ Add NewData to Top of stack.                   }
{************************************************}
PROCEDURE Push( VAR Top : Stack;
                NewData : DataType );
{
  PRECONDITION:
  Top has been initialized.

  POSTCONDITION:
  NewData has been added to top of stack.
}
```

```
{***********************************************}
{ Pop top of stack into PoppedData.             }
{***********************************************}
PROCEDURE Pop( VAR Top        : Stack;
               VAR PoppedData : DataType );
{
  PRECONDITION:
  Top is not empty.

  POSTCONDITIONS:
  Top of stack has been copied into PoppedData;
  top node of stack has been deleted.
}

{***********************************************}
{ Copy top of stack into TopData.               }
{***********************************************}
PROCEDURE RetrieveTop( Top         : Stack;
                       VAR TopData : DataType );
{
  PRECONDITION:
  Top is not empty.

  POSTCONDITIONS:
  TopData contains a copy of the top item in the
  stack. The stack is unchanged.
}
```

Note that, according to these declarations, it is an error to call `Pop` or `RetrieveTop` when the stack is empty. When the stack is empty, we can expect these procedures to issue error messages.

Also note that `Pop` and `RetrieveTop` are procedures and not functions because they return `DataType`, which may be composite. Pascal functions are not allowed to return composite types.

Implementing the stack ADT operations

The operations are all similar to, or written in terms of, the list operations of Sections 20.3 and 20.4. This means that the declaration of `List` itself, and the procedures `InsertAtHead` and `DeleteHead`, are used by our new ADT. In other words, we are using one ADT to build another, as we did with strings in Section 20.4. Again, several of the procedures and functions are trivial:

```
PROCEDURE CreateEmptyStack( VAR Top : Stack );
BEGIN

   CreateEmptyList( Top )

END; { CreateEmptyStack }


FUNCTION StackIsEmpty( Top : Stack ) : Boolean;
BEGIN

   StackIsEmpty := ListIsEmpty( Top )

END; { StackIsEmpty }


FUNCTION StackIsFull( Top : Stack ) : Boolean;
BEGIN

   StackIsFull := ListIsFull( Top )

END; { StackIsFull }


PROCEDURE Push( VAR Top : Stack;
                NewData : DataType );
BEGIN

   IF NOT ListIsFull( Top ) THEN
      InsertAtHead( Top, NewData )

   ELSE
      WriteLn( 'STACK IS FULL' )

END; { Push }


PROCEDURE Pop( VAR Top        : Stack;
               VAR PoppedData : DataType );
VAR
   Found : Boolean;

BEGIN

   IF NOT ListIsEmpty( Top ) THEN
   BEGIN
      RetrieveNth( Top, 1, PoppedData, Found );
      DeleteHead( Top )
   END

   ELSE
      WriteLn( 'ATTEMPT TO POP EMPTY STACK.' )

END; { Pop }
```

```
PROCEDURE RetrieveTop( Top        : Stack;
                       VAR TopData : DataType );
VAR
   Found : Boolean;

BEGIN

   IF NOT ListIsEmpty( Top ) THEN
      RetrieveNth( Top, 1, TopData, Found )

   ELSE
      WriteLn( 'STACK IS EMPTY' )

END; { RetrieveTop }
```

21.2 CASE STUDY: EVALUATING POSTFIX EXPRESSIONS

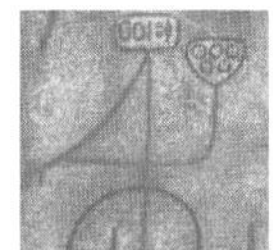

The algebraic notation commonly used for numeric expressions places a binary operator between its two operands. For example, in the expression A * (B + C), the operands of + are B and C, while the operands of * are A and the result of B + C. This notation, with the operators between the operands, is called **infix notation**.

Unfortunately, this notation is often ambiguous. What, for example, is the value of A * B + C? Are the operands of * A and B, or A and the result of B + C? Of course, we resolve this ambiguity by establishing an order of precedence of operators. Taking * to have higher precedence than +, we say that A * B + C should be evaluated as though it were written (A * B) + C. In other words, in expressions of this kind, we often have ambiguity that must be solved with the help of additional rules, or we have parentheses that serve to force some operations to be performed before others.

But there are other ways to write expressions. We can adopt a *postfix notation*, in which an operator is immediately preceded by its operands. In this notation, the expression AB+ means to add A and B; the expression AB* means to multiply A and B. Continuing on, AB+C* means that A and B should be added, then the result should be multiplied by C. Table 21.2.1 shows some more examples, using single-digit numbers as operands.

Examples of postfix expressions. **Table 21.2.1**

Postfix expression	Meaning	Value
5 2 3 * +	Multiply 2 and 3, then add the result to 5.	11
5 2 * 4 2 / –	Multiply 5 and 2, divide 4 by 2, then subtract the second result from the first.	8

We can also extend this notation to include unary operators. We can use, for example, ~ to mean unary minus, understanding that this special operator takes only one operand. Then the postfix expression 6 ~ 2 * 3 / would mean to "multiply –6 by 2, and then divide the result by 3," giving the value –4.

The advantage of postfix notation is that it is completely unambiguous, without the need to use precedence rules or parentheses. For this reason, high-level language compilers translate numeric expressions to postfix notation before generating machine-level object code to carry out the operations.

To carry out the operations in the correct order, the computer stores the operands in an **operand stack**. A stack is needed because an operator operates on the previous two operands—the most recent operands, so to speak. To see how this works, consider the steps in the evaluation of 5 2 3 * +. As the computer starts to scan the expression, it first finds three operands. At this point, no operators have been found, so the operands must be stored until an operator happens along. The computer pushes them onto a stack:

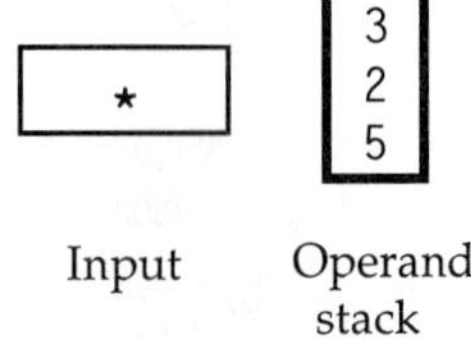

Then a * operator is encountered. We know that the * must multiply the last two operands, so we pop two operands—3 and then 2—from the stack and multiply them, obtaining the product 6. Since we don't yet know what to do with the 6, we push it onto the stack:

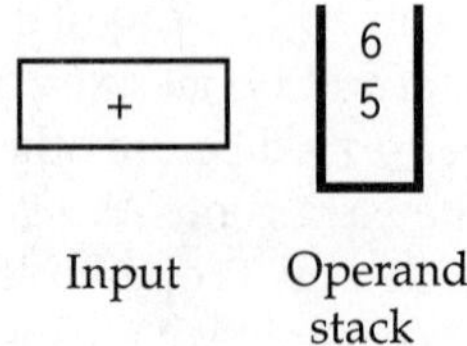

Then, continuing to scan the expression, we encounter a + operator. It must operate on the two previous operands, so we pop a 6 and then a 5 from the stack and add them together. We push the sum, 11, back onto the stack:

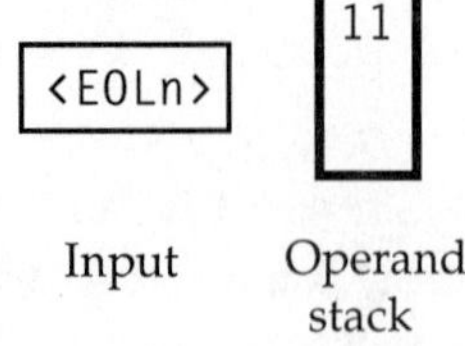

When we continue to scan the expression, we find that we are finished. This means that the number on top of the stack must be the value of the expression, so we pop it:

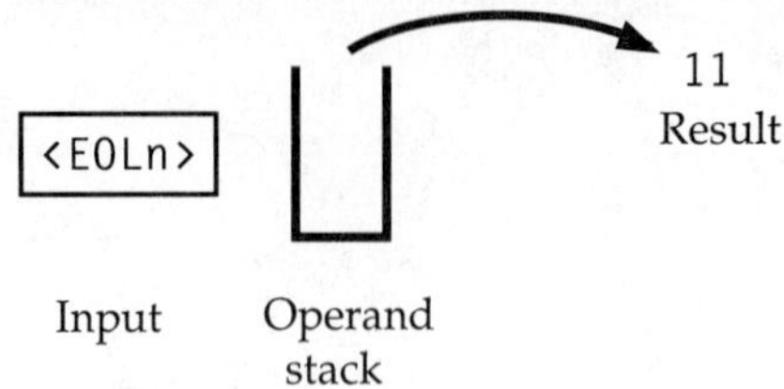

We can extend this method to include unary minus by adopting the special symbol ~ to mean a minus sign, and agreeing to pop only one operand for this operator.

A procedure to evaluate a postfix expression

Because it is completely unambiguous, postfix evaluation is easy to program. We need a stack for storing operands, the ADT operations shown in Section 21.1, and some conventions regarding the nature of operands. For the sake of a simple illustration, let's limit ourselves to single-digit numbers, stored as real values, and let's avoid embedded spaces in expressions. With these simplifications, each character in a postfix expression represents either an operand or an expression. The procedure below uses a stack of real numbers:

```
FUNCTION NotAnOperator( Op : Char ) : Boolean;
{ Used by EvaluatePostfix. }
BEGIN

   NotAnOperator :=
      ( ( Op <> '+' )
           AND ( Op <> '-' )
              AND ( Op <> '*' )
                 AND ( Op <> '/' )
                    AND ( Op <> '~' ) )

END; { NotAnOperator }


PROCEDURE EvaluatePostfix;
{
  Reads a one-line postfix expression from the
  keyboard and displays its value.

  WARNING: NO ERROR-CHECKING IS PERFORMED ON THE
  EXPRESSION.

  FUNCTION REQUIRED: NotAnOperator.
}
VAR
   Ch : Char;
   Operand1, Operand2, Value : Real;
   OperandStack : Stack; { Stack of reals }

BEGIN

   CreateEmptyStack( OperandStack );
```

```
WHILE ( NOT EOF ) AND ( NOT EOLn ) DO
BEGIN

   Read( Ch );

   IF NotAnOperator( Ch ) THEN
   BEGIN
      {
       -- Ch represents an operand:
          push its real value onto stack.
      }
      Value := Ord( Ch ) - Ord( '0' );
      Push( OperandStack, Value )
   END

   ELSE
      {
       -- Ch represents an operator: pop its
          operand(s), perform the operation, and
          push the result back onto the stack.
      }
      CASE Ch OF

      '+':
           BEGIN
              Pop( OperandStack, Operand2 );
              Pop( OperandStack, Operand1 );
              Push( OperandStack,
                    (Operand1 + Operand2) )
           END;

      '-':
           BEGIN
              Pop( OperandStack, Operand2 );
              Pop( OperandStack, Operand1 );
              Push( OperandStack,
                    (Operand1 - Operand2) )
           END;

      '*':
           BEGIN
              Pop( OperandStack, Operand2 );
              Pop( OperandStack, Operand1 );
              Push( OperandStack,
                    (Operand1 * Operand2) )
           END;
```

```
        '/':
            BEGIN
               Pop( OperandStack, Operand2 );
               Pop( OperandStack, Operand1 );
               Push( OperandStack,
                     (Operand1 / Operand2) )
            END;

        '~':
            BEGIN
               Pop( OperandStack, Operand1 );
               Push( OperandStack,
                     (-Operand1) )
            END
      END { CASE }
   END; { WHILE }
   {--Display final result }
   Pop( OperandStack, Value );
   WriteLn( 'Value is ', Value:10:4 );
   IF EOLn THEN
      {--Flush the remainder of the input line }
      ReadLn;
END; { EvaluatePostfix }
```

Exercises

1. In your own words, explain the conceptual difference between a stack and a list.
2. Draw a diagram of stack S and variable Dat after the following sequence of operations. Assume that Dat is of type Char and that S is a stack of characters.

   ```
   CreateEmptyStack( S );
   Push( S, 'P' );
   Push( S, 'O' );
   Push( S, 'T' );
   Pop( S, Dat );
   Push( S, 'P' )
   ```

3. Eliminate the NotAnOperator function by rewriting the EvaluatePostfix procedure to use a *set* of operators rather than a hard-wired list.
4. Draw a diagram of stack S and variable Dat after the following sequence of operations. Assume that Dat is of type Char and that S is a stack of characters.

   ```
   CreateEmptyStack( S );
   Push( S, 'W' );
   Pop( S, Dat );
   Push( S, 'E' );
   Pop( S, Dat );
   ```

5. Write a procedure that flushes a dynamic stack by de-allocating all its nodes and setting Top to empty. Do not use pointer operations directly; instead, make calls to operations defined in the list ADT.

6. Write a `Reverse` procedure that reverses the items in a list by using a stack. Do not use pointer operations directly; use only operations from `StackADT`.

21.3 QUEUES

Queue: A list in which items are inserted at one end and retrieved at the other end. In other words, a first-in, first-out list.

Another special kind of list is called a *queue*. A queue is a first-in, first-out list. In other words, the first item stored in the list is the first to be removed. To accomplish this, data values are inserted at one end of the list, called the **back**, but removed from the other end, called the **front**. The data are treated like people waiting in line, or queue, as it is called in Britain. That's the origin of the term.

When we insert an item in a queue, we are said to **enqueue** it; when we delete an item, we are said to **dequeue** (pronounced "dee-kyoo") it. These operations are shown in Figure 21.3.1.

Specifying a queue ADT

Like a stack, a queue is a specialized list in which insertion and deletion are defined only at specified ends of the list. But unlike a stack, a queue inserts data at the end opposite to that from which data are removed.

The queue operations are analogous to those we defined for stacks:

Figure 21.3.1 *Enqueuing adds data at the back of the queue; dequeuing removes data from the front.*

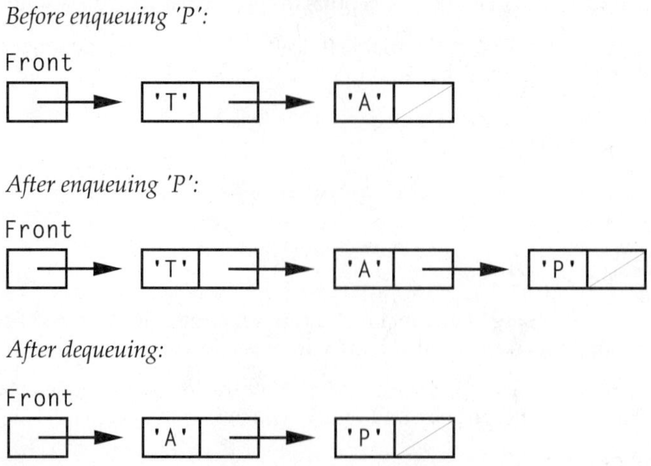

Before enqueuing 'P':

Front

'T' → 'A'

After enqueuing 'P':

Front

'T' → 'A' → 'P'

After dequeuing:

Front

'A' → 'P'

Queue ADT Specification

Data structure:

A list with insertion at one end, called the back, and deletion at the other end, called the front. A queue is therefore a first-in, first-out list.

Operations:

- Create an empty queue.
- Check whether a given queue is empty.
- Check whether a given queue is full.
- Determine the number of items in a queue.
- Enqueue (insert) a given item at the back of a given queue.
- Dequeue (delete) the front item in a given queue by making a copy of it, and then removing it from the front of the queue.
- Inspect the item at the front of the queue without dequeuing it.

Declaring a queue ADT

Typical Pascal declarations for queue operations are shown below:

```
{************************************************}
{ Create an empty queue.                         }
{************************************************}
PROCEDURE CreateEmptyQueue( VAR Front : Queue );
{
  POSTCONDITION:
  Front is an empty queue.
}

{************************************************}
{ Report whether a given queue is empty.         }
{************************************************}
FUNCTION QueueIsEmpty( Front : Queue ) : Boolean;
{
  PRECONDITION:
  Front has been initialized.

  POSTCONDITIONS:
  Returns True if Front is empty; otherwise, returns False.
}
```

```
{**************************************************}
{ Report whether a given queue is full.            }
{**************************************************}
FUNCTION QueueIsFull( Front : Queue ) : Boolean;
{
  PRECONDITION:
  Front has been initialized.

  POSTCONDITIONS:
  Returns True if Front cannot accept more data;
  otherwise, returns False.
}

{**************************************************}
{ Report number of items in a given queue.         }
{**************************************************}
FUNCTION QueueLength( Front : Queue ) : NonNegInt;
{
  PRECONDITION:
  Front has been initialized.

  POSTCONDITIONS:
  Returns number of items in queue if nonempty;
  if queue is empty, returns zero.
}

{**************************************************}
{ If given queue is not full, add NewData to the   }
{ back of a given queue. If full, do nothing.      }
{**************************************************}
PROCEDURE Enqueue( VAR Front    : Queue;
                       NewData  : DataType );
{
  PRECONDITIONS:
  Front and NewData have been initialized.

  POSTCONDITIONS:
  A copy of NewData has been appended at the back of the
  queue unless queue is full, in which case the queue
  is unchanged.
}
```

```
{************************************************}
{ Remove front item from queue, if not empty;     }
{ if queue is empty, do nothing.                  }
{************************************************}
PROCEDURE Dequeue( VAR Front     : Queue;
                   VAR FrontData : DataType );
{
  PRECONDITION:
  Front is not empty.

  POSTCONDITION:
  The front item in the queue has been copied
  into FrontData and then removed from the queue.
}

{************************************************}
{ Copy the front item from a given queue,         }
{ if there is a front item.                       }
{************************************************}
PROCEDURE RetrieveFront( Front         : Queue;
                         VAR FrontData : DataType );
{
  PRECONDITION:
  Front is not empty.

  POSTCONDITION:
  Copies into FrontData the item at the front of
  the queue, without changing the queue. If queue
  is empty, does nothing.
}
```

Implementing a queue ADT

As with stacks, the queue ADT can be written easily in terms of the List ADT from Sections 20.2 and 20.3.

```
TYPE
   { Uses the List ADT of Sections 20.2 and 20.3. }
   Queue = List;


PROCEDURE CreateEmptyQueue( VAR Front : Queue );
BEGIN

   CreateEmptyList( Front )

END; { CreateEmptyQueue }
```

```
FUNCTION QueueIsEmpty( Front : Queue ) : Boolean;
BEGIN

   QueueIsEmpty := ListIsEmpty( Front )

END; { QueueIsEmpty }


FUNCTION QueueLength( Front : Queue ) : NonNegInt;
BEGIN

   QueueLength := ListLength( Front )

END; { QueueLength }


PROCEDURE Enqueue( VAR Front : Queue ;
                   NewData   : DataType );

BEGIN

   IF NOT ListIsFull( Front ) THEN
      InsertAtTail( Front, NewData )

END; { Enqueue }


PROCEDURE Dequeue( VAR Front     : Queue;
                   VAR FrontData : DataType );
VAR
   Found : Boolean;

BEGIN

   IF NOT ListIsEmpty( Front ) THEN
   BEGIN
      RetrieveNth( Front, 1, FrontData, Found );
      DeleteHead( Front )
   END

END; { Dequeue }


PROCEDURE RetrieveFront( Front     : Queue;
                         VAR FrontData : DataType );
VAR
   Found : Boolean;

BEGIN

   IF NOT ListIsEmpty( Front ) THEN
      RetrieveNth( Front, 1, FrontData, Found )

END; { RetrieveFront }
```

The QueueIsFull function is system-dependent in this implementation and therefore is not shown. Check your reference manual for nonstandard ways of determining whether memory is available to be allocated.

Exercises

7. Diagram the state of Q and Dat after the following sequence of operations. Assume that Dat is of type Char and Q is a queue of characters.

```
CreateEmptyQueue( Q );
Enqueue( Q, 'H' );
Enqueue( Q, 'I' );
Enqueue( Q, 'S' );
Dequeue( Q, Dat );
Enqueue( Q, 'H' );
```

8. The implementation shown above is very inefficient when enqueuing data, because the Enqueue procedure must traverse the existing queue to find the back node. This inefficiency is caused by our implementation of lists in Section 20.3. However, Section 20.5 described a solution to this problem: using both Head and Tail pointers in a list. Build a queue ADT that uses such an implementation for lists, and then test it.

9. Consider implementing a queue as an array of DataType, as in the following declarations:

```
CONST
   MaxQLen = 20; { or whatever }
TYPE
   DataType = Char; { or whatever }
   DataArray = ARRAY [ 1..MaxQLen ] OF DataType;
   SubscriptRange = 1..MaxQLen;
   AugmentedRange = 0..MaxQLen;
   Queue = RECORD
               Items : DataArray;
               Front : SubscriptRange;
                  Back  : AugmentedRange
           END;
```

Front and Back are initially 1 and 0, respectively. Each time a datum is enqueued, Back is incremented. Each time a datum is dequeued, Front is incremented. When Back is less than Front, the queue is empty. Consider using this implementation, and explain what shortcomings it has. Can you think of any solutions?

10. In the array implementation of queues described in Exercise 9, show how to implement the queue operations listed in the interface in the text.

21.4 CASE STUDY: SIMULATING TRAFFIC AT AN INTERSECTION

Computing can often simulate a real-world situation with an abstract model, allowing the situation to be examined and analyzed without taking the time or expense to set up an actual experiment. This is particularly important when analyzing situations that might be dangerous for the experimenter or extremely expensive.

As an example of a simple (and safe) **simulation** requiring queues, consider the traffic pattern at a T-intersection where one road enters another at a stop sign. Our goal is to estimate how much traffic can flow on the bigger street before stopped cars line up more than three-deep at the stop sign (Figure 21.4.1).

On the bigger street, cars roll by in both directions without stopping. They never turn into the side street because the side street is one-way. At the stop sign, a car waiting to turn right must continue to wait until no cars are imminent from the left. A car waiting to turn left must wait until no cars are imminent from either the left or the right. On both streets, cars arrive at the intersection at random intervals.

To simulate this situation, we first need a way to represent the passage of intervals of time. For this, we will use a loop. Each trip through the loop will represent one interval of time, during which cars may approach the intersection from any of the three directions. We assume that there is no pattern to this—cars enter the directions of approach at random intervals.

The randomly timed cars approaching the intersection from either left or right on the bigger street can be represented as queued items. A queue can be thought of as a sort of tunnel, extending from off in the distance, and ending at the intersection. During any given interval of time, the queue receives either a car or the absence of a car. In other words, we either enqueue a car or we enqueue the lack of a car, and we decide on this randomly, by means of a random-number generator like the one in Appendix I. At the other end of the queue during that same interval, we dequeue whatever is there: a car or the lack of a car. Thus, the contents of a queue move forward one car length during each interval. Such a queue simulates random flow of traffic toward the intersection from a single direction. Of course, we will have two such queues, representing the flow of traffic from left and right, respectively. Cars coming from these directions just pass

Figure 21.4.1 *Traffic at an intersection where a one-way street enters a larger street at a stop sign.*

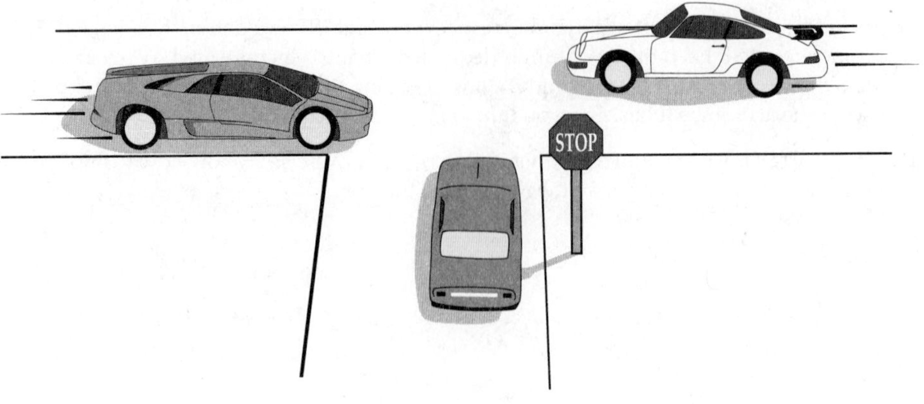

on through the intersection without stopping, so we will dequeue them as they arrive, and then discard them.

But cars coming up to the stop sign on the smaller street are a different matter because they must wait until it is safe to turn right or left. During each interval, we will randomly decide whether another car is arriving at the stop sign. We will use a third queue to hold the cars waiting at the stop sign. If a waiting car wants to turn right, we will allow this only if there are no cars in the front three positions of the queue approaching from the left. A waiting car will be allowed to turn left only if there are no cars in the front three positions of the queues approaching from both left and right. We will decide randomly which way a waiting car wants to turn at the stop sign.

Now we have a picture of the major features of the simulation. Here's an outline of the algorithm so far:

Initialization:

> Start out with empty queue of cars coming from the left and right on the big street. These queues are called `ComingFromLeft` and `ComingFromRight`.
>
> Start out with one car waiting at the stop sign: Enqueue one car in the `WaitingAtStopSign` queue.
>
> Ask user for a `TrafficDensity` number between 0.0 and 1.0. This number will be the probability that a car enters the main street from the left or right during one interval of time.
>
> Seed the random-number generator. (See Appendix I.)

Simulation loop: Each trip thru loop represents one interval of time. For all values of `Time` from 1 to `NumIntervals`, do this:

> Are cars entering big street from left or right horizon? Randomly decide whether a car enters the `ComingFromLeft` queue and whether a car enters the `ComingFromRight` queue. The probability that cars enter these queues is given by the `TrafficDensity` number.
>
> Has another car arrived at stop sign? Randomly decide whether another car should enter the `WaitingAtStopSign` queue.
>
> If there are cars waiting at the stop sign, then do this:
>
> > If the first waiting car wants to turn right, then allow it to turn right if no cars are imminent from the left.
> >
> > Otherwise, the first waiting car wants to turn left, so allow it to turn left if no cars are imminent from either the left or the right.
>
> Allow the cars coming from left and right to move forward one position in their respective queues.
>
> End of simulation loop.

If ever there was a program needing top-down design, this is it. Let's sketch the main program and its declarations before tackling the various subprograms. Here is the Pascal for the outline shown above:

```
PROGRAM TrafficFlow (Input, Output);
{ Simulates traffic at a T-intersection with stop sign. }

CONST
   NumIntervals   = 2000; { Number of time intervals simulated. }
   InitialQLength = 2;    { Initial length of queues.           }

TYPE
   NonNegInt   = 0..MaxInt;
   RightOrLeft = ( RightTurn, LeftTurn ); { For turns at stop sign }
   CarOrNot    = ( Car, NoCar );  { A car or the absence of a car. }

   {
     The queue declarations from Section 21.3 are
     modified as follows:
   }
   DataType  = CarOrNot;
   Queue     = ^Node;
   Node      = RECORD
                  Data : DataType;
                  Link : Queue
               END;

VAR
   ComingFromLeft, ComingFromRight, WaitingAtStopSign : Queue;
   Time           : Integer;     { Time interval number.          }
   Turn           : RightOrLeft; { Direction of car turning next. }
   TrafficDensity : Real;     { Probability of car appearing      }
                              { from left or right on main street. }

   Seed           : Real;     { For pseudorandom number generator. }

{
  The QueueADT procedures Enqueue, Dequeue from Section 21.3 must
  be included or imported. See Appendix H for ways to do this.
}

BEGIN { main program }

   {
     Start out with no cars from left or right,
     and one car at stop sign.
   }
   Initialize( ComingFromLeft, ComingFromRight, WaitingAtStopSign,
               Turn, TrafficDensity, Seed );
```

```
   { Start the simulation. }
   { Each trip thru loop represents one unit of time. }
   FOR Time := 1 TO NumIntervals DO
   BEGIN

      {--Are cars entering big street from left or right horizon? }
      TrafficAtHorizon( ComingFromLeft );
      TrafficAtHorizon( ComingFromRight );

      {--Has another car arrived at stop sign? }
      CheckForAnotherCar( WaitingAtStopSign );
      WriteLn(
           QueueLength(WaitingAtStopSign):2, ' cars waiting... ' );

      IF QueueLength( WaitingAtStopSign ) > 0 THEN
      {--Cars are waiting at the stop sign }
      BEGIN

         IF Turn = RightTurn THEN
         BEGIN
            IF NoCars( ComingFromLeft ) THEN
                CarTurns( WaitingAtStopSign, Turn )
         END

         ELSE { Turn = LeftTurn }
            IF NoCars( ComingFromLeft )
                     AND NoCars( ComingFromRight ) THEN
                CarTurns( WaitingAtStopSign, Turn )

      END; { IF }

      CarsMove( ComingFromLeft, ComingFromRight );
      WriteLn

   END { FOR }

END.
```

Making random decisions

The simulation uses random numbers to decide when cars enter the main-street flow from left or right, when cars arrive at the stop sign, and which way a given car wants to turn at the stop sign. In many Pascal systems, random numbers in the range $0 \leq$ number < 1 can be generated by means of a built-in `Random` function. This function uses the number initially stored in a global `Seed` variable to generate another number having no obvious relationship to the first. `Numbers` related in this way are said to be pseudorandom. For a given initial `Seed` value, a number of calls to the `Random` function will always generate the same sequence of pseudorandom numbers. To keep our program from behaving the same way every time we run it with the same `TrafficDensity` parameter, we must have some way to "randomize" the pseudorandom-number generator. For this purpose, many Pascal systems provide a `Randomize` function that gets an initial seed from the system clock.

If your Pascal system does not provide built-in `Randomize` and `Random` functions, you can use the ones provided in Appendix I. A more complete explanation of their operation is given there.

Initializing the global variables

The main program calls an Initialize procedure to perform the following initializations. The choices described below are somewhat arbitrary, and you might be interested in studying the effects of changing them:

- We get an initial seed for the pseudorandom generator.
- No cars are coming from the left on the main street.
- No cars are coming from the right on the main street.
- One car is waiting at the stop sign.
- We decide randomly which way the car wants to turn.
- We ask the user for the traffic density on the main street. This will be a number in the range [0, 1].

The following code performs these six tasks:

```
FUNCTION TurnDirection : RightOrLeft;
{ Allows a 50-50 chance for each turning direction. }
BEGIN
   IF Random > 0.5 THEN
      TurnDirection := LeftTurn
   ELSE
      TurnDirection := RightTurn
END; { TurnDirection }


PROCEDURE Initialize ( VAR ComingFromLeft     : Queue;
                       VAR ComingFromRight    : Queue;
                       VAR WaitingAtStopSign  : Queue;
                       VAR Turn               : RightOrLeft;
                       VAR TrafficDensity     : Real;
                       VAR Seed               : Real );
VAR
   Count: Integer;
BEGIN
   {--Initialize the random-number generator's global Seed }
   Randomize;
   {--Start out with no cars coming from left or right }
   CreateEmptyQueue( ComingFromLeft );
   CreateEmptyQueue( ComingFromRight );
```

```
    FOR Count := 1 TO InitialQLength DO
    BEGIN
       Enqueue( ComingFromLeft, NoCar );
       Enqueue( ComingFromRight, NoCar )
    END;

    {--Start out with one car waiting at the stop sign }
    CreateEmptyQueue( WaitingAtStopSign );
    Enqueue( WaitingAtStopSign, Car );

    {--Get turning direction for car at stop sign }
    Turn := TurnDirection;

    { Get traffic density on busy street }
    REPEAT
       WriteLn( 'Traffic density' );
       Write( 'on main road (Between 0 and 1): ' );
       ReadLn( TrafficDensity )
    UNTIL ( TrafficDensity >= 0.0 ) AND ( TrafficDensity <= 1.0 );
    WriteLn

END; { Initialize }
```

How the cars appear in the traffic streams

Cars will "pop up" at random in the streams of traffic coming from left and right on the main street, and will appear randomly at the stop sign on the side street. To make cars appear randomly, all we have to do is generate a random number and use it to decide whether to enqueue a car in the appropriate queue. If we don't enqueue a car, we enqueue the absence of a car. Thus a queue contains `Data` fields of the type `CarOrNot`, which can have the value `Car` or `NoCar`.

Traffic density is controlled on the main street by the `TrafficDensity` parameter, which the user supplies from the keyboard. During each interval of time, we generate a random number for cars coming from the left. If this number is less than `TrafficDensity`, we enqueue a `Car` in the `ComingFromLeft` queue; otherwise, we enqueue `NoCar`. Thus the lower the supplied value of `TrafficDensity`, the less likely it is that a car will be enqueued during each interval of time. The `ComingFromRight` queue is treated the same way. In both of these queues, enqueuing is handled by the `TrafficAtHorizon` procedure:

```
PROCEDURE TrafficAtHorizon( VAR Q : Queue );
BEGIN

    IF Random < TrafficDensity THEN
       Enqueue( Q, Car )

    ELSE
       Enqueue( Q, NoCar )

END; { TrafficAtHorizon }
```

Traffic on the side street is not controlled by the `TrafficDensity` parameter. Instead, let's say there is a 50–50 chance that a car will appear at the stop sign during a given interval:

```
PROCEDURE CheckForAnotherCar( VAR WaitingAtStopSign : Queue );
BEGIN

   IF Random < 0.5 THEN
      Enqueue( WaitingAtStopSign, Car );

END; { CheckForAnotherCar }
```

When a car is able to turn right or left from the stop sign, it must be dequeued from the `WaitingAtStopSign` queue. A `CarTurns` procedure is used for this. The dequeued car is simply discarded by dequeuing it into an `OnDownTheLine` variable, which is never used. In other words, the car merely moves "on down the line":

```
PROCEDURE CarTurns( VAR WaitingAtStopSign : Queue;
                    VAR Turn              : RightOrLeft );
VAR
   OnDownTheLine: DataType;

BEGIN

   IF Turn = RightTurn THEN
      WriteLn( ' A car turns right.' )

   ELSE
      WriteLn( ' A car turns left.' );

   {--Discard car at front of queue }
   Dequeue( WaitingAtStopSign, OnDownTheLine );

   {--Get direction for next turning car }
   Turn := TurnDirection

END; { CarTurns }
```

Similarly, when cars move forward on the main street from right or left, they are merely dequeued and discarded:

```
PROCEDURE CarsMove( VAR ComingFromLeft  : Queue;
                    VAR ComingFromRight : Queue );
VAR
   OnDownTheLine : DataType;

BEGIN

   {--Move cars forward one position and discard them }
   Dequeue( ComingFromLeft, OnDownTheLine );
   Dequeue( ComingFromRight, OnDownTheLine )

END; { CarsMove }
```

Finally, we come to the only tricky subprogram. A car will be allowed to turn right at the stop sign only if no cars are coming on the main road from the left. A car will be allowed to turn left at the stop sign only if no cars are coming on the main road from either the left or the right. In either case, we need a way to determine if any cars are coming from a given direction. Let us agree that the turning car is in danger if main-street cars are within three car lengths of the intersection. (These are very slow streets!) Here is a function that checks whether no cars are coming:

```
FUNCTION NoCars( Q : Queue ) : Boolean;
VAR
   Pos1, Pos2, Pos3 : DataType;

BEGIN

   {--Copy front three queue positions without changing the queue.}
   RetrieveFrontThree( Q, Pos1, Pos2, Pos3 );

   NoCars := NOT( (Pos1 = Car) OR (Pos2 = Car) OR (Pos3 = Car) )

END; { NoCars }
```

Running the simulation

This requires a `RetrieveFrontThree` procedure that can copy the front three positions of a queue into three variables of `DataType`. There is no such subprogram in the `Queue ADT` of Section 21.3, so we leave this as Project 6.

The reason for making `NoCars` a function and for giving it such a peculiar name is so that we can call it with syntax like this:

```
IF NoCars( ComingFromLeft ) THEN
```

When the above pieces are assembled, we have a program with rather spartan I/O, but it makes a nice starting point. Here is some typical output:

```
Traffic density
on main road (Between 0 and 1): 0.2

 1 cars waiting...
 A car turns left.

 0 cars waiting...

 0 cars waiting...

 0 cars waiting...

 1 cars waiting...
 A car turns right.

 1 cars waiting...

 2 cars waiting...

 2 cars waiting...
```

It should be fun to add some simple graphics to this, as suggested in the projects at the end of the chapter.

This completes our example of queues being used to aid the simulation of real-world events. As usual, the queues were used to represent data "waiting in line for something to happen." Other examples are described in the projects.

LOOKING BACK

This chapter has briefly discussed two special cases of lists in which only the ends of the list are accessed:

- In a *stack*, data are inserted and deleted at the same end, which is called the *top* of the stack. The insertion process is called *pushing* and the deletion process is called *popping*. A stack is a last-in, first-out (LIFO) list.
- In a *queue*, data are inserted and deleted at opposite ends. The end at which data are inserted is called the *back* of the queue; the end at which data are removed is called the *front*. The insertion process is called *enqueuing* and the deletion process is called *dequeuing*. A queue is a first-in, first-out (FIFO) list.

We built ADTs for stacks and queues, using the list ADT we developed in Sections 20.2 and 20.3. Since stacks and queues are just specialized lists, the new ADTs were easy to write in terms of the old one.

There were two sizable applications of these data types. We wrote a procedure to evaluate postfix expressions, using a stack to store operands until we found the corresponding operator. We wrote a program to simulate traffic at a T-intersection, using queues to represent the three streams of oncoming cars.

TERMS EMPHASIZED IN THIS CHAPTER

Dequeue 764
Enqueue 764
Evaluating postfix expressions 759–63
First-in, first-out (FIFO) 753
Infix notation 759
Last-in, first-out (LIFO) 753
Operand stack 760
Pop 754
Postfix notation 759–60
Precedence 759
Pseudorandom numbers 773–74
Push 754
Queue ADT 764–69
Queue back 764
Queue front 764
Random 773–74
Seed 773
Simulation 770–77
Stack ADT 754–59
Stack top 754
Unary operator 760

PROJECTS

1. Using stack operations, write a program that checks arithmetic expressions for balanced parentheses. That is, your program should check expressions to see if each left parenthesis has a matching right parenthesis. Push each left parenthesis onto the stack when encountered; pop the stack on encountering a right parenthesis. If there is never any attempt to pop an empty stack, and if no parentheses are left on the stack when the program terminates, the parentheses must have been balanced.
2. Write an array implementation of the stack ADT, and test your code.
3. Rewrite the maze program of Project 13, Chapter 14, using stacks. Whenever the program encounters a fork in the path, it should push all but one path onto a stack while it tries the remaining path. If that path is blocked, the program should backtrack to the fork, pop the stack to get a new path, and then try that one.
4. When a Pascal program unit calls another, it pushes its currently active variables onto a stack, followed by the arguments of the called procedure or function, and then executes the called subprogram. When this has terminated, execution returns to the caller, where the values on the stack are popped to recover the values that existed before the call. This means that a recursive call is equivalent to

   PushVariables;
   ExecuteRecursiveCode;
   PopVariables;

   Use a stack in this way to write an iterative version of the Towers of Hanoi procedure from Section 12.5. Test your work.
5. Write a complete program for running `EvaluatePostfix` (Section 21.2) in a user-friendly environment. Add error checking to protect `EvaluatePostfix` from illegal expressions.
6. Write a `RetrieveFrontThree` procedure for the queue ADT, as discussed in the description of the traffic simulation program. Then put all the pieces of the simulation together to build a working program. Test your program and use it to determine how the average number of cars waiting at the stop sign depends upon the `TrafficDensity` parameter.
7. Embellish the traffic simulation program by adding rudimentary graphics to show the flows of cars from the three directions, and how many cars are waiting at the stop sign at a given moment.
8. Write a program that simulates customers waiting for service at an airport ticket counter. Assume that customers arrive in the back of the line at random intervals, and that customers are being served by a single ticket agent, who has a fixed serving time. Use your program to determine, for given values of the parameters, the average number of people waiting in line at a given time and the average time a customer waits in line before being served.

REFERENCES

Good references for stacks and queues include Daniel F. Stubbs and Neil W. Webre, *Data Structures with Abstract Data Types and Pascal*, second edition (Brooks/Cole, 1989), and Robert L. Kruse, *Data Structures and Program Design*, second edition (Prentice Hall, 1987).

APPENDIX

Reserved Words

Reserved words have special meanings in the Pascal language and cannot be used as identifiers.

AND	DO	FUNCTION	NIL	PROGRAM	TYPE
ARRAY	DOWNTO	GOTO	NOT	RECORD	UNTIL
BEGIN	ELSE	IF	OF	REPEAT	VAR
CASE	END	IN	OR	SET	WHILE
CONST	FILE	LABEL	PACKED	THEN	WITH
DIV	FOR	MOD	PROCEDURE	TO	

Note: Some Pascal compilers treat `FORWARD` as a reserved word.

APPENDIX

B

Required Procedures and Functions

Procedures

Pascal provides 13 standard procedures that are predefined and therefore can be called without first declaring them in your program.

Procedure	Description
`Dispose(` *Pointer* `)`	De-allocates the storage cell pointed to by *Pointer*. The *Pointers* value is then undefined.
`Get(` *FilePointer* `)`	Moves the *FilePointer* forward, so that it points to the next element in the file. It is an error to use this procedure if the file is not open for reading.
`New(` *Pointer* `)`	Allocates a storage cell of the type pointed to by *Pointer*, and stores its address in *Pointer*.
`Pack(` *UnpackedArray*, *FirstSubscript*, *PackedArray* `)`	Copies the elements of *UnpackedArray* into *PackedArray*. The *FirstSubscript* element of *UnpackedArray* copied into the first position of *PackedArray*, and so on.
`Page(` *FilePointer* `)`	Advances the output device to a new page before printing the next line of the named file. If the file is not specified, the standard `Output` file is "paged," producing a system-dependent effect, often clearing the screen.
`Put(` *FilePointer* `)`	Appends the buffer variable *FilePointer*^ to the file. It is an error to use this procedure if the file is not open for writing, if *FilePointer*^ is undefined, or if *FilePointer* is not positioned at the end of the file.

Procedure	Description
`Read(` *FilePointer*, *VariableList* `)`	Reads data from the specified file into the listed variables. If the file pointer is not given, the standard `Input` file is read. It is an error to use this procedure if the file is not open for reading.
`ReadLn(` *FilePointer*, *VariableList* `)`	Reads data from the specified file into the listed variables. If the file pointer is not given, the standard `Input` file is read. Extra data on the last line are discarded. It is an error to use this procedure if the file is not open for reading, or is not a `Text` file.
`Reset(` *FilePointer* `)`	Opens the file associated with *FilePointer*, placing the file pointer at the beginning of the file. The file is *read-only*: it can be read but not written. Therefore a file must already exist before it can be opened by `Reset`.
`Rewrite(` *FilePointer* `)`	Opens the file associated with *FilePointer*, placing the file pointer at the beginning of the file. The file is *write-only*: it can be written to, but not read. If the file already contains data, they will be overwritten as the file pointer passes over them. Thus, every file opened by `Rewrite` is effectively empty.
`Unpack(` *PackedArray*, *UnpackedArray*, *FirstSubscript* `)`	Copies the elements of *PackedArray* into *UnpackedArray*. The first element of *UnpackedArray* will be copied into the *FirstSubscript* position of *UnpackedArray*, and so on.
`Write(` *FilePointer*, *ExprList* `)`	Writes the values of the listed expressions to the specified file. If the file pointer is not given, the values are written to the standard `Output` file. It is an error to use this procedure if the file is not open for writing.
`WriteLn(` *FilePointer*, *ExprList* `)`	Writes the values of the listed expressions to the specified text file. If the file pointer is not given, the values are written to the standard `Output` file. The data are written to a single line, then the line is terminated. It is an error to use this procedure if the file is not open for writing, or if the file is not a `Text` file.

Arithmetic functions

The following functions can accept either `Integer` or `Real` parameters.

Function	Computes	Comments
`Abs( X )`	Absolute value of `X`.	Result is same type as `X`.
`Arctan( X )`	Principal value of arctangent	Result is Real and in radians.
`Cos( X )`	Cosine of `X`.	`X` is assumed to be in radians. Result is Real.
`Exp( X )`	*e* to the `X` power.	Result is Real. It is an error if the result overflows.

Function	Computes	Comments
`Ln( X )`	Natural (i.e., base *e*) log of `X`.	It is an error if $X \le 0$.
`Sin( X )`	Sine of `X`.	Result is `Real`. `X` is assumed to be in radians.
`Sqr( X )`	`X * X`.	Result is same type as `X`. It is an error if `X * X` overflows.
`SqRt( X )`	Square root of `X`.	Result is Real. It is an error if the result overflows.

Transfer functions

The following functions transfer a value from one type to another, in cases where this makes sense.

Function	Parameter Type	Result Type	Computes
`Chr( I )`	`Integer`	`Char`	The character with ordinal value `I`, according to the system's character code set. (See Appendix C.)

`Ord( P )`	Any ordinal type	`Integer`	Ordinal value of `P`. For example,
			`Ord( False ) = 0`
			`Ord( True ) = 1`
			The `Ord` of a character depends on the character code used.

`Round( X )`	`Real`	`Integer`	Nearest integer to `X`. For example,
			`Round( 2.7 ) = 3;`
			`Round( -2.7 ) = -3.`

`Trunc( X )`	`Real`	`Integer`	Integer part of `X`. For example,
			`Trunc( 2.7 ) = 2;`
			`Trunc( -2.7 ) = -2.`

Ordinal functions

These functions increment or decrement an ordinal value.

Function	Computes	Comments
`Pred(` *OrdValue* `)`	The predecessor of *OrdValue*: that is, that value of the same type having an ordinal value one less.	It is an error if the predecessor does not exist.
`Succ(` *OrdValue* `)`	The successor of *OrdValue*: that is, that value of the same type having an ordinal value one greater.	It is an error if the successor does not exist.

Boolean functions

These functions compute Boolean values.

Function	Computes	Comments
`EOF(` *FilePtr* `)`	`True` if *FilePtr* points at the end of file; `False` otherwise.	It is an error if *FilePtr* has not been associated with a file. If *FilePtr* is not specified, the `Input` file is used.
`EOLn(` *FilePtr* `)`	`True` if *FilePtr* points at the end of a line; `False` otherwise.	It is an error if *FilePtr* has not been associated with a file, or if *FilePtr* is associated with a non-`Text` file. If *FilePtr* is not specified, the `Input` file is used.
`Odd( I )`	`True` if `I` is odd; `False` if `I` is even. (Zero is even.)	`I` must be `Integer`.

APPENDIX

C

Character Codes

Most computer systems use the International Standards Organization (ISO) character code, of which the American variant is the **American Standard Code for Information Interchange** (ANSI X3.41977), called ASCII (ass'-key) for short. ASCII is a seven-bit code, yielding 128 possible values from 0 through 127 decimal. The eighth bit, the most significant bit, is either set to zero, used as a parity (error-checking) bit, or used for some system-specific purpose. The characters with ordinal values 0 through 31 decimal are nondisplayable and are used to control hardware. They are called *control characters*.

Many IBM mainframes, and some competing mainframes, use the **Extended Binary-Coded Decimal Interchange Code**, called EBCDIC (ebb'-sih-dick') for short. This code is almost never used on microcomputers. EBCDIC is an 8-bit code, yielding 256 possible values from 0 through 255 decimal. Some of the 256 codes are currently unspecified. In EBCDIC, the control characters have ordinal values 0 through 63.

On the following pages are listed character code numbers in decimal (base 10), octal (base 8), and hexadecimal (base 16) notation, along with the corresponding characters. As an example of the use of these tables, on systems using ASCII, `Chr(65)` is the letter `'A'`, so that `Ord('A')` is `65`, while on systems using EBCDIC, `Chr( 193 )` is the letter `'A'`, so that `Ord('A')` is `193`.

ASCII: AMERICAN STANDARD CODE FOR INFORMATION INTERCHANGE

Dec	Oct	Hex	Char	Dec	Oct	Hex	Char
0	000	00	Null	64	100	40	@
1	001	01	^A = SOH	65	101	41	A
2	002	02	^B = STX	66	102	42	B
3	003	03	^C = ETX	67	103	43	C
4	004	04	^D = EOT	68	104	44	D
5	005	05	^E = ENQ	69	105	45	E
6	006	06	^F = ACK	70	106	46	F
7	007	07	^G = BEL	71	107	47	G
8	010	08	^H = Backspace	72	110	48	H
9	011	09	^I = Horiz Tab	73	111	49	I
10	012	0A	^J = Line Feed	74	112	4A	J
11	013	0B	^K = Vert Tab	75	113	4B	K
12	014	0C	^L = Form Feed	76	114	4C	L
13	015	0D	^M = Car Return	77	115	4D	M
14	016	0E	^N = Shift Out	78	116	4E	N
15	017	0F	^O = Shift In	79	117	4F	O
16	020	10	^P = DL Esc	80	120	50	P
17	021	11	^Q = Dev Ctl 1	81	121	51	Q
18	022	12	^R = Dev Ctl 2	82	122	52	R
19	023	13	^S = Dev Ctl 3	83	123	53	S
20	024	14	^T = Dev Ctl 4	84	124	54	T
21	025	15	^U = Neg Ack	85	125	55	U
22	026	16	^V = Synch Idle	86	126	56	V
23	027	17	^W = ETB	87	127	57	W
24	030	18	^X = Cancel	88	130	58	X
25	031	19	^Y = EM	89	131	59	Y
26	032	1A	^Z = Substitute	90	132	5A	Z
27	033	1B	Escape	91	133	5B	[
28	034	1C	File Sep	92	134	5C	\
29	035	1D	Group Sep	93	135	5D	]
30	036	1E	Record Sep	94	136	5E	^
31	037	1F	Unit Sep	95	137	5F	_
32	040	20	Space	96	140	60	`
33	041	21	!	97	141	61	a
34	042	22	"	98	142	62	b
35	043	23	#	99	143	63	c
36	044	24	$	100	144	64	d
37	045	25	%	101	145	65	e
38	046	26	&	102	146	66	f
39	047	27	'	103	147	67	g
40	050	28	(	104	150	68	h
41	051	29	)	105	151	69	i
42	052	2A	*	106	152	6A	j
43	053	2B	+	107	153	6B	k
44	054	2C	,	108	154	6C	l
45	055	2D	-	109	155	6D	m
46	056	2E	.	110	156	6E	n
47	057	2F	/	111	157	6F	o
48	060	30	0	112	160	70	p
49	061	31	1	113	161	71	q
50	062	32	2	114	162	72	r
51	063	33	3	115	163	73	s
52	064	34	4	116	164	74	t
53	065	35	5	117	165	75	u
54	066	36	6	118	166	76	v
55	067	37	7	119	167	77	w
56	070	38	8	120	170	78	x
57	071	39	9	121	171	79	y
58	072	3A	:	122	172	7A	z
59	073	3B	;	123	173	7B	{
60	074	3C	<	124	174	7C	|
61	075	3D	=	125	175	7D	}
62	076	3E	>	126	176	7E	~
63	077	3F	?	127	177	7F	Delete

EBCDIC: EXTENDED BINARY-CODED DECIMAL INTERCHANGE CODE

Dec	Oct	Hex	Char	Dec	Oct	Hex	Char
0	000	00	Null	64	100	40	Space
1	001	01	SOH	65	101	41	Req Space
2	002	02	STX	66	102	42	
3	003	03	ETX	67	103	43	
4	004	04	Select	68	104	44	
5	005	05	Horiz Tab	69	105	45	
6	006	06	Req new line	70	106	46	
7	007	07	Delete	71	107	47	
8	010	08	Graphic esc	72	110	48	
9	011	09	Superscript	73	111	49	
10	012	0A	Repeat	74	112	4A	¢
11	013	0B	Vert Tab	75	113	4B	.
12	014	0C	Form Feed	76	114	4C	<
13	015	0D	Car Return	77	115	4D	(
14	016	0E	Shift Out	78	116	4E	+
15	017	0F	Shift In	79	117	4F	OR
16	020	10	DL Escape	80	120	50	&
17	021	11	Dev Ctl 1	81	121	51	
18	022	12	Dev Ctl 2	82	122	52	
19	023	13	Dev Ctl 3	83	123	53	
20	024	14	Restore	84	124	54	
21	025	15	NL Ack	85	125	55	
22	026	16	Backspace	86	126	56	
23	027	17	POC	87	127	57	
24	030	18	Cancel	88	130	58	
25	031	19	EM	89	131	59	
26	032	1A	Unit BS	90	132	5A	!
27	033	1B	Cust Use 1	91	133	5B	$
28	034	1C	Int File Sep	92	134	5C	*
29	035	1D	Int Grp Sep	93	135	5D	)
30	036	1E	Int Rec Sep	94	136	5E	;
31	037	1F	Int Unit Sep	95	137	5F	NOT
32	040	20	Digit Select	96	140	60	-
33	041	21	Start Signif	97	141	61	/
34	042	22	Field Sep	98	142	62	
35	043	23	Wrd Undersc	99	143	63	
36	044	24	Bypass	100	144	64	
37	045	25	Line Feed	101	145	65	
38	046	26	ETB	102	146	66	
39	047	27	Escape	103	147	67	
40	050	28	Reserved	104	150	68	
41	051	29	Reserved	105	151	69	
42	052	2A	SMS	106	152	6A	|
43	053	2B	Format	107	153	6B	,
44	054	2C	Reserved	108	154	6C	%
45	055	2D	Enquiry	109	155	6D	_
46	056	2E	Ack	110	156	6E	>
47	057	2F	Bell	111	157	6F	?
48	060	30	Reserved	112	160	70	
49	061	31	Reserved	113	161	71	
50	062	32	Synch	114	162	72	
51	063	33	Index	115	163	73	
52	064	34	Present Pos	116	164	74	
53	065	35	Transparent	117	165	75	
54	066	36	Num BS	118	166	76	
55	067	37	EOT	119	167	77	
56	070	38	Subscript	120	170	78	
57	071	39	Indent	121	171	79	`
58	072	3A	Required	122	172	7A	:
59	073	3B	Cust Use 3	123	173	7B	#
60	074	3C	Dev Ctl 4	124	174	7C	@
61	075	3D	Neg Ack	125	175	7D	'
62	076	3E	Reserved	126	176	7E	=
63	077	3F	Substitute	127	177	7F	"

EBCDIC, continued

Dec	Oct	Hex	Char
128	200	80	
129	201	81	a
130	202	82	b
131	203	83	c
132	204	84	d
133	205	85	e
134	206	86	f
135	207	87	g
136	210	88	h
137	211	89	i
138	212	8A	
139	213	8B	
140	214	8C	
141	215	8D	
142	216	8E	
143	217	8F	
144	220	90	
145	221	91	j
146	222	92	k
147	223	93	l
148	224	94	m
149	225	95	n
150	226	96	o
151	227	97	p
152	230	98	q
153	231	99	r
154	232	9A	
155	233	9B	
156	234	9C	
157	235	9D	
158	236	9E	
159	237	9F	
160	240	A0	
161	241	A1	~
162	242	A2	s
163	243	A3	t
164	244	A4	u
165	245	A5	v
166	246	A6	w
167	247	A7	x
168	250	A8	y
169	251	A9	z
170	252	AA	
171	253	AB	
172	254	AC	
173	255	AD	
174	256	AE	
175	257	AF	
176	260	B0	
177	261	B1	
178	262	B2	
179	263	B3	
180	264	B4	
181	265	B5	
182	266	B6	
183	267	B7	
184	270	B8	
185	271	B9	
186	272	BA	
187	273	BB	
188	274	BC	
189	275	BD	
190	276	BE	
191	277	BF	

Dec	Oct	Hex	Char
192	300	C0	{
193	301	C1	A
194	302	C2	B
195	303	C3	C
196	304	C4	D
197	305	C5	E
198	306	C6	F
199	307	C7	G
200	310	C8	H
201	311	C9	I
202	312	CA	
203	313	CB	
204	314	CC	
205	315	CD	
206	316	CE	
207	317	CF	
208	320	D0	}
209	321	D1	J
210	322	D2	K
211	323	D3	L
212	324	D4	M
213	325	D5	N
214	326	D6	O
215	327	D7	P
216	330	D8	Q
217	331	D9	R
218	332	DA	
219	333	DB	
220	334	DC	
221	335	DD	
222	336	DE	
223	337	DF	
224	340	E0	\
225	341	E1	
226	342	E2	S
227	343	E3	T
228	344	E4	U
229	345	E5	V
230	346	E6	W
231	347	E7	X
232	350	E8	Y
233	351	E9	Z
234	352	EA	
235	353	EB	
236	354	EC	
237	355	ED	
238	356	EE	
239	357	EF	
240	360	F0	0
241	361	F1	1
242	362	F2	2
243	363	F3	3
244	364	F4	4
245	365	F5	5
246	366	F6	6
247	367	F7	7
248	370	F8	8
249	371	F9	9
250	372	FA	
251	373	FB	
252	374	FC	
253	375	FD	
254	376	FE	
255	377	FF	

APPENDIX D

Operator Precedence

Operators	**Category**	**Precedence Level**	
`( )`	Parentheses	Highest:	1
`NOT`	Negation		2
`*, /, DIV, MOD, AND`	Multiplicative		3
`+, -, OR`	Additive		4
`=, <>, <, <=, >, >=, IN`	Relational	Lowest:	5

APPENDIX

E

Type Compatibility

Strict compatibility

Types T1 and T2 are said to be *strictly compatible* if they are declared in *exactly* the same way.

Assignment compatibility

A value of type T2 can be assigned to or read into a variable of type T1 if

- T1 and T2 are the same type, but not a file type.
- T1 is a subrange of T2 or T2 is a subrange of T1 or they are both subranges of the same host type, and T2's value falls within the range of T1.
- T1 is real and T2 is integer.
- T1 and T2 are set types for which the corresponding base types are ordinal and assignment compatible, and the values stored in T2 belong to the base type for T1. The base types must both be packed or unpacked.
- T1 and T2 are string arrays with the same number of components.

Parameter compatibility

A *variable* (VAR) formal parameter must be associated with an actual parameter that is *strictly compatible.* A *value* formal parameter may be associated with any actual parameter that is *assignment compatible.*

APPENDIX

Syntax Diagrams

(in the order of presentation in the book)

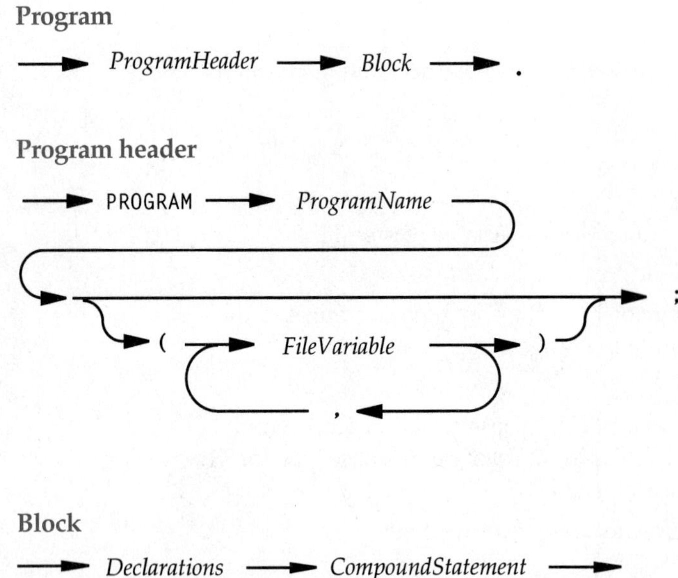

Declarations

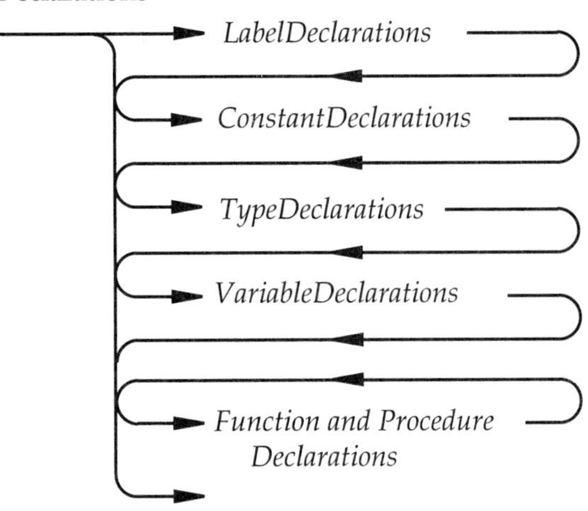

Compound statement

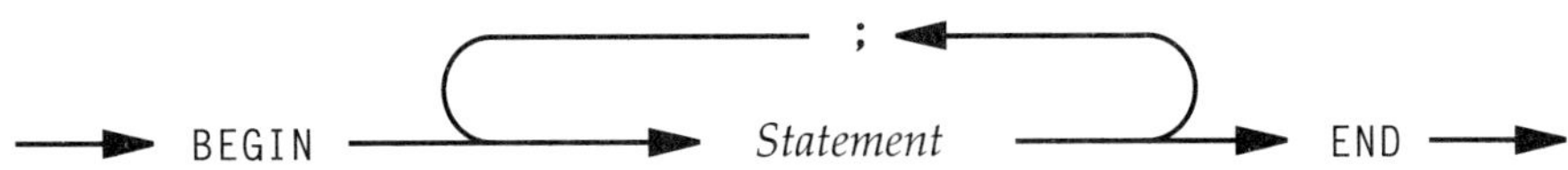

Statement

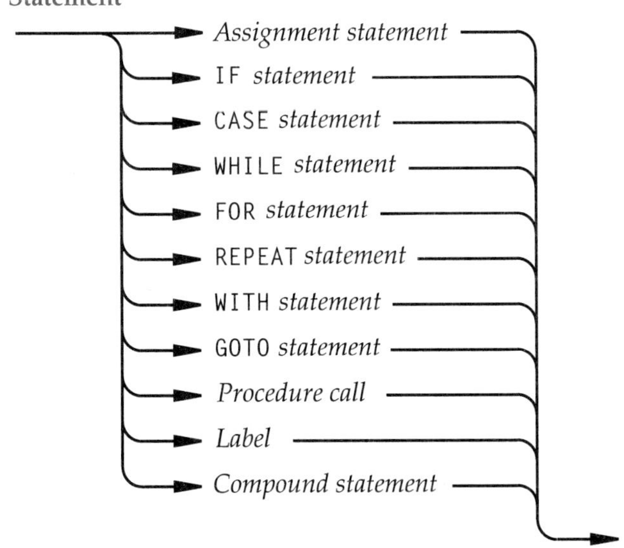

Identifier

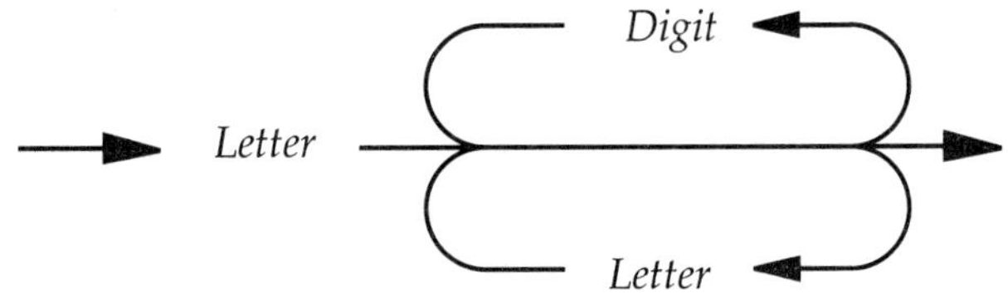

Declaring a parameterless procedure

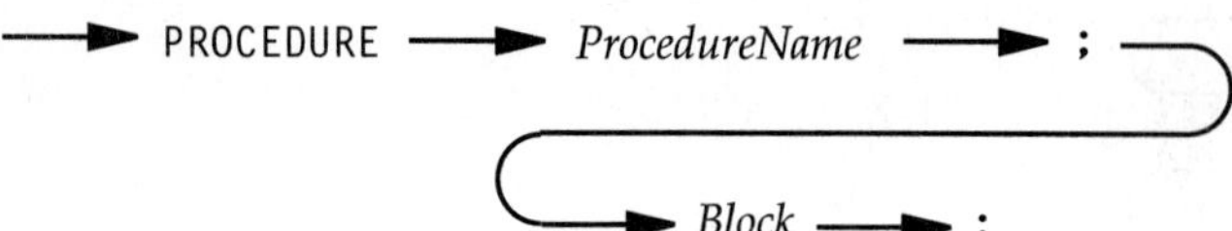

Real number

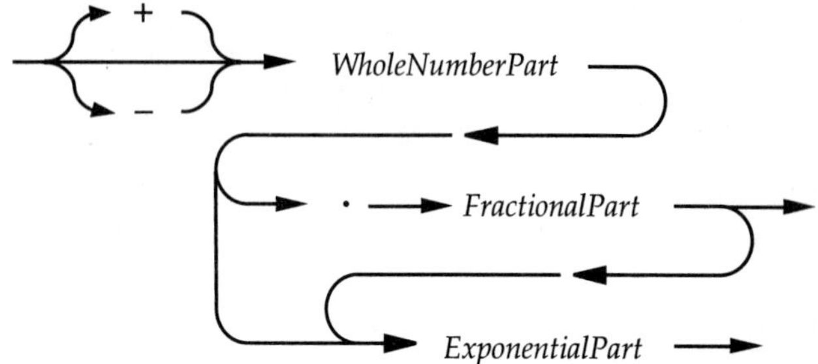

Constant declaration

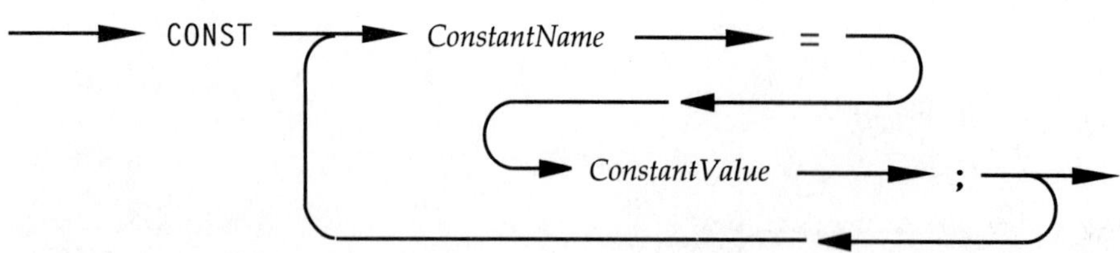

Variable declaration

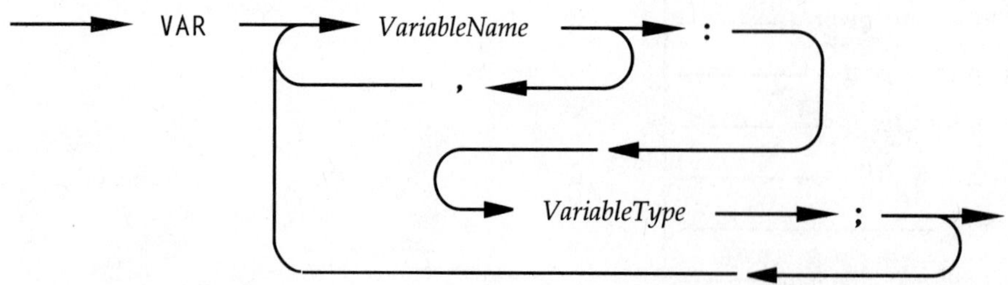

Calling the Write and WriteLn procedures, sending to Output file

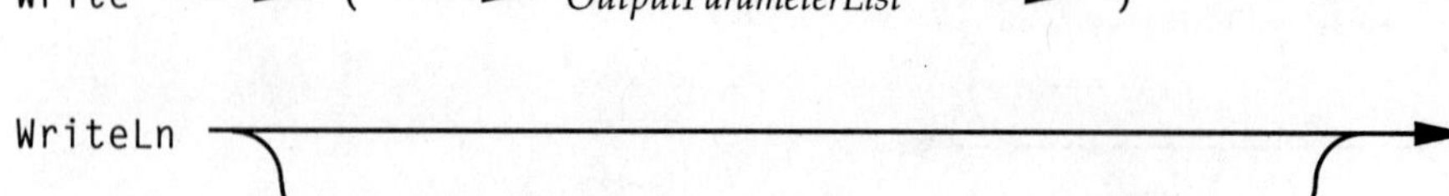

Calling the Read and ReadLn procedures, reading from Input file

Read → (→ *InputParameterList* →)

ReadLn → (→ *InputParameterList* →) →

Procedure declaration

→ *ProcedureHeader* → *Block* → ;

Procedure header

→ PROCEDURE → *ProcedureName* → (→ *Parameter-Declaration* →) → ;
;

Value parameter declaration

→ *ParameterName* → : → *ParameterType* →
,

Variable parameter declaration

→ VAR → *ParameterName* → : → *ParameterType* →
,

Function declaration

→ *FunctionHeader* → *Block* → ;

IF . . THEN . . ELSE (simple form)

→ IF → *TrueOrFalseExpression* → THEN → *Statement1* →

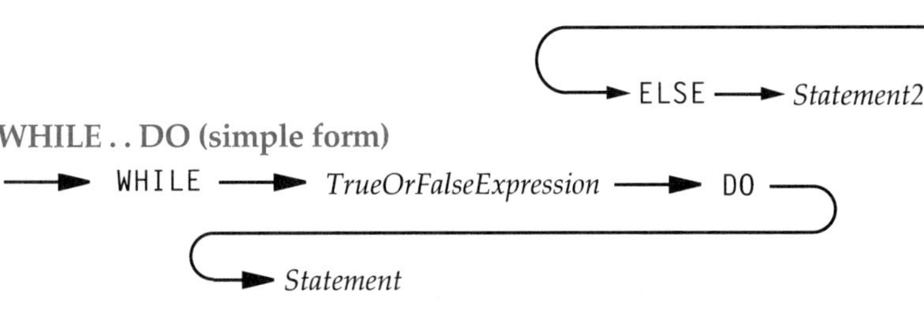

Function header

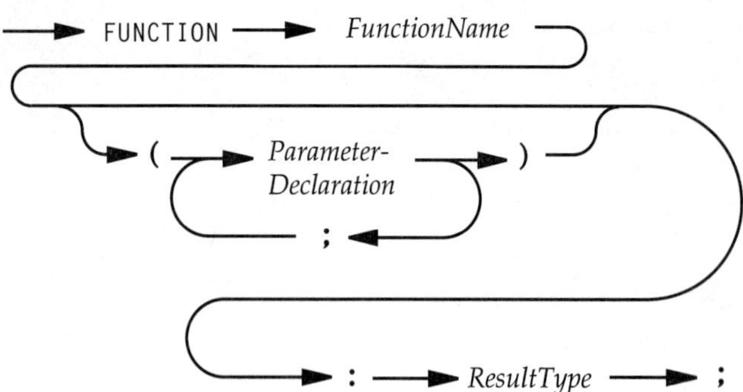

Type declaration

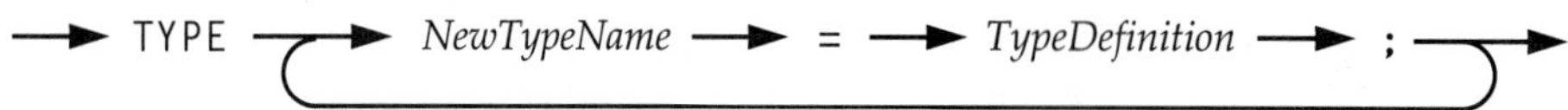

IF . . THEN . . ELSE

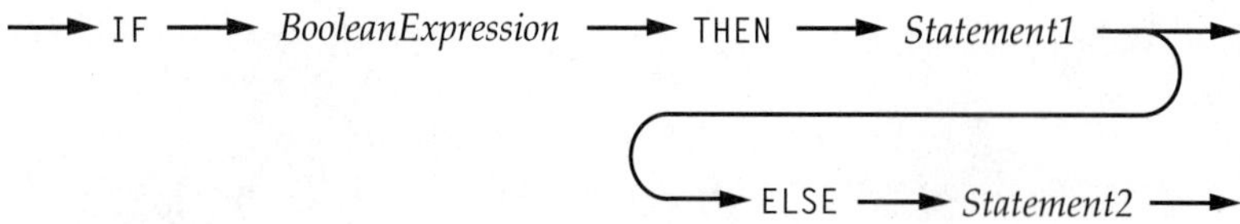

CASE

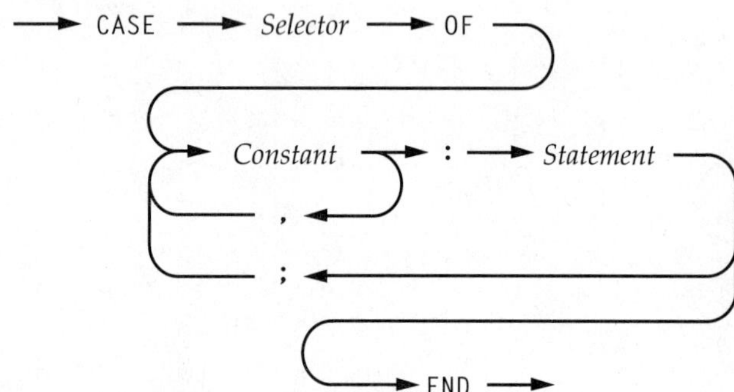

WHILE . . DO

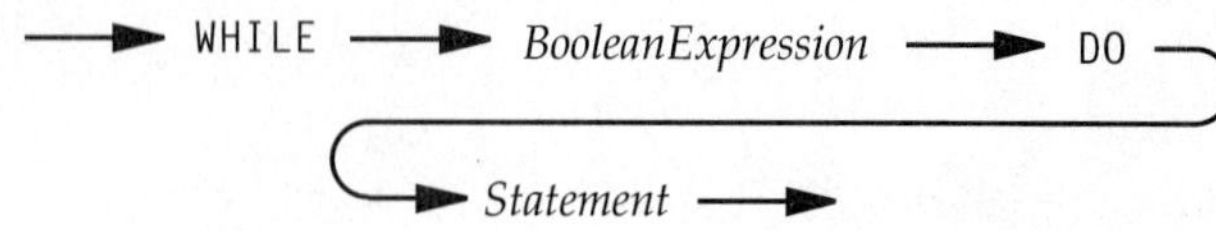

FOR structure, counting upward

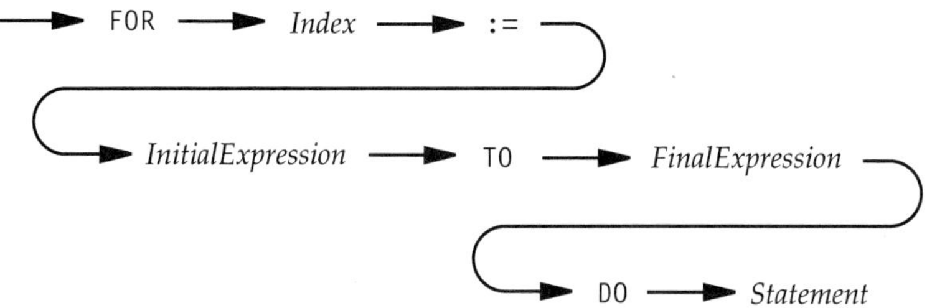

FOR structure, counting downward

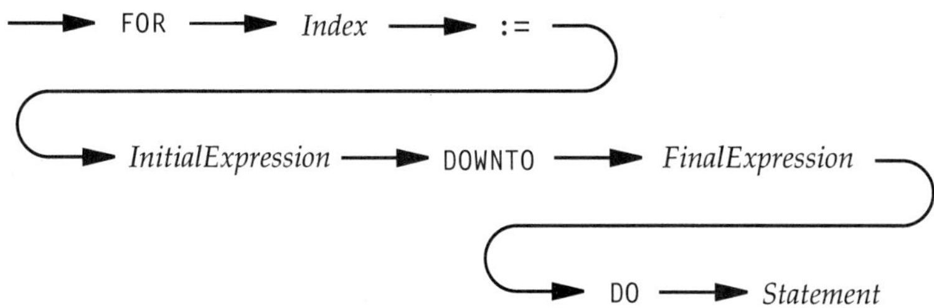

REPEAT . . UNTIL

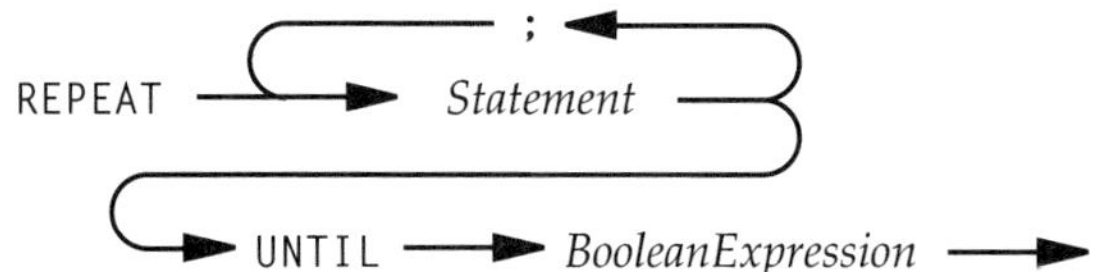

Subrange type and variable declarations

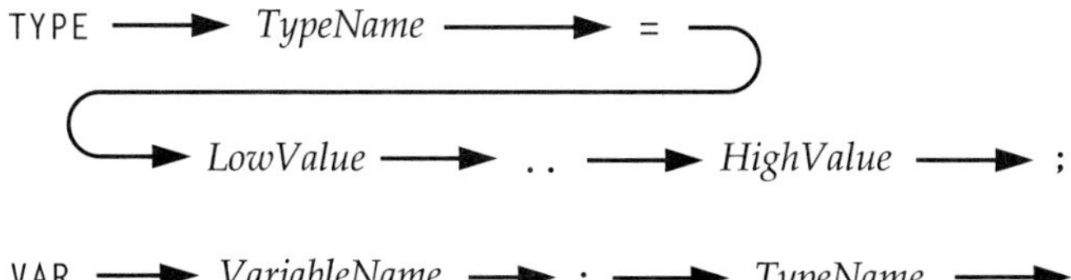

Enumerated type and variable declarations

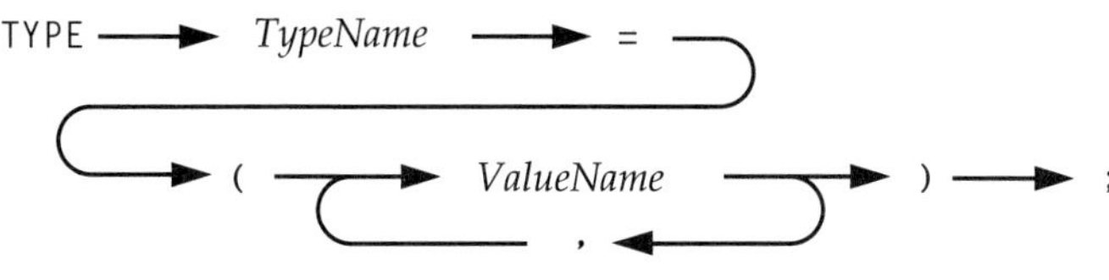

Array type and variable declaration

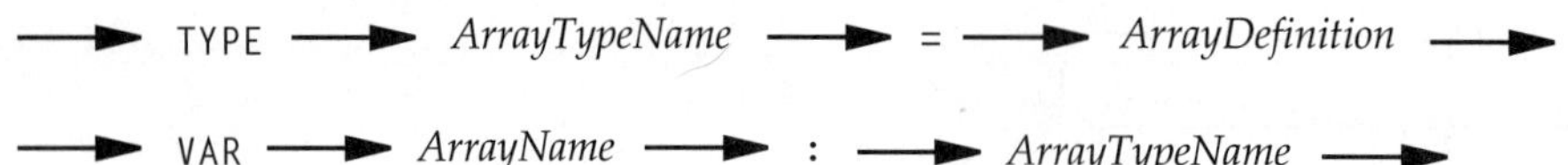

One-dimensional *ArrayDefinition*

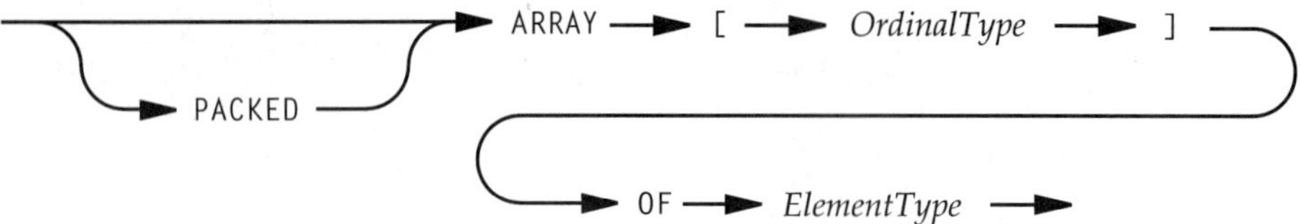

Multidimensional *ArrayDefinition*

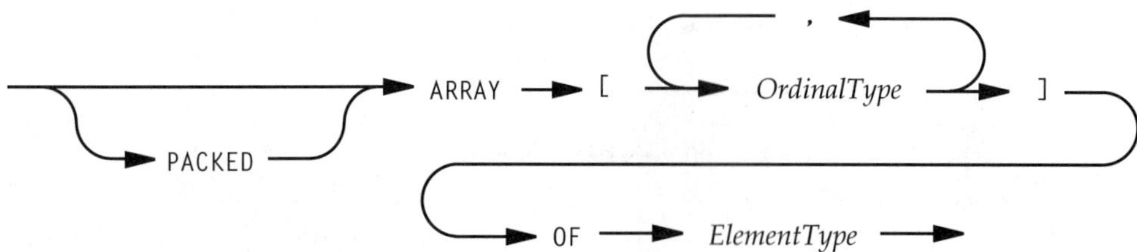

Record

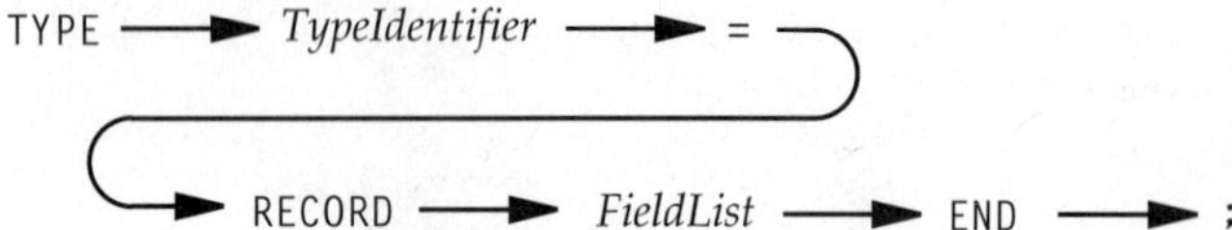

Record *FieldList*

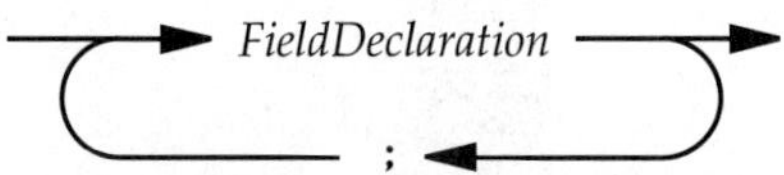

Record *FieldDeclaration*

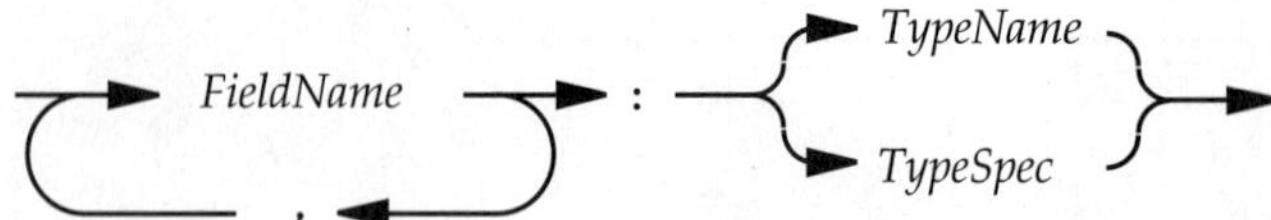

WITH structure

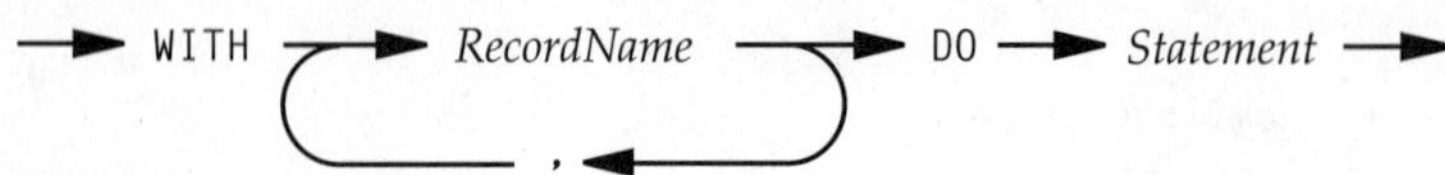

Variant record

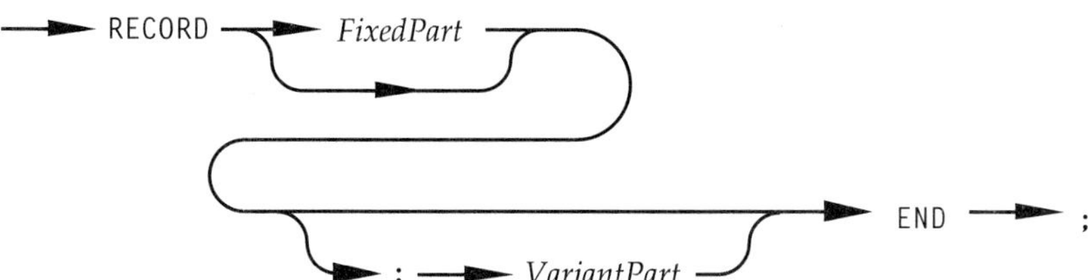

***FixedPart* of variant record**

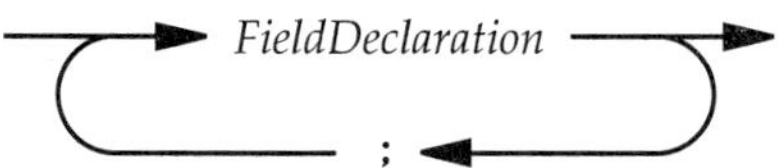

***VariantPart* of variant record**
(discriminated union)

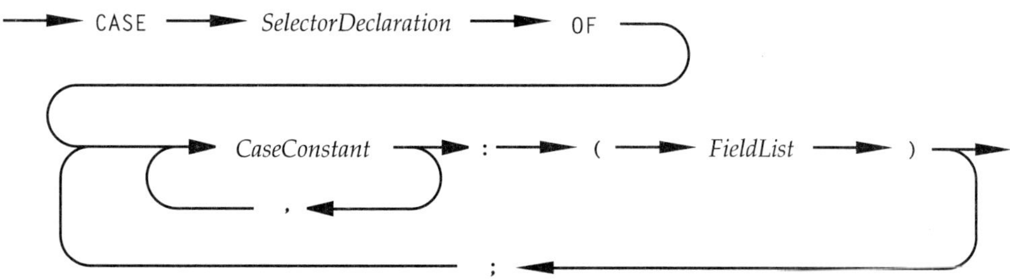

***VariantPart* of variant record**
(undiscriminated union)

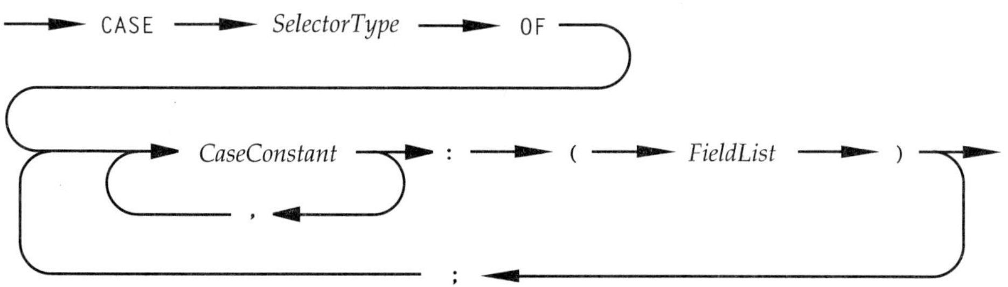

Calling Write and WriteLn, output to a file

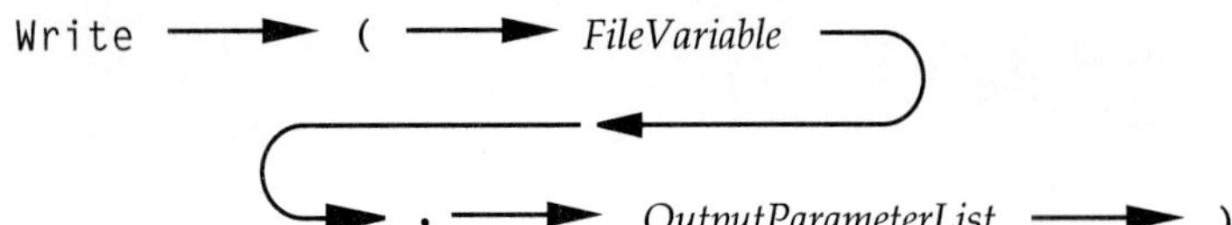

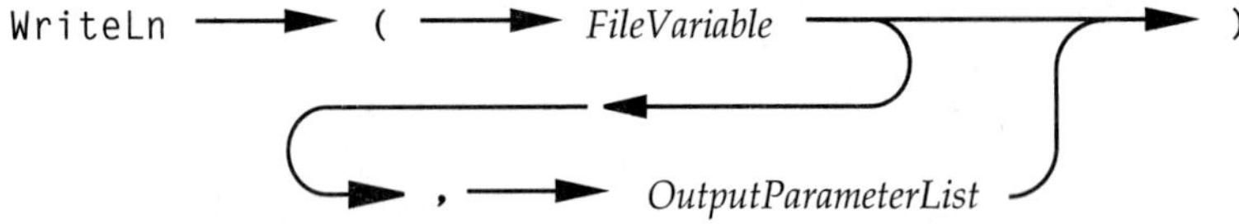

Calling Read and ReadLn, input from a file

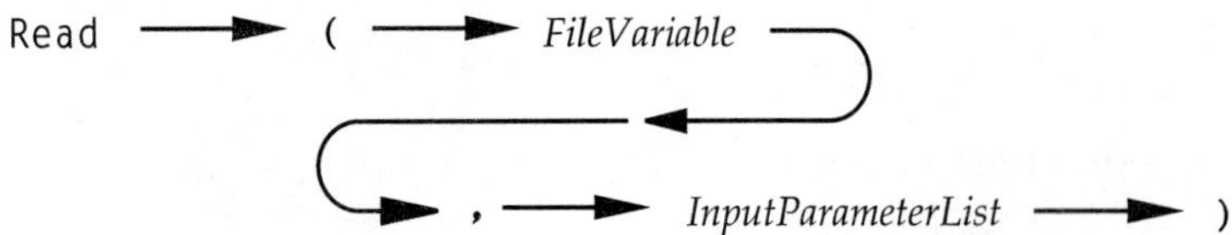

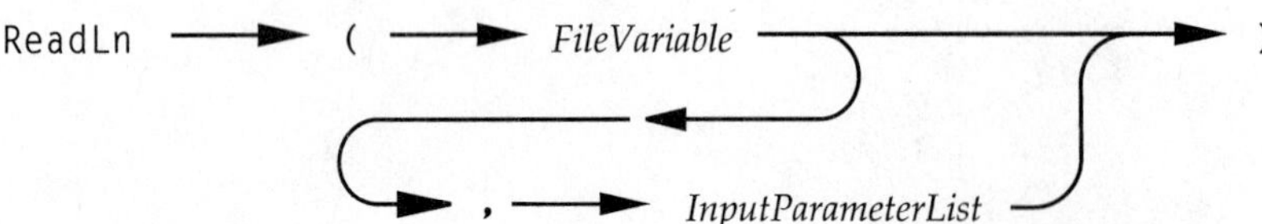

Set type declaration

→ TYPE → *SetTypeName* → = → SET OF *OrdinalBaseType* → ; →

→ VAR → *SetVariableName* → : → *SetTypeName* → ; →

Pointer type declaration

→ TYPE → *PointerType* → = → ^ → *TypeName* → ;

APPENDIX

G

Inductive Proofs

In computer science, we often need to prove mathematical assertions that are said to be true not just for one value of an independent variable, but for infinitely many. One of the most common examples arises in Sections 14.4 and 19.4, where it is asserted that

$$1 + 2 + 3 + \cdots + N = N(N+1)/2 \quad \text{for } N \geq 1$$

It is easy to confirm that the assertion is true when $N = 1$, when $N = 2$, and when $N = 3$, but it soon becomes tiresome to work such cases, and no matter how many we check, there will always be more because *the assertion is made for infinitely many values of N.*

To prove such an assertion for all positive integers N requires a technique that generalizes from particular cases to the general case, using a process called *induction*. Applied to the above example, the method is this:

1. When $N = 1$, the left side of the equation is a sum containing only the first term, 1. The right side is $1(1+1)/2 = 1$. Therefore the assertion holds when $N = 1$.

2. Assume that the assertion holds when $N = k$, where $k \geq 1$; that is, assume that

$$1 + 2 + 3 + \cdots + N = 1 + 2 + 3 + \cdots + k = k(k+1)/2$$

Then when $N = k + 1$, the sum $1 + 2 + 3 + \cdots + N$ is

$$\begin{aligned}1 + 2 + 3 + \cdots + N &= 1 + 2 + 3 + \cdots + (k+1)\\ &= [1 + 2 + 3 + \cdots + k] + (k+1)\\ &= k(k+1)/2 + (k+1)\\ &= [(k/2) + 1](k+1)\\ &= (k+1)(k+2)/2\\ &= N(N+1)/2\end{aligned}$$

Therefore, if the assertion holds for $N = k$, with $k \geq 1$, the assertion necessarily holds for $N = k + 1$.

3. Since the assertion holds for $N = 1$, step 2 shows that it necessarily holds also for $N = 2$. But this in turn implies that it holds for $N = 3$, and so on, for all positive N. Therefore the assertion holds for all $N \geq 1$.

APPENDIX H

Building ADTs as Units or Include Files

Units are provided as nonstandard extensions to the language in many commercial Pascal systems. A unit is a separately compiled body of code that cannot run alone. Its purpose is to provide declarations, implementations, and sometimes initialization code that can be imported into client programs. The concept was discussed in Chapter 14.

Although the syntax for units is not standardized and therefore depends somewhat on the system being used, the syntax is generally like this:

UNIT *UnitName*;

INTERFACE

Public Constant Declarations
Public Type Declarations
Public Variable Declarations
Public Procedure and Function Declarations

IMPLEMENTATION

Private Declarations
Procedure and Function Implementations

END.

As explained in Chapter 16, the interface part is intended to be the documentation for the ADT. It consists of all public declarations of constants, types, variables, procedures, and functions, showing client programmers all that needs to be known in order to use the ADT. The source code for the interface is provided separately to client programmers as part of the documentation for the ADT.

The implementation part contains the implementations of procedures and functions, together with any "secret" declarations that are needed by the implementation, but not to be revealed to client programmers. The source code for the implementation part is not usually provided to users of the ADT.

The exact details of ADT syntax depend a little on your Pascal system, so you should check your system reference manual for further information. The following notes describe how ADTs are compiled and used in two widely used Pascal systems: Borland International's Turbo

Pascal® and Symantec Corporation's THINK Pascal™. The instructions are written in terms of the `FractionADT` of Section 16.2.

Building and using a library in Turbo Pascal 7.0 (under MS-DOS)

1. Store the `FractionADT` unit in a file named `FRACTION.PAS`. (The filename *must* be the first eight characters of the unit's name.)
2. Compile (Alt-F9) the `FRACTION.PAS` file, with the `destination disk` option selected. (The default is `destination memory`.) The compiler will automatically notice that this is a unit rather than a program, and will therefore create an object code file named `FRACTION.TPU`. (`TPU` means "Turbo Pascal Unit.")
3. Your client program must contain, right after the program header, a statement of the form

   ```
   USES FractionADT;
   ```

   This causes the client program to import all the identifiers from `FRACTION.TPU`.
4. Then compile, link, and run (Ctl-F9) your client program in the normal way. It will automatically link to `FRACTION.TPU` if this filename is the same as the first eight letters of the unit name specified in the `USES` statement.

Building and Using a library in THINK Pascal 4.0 (on Apple Macintosh)

The easiest way to use an ADT in THINK Pascal is to include the entire ADT source code file in the client project, before the client program. This is useful when testing the ADT, but does not conceal the ADT's implementation from curious clients. Therefore, the commercial use of ADTs requires the following more complicated process:

1. **Building a FractionADT library:** Create a new project called `Fraction.PROJ`. Remove the `Runtime.lib` and `Interface.lib` files from the project, but add the `FractionADT.pas` file to it. Select *Build Library* from the *Project* menu. Build a library called `FractionADT.lib`.

   Notes:

   - In THINK Pascal, a library may contain more than one unit.
   - A library should not contain `Runtime.lib` and `Interface.lib` because, if they are included, any project that uses the library will again contain these as multiply defined symbols.
2. **Creating an Interface file:** Any client program that uses the `FractionADT.lib` library will need source code for the interface to the library. Take the `FractionADT.pas` file, remove all the procedures and functions from the implementation part, leaving an empty implementation part, and save the resulting file under a name like `FractionADTIntf.pas`. This new file is now the public statement of the declarations for the Fraction library, and must be included in any client project, together with the compiled library file created in step 1.
3. **Using the Fractions library:** Create a new project called `TestFractions`. This project will automatically contain `Runtime.lib` and `Interface.lib`. Add to the project the `FractionADT.lib` file created in step 1. Also add the `FractionADTIntf.pas` file created in step 2. Finally, add the source code for a client program that can test the Fractions library. This source code file must contain, right after the program header, a statement of the form

   ```
   USES FractionADT;
   ```

   This causes the client program to import from `FractionADT.lib` all identifiers listed in the `FractionADTIntf.pas` interface file. Now compile and run your project as usual.

Notes:

- The `FractionADT.lib` and `FractionADTIntf.pas` files must be listed in your project *before* the source code file for the client program; otherwise, you will get the Wrong build order error message.
- Your client program source code imports all of the `Fraction` library's identifiers. Therefore, your client program must not contain redeclarations of these identifiers.

Include files

An *include file* is simply a source code file that is to be automatically copied into client source code. The copying is commanded by a special compiler directive embedded in the client program, usually taking a form similar to this example, which commands that the compiler copy the source code file `Fraction.pas` into the client source code before compilation:

```
{ $INCLUDE Fraction.pas }
```

Unfortunately, this means that the `Fraction.pas` source code must be available to the client program, so its implementation cannot be kept secret from client programmers, who may misuse it or (Heaven forbid) modify it. This subverts the whole purpose of data abstraction.

APPENDIX I

Generating Pseudorandom Numbers

In various applications we need to generate a sequence of random real numbers uniformly distributed over the interval from 0.0 to 1.0. Many computer systems therefore provide a so-called random-number generator, a procedure intended to do this. Unfortunately, not all computer systems provide such a generator, and many of the commercial generators are defective. (See Project 7 at the end of Chapter 10.) We therefore provide one here.

It seems paradoxical that a machine can generate random numbers by means of an algorithm. After all, an algorithm is not random. Although a computer cannot truly generate randomness, it can generate a sequence of numbers in which there is no obvious relation between one number and the next, and in which the numbers are uniformly distributed over an interval. Such numbers are said to be *pseudorandom*. It is not nearly as easy to generate pseudorandom numbers as many programmers have thought. The most studied technique was first described by D. H. Lehmer in 1951 and is known as *linear congruence*. The process starts with a positive number chosen at random, called the *seed*. This number is used to begin the repeated process

Seed = (A • Seed) mod M;
RealNum = Seed / M

At each stage, the resulting Seed is then the seed number for generating the next real number; the numbers $\text{RealNum}_1, \text{RealNum}_2, \ldots,$ constitute the sequence of pseudorandom real numbers in the half-open interval [0.0, 1.0). Note that, because of the mod operation, the right endpoint of this interval is not generated.

The key to this method is to choose the multiplier, A, and the modulus, M, correctly. Much study has revealed proper choices for these numbers. A good analysis and summary of results were given in an article by S. Park and K. Miller in *Communications of the ACM* **31**, 1192–1201 (1988). The reader is referred to that article for further details;. Here is the Pascal:

```
VAR
   Seed : Real;  { global variable; 0 < Seed <= 2147483646.0 }

PROCEDURE Randomize;
BEGIN
   REPEAT
      Write('Seed for pseudorandom generator? ' );
```

```
      ReadLn( Seed );
      Seed := Abs( Seed )
   UNTIL Seed <= 2147483646.0
END; { Randomize }

FUNCTION Random : Real;
{ Requires 46-bit significand in real storage, plus sign bit. }
{ Works when MaxInt > 16806. }
CONST
   A = 16807.0;
   M = 2147483647.0;

VAR
   Temp : Real;

BEGIN
   Temp   := A * Seed;
   Seed   := Temp - ( M * Trunc( Temp / M ) );
   Random := Seed / M
END; { Random }
```

The first step in `Random` can produce a product as large as $16807 \times 2147483646 = 3.609 \times 10^{13} = 1.025 \times 2^{45}$. Therefore this version of `Random` requires that real numbers are stored with at least 46 bits in the significand, or overflow errors will occur. On the other hand, the `Trunc` operation in the second step never produces an integer larger than `Trunc(` (16807)(2147483646) / 2147483647 `)` = 16806. As long as `MaxInt` is greater than this, there will be no integer overflow.

When dealing with a Pascal system that does not store 46-bit real significands, `Random` must be modified as follows:

```
FUNCTION Random : Real;
{ Requires 32-bit significand in real storage, including sign bit. }
{ Works when MaxInt > 16806. }
CONST
   A = 16807.0;
   M = 2147483647.0;
   Q = 127773.0;       { M DIV A }
   R = 2836.0;         { M MOD A }

VAR
   Low, High, Test : Real;

BEGIN

   High   := Trunc( Seed / Q );
   Low    := Seed - ( Q * High );
   Test   := ( A * Low ) - ( R * High );
   IF Test > 0.0 THEN
      Seed := Test
   ELSE
      Seed := Test + M;
   Random := Seed / M

END; { Random }
```

These two versions of Lehmer's algorithm are taken from the paper by Park and Miller cited previously. A worthwhile embellishment of this procedure can be found on page 513 of Robert Sedgewick's *Algorithms*, second edition (Addison-Wesley Publishing, 1988). It breaks the multiplication into pieces and keeps only the most random digits of the product.

APPENDIX

J

Review of Binary Number Representations

For the reasons explained in Chapter 1, computers store numbers in formats that involve binary notations. Here we review such notations. In particular, we will review base 2, base 8, and base 16 notations by comparing them to the more familiar base 10 notation.

Base 10 notation

The base 10 number 123.45 is written in the usual place system based on powers of 10. Because the number is built from powers of 10, the digits range from 0 up to (10 – 1) = 9. Each digit in the number occupies a column or *place*, as indicated in the following diagram:

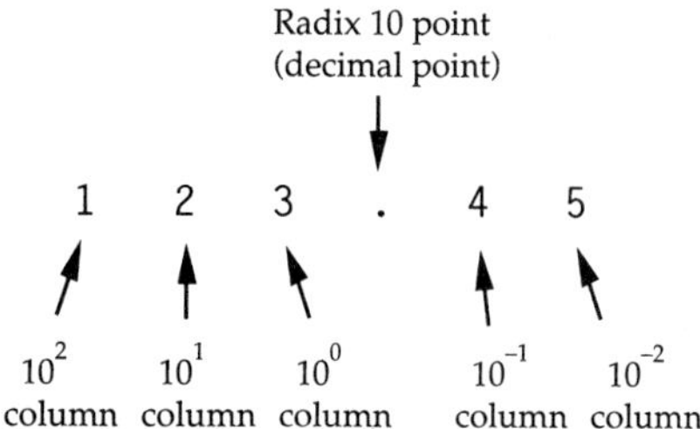

Thus the value of the number 123.45 is

$$
\begin{aligned}
&(1 \times 10^2) + (2 \times 10^1) + (3 \times 10^0) + (4 \times 10^{-1}) + (5 \times 10^{-2}) \\
&= (1 \times 100) + (2 \times 10) + (3 \times 1) + (4 \times 0.1) + (5 \times 0.01) \\
&= 100 + 20 + 3 + 0.4 + 0.05 \\
&= 123.45
\end{aligned}
$$

Base 2 notation (binary notation)

The base 2, or binary, system is similar, but with powers of 2 instead of powers of 10. Because the base is 2, the digits can only have the values 0 or 1. A binary digit is called a **bit** for short.

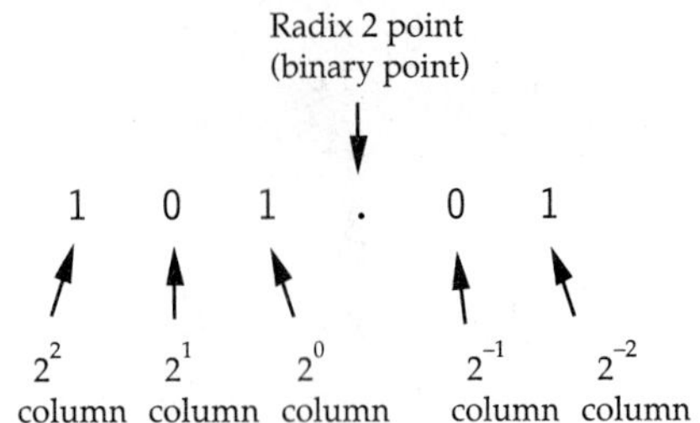

Thus the notation 101.01_2 (the subscript indicates base 2 notation) means

$$(1 \times 2^2) + (0 \times 2^1) + (1 \times 2^0) + (0 \times 2^{-1}) + (1 \times 2^{-2})$$
$$= (1 \times 4) + (0 \times 2) + (1 \times 1) + (0 \times 0.5) + (1 \times 0.25)$$
$$= 4 + 0 + 1 + 0.0 + 0.25$$
$$= 5.25$$

That is, the binary notation 101.01_2 means the same thing as the decimal notation 5.25_{10}.

Common binary numbers

Many whole-number patterns are so common in computer science that students should memorize them. It should be easy, for example, to recognize the binary notation for various powers of 2. The following eight-bit patterns are shown in four-bit groups to make them easier to read:

$0000\ 0001_2$	=	1_{10}	$0001\ 0000_2$	=	16_{10}
$0000\ 0010_2$	=	2_{10}	$0010\ 0000_2$	=	32_{10}
$0000\ 0100_2$	=	4_{10}	$0100\ 0000_2$	=	64_{10}
$0000\ 1000_2$	=	8_{10}	$1000\ 0000_2$	=	128_{10}

Other common patterns that should be easy to recognize are those representing numbers one less than a power of two:

$0000\ 0011_2$	=	3_{10}	$0001\ 1111_2$	=	31_0
$0000\ 0111_2$	=	7_{10}	$0011\ 1111_2$	=	63_{10}
$0000\ 1111_2$	=	15_{10}	$0111\ 1111_2$	=	127_{10}

Base 8 notation (octal notation)

Long binary bit patterns like 010110110_2 are hard to read and interpret. They are also hard to speak. To aid the verbal description of long bit patterns, and to make it easier to interpret them, computer scientists often represent the numbers in a base that is itself a power of 2. One of the most common is base 8, which is called **octal**. Octal notation uses digits that range from 0 up to $(8 - 1) = 7$.

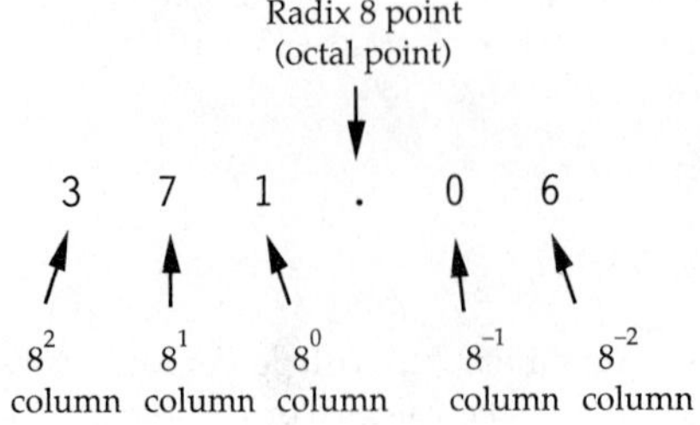

Thus the value of the number 371.06_8 is

$$(3 \times 8^2) + (7 \times 8^1) + (1 \times 8^0) + (0 \times 8^{-1}) + (6 \times 8^{-2})$$
$$= (3 \times 64) + (7 \times 8) + (1 \times 1) + (0 \times (1/8)) + (6 \times (1/64))$$
$$= 192 + 56 + 1 + 0.0 + 0.09375$$
$$= 249.09375_{10}$$

The translation between octal and binary is easy because each octal digit acts as shorthand for a group of three bits, according to the following table:

111_2	=	7_8	011_2	=	3_8
110_2	=	6_8	010_2	=	2_8
101_2	=	5_8	001_2	=	1_8
100_2	=	4_8	000_2	=	0_8

Thus, to translate octal notation to binary, just replace each octal digit by the corresponding three-bit binary notation:

$$7734_8 \quad = \; 111\ 111\ 011\ 100_2 \quad = \; 111111011100_2$$

Similarly, to translate binary to octal, just replace each three-bit group, starting from the right, with the corresponding octal notation. If necessary, pad the left end with zeros so that the leftmost group will have three bits:

$$10110010100_2 \quad = \; 010\ 110\ 010\ 100_2 \quad = \; 2624_8$$

Base 16 notation (hexadecimal notation)

Another common notation uses base 16 and is called **hexadecimal**. Hexadecimal notation uses digits that range from 0 up to (16 – 1) = 15. This raises a new problem: How can we have a two-digit digit? The hexadecimal system gets around this problem by using letters to augment the usual digits 0, 1, 2, . . . , 9:

F_{16}	=	15_{10}	B_{16}	=	11_{10}	7_{16}	=	7_{10}	3_{16}	=	3_{10}
E_{16}	=	14_{10}	A_{16}	=	10_{10}	6_{16}	=	6_{10}	2_{16}	=	2_{10}
D_{16}	=	13_{10}	9_{16}	=	9_{10}	5_{16}	=	5_{10}	1_{16}	=	1_{10}
C_{16}	=	12_{10}	8_{16}	=	8_{10}	4_{16}	=	4_{10}	0_{16}	=	0_{10}

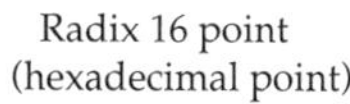

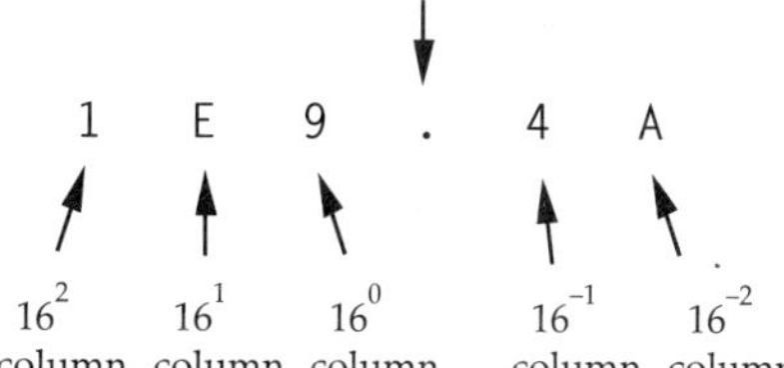

Thus the value of the number $1E9.4A_{16}$ is

$$(1 \times 16^2) + (14 \times 16^1) + (9 \times 16^0) + (4 \times 16^{-1}) + (10 \times 16^{-2})$$
$$= (1 \times 256) + (14 \times 16) + (9 \times 1) + (4 \times (1/16)) + (10 \times (1/256))$$
$$= 256 + 224 + 9 + 0.25 + 0.03906$$
$$= 489.289_{10}$$

The translation between hexadecimal and binary is easy because each hexadecimal digit acts as shorthand for a group of four bits, as shown in the following table:

1111_2	=	F_{16}	1001_2	=	9_{16}	0011_2	=	3_{16}
1110_2	=	E_{16}	1000_2	=	8_{16}	0010_2	=	2_{16}
1101_2	=	D_{16}	0111_2	=	7_{16}	0001_2	=	1_{16}
1100_2	=	C_{16}	0110_2	=	6_{16}	0000_2	=	0_{16}
1011_2	=	B_{16}	0101_2	=	5_{16}			
1010_2	=	A_{16}	0100_2	=	4_{16}			

Thus to translate hexadecimal notation to binary, just replace each hexadecimal digit by the corresponding four-bit binary notation:

$$3BA0_{16} = 0011\ 1011\ 1010\ 0000_2 = 0011101110100000_2$$

Similarly, to translate binary to hexadecimal, just replace each four-bit group, starting from the right, with the corresponding hexadecimal notation. If necessary, pad the left end with zeros so that the last group will have four bits:

$$10110011100_2 = 0101\ 1001\ 1100_2 = 59C_{16}$$

APPENDIX K

Data Storage Representations

When an integer is stored in four bytes, there are 32 bits to represent it, each of which can be either on or off. Thus there are $2^{32} = 4{,}294{,}967{,}296$ distinct bit patterns available for symbolizing integers. In other words, only a finite subset of the mathematical integers can be symbolized in the computer. If we represent only nonnegative integers, the association between bit patterns and integers might be as shown in Table K.1.

But for many purposes, negative integers are just as important as positive ones, so we usually divide the computer's integer bit patterns more or less equally between positive and negative representations. The simplest scheme would be to use one bit—the leftmost one, let's say—to represent the sign of the integer. If the leftmost bit is turned on, we will say that the integer is negative; otherwise, it is positive. With this scheme, the maximum magnitude represented is necessarily half as big as before, as shown in Table K.2.

As you can see, this scheme gives us distinct bit patterns for +0 and –0, which is computationally awkward. Rather than designing a special arithmetic to deal with two zeros, modern computer system designers usually choose a different scheme of representation, called **two's-complement notation**, in which a negative integer's bit pattern is computed from that of the corresponding positive bit pattern by the algorithm

1. Invert all the bits. (I.e., change each 1 to a 0 and vice versa.)
2. Then add 1.

Thus with the bit pattern

```
00000000 00000000 00000000 00000011
```

Table K.1 *Nonnegative integers represented by bit patterns.*

Bit pattern	Integer represented
11111111 11111111 11111111 11111111	4,294,967,295
11111111 11111111 11111111 11111110	4,294,967,294
11111111 11111111 11111111 11111101	4,294,967,293
⋮	⋮
10000000 00000000 00000000 00000011	2,147,483,651
10000000 00000000 00000000 00000010	2,147,483,650
10000000 00000000 00000000 00000001	2,147,483,649
10000000 00000000 00000000 00000000	2,147,483,648
01111111 11111111 11111111 11111111	2,147,483,647
01111111 11111111 11111111 11111110	2,147,483,646
01111111 11111111 11111111 11111101	2,147,483,645
⋮	⋮
00000000 00000000 00000000 00000011	3
00000000 00000000 00000000 00000010	2
00000000 00000000 00000000 00000001	1
00000000 00000000 00000000 00000000	0

representing +3, the corresponding bit pattern for –3 would be computed by inverting the bits to get

11111111 11111111 11111111 11111100

and then adding 1 to get

11111111 11111111 11111111 11111101

Table K.2 *One scheme for representing all integers by bit patterns.*

Bit pattern	Integer represented
11111111 11111111 11111111 11111111	-2,147,483,647
11111111 11111111 11111111 11111110	-2,147,483,646
11111111 11111111 11111111 11111101	-2,147,483,645
⋮	⋮
10000000 00000000 00000000 00000011	-3
10000000 00000000 00000000 00000010	-2
10000000 00000000 00000000 00000001	-1
10000000 00000000 00000000 00000000	-0
01111111 11111111 11111111 11111111	2,147,483,647
01111111 11111111 11111111 11111110	2,147,483,646
01111111 11111111 11111111 11111101	2,147,483,645
⋮	⋮
00000000 00000000 00000000 00000011	3
00000000 00000000 00000000 00000010	2
00000000 00000000 00000000 00000001	1
00000000 00000000 00000000 00000000	0

Table K.3

Two's-complement scheme for representing integers by bit patterns.

Bit pattern	Integer represented
11111111 11111111 11111111 11111111	−1
11111111 11111111 11111111 11111110	−2
11111111 11111111 11111111 11111101	−3
⋮	⋮
10000000 00000000 00000000 00000011	−2,147,483,645
10000000 00000000 00000000 00000010	−2,147,483,646
10000000 00000000 00000000 00000001	−2,147,483,647
10000000 00000000 00000000 00000000	−2,147,483,648
01111111 11111111 11111111 11111111	2,147,483,647
01111111 11111111 11111111 11111110	2,147,483,646
01111111 11111111 11111111 11111101	2,147,483,645
⋮	⋮
00000000 00000000 00000000 00000011	3
00000000 00000000 00000000 00000010	2
00000000 00000000 00000000 00000001	1
00000000 00000000 00000000 00000000	0

The resulting two's-complement representations are shown in Table K.3. This scheme retains the advantage of easy recognition of negative bit patterns, while getting rid of the second representation of zero. It also simplifies arithmetic operations, and is the most common representation of integers in digital computers.

Bit patterns can symbolize real numbers, but . . .

As explained in Section 1.3, a real number is represented in memory by a sign, a binary significand, and a power-of-2 exponent. For example, the number −1.75 is stored as −(1 + 1/2 + 1/4), which is binary −1.11. Normalizing the significand so that it is completely to the right of the binary point, we write the number as $-.111 \times 2^1$, which is stored as

−	.111	1
Sign	Significand	Exponent

Storing the negative sign as an "on" bit, we have the following bit pattern:

1	11100000000000000000000	00000001
sign	23-bit significand	8-bit exponent with sign

Let's suppose these three pieces are actually stored in the order shown. (Some machines store them in a different order.) Regrouping bytewise from the left, we have

```
11110000 00000000 00000000 00000001
```

Now consider numbers of very small magnitude. We would store a zero as $+0.0 \times 2^0$, or the bit pattern

```
00000000 00000000 00000000 00000000
```

(This happens to be the same as the bit pattern for integer zero.)

Now here's an interesting question: What bit pattern represents the next-higher number above zero? Although this question makes no sense in mathematics, it makes sense in computing. Assuming normalization as described, the bit pattern representing the next number above zero is the one that has a 1 at the left end of the significand, all other significant bits zero, and the most negative exponent possible. If exponents are stored in an eight-bit two's-complement notation, the whole bit pattern would be

```
01000000 00000000 00000000 10000000
| ------------- significand ---------- exponent
sign bit
```

which represents the binary number

$+0.10000000000000000000000 \times 2^{-128}$

which is the same as 2^{-129} or decimal 1.47×10^{-39}. This means that 1.47×10^{-39} is the smallest positive nonzero number that can be stored in the computer by means of the normalized representation described. If the computer attempts to calculate a positive number less than this, we have what is called an **underflow error**, and the computer system either stores a zero (losing all significant figures in the result), or issues an error message, or both.

Similarly, the bit pattern representing the highest storable real number is the one with the largest significand and largest positive exponent:

```
01111111 11111111 11111111 01111111
```

This bit pattern represents the number $1.0 \times 2^{127} = 1.70 \times 10^{38}$. If the computer calculates a result larger than this, the result will not be storable and we will have what is called an **overflow error**. The computer either stores 1.70×10^{38}, losing all significant figures in the result, or issues an error message, or both.

Underflow and overflow are examples of a more general problem. Only finitely many real numbers can be stored in a computer, and other real numbers must be rounded to one of the storable values before they can be represented in computer memory. This means that *real numbers are usually not stored exactly*. The resulting **roundoff error** is frequently important in real-world applications, and is examined briefly in Section 4.2.

Storing characters

As explained in Section 1.3 and Appendix C, a character is stored as a one-byte bit pattern determined by the character codes used by the computer system. See Appendix C for examples.

Storing arrays and records

Chapters 14 and 15 describe arrays and records, respectively. These are examples of composite data types, in which a collection of values are stored together under a single name. Section 14.1 describes storage for one-dimensional arrays, while Section 14.7 explains how multidimensional arrays are stored. Similarly, Section 15.1 explains the storage of records. In particular, see Figures 15.1.1, 15.2.1, and 15.6.1.

Answers to Selected Questions and Exercises

These answers were prepared by Bill Salmon and Dave Hanscom at the University of Utah.

1-1. An algorithm is a list of steps that must be followed in order to accomplish some task. A program is an algorithm written in a language that is understandable (or can be made understandable) to a computer.

1-6. To be manipulated by a digital computer, symbols must differ discretely from other symbols and be storable in a finite number of bits.

1-10. Hardware elements in the list are floppy disk, CPU, RAM, ROM, and secondary storage. Program, data, and bit patterns are software.

1-11. Bits, whole numbers, and traffic signals are digital. Sound waves and colors are analog, since they can take on any values within some range; that is, they are not constrained to have specific discrete values. (Colors and sounds can be approximated by discrete values, however, and these approximations can be stored in a digital computer.)

2-4. *Bicycle:* A human-propelled vehicle with two wheels, one in front of the other. The rear wheel is driven by a roller chain which, in turn, is driven by a chainwheel gear turned by foot pedals. The vehicle is steered by a cross-vehicle handlebar that turns the front wheel. Procedures used in riding a bicycle:

Stepping over the frame.
Mounting the saddle.
Pushing off.
Pedaling.
Turning right.
Turning left.
Changing gears.
Braking.
Dismounting.
And so on.

2-6. Procedure for adjusting water temperature with single-knob faucet:

Grasp faucet knob with one hand.
Push knob away from you.
Put free hand in water flow below faucet.
Repeat following actions until flow rate is correct:
    If flow is too little, then
        Push knob slightly away from you;
    otherwise, if flow is too great, then
        Pull knob slightly toward you.
Repeat following actions until water is correct temperature:
    If water becomes too hot, then
        Push knob slightly to right;
    otherwise, if water becomes too cold, then
        Push knob slightly to left.

2-P4. This algorithm assumes that the user is able to add two single-digit decimal numbers, and that the user is able to add 1 to any number. Let the two 3-digit numbers that are to be added be called NUM1 and NUM2, and let the sum be called SUM.

a. Initialize a number called CARRY to 0.

b. Starting with the least significant (rightmost) digit, perform the following operations on successive digits of NUM1 and NUM2 to generate the corresponding digit of SUM.

i. Add the current digit of NUM1 to the current digit of NUM2. (If either number has fewer than three digits, extend it by appending preceding zeros.)

ii. Add CARRY to that value.

iii. If the result of Step ii exceeds 9 (i.e., if it has two digits), assign 1 to CARRY; otherwise, assign 0 to CARRY.

iv. Assign the least significant digit of the result of Step ii to the current digit of SUM.

c. If CARRY is 0, SUM contains the correct value for the sum of NUM1 and NUM2. If CARRY is 1, however, the result requires four digits. In the latter case, the fourth (most significant) digit of SUM is 1.

3-1. Only the reserved words cannot be used as names for variables and constants. (Actually, depending upon the sensitivity of your teacher, profane or sexist words may not be allowed either.)

3-3. `END.`

3-5. The Pascal compiler makes no distinction between lower- and uppercase, so `Monolithic` and `MONOlithiC` are the same as far as the compiler is concerned.

3-7. Procedures and functions.

3-9. A program header contains the reserved word `PROGRAM`, followed by the name of the program, an optional parameter list, and finally, a semicolon. The optional parameter list consists of a pair of parentheses containing one or more file-variable names, separated by commas. Right after the program header comes a block.

3-11. Infinitely many. (Of course, we don't actually have the time to write a program with infinitely many statements, let alone compile one!)

3-15. `4Dimensional` and `2X` are illegal because they start with numerical characters. `Begin` and `Char` are illegal because they are reserved words. Other identifiers that contain illegal characters are `X_Squared`, `e.e.cummings`, and `Yes/No`. It should be noted that the underline character, though nonstandard, is accepted by many Pascal compilers.

3-26. The four errors are

a. Missing semicolon at the end of the first line.

b. `BEGIN` is misspelled.

c. Missing period after `END`.

d. There are only three syntax errors in this program; the fourth error is that the output message is wrong! (Arrggghh!!!)

4-6. Real variables may be initialized in Pascal, but you should not count on it. This is a system-dependent characteristic, and not standard. All variables should be initialized deliberately in a program, since their values will initially be unknown. If you use them without assigning a known value, the results will not be predictable.

4-8. The constants with illegal syntax are `1.e-2`, `.5`, `2.`, and `1,000.50`. The first has an incomplete fractional part; the next two lack a whole number part; the last contains a comma.

4-10.

a. `8.0 - ((4.0 * 1.0) / 2.0) = 6.0`

b. `(((1.0 / 2.0) * 2.0) / 1.0) = 1.0`

4-13. Here are some hints:

a. For what value of x is $\ln x$ undefined? The calculator's ln function is likely to be inaccurate near this value, and presumably $\exp(\ln x)$ will differ noticeably from x.

b. Similar to **a.**

c. When x^2 contains more significant figures than can be stored, the square root of x^2 will become noticeably different from x.

4-14. Hint: x will be a very small nonnegative number. Try a value of x, chosen at random. If this is big enough that $1.0 + x$ differs from x, halve your value of x and try again. Keep this up until your x is so small that it makes no difference when added to 1.0. Then home in on the value of the machine epsilon from there.

4-15. Hint: Will the computed value of $(x_1 / n) + (x_2 / n) + \ldots + (x_n / n)$ be the same as the sum shown in the exercise?

4-17. When the variable `Two` is written to the screen, the characters that go to the screen are a symbolic representation of the value of that variable. The format of the information written depends on the syntax of the `Write` statement and the Pascal compiler. When `'Two'` is written to the screen, only the three characters `'T'`, `'w'`, and `'o'` go are written.

4-19.

```
Key F for first name
or  L for Last name
_
```

4-21. Your system may not format the numbers the same as mine, but you should see something like this:

```
FREQUENCY-ENERGY RELATION:

For a frequency of  6.000E+14/sec, energy = 3.97571E-19 Joules
```

4-25. The parameters of a `Read` or `ReadLn` procedure must each be a variable of some predefined type. The code checks the type of each parameter in turn and expects data of that type to be entered. The procedure then tries to convert the string of characters arriving from the keyboard to a value of the same type as the receiving parameter.

4-29. The program header should declare `Output` as well as `Input`. The `VAR` declaration should contain a colon, not an equality. The `ReadLn` should not attach format specifiers to the name of the `Millimeters` parameter.

5-1. `Ready( Set, Go );`

5-3. A value parameter is used only for passing a value into a procedure. It cannot be used for returning a value to the actual parameter in the calling statement.

5-5. The actual parameters are separated by commas. The formal parameters have types as well as identifiers, and are separated by semicolons.

5-14. The error that prevents this program from compiling is the use of the variable `Junk` in the main program. `Junk` was declared locally in the procedure. (Incidentally, Jackson is also in major semantic trouble.)

5-16. The first actual parameter will be `Celsius`, which will contain garbage. This garbage value will be sent to `ConvertToCelsius` and used to calculate another garbage value. This second garbage value will be returned to the `Fahrenheit` variable in the main program. As a result, a garbage value of `Fahrenheit` will be printed by `ShowTemperature`.

5-21a. The scope of `X` in each of the procedures is over the one procedure that does the declaring. `Y` is declared globally, however. Its scope extends over the whole program.

5-22a. The scope of `One` and `Two` in a procedure is over just the procedure itself. `X` and `Y` are declared globally, however. Their scopes extend over the whole program.

6-2. The structures shown in **c** and **d**.

6-5. `I'm quite communicative for my age.`

6-9. If `Fahrenheit` is less than `AbsoluteZero`, code fragment **a** executes the `Write` and `ReadLn` once. On the other hand, code fragment **b** executes the `Write` and `ReadLn` repeatedly, as long as `Fahrenheit` is less than `AbsoluteZero`.

6-10.

```
Tomorrow,
and tomorrow,
and tomorrow,
Creeps in this petty pace from day to day
```

6-12a. Twice.

6-14. The *state* of the program is the condition of all variables and files associated with the program; that is, the set of values stored in all those variables and files.

6-16. The precondition of a procedure is the program state existing just before the procedure is executed.

6-20. A procedure must be declared before it is used. If `Swap2Reals` is declared after a procedure that calls it, the program won't compile. The compiler will issue an error message saying that the `Swap2Reals` identifier is unknown.

6-22.
```
7.0000000000E+00
8.0000000000E+00
13.0000000000E+00
13.0000000000E+00

3.0000000000E+00 7.0000000000E+00
```

7-1. A function returns a single value, associated with the name of the function. A procedure may or may not return any values to its caller; if it does, these values are associated with `VAR` parameters, not with the name of the procedure. A procedure can return multiple values in this way.

7-3. A function call can appear in any expression of a compatible type.

7-5.
```
FUNCTION CToF( C : Real ) : Real;
BEGIN

   CToF := ( 1.8 * C ) + 32.0

END; { CToF }
```

7-14.
```
49.0000000000E+00
```

8-1. The only legal integer constants are `14`, `0`, and `MaxInt`. The others have either a decimal point, a comma, or alpha characters.

8-2.
a. `(4 + (2 * 3)) - 1 = 9`
b. `(4 * 2) + (3 div 1) = 11`

8-6.
```
FUNCTION FractionalPart( RealNum : Real ) : Real;
BEGIN

    FractionalPart := RealNum - Trunc( RealNum )

END; { FractionalPart }
```

8-12. Character constants must be single characters enclosed in single quotes. In this question, only `'a'`, `'7'`, and `'?'` meet this requirement. The rest are illegal.

8-15. `Chr(7)` in a system that uses the ASCII code is called `Bell`. It usually will cause a computer to beep.

8-19.
a. `( ( 1994 - 1988 ) <> 4 ) = True`
b. `( ( (1994 - 1988) * 32.75 ) <= 200.0 ) = True`

8-26. "I don't drink and drive" is understood to mean, "I don't do both," so this matches **d**. "B1 but not B2" means "B1 and not B2," which is **c**.

8-28. Assuming ASCII codes,

a. `Error := NOT( (Number >= 0.0) AND (Ch = 'C') );`

b. `Fast := (Angle > 0.0) AND (Velocity > 100.0);`

8-31. **a.** `True AND ( NOT False ) = True AND True = True`

b. `NOT( True AND False ) = NOT( False ) = True`

9-1a.

```
FUNCTION EvenNegative( Num : Integer ) : Boolean;
BEGIN

   EvenNegative := ( Num < 0 ) AND ( (Num MOD 2) = 0 )

END; { EvenNegative }
```

9-4. If you look carefully at the locations of the semicolons, you will see that the **a** and **b** procedure outputs are as follows:

```
J <= I
J > I
```

9-5a. Remove the semicolon after the first `WriteLn` and insert the keyword `THEN` in the second `IF`.

9-6a. `Phase` is not less than 4, so the `ELSE` clause is executed, writing 6. The following `IF` statement then writes 4, so the output looks like this:

```
6
4
```

9-10.

```
CASE Choice OF
   'A' : Total := Total + 1;
   'D' : Total := Total - 1;
   'P' : WriteLn( Total )
END;
```

10-1. The procedure will fail. In fact, the program will terminate with a message informing the user that input has been prematurely terminated. The problem is that `<EOF>` is not treated as a character in Pascal. Thus the first `ReadLn` will not be successful.

10-2. The `CountChars` procedure requires that the user press RETURN after every character because it uses a `ReadLn` statement rather than a `Read`. If the user did not press RETURN after each character, only one character per line would be used. Not only would the character count be incorrect, but the sentinel might be missed.

10-3 **a.** Once. **b.** Not at all.

10-5a. `Count` is not a `Boolean` expression.

10-6. **a.** Once. **b.** Not at all.

10-7a. It prints 16 lines in all:

```
0  0
0  1
0  2
0  3
```

```
1  0
1  1
1  2
1  3
.
.
.
3  3
```

10-9. It would run more slowly because each iteration of the loop body would perform a multiplication as well as a subtraction. The original version of the loop performed only an addition, which takes the same time as a subtraction.

10-13. It prints 12 lines in all:

```
 Num   SqRt( Num )

 1.0      1.000
 2.0      1.414
  .         .
  .         .
  .         .
10.0      3.162
```

10-15a. There are 26 trips through the loop: one trip for every lowercase letter.

10-16a. When `Ch1` is `'a'`, the `Ch2` loop makes one trip. When `Ch1` is `'b'`, the `Ch2` loop makes two trips, and so on, until when `Ch1` is `'z'`, the `Ch2` loop makes 26 trips. Therefore the total number of trips through the inner loop is $1 + 2 + \ldots + 26 = 26 * 27 / 2 = 351$.

10-19a. Five times.

10-20a.

```
REPEAT
   Write( 'What number am I thinking of? ' );
   ReadLn( Num )
UNTIL Num = MyNumber;
```

11-6. Hints:

Are the preconditions listed at the correct place in the code? That is, are they preconditions of the entire code segment, or are they preconditions of the loop?

The loop invariant asserts what is true at the beginning and end of every trip through the loop. Therefore the loop invariant must be consistent with the loop's preconditions. Is that true of Jackson's invariant?

What is the final value of `N` as the loop terminates? Is this consistent with the loop invariant as Jackson has written it?

11-8a. Preconditions: `Int = 0; Product = 1 = 0!`

Invariant: `0 <= Int <= 10;`
`Product = Int!`

Postconditions: `Int = 10; Product = 10!`

11-9. The zeroth power of any real number is 1.0. The `IntPower` function begins by initializing `Product` to 1.0, which is the zeroth power of `Number`, no matter what value `Number` has. Then if `Power` is zero, the loop is skipped, and the function is assigned the value 1.0, which is the correct value. The loop invariant covers this possibility because it shows that when `Mults = Abs( Power )`, we have `Product = (Number ** Mults)`, which would be the same as `( Number ** Abs(Power) )`.

11-11.

```
FUNCTION RealPower( Number, Power : Real ) : Real;
BEGIN

    RealPower := Exp( Power * Ln( Number ) )

END; { RealPower }
```

The accuracy of this function will not be as good as that of the `IntPower` function because natural logarithms and exponents are approximated by a series expansion.

11-14. Within the body of the loop, `Smaller` is assigned to `Larger`, so the two variables become equal in value. Then the second assignment statement calculates `Larger MOD Smaller`, which is the same as `Larger MOD Larger`, which is 0, and assigns this result to `Smaller`, terminating the loop. Thus only one trip is made through the loop, after which the function always returns the original value of `Smaller`.

11-20. The loop invariant says that the new estimate tends to be closer to the true root than the old estimate, and is never farther from the true root. Therefore, unless the new estimate always equals the old estimate, the iterative process will home in on the true root.

11-22. Substituting g for g' in the equation given in the problem:

$$\begin{aligned} g &= (g + N / g) / 2 \\ 2g &= g + N / g \\ g &= N / g \\ g^2 &= N \\ g &= \text{SqRt}(N) = r \end{aligned}$$

11-28. The time required for these code fragments is directly related to the number of `Write` statements that are executed. Fragment 11.5.3 has only three outputs for each value of `N`, while fragment 11.5.1 has `N–1` outputs for each `N`. If `N` is much larger than `4`, the latter will take much longer to execute.

11-29b.

```
1  1
1  2
1  3
1  4
2  1
2  2
```

11-31a. Outer loop: N times.
Inner loop: $(N-1)$ times each.
Total: $N(N-1)$.

12-3. In order to prevent infinite repetition, the recursive call must be conditional, and that condition must ultimately become false.

12-6. If the sun set recursively, our calendars would have to be printed backwards.

12-9.
```
FUNCTION IntPower( Number : Real;
                   Power  : Integer ) : Real;
BEGIN

   IF Power = 0 THEN
      IntPower := 1
   ELSE IF Power = 1 THEN
      IntPower := Number
   ELSE IF Power > 1 THEN
      IntPower := Number * IntPower( Number, Power - 1 )
   ELSE
      IntPower := 1.0 / IntPower( Number, -Power )

END; { IntPower }
```

12-15. `Mystery` returns the factorial of `Number`.

12-18a.
```
FUNCTION Mystery( Number : Integer ) : Integer;
VAR
    Fact : Integer;
BEGIN

   Fact := 1;
   While Number > 1 DO
   BEGIN
      Fact := Fact * Number;
      Number := Number - 1
   END;
   Mystery := Fact

END; { Mystery }
```

13-1. A subrange type is a programmer-defined type whose values can range over a subset of the values allowed for some predeclared ordinal host type. Thus the subrange type is derived from the host type.

13-8a. `255`

13-9. Only **a** is legal. `127` has a predecessor, `126`, that belongs to the subrange `1..127` but no successor that belongs to the subrange. `0` lies outside the subrange and `1.1` is a real number, and therefore cannot belong to a subrange type.

13-10. All of these types consist of nonconsecutive values. Pascal subranges are defined only by a low and a high value.

13-11. Loop invariant: `0 <= Power <= 128;`
`0 <= Remainder < 2 ** Power;`
`log( 128 DIV Power )` digits already printed.
(These are base 2 logarithms and ** indicates exponentiation.)

13-13. The enumeration constant `Blue` is an identifier associated with the integer value 2, and it is stored as a single integer. `'Blue'` is stored as a string of four individual characters, each of which requires one byte of memory.

13-16. It is legal to declare a subrange of an enumeration type, but not vice versa.

13-17. **d** is most suitable for storing the suit of a playing card (yes, that was a pun) because the identifiers are very descriptive. This is a good application for the enumerated type in Pascal. If a numerical value is needed in some part of the program, the `Ord` function may be used to convert an enumerated value to an integral value.

14-2. The subscripts of `RealOrNot` in the code fragment are not legal. They must be either `True` or `False`, rather than the integers `1` and `2`, since they are of type `Boolean`.

14-4a.
```
TYPE
   LowerCase = 'a' .. 'z';
   SubType   = 0 .. 99;
   CharArray = ARRAY [ SubType ] OF LowerCase;
VAR
   TheRealThing : CharArray;
```

14-5. The values in `Salary[1]` through `Salary[8]` are 100.00, 150.00, 250.00, 450.00, 850.00, 1650.00, 3250.00, and 6450.00. `Salary[ 9 ]` and `Salary[ 10 ]` contain garbage.

14-16. `Index` is out of range in the first pass through the loop, since it will take on the value `Low - 1`. The range of values for the loop should be from `(Low + 1)` to `(High - 1)`.

14-20. In the statement `IF Key[LatestUnsorted] < Key[PositionOfLowest] THEN`, the name of the `PositionOfLowest` function is used as though it were a variable, as an array subscript. This is not allowed.

14-21. Change the "less-thans" to "greater-thans."

14-22.

At beginning of first trip:	`GIBBERISH`
At beginning of second trip:	`BIGBERISH`
At beginning of third trip:	`BBGIERISH`

14-28. `Gerald` is not a string array because its subscript range includes `0`.
`Ronald` is not a string array because it contains only one element and because it is not an array of `Char`.
`George` and `Bill` are not string arrays because they are not `PACKED`.

14-30. The assignment statement assigns a string constant of length 5 to a string array that holds eight characters; this is illegal. In Standard Pascal, a string array cannot be a parameter of a `ReadLn`. In the `IF..THEN` structure, `S` cannot be compared to `'Knuth'` because these have different lengths.

14-33. The problem with this function is that the loop executes one time too many. It compares `A[N]` to `A[N+1]` the last time through, but it should only compare `A[N-1]` to `A[N]`. The final value for the loop should be `N-1` instead of `N`. Also, there is no check for `N` exceeding `Limit`. Here is code that takes care of both problems:

```
IF N > Limit THEN
   N := Limit;
InIncreasingOrder := True;
FOR Index := 1 TO N-1 DO
   IF A[ Index ] > A[ Index + 1 ] THEN
      InIncreasingOrder := False;
```

14-38. `Scores` is illegal because the subscript ranges are separated by a semicolon instead of a comma. `Strike` is illegal since the lower bound on the subscripts is greater than the upper bound.

15-1. An array is a data structure in which all the components, called elements, have the same type, and in which these elements are numbered. In a record, on the other hand, the various components, called fields, can have different types, and they are given names.

15-3. A homogeneous data structure is one in which all the components have the same type. In a heterogeneous data structure, the components can have differing types.

15-4. `ThisLight` has the type `TrafficLight`—that is, it is a record containing two fields. `ThisLight.Color` has the type `SignalColor`—an enumerated type. `ThisLight.Duration` is a `Real` number.

15-6.
```
PB
CH
```

15-9.
```
TYPE
   String4      = PACKED ARRAY [ 1..4 ] OF Char;
   String20     = PACKED ARRAY [ 1..20 ] OF Char;
   Registration = RECORD
        Brand        : String4;
        Model        : String20;
        Year         : Integer;
        Cylinders    : Integer;
        Displacement : Real;
        Tax          : Real
   END;

VAR
    MyCar : Registration;
```

15-18. **a.** `Student[ 2 ].Name` is a 40-character string containing the second student's name.
b. `Student[ 2 ].Name[ 3 ]` is the third character in the second student's name.

15-27.
```
2
1.23
1
4.32
```

15-42.
```
ade
```

16-1. An abstract data type packages the data type itself together with a set of operations that make the data type useful. Pascal does not provide its predefined arrays and records with very complete sets of operators.

16-5. *Information hiding* is the principle of supplying information only as it is needed. An abstraction simplifies the perception of a complex entity by ignoring (hiding) the minute details of the entity. For example, if we think of "car" in the usual sense, we think only of the car's outward appearence (data abstraction) and the way the car is used (procedural abstraction), but not in terms of the inner construction and detailed mechanical function of the car.

16-6. The code implementing the various procedures and functions in an ADT implementation is distinct from the ways in which these procedures and functions are called. Thus the code within the procedures and functions can be changed without necessarily affecting the interface's declarations of the subprograms. On the other hand, the procedures and functions interact with their callers because the subprograms exchange data with the callers. Thus the code within the subprograms depends to some extent on the ways in which these subprograms are declared in the interface.

16-10. Here's the code for `MultiplyFr`:

```
PROCEDURE MultiplyFr( Fr1, Fr2 : Fraction;
                      VAR Prod : Fraction );
BEGIN

   Prod.Numerator   := Fr1.Numerator * Fr2.Numerator;
   Prod.Denominator := Fr1.Denominator * Fr2.Denominator;

END; { MultiplyFr }
```

16-14. The slope of the line is defined to be `DeltaY / DeltaX`. If that value is less than 1.0 (i.e., if `DeltaY < DeltaX`), the algorithm plots y as a function of x (i.e., `NumSteps = Round(DeltaX)` and `XStep = 1.0`). If the slope exceeds 1.0, however, the algorithm plots x as a function of y (i.e., `NumSteps = Round(DeltaY)` and `YStep = 1.0`).

16-15.

```
PROCEDURE DrawRect( Side1, Side2 : NonNegInt );
BEGIN

   MoveForward( Side1 );
   Right( 90 );
   MoveForward( Side2 );
   Right( 90 );
   MoveForward( Side1 );
   Right( 90 );
   MoveForward( Side2 );
   Right( 90 )

END; { DrawRect }
```

17-1. A stream of characters is simply a sequence of characters, one followed by another. A text file is such a stream of characters, divided into "lines" by so-called end-of-line signals (symbolized in the book as `<EOLn>`) inserted among the characters. A "line" of text is therefore a sequence of characters beginning with the start of the file or the last `<EOLn>`, and extending to the next `<EOLn>`.

17-3. The bit pattern used to store a real number in main memory—with a sign, significand, and exponent encoded in binary—is not written to a text file. Text files contain only characters, so if a real number is written to such a file, what gets written is a stream of characters symbolizing the decimal notation for the number. Often this is more bytes than would be required to store the number in main memory.

17-6. Indicating the end-of-line signal by `<EOLn>` and end-of-file signal by `<EOF>`, the output to the file would be

```
VOLUME OF A CONE<EOLn><EOLn>Radius =  1.5<EOLn>Height =  2.0<EOLn>
Volume =      4.71<EOLn><EOF>
```

17-11. The `Read` or `ReadLn` procedure that processes the input data knows what type of variable is to be the destination for the data. It converts the string of input characters to a datum of this type. If the conversion is impossible, the procedure issues an error message.

17-12. `Read` and `ReadLn` return values to their callers, so they make use of `VAR` parameters. `Write` and `WriteLn`, on the other hand, use value parameters. Furthermore, `Read` and `ReadLn` cannot accept string-array inputs in Standard Pascal.

17-14. The `VAR` declaration should use a colon, not an equality.
`OutFile` is not declared to have type `Text`.
The `ReadLn` is not allowed to contain format specifiers.

17-18. `False`, because the file pointer cannot point to `<EOLn>` and `<EOF>` simultaneously.

17-19. `False`, because the file pointer cannot point to `<EOLn>` and `<EOF>` simultaneously.

17-20. No, because the file pointer cannot point to `<EOLn>` and `<EOF>` simultaneously.

17-21. Because it performs I/O as well as returning a value.

17-23. One problem is that the `Read` procedure is not getting its input from `InFile`. Another problem is that the tests for `EOLn` and `EOF` are done in the same expression, and Pascal does not shortcircuit evaluations of logical `AND`s and `OR`s. The code must first make sure that `EOF` is `False` before testing for `EOLn` because `Read( InFile, Ch )` cannot be executed and `EOLn( InFile )` cannot be evaluated if `EOF( InFile )` is `True`.

17-28. A file variable does not contain the components of a file; it contains only the address of the file buffer. Therefore, if the value of one file variable is assigned to another, only a buffer address is copied, and not the contents of the file.

17-36.

```
VAR
   OldFile, CopyFile : FILE OF Real;
   Temp              : Real;

BEGIN

   Reset( OldFile );
   Rewrite( CopyFile );
   WHILE NOT EOF( OldFile ) DO
   BEGIN
   Read( OldFile, Temp );
   Write( CopyFile, Temp )

END;
```

18-3. The first three of the examples in this problem are finite sets, but the last two are infinite.

18-5. The difference { } - *S* is { } for any *S*. Removing values from an empty set leaves an empty set, since there is nothing to be removed.

18-8. All but **a** are proper subsets of the set of all American presidents.

18-12. **a.** True. **b.** False.

18-13. **a.** `{2}` **b.** `{1,2,3,6}`

18-16.
a. Illegal. Pascal uses brackets `[]`, not braces {}, for sets.
b. Legal.
c. Illegal. The 3 must be in apostrophes, since the set contains characters.
d. Illegal. The 3 must be in apostrophes and brackets.
e. Illegal. `S4` is a set variable, but the value assigned is `Boolean`.

18-17.
a. `WriteLn( S0 <= S2 );`
b. `WriteLn( 5 IN S3 );`
c.
```
FOR Int := 0 TO 255 DO
    IF Int IN ( ( S2 * S4 ) - [ 32, 64, 128 ] ) THEN
        Write( Int:4 );
    WriteLn;
```
d.
```
FOR Int := 0 TO 255 DO
    IF Int IN ( ( S2 * S3 ) + [ 32, 64, 128 ] ) THEN
        Write( Int:4 );
    WriteLn;
```
e. `WriteLn( ( S1 <= S2 ) AND NOT ( S1 = S2 ) );`

19-1. Using the `Succ` function to increment `Index` allows the code to be used for an index of any ordinal type. If `Index` is incremented by adding 1, the code can be used only for an index of integer type.

19-5. The key values in the array are not in increasing order. This violates the precondition of the binary search procedure.

19-6. Binary search requires an ordered array. If the `SearchKey` is larger than the last element in the array, `First` will be ultimately assigned the same value as `Last`. The next time through the loop, `Location = ( Last + Last ) DIV 2 = Last.`

19-7. Each time through the loop (in the iterative case) or through the procedure (in the recursive case) there are at most two comparisons made between the `SearchKey` and the listed names. The number of names left to search is cut in half after each iteration or recursion. The worst-case situation for comparisons occurs when the `SearchKey` is smaller than the first name in the array. After 16 times through the loop, requiring 32 comparisons, `First` and `Location` both equal 1. The first element in the array is compared to the `SearchKey` twice more, and `Last` is assigned a value of 0.

19-17. The big-oh order in these solutions is that power of the independent variable that increases most rapidly:
a. $n(n+1)/2 = (n^2+n)/2 = (n^2/2)+(n/2) = O(n^2)$
b. $(1/n) - n(n+1) = (1/n) - n^2 - n = O(n^2)$

19-23. After the first loop, the lowest key has been swapped down to the first position:

`A E F F H L U M P`

Then, during the first four passes through the second loop, in which elements 3, 4, 5, and 6 are compared with `'E'`, no elements are swapped because the elements considered are greater than `'E'`.

19-27. If the `Partition` procedure returns a `PivotPos` equal to the lowest subscript in the array, the succeeding call to `QuickSort( Key, First, PivotPos-1 )` will take `Last` beyond the lower limit of the array subscripts. Similarly, if the `Partition` procedure returns a `PivotPos` equal to the highest subscript in the array, the succeeding call to `QuickSort( Key, PivotPos+1, Last )` will take `First` beyond the upper limit of the array subscripts.

19-33. If a single array element is chosen at random, there is an equal probability that it is greater than or lower than the median value in the array (assuming array elements are unique). If three elements are chosen at random, there are several possibilities for the median of those three. (a) The first one chosen is the median of the three, in which case there is no improvement over selecting only one. (b) The first one chosen is not the median of the three, but that median is farther from the actual median of the array than the first number. (c) The first one chosen is not the median of the three, but that median is a better estimate of the actual median of the array. The probability of (a) is 0.33. The probability of (b) is 0.25 * 0.67. The probability of (c) is 0.75 * 0.67. Thus the probability of an improvement using this algorithm is that of (c), which is 0.50.

20-1. **a.** `IPtr` contains garbage because it has not yet been initialized.
b. `IPtr` contains a pointer to a storage location that contains 2 and `IPtr^` contains the value 2.

20-2. Only `TPtr` and `TTPtr` contain valid information. The other variables have not yet been initialized, so they contain garbage. In fact, `TPtr^` is an illegal reference since `TPtr` contains `NIL`.

20-7.

```
B
B
```

20-9. This function always returns `NIL`. The termination condition must occur when there is still one node in the list, so that a pointer to that node may be returned. The correct function is as follows:

```
FUNCTION Tail( L : List ) : List;
BEGIN

   IF L = NIL THEN
      Tail := L
   ELSE IF L^.Link = NIL THEN
      Tail := L
   ELSE
      Tail := Tail( L^.Link )

END; { Tail }
```

20-10.

```
PROCEDURE DeleteHead( VAR Head : List );
VAR
   First : List;
BEGIN
   IF Head <> NIL THEN
   BEGIN
      First := Head;
      Head  := First^.Link;
      Dispose( First )
   END

END; { DeleteHead }
```

20-25. If the binary search tree is full, the maximum height of the tree is approximately the log of the number of nodes in the tree. The maximum number of comparisons required to find a value, or to discover that the value is not in the tree, is the height of the tree. If, on the other hand, the tree is not full, it could actually be one long string of elements as shown in Figure 20.6.6. The number of comparisons required to search that tree could be the number of nodes in the tree. Hence the search process would be $O(N)$.

20-28. `RetrieveRoot` returns a value of `DataType`, which may be a composite type. Pascal functions can return only simple values, not composite values.

21-5.

```
PROCEDURE FlushStack( Top : Stack );
BEGIN

   WHILE NOT ListIsEmpty( Top ) DO
      DeleteHead( Top )

END; { FlushStack }
```

21-6.

```
PROCEDURE Reverse( Head : List );
VAR
   Top      : Stack;
   TempData : DataType;

BEGIN

   CreateEmptyStack( Top );
   WHILE NOT ListIsEmpty( Head ) DO
   BEGIN
      RetrieveNth( Head, 1, TempData, Found );
      DeleteHead( Head );
      Push( Top, TempData )
   END;

   WHILE NOT StackIsEmpty( Top ) DO
   BEGIN
      Pop( Top, TempData );
      InsertAtTail( TempData )
   END

END; { Reverse }
```

Glossary

ABSTRACT DATA TYPE (ADT) A data type packaged together with meaningful operations in such a way that the type can be used without concern for the internal storage representation or the implementations of the operations.

ABSTRACTION Separating the use of an object from its internal construction by encapsulating the object and giving it a name by which it can be invoked.

ACCESS To read from or write to a storage device.

ACTUAL PARAMETER An actual value sent to or from a subprogram's formal parameter.

ALGORITHM A sequence of step-by-step instructions for performing some task, usually a computation.

ALLOCATE To set aside memory for use in a variable.

ANALOG Smoothly variable; capable of continuous variations of physical state.

ANONYMOUS TYPE OR VARIABLE A type or variable created implicitly by a program, and to which no name has been explicitly associated.

ARRAY A composite data structure in which one or more subscripts are used to identify the individual elements stored, and in which the elements can be accessed in any order.

ASCII American Standard Code for Information Interchange; a seven-bit character code widely used in the United States. The American version of the International Standards Organization (ISO) character code.

ASSERTION A comment that specifies the program state at a particular point in execution.

ASSIGN To copy a value into a variable.

ASSIGNMENT COMPATIBILITY Compatibility that allows a given value to be assigned to a given variable.

BASE CASE (in recursion) A nonrecursive and therefore terminating case that is eventually reached by a process of recursion.

BASE TYPE See *host type*.

BINARY FILE See *nontext file*.

BINARY NUMBER A number written in base 2 notation.

BINARY OPERATOR An operator acting on two operands.

BINARY SEARCH TREE A binary tree organized to facilitate data searches.

BINARY TREE A tree structure in which each node is linked to two subtrees.

BIT 1. The most fundamental unit of data as represented in a computer; a single on/off signal. **2.** A binary digit.

BIT PATTERN A pattern of on/off signals in a digital memory device, symbolizing a data value.

BLOCK A set of declarations together with an associated compound statement in which the declarations take effect.

BOTTOM–UP CONSTRUCTION A construction technique in which the lowest-level subprograms are built and tested first, then the next-level subprograms are built and tested, and so on, moving upward in the hierarchy.

BREAKPOINT A point marked in a program at which a debugger will automatically halt execution to allow inspection of variables.

BYTE A unit of computer storage usually consisting of eight bits.

CALL To command that a subprogram be executed.

CALLER The program unit invoking a subprogram.

CARDINALITY The number of members in a set.

CHARACTER CODE The character set available in a given Pascal system, together with the ordinal values associated with the characters.

CODE A sequence of program instructions.

COMPILER A program that translates instructions in a high-level programming language to instructions in machine language or other low-level language.

COMPILE–TIME ERROR An error that occurs during compilation of a program; a syntax error. Also sometimes used loosely to include linking errors, in which a referenced external identifier is not found.

COMPOSITE TYPE A data type containing more than one simple variable; a data structure.

CONDITIONAL EXECUTION Executing a statement or sequence of statements only if some condition prevails.

CONSTRUCTOR A procedure used to initialize an object that uses virtual methods.

CONTROL STRUCTURE A program instruction or group of instructions that control the execution of statements. Examples include *decision structures* and *iteration structures* (loops).

COUNTER–DRIVEN LOOP A loop in which a counter variable is used to specify, directly or indirectly, the number of iterations.

DATA A sequence of symbols.

DATA ABSTRACTION Packaging a data type together with its operations, so that the type can be considered in terms of its use, without concern for its representation in memory or the implementation of its operations.

DATA STRUCTURE A composite data type; that is, a data type containing more than one simple variable.

DATA TYPE A class of data storage specified by defining both the allowed values and the allowed operations.

DE-ALLOCATE To release main memory from use by a variable or data structure so that the memory can be reused.

DECISION STRUCTURE or **SELECTION STRUCTURE** A statement or group of statements that controls the sequence of execution in a program, deciding at runtime which statements to execute.

DECLARATION A notice to the compiler, associating an identifier with a constant, type, variable, procedure, or function. The declaration of a variable also causes the compiler to generate code allocating storage for the variable when the declaring block becomes active.

DECREMENT To subtract from the value of a variable.

DEREFERENCE To derive from the name of a pointer the variable pointed to.

DIGITAL Capable of assuming only distinct states, as opposed to a continuous range of states.

DIMENSIONS The number of subscripts in an array.

DISCRETE Having distinct and separate values, not continuously spread.

DRIVER A main program used in testing a subprogram.

DYNAMIC ALLOCATION Allocation of memory for variables that occurs during execution of a program.

DYNAMIC DATA STRUCTURE A data structure that can grow, shrink, or go out of existence under program control, during execution.

ECHO To print out or display an input value.

EDITOR A text processing program that makes it easy to create, modify, and save text.

ELEMENT An item stored in an array and identified by a subscript.

ENUMERATE To list individually, as in counting.

ENUMERATED TYPE A data type specified by enumerating the allowed values.

EXECUTE To carry out actions; to run a program.

EXPRESSION A combination of operands and operators, having an overall value.

EXTERNAL FILE A file that is stored on a mass storage medium.

EXTERNAL SORTING METHOD A sorting method in which most of the data reside on a mass storage device at any time during sorting.

FENCEPOST ERROR An off-by-one error; that is, an error that causes a result to be incorrect by one unit or a loop that makes one too many or one too few iterations.

FIELD **1.** One of the items in a record. **2.** The area within a display or printout in which a value is shown.

FIFO Acronym for first-in, first-out, referring to a data structure in which the first item stored is the first to be retrieved.

FILE A sequence of data of one type (either characters or internal bit patterns) and accessible only in sequence. External files reside in mass storage; internal files reside in main memory.

FILE BUFFER VARIABLE In a file buffer, the storage cell pointed to by the file pointer, and therefore the currently accessed cell in the file. Also called the file window.

FILE COMPONENT One of the data values stored in a file.

FILENAME The name associated with an external file by the operating system, not to be confused with the name of the file pointer.

FILE POINTER A variable containing the memory address of the buffer for a file. Sometimes called a file variable.

FILE WINDOW See *file buffer variable.*

FINITE Limited in size; neither infinite nor infinitesimal.

FIXED PART In a variant record, the optional part whose type is not affected by the value of the selector.

FORMAL PARAMETER A variable appearing in the parameter list of a subprogram declaration, acting as a placeholder or dummy variable for the actual value to be transmitted to or from the calling program unit.

FORWARD REFERENCE A reference to an identifier that has not yet been declared. In Pascal, such references are allowed only in the case of mutually recursive declarations of dynamic data structures or mutually recursive subprograms. The latter situation requires an explicit `FORWARD` directive.

FUNCTION A subprogram that returns a resulting simple data value by associating it with the subprogram's name. A function can be regarded as a special kind of procedure.

GARBAGE Meaningless data; gibberish.

GLOBAL IDENTIFIER An identifier that can be referenced beyond the scope of a single block.

GLOBAL SCOPE Scope extending over more than a single block.

GLOBAL VARIABLE A variable that can be referenced beyond the scope of a single block.

HARDWARE The physical parts of a computer system, as opposed to data and programs.

HETEROGENEOUS DATA STRUCTURE A composite data type in which the stored items are of differing types.

HEXADECIMAL Base 16 number representation. See Appendix J.

HIERARCHICAL DESIGN The planning of a *hierarchy*, in which items are ranked one above another.

HIERARCHY A layered structure, in which items are ranked one above another.

HIGH–LEVEL LANGUAGE A programming language like Pascal, in which instructions are written in a form relatively understandable to humans.

HOMOGENEOUS DATA STRUCTURE A composite data type in which the stored items are all of the same type.

HOST TYPE or **BASE TYPE** The ordinal type in which we construct a subrange type.

I/O Input and output.

IDENTIFIER A name. In Pascal, identifiers are given to programs, procedures, functions, constants, types, and variables.

IMPLEMENTATION The instructions within a subprogram or set of subprograms.

INCREMENT To add to the value of a variable.

INCREMENTAL TESTING A process in which a code skeleton is first tested, then a little more code is added and tested, and so on.

INDEX **1.** An array subscript. **2.** The counter in a loop.

INFINITE LOOP A loop that iterates forever or until interrupted by outside control.

INFIX NOTATION Notation in which binary operators are written between their operands.

INFORMATION The human significance of data.

INFORMATION HIDING A software engineering practice in which lower-level implementation details are hidden while viewing higher-level modules.

INHERITANCE Process by which one object can be defined in terms of another, from which it acquires fields and methods.

INITIALIZE To store an initial value in a variable.

INORDER TRAVERSAL Traversal of a binary tree, in which the left subtree is traversed, followed by the root node and then the right subtree.

INPUT Data transferred into a program or computer from a peripheral device.

INTEGER A whole number in the range from –`MaxInt` to +`MaxInt`, to which integer arithmetic operations can be applied.

INTERFACE The declarations of the parameters and names of subprograms, as distinct from the instructions within the subprograms.

INTERIOR NODE A tree node having at least one descendent.

INTERNAL FILE A file that is stored in the computer's main memory.

INTERNAL SORTING METHOD A sorting process during which the data reside in main memory.

INVARIANT See *loop invariant*.

ITERATION The process of repeatedly executing the same sequence of instructions, performing the same actions in the same order. The term *an iteration* is also used to refer to one such repetition.

ITERATION STRUCTURE A control structure that iterates (loops); a loop structure.

ITERATIVE METHOD A computational method in which a result is found by a process of successive, iterated approximations.

KEYS The fields that are being operated upon in a collection of data.

LEAF A tree node having no descendents.

LEXICAL SCANNER A parser.

LIFO Acronym for last-in, first-out, referring to a data structure in which the last item inserted is the first one retrieved.

LINKED LIST A list in which each item is associated with information about the location of its successor and/or predecessor.

LINKER A program that links the object code for a program to the referenced library modules to create a complete, executable program.

LIST A sequence of data. This is a more general concept than *file*, because in a list, access is not necessarily sequential.

LOCAL SCOPE Scope that extends over only a subprogram.

LOCAL VARIABLE A variable that can be referenced only within a single block.

LOOP A control structure in which the same instructions are executed repeatedly.

LOOP BOUND A function of the loop variables indicating the amount of work remaining to be performed by the loop. As the loop runs, this function decreases monotonically, reaching zero when there is no more work to be done. At this point, the loop should terminate.

LOOP INVARIANT An assertion of a constant property of the program states at the beginnings and ends of every iteration of a loop structure.

LOOP STRUCTURE A control structure that directs the repeated execution of the same sequence of instructions, performing the same actions in the same order each time.

LOOPING See *iteration*.

MACHINE CODE Instructions expressed in a form that can be understood directly by the CPU.

MACHINE LANGUAGE The language of instructions understood directly by a CPU, and written in bit patterns.

MAIN MEMORY The internal electronic storage of a computer.

MAIN PROGRAM The program unit that executes first in a program.

MASS STORAGE Storage external to main memory and typically much larger. Such storage is usually nonvolatile.

MaxInt A predefined constant—the largest allowed `Integer` value in a given Pascal system.

MEDIAN VALUE That value chosen from a set such that there are equally many values in the set higher and lower than the chosen value. (Note that the median is not in general the same as the mean; the mean is the arithmetic average.)

MEMBER An item stored in a set or belonging to a set.

MENU A list of choices available to the user of an interactive program.

MODULAR CONSTRUCTION or **MODULARITY** Construction from individually distinct program units, treated as plug-together building blocks.

MONTE CARLO METHOD A probabilistic computational method.

MULTIDIMENSIONAL ARRAY An array with more than one subscript.

NESTING Placing one control structure or program structure within another.

NODE A component data structure within an overall dynamic data structure.

NONTEXT FILE or **BINARY FILE** A file whose components are stored as the same bit patterns used to store these values in main memory.

NULL STATEMENT or **EMPTY STATEMENT** A statement containing no instruction and doing nothing. Null statements are created by the presence of unnecessary semicolons in the code.

OBJECT CODE The result of compilation; the low-level translation of a program unit or complete program, often in machine language.

OCTAL Base 8 number representation. See Appendix J.

ONE-DIMENSIONAL ARRAY An array with only one subscript.

OPAQUE TYPE A type whose structure or representation is not revealed.

OPERAND A data object acted on by an operator.

OPERATING SYSTEM The set of programs that manages the computer hardware resources, carries out commands, and controls the user interface.

OPERATOR A symbol specifying an action to be performed.

OPERATOR PRECEDENCE The order in which operators are applied in the absence of overriding parentheses. (See Appendix D.)

ORDER OF PRECEDENCE See *operator precedence.*

ORDERED LIST A sorted list; that is, a list in which the keys are arranged in some order.

ORDINAL TYPE A data type whose allowed values can be enumerated, with each such value except the first having a unique predecessor, and each except the last having a unique successor. In Pascal, the ordinal types are `Integer`, `Char`, `Boolean`, subrange types, and enumeration types.

OUTPUT Data transferred out of a program to a peripheral device.

OVERFLOW ERROR An attempt to store a value too large for storage.

OVERLOADED OPERATOR An operator symbol whose interpretation depends on the type(s) of its operands; a context-sensitive operator.

PACKED DATA Data that are stored in the fewest possible bits.

PARALLEL ARRAYS Arrays in which similarly subscripted elements are related conceptually.

PARAMETER An argument of a procedure or function.

PARSE To analyze the syntax of text, determining the grammatical structure.

PERIPHERAL DEVICE An I/O or storage device external to the CPU and main memory.

POINTER A variable that stores memory addresses.

POLYMORPHIC OPERATOR See *overloaded operator*.

POP To remove a data item from the top of a stack.

PORTABLE SOFTWARE Software capable of being used on a wide range of computers.

POSTCONDITION The program state existing after a specified action.

POSTFIX NOTATION Notation in which operators are written after their operands.

POSTORDER TRAVERSAL Traversal of a binary tree, in which the left subtree is traversed, followed by the right subtree and then the root node.

POSTTEST LOOP A loop structure in which the loop termination test is performed after each iteration.

PRAGMATIC ERRORS Design or stylistic faults that make a program inconvenient or impractical for users or programmers.

PRECONDITION The program state existing before a specified action.

PREFIX NOTATION Notation in which operators are written before their operands.

PREORDER TRAVERSAL Traversal of a binary tree, in which the root node is traversed, followed by the left subtree and then the right subtree.

PRETEST LOOP A loop structure in which the loop termination test is performed before each iteration.

PROCEDURAL ABSTRACTION Grouping together the statements that perform a distinct task, giving the overall action a name. This is accomplished by incorporating the statements in a procedure. The resulting procedure can be used without knowledge of its implementation.

PROCEDURE A subprogram in which data are transferred in and out by means of a parameter list. The actions of the procedure are invoked by simply calling upon it.

PROGRAM The expression of an algorithm in the unambiguous syntax of a programming language.

PROGRAM STATE The condition, at a particular point in the execution of the program, of the values stored in all variables, together with the conditions existing in all files connected to the program.

PROGRAM UNIT A module in a Pascal program; that is, the main program or a subprogram.

PROMPT *(verb)* To ask the user for input. *(noun)* A message asking for input.

PSEUDORANDOM NUMBERS A sequence of apparently random numbers generated in a computer. Such numbers are not really random, but they have no obvious correlation and are uniformly distributed over some interval.

PUSH To add a data item to the top of a stack.

QUEUE A list in which items are extracted in the same order they were inserted; that is, a first-in, first-out list.

RANDOM ACCESS Accessing stored items in any order whatever, as contrasted, for example, to *sequential access*.

RANDOM–ACCESS DATA STRUCTURE A data structure in which data can be written or read in any order. Arrays, records, and sets are examples.

RANGE-CHECKING Checking performed by the Pascal runtime system to determine whether values have gone beyond their declared ranges.

RANGE ERROR An attempt to store a value outside the declared range for its type.

READ To accept input, copying it into main memory.

REAL NUMBER In Pascal, a number having a fractional part and/or an exponent.

RECORD A heterogeneous data structure in which the individual items, called fields, are accessed by name.

RECURSION Repetition by self-reference, when a subprogram invokes itself. Such a process will repeat forever unless terminated by a control structure.

REFERENCE *(verb)* To refer to something by name.

RESERVED WORD A predefined word in the Pascal language that cannot be redefined by a program.

RETURNED VALUE **1.** The value produced by a function and passed back to the calling program unit in association with the function's name. **2.** A value produced by a subprogram and passed back to the calling program unit as a parameter.

ROOT NODE In a tree, the node from which all other nodes are descended.

ROUNDOFF ERROR The approximation that results when a real number is rounded off for computer storage. Most real numbers suffer roundoff error when stored in a computer.

RUNTIME ERROR An error that occurs during the execution of a program. Such an error may or may not cause an error message to appear.

SCOPE The region of a program over which an identifier is defined.

SECONDARY STORAGE Mass storage.

SELECTION STRUCTURE A decision control structure.

SELF–REFERENCING CODE Code that calls itself; recursive code.

SEMANTIC ERROR An error in the meaning of a program, as opposed to its syntax. These do not keep a program from compiling, but produce incorrect results when the program is executed.

SEMANTICS The meaning expressed in a language.

SENTINEL A data value serving as a marker, for example, marking the end of input.

SEQUENCE OF EXECUTION The order in which program instructions are executed.

SEQUENTIAL ACCESS Accessing stored items in order, from first to last.

SEQUENTIAL–ACCESS DATA STRUCTURE A data structure in which data can be written or read only in sequence. In Standard Pascal, all files are sequential-access data structures.

SET A collection of data of the same type.

SIDE EFFECT An effect of a subprogram other than the effect that was obviously intended.

SIGNIFICAND The bits or digits of a numeric magnitude, independent of sign or exponential scaling factor. Formerly called the mantissa.

SIMPLE TYPE An unstructured data type, either `Real`, `Integer`, `Char`, `Boolean`, or a subrange or enumerated type.

SOFTWARE The data and instructions used by a computer system, and provided to the computer in symbolic form.

SOFTWARE ENGINEERING The careful design and development of software by methods similar to those used in designing hardware. The emphasis is on correctness, reliability under all circumstances, and ease of maintenance.

SOFTWARE LIFE CYCLE The lifetime of a program, consisting of six phases: planning, requirements analysis and specifications, design, coding, validation, and maintenance.

SORTING Arranging a list of items in a desired order.

SOURCE CODE A program written in a high-level language. The source code is supplied to a *compiler* to be translated into *object code.*

SPECIFICATION A detailed, precise statement of the operational and interface characteristics of a program or program unit.

STACK A list in which items are retrieved in the reverse of the order in which they were inserted; that is, a first-in, last-out list.

STANDARD PASCAL The Pascal language as specified by the International Standards Organization (ISO).

STATE See *program state.*

STATIC ALLOCATION Storage allocation for variables that occurs before the program begins execution, and which is therefore unchanging during execution.

STRING A sequence of characters.

STRING ARRAY In Standard Pascal, a packed array of characters in which there are at least two characters, the first of which has subscript 1.

STUB A skeletal subprogram written for first-stage testing. After the stub is tested, it is fleshed out to a complete subprogram.

SUBPROGRAM A program unit that cannot be executed by itself; in Pascal, a procedure or function.

SUBRANGE TYPE A data type in which the allowed data values are specified as a subrange of the allowed values for some ordinal host type.

SUBSCRIPTED VARIABLE An algebraic variable containing a number of closely-related values distinguished from one another by numeric subscripts attached to the variable name (for example, x_1, x_2, x_3).

SYMBOL A stimulus or signal used to represent something else. In this book, symbols are the units that make up data, to which humans may ascribe meanings.

SYNTAX The vocabulary and grammar of a language.

SYNTAX ERROR An error in the vocabulary or grammar of a program. Such errors make it impossible for the compiler to translate the program into machine language.

SYSTEM DEPENDENT Depending on the Pascal system being used.

TAG FIELD The selector field in a variant record.

TAIL RECURSION Recursion that occurs as the last action in a procedure.

TEXT FILE A file consisting of lines of characters; that is, a file of characters in which there is an end-of-line signal after the last character, and perhaps other end-of-line signals among the characters.

TIMESHARING A system for allocating computer resources in which a number of people use the same computer at the same time, with the CPU time split among the users. Each user has access to a unique portion of memory.

TOGGLE To switch on and off, as if with a toggle switch.

TOP–DOWN DESIGN A design technique in which the main program is designed first, followed by the highest-level subprograms, and so on, moving downward in the hierarchy.

TRACE Using a debugger to single-step through a program, watching the values change in the variables.

TRAVERSE To travel from node to node in a linked data structure.

TREE A recursive data structure in which a single node, called the root, is linked to zero or more nodes, which are themselves disjoint trees.

TYPE A data type; a class of data storage, specified by defining both the allowed values and the allowed operations.

TYPE SUBVERSION Treating a data item as though it sometimes had one type and sometimes another.

TYPE–TRANSFER FUNCTION A function that converts a value of one type to a value of another type.

UNARY OPERATOR An operator that acts on a single datum.

UNDEFINED Having an unpredictable value.

UNDERFLOW ERROR An attempt to store a nonzero numeric magnitude too small for storage.

UNIT A separately compiled body of code that is used only to declare data items and operations for client programs and perhaps to initialize them. *See* Appendix H.

USER INTERFACE The way in which a program interacts with the user while running.

VALUE PARAMETER A parameter that transmits a value into a subprogram, but does not transmit new values back out even if the subprogram attempts to change the value of its formal parameter. A value parameter is also called an *in-only parameter*.

VARIABLE A named storage cell in main memory, in which the value can be changed during execution of the program.

VARIABLE (VAR) PARAMETER A parameter that transmits a value both into and out of a procedure. If the procedure changes the value of the formal `VAR` parameter, these changes appear in the value of the corresponding actual parameter in the calling program unit. A `VAR` parameter is also called an in/out parameter.

VARIANT RECORD A record in which at least one field's type depends on the value of a selector field.

VOLATILE STORAGE Storage that is erased on loss of power or after a program terminates.

WORD A unit of computer storage larger than a byte, of a size depending on the system being used.

Index